TARGET
LONDON

TARGET LONDON

UNDER ATTACK FROM THE
V-WEAPONS DURING WWII

CHRISTY CAMPBELL

Little, Brown

LITTLE, BROWN

First published in Great Britain in 2012 by Little, Brown

Copyright © Christy Campbell 2012

The moral right of the author has been asserted.

A CIP catalogue record for this book
is available from the British Library.

Hardback ISBN 978-1-40870-292-5
C format ISBN 978-1-40870-293-2

Typeset in Caslon by M Rules
Printed and bound in Great Britain by
Clays Ltd, St Ives plc

Papers used by Little, Brown are from well-managed forests
and other responsible sources

MIX
Paper from
responsible sources
FSC® C104740

Little, Brown
An imprint of
Little, Brown Book Group
100 Victoria Embankment
London EC4Y 0DY

An Hachette UK Company
www.hachette.co.uk

www.littlebrown.co.uk

To Miss M. Moss, Foreign Office civilian,
Broadway and War Station, 1938–9

'In their obsession with this new type of war, the Germans lost their sense of reality. In reaching out after the future, they sacrificed the present.'

Stuart Milner-Barry, *The V-Codes*

'Those damn silly rockets.'

Air Marshal Sir Arthur Harris,
AOC Bomber Command

Central London: Summer 1944

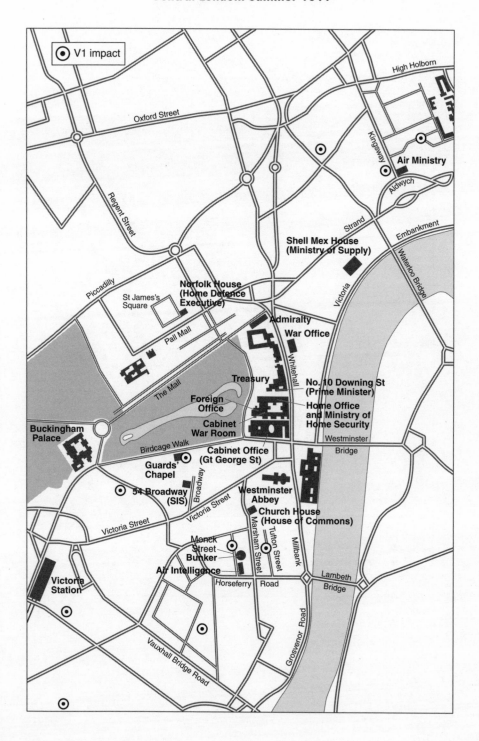

- V1 impact

High Holborn

Oxford Street

Kingsway

Air Ministry

Aldwych

Regent Street

Strand

Embankment

Shell Mex House
(Ministry of Supply)

Waterloo Bridge

Piccadilly

Norfolk House
(Home Defence
Executive)

St James's
Square

Victoria

Pall Mall

Admiralty

War Office

The Mall

Treasury

Whitehall

No. 10 Downing St
(Prime Minister)

Foreign
Office

Home Office
and Ministry of
Home Security

Buckingham
Palace

Cabinet
War Room

Birdcage Walk

Cabinet Office
(Gt George St)

Westminster

Guards'
Chapel

Bridge

Broadway

54 Broadway
(SIS)

Victoria Street

Westminster
Abbey

Church House
(House of Commons)

Victoria Street

Marsham Street

Tufton Street

Millbank

Monck
Street
Bunker

Air Intelligence

Horseferry Road

Lambeth
Bridge

Victoria
Station

Grosvenor Road

Vauxhall Bridge Road

The V-Weapon Complex, Western and Central Europe, 1943–5

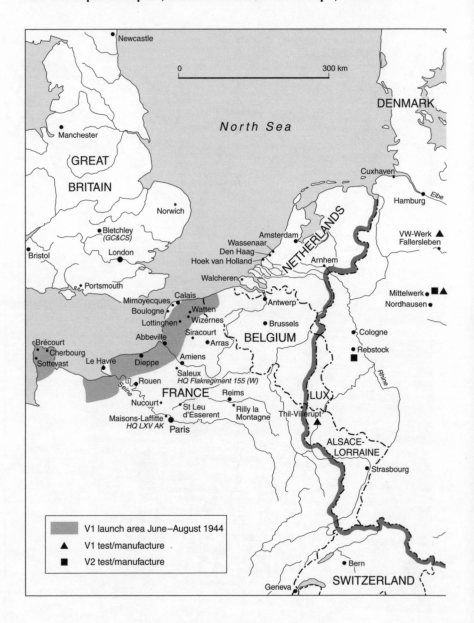

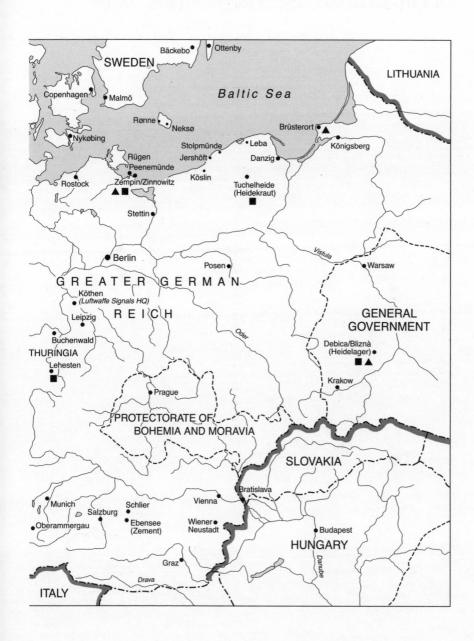

PREFACE

This is a story of science in the service of war. It is the story of how London suffered as a result, and how intellect, moral bravery and cunning were engaged to save it from greater destruction.

As a child, as for many of my 1950s-born generation, the war was the presiding mystery. Our central-London neighbour was a veteran character actor who played Germans in the many war films and TV shows of the period. He played the 'Reichsführer' in a movie called *The Battle of the V1*, which we all went to see. Such yarns were my education.

Many years later, as an aviation writer in my twenties, I reported on the inception of the National Air and Space Museum in Washington, DC. At its conservation facility in Maryland a German jet aircraft captured at the end of the war was being restored. It was a Messerschmitt Me 262A-1a.

The beautiful shark-like plane had always fascinated me. I watched the technicians popping the rivets and peeling back the aluminium wing panels. There was writing scrawled inside. The inscriptions were in Russian, Polish, Serbo-Croat – one of them read in French: 'My heart is not in it.' These were messages left by the slave workers who had built the plane thirty-three years before in some underground factory. After thousands of hours of restoration work the machine would go to the fine museum for new generations to wonder at. But the real story was already inside.

The NASM collection includes two 'revenge weapons', an A-4 (V2) rocket and a Fi 103 (V1) flying bomb ('V' stands for *Vergeltung*, revenge), the long-range weapons developed in turn by the German army and air force. No serious war museum is complete without them, although the flying bomb is now a period curiosity while the rocket still looks timelessly fit for purpose.

But contemporary museum curators 'interpreting' the rocket have to acknowledge the circumstances of its making, as well as what it did to those it fell on. Production versions were assembled in an underground factory called the 'Mittelwerk' (Central Works) in the Harz Mountains of central Germany, with a slave labour camp known as Dora at the entrance to its tunnels. There were more camps beyond. Many thousands died in the making of these revenge weapons – far more than those they actually killed on war-like operations.

The Washington rocket was seized from the Mittelwerk and brought to the US in extraordinary circumstances. At Peenemünde on the Baltic, meanwhile, another preserved A-4 points skywards – outside the splendid Historisch-Technisches Museum. It is accommodated largely in the research centre's purpose-built power station, untouched by the famous RAF raid of August 1943. The site, which was sealed off as an East German military base, was restored post-reunification and fitted out as a museum in a cool and candid way that even a Londoner finds it hard to find fault with.

In October 1992, on the fiftieth anniversary of the first successful A-4 launch, veterans of the era returned to the Baltic, where the German Aerospace Industry Association had arranged an official function to mark 'the birth of space travel'. When British newspapers found out there was outrage. The German Chancellor, Helmut Kohl, called it an 'unwise arrangement'. An unofficial commemoration went ahead, while at roughly the same time a statue of Air Marshal Sir Arthur 'Bomber' Harris was ceremoniously unveiled in central London by the Queen Mother amid some fatuous controversy – which I, as a newspaper journalist, was bidden by my editor to stoke up.

North of London there is another museum, Bletchley Park, where wartime codes were broken. In the same year that the restoration of Peenemünde began, a move was made to raze the site in Buckinghamshire with its late-nineteenth-century mansion and rickety huts, to make way for a supermarket. The local historical society appealed for wartime veterans who had worked there to come forward, and four hundred did so for a celebration and commemoration in 1992. At the same time a fight began to save the place. The supermarket plan was dropped and the Park has limped along gallantly since as a charitable trust with the help of the National Heritage Fund and some corporate donations, acknowledging its status in the story of the birth of computing via the electromechanical computers, called 'bombes', used to break the German codes.

The story of the Park had been kept secret until the mid-1970s. Once it came out, Ultra joined the grand narrative of how Anglo-American scientific and technical intellect joined forces to achieve victory, climaxing in the atom bomb. Meanwhile the *Official History of British Intelligence in the Second World War* was published and the Park's wartime files were placed in the National Archives for public access. With the unveiling of the Ultra secret, those who had worked at Bletchley, to their own general astonishment, found themselves free to tell their story. A tide of revelations ensued – factual accounts, novels and films.

As the 'revenge weapon' story began to pass out of living memory, accessing it became increasingly a question of official files, personal documents and diaries. In the course of exploring this narrative – the German offensive on southern England by long-range weapons and the Allied attempts to defeat them – I made used of many such primary sources, but one seemed to have been hitherto overlooked. In the National Archives at Kew in south-west London are eleven bound volumes of Ultra decrypts. Called the 'Most Secret Source J Series' (CX/MSS/J), they contain many hundreds of messages about 'secret weapons', decrypted and analysed from spring 1943 to the end of the war in Europe. The shorter SJ series added background commentary. The messages range from the highest 'secret command matters', to the most mundane items of housekeeping. To read them is to eavesdrop on the eavesdroppers. As an internal history of the operation compiled in 1945 put it:

Under the ill-considered belief that we should put in every reference to everything that had ever been contextually associated with secret weapons, even when the association was fully under-stood by us and known to be trivial, we reported large quantities of conspicuously irrelevant matter. Because members of the LN-Versuchsregiment [radar specialists] were plotting flying bombs and rockets, we reported details of their bicycles and marriages in enormous volume.

It is these soap-opera details (and soap would prove important) that make the story so fascinating, and it began with the most inconsequential-seeming clues. Take this Ultra decrypt from early April 1943:

Source found a circular dated 6/4 ... addressed to Luftgaustab Centre, Crete. GAF Signal Experimental Regt. is taking over the GAF Signals Equipment Office in Tempelhof [Berlin] and is delivering ... Würzburg 1076 for experimental station Peenemünde.

It was deeply obscure, but it marked the beginning of it all: the point at which an already remarkable partnership between a London-born physicist and a professor of German linguistics turned to the dark matter of long-range secret weapons. They were Dr Reginald Victor Jones, Assistant Director Intelligence (Science) at the Air Ministry, and Professor Frederick Norman of King's College London, the wartime head of Section 3G(N) at Hut Three, the Government Code and Cipher School, Bletchley Park. A linguist ignorant of science and a scientist with no German – they were the perfect partnership.

The brilliant, hubristic, exasperating, impossible – and in the end indispensable – Dr Jones told the British War Cabinet on the very eve of the rocket attack on London in late summer 1944: 'The German Army has produced a great technical achievement in the Rocket ... and the Nazis have been carried away by the romantic prospect of operational consummation. There is no deeper policy behind the Rocket.'

It was a wonderful line. And it was true. But how did it come about? It was via Hitler himself, who sidelined fundamental research in favour of the gadgetry that he could see being paraded in front of him. Sceptical at first, he became enraptured as the wider war spun out of his control. And it came about, as the historian Richard Overy wrote, 'because of the extreme compartmentalisation of function that denied [German] scientists access to the working of the war itself'. The rocket prospered in supposedly secret isolation while other initiatives – nuclear research, for example – pottered along in academic crevices. There was no atomic equivalent of Peenemünde – no reactor on the Baltic. The rocket focused all those clever minds, as it turned out, in the wrong direction.

Walter Dornberger, the artilleryman who worked on the military rocket from start to finish, claimed that because of the Führer's early doubts the programme was delayed by two years – it came too late. But others have pointed out that the German rocket in fact appeared too early. It went into action before its accuracy could be perfected, before it could make a truly decisive bang. And it cost an estimated equivalent of twenty-four thousand defensive fighter aircraft.

The V2's baleful promise kept the Gothic dream of final victory alive. Military realists in Germany could see the absurdity, but the true believers exulted. The wonder-weapon chimera caused far more damage to its creators than for those it fell upon. It prolonged the agony and deepened its intensity. As a wickedly cynical Whitehall memo of October 1944 put it, 'The wide dispersion and variety of [V-weapon] plants which might be working on various components and supplies means that devastating air attacks are possible on unexpected and (apparently) harmless targets.'

Between January and May 1945, Dresden, Pforzheim, Potsdam, Chemnitz and many more German cities would suffer Anglo-American air attacks, the numbers killed in which made the endgame, such as the rocket-inflicted tragedies of Farringdon Road (close to my own childhood home) and Hughes Mansions, Stepney, seem trivial. Which is not to say that the people of London did not suffer grievous hurt, but rather that, unlike the Blitz of 1940–1 and its narrative of defiant heroism, during the V-weapon episode the Anglo-American allies possessed in their bomber fleets the means to terribly punish the German civil population for their folly in staying loyal to the Nazi regime. And they used it. And they would have used it more.

The intelligence struggle waged in much of the story that follows was to determine not how fearsome was the threat, but how ultimately impotent. Any member of Britain's Joint Intelligence Committee possessing a sense of history, bidden to sign off the 'Iraq Dossier' of 2002, might have profited by looking at its equivalents in 1943–4, which spoke of bacteria bombs and atom-splitting warheads ready to rain down on London by monster rocket at the whim of a dictator. The Home Secretary urged that the capital be evacuated. Apocalyptic retaliation plans against German cities were ready to launch. The Americans caught the same panic. But the reality was different. The struggle in that febrile doodlebug summer of 1944 was to perceive that reality. It became very dangerous indeed until all-source intelligence got to the truth.

In spite of Bletchley Park's magical-seeming insight, Ultra could get it wrong. Decrypts were fragmented and technically opaque. It was a question of interpretation. There were grave misconceptions throughout, and as an internal history of the section most involved put it, 'The extremely strict security placed on all information about secret weapons ... meant a great deal of subterfuge in dealing with other departments both inside and outside BP.' Furthermore:

> There was intense political activity in London. The threat was deemed sufficiently serious to warrant the creation of a special committee to deal with it, in addition to the office ... already responsible for routine intelligence cover. The effect was that two political parties came into being, between which there was rivalry. This was not without influence in our approach to Source.

Bletchley and Peenemünde were high-level secret concentrations of militarised intellect, both with mathematics at their heart. One produced teleprinter message forms, the other produced rockets. Both employed electromechanical computing devices of which the other side knew nothing. In Buckinghamshire it was the 'bombe'. Beside the Baltic it was the integrating accelerometer. In the outcome, the bombe was by far the deadlier weapon.

There were more similarities. Both enterprises recruited the necessary talent through clandestine means. Both had formidable secrecy oaths. Exhortations to keep quiet were everywhere to be seen: *Feind Hört Mit* – 'The Enemy is Listening', Careless Talk

Costs Lives. Canteen talk was about anything except what people were actually doing.

Peenemünde had a string quartet, with Wernher von Braun on cello, while the Park had a little orchestra. A Park veteran recorded: 'According to RAF regulations, all musicians were Aircraft Hands and were expected to do menial jobs when not rehearsing. They also had to play selections from "The Desert Song" and "Rose Marie" when the camp commandant had visitors.'

There were two other presiding differences: there were no slave labourers at Bletchley. And the British found Peenemünde pretty quick, but the Germans never found the Park.

ABBREVIATIONS, TECHNICAL AND OTHER TERMS

This story is of necessity infused with an alphabet soup of abbreviations, acronyms and technical terms, many in German. Bletchley Park logged thousands of them.

AA anti-aircraft
Abteilung battalion or department
Abwehrstelle military intelligence station
ACAS (I) Assistant Chief of the Air Staff (Intelligence)
ADGB Air Defence of Great Britain
ADI (K) Assistant Director of Intelligence (Air) (prisoners of war)
ADI (Sc) Assistant Director of Intelligence (Science)
AEAF Allied Expeditionary Air Force
AI Air Intelligence
AK Armee Korps
AK Armia Krajowa, Polish Home Army
AKzV Armee Korps zur Vergeltung, army corps for revenge
ARP Air Raid Precautions
ATS Auxiliary Territorial Service, women's branch of British army
Big Ben codename for rocket
Bodyline codename for 1943 investigation into the German long-range rocket
Bois Carré village in France where first 'ski site' identified
bombe electromechanical code-breaking device

BP Bletchley Park

Brennschluss rocket motor shut-down

'Brown' Luftwaffe Enigma key

BzbV Beauftragter zur besonderen Verwendung, Officer for Special Duties

C Chief of British Secret Intelligence Service (MI6)

CAS Chief of the Air Staff

CIU Central Interpretation Unit, Medmenham

'Corncrake' German army Enigma key

cover photographs produced by aerial reconnaissance missions

Crossbow UK umbrella term for German long-range weapons and countermeasures against them. After D-Day the term included attacks against Continental targets

CSDIC Combined Services Detailed Interrogation Centre

CX agent-derived intelligence

DCAS (Ops) Deputy Chief of the Air Staff (Operations)

Diver codename for flying bomb

DMI Director of Military Intelligence

ETOUSA European Theater of Operations, United States Army

Flak anti-aircraft (troops, etc)

Flieger airman

Funkmeister radio operator

GAF German air force

GC&CS Government Code and Cipher School, Bletchley Park

IID scientific adviser to Secret Intelligence Service

integrating accelerometer on-board device to determine distance travelled and trigger A-4 rocket engine shut-down

JCC Joint Crossbow Committee

'Jerboa' Luftwaffe flying-bomb unit Enigma key

JIC Joint Intelligence Committee

J-series series of Ultra messages plus accompanying analysis concerning V-weapons produced by Section 3G(N) at Bletchley Park from 1943 to 1945

KdF Strength through Joy

key Enigma system shared by a group of users (the coding of which would change daily); a 'cryptonet' in American usage; some lasted a few weeks, others for years

'Klavier' Luftwaffe flying-bomb unit low-level signals key

Kommandantur command, headquarters

KZ Konzentrationslager, concentration camp

lox liquid oxygen

Luftgau military air district

Luftnachrichten-Versuchs Regiment experimental signals regiment

MI14 Military Intelligence section 14 (information about Germany)

MPI mean point of impact

MSS Most Secret Source

NASA National Air and Space Administration

NASM National Air and Space Museum, Washington, DC

Oberkommando der Wehrmacht Supreme Command of the Armed Forces

OT Organisation Todt (construction corps)

P/W prisoner of war

PI photo-interpreter

Pingpong SIS term for agent-derived V-weapon intelligence

PR photo-reconnaissance

Queen Bee British radio-controlled gunnery target drone

'Quince' German Police (SS) Enigma key

réseau French Resistance network

RFSS Reichsführer-SS (Heinrich Himmler)

SD Sicherheitsdienst, SS security service

SIS Secret Intelligence Service

SOE Special Operations Executive

TA Territorial Army

TAF Tactical Air Force

T-Stoff hydrogen peroxide

USAAF US Army Air Force

USSAFE US Strategic Air Force Europe

'Vera' V-2 launch unit low-level signals key

Vergeltung revenge

versuchs experimental

VKN Versuchs Kommando Nord, military unit at Peenemünde-Ost

Waffenamt weapons department, German War Ministry

W/T Wireless Telegraphy

XX Double-Cross (deception), hence the Twenty Committee

Z-Stoff sodium permanganate

PEOPLE

Politicians

WINSTON CHURCHILL Prime Minister and Minister of Defence
SIR STAFFORD CRIPPS Minister of Aircraft Production
HERBERT MORRISON Home Secretary and Minister of Home Security
CLEMENT ATTLEE Deputy Prime Minister
DUNCAN SANDYS, Junior Minister, Ministry of Supply; chairman of
  Bodyline (investigation into the German long-range rocket) and
  later Crossbow Committee
LORD CHERWELL (Professor F. A. Lindemann) Paymaster-General,
  scientific adviser to Winston Churchill

Intelligence Officers

DR R. V. JONES Assistant Director Intelligence (Science), Air Ministry;
  scientific adviser to the Secret Intelligence Service
DR CHARLES FRANK deputy to R. V. Jones
PROFESSOR H. P. 'BOB' ROBERTSON professor of mathematics at
  Princeton, seconded to ADI (Science), 1944
PROFESSOR FREDERICK NORMAN head of Section 3G(N), Hut Three,
  Bletchley Park, former professor of German linguistics
BRIGADIER STEWART MENZIES 'C', Chief, Secret Intelligence Service

SQUADRON LEADER DENYS FELKIN ADI(K), prisoner-of-war interrogator

LIEUTENANT-COLONEL MATTHEW PRYOR MI14, first to draw attention to the German long-range rocket

MAJOR-GENERAL FRANCIS DAVIDSON Director of Military Intelligence
1940–4

MAJOR-GENERAL JOHN SINCLAIR Director of Military Intelligence
1944–5

FLIGHT LIEUTENANT DAVID NUTTING Air Intelligence, attached to
30 Assault Unit, Royal Marine Commando

VICTOR CAVENDISH-BENTINCK chairman Joint Intelligence
Committee

STUART MILNER-BARRY Bletchley Park Hut Six codebreaker

GORDON WELCHMAN Cambridge mathematician, Bletchley Park Hut
Six code-breaker

WING COMMANDER DOUGLAS KENDALL senior photo-reconnaissance
interpreter, CIU

FLYING OFFICER CONSTANCE BABINGTON SMITH interpreter
Aircraft, CIU

FLIGHT LIEUTENANT ANDRÉ KENNY interpreter Industry, CIU

FLIGHT LIEUTENANT CLAUDE WAVELL interpreter RDF (radar),
CIU

Patriots

PIERRE GINTER Luxembourg telephone operator: transmits early
intelligence about Peenemünde to London

JEANNIE ROUSSEAU French agent 'Amniarix': transmits flying bomb
and rocket intelligence to London

MICHEL HOLLARD French patriot: Bois Carré 'ski site' information to
London

AAGE ANDREASEN Danish chemical engineer, agent 'Elgar': first
rocket information to London

LIEUTENANT-COMMANDER CHRISTIAN HASAGER CHRISTIANSEN
Danish naval officer: flying bomb intelligence to London

JERZY CHMIELEWSKI Polish Home Army operative flown to London
with rocket parts

Deceivers

LIEUTENANT-COLONEL J. H. BEVAN head of London Controlling
Section

SIR SAMUEL FINDLATER STEWART chairman Home Defence
Executive

J. C. MASTERMAN chairman Twenty (Double-Cross) Committee

JOHN DREW Home Defence Executive

FLIGHT LIEUTENANT CHARLES CHOLMONDELEY MI5's B1a (double-
agent) section

JUAN PUJOL agent 'Garbo', London-based double agent

Scientists

ISAAC LUBBOCK UK pioneer of the liquid-fuelled rocket

GEOFFREY GOLLIN UK pioneer of the liquid-fuelled rocket

DR HAROLD J. PHELPS scientific adviser to the Ministry of Economic
Warfare

PROFESSOR CHARLES DRUMMOND ELLIS scientific adviser to the
Army Council

DR ALWYN CROW Controller of Projectile Development, Ministry of
Supply

WILLIAM COOK Assistant Controller of Projectile Development,
Ministry of Supply

Airmen

AIR MARSHAL SIR CHARLES PORTAL Chief of the Air Staff

AIR MARSHAL SIR DOUGLAS EVILL Vice Chief of the Air Staff

AIR MARSHAL SIR RODERIC HILL AOC Air Defence of Great Britain

AIR MARSHAL SIR ARTHUR 'BERT' HARRIS AOC Bomber Command
1942–5

AIR VICE MARSHAL FRANK INGLIS Assistant Chief of the Air Staff
(Intelligence)

AIR VICE MARSHAL NORMAN BOTTOMLEY Deputy Chief of the Air Staff (Operations) 1943–5

AIR COMMODORE SIDNEY BUFTON Director of Bomber Operations, Air Ministry

AIR COMMODORE CLAUDE PELLY Director of Operations (Special Operations)

AIR COMMODORE COLIN MCKAY GRIERSON Director of Operations (Special Operations)

GROUP CAPTAIN JACK EASTON Director of Intelligence (Research), Air Ministry

AIR CHIEF MARSHAL TRAFFORD LEIGH-MALLORY AOC Allied Expeditionary Air Force

Soldiers

FIELD MARSHAL SIR ALAN BROOKE Chief of the Imperial General Staff (head of the army)

GENERAL SIR HASTINGS ISMAY secretary of the Chiefs of Staff Committee

LIEUTENANT-GENERAL SIR FREDERICK PILE commander anti-aircraft artillery defences

LIEUTENANT-GENERAL ARCHIBALD NYE Vice Chief of the Imperial General Staff

BRIGADIER LESLIE HOLLIS Senior Military Assistant Secretary to the War Cabinet

BRIGADIER IAN JACOB Military Assistant Secretary to the War Cabinet

LIEUTENANT-COLONEL TERENCE SANDERS leader of August 1944 Anglo-US mission to Moscow and Blizna

Germans

MAJOR OTTO STAHMS commander of the Luftwaffe experimental station at Peenemünde-West

GENERALMAJOR JOSEF ROSSMAN commander of army experimental station at Peenemünde-Ost

OBERST GERHARD STEGMAIER commander Köslin rocket school

OBERST WALTER DORNBERGER veteran artilleryman, head of Waffen Prüf Amt 10, War Ministry department concerned with rocket development

HERMANN OBERTH rocket pioneer and Peenemünde scientist

WERNHER VON BRAUN rocket pioneer, technical director of the military rocket programme

ALBIN SAWATZKI engineer, manager of rocket production at the Mittelwerk

LEUTNANT MUETZE Luftwaffe officer commanding Baltic 'Insect' radar tracking detachment, XIV Kompanie, Luftnachrichten-Versuchs [Experimental Signals] Regiment

REICHSMINISTER ALBERT SPEER Ministry of Armaments

GENERALFELDMARSCHALL ERHARD MILCH General Inspector of the Luftwaffe, in charge of air armaments

GENERALLEUTNANT ERICH HEINEMANN commander LXV Armee Korps

LUFTWAFFE OBERST EUGEN WALTER second-in-command LXV Armee Korps

GENERALMAJOR RICHARD METZ A-4 rocket commander, LXV Armee Korps

OBERST MAX WACHTEL commander 155(W) Flakregiment, LXV Armee Korps

GENERAL DER FLAKARTILLERIE WALTHER VON AXTHELM Flak troops commander

SS-OBERGRUPPENFÜHRER HANS KAMMLER commander Revenge Division

OBERST GEORG THOM Chief of Staff, Revenge Division

HAUPTMANN CLEFF 'fantasist' Panzer captain (captured 1943)

HAUPTMANN LAUTERJUNG anti-Nazi architect (captured D-Day)

FELDWEBEL HELMUT MÜLLER ex-Peenemünde technician (captured in Italy 1944)

Americans

LIEUTENANT-GENERAL CARL SPAATZ commander US Strategic Air Forces in Europe (USSAFE)

BRIGADIER-GENERAL CHARLES P. CABELL Director of Plans USSAFE

BRIGADIER-GENERAL GEORGE McDONALD Director of Intelligence USSAFE

MAJOR-GENERAL FREDERICK L. ANDERSON deputy commander USSAFE

LIEUTENANT-GENERAL IRA EAKER commander 8th Air Force, 1943–4

LIEUTENANT-GENERAL 'JIMMY' DOOLITTLE commander 8th Air Force

COLONEL RICHARD D'OYLY HUGHES Chief of Plans 8th Air Force

CAPTAIN WALT ROSTOW US army, member of Enemy Objectives Unit, London; secretary Joint Crossbow Committee, July–August 1944

Russians

MAJOR-GENERAL P. I. FEDOROV director of NII-1, Scientific Research Institute 1, Moscow

BORIS CHERTOK engineer with NII-1

MIKHAIL TIKHONRAVOV rocket scientist, Blizna investigator

PART I

WHISPERS FROM THE BALTIC

CHAPTER 1

Greifswalder Oie, 20 November 1943

It was the doomed love affair of a German air force radar technician that gave the listeners the clue. It was not why he had chosen
to kill himself, but where – on an island in the Baltic Sea.

A little after lunch on a cold November day, Obergefreiter*
Wilde had left the mess hut and taken the path that led to the
strand beneath the cliffs near the tiny harbour. The gunshot
echoed down the cliff face, setting a gaggle of seabirds wheeling
and shrieking out to sea. It was this that alerted the aircraftman's
comrades, and they found him on the pebbly beach. Somehow he
must have manipulated the carbine that lay bloodied beside him
under his chin and pulled the trigger. He had blown the top of his
skull off. Leutnant Muetze, the detachment commander, came to
see for himself. This was all very inconvenient.

A submarine telephone cable linked the Leutnant's little command post to the much larger island of Usedom close to the
mainland. Major Otto Stahms, commander of the Luftwaffe
Erprobungsstelle (experimental station) at Peenemünde-West,
expressed weary irritability at the news of the wretched
Obergefreiter. Was it suicide? By the state of him, it could not be

* Equivalent to leading aircraftman in the Royal Air Force.

anything else. No raiding party had penetrated the station's secrets, and in any case would the enemy attempt such a thing in this weather? A storm was raging in the nearby Greifswalder Bodden. The Fieseler Storch liaison aircraft could not fly in this murk. Sometimes in the depths of winter the sea froze and you could walk all the way to Usedom, or so it was said by the older hands.

Oberstabsarzt Bahr was dispatched from Usedom by boat. The doctor examined the body and later that evening, 20 November 1943, he signed the death certificate. Cause of death: gunshot, self-inflicted. Self-inflicted wounds were a serious offence under the Luftwaffe's disciplinary code, even if this prosecution was clearly not going to go very far. There would have to be a wider inquiry – the Feldgericht (military court) at Wismar would get agitated – and there would doubtless be a further investigation by the military air district Luftgau XI covering Mecklenburg-Vorpommern. The death certificate would have to be sent to the Air Ministry. God knows what all those hundreds of lawyers in uniform at the Reichsluftministerium legal department in Berlin would make of it. God knows what they actually did, anyway.

They were nowhere near any front line, but what Leutnant Muetze's men were engaged in on their Baltic island was very sensitive. It was supposed to be the most secret place in the whole Reich. Heinrich Himmler, the Reichsführer-SS, had been here this summer. Now the love-struck airman had attracted all this attention. Why did Aircraftman Wilde have to fall for someone else's wife?

Leutnant Muetze had to radio a report to Hauptmann Gust, officer commanding XIV Kompanie of the Luftnachrichten-Versuchs [Experimental Signals] Regiment at Köthen, the airbase three hundred kilometres to the south near the city of Halle. It was the administrative HQ of the German air force's specialists in ground-based navigation systems and radar. The regiment's technical companies were spread all over Europe from Arctic Norway to the Aegean. And here were Leutnant Muetze and his Kommando on their island in the Baltic where, since arriving six months ago to start setting up their aircraft-tracking radars, they had been engaged on a task that would win the war for Germany. Or so they had been told.

The call-sign of Köthen's radio-transmitter was 'Control'. The apparent location of Muetze's detachment had already been allotted a call-sign – it was Heuschrecke, 'cricket'.

What should he tell Control about yesterday's tragedy? It must all be done with the utmost correctness. He pencilled a few carefully considered words on a message form. In the radio bunker, Funkmeister Eckhardt sat ready by his set. The two duty cipher clerks stood loosely to attention by the Enigma machine placed on a folding table. It looked like an oversized portable typewriter in its black, crackle-finish metal case set in a wooden box.

Following standard orders, one of the cipher clerks had already set it up at midnight. He had read across from the *Sonder-Maschinenschlussel*, a closely guarded book of tables which were delivered on the last day of every month by special messenger to Luftwaffe units wherever they might be. The books were issued by the Chiffrier-Stelle, the air force signals intelligence agency, with its headquarters at Potsdam.

The instruction for that day gave the choice and position of the rotors (three out of a choice of five) with twenty-six letters of the alphabet engraved on their circumference, their internal 'ring-settings', the cross-wiring of the plugboard and the 'discriminant', the three-letter code at the head of the signal which indicated to the recipient which key* the message was written in.

The cipher clerk now moved to the second stage of encryption, turning the three rotor positions at random and then typing an equally unscripted three-letter code to give what was called the 'indicator'. It would be unique to this message. All other users of their particular 'key' would have followed the printed instructions at 00:00 so as to give the Enigma's wiring an identical set-up. The settings would change again on the midnight to come. With 159 million billion possible daily set-ups, Enigma was a mathematical miracle. Messages could be put on air with complete confidence, from the most 'secret command matter' to requests for bicycle inner tubes.

The cipher clerk propped the Herr Leutnant's message upright

---

* 'Key', defined in Enigma terms as the set-up of the machine used in common by a group of users on a particular day or for a fixed time. All of the far-flung users of that key were given the same instructions in the same preprinted table that contained the daily Enigma-machine settings for the month ahead. They could therefore engage in a closed conversation that was meaningless to those without the key. Although the set-up might change every twenty-four hours, the user group stayed the same. See Alan Stripp, 'The Enigma Machine, Its Mechanism and Use', in *The Codebreakers* for an accessible technical description of a complex process.

in the open lid of the Enigma's case. He then tapped the words out in Morse on the keyboard. Lights glowed on the machine's lamp board in sequence. The second signaller wrote them down in pencil on a flimsy message form, a stream of five-letter groups on a pre-printed grid reading left to right in columns and rows. He counted the number of characters, and scribbled down the total. Funkmeister Eckhardt, meanwhile, tuned the transmitter to 4778 kilocycles and sent an 'are you ready to receive?' three-letter Q-code* in Morse to Control. The reply was positive: reception good. He then tapped out in clear his call-sign, the time of origin and the number of letters in the text, and the indicator setting. After that he keyed in the three-letter 'discriminant' and the indicator itself.

Then he began to tap out the coded sequence from the message form in its five-letter groups telling the sad story of Obergefreiter Wilde. There was no rush. Procedure had been followed. All was secure.

RAF Cheadle, 21 November 1943

In the gathering gloom of a late-autumn evening, the second watch of the day reported for its eight-hour shift at Woodhead Hall, a redbrick mansion on the Staffordshire moors built for a late-nineteenth-century Manchester mill owner. At 16:00 a cheerful gaggle of WAAFs (Women's Auxiliary Air Force members) arrived by bus from billets in the town of Cheadle. Snatches of laughter, a dab of lipstick, a quick cigarette, then it was down to work.

The house was one of the chain of listening stations that straddled Britain in a three-hundred-mile arc. They all reported more or less to the same place. Their uniformed inhabitants, mostly young women, strained without cease to hear the whispers from the east. Out on the moors the cable stays and metal lattice of the aerial farm shivered and sang in the wind, a net strung to catch tiny pulses of electromagnetic energy as they rippled out from their point of transmission. Inside, the Hall's former billiard room had

---

* The standardised collection of brief operational messages adopted internationally soon after 'wireless' began.

been crammed with plain wooden tables set out in rows as if for a church-hall whist drive. Two operators sat at each table, each with her own wideband receiver – Hallicrafter SX-28 Super Skyriders, beloved of radio amateurs, which had been urgently acquired from America by the Air Ministry in 1941.

By now they had become very skilled at chasing up and down their target stations' frequencies, listening for the string of dits and dahs of a signal being sent in Morse. They had learned especially to recognise the keying techniques of the message-senders – tap-tapping far away, so certain of their immunity.

The operator transcribed the Morse she was hearing in her headphones into a stream of letter groups onto a signal pad. There was no recording, no second chance. She might pick up only fragments. Quite often, reception would break off completely. There was nothing but this real-time paper record – although other intercept stations might pick up the same transmission and contribute a second or third source for the decrypt. But it must be true to what was being sent, especially in its opening sequence, for a cryptanalytical attack to work.

When the message had clearly finished, the operator pressed a button that switched on a light at the front of the table to alert the duty sergeant, who then came and collected the slip of paper. To the operator herself, what she had just written down was meaningless. All she knew, as all of them knew, was how much it mattered.

And that is how it was when station Heuschrecke came on air on the evening of 21 November 1943 with its 'are you ready to receive?' Q-code protocol for Control. Time of intercept: 18:05; a stream of dits and dahs on 4778 kilocycles. The sender's keying technique was familiar. Reception good. A string of five-letter groups – the final message was a little longer than usual. Then the transmission ended. The operator pressed her button and the message was spirited away by the duty sergeant.

In the teleprinter room the intercepted signal pencilled on its slip of paper was keyed into a Typex machine (the UK Air Ministry-developed version of the same commercial pre-war Enigma machine) to be sent by Post Office landline to Hut Six of the Government Code and Cipher School at Bletchley Park, Buckinghamshire, some forty miles north of London.

Bletchley Park, 21 November 1943

The Government Code and Cipher School operated from a late-Victorian stockbroker's mansion in vulgar neo-Tudor style, from which it had long since overflowed, first into a collection of wooden huts dotting the grounds, then from 1942 into a clutch of utilitarian brick buildings. Bletchley was also referred to as 'War Station', 'Station X', 'BP' or simply the 'Park'. Wags called it the 'Golf, Chess and Crossword Society'.

In the first winter of the war the Park, nominally an out-station of the Secret Intelligence Service (SIS), had begun to tentatively eavesdrop on a proliferating conversation. By now it had become a babel – the German political leadership, army, navy, air force, police, SS, railways, intelligence, diplomats, all talking to each other in a host of encoded wireless messages from the highest to the humblest and in many and various 'keys'. The first important breaks – into Luftwaffe signals – had been made in January 1940.

The Park was a combination of human and machine intellect – the latter in the shape of electromechanical computers called 'bombes', that were used to unravel the coding of enemy signals. A string of familiar stereotyped phrasing or a lazy operator neglecting to change the settings, could provide a 'crib' that would supply the bombes with a 'menu' via which to get a full solution to the daily midnight change in the Enigma machine's programming set-up on whichever of a range of keys was the target. The main thing was to achieve the break as soon after 00:00 as possible.

Sometimes that new day's configuration might take just a few minutes to break: more often it took many hours. Sometimes the window went dark for months on end, as happened with naval Enigma keys in early 1942. Although some keys would never be broken, all Enigma traffic was vulnerable. Once Bletchley had learned how to crack one basic system, any trivial chit-chat could compromise traffic of great significance.

In the early days the intelligence establishment in Whitehall had deeply resented that the Park should have any role beyond producing intercepts. But there was such a mass of raw intelligence being scooped up at Bletchley that some sort of on-site assessment was inevitable. Thus the analysis side of the Park blossomed alongside the cryptographic, and along with means to get its output securely to those who needed it.

Since the start, the Park had divided its decoding activities into discrete areas, to be kept secure from each other unless it would help for an insight to be shared, at which point the 'fusion' of intelligence was actively promoted. One of the founding mathematicians, Gordon Welchman, had devised the step-by-step process that moved the raw intercept through traffic analysis, decryption, than what was called 'emendation', and on through translation and elucidation. There were many working on such material at the Park and beyond who knew neither how the source material was derived, nor the secret at the heart of it – namely, that Enigma codes were being broken by machine. Those who did know were said to be 'in the picture'.

Hut Six targeted German army and air force code-breaking. Hut Eight did the same for naval Enigma. Another section of the Park dealt with the Abwehr, the intelligence service of the German High Command. Hut Three (by mid-1943 housed in an industrial-style building, the 'hut' tag enduring as a cover name) handled the translation into English and subsequent analysis of the German air force and army intercepts that flowed from Hut Six.

For months after those first successful breaks, the code-breakers and the analysts had held their breath. The enemy seemed to be sleepwalking. He must surely wake up. After the fall of France the Luftwaffe breaks were a lifeline. On 5 June 1940, the day the last British troops were evacuated from Dunkirk, a 'Brown' key (the Park's codename for it) message was intercepted by the army listening station at Chatham in Kent and sent to the Park. It took four days to break. It came from the signals traffic of the German air force's Luftnachrichten-Versuchs [Experimental Signals] Regiment, headquartered at Köthen in Saxony, and it mentioned three things: the word *Knickebein*, which translated as 'crooked leg', the town of Kleve, and a set of compass bearings. *Knickebein* was a novel electronic system for guiding bombers at night to make precision attacks on British targets.

To begin with the 'Brown' intercepts did not even need the intervention of machines in order to be read. The key was broken by Hut Six in the use of 'cillies' – the code-breakers' name for transmitters' mistakes, named supposedly after a Luftwaffe radio operator's girlfriend with the initials 'CIL', that were used repeatedly in the keying of the message indicator. The Chatham listeners noted at the time in a memorandum about Brown: 'Operators ... constantly address to each other remarks of a private nature, often in a form of abbreviated clear, and are occasionally guilty of remarks of a less personal nature which are of great use.'

The breaking of Brown would give the defenders a crucial edge in the 'Battle of the Beams' in the winter of 1940–1, which was won just in time by hastily developed electronic countermeasures. The meaning of the cryptic messages, even when deciphered, defied interpretation until a young scientist already working for the Secret Intelligence Service and now attached to the Ministry of Aircraft Production (he would later be transferred to the Air Ministry) worked out how German bombers were being directed to their targets. He was Dr Reginald Victor Jones.

The enemy still did not wake up. Here was a seeming miracle on which an outcome that averted obliteration by bombing, starving by U-Boat or outright invasion might turn.

In summer 1941 the Soviet Union entered the fight. Germany declared war on the United States. Ultra, by now reading the enemy's higher strategic intentions, began to open up. What the tiny political and military circle indoctrinated into Ultra's existence received were English-language messages with brief, well-informed annotations indicating their possible significance. The Prime Minister received a daily stream of them with a covering note from Brigadier Sir Stewart Menzies – 'C', the head of the Secret Intelligence Service.

Ultra had direct links with the second-closest-held secret of the war – strategic deception. The Security Service (MI5) had begun running double agents soon after the outbreak of war. In 1941 the operation had budded the so-called Twenty Committee (XX, Double-Cross) which, because Ultra told them so, could give an assurance that every one of the Abwehr's agents in Britain was under their control. Thus an orchestrated stream of disinformation could be fed back to Berlin.

Security was everything. The secrecy oath was for life. The most contentious issue, perhaps, was who in the leadership of Britain's war effort should or should not be informed. A file of correspondence from late 1940 between the Prime Minister and

Menzies survives. Each service chief sent in a list of indoctrinated officers and a report on how the special messages were handled once they arrived from the Park. Churchill was 'astounded at the vast congregation who are invited to study these matters'. Thus it was, according to one authority, that 'the number of recipients on the Prime Minister's insistence was restricted to some thirty of those most closely concerned with the direction of the war – and of these thirty, only six of thirty-five Cabinet Ministers were included'. That figure would inevitably grow, but the fact that some very senior British military commanders were not in the picture, while less senior ones (including Americans) were, served to make things delicate.

It was the same with ministers. Some knew, some did not. Some were told deliberate untruths. Some suspected but did not want to know more. As with an extramarital affair, when everyone in the room knows what's going on except the cuckolded husband, things could get very scratchy. The resulting dysfunctions fuelled the jealousy, the suspicion and the tantrums – among the British, let alone the Germans – that punctuate so much of this story.

In the early days, 'source' was passed off as an omnipresent spy called Boniface, who seemed to be peering over every shoulder in Berlin. Boniface had to be represented as subordinate to C and the information he provided was cast as an 'agent's' report, to be judged by those not in the picture alongside SIS's general output. The pretence was never altogether dropped, although it wore increasingly thin. The secret conversation had its side channels. Peter Calvocoressi, head of Hut Three Air Section, recalled years later: 'It is impossible to imagine Hut 3 without the scrambler telephone. Its invention [in the US in 1941] meant we could discuss the latest puzzle with colleagues in the Air Ministry in the same way we discussed these matters amongst ourselves.'

There would be a lot for Hut Three to discuss with the Air Ministry on the night of 21 November: a decrypt made by Hut Six that evening of a signal concerning events on a Baltic island.

The message from Heuschrecke to Köthen sent at 18:05 had been easy to break. That day's machine set-up had already been solved in a message about a new lamp for the island's lighthouse, timed at 08:00. It was in the key known as 'Brown'. And so it was with this latest message. The decode went from Hut Six to Hut Three within ninety minutes of having been first transmitted by radio operator Eckhardt. The matter of a German airman's suicide was about to be forensically examined, but not by a Luftwaffe court of inquiry.

Hut Three was a very different realm from Hut Six. The personnel were older, tweedier, in contrast to the brilliant young mathematicians in the front line of cryptanalysis. At its head was an RAF Volunteer Reserve officer, Wing Commander Eric Jones, latterly the manager of a Midlands textile company. This was where the raw intercepts were 'translated and elucidated' while being further analysed and sifted for every scrap of information. It had an army and an air section and a smaller naval contingent, their duty officers grouped round a horseshoe-shaped table with the 'head of the watch' sitting at top centre. He had the first take at the material flowing from 'DR' (the decoding room) and sorted it into four piles in perceived order of urgency, then those working down-table would help themselves.

Anyone familiar with a pre-digital newsroom would recognise the layout, designed to take the raw input, 'copy-taste', prioritise, check for accuracy, pass for expert comment, process, rewrite and distribute into its appropriate place, and all against a deadline. Libraries and indexes were in back rooms, within easy reach. Only the libel lawyer was missing.

There were three eight-hour shifts. No sleep on the night watch and no provision for it. The daily rhythm was determined by Hut Six's success in producing decrypts.

The enemy's use of abbreviations (typical of in-group chatter), acronyms, technical neologisms and obscure place names was always problematic. As a Park veteran described it: 'Even when German words were extracted from their code, it was still very often a problem to extract the meaning from these words – they *bristled with obscurity*. There were unintentional obscurities – things obscure simply because we were eavesdroppers, strangers reading stolen scraps of other people's correspondence. Then there were intentional obscurities in which things were made deliberately incomprehensible.'

A special 'Abbreviations and Equivalents' index was established, which included terms and clarifications drawn from sources as well as from Ultra to make it more than a technical glossary. No individual German serviceman might be acquainted with more than a fragment of this huge vocabulary, while a youthful indexer at the Park might have them at her fingertips. Dr R. V. Jones would say: 'The obvious needs carding as much as the obscure.'

The tiniest scrap could be a breakthrough. The Germans, bless their thoroughness, put every intimate detail on air. What should be made of the fact that a large number of female signal auxiliaries were expected to arrive at a Baltic seaside resort and suitable accommodation must be found at short notice? What should be made of the Enigma-encoded news that Obergefreiter Dzerzhinsky at aircraft reporting station Ameise was especially anxious to ring up his fiancée in Halle and pass on instructions for her intended visit? Higher Command agreed that 'she is to go by train to Schlawa and by bus from there'. That signal very usefully showed the location of 'Ameise' – it was on the Baltic coast at Jershöft.

The Number One of B watch in Hut Three on that evening of 21 November 1943 received the Brown-key decode at around 19:35. On one side of the message form was the original encoded text as taken down by the listening station. On the other side was a gummed strip with the machine decode in plain text, still in five-letter groups. The first step in its processing was called 'emending', splitting the letter groups into meaningful German words and numbers. Gaps could be filled by informed guesswork if necessary, with an indication appended as to the degree of speculation employed. Next, the emended signal was translated from German into English, written out by hand on a simple form then handed back to the Number One, who checked it for accuracy. He then passed it down-table to the appropriate service adviser, who must judge its significance and prepare an annotated, amplified version.

In the normal course of operations this was passed to the duty officer, who checked it again and was responsible for its release (stripped of any indication of its true source and time of origin) to the appropriate customer. The duty officer had also to decide its urgency, whether it had any 'direct and immediate value', in Park phraseology, to an operational command, or whether it was merely 'of interest'. It was the time-frame that mattered, not the implications of its contents. Otherwise, it went straight by secure teleprinter to the appropriate intelligence section in Whitehall.

Several matters required different procedures in Hut Three. Anything that touched on deception operations was extracted at the preliminary scanning stage; so was any signal of an overtly scientific or technical nature.

The emending and translation of the Heuschrecke-Köthen Brown-key signal took just a few minutes. This message concerned a lovelorn Luftwaffe airman's suicide. What did that signify? But a part of Hut Three had been taking the deepest interest in Köthen traffic for the past six months. To them, everything to do with the girlfriends and bicycles of XIV Kompanie of the IV Abteilung of the Luftnachrichten-Versuchs Regiment was absolutely riveting.

Section 3G (General) had been set up early in the Park's existence as a deep intelligence resource available to all three service sections. To pursue the newspaper analogy, this was its cuttings library, overflowing with arcane snippets from intercepts past. By 1943 Section 3G had grown to a forty-strong staff of whom most were civilians, subdivided into six smaller sections. One specialised in cover names and codes occurring within Enigma texts liberally used by the Luftwaffe. A second specialised in the Luftwaffe's own signals intelligence operation, its call-signs and abbreviations – conjoined in the so-called 'Mustard' key. Another section tended a sprawling index of geographical references and place names. Its head, Morris Hoffman, had bought old Baedeker guides from a second-hand shop in London and scrabbled around for captured maps and telephone directories. The system worked. Another section monitored enemy terminology, technical terms and abbreviations. 'Bristling with obscurity' it certainly was.

A fifth subsection of General Intelligence covered enemy Field Post Office (very important for compiling an order of battle) and railway organisation. The sixth, with its own section head and small, dedicated clerical staff, kept watch on enemy radar, night fighters, ground-controlled interception, navigation, signals and other technical matters. Its focus was thus almost entirely on the Luftwaffe.

Each section was named after its head. The section dealing with radar was called 3G(N), its head being Professor Frederick Norman, universally known for some obscure childhood reason as 'Bimbo'.

On that November evening Professor Norman took the German-language plain text, the emendation and the duty translation watch's first stab. There were some place names and personalities not previously encountered and some contentious abbreviations and codenames. He must consult his colleagues. Why did the Germans always do it – come up with cover names that were so obvious, or achingly unfunny puns? It was as if they wanted to give the game away. The message to Köthen read:

For Abt[eilung] via 14th Company. Obergfr[eiter] Wilde shot himself at 1305/20/11 on island OIE. Reason probably investigation by technical company on 19/11 into his relations with a married woman. Death certificate has been sent to Air Ministry, and a report to Luftgau XI and the military court at Wismar. This was done by order of the Kommandeur of the EDL [?]. Further details will be elicited on 21/11 or as soon as the weather permits. Full details will follow. Send any further orders.

From Muetze, Leutnant.

In the unfortunate airman and his violent end Professor Norman showed no interest. Nor did he pause to consider how he had managed to have an affair with a married woman on an island which apparently had no civilian population other than a lighthouse keeper and a couple of highland croft-like smallholdings. It was the word 'Oie' that caught his attention, meaning 'islet'.

Hut Three's Topography Section produced Admiralty pilot charts of the Baltic. The Park's Air Index had some recent aerial photographs and an interpretation report from photo-reconnaissance sortie N/853 taken of the Greifswalder Oie in June that year: 'At the top of the small cliff there are some farm buildings, on the north east tip of the island there is a lighthouse with associated gardens and dwelling places. There are structures in the middle of the island which look like unoccupied flak towers. There are tracks which do not seem much used. Apart from a 60 foot vessel in the fishing harbour, there is no activity evident.' In fact there was a great deal of activity.

Professor Norman wrote his first observation to append to the translated signal: 'NOTES (1) This is the first mention in [Ultra] of the GREIFSWALDER OIE. The island lies about 10 km NE of the PEENEMUENDER HAKEN. The island probably houses the HQ of the insect group [the radar tracking detachment of XIV Kompanie] and its cover name is HEUSCHRECKE. HEU = OIE! Cf FLIEGE at HORST = Fliegerhorst.'

There had been a clutch of Brown-key messages in the past month. The first had popped up on a routine search for keywords. On 12 October there was one saying: 'Traffic can come live at 08:00 tomorrow.' And so it had, in an ever increasing number of signals on as yet unreported call-signs. To begin with, a Leutnant Kubitza began sending urgent messages to the SS artillery school at Glau, south of Berlin, about the transfer of special equipment. On 14 October there had been a signal concerning ration cards and field post stamps for something referred to as the 'Lehr und Erprobungskommando Wachtel', based at Zempin on the island of Usedom. It translated as demonstration and experimental command. Another message indicated that a subdetachment of the XIV Kompanie was staying at the 'Hotel Baltic,' at Hasselø on the island of Falster in Denmark.

By the third week of October more call-signs had begun popping up – Ameise, Grille, Termite, Spinne, Fliege, Muecke, Libelle (ant, cricket, termite, spider, fly, mosquito, dragonfly) – apparently linked to geographical locations that seemed to be strung out along the Baltic coast all the way to East Prussia. One was on the Danish island of Bornholm. The busy Leutnant Muetze appeared to be hopping around from one to the next in an aircraft. Where they actually were remained a mystery. They were being described as 'aircraft reporting stations'.*

On the 25th, the notice of the approval of the award of the Afrika cuff title to an Oberstleutnant Dittrich was sent to a unit called Flak Regiment 155 (W) based at a place called Brüsterort.

---

*Station Spinne would be discerned by Bletchley Park as the wireless reporting centre of the Insect 'circle' and their link to Köthen. Very usefully, the Enigma operator at Spinne decoded incoming messages and re-encoded them using the same three letters for indicator and message settings. The name of the operator at Fliege, meanwhile, Feldwebel Klussendorf, with which he always signed, was long enough to provide a way in. And when auxiliary female signallers – Helferinnen – arrived by the Baltic they 'caused more log chat, not less'.

Why was the Reich's greatest secret so carelessly guarded? Because, according to the man who broke their codes, 'no operator was ever posted away ... they were a group on their own who knew their recipients with no official interference ... and the officers were more interested in science than discipline'.

Morris Hoffman found it in the Park's Air Index, a small naval airbase on the eastern flank of the Gulf of Danzig. The signal seemed to connect it to the Wachtel operation at Zempin, whatever that might be. The next day there had been a message from a mysterious Hauptmann Lippold based at Zempin: 'To the usual four outstations ... there will be shooting every day on a bearing of 52 degrees from the catapult at Zempin. Later there will be angle shots [Winkelschüsse], the body [Körper] will leave its original direction after 6 km and return to the old course ... target will then be in an area where it can be monitored by all the apparatus.' Long strings of numbers had begun to turn up in messages from 28 October onwards. As the standard Enigma machine had no number keys, the number signals were sent in a simple letter-substitution code that could be broken easily. In the accompanying Brown-key-coded messages there were mentions of 'departure and impact', and 'explosive trials'. The numbers seemed to be the measures of bearing, height and distance flown of an airborne object.

On 7 November, reporting station Spinne had told Heuschrecke that the 'Fi 76 flew past apparatus position to about 100 kilometres inland'. But until the affair of the lovesick Obergefreiter was discovered it was impossible to pin down where Heuschrecke actually was. But if 'Fliege' was at Horst (*Fliegerhorst* meant 'airfield'), 'Heu' was at Oie! It was that dreadful German love of puns again. Everything fell into place. As Dr Jones would tell the War Cabinet later: 'When we had fixed one station, that on the Greifswalder Oie, the others could be fixed station by station, thus we could build up the plotting framework.'

Pretty soon something else would turn up on the Brown key. Along with the 'flying body', the Insect radar operators were now told to pick up something that 'ascended vertically' and hold it 'for as long as possible'. It was called 'A-4' and was coming from 'Ost'. There had been lots of rumours, cryptic photographs, garbled agents' reports. The whole striking force of Bomber Command had been sent to attack Peenemünde on the strength of them. But there had been nothing yet via Enigma. Now there was.

Although they did not know it quite yet, on 10 December 1943 Bletchley Park would find the rocket. On that day Professor Norman picked up the phone, went to scramble, and put a call

through to the Assistant Director Intelligence (Science) at the Air
Ministry, Dr R. V. Jones. The two men had first discussed such a
prospect in 1939. The German rocket had been a much longer
time in the making than that.

CHAPTER 2

Berlin, October 1929

All over Berlin could be seen brightly coloured posters featuring flame-tailed rockets reaching for the heavens. One outfitter had created a shop-window tableau of mannequins in outsize woolly cardigans stepping down a ladder from what looked like a giant cigar tube, against a backdrop of papier-mâché mountains and twinkling stars. It was the 'surface of the moon'. Outside Wertheim's department store on Leipziger Platz strutted men in high boots and peaked caps carrying placards saying, 'Don't Buy from Jews'. The store's main entrance, with its optimistic murals of peace and plenty from the time of the Kaisers, sported a new embellishment. From a distance it looked like a pipe organ. Closer up, a very few might have recognised it as a display of model 'rockets' – shiny tubes with fins at one end and a pointy nose at the other.

A young man with pale-blue eyes and blond hair tended them. As he would tell an interviewer many years later, 'I stood on the stand there for eight hours a day telling shopping housewives how an interplanetary rocket would cost seven thousand marks and take a year to build . . . I told them: "I bet you that the first man to walk on the Moon is alive today somewhere on this earth."' The housewives beamed. And they loved the attentions of this handsome young man with his fine manners and infectious enthusiasm. His name was Wernher von Braun.

The new Wertheim display was all to do with a movie, *Frau im Mond – The Woman in the Moon* – the fabulous new production from the Universum Film AG studios to be premiered by the Am Zoo station at the UFA-Palast, the biggest cinema in Germany. The Germans were the most enthusiastic cinema-going nation on earth, and what they loved to see most was science fantasy.

Two years earlier UFA had nearly gone bust making *Metropolis*, the city-of-the-future epic featuring a duplicitous female robot, a cowed proletariat toiling in an underground factory, and television. The most expensive film of its time had been a national and international sensation – Adolf Hitler had gone to see it in a provincial cinema and was said to have been enraptured – but it had bankrupted the studio, which was quickly snapped up by the ultra-conservative media magnate Alfred Hugenberg. The press baron now produced the finance for *Metropolis*'s director Fritz Lang and his scriptwriter wife Thea von Harbou to make an even bigger science fiction epic.

Science popularisers were having a terrific time. They called it the *Raketenrummel* – the 'rocket craze' – in which any eccentric could gird himself or some vehicle (a bicycle or a car would do – even a pair of ice-skates) with a battery of solid-fuel rockets and blast off into the nearest casualty department. An amateur astronomer named Max Valier persuaded Fritz von Opel, heir to the car manufacturing fortune, to fund the experimental stunts.

Some in Germany were taking all this very seriously indeed – men like the Berlin-born science writer Willy Ley, who after publishing *Die Fahrt ins Weltall* ('Travel in Outer Space') in 1926, became along with Max Valier one of the first members of Germany's amateur rocket group, the Verein für Raumschiffahrt (Space Travel Society), and wrote extensively for its journal *Die Rakete* ('The Rocket'). Willy Ley's mentor was the slightly older Hermann Oberth, who by 1929 through a series of books and articles had made himself the world's leading authority on what he called – in his most influential work, of the same name – 'ways to spaceflight'. It would be achieved by launching man-carrying craft into orbit and beyond, by means of multi-staged boosters powered by propellants such as liquid oxygen and alcohol which would develop enough thrust to overcome the Earth's gravity.

The latest in his series of books raised the prospect of showering poison gas on some unfortunate city at intercontinental range by means of a powerful rocket. Oberth said later that he mentioned this possibility because of the huge number of (one assumes enthusiastic) inquiries he had had from the German public on the theme. It was not technically feasible, he said, 'for at least a decade' because of problems in making sure the missile hit the target.

With *Frau im Mond* in production at UFA, it was inevitable perhaps that Oberth should be brought in as technical adviser. And with Hugenberg money behind it, a celluloid space epic seemed set for commercial success. Halfway through begins the visionary part of the film – a remarkable sequence which takes the audience from launch to landing. Oberth possessed enough expertise to make the rocket science both fabulously innovative and technically plausible (especially to a later generation.) It was in this move that the countdown was invented, and en-route course corrections were effected by means of two wheels arranged at right-angles, serving as a gyroscope. Interplanetary weightlessness featured, too.

UFA and then Lang proposed that Oberth make and launch a real rocket, powerful enough to broach the stratosphere. He was given a workshop on the UFA backlot and a budget. When he advertised for assistants in the Berlin newspapers, schoolkids clamoured to get in on the excitement (the film's storyline shrewdly featured a Tintin-like adventurer). At his boarding school on the Baltic island of Spiekeroog, sixteen-year-old Wernher von Braun had already filled notebooks with visions of space travel inspired by the writing of Oberth, Valier and Ley. At the family home in Berlin he celebrated Christmas 1928 by strapping a dozen black powder rockets to an old pram, lighting up and letting go.

In autumn 1929, when von Braun was seventeen, he left Spiekeroog, bound for the Institute of Technology in Charlottenburg, Berlin. His rocket fever unabated, he presented himself uninvited at Willy Ley's house and asked to be inducted into the little brotherhood of the Space Travel Society. Oberth took him on as a volunteer fund-raiser. 'My first job with Hermann Oberth,' he would recall long afterwards, 'was helping him with a little display of interplanetary rockets in a Berlin department store.'

UFA leaked press stories about the project's astonishing

progress as the film's premiere approached. Oberth thought he had found a place to launch his real rocket, an obscure island in the Baltic called the Greifswalder Oie. But the local authorities were fearful it would damage the lighthouse there, and anyway, the rocket when tested refused to take off. The motor assembly was too unstable.

So although the premiere went ahead with no fireworks by the sea, the movie-show lit up the Berlin sky. For its British readers, *The Times* reported the screening of 'the most ambitious German film ever made', in breathless tones.* And on a cold, still autumn evening a stream of black limousines drew up to disgorge Berlin's elite. Searchlights stabbed the air, flashbulbs popped and movie starlets waved coyly under the cardboard stars that studded the front of the UFA-Palast. The final credits were greeted by 'thunderous applause' from the ebullient audience. Germany was heading for the stars.

On 29 October, the Wall Street stock market crashed. US institutions called in their short-term German loans. Unemployment soared from half a million to two and half. In September 1930 the National Socialist German Workers' Party (the Nazi party) won over a hundred seats in the Reichstag. Germany was heading for the abyss.

Hermann Oberth went homewards to resume school-teaching. But the Berlin rocket enthusiasts did not let go, and the youthful von Braun, Rudolf Nebel, Willy Ley and others kept the Space Travel Society afloat. They would meet at an old artillery proving ground of the Imperial Army at Reinickendorf in the north-west suburbs of the capital, which they grandly named Raketenflugplatz (Rocket Launch Site) Berlin. Nebel proved an adept showman, staging public displays on Sundays. Rocket misfires and premature explosions proved especially popular. The Nazis didn't take much interest. Berlin's 'space port' was in the Wedding district of the capital, a Communist Party stronghold and a place where men in brown shirts did not go.

The time of innocence was about to end, however. One obvious source of money for rocket experiments had always been the

---

* The first public event of the American Interplanetary Society, founded in 1930, was a showing of *Frau im Mond* with English subtitles at the Manhattan Museum of Natural History.

military. The Reichswehr, the postwar army prescribed by the 1919 peace treaty, was forbidden to develop or possess heavy artillery, but rockets were not mentioned in the Versailles diktat. Nebel was in touch with one Oberst Karl Becker of the Ordnance Office, who offered a small sum of money for continuing experiments. But Nebel wanted publicity – he was still the fund-raising showman who cared little for authority or secrecy. So it was von Braun at the tender age of twenty who would eventually make the deal.

One day in the early spring of 1932 a Horch saloon bearing Reichswehr number plates arrived at the scruffy entrance to the Raketenflugplatz. Three men got out, muffled up in tweeds and hats as if going on a fishing expedition. They were Oberst Becker, a Major von Horstig who was an ammunition specialist, and Hauptmann Walter Dornberger, in charge of developing powder rockets as battlefield weapons. Captain Dornberger's subsequent career would be at the heart of the story to come.

Von Braun recalled the moment for an American interviewer some twenty years later:

> Rocketry offered an approach to the long-range weapon unrestricted by the Versailles Treaty. It was no particular surprise we recognised three inconspicuous civilian visitors who called on us as representatives of the [army] ordnance department ... [whatever might be said] there was no sell-out of the Raketenflugplatz to the Nazis. To us Hitler was a pompous fool with a Charlie Chaplin moustache.

Von Braun accepted the challenge eagerly. It was autumn 1932, he was now a servant of the state, the German Reich, and under military discipline. Soon the young man and his military superiors, Becker, Dornberger – all of them – would have a new master.

CHAPTER 3

London, May 1958

At the Athenaeum Club on a spring day in London, two middle-aged academics were contemplating a scheme for mutual enrichment that some people at the time might have considered to border on treason. The younger of them, Reginald Victor Jones, was a fifty-one-year-old physicist, professor of natural philosophy at the University of Aberdeen. The other, older by ten years, was Frederick Norman, a scholar of heroic German poetry, director of the Institute of Germanic Studies at London University, ornament of King's College and expert among much else on the ninth-century 'Lay of Hildebrand'. Both were laden with honours and both were members of the cerebral Athenaeum Club. They were of the Establishment, but not quite part of it.

Between them, the two men knew the greatest secret of the Second World War. It was still secret. In the phraseology of the time they had been 'in the picture'. And like many thousands of others they had made a solemn declaration that they would never reveal what they had been up to on behalf of HM Government at the time when Britain had been fighting for its life.

Their partnership had begun at the very outset of the conflict and had lasted until its end. The intellectual tools each had brought to the task were as different as their personalities. If they shared one thing, it was a love of practical jokes.* They had acted within orthodox intelligence channels as well as a long way outside them in order to confront a lethal threat facing Britain and its capital. It was a war fought in their heads, with card indexes, reference books, late-night scrambled phone calls and sheer intellectual firepower. And they had succeeded. Now, almost thirteen years since their wartime collaboration had ended, perhaps it was time, suggested the older man, to tell the world the truth. Or at least confide their story to a big-spending newspaper with an appetite for sensational revelations. Or perhaps they should do it just for the hell of it.

Professor Norman was particularly excited. On a trip to Berlin he had just come across a German magazine publishing revelations about the development of flying bombs and rockets at the Peenemünde research station on the Baltic coast, and their use in the bombardment of London in 1944–5. The article's authors seemed to be well informed about some things but wildly inaccurate on others. Who were these people? Presumably someone was being paid for it. As Professor Norman suggested: 'Most of the things we know are probably known to the people who ought not to know them – although they would not admit it – so why not tell the general public? Don't you think we ought to write a dozen articles ourselves, bank the cash which would be considerable ... and then take the rap? I feel we are being far too scrupulous.'

Bimbo Norman had always had a mischievous streak. As a child of British parents in pre-1914 Hamburg, his teenage years were spent at Ruhleben, the racecourse outside Berlin which on the outbreak of the First World War had been turned into an internment camp for civilian enemies of the Kaiser. He loved German culture dearly, but spending his youth as a prisoner had imbued in him a very unteutonic defiance of authority. A colleague called him 'a born rebel'. On his death it would be said: 'There is a sense in which he remained a small boy all his life. He preserved until the

---

* Which never abated. Jones and Norman were founder members of the Crabtree Foundation, which honoured in a series of orations the great polymath Joseph Crabtree (1754–1854), whose 'achievements have been erased from history'. The orations went on (and on) into the 1980s.

end the gusto, the quickness of wit, the intellectual curiosity of the formidably intelligent schoolboy.' What he had done in the late war, however, remained opaque. When he was made a Companion of the Order of the British Empire in June 1947 the *London Gazette* stated simply that he had been 'employed in a Department of the Foreign Office'.

He had done a little more than that. At the very climax of their wartime exploits, in April 1945, Professor Norman had been given a temporary commission as an RAF wing commander, outfitted in air-force-blue battledress and steel helmet and urgently airlifted into a place called Haigerloch, situated in a narrow limestone valley fifty kilometres south-west of Stuttgart. He was reportedly 'horrified' to be begged by the villagers to ensure the surrender of some fanatical 'Werwolfen' Nazi resisters.

In a beer cellar burrowed into a cliff at a bend in the River Neckar, the Germans had two months earlier installed an experimental reactor, the last of a string of thus far unsuccessful attempts to achieve criticality as a step towards making an operational nuclear weapon. That fact was well in the public domain by 1958. But it was what happened after the reactor's discovery that was still far too sensitive to be revealed in the jittery ban-the-bomb 1950s.

Frederick Norman had been sent to retrieve German-language scientific documents from the cave, but instead the haul was put into a truck by an American team and flown across the Atlantic for US eyes only. (Very much later, Jones would put the episode down to double-dealing within Whitehall intelligence departments.)

In 1958 much more of his friend Reg Jones's now distant wartime career was in the public domain than of Norman's. Jones's life story thus far was remarkable enough. The son of a regular army Grenadier Guardsman, young Reg went to the Sussex Road Elementary School at Loughborough Junction in south London, from where, in spite of the school being 'rough', he won a London County Council junior scholarship to Alleyn's School in Dulwich. Thence in 1929, aged eighteen, to Wadham College, Oxford, to graduate with first-class honours in physics. He was awarded a research studentship, and at the suggestion of Professor Frederick Lindemann (later Lord Cherwell, and a Cabinet Minister (Paymaster-General) in 1942) he began developing infrared detectors at the Clarendon Laboratory.

He would prove a powerful patron. Unmarried, vegetarian, teetotal – in contrast to Churchill – the strongly Conservative Lindemann made the politician his hero. When Churchill came back into government in September 1939, he brought his friend with him. 'It was this personal connection alone that made Lindemann scientific dictator during the war,' in the judgement of the historian A. J. P. Taylor, and which would determine the course of so much of this story.

Soon, with Lindemann's encouragement, Dr Jones (title awarded in 1934) was experimenting with infrared as a means of detecting aircraft. Science was gearing up for war. The Air Ministry's Committee on Air Defence, chaired by the chemist Sir Henry Tizard, employed Jones from January 1936 to work at the Clarendon Laboratory on the development of an airborne detector that could be mounted on night fighters. That October he became a member of the Air Ministry staff as a 'scientific officer'.

In January 1938 the infrared project championed by Lindemann was terminated: it was radar that would turn out to be the key to air defence. Jones was posted to the Admiralty Research Laboratory west of London which he viewed as 'exile' but it was here he was to meet Vera Cain when she chased away a squad of physicists who were trying to dig air-raid-shelter trenches on her hockey pitch. They married a little later.

In May 1939 the secretary of the Tizard Committee made a discreet approach to Jones, asking him to explore something that seemed a great unknown – 'how the Germans [are] applying science to air warfare' – something the intelligence services had signally failed to discover. To save money, Jones was given the job and would report to SIS while still an Air Ministry civil servant. This amphibian existence would continue for the duration. Then, like many other academics, Jones disappeared from public life in September 1939.

The Companionship of the Order of the Bath (third degree, for civilian service) had been gazetted thus on New Year's Day 1946: 'Reginald Victor Jones, Esq., Assistant Director of Intelligence (Science), Air Ministry. In recognition of distinguished service.'

In 1945 Dr Jones had gratefully returned to academia. His first-year natural philosophy course at Aberdeen was taken by all science, engineering and medical students, and was hugely popular. So he had continued his distinguished academic career (punctuated by an unhappy time (1952–3) spent as Director of Scientific Intelligence at the Ministry of Defence, when called back by Churchill) in Scotland, remote from the feuds and jealousies of London officialdom. He resisted blandishments urging him to say more about his wartime adventures, although it was tempting. He would later tell a story against himself – namely that when new students were shown around his department they were cautioned: 'Whatever you do, be careful around Professor Jones. He thinks he won the war by himself.' Well, not quite, but it would be a shame if his real story stayed untold because of official secrecy.

If spilling the beans on Hun-baffling wartime stunts was acceptable, though, colluding in Bimbo Norman's proposal to reveal national secrets would have landed the pair in the hottest water that their former employers might consider fitting. With the end of the Second World War there was a public hunger to know more of the reasons why wartime leaders had taken the decisions they had, and the intelligence on which they were based. There was an equal inquisitiveness on the part of journalists, novelists and screenwriters to get under the skin of wartime secrets. There was money in it.

In Britain, the Whitehall establishment was concerned to ensure the opposite. There was a presiding secret that must not be revealed, not for years. The curious must wait for the Cabinet Office-sponsored *Official Histories* that would put the sober stamp of authority on whatever they chose to say, rather than on any politically embarrassing narratives that might be advanced by outsiders.

But, appearing as they did in majestic sequence, those histories made no reference to the extraordinary code-breaking operation conducted at Bletchley Park in Buckinghamshire. Neither did they mention the strategic deception undertaken, through turned double agents and other means, on which the outcome of the invasion of Normandy might be said to have depended; or the 'Ultra'-aspect of the campaign against the 'V-weapons' which also depended on a combination of such operations. These sanitised publications have been called 'the last deception operation of the Second World War'.

This particular operation was set in motion before the war even ended. In July 1945 the Joint Intelligence Committee, the main Whitehall forum for discussing high-level secret matters, met under its chairman Victor Cavendish-Bentinck to discuss 'the use of special intelligence by historians'. It informed the Chiefs of Staff that it was 'imperative that the fact that such intelligence was available should *never* be disclosed'.

'Special intelligence' was what came out of Bletchley Park. For wider consumption, it had been served up as coming from a mysterious all-seeing agent called 'Most Secret Source' (MSS), of whose existence the enemy must never know and whose discoveries must be seen to have been made by other means. As an American code-breaker on a revelatory induction to the Park in summer 1943 noted: '[It must be] ensured that operational action is never obviously undertaken from information solely derived in signals from BP. [The Park's representative] must insist that reconnaissance be made evident to the enemy so as to make it appear that the action taken was based on this ... and not upon MSS.' That stricture applied to the V-weapons.

The great secret had been tightly held throughout. With the war over, there was no imperative to reveal Ultra – in fact, quite the opposite. It had contributed immeasurably to the defeat of the Axis powers, and now it was the Soviets and their satellites that might be similarly snooped upon. To some it might look like cheating – eavesdropping, hoaxes, plants, black propaganda, disinformation, double agents – Don't mention *this* war. If you do, you face an in camera prosecution under the Official Secrets Act. One arena was especially difficult to police: stories from the war fought by resistance groups who had been aided by the Special Operations Executive (SOE). Such stories started appearing from 1945 onwards, in particular from French and Polish sources, and were clandestinely promoted by Whitehall whenever they countered the narrative that the only effective resistance to the Nazis had been organised by the Communists.

One outlet for such yarns was the *Now It Can Be Told* drama-documentary series that went out on Sunday nights via the Home Service of the BBC and was syndicated around the world. Number 16, broadcast on 28 February 1951, revealed how 'British Intelligence' learned from Polish 'housemaids' about the supposed secret weapons development base at Peenemünde in the Baltic, thus priming the RAF attack against it on the night of 18–19 August 1943.

The script was written by the spy novelist Bernard Newman, who would bring out a strange book in 1952 called *They Saved London*, part fact, part fiction, that included the story of how Poles of the London-backed Home Army got information about long-range weapon experiments to Whitehall. In the book the cleaning girls of his BBC radio play were supplanted by the forced labourers 'Tadeusz' and 'Stefan', who found secret plans while working as latrine cleaners at Peenemünde.*

In fact some of the truth had been made public five years earlier, in February 1947, when an obscure academic called Dr Jones had given a well-attended lecture on 'scientific intelligence' at the Royal United Services Institute in Whitehall. The lecture offered a fleeting glimpse into some very unusual wartime goings-on, and was printed in the *RUSI Journal* and summarised in *The Times*. Dr Jones had revealed details of the 'Oslo report' (see p. 39), the battle against German night-bomber navigation systems in 1940–1 and the Bruneval raid, when components of the Wurzburg night fighter control radar were snatched in a daring raid on a French coastal station. And he also gave his audience, for the first time, a glimpse into the feuds that had smouldered in London in early 1943 concerning the threat of attack by novel weapons:

> Another intelligence section, while correctly interpreting the early intelligence reports as indicating a long range weapon, nevertheless caused unending trouble by 'barking' too soon.
>
> As a result ... it was widely believed in May, 1943, that London would within a few weeks be attacked by rockets weighing 80 tons with a 10-ton warhead. We, having the same facts, had raised no alarm at all ... The thing to do was to seek fresh facts ...

---

* After years of misinformation the contribution that Polish patriots made to alerting London is covered in 'Polish Intelligence and the German Secret Weapons' (chapter 48) by Rafal Wnuk in the monumental *Intelligence Co-operation Between Poland and Great Britain* (2005).

By a very long shot* we got right into the heart of German long range weapon development ... Peenemünde was photographed from the air and secret agents were insinuated into the army of foreign workers at that place.

Thus it was that the narrative that emerged about one of the most dramatic episodes of the war had a deception at its heart. Ultra was completely excised from it, and it would stay that way for decades. Churchill's account of 'German secret weapons' in volume 5 of his semi-autobiographical history of the war (published in 1951) gave no hint. And nor did *The Official History of the Defence of the United Kingdom* that appeared six years later (after much internal Cabinet Office anguish about the depiction of a certain politician's role).

Like the official historians, the former wartime Prime Minister had to grumpily submit his huge manuscript in instalments to a security committee. Churchill, unlike other senior figures of the wartime leadership, had been indoctrinated into the great secret from the start. He knew what he might reveal and what he must not – as was the case with those from whom he had solicited papers and recollections and the six-member team of writers, who actually completed his own epic history of the war.

The V-weapon chapter in Churchill's volume 5 had originally been drafted by Duncan Sandys, his politician son-in-law, who had been in charge of the committee responsible for counter-measures. His effort was not quite up to it, so Reginald Jones was brought in. In spring 1951 the seventy-seven-year-old Churchill sent him the draft manuscript for comment and corrections, eliciting a detailed fifteen-page response in which references to Ultra had been blanked out – but it was clear from the context what was intended. Jones said this: 'We in scientific intelligence had pretty rough handling in this period ... and I was very glad that in spite of it all, we came so near the truth.' Churchill understood.

This stately approach was applied both to those accounts

---

* The CIA website posts the 1947 lecture as 'a classic of intelligence'. The apparently all-seeing US agency footnotes this line: 'We have no information on the nature of this "very long shot".'

officially laid down by the approved historians and to those given, with careful vetting, by high military and political leaders; and it was all rather dull.

Meanwhile, an unlikely popular hero had emerged, the cardigan-wearing boffin exemplified by the actor Michael Redgrave's depiction of the bouncing-bomb designer Dr Barnes Wallis in *The Dam Busters*, the biggest British cinema box-office hit of 1955. The element of cleverness was all-important. If torching German cities by firestorm was difficult to depict as clever – which it certainly was – then flooding the Lower Ruhr valley by means of innovative aerial attack could be made to seem so. Water was so much more sporting than fire.

In America, in the meantime, a different story was being told. The rocket scientists snatched from central Germany in 1945 and spirited to the US to work on military rockets were now stepping into the limelight as patriots whose work was essential to the Free World. Wernher von Braun was now a lovable eccentric, known to children as 'Doctor Space'. It was said he got more fan mail than Elvis, and he was a friend of Walt Disney. Von Braun frenzy peaked in January 1958, when Explorer I, the Soviet Sputnik-trumping satellite, was sent into orbit atop a multi-stage booster rocket. Patriotic family magazines ran glowing biographies, telling how 'von Braun and his fellow rocketeers outsmarted both the Nazis and the Russians, to surrender themselves and their scientific know-how to the Americans'. A Hollywood biopic of the aristocratic rocket scientist was in pre-production (the Pentagon was fully cooperating), called *I Aim for the Stars*.

Fifteen years since the last V2 fell on London, the revenge-weapon story was thus being wrapped up in a double layer of misinformation: the rocket scientists had been anti-Nazis, diverted from their dream of space travel, while their destructive wartime plans had been scuppered by intelligence gathered by gallant Allied agents and photo-reconnaissance.

The dilemma of the professors-who-knew-too-much was exquisite, and for Bimbo and Reg the temptations mounted. The real story was going to come out, surely? And so it almost did. On 20 January 1958 Professor Frederick Norman wrote on King's College headed paper to his former wartime colleague:

Dear Reg

I have just come back from Berlin. Sitting in the train
yesterday I opened a German rag and what should I find . . .
You occur on page 3 at a famous Cabinet meeting when we
decided to bomb Peenemünde. Your antagonist is said to be
the dear old Prof. There is much nonsense in this article but
there is a great deal that puzzles me.

Where could the authors possibly have got their
information? They know about Duncan Sandys though they
do not know that he joined us much later and what a damned
nuisance he was.

You will see an extremely sympathetic photograph of a fat
chap looking rather like me, namely our old friend Col.
Wachtel. They know that he had four names during the war
which you will remember was a bit of a puzzler and they tell
us that he is head of Hamburg airport. I feel very much
inclined to go to Germany and have a talk with the old boy. It
would be great fun.

Colonel Wachtel was indeed an old friend. Jones and Norman had
had their first encounter with him in 1943 when he popped up in
an agent's report from Paris. He was the Luftwaffe officer who had
been charged with nothing less than the destruction of London.

The 'dear old Prof' – the eminent physicist Professor Frederick
Alexander Lindemann, Lord Cherwell from 1941 – had been
Jones's mentor at Oxford and involved in pre-war research on air
defence. After his death in 1957, his reputation came in for a hammering. According to one wartime contemporary, 'He had an
almost pathological unsoundness of judgment . . . if two versions
were possible he almost invariably supported the wrong one.' But
he got one thing right: 'His support of R. V. Jones was probably the
most useful thing he did during the war.'

And Duncan Sandys? At the time of Professor Norman's letter
he was the fifty-year-old Conservative MP for Streatham, Minister
of Defence in Harold Macmillan's government and latterly the
force behind a radical review of Britain's defence strategy which
predicated much on the dominance of guided missiles. And
indeed, fifteen years before, he had been a damned nuisance.

The Professor's letter continued: 'Who is Babington Smith? Is this perhaps the child we had at Kingsdown [a wireless intercept station in Kent] whose name certainly ended in –ington?'

Constance Babington Smith was no child. Born in 1912, she was the offspring of an eminent Edwardian civil servant and the aristocratic daughter of the Viceroy of India (to whom Papa had been private secretary). She had already caused a small sensation when the year before, in 1957, she published her wartime memoir of service as a flight officer in the Women's Auxiliary Air Force. The book was called *Evidence in Camera* and was about intelligence gleaned by poring over images secured by aerial reconnaissance at the Central Interpretation Unit (CIU) based at Danesfield House, at Medmenham in Buckinghamshire. She had been a photographic interpreter (PI) in the Aircraft Section, looking for new Luftwaffe technical developments. It was a bestseller.

Miss Babington Smith's story had also been a big hit in America, where it had been serialised in *Life* magazine, for which she had worked in the immediate post-war years. The award of the US Legion of Merit in 1946 had brought newspaper claims on both sides of the Atlantic that not only had she delayed 'the full force of the V1 attack [on London] for six months', but that she had saved New York City from a similar fate. Babs had won the war on her own. There had been much tut-tutting at the time by those in the know. This time her editors had chosen the exciting bits about the detection from the air of 'German V-Bombs' and other 'secret weapons'. Her writing read like a film script of the period, turning an arcane and solitary preoccupation into intense human drama. Furthermore, the entrepreneurial publishers of the journal that so excited Professor Norman in Berlin had lifted Miss Babington Smith's revelations about 'Nazi V-bombs', added a dash of the von Braun eulogies now appearing in the American press and gone in search of German participants in the story, now in middle age, with whose reminiscences they might intercut. One of them was Luftwaffe Colonel Max Wachtel, the 'fat chap' that Professor Norman thought it would be great fun to look up in Hamburg.

Norman was gripped by these latest revelations. He told Jones on 4 February: 'The second instalment stops at the exciting moment when Wachtel flying his Heinkel up to his ski sites [missile launchers] is suddenly diverted to Paris by a wireless message saying that a mysterious English Colonel by the name of Kenney [sic] is after him. I have never heard of Kenney. Who is he? I don't suppose you have either.' The story was getting a bit garbled. Flight Lieutenant André Kenny was a Medmenham photo interpreter, head of the Industrial Section which looked for factories to bomb. In autumn 1943 he was indeed after the colonel, but only in a metaphorical sense. After the war, Wachtel and Kenny would encounter each other in the most unusual circumstances.

A week later, Professor Norman awoke with the mildest of hangovers after an agreeable dinner with Professor Jones the night before, and made his way to Soho where he bought the latest issue of the German news magazine in a Continental newsagent. There was more about Wachtel and his V-weapons. This time the professor could not restrain his excitement. He dispatched an urgent note to his friend suggesting 'a book by you with possibly me as a minor star would not be an unattractive selling proposition. I am sure we could get round the Official Secrets Act … Perhaps we could meet sometime and plan an outline.'

More episodes appeared – 'Getting a little dreary, not much new,' commented Professor Norman. 'The story of the interference of the Gestapo and the arrest of various people is largely taken from Dornberger's book,' he said. (Walter Dornberger's own memoir *V2 – Der Schuss ins Weltall* ('The Shot into Space') had been published in Germany in 1952, and in translation. It was the first published account by a major participant in the Nazi-secret-weapons saga and became an instant classic.

'The thing has fizzled out and these journalists obviously don't know much,' Professor Norman concluded. It was then that he suggested they should go public, bank the cash and take the rap. And what a story it would have made! But of course they could not tell it – not yet, anyway.

CHAPTER 4

London, autumn 1939

Reg Jones and Bimbo Norman had gone into business together in the earliest days of the war. It was Adolf Hitler who did the match-making, when on 19 September 1939 the Führer broadcast a speech in Danzig announcing, it seemed, that he was 'sitting' in some sort of weapon within which he could not be attacked. Or perhaps he had a weapon 'against which no defence would avail'. There was great confusion in London about just what was meant. 'Hitler's Secret Weapon' became a big news story, to be debunked by the popular press and music-hall acts as best they might.

For many years, 'future war' fiction writers – and politicians – had assumed that a conflict would begin with cataclysmic gas and bomb attacks on cities, delivered from the skies. So when nothing more terrifying than Heinkel He 111 bombers came up the Thames estuary late that year, it was time for general hilarity. From their exquisitely remote viewpoint, *Astronautics*, the journal of the American Rocket Society of New York, commented: 'Adolph Hitler ... in a recent speech remarked that if the war continued, Germany would have access to a weapon now under development that would not be available to other nations. Rocket experimenters naturally wonder if that is not an allusion to military rockets.'

Very soon after the outbreak of war, Dr R. V. Jones had found himself attached to AI1(c), the Air Ministry section run by the energetic Wing Commander F. W. Winterbotham, responsible for liaison with the Secret Intelligence Service (MI6). After Hitler's Danzig speech, the section had been asked by the Prime Minister Neville Chamberlain to find out what his mysterious 'weapon' might be. Winterbotham gave the task to Jones. As the physicist would reveal later: 'This was a great stroke of luck ... I was taken to the very heart of Intelligence and its secrets were laid bare to me. After a day or two at MI6 headquarters at 54 Broadway [Westminster] I was told to go to Bletchley Park ... which was to be the evacuation headquarters of MI6 and where all its pre-war files now rested.'

And so Dr Jones was one of the Park's earliest adepts. His memoir continued: 'The following day I found myself sitting opposite a decidedly excitable professor of German who turned out to be Frederick Norman of King's College ... he seemed to have no technical knowledge whatsoever.' Jones then went through MI6's pre-war files on mysterious rays, bacteria bombs and gas clouds that stopped aero-engines. Older hands in the service remembered the time a decade before when the eccentric inventor Harry Grindell-Matthews had promoted his 'death ray' to bemused officials.* Jones discovered from the files that the service was itself funding the development of a 'death ray', one by an inventor who, after much trying, could not quite get his device to work. In intelligence circles, scepticism about 'secret weapons' was, unsurprisingly, high.

Jones managed to get a recording of Hitler's Danzig speech from the BBC. He could not speak German, so asked Norman what it meant. Writing at the end of the war (in the third person) the language scholar said: 'It was possible to prove by linguistic parallels that Hitler was talking Austro-Bavarian dialect and not German. The famous weapon he was talking about was nothing more than the Luftwaffe. What Jones and Norman did not realise at the time was that this, their earliest collaboration, was destined to grow into a linguistic/scientific collaboration that would last until VE-Day.'

---

* Having had his death ray turned down, the inventor took up a new obsession, having joined the British Interplanetary Society – promoting his space-travelling 'stratoplane', to general official disinterest.

Ensconced in MI6 headquarters in London, with a line to Frederick Norman at the Park, Reginald Jones of AI1(c) became a Whitehall clearing-house for all kinds of interservice scientific intelligence. Thus it was that a report about some sort of 'rocket shell' being developed by a certain Professor Schmidz came his way on 17 October 1939. As with the 'death ray', there were agent reports in the files on German experiments with 'gliding bombs and pilotless aircraft' going back to 1937. 'A long range rocket to be aimed at England from the Rhineland is within the bounds of possibility,' Dr Jones reported. Britain itself was working on anti-aircraft rockets he pointed out, 'and these had already been tested at a range in the West Indies'. If the Germans were testing such a device then some might surely have strayed, but perhaps they would be taken to be falling meteorites, he suggested. Sir Henry Tizard, chairman of the Air Defence Committee, minuted on the file that a practical long-range rocket weapon would be more of a danger to Germany than to Britain.

Two weeks later Wing Commander Winterbotham came into Jones's office with a small parcel forwarded by the Admiralty. It contained seven sheets of typescript and a box with a glass tube inside, a bit like a radio valve. The story of the parcel's provenance was as strange as its contents.

At the beginning of November the naval attaché at the British embassy in Oslo, fifty-eight-year-old Rear Admiral Hector Boyes RN, had found a letter in his mailbox asking whether the British would like to receive information on technical research going on in Germany. On 4 November a parcel was left on a window ledge outside the embassy, at Drammensveien 79, a fine old house in neoclassical style screened by plane trees. The German Legation was across the way. The parcel contained a technical manual within which was the short page typescript in German and the valve (it would turn out to be a prototype proximity fuse).

The document was flown to London, where it was translated at the Admiralty by a Mr W. Todhunter for the attention of a Mr Knight. Then it reached Dr Jones. It was a strange mix of ama-teurish gossip and the very precise details of an electronic apparatus. The document said: 'Remote-controlled missiles (or projectiles). The Heereswaffenamt is the [weapons] development centre for the Army. This centre is developing missiles of 80 cm calibre. Rocket propulsion is used; stabilization is by means of built-in gyroscopes.' The German navy, it said, was to be working on 'remote control gliders. The code number is FZ 21 ... The test site is at Peenemünde, at the mouth of the river Peene, near Wolgast in the vicinity of Greifswald.'

It seemed too good to be true, and the service ministries in London all declared it to be a hoax. The Admiralty was especially hostile. It was propaganda. How could a single person know so much? The Oslo report, in its few cyclostyled copies, went into Whitehall incinerators. At the end of 1939 Jones filed his copy away. There were immediate perils to face, acoustic-fused torpedoes, beam-guided night bombers. What might be significant about some test site 'in the vicinity of Greifswald'?

But Peenemünde was real. By the time the Oslo report was written, it was the well-established centre of some very secret military developments. Since 1935 the windblown site had been the ever expanding home of army weapons experiments.

The early rocket work had been done at a gunnery range at Kummersdorf, south of Berlin. But within a couple of years it had become too constricted – somewhere big and remote was needed.

While he was visiting his parents in Silesia in 1936, Wernher von Braun's mother had suggested he look at the wilderness around Peenemünde. She told him her own father used to go duck-hunting there on her von Quistorp family estates. Various uncles lived conveniently nearby. It would be perfect for his rocket experiments – they could make as many bangs as they liked. As Walter Dornberger wrote:

> The place was far from any large town. Pomeranian deer with dark antlers roamed through the bilberry bushes ... swarms of duck, crested grebes and swans inhabited this beautiful spot ... We had an immeasurable advantage in the shape of a small island which faced the Peene estuary, the Greifswalder Oie. There we could carry out our experiments unnoticed throughout the year. We had a firing range of over 250 miles seaward along the Pomeranian coast.

In April 1936 General Karl Emil Becker, head of the army Waffenamt (weapons department), met the Luftwaffe commander Albert Kesselring with Dornberger and von Braun to agree on the acquisition and joint development of Peenemünde. That August the first construction workers arrived to lay roads and make an airstrip. The fishing village of Peene was evacuated. The first 350 technicians moved from Kummersdorf to the Baltic at the end of April 1937. The Heeresversuchsanstalt-Peenemünde, the army experimental establishment, was in business, with von Braun as technical director, while Dornberger, a soldier not a scientist, stayed as head of the Waffen Prüf Amt (weapons development office) 10, in charge of army guided-missile development and with his primary office in Berlin.

The establishment began to spread mainly along the eastern shore of the island. Usedom was separated from the mainland by the Stettin lagoon to the south, the Peene River to the west and the Swine Channel to the east at Swinemünde, but was accessible by three closely guarded bridges. North of the small resort village of Karlshagen, new housing for three thousand elite workers and their families was to be built in garden-city style. To the north were the experimental works with laboratories and workshops, which would become more familiarly known as Peenemünde-Ost (East). On the sandy meadows of the western tip of the peninsula a full-size airfield was laid out – Peenemünde-West. (It would also be known as the Luftwaffe (Karlshagen) Erprobungsstelle [experimental station].)

A big coal-powered electricity-generating plant was built on the west side of the peninsula. Along the eastern shore between the strand and the trees nine test stands (*Prüfstände*) were built, the most important of which was test stand VII, surrounded by an oval earth wall to provide a windbreak against the Baltic storms.

Here was more than a weapons-testing range. It was a model of Aryan genius, a community of elite weapon designers in the service of the National Socialist state. The closed science city would become a staple of the twentieth-century imagination. An architect was appointed, Hannes Luehrsen, and a generous budget allocated. Luehrsen raised the assembly building, power plant, liquid-oxygen plant and laboratories in functional red brick, while lavishing a pitched-roof whimsicality on the the housing estate.

Eventually a Berlin-style S-Bahn electric railway would link the miniature suburb with the burgeoning rocketeering complex, all the way to the resort of Zinnowitz outside the southern security boundary to where the state railway (the *Reichsbahn*) ran a branch line.

Once this area had been the Reich's Riviera, a place of genteel bathing resorts, white stucco hotels and villas where families would gather on the beach, sheltering in their ornate beach chairs from the Baltic wind that sent the Imperial flags staked in the sand fluttering. In 1936, on the nearby island of Rügen, construction of the extraordinary monumental resort of KdF-Bad Prora began, five kilometres of brutalist concrete apartment blocks facing the sea, designed as a 'strength through joy' (the Nazi 'holiday' organisation) camp to reward deserving workers.

But the research centre on Usedom was a place of intense scientific purpose. The German army's rockets were at the forefront of technology. It was not just the development of the liquid-fuelled motor, mixing propellant with an oxidant, that had brought back to life the ancient idea of a military rocket, a projectile that propelled itself with an on-board thrust source. It was the simultaneous advent of new testing technologies – the photo-theodolite, for example – that could be used for measuring precise distances and elevation angles of a body in flight; while wind-tunnel droplet photography could be used to explore the ideal aerodynamic shape of high-speed vehicles.

Guidance control was the key. Without the spin imparted to an artillery shell fired from a gun, how could a rocket's flight be stabilised? Radio control was one way, as was a development of the gyroscope-based 'autopilot', which by the late 1930s was an everyday aviation reality. The A-3 experimental rocket of 1937 had a three-axis gyroscopic assembly (developed by Kreiselgeräte (Gyro Devices) of Berlin) which controlled rudders acting in the rocket's jet stream plus additional rudder actuators on the stabiliser fins. This was a principle that British intelligence failed to grasp until almost the eve of the attack on London, seven years later. There was also an on-board electric power system plus a radio receiver, which allowed engine shut-off by command from the ground.

It was very clever, except that it didn't work. In summer 1937 four attempted A-3 launches in a row from the Greifswalder Oie went wrong, toppling in the wind or prematurely ejecting the parachute. The gyro was not up to it. To test a new control system, a new – A-5 – rocket was proposed, while the designation A-4 was reserved for an operational military projectile. Meanwhile, a sophisticated wind tunnel which would ultimately simulate a flight speed of Mach 4+ was built in the laboratory area of Peenemünde-Ost.

The rocket programme had its opponents in Berlin. It was all hugely expensive. Who were these dreamers sunbathing by the sea? Fritz Todt, Minister for Armaments (until his death in an aircraft crash in February 1942), would write disapprovingly to General Fromm, head of army weapon development: 'In Peenemünde they have created a paradise. The accommodations, the social provisions, clubs and apartments, factory halls, warehouses, all exhibit the highest degree of expense that one can possibly imagine.'

The rocketeers had to fight for political favour at the highest level. On 23 March 1939 the Führer was invited to Kummersdorf to see a static motor test. Dornberger recorded meeting Hitler 'on a cloudy overcast day with water dripping from the rain drenched pines ... while I spoke he kept his eyes fixed on me. I still don't know whether he understood what I was talking about. Certainly he was the only visitor who had ever listened to me without asking questions.' The rocket motor fired, but in spite of the majesty of the demonstration, 'the radiating shock waves, the luminous colours, the thunderous rumble of power', Hitler was not impressed.

Over lunch in the mess afterwards at which he ate mixed vegetables and drank Fachingen mineral water, the Führer chatted with General Becker. 'He asked casually about how long it had taken to develop; and about the range.' He said he had known the rocket pioneer–showman Max Valier in Munich, Dornberger recorded. Hitler described him as 'a dreamer'. And that was it.

Hermann Goering, head of the Luftwaffe, was treated to the same rocket show a few weeks later, and was 'laughing and roaring, full of fantastic prophecies'. The Reichsmarschall's dreams were certainly not about space travel. The A-5, next in the experimental series, was to be a pilot for the A-4, the war rocket. It built on the A-3 experience but with a more robust guidance control from the Siemens Company of Berlin.

In Germany's time of triumph from 1939 onwards, Peenemünde pottered away, remote from events, its priority to the Nazi weapons-state slipping. The head of the army, Generalfeldmarschall Walther von Brauchitsch, kept it afloat by finding funding for a 'smoke trial device'. Heinrich Himmler kept an eye on the goings-on. As a token of his interest, he sent an SS-Standartenführer (Colonel) Müller from Greifswald to see Wernher von Braun on 1 May 1940, bearing his personal offer of the honorary rank of Untersturmführer in the SS. The scientist did not refuse.

There was enough funding, meanwhile, to progress from the experimental A-5 towards the planned-to-be-operational A-4. The rocket motor presented the outstanding problem: how to produce more power by getting more fuel to the combustion chamber in less time. The existing method, using pressurised tanks to feed in liquid oxygen and alcohol via valves, was insufficient. Dr Walter Thiel's breakthrough was to use a second motor to achieve the necessary surge, a turbo-pump using steam derived from the catalytic decomposition of hydrogen peroxide. The Helmuth Walter Company at Kiel was already experimenting with this system for U-Boat propulsion. The clever pump with the gyro-controlled jet rudders would be the key to the rocket.

The German air force watched the army's progress on its long-range weapons systems with a growing jealousy. After an initial sweeping tactical success, by 1940 it had failed to subdue Britain. From summer 1941 its attention focused on the Balkans and the Soviet Union. Novel technologies continued to be explored at Peenemünde, meanwhile, including jet and rocket propulsion, but the concept of a cheap, throw-away bombardment system was to come from outside the air force.

Paul Schmidt, a Munich-based inventor, had promoted an improved version of the pulse-jet principle, known since the early twentieth century. The Argus motor company took it up under its director Dr Fritz Gosslau, and in April 1941 it was tested, mounted under a Gotha Go 145 biplane, at Peenemünde-West. What was to be made of this very noisy device that would run on any grade of fuel but would only last an hour or so before its shutter array burned out? It also needed an initial kick to get any airframe airborne. The Argus Company sent a proposal for a remote-controlled aircraft carrying a payload of 1000 kilograms over a distance of 500 kilometres to the technical office of the Reich Air Ministry, the Reichsluftministerium, in Berlin. It was filed and forgotten.

Hitler had not forgotten his visit to Kummersdorf. On 20 August 1941, Walter Dornberger showed him a film of the progress achieved thus far at Peenemünde with the rockets. The Führer, warming to the project, fantasised about hundreds of thousands of such devices bringing the absurdly defiant enemy across the Channel to heel. On 15 September the rocket was awarded a degree of spending priority for development work and pilot production. The goings-on by the Baltic went up a gear.

Professors were tipped off to send their best graduates to attend interviews for places at an 'electromechanical institute somewhere in northern Germany'. It was all rather jolly by the sea. There were four cinemas on Usedom. The one at Karlshagen 'showed old films with nothing to do with the war', and Zinnowitz had retained its bourgeois charm. There were 'festive parties at the houses and hotels' where waiters in white tie tended tables of revellers with starched napkins. A military unit, the Versuchs Kommando Nord (VKN) was established to bring the scientific incomers under some sort of discipline. They were housed in the former KdF camp at Karlshagen, the layout of whose distinctive horseshoe-shaped site would show up clearly on later reconnaissance photographs.

But few were aware that the good life by the Baltic depended on the brutal exploitation of others. Since 1940 a thousand Polish workers employed by the Organisation Todt (construction corps) had sweated blood to get the rocket stands functioning, and their numbers were increasing. They were first housed in a group of huts near the VKN barracks at Karlshagen, then from 1942 in a much bigger, guarded camp near the village of Trassenheide. The semi-prisoners managed to form a band and hold dances, which the Polish girls working on farms around were allowed to attend, though the signs on the nearby beach read 'No Poles or Dogs'. At Wolgast on the mainland there were three hundred Soviet army prisoners, some of them technical specialists who were set to work on blueprint-drafting and electronic assembly or employed in the graphite shop making the servo-controlled jet rudders.

By 25 February 1942, the first test rocket was complete. On

18 March the A-4/V1 was wheeled out, featuring a steel corset to fix the missile to the test stand. But when freezing liquid oxygen was pumped in, the metal contracted, the missile slipped, then crumpled in a heap. Undaunted, Dornberger wrote a memo to the High Command headed 'Proposals for Employment of the Long-Range Rocket'. It referred to London as a 'profitable target ... the moral and physical effects of such a defenceless bombardment over a number of months cannot be stressed enough'. London, the sprawling imperial city, with its millions of people now within rocket range of German-occupied territory – and the enemy did not even know about the missile's existence! What a glorious opportunity for the German army! Dornberger's paper spoke of finishing the war. No one in Berlin paid it much attention.

Then the Royal Air Force intervened.

Lübeck, north Germany, 28–29 March 1942

On a cold, moonlit spring night in 1942, over 240 RAF bombers attacked the city of Lübeck. The raid was artfully planned. Blast bombs took the roofs off the humpbacked streets of the old town, then incendiaries rained into the exposed interiors. Beautiful, venerable Lübeck was hollowed out by fire.

The city had no real significance as a target. It was attacked because the area bombing directive issued by the British Air Staff on 14 February had focused on 'attacking the morale of the enemy civil population'. The enterprise was backed by Professor Lindemann's statistics-based rationale for 'dehousing' the German working class and thus crippling the country's war production. Lübeck was chosen because it was built of wood and was close to the coast and thus easy to find.

The German leadership was chastened. According to Joseph Goebbels's diary: 'The Führer ... absolutely shares my view that ... it is now necessary to return terror for terror. There is no other way to bring the English back to reason.' That word 'terror' would become ever more significant.

On 23–24 April the 'Baedeker raids', named after the famous tourist guide books, were launched by Luftwaffe medium-range bombers. These raids were *Vergeltungsangriffe*, 'revenge attacks', on historic British cities, and were laden, like the raids on Lübeck, with cultural baggage. They had no military–industrial purpose.

Hitler clearly had even more destructive visions. On 14 April he ordered 'terror attacks of a retaliatory nature' – five thousand rockets to be fired in one salvo – plus the production of fifty thousand more thereafter. And the Luftwaffe was not to be left out. After Lübeck, the Air Ministry woke up to the Argus pulse-jet-powered device and asked for a new proposal for the 'distance firing' project, which was submitted in June 1942 with an airframe designed by Robert Lusser of the Fieseler company of Kassel and an autopilot from the Askania company of Berlin. On 12 June development of the Fi 103, as it was now type-named, was given high priority by Feldmarschall Erhard Milch, Secretary of State for Aircraft Production, after a 'rough drawing' had been submitted. It was codenamed 'Kirschkern' (Cherrystone).*

The trials were to be conducted at Peenemünde-West. At the north corner of the airfield just behind the foreshore a launching site was cleared, pointing out to sea, for launches parallel to the coast. The Rheinmetall-Borsig company was commissioned to make a rocket sled catapult to achieve the 15G punch needed to get the little Fi 103, with its stubby wings, into the air.

By 30 August 1942 a prototype fuselage was complete, and the first unpowered flight of the Fi 103 V7 took place on 10 December when it was air-dropped over Peenemünde-West by an Fw 200 Kondor patrol bomber. On Christmas Eve, late in the afternoon, the first ground-launched bomb was shot into the air by a battery of six solid-fuel rockets. With the Argus duct running at full power the rockets accelerated the sled carrying the bomb up the ramp. Then the bomb departed, gained a bit of height, flew a short distance and fell into the sea. The sled had disintegrated. It was regarded as a success, all the same.

---

* The German 'flying bomb' would be given multiple names on both sides. To British officialdom it was the 'pilotless aircraft', 'PAC', 'Fly' and 'Diver'. To Londoners it was the 'doodlebug'. To Americans, the 'buzz-bomb'. Pursuing pilots had all sorts of names for it, including some very rude ones. To the Germans it was the Fieseler Fi 103, Flak Zielgerät 76 (FZG 76), Maikäfer (Maybug), Krähe (Crow) and eventually Vergeltungswaffe Eins or V1 (Revenge Weapon One).

Army Research Centre, Peenemünde-Ost, October 1942

Nothing would go right with the rocket. Three launches during the summer were spectacular flops. On 16 August, shortly after midday, A-4/V3 rose ponderously from rest stand 7, broke the sound barrier and then, after a forty-five-second flight, the engine suddenly stopped. The newly appointed armaments minister, Albert Speer, was due to witness the shoot, but he was late and glimpsed the doomed demonstration as his aircraft was coming into Karlshagen airfield. They would try again.

On 3 October, A-4/V4 stood ready on test stand 7, painted black and white for the camera telemetry, a semi-nude woman in black stockings swinging on a new moon emblazoned at its base. *Frau im Mond.* At two minutes before four in the afternoon, the rocket lifted off – and this time flew straight until all that was visible was a glowing dot at the end of a white exhaust plume. At fifty-eight seconds the radio signal for *Brennschluss*, engine shutdown, was transmitted.

A-4/V4 plunged into the sea about 190 kilometres down-range, having brushed the edge of space at an altitude of nearly 80 kilometres. The guidance expert Ernst Steinhoff was already airborne in a Heinkel He 111, looking for the patch of green in the darkening Baltic. They found it after an hour. It was just ten kilometres from its computed point of impact. That night Dornberger held a little party; the toast was 'To space travel'. Thirteen misfires followed, and it looked as if the rocket was going nowhere again.

On 11 December Heinrich Himmler visited Peenemünde for the first time. Leather-coated against the Baltic chill, he arrived by aircraft. About four seconds after ignition, A-4/V9 rose from test stand 7, toppled and exploded. The party retired to the snug in the officers' club, and according to Dornberger's account Himmler told him: 'Soon your work will become the concern of the German people and no longer the affair of the Army Weapons Office ... The Führer is about to give your project his support and that is why I came ... I will protect it from sabotage and treason.'

Hitler's mood at this time was conditioned by affairs far to the east where the cataclysm of the siege of Stalingrad was about to reach its climax. Hitler's army adjutant, Gerhard Engel, reported a conference with the Führer, Speer and the chief of the Oberkommando der Wehrmacht (The Supreme Command of the Armed Forces) Field Marshal Keitel on 18 December, when he 'seriously wonder[ed] whether one should spend money on play and rubbish, war is too serious for playing around ... he would prefer one hundred fighter planes and five hundred tanks to one rocket'.

Dornberger was convinced that if he could only see Hitler personally, then the project would take off. 'I expected that Speer, a special favourite of Hitler's, would be able to persuade the Führer to come to a decision,' he wrote later. Or perhaps Himmler might intercede.

The A-4 and the 'Cherrystone' were still far from being practical weapons. But it might be assumed that they soon would be, and that forces would be raised and trained to operate them. From where and how would the rocket be fired? Proposals for gigantic bunkers began circulating. Von Braun liked it – an extension of men in white coats in a laboratory, only buried under ground. Dornberger favoured the concept of mobile launchers, which would shoot and move like artillery. Hitler, meanwhile, had been shown by Speer a curious cardboard model of a giant bunker, and he leapt at it.

On 22 December 1942 Lt-Colonel Georg Thom, Dornberger's chief of staff, and Dr Steinhoff were ordered by Speer to reconnoitre northern France for suitable sites. More definitive bunker models were constructed at Peenemünde to 1:100 scale, along with miniatures of the proposed motorised detachments with their prime movers, command vehicles and special trailer-erectors, the design of which was already in hand.

The Luftwaffe got in on the bunker building. Unlike A-4, the Cherrystones were tied to ground catapults anyway (much later some would be dropped from converted bomber aircraft). Feldmarschall Milch was keen on gigantic bomb-proof installations (he knew that Hitler would approve) as well as on dispersed launching sites. A compromise was reached. The initial air force plan envisaged six big bunkers grouped in the Pas-de-Calais and on the Cotentin peninsula in the west, plus between thirty and fifty smaller field sites extending in an arc across northern France and with London and Britain's south coast ports in range.

During Christmas leave in Berlin, Speer told Dornberger about the great bunker plan, but his little models of mobile launchers seemed far less impressive. Meanwhile, the test launch programme had been sputtering on by the Baltic. On 8 January 1943 Dornberger was suddenly summoned back to the capital and introduced to the man who was going to galvanise the whole programme and propel the A-4 from an experiment into a mass-produced weapon that would win the war for Germany. His name was Gerhard Degenkolb, the industrial 'genius' who had transformed steam locomotive construction for the demands of war. Dornberger was appalled. His new master was 'completely bald with a spherical head, soft, loose cheeks, bull neck and fleshy lips [which] revealed a tendency towards good living and sensual pleasures,' he wrote. What he was really offended by, however, was the fact that he was a civilian. The relationship would be stormy.

As Dornberger realised, the rocket's progress depended entirely on the will of Adolf Hitler. A British army intelligence report compiled by MI14 at the end of the war would examine how 'Hitler's enthusiasm or lack of it' had influenced events in early 1943. It concluded that the Führer's whims 'reflected fairly closely the successes and setbacks which occurred at Peenemünde, while throughout the period there is more than a suggestion that his comprehension of the technical problems ... involved in a weapon of the originality and complexity of the A-4 was far from complete'. In early March, the report revealed, Speer had told Dornberger that 'the Führer had had a dream that the A-4 would never be used against England and accordingly had lost interest in the project'. It did not record the armaments minister's opinion on such metaphysical interventions.

Hitler's dream-induced indifference did not last long. He ordered a body called the Development Committee for Long-Range Bombardment – an umbrella organisation chaired by Professor Waldemar Petersen, the elderly former director of AEG – to decide on the continued development of one or other or both of the projects. Petersen was impressed by what he saw of the rocket. According to MI14, he had 'returned [from an inspection of Peenemünde] full of enthusiasm ... this appears to have had some effect, because on 29 March the Führer gave permission for the building of an A-4 launch bunker at a proposed site at Watten [in the Forêt d'Éperlecques, south-east of Calais]'.

In early April, the Speer ministry backed the Degenkolb programme. It was wildly ambitious, providing for the assembly by December 1943 of a monthly total of 900 A-4s at three factories – at Peenemünde itself, at the airship builders Luftschiffbau Zeppelin at Friedrichshafen on Lake Constance, and at the Henschel-Rax locomotive works at Wiener Neustadt in the Ostmark (the former Austria).

It was not to be. There were those in the line of fire who were waking up to what was coming London's way. There had been a leak.

CHAPTER 5

In the personal papers of Professor R. V. Jones there are two carbon flimsies of messages printed in blue ink on thin wartime Utility paper. They had come clattering out of a secure teleprinter at 54 Broadway, the headquarters of the Secret Intelligence Service in London, a few minutes apart late on the evening of Sunday 18 December 1942. It was the day Hitler had reportedly said that the war was too serious for playing around with toys like the rocket, the day the German attempt to break through and relieve the encircled Sixth Army at Stalingrad stalled, and the day the war on the Eastern Front turned.

The cables, from the SIS station chief in Stockholm, concerned more mundane affairs: gossip 'overheard' in a Berlin restaurant. But the arrival of the cables in London was also a turning point. The first message said:

> Source overheard conversation between professor Fauner of Berlin Technische Hochschule and engineer Stephan Szenassy on new German weapons. Weapon is a rocket containing five tons explosive with a maximum range of 200 kilometres with a danger area of 10 km square. Further limited details follow in bag but I am seeing source about January 6th. Please telegraph before that date any details you want asked.

The second flimsy gave the name of the source: Aage
Andreasen of Copenhagen. It is what Jones scribbled on the
second of them in pencil that is fascinating: 'This signal important – start of rocket flap.'*

The telegrams were indeed the start of what would be the most
tremendous rocket flap, though Jones did not know it when he first
got sight of them. He was, however, one of the very few people in
London who could see that the information might be significant.
The intelligence services employed him in two capacities: he was
both scientific adviser to the SIS ('IID' in the wartime military-
civil-service initialisms) and for the past two years had been
Assistant Director Intelligence [ADI] (Science) at the Air Ministry.
He was Ultra-enwised and knew its deepest secret.† When his
information was later presented to the War Cabinet, Mr Andreasen
would be described as 'a new source, a neutral armaments engineer'. He was a chemical engineer from Denmark who travelled
freely to Germany. The Secret Intelligence Service would give him
the codename 'Elgar', and great things were expected of him. But
his career as a spy would turn out to be turbulent.

Dr Jones did not have much to go on. The Berlin Technische
Hochschule reference was good – the institution was a centre of
primary research on new weapons for the Germany army. A
'rocket' containing five tons of explosive. That could not be
ignored. Just who the gossiping engineers in a Berlin café might be
was utterly mysterious.

On 1 January 1943 an amplification of the same overheard conversation came from Stockholm. There was further mention this
time of an 'automatic steering apparatus', which meant that the
previously mentioned rocket could be fired from a ship in the
roughest weather and that its 'course and range were determined
by a metal body inserted into it before firing'.

---

* The pencilled annotation seems to have been made when Dr Jones was clearing his ministry files after the war, when special papers were marked up and saved for the record. The
cables ended up unofficially in his personal possession, along with much else.
† Professor Norman got into big trouble in early 1942 when he very unofficially showed
Jones and his assistant Charles Frank a bombe in operation on a visit to the Park. In an
abject letter of apology to the Director, Norman said he had 'solemnly stressed that this was
the one big defeat the Germans had suffered and continued to suffer and if any one of them
opens his mouth on the subject they deserved to be boiled in oil'. Jones got the message.

Dr Jones's memoirs describe the receipt of the telegram (but not the identity of its author) and how it had 're-sensitised' his tiny scientific intelligence directorate to the possibility that the Germans were developing long-range rockets. He also explained his dilemma when presented with such material, which could only be verified with great difficulty, if at all. 'I regarded myself as a watchdog,' he wrote. 'If he barks too late it is fatal, but if he barks too early his master will get tired of responding to false alarms. My duty over the rocket was clear, to pursue the intelligence case energetically and let men in key positions know that we were on to something... which I did.' By his account, the first person he told about the intelligence from Stockholm was his old Oxford mentor, Professor Lindemann, by now Lord Cherwell and member of the Cabinet.

On 12 January there was another whisper from Sweden, this time from 'Source 36966', described as 'well versed in examining his informants and sifting their information'. The message said: 'The Germans have constructed a new factory at Peenemünde near Bornhoft where new weapons are constructed. Foreign workers are not allowed to work longer than two days on the same site. The new weapon is in the form of a rocket which has been seen fired from the testing ground. It has previously been tested somewhere in South America.' That last line was unhelpful.

The SIS digest of 8 February read: 'On the peninsula of Usedom near the island of Rügen a very large aerodrome is being built near the village of Wolgast. Tests are being made with rockets. One was seen to rise vertically and disappear in a horizontal direction.' Then six days later, 'from a neutral source': 'Experiments are being made at a big factory at Peenemünde west of Greifswald with a new rocket with a range of 100km which contains 10 tons of high explosive. These rockets will shortly be used from the French coast against England.' On receipt of such information SIS was expected to put it in the appropriate in-trays. As Dr Jones's memoirs explain: 'All the information that had come to me had also gone to the War Office and a very able intelligence officer there had come to the same conclusion that [Dr Charles] Frank and I had about the reality of rocket development.'

The army officer who raised the alarm was Captain (later Lt-Colonel) Matthew Pryor who worked for MI14, the branch of War

Office intelligence that dealt with German military organisation. But Captain Pryor, a TA artilleryman, was not going to bark until he had done some checking himself. Were there really rockets by the Baltic? He would obtain some photographs before declaring that there might be.

Photo-reconnaissance was an Air Ministry responsibility (up to 1939 it had been the preserve of the SIS). Two sections of its Intelligence Directorate, the PRU (photo-reconnaissance unit) and the PIU (photo-interpretation unit), were responsible for mounting the airborne camera-carrying missions and interpreting the resulting 'covers'.

A key figure at Medmenham was the pre-war aerial survey pilot Wing Commander Douglas Kendall, head of the Technical Control Section. Kendall was Ultra-cleared (the only one at Medmenham who was) and also received CX (agent) material in the highly secret briefing that came from Whitehall. The CIU had a sophisticated model-making and reprographic operation, and organised its efforts in specialised sections with ever more expert interpreters.

Its 'customers' were meant to apply to the Joint Photographic Reconnaissance Committee, a subcommittee of the JIC answerable to the chiefs, to get approval for a mission. But in the heat of action, according to the Medmenham photographic interpreter Ursula Powys-Lybbe, 'a by-pass route for requests came into existence, which allowed certain customers to approach Medmenham direct through the front door'. The surviving documentation is minimal, but this is clearly the route that Matthew Pryor took. In fact there had already been a cover of the area, made on 15 May 1942 (Sortie A/762) by a camera-carrying Spitfire sweeping eastward along the coast from Kiel to the seaplane base at Swinemünde. The pilot had turned on his cameras above Usedom. The images had been duly processed, eventually reaching Constance Babington Smith of the Aircraft Section for a third-stage search* for anything of interest that

---

* First phase was time-sensitive immediate intelligence on the presence of aircraft or mobile formations, initial bombing effects etc. Second phase, due out within twenty-four hours of a mission, looked at the scope of the whole day's operations. Third phase was specialist, comparative intelligence that might take weeks to produce.

she, as an expert on the Luftwaffe, might find. She recalled in her memoirs: 'Something unusual caught my eye. I stopped to take a look at some extraordinary circular embankments. I glanced quickly at the plot to see where it was and noticed the name Peenemünde. Then I looked at the prints again. I thought those don't belong to me ... someone must know all about them.'

The prints had been filed away along with an interpretation report noting 'heavy constructional work' and little else. Now they were re-examined, to show big circles in the ground with no explanation and 'a lattice crane over a trench'. It was time to take another look. The first deliberately targeted photo-reconnaissance of Peenemünde was thus made, on the British army's urging, on 19 January 1943. It showed the circles again, but the ground was covered in snow and there was no stereo pair – which would make a 3D image in a viewer.* 'Detailed interpretation was therefore difficult.'

On Pryor's urgent suggestion, Sortie N/756 was flown on 1 March – again with the sketchiest of briefings – to take another look. The third-stage interpretation was presented to the War Office on 27 March, calling particular attention to the three circular earthworks with what looked like 'scaffoldings rising at their centres'. The crane and trench were seen again, and it was noted that material was being dumped on a fan-shaped area of the foreshore seaward of the elliptical embankments by a pipe attached to a 'suction dredger'. The cover was admittedly 'poor and much obscured by cloud'. But a comparison of old with new imagery showed that several large buildings had been completed in the time that had elapsed. No rockets could be seen, or anything resembling what anyone in London might consider a rocket to look like. MI14 meanwhile issued more guidance on 19 March, suggesting unhelpfully that a search be made for a 'two stage compound rocket around 95 feet in length, total diameter 30 inches. It would be associated with some sort of projector with a length of 100 yards.'

As well as mentioning Peenemünde, several agent reports had referred to the French coast as the place from where whatever it was that might be being developed in the Baltic might be

---

* See Taylor Downing, *Spies in the Sky*, pp. 86–7, for the technique and importance of 3D stereoscopy in aerial reconnaissance.

launched. Captain Pryor had thought it worthwhile looking there as well. On 13 February he had urged the army section at Medmenham to watch the vast hinterland of northern France for 'projectors', which might be indicated by 'suspicious erections of rails or scaffolding'. It had been the start of a hunt that would expend a huge effort to find anything at all. With nothing certain by the Baltic, a wider search was pointless. A report by Wing Commander Hamshaw-Thomas, in charge of all third-phase interpretation at Medmenham, concluded on 22 April: 'No evidence has been found ... which would connect the Peenemünde area with rocket development, [but] no evidence has been found that could rule it out. No definite evidence has been found of the type of projector that may be used and hence no guide is available for the search for rocket projectors in the N. of France.'

The haystack was vast, and the needle might not even exist. There were, however, clues closer to home.

Combined Services Detailed Interrogation Centre, spring 1943

Military Intelligence Section 10, responsible for watching enemy land warfare technical developments, had tapped a seemingly wondrous source of rocket intelligence: namely, a German officer captured in North Africa in November 1942, a 'tank expert' who would be known henceforth as 'P/W 164'.

MI10 wanted to know about enemy armoured fighting vehicles, of which P/W 164 had already told them much. But he had lots more to say. He had 'seen experiments' and so, 'given the current interest in rockets,' said a memorandum of 26 March addressed to MI's deputy scientific adviser, the interrogating officer thought it right that 'he should see his story'. He warned, however, that 'when he turns loose he gives his imagination full rein'.

He certainly did. P/W 164's version of the supposed long-range rocket was 'propelled by hydrogen', and weighed 120 tons, half of which was the explosive warhead. It was guided by a combination of radio beam and gyroscope and could 'wipe out ... everything within a radius of 30 kilometres'. One hundred and fifty projectors

were reported to be in position already, firing three missiles each –
thus an area of 800,000 square kilometres could be devastated. In
all the febrile reporting of 'rockets' in the spring of 1943 this was
by far the most bizarre. MI10's dubious dossier was not going to do
their reputation much good in the Whitehall battle for intelligence
supremacy that was to come.

An army psychiatrist was asked for an opinion. He judged the
prisoner to be a 'Frankenstein personality almost devoid of human
feeling . . . a morbid genius very close to insanity . . . [He is] someone who invents destructive apparatus having no saner means of
getting fun out of life.'

There were many like him in Peenemünde. P/W 164 was
Hauptmann Herbert Cleff, aged thirty-two, a graduate of the
Berlin Technische Hochschule. Once he had started, Captain Cleff
would not stop. Daring missions would be sent deep into hostile
territory on the strength of his ever stranger fantasies. His notions
of huge rockets fired from underground caverns would pervade the
entire hunt for the real rocket, and live on for decades in movie art-
direction fantasies.

On 31 March the Danish engineer Aage Andreasen came back in
contact from the SIS station in Stockholm. He could report that
the rocket's 'blast effect was considerable' and that 'a large area
had been cleared when it was first tested between 30 November
and 2 December the previous year near Swinemünde on the Baltic
coast'. It was being manufactured at the Adam Opelwerk,
Rüsselsheim, near Frankfurt-am-Main.

Broadway had just then got news from closer to home, near
Cockfosters in north-east London. This was prisoner-of-war camp
11, at Trent Park, a suburban English Colditz, once the residence
of a tea magnate, which since early 1942 had been home to high-
ranking Axis prisoners. It was where Squadron Leader Denys
Felkin practised the subtle arts of extracting information by interrogation – and by bugging. Felkin's trick was to stage-manage
encounters and plant material likely to stimulate a usefully eaves-
droppable conversation.

Two of his prize captives that spring of 1943 were General der
Panzertruppe Wilhelm Ritter von Thoma, who had been captured
in North Africa the previous November, and General Ludwig

Crüwell, Rommel's deputy, captured in Libya when his aircraft landed on the wrong side of the lines. The two men had been brought together on 22 March, and rockets were soon under discussion. Felkin had bugged the room with clever GPO-developed microphones. A short abstract that appeared in the intelligence digest being circulated in Whitehall in early April reported von Thoma as saying to his fellow prisoner: 'There's a special proving ground near Kunersdorf [Kummersdorf]. They've always said these things would go 15 kilometres up into the stratosphere. You can only aim at an area ... it's very unpleasant but they can't have made any progress.'

The captive generals presumably knew they were being held somewhere close to London, which seemed surprisingly intact. The rocket programme must have stalled. Felkin gave the transcript to Jones's deputy Charles Frank, who brought it to Broadway on the 27th. As Jones said in his memoirs: 'This changed the situation completely.'

Jones and Frank saw the road ahead clearly. With Bimbo Norman at Bletchley Park, Denys Felkin at Trent Park and their sympathetic photo interpreter Claude Wavell at the Central Interpretation Unit, this tight band, battle-hardened by many encounters past, would face down the new threat as resolutely as any other. Dr Jones, being of both the Air Ministry and the Secret Intelligence Service, had unique access to multiple sources. He could tell agents what to look for via SIS station chiefs and gain immediate access to their reports. The line to Hut Three at the Park was always open. He could advise on and direct the code-breaking attack.

Furthermore, his relationship with Lord Cherwell was unencumbered by any political or personal jealousy. His small directorate at the Air Ministry would surely rise to the challenge, assess it scientifically, and 'bark' only when appropriate.

CHAPTER 6

London, April 1943

There had been political developments. It was his old mentor Lord Cherwell who gave Dr Jones the news. The task of coordinating intelligence on the threat to London by German long-range weapons had been given to a politician: Duncan Sandys, the Prime Minister's son-in-law. Jones was appalled, Cherwell even more so. Up to now Churchill had depended on the Prof absolutely for advice on the application of science to the war. Now there was a rival. Henceforth it would be said that 'within the Prof's circle what they were doing with "their" rocket referred not to the Germans but to Mr Sandys and his camp'.

It had happened like this. In January Matthew Pryor had told the bemused RAF to go looking for some sort of rocket projector in the Baltic. Along the way he had flagged up his slim file on the subject to the Director of Military Intelligence, Major-General Francis Davidson. Thus it was that around 6–7 April an ill-defined alarm had been transmitted to the Vice Chief of the Imperial General Staff (the number two in the army command), Lt-General Archibald Nye. Nye could see that the information was significant, and had quickly summoned Professor Charles Drummond Ellis, scientific adviser to the Army Council, and Dr Alwyn Crow, Controller of Projectile Development at the Ministry of Supply – Britain's very own rocket specialist. They quickly put together a speculative account of such a device and its imagined method of launching.

On 9 April Nye circulated a paper for the attention of the chiefs of staff army, navy and air force, informing them that they 'should be made aware of reports received in the War Office since the end of 1942'. The paper contained a speculative technical outline plus a summary of the various SIS-originated reports that had been circulating in Whitehall since December. The supposed rocket would require 'a projector about 100 yards long, unless an extremely advanced method of directional control in flight had been developed'. Dimensions were for the same etiolated, 95-foot-long, 30-inch-diameter device that had been described by Captain Pryor to Medmenham in early January. The weight of the warhead was of the order of 1600 pounds.

The paper concluded: 'Indications are sufficient to justify taking certain actions in view of the powerful morale and surprise effect of such weapons.' Now the Air Ministry was formally in the picture – but was 'a rocket' any more its business than the War Office's? The senior airmen seemed baffled. The Vice Chief of the Air Staff, Air Marshal Sir Douglas Evill, noted on 11 April that 'although it is not inconceivable that this is propaganda, the enemy would not be working on such a scheme for fun'. 'Whether the rocket could be detected by RDF [radar], or otherwise be the subject of some kind of electronic countermeasures should be investigated,' he wrote. He advised that it was wiser not to brief the Observer Corps (the civilian aircraft-plotting organisation) to be on the lookout because 'they are part of the general public who [are] not to be informed at this stage'.

The chiefs met on the 12th (Sir Charles Portal was in America and so was represented by Evill) and agreed to present the report to the Prime Minister. On the 14th, Brigadier L. C. Hollis, Senior Military Assistant Secretary to the War Cabinet, advised that in addition to the War Office intelligence branch, now aided by Professor Ellis and Dr Crow, there 'were a number of other agencies that should be brought in ... including the Joint Intelligence Committee and the scientific advisers to the Air Ministry and Ministry of Aircraft Production'. He noted that it might be recommended to the PM that one individual 'who could devote a considerable amount of his time to the investigations should be appointed to take charge'. Who might that be?

It was not R. V. Jones, who in retrospect assumed grandly that he was overlooked because his military master, Sir Charles Portal, was 'in America at the time'. General Sir Hastings 'Pug' Ismay, Secretary of the Chiefs of Staff Committee, wrote his defining memo to the Prime Minister on 15 April: 'The Chiefs of Staff feel you should be made aware of reports of German experiments with a long range rocket.' It suggested the employment of one man to get the best and quickest result in establishing the reality of the threat: 'Mr Duncan Sandys would be very suitable if he could be made available.'

Duncan Sandys was thirty-five, an MP (like his father), and had been educated at Eton and Magdalen College, Oxford, where he had read modern history. His parents had divorced, and 'young Sandys [had] behaved very well and shown good feeling towards both', according to his tutor. He had gone into the Foreign Office and served in Berlin in 1932. He was exceptionally good-looking, according to one account. Elected Tory MP for Norwood in south London, in the general election of November 1935, he had met the recently-divorced Diana Churchill on the hustings and soon after married her.

Sandys had been one of the few Conservative members to back Churchill's call in 1936 to take military action to oppose Hitler's ambitions, and he almost became the first Churchill martyr two years later when he invoked parliamentary privilege against an attempt to prosecute him under the Official Secrets Act (he was then a Territorial Army artillery officer) for using classified information in a parliamentary question about the nation's anti-aircraft defences. He had seen action during the disastrous 1940 Norwegian campaign, then worked briefly in the War Cabinet secretariat on tedious blackout regulations. When he wrote to his father-in-law ('My Dear Winston') seeking permission 'to take a more active part in the war', he had been sent to Aberporth on Cardigan Bay to command an experimental anti-aircraft rocket battery.

Having proved the battery's potential and seen his men trained, two operational batteries were moved to aid the night defence of Cardiff, while training continued at Aberporth. One night in transit between the two, his driver fell asleep and crashed the staff car into a wall. After three months in hospital Major D. E. Sandys RA (TA), a parliamentarian in uniform, was back in pinstripes.

In February 1943 he had been appointed a junior minister, Joint Parliamentary Secretary at the Ministry of Supply, with wide-ranging responsibility for weapon research, development and production. On 19 April Sandys was given his brief, which he accepted willingly. He was no technocrat, but he actually did know a bit about rockets. His first task was to establish whether the intelligence thus far acquired on German long-range rockets was reliable.

That same day Medmenham got its first instructions from the Air Ministry rather than from the War Office. Dr Jones would tell an interviewer later that it was he who had conveyed them – 'verbally by telephone' – in a briefing to his friend, the interpreter Claude Wavell, with whom he had worked before on radar intelligence. This one was vaguer even than the War Office briefing of February–March; Peenemünde was not mentioned at all. An aerial search was to be made of north-west France within a 130-mile radius of the area between London and Southampton, looking for a long-range gun or some sort of 'tube or mineshaft from which a rocket could be squirted'. The photo interpreter Ursula Powys-Lybbe thought the briefing 'as useful as telling a blind man to cross the road without a stick'. Wing Commander Kendall instructed Squadron Leader Hamshaw-Thomas and the army interpreter, Major Norman Falcon, to set up two sub-sections, with Flight Lieutenant André Kenny scouring the Baltic and Captain Robert Rowell doing the same for northern France.

Every photograph taken since January 1943 should be put under the stereoscope again, it was suggested, and where there were gaps the photo-reconnaissance unit at Benson in Oxfordshire should be ordered to fly missions to fill them. Getting the imagery was comparatively straightforward. Making sense of it would not be.

Whitehall had opened its eyes to the threat of German long-range weapons and no one was going to be caught napping while RAF camera-carrying Mosquitos could roam unmolested above the Baltic. But what was really going on on the ground?

On 20 April Duncan Sandys set up an office on the fourth floor of Shell Mex House, the art deco block on the north bank of the Thames topped by what looked like a giant mantel-clock, the seat of the Ministry of Supply. Where were the files? Who knew what? William Cook, Assistant Controller of Projectile Development at the ministry, and Dr Harold J. Phelps, an explosives expert and scientific adviser to the Ministry of Economic Warfare, were seconded to help Mr Sandys find out. Also drafted in was Lt-Colonel Kenneth Post, a friend from Oxford who had been Sandys's second-in-command in Norway. He would act as the new minister's 'military assistant'. A good opening move, it was suggested, would be to prepare a questionnaire to be circulated to interested parties (a circle that would get ever wider).

Whitehall's intelligence establishment was not at all sure how to react to this ministerial inquisitor married to the Prime Minister's daughter. In any event, Sandys was wasting no time. First on the list was the Joint Intelligence Committee,* from whom he requested an 'assessment of the reliability of reports thus far and sight of all additional reports on German long range rockets'. The JIC's secretary Lt-Colonel Denis Capel-Dunn promised him silkily on 21 April to do 'everything to meet your wishes'.

Next, Sandys opened direct communications with C, seeking guidance from the SIS director on the 'reliability of reports from Continental sources'. Brigadier Menzies was 'required and requested' to mount an intelligence offensive, and his deputy, the veteran spy-runner Lt-Colonel Claude Dansey, duly briefed station chiefs with requests to look out for anything unusual. Then the Directors of Intelligence at the War Office and Air Ministry were canvassed. MI10 (Military Intelligence Germany (Technical)) offered the fullest cooperation, as did the prisoner-of-war section, which effusively promised to make interrogation reports available to the inquiry.

The Air Ministry, for now, decided to keep its best card up its sleeve. Maurice Dean, Chief of the Air Staff Secretariat (a civil servant), advised on 21 April: 'So far as the intelligence side is concerned, it would seems best for Mr Sandys to deal with the Joint Intelligence Committee to start with, rather than to make

---

* Comprising the service intelligence heads, with a Foreign Office diplomat as permanent chairman.

individual contacts e.g. with ADI (Sci).' That was Jones. For weeks to come, Sandys would have no idea that his technical intelligence operations either at the Air Ministry or at 54 Broadway even existed. When he did find out, there would be trouble.

The person most put out by the Sandys appointment was Cherwell. He set his thoughts down on 22 April in a typed two-page memorandum for the Prime Minister: 'German Long Range Rockets: Although their possibility cannot be ruled out a priori, the technical difficulties would be extreme, and I should be rather surprised if the Germans had solved them.' He also questioned whether the rocket could be stabilised immediately after lift-off. It would surely need some sort of launcher to put it into the air. And it was powered, he assumed, by the standard shell-filler – cordite. In spite of what could be gleaned from the scientific literature there was little understanding in Britain of liquid-fuelled rockets, or of how take-off and flight could be controlled. So the terms 'rocket gun' and 'projector' crept in at the earliest stage – terms that were to plague the investigation throughout.

Cherwell summoned Dr Jones to ask his opinion. The young physicist thought a German long-range rocket was very possible. The Sandys appointment was unfortunate – the two men could agree on that. But Cherwell was in the most enormous sulk, whereas Jones was in a mood to just get on with it. Sandys, meanwhile, was a whirl of activity.

In the slim file made available by the Secret Intelligence Service there were references to places called Peenemünde and Kummersdorf; Military Intelligence had already pointed its photo-reconnaissance missions in the direction of Peenemünde, but without any real idea of what they were after.

The answer lay at Medmenham. On Easter Sunday, Flight Lieutenant André Kenny, head of the Industrial Section, was summoned to meet two of Mr Sandys's experts who, like MI14 officers before them, had arrived urgently from London to look at the very latest covers of the Baltic. Ursula Powys-Lybbe remembered later: 'The experts from the Ministry of Supply descended on us on 24 April wanting to know everything there was to know about Peenemünde – which wasn't very much.' In fact there had been an unexpectedly fruitful mission over Usedom two days before (sortie N/807), on 22 April, by a Mosquito from Leuchars in

Scotland looking for bomb damage at the Stettin railyards. They had left their cameras running, and when the film was developed, it was found to contain pictures of Peenemünde.

Kenny guided the visitors around a mosaic of photographs. What should they make of it? Industrial buildings, a power station with coal stocks, an elliptical earth bank, mysterious circular emplacements. At the northern end of the peninsula there was clearly an airfield, on the shoreline of which land reclamation seemed to be in progress. One item, a long thin shape pointing out to sea, baffled them. Kenny had an answer: '[A]t the extreme NE of the area being reclaimed can be found a length of pipe supported on a movable trestle carriage. This is used for pumping the material dredged by the suction dredgers over the banks of the enclosures into which the reclamation area is divided.'

It would turn out to be something rather different.

On the 25th, the JIC came back as requested to give Sandys their considered opinion: that it was likely that Peenemünde was indeed a rocket development site, but anything being worked on was a still a long way from being operational. In the meantime the results of the 22 April Mosquito sortie N/807 were being rushed through the interpretation process. Flight Lieutenant Kenny and the Medmenham PI, Section Office Bartindale, were summoned to Shell Mex House on the 29th along with Cook and Phelps; Sandys was in the chair. Lt-Colonel Post and the scientific advisers Professor Garner and Sir Edward Bullard hovered in anticipation. Kenny's briefcase bulged with papers and prints – he talked his audience through them enthusiastically. There was clearly a factory area, and a power station that showed 'no sign of activity at the time of photography, apart from the stores of fuel present in the coal yard. Not one of the six chimneys of the boiler house is smoking.' Kenny further noted:

A large cloud of white smoke or steam can be seen drifting in a north-westerly direction from the area. In photograph 5010, an object about twenty-five feet long can be seen projecting in a north-westerly direction from the seaward end of the building. When photograph 5011 was taken four seconds later this object had disappeared, and a small puff of white smoke or steam was issuing from the seaward end of the building.

In the embankment area a mysterious tall object showed up on the stereo pairs, and there was a large structure south-east of the powerhouse described as a large building 220 feet by 140, but without further comment. In fact it was the on-site liquid-oxygen plant – a vital clue to how the rocket was powered (along with the power station this is one of the big rocket-era buildings on Usedom that survives). The nearby Luftwaffe airfield with its scattering of standard aircraft types appeared to have no connection with novel weapons. These objects on the foreshore were the usual dredging equipment.

By that evening Duncan Sandys had concluded that the mysterious site on Usedom was probably an experimental station but in view of the absence of power-station activity it was not yet in full use. The area must continue to be watched, however.

London, April–May 1943

'Somehow,' Jones recalled of the weeks of April–May 1943, 'Sandys must have found out about me ... there was no contact between us, but I sensed a move to corner all the information.'

And he was right. His friend Group Captain Peter Stewart, Assistant Director of Intelligence (Photographic), told him at the time that he had been discreetly ordered that covers of Peenemünde were to go 'nowhere outside of Mr Sandys's party'. Jones told an interviewer in 1964 that Sandys would have had 'difficulty in explaining why he did not get in touch with me ... At first he may have been unaware of my existence, but he certainly had had an instruction from Mr Churchill to talk to me for some weeks.'

There is another explanation that emerges from the archives: that the Air Staff were waiting to see which way the political wind would blow before turning their best asset over to the ambitious junior minister. And it is clear from the carefully phrased correspondence of the time that there were some who wanted to stay well away from the rocket until it was apparent exactly what they were up against. Was not a rocket just a big gun and thus an army affair?

When it was suggested the Air Ministry should be responsible for all public security and information in the event of a rocket attack, Air Marshal Sir Richard Peck, who had been instructed since the beginning of the war to act as the anonymous 'Air Ministry spokesman' for portentous press pronouncements, minuted: 'I am anxious to guard the Air Ministry against the onus and possibly the *odium* of dealing with this matter. This is no more an air attack than invasion would be. I think that its nature is more appropriate to the War Office.' If it ended in disaster, let the army take the blame.

Dr Jones was not going to do nothing. He got a back channel into Medmenham to see what was being sent to Shell Mex House, by means of an unusual arrangement with the father of the station commander, Squadron Leader 'Pop' Stewart, who worked at the Central Interpretation Unit under the command of his son Group Captain Stewart, Jones's friend. The arrangement rested on the suppression of any reference in writing to long-range weapons. Dr Jones was concerned only with a certain wireless telegraphy station. There is an otherwise inexplicable note in Air Intelligence archives, dated 10 May from Medmenham to Jones, 'enclosing photographs from Sortie N/807 [the Mosquito mission of 22 April] of the W/T [wireless telegraphy] station at Wolgast/Peenemünde'. The last line explains it: 'Also sent at your request are photographs covering the peninsula on which the station stands.'

The same subterfuge was used to get him images from sortie N/825 of 14 May. Jones saw them on the 20th and was able to compare like with like. What changes had there been? Handwritten annotation reads: 'Along the shore line are lots of new gadgets – all very small and identifiable.'

In spite of Mr Sandys, Jones was managing to see the photo-reconnaissance covers of the Baltic, even if only by stealth. Jones in his other hat as IID, scientific adviser to SIS, still gave him first sight of agent reports. But the Stockholm station, thus far the most productive on Baltic matters, had been quiet since March. Other material from agents was proving erratic and repetitive. The generals of Cockfosters, however, could not be doubted in what they had unwittingly revealed.

Dr Jones's line was open to Bimbo Norman at Bletchley. It was highly probable that rocket development at Peenemünde was a

German army operation. Breaking army Enigma traffic was problematic, but there might be a way. By his own account, it was his 'longest long shot of the war'. He first told the story in a history compiled in 1945 for internal use only, preserved in the Bletchley archives:

> The plan of attack was simple. Peenemünde could be photographed and agents could be briefed. Our long study of German radar gave us a faint chance of enfilade. The argument was this: If the Germans were developing long range missiles be it a rocket or pilotless aircraft, they would want to follow its flight ... probably ... by radar. They would want the most experienced observers. These we knew were in two companies of the GAF [German air force] Signals Experimental Regiment and by looking for their W/T traffic, GC&CS [Government Code and Cipher School] might gain some sidelight into their activities. This oblique line of investigation was followed quietly for several months.

Thus it was that Bimbo Norman got the brief. Keep watching the air force Brown key. Should their old friend the Luftnachrichten-Versuchs Regiment, the XIV and XV Kompanien in particular, be encountered on the airwaves, would he kindly let Dr Jones know immediately?

CHAPTER 7

The Baltic, May 1943

There was not long to wait. On 8 May a certain Unteroffizier Karnofsky of the XIV Kompanie sent the air force signals HQ at Köthen a message. It seemed inconsequential: the new address of 'Kommando Rügen' was the Villa Sirene, it said, a hotel at Bad Göhren, a seaside spa on the Baltic island near the gigantic KdF-Bad Prora holiday camp. Unusual items of equipment were requested. 'Newly arising measurement work' was mentioned in a subsequent message, along with the names of personnel ordered to report to Rügen. An Oberleutnant Weber seemed to be in command. On 27 May he asked for petrol and oil coupons for an Opel P4 truck with Luftwaffe serial number WL 298634. Then he put in a request for bicycle-tyre repair kits. You could not have a war without those.

Not far from Rügen, at Rerik on the Baltic coast, the senior instructor at the Luftwaffe Flak artillery school was lecturing students on the 8.8cm dual-purpose gun. As the former Oberst Max Wachtel recalled twenty years later, 'An orderly interrupted my lecture to say: "The Colonel is required urgently in the communications hut."'

It was Berlin on the line – Oberst Stahms, chief of staff to General der Flakartillerie Walther von Axthelm, the most senior man in the whole business. He had been Wachtel's brigade commander during the triumphant invasion of France in 1940. Wachtel, the tough veteran artilleryman of the Great War, born in the Baltic port of Rostock, had gone on to distinguish himself commanding a detachment of 8.8cm guns mounted on Siebel ferries on Lake Ladoga outside Leningrad in summer 1942. Now aged forty-two, he taught younger men his warlike skills.

The Herr Oberst was to present himself at Flak headquarters in Fasanenstrasse at 16:00 hours that afternoon. Wachtel's driver was summoned. 'Ten minutes later, our dark-blue, six-seat, open Horch swept out of the barracks.' The colonel continued to tell the story with novelistic detail. They swept across north Germany and through the capital's northern suburbs, to arrive at their destination just off the Kurfürstendamm with five minutes to spare.

Berlin in April 1943 bore few scars of war. The general's secretary was a 'lovely person, but was wearing a little too much make-up for my taste, nevertheless very charming', according to the colonel. On this spring evening, sparrows were chattering in the lime trees.

As Wachtel told the story, von Axthelm brought him into the secret over a glass of cognac: 'In Peenemünde on Usedom they are experimenting with something with which it is intended to bombard London. This device actually exists, but is not operational – not yet.' It had been developed by the Fieseler and Argus companies, the general told him. It resembled a small pilotless aircraft, and could carry an explosive charge of one ton over a distance of 250 kilometres. The first test had taken place last Christmas. In early January, von Axthelm had himself witnessed a second flight trial. Since then, the new weapon had been given the highest priority. The industry type name Fi 103 had soon been replaced in general use by 'Cherrystone', and then on Axthelm's own initiative had very recently been changed to FZG 76, short for Flak Zielgerät. It was an attempt to confuse the English, you see. Wachtel was not stupid. There would be a lot more deception before this was over.

The experimental station at Peenemünde-West was already busily engaged in trials. A new catapult had been set up which could be turned five degrees in either direction: not the Rheinmetall rocket sled, but a product of the Hellmuth Walter Company of Kiel – one of their astonishing chemical steam-generating devices. It accelerated to 350 kilometres an hour in one second. The FZG 76 should be made into an effective military weapon as soon as possible. An experimental command must be set up which in due course would become the operational regiment – no later than by the end of the year. 'Its commander would get all sorts of powers.'

Wachtel leapt at it.

On 12 May he took up residence at the Hotel Preussenhof in Zinnowitz. 'The spa hotel is plastered white,' he wrote. 'My room has a balcony and a lake view.' How very pleasant. 'I had complete power,' he recalled later, 'to recruit from the entire Luftwaffe, apart from trained aircrew ... Who should I get? Where are the kind of men who know what I expect of them and that I can rely on completely?' He found old comrades from the 1940 French campaign and from the 'ferry war' outside Leningrad. As Wachtel recalled those days in late May 1943: 'Each of these men is now committed to the highest level of secrecy. Every day we go to Peenemünde-West, to familiarize ourselves with the launcher for the new weapon. And every day we experience disappointment.'

He described the launcher: 'a catapult 42 metres long composed of seven six-metre sections. At the base of the catapult there is a steam generator where a mixture of *T-Stoff* and *Z-Stoff* [hydrogen peroxide and sodium permanganate], which is delivered in the equivalent of large milk churns, is ignited electrically. Immediately after ignition this generator develops a force of a million horsepower, to punch a heavy bolt through the groove of the catapult.'

But it didn't work. 'They fly at most a hundred metres and then go plop into the Baltic.'

The Luftwaffe were getting on with their project as best they could. But what was the plan of their rival the German army, as envisaged in the spring of 1943, for the destruction of London by rockets? MI14 would note at the end of the war: 'It seems unlikely that such a plan was ever embodied in a single operational instruction.' Or if it had been, they could not find it. But it could be conjectured that the army had planned to start with a stock in hand of two thousand rockets and a monthly production of nine hundred thereafter – the launch rate limited by among other things the amount of fuel alcohol allotted from the total national production, which was dependent on the potato crop.

The rate of fire was based on there being two mobile motorised battalions, each with three batteries, each battery having three firing sections – giving a total of eighteen firing platforms capable of putting fifty-four rockets into the air per day. A third unit was the planned 'bunker' battalion, with two firing and one technical battery. This unit, a kind of Peenemünde under concrete, supplied by rail direct from Germany, bypassing the planned main dump and the field-supply system intended for the mobile batteries, was also supposed to generate fifty-four rocket firings a day – a figure regarded as wildly overoptimistic by the commander designate, Oberst Georg Thom. The mobile batteries were to be spread out in an arc across northern France from Dunkirk to Normandy, the primary target being London. Operations were projected to begin in January 1944.

A survey team was sent to France in May-July to find firing sites near suitable roads for the mobile batteries; these sites would have the required visual link between the firing points and mobile radio control units.* Sites for field stores, each to contain two days' supply of rockets, plus technical facilities, were surveyed, as were suitable caves and tunnels near rail lines capable of holding up to a hundred rockets. A framework for the production and supply of liquid oxygen via rail tankers was put in hand. Development and pre-production work began on specialist vehicles and launchers.

On 4 May Generaloberst Friedrich Fromm, head of army weapons development, wrote to Walter Dornberger that 'in view of the imminent mass production of A-4 missiles' he would require the bunker at Watten, twenty kilometres south-east of Calais, to be operational by 1 November. At which time, it might be presumed, in the same way that Paris had been shelled from long range by a naval gun crew in 1918, the German army would begin its bombardment of the capital of the British Empire. Then on 13 May Fritz Sauckel, Reich Plenipotentiary for Labour Deployment, came at Dornberger's instigation to Peenemünde-Ost, to be given a grand tour of the place where the final victory of National

---

* At this stage, the engine cut-off command that determined range was sent by radio signal from the ground. Later it would be via the on-board integrating accelerometer.

Socialism was being forged. The next day he witnessed a faultless A-4 launch.

Hitler approved Albert Speer's suggestion that more ministers should see for themselves the wondrous weapons by the Baltic. On the 26th, under brooding, humid skies, a glittering array of military and political dignitaries gathered at Peenemünde. They had come to witness a fly-off between the rival army and air force projects. The nominal purpose was for the long-range bombardment commission to compare the performances of the two weapons and decide whether to proceed with one, or both.

Two rockets were fired. The first lifted off at noon precisely and vanished into the low cumulus cloud. It flew for two hundred seconds, then fell twenty-seven kilometres down-range. The second, A-4 V-026, flew for a much a more convincing 265 kilometres. Then the Luftwaffe catapulted two Fi 103s from the north-eastern corner of Peenemünde-West. One crashed soon after launching and the other merely buzzed angrily on its catapult.

The commission's decision was to proceed with both. The crude Cherrystone was cheaper but needed fixed catapults, which were vulnerable to air attack. The very much more labour- and material-intensive ballistic missile promised to be more accurate and, as Dornberger insisted, need not be tied to immobile launchers. So on 2 June the Armaments Ministry issued the necessary order, and a follow-up document from 11 June stated: 'The Führer has ordered that the A-4 programme rates in priority before all other armaments production.' More dignitaries streamed into Peenemünde, including Himmler, the chemical-industry leader Dr Carl Krauch and Field Marshal Keitel. It was the must-see fairground attraction of the Third Reich – and the only Nazi leader not to see a live launch was Hitler.

On 17 June the first two hundred prisoners from Buchenwald arrived with sixty SS guards. They were confined in the basement of the assembly building, their first task to ring it with concrete posts and barbed wire. The mix of prisoners with civilians and military led to 'a partly bearable situation', according to a survivor.

The next day Dornberger gave a rousing address to more than six thousand workers gathered, party-rally style, in the main hall of the 'F1' (Fertingungshalle 1) pilot production plant. 'German industry works tirelessly to put the best weapons in the hands of the best soldiers in the world,' he said. 'We will pay the English back for the terrible sorrow they have caused ... to our women and children with their terror attacks.'

Did they know as they exulted that retribution was coming? Did they know the 'English' had already found what Dornberger was calling 'our model National Socialist factory'? According to him, they did. 'We did not doubt the Allies would find out about us before very long,' he wrote in his memoirs. 'Agents could call attention and one day the keen eye of an Allied camera would spot us from the air.'

From the spring of 1943 'everyone expected a raid', wrote Dornberger, especially 'when one of my employees found the location and business of Peenemünde concealed in a magazine crossword'. He did not elaborate. The Abwehr, the High Command's intelligence service, sent soothing messages 'telling us that we were worrying unnecessarily'. Dornberger, meanwhile, found the waiting 'nerve-racking'. But he would not have to wait for long.

CHAPTER 8

London, May–June 1943

Duncan Sandys's first interim report was delivered to the chiefs on 15 May. Its short preamble warned that nothing was final and that the evidence was conflicting. Its opening remarks unequivocally proclaimed: 'The Germans have for some time past been developing a heavy rocket capable of bombarding an area with High Explosive or gas over a long range.' Very little information was available, but what there was suggested that development was 'far advanced'. The rocket he presented was now substantially bigger than the War Office's flying pencil of January–February – it had metamorphosed into a multi-stage device twenty feet long by ten in diameter, with a 'new fuel with at least twice the calorific content of cordite'. Estimated weight was seventy tons, of which the warhead comprised potentially ten. 'The possibility that projectors for such a weapon [have] already been installed in northern France [can] not be excluded,' said the report. London was the most likely target.

More information from agents and prisoners should be urgently sought. A counter-bombing programme should be made ready, to be aimed at development and production sites, while those concerned with home security should examine the civil defence, censorship and public-order aspects of the threat.

The report was approved. Sandys's recommended actions were sanctioned by the chiefs and it was agreed to set up an Air Ministry subcommittee to pursue the recommendations on reconnaissance, pre-emptive attack, and possible technical means to trace the source of fire should the rocket materialise. It should further, 'with other appropriate authorities, attempt to evolve a deception plan'. The first Sandys report went to the relevant desks in Whitehall, but not to Dr Jones.

Photo-reconnaissance missions were flown on 14 and 20 May. The interpretation of these and continuing examination of the April covers revealed vehicles and railway trucks inside and near the mysterious ellipse, along with a 'traverser' conveying an unidentifiable 'cylindrical object measuring an estimated 40 feet long and 8 feet in diameter'.

On 24 May Sandys wrote to Air Marshal Sir Douglas Evill with an even more ambitious menu of what to cover: not only Peenemünde, but the area of German-occupied Europe within 130 miles of London, or at least 'those parts that had not been covered since January'. And there was something new. An agent report dated 9 May had reached Shell Mex House mentioning Wissant, a place on the Channel coast near Calais where 'long-range guns were to be emplaced'. Sandys gave Evill a list of targets, to be not just watched but physically attacked: Peenemünde itself, and the IG Farben plants at Leuna and Ludwigshafen, where 'a new kind of fuel was being manufactured'. Evill was most put out, writing marginal notes on the correspondence about 'wasting bomber effort' and 'giving away our interest to no purpose'. Meanwhile Lt-Colonel Kenneth Post, Sandys's 'military assistant', had been seconded directly onto his operations staff.

A politician was dictating operations! The air staff must get a grip. And who better to do so than the substantial figure of Air Vice Marshal Norman Howard Bottomley, Assistant Chief of the Air Staff (Operations), the Yorkshire-born Royal Flying Corps fighter pilot and career airman, effectively the RAF's chief executive. Bottomley was the natural choice to chair the ministry's very own Ad-hoc Long-Range Rocket Committee, which met that same day. How compliant the air force was being is revealed by the minutes of its first meeting. It heard the Director of Intelligence (Operations) Group Captain Lawrence Pendred explain that the Air Ministry had 'no direction over mounting reconnaissance missions', which were effected 'solely as the result of requests from the Duncan Sandys

committee'. Pendred could reassure his colleagues that close contact
was being maintained with ADI (Science) as well as with Wing
Commander Felkin and his prisoner interrogation operation.

It was also noted at this meeting that Sir Henry Tizard (who had
taken British defence secrets to the then neutral America in 1940)
had recommended that all reports and photos received thus far
should be forwarded to the US authorities. The committee could
only agree, but such a move would now have to be the decision of
the Sandys operation. What and what not to tell the Americans
would become ever more contentious.

As far as offensive action was concerned, the newly appointed
Director of Bomber Operations, Air Commodore Sidney Bufton,
confessed to being only 'generally aware of locations', including
Peenemünde and the supposed fuel plant at Leuna, and was waiting for guidance from the Sandys committee.

The Bottomley committee also picked up Sandys's suggestion to
the chiefs of staff made on 15 May that the Air Ministry should
'develop a deception plan' and 'make the observation of fire by the
enemy difficult, both from the air and from the ground'. It was
judged that London could not be entirely shielded from German
air reconnaissance and that ground sources were going to leak information whatever the degree of censorship imposed. Therefore a
physical decoy plan should be considered along with a more con-
ceptual deception plan, to be – 'dealt with in conjunction with "the
Controller in the Cabinet Office".'*

It looked as if the Air Staff had entirely given in to the junior
minister. Or perhaps they were minded to let Mr Sandys get it cat-
astrophically wrong before they were inevitably called in to put
things right.

The next day, 25 May, Sandys's adviser Dr Harold Phelps drafted
his own report on what he could make of the photographic covers

---

* The London Controlling Section was set up in June 1942 in the Cabinet Office under
prime-ministerial control to develop and run deception operations. The controlling officer
in 1943 was fifty-year-old Lt-Colonel J. H. Bevan. The LCS liaised with the Park (which
had broken the Abwehr hand cipher and machine codes and thus could read the traffic with
their agents in Britain), with Section B1a, the double-agent specialists within MI5 (the
Security Service), and with the multi-agency Twenty (XX, Double Cross) Committee
formed in January 1941 to run strategic-deception operations via double agents.

of Usedom produced earlier that month. He noted of the images
of 14 May: 'A large object can be observed on a flatcar near the
elliptical mounded site which could conceivably be related to
some descriptions of the long range rocket which we have.' On the
cover of 20 May he noted:

> A train of first class main line rolling stock believed to include
> four sleeping cars and a dining car appeared and was parked on
> a curved track between two sections of the so-called factory area.
> At the same time certain large and highly polished motor cars
> made their appearance – a distinguished gathering was visiting
> the station to witness some sort of demonstration ... or in the
> immediate following days.

From a viewpoint of thirty thousand feet, he was being remarkably perceptive.

Dr Phelps concluded that no more fundamental information
could be extracted from the photographs. More vigorous prisoner-
of-war interrogations were needed, plus more secret-source reports
from agents.

The imaginative Captain Herbert Cleff had been passed, meanwhile, into the hands of the Air Ministry prisoner-interrogation
branch, ADI (K). On 25 May, Phelps wrote to Lt-Colonel Post
asking him to encourage Sandys to 'ginger up' the interrogation.
'Felkin has had long enough, P/W 164 could certainly fall for psy-
chology applied by civilians!' he wrote.

Denys Felkin, in fact, was doing rather too well in getting more
information from the talkative captain. Britain's gas turbine expert,
Wing Commander Frank Whittle (who had been working on a jet
aero-engine for a decade), had been drafted in to help with the
technical questions. There was a stream of new revelations about
something called an 'athodyd', or aero-thermo-dynamic duct, a
novel power source for missiles and aircraft which he had seen
being tested at the Lettstadter Hohe, a mountain in the Black
Forest. This development was so secret that a hillside had been
hollowed out and fitted with a sliding armoured roof to conceal
what was going on. A technical drawing was prepared showing
little more than a comic-book rocket – it was all fantasy.

Sandys's ambition was becoming boundless. He now asked the

War Cabinet Secretary Brigadier Hollis to keep him 'generally in the picture with any action being taken by other government departments'. Whitehall feathers were already ruffled. It was noted by the JIC secretary that this 'could be tricky as DS likes to deal direct and has already done so'.

Another request was dispatched to Air Marshal Evill on the 26th, this time that the island of Rügen be added to the target list on the strength of a report about 'hydrogen fuel experiments'. The next day Evill replied with undisguised sarcasm: 'I am anxious that anything we do shall fit in with whatever system you are adopting in performance of your mandate from the Chiefs of Staff.' There was no system. The resulting effort to cover Rügen exhausted both pilots and interpreters, who could find nothing except pine forest, beaches and holiday villas.

Herbert Cleff's super-fuel story kept changing. On 1 June Felkin could report: 'The previous statements about uranium or lithium being used as catalysts were momentary ideas of the P/W, having no foundation in fact.' A digest of the material was passed to William Cook, assistant to Dr Crow, the British rocket expert. He forwarded extracts to the chief chemist of the Shell Petroleum Company, a Mr J. A. Oriel. The prisoner might be making it all up, but the contact served to bring Britain's tiny band of liquid-fuelled-rocket experts into the story. It was timely.

Oriel sent the Cleff ramblings to Isaac Lubbock, an engineer working for the Asiatic Petroleum Company (a Shell International Petroleum subsidiary) who had been in charge of the first British liquid-fuel rocket motor, originally designed as an assisted take-off unit for the Wellington bomber. Lubbock and his assistant, the forty-three-year-old Liverpool-born engineer Geoffrey Gollin, had been experimenting since 1941. Now they had been brought to the fringe of the Sandys investigation, although the Cherwell loyalist Dr Crow would keep them at arm's length for as long as he could.

Duncan Sandys was already moving towards getting a grip not just on intelligence and the means of acquiring it, but on the means to strike at whatever it turned up. Douglas Evill agreed on 4 June that the junior minister would present Air Vice Marshal Bottomley with a list of objectives such as 'experimental establishments ... which in his view merit attack'.

Two days later Sandys came back with a memorandum advocating that they go after Peenemünde, where there was 'reason to suppose that some equipment may be ready for despatch to operational sites'. It was urgent. A spoiling attack should be mounted immediately, one aim of which would be to 'kill or injure technical personnel'. By day, these people were to be found in the factory area with its administration block and canteen for high-level and specialist workers, said Sandys. The bomber specialist Air Commodore Sidney Bufton pointed out that a hastily put-together attack at dusk at medium level, as was being suggested, would not do enough damage. And it would give away the fact that Peenemünde had been discovered. They had one chance: a large-scale night attack by heavy bombers, in one decisive blow.

Cherwell was exuding calm. He told Churchill by letter on 11 June that the rocket was 'a remote contingency, a scare started by this prisoner of war [Cleff] worthy of the late lamented Grindell-Matthews'. He did suggest, however, that 'the old scheme of a radio directed aeroplane, jet-propelled or otherwise, would seem more feasible'. He added another reason not to panic: 'Jones, who you may remember is in charge of air intelligence, has been following these developments closely and I do not think there is any great risk of our being caught napping.'

CHAPTER 9

London, June 1943

Throughout early June, Duncan Sandys received the first fruits of aerial reconnaissance, but Dr Jones got first look at the secret reports reaching London about whatever it was that might be going on in the Baltic.

On 2 June a microfilm arrived at 54 Broadway from the SIS station in Berne, Switzerland. Under magnification it was nothing less than an annotated sketch map of Usedom. It was 'dirty and ragged', but showed points of interest from a location called 'P7' on the north-east coast to as far round as Swinemünde. It was accompanied by a handwritten message giving information about 'a cigar shaped projectile ten metres long which could be seen in flight', which had a range of perhaps 250 kilometres. The information's currency was of mid-April. The airfield on the left tip of the peninsula was marked distinctly as a test centre for 'aircraft and submarines'. Berne was congratulated and requested that 'anything further on this subject should be telegraphed Most Immediate'.

The microfilm's origin, it would be established later, was a Luxembourger called Pierre Ginter. At the beginning of January 1943 after going home on leave, he had recreated what he knew for Dr Fernand Schwachtgen, a physician, who under the codename Jean l'Aveugle was head of a tiny underground organisation that by four different routes had got the Usedom report to London.

One of those routes was via Switzerland. When the SIS station chief in Geneva found out that it had been forwarded to London by his deputy, he called him 'a fool for believing such nonsense'. A second message arrived in London that spring, also from a Luxembourg source, speaking of a 'torpedo' that had been under test since 20 November the previous year. It was 'started from a catapult and flew over the beach making a noise like a squadron of aircraft at low altitude'. That message, it would be established, had come from a young man called Léon-Henri Roth, a twenty-year-old student expelled from college for starting a resistance cell. He had ended up on Usedom as a lowly, though not yet slave, labourer.

The censor's eagerness to blot out where the letter-writer was alerted his patriotic father, who was already in contact with the Belgian underground group Service Clarence. Coded references from his son got through in later letters and were transmitted to London.

There were more reports. Some merely repeated what had been said before, some were wildly speculative. On 22 June would arrive a message much closer to the matter, one that seemed to originate from within the German army weapons-development branch itself, the Heereswaffenamt, of which Dornberger's Waffen Prüf Amt 10 was a subdirectorate. It spoke of winged rockets with remote control launched by catapult, which Hitler was urging be used imminently. The target was London.

The notion of somehow defending the capital by trickery against the still vague threat was being taken very seriously. A meeting at the Air Ministry on 3 June brought together a swarm of would-be hoaxers, including Lt-Colonel J. H. Bevan, head of the London Controlling Section (deception), Lt-Colonel Sir John Turner, master of 'Starfish' (physical deception such as phoney airfields and factories) and the novelist Flight Lieutenant Dennis Wheatley. Colonel Bevan suggested that supplying false reports to the enemy could be arranged, but they would quickly be disproved by air reconnaissance, so more original thinking was required.

Sir Samuel Findlater Stewart, chairman of the Home Defence Executive, was now brought into the proceedings. Sandys himself, keen to be informed about deception planning as about everything else, attended a meeting at Shell Mex House with Bevan, Turner et al. The meeting ended by recommending yet more committees, one in Findlater Stewart's department coordinating deception and security and another at the Ministry of Home Security to look at passive protection measures. Both would report to Mr Sandys, with the ubiquitous Lt-Colonel Post sitting on both.

The photo-reconnaissance coverage of northern France, meanwhile, was continuing on an industrial scale. Another meeting at the Air Ministry on 3 June heard that it would take at least four weeks to cover the huge area for which as yet no cover existed. Coverage inland of the coastal strip would take several months. The meeting's chairman asked if anyone knew how long it took to dig an emplacement or erect the necessary workings for the 'rocket'. Captain Pryor of MI14 estimated 'five to six weeks'. In view of that, older existing covers 'were practically useless'.

Dr Jones, in the meantime, was receiving more relevant covers via his confidant at Medmenham. He told one story with special relish in his memoirs. On a clear summer day Sortie N/853, flown on 12 June from Leuchars, covered the area of interest at Peenemünde. The typed-up third-stage interpretation report was ready four days later. Jones got to see a copy of it at the Air Ministry on the 18th, and the imagery itself the day after that. He went over the covers with a stereoscopic viewer: 'Suddenly I spotted on a railway truck something that could be a whitish cylinder about 35 feet long and five feet or so in diameter with a blunt nose and fins at the other end.' It was a question of attribution, the true expert discovering the Old Master under the layers of varnish. Kenny, Cook, Phelps, Sandys – they had all missed it. To them it was just 'an object'. To Jones it was a rocket.

Jones telephoned Lord Cherwell, who suggested he should send Sandys a note before he told anyone else. The carbon flimsy dated 19 June 1943, mocking in its icy politeness, is preserved among Jones's working papers: 'Lord Cherwell has asked me to draw your attention to the fact, should you not have already noticed it, that a rocket seems to be visible on Sortie N/853 of Peenemünde; it is about 35 feet long.' The scorn was aimed equally at the Sandys fan club at Medmenham. In defence of her colleagues, the photo-interpreter Ursula Powys-Lybbe wrote in retrospect: 'André Kenny assured me that none of the highly

trained PIs who had studied the photographs ever doubted that
the objects were rockets – it was up to the authorities to confirm
it.' Hence they stayed 'objects'.

Sandys chose not to reply to Jones's note, but it would seem he
contacted Medmenham demanding urgent answers. Kenny issued
an addendum that said simply: 'This object is thirty-five feet long
and appears to have a blunt point at the end … The appearance
presented by this object is not incompatible with it being a cylinder tapered at one end and provided with three radial fins at the
other.'

Sandys moved now to consolidate his position, effectively as
executive director of operations. He formulated a statement on the
'division of responsibilities in connection with the German Long
Range Rocket', which he sent to the Chiefs of Staff Committee on
19 June, the day of Jones's sarcastic note. The intelligence direc-
torates would continue to supply him with reports from agents and
prisoners. 'The Air Ministry will receive from Mr Sandys recommendations for action: for reconnaissance flights and bombing
attacks on development establishments, factories or projector
emplacements [and] fighter interception of enemy reconnaissance
planes,' the statement said. Deception, security and civil defence
would be the responsibility of a special committee of the Home
Defence Executive under Findlater Stewart, and radio location of
rockets would be charged to a special committee of the Ministry
of Aircraft Production chaired by Sir Robert Watson-Watt. Sandys
did not demand executive oversight of these last two, but he
wanted responsibility for coordinating action across the whole
counter-rocket operation, on the progress of which he would report
periodically to the chiefs.

The sensible thing to do was take another look at Peenemünde.
The briefing this time came direct from Shell Mex House. At first
light on Wednesday 23 June a photo-reconnaissance Mosquito
took off from Leuchars. Peenemünde was six hundred miles distant, just under two hours' flying time. The sky was clear, the
sunshine bright; the mission had timed its double overpass for
when the morning sun was bright but shadows were long on the
ground – sortie N/860 could not have had better conditions.

The aircraft, flying at thirty-five thousand feet, made its two
passes, then turned for home. No attempts at fighter intercept, no

gunfire from the ground. By late afternoon the film was on its way south from Scotland, flown by liaison aircraft to Medmenham.

Cherwell was moving in the background to advance his protégé to the high table. His 'Jones won't let us be caught napping' note had gone to Churchill on 11 June. On the 23rd, as the Mosquito was making its double pass over Usedom, at a meeting in the Cabinet Room at 10 Downing Street* the premier had called Dr Jones aside and asked: 'Has Mr Sandys seen you yet?' He had not, but in that moment Jones could see that he was back in the picture. Churchill asked the physicist to 'hold himself in readiness'. He sat up that night till the early hours drafting his own report on the rocket, without reference to Sandys or his attendant experts. There would be a War Cabinet Defence Committee (Operations) meeting on the following Tuesday to take Sandys's latest assessment. The Prime Minister seemed minded that Dr Jones should also be present (Cherwell had urged him to hear Jones's views, even if they were to differ from his own). As Jones told an interviewer twenty years later: 'In fact, from what Mr Churchill said to me, he called that meeting specifically because he was impatient that Mr Sandys had not made contact.'

Sandys got to hear of Jones's intended attendance via a mischief-making Cherwell. The summons for a personal pre-emptive meeting between Jones and Sandys came from Shell Mex House, and a frosty encounter took place on the afternoon of 26 June, a Saturday. Both men could agree the rocket was real. Both men could agree that it presented a danger. They traded what they knew. Jones went over the latest agent-derived intelligence, the messages from the Luxembourgers and the extraordinary leak of a few days before apparently from inside the Heereswaffenamt, the weapons-development centre, in Berlin. The conversation turned to the rocket's size and weight. Sandys was assuming around eighty tons – Jones was astonished. Sandys invited him to talk by telephone with Dr William Cook, his inquiry's adviser, who

---

* The Defence Committee (Technical Devices) meeting had been called to discuss the use of the ground-intercept radar-confusing device codenamed 'Window' for the first time in the mass RAF raid being planned on the German port of Hamburg – hence the presence of Dr Jones. Opinion was balanced as to whether revealing the existence of the device (via packets of reflective tinfoil strips dumped in the airstream) might invite its counter-use by the enemy.

would explain the reasoning. The rocket casing must be strong enough to resist the power of the burning propellant, and at least 50 per cent of the weight would be structure.

Jones went back to his office, where Joan Stenning, his secretary, had just finished cutting the stencil for his own report, for cyclostyling. He told her: 'They say it's sixty to one hundred tons. They seem to know what they're talking about. Even so, I can't just put my figure up to eighty.' The stencil was recut, changing '20–40' to '40–80 tons'. The change is clearly visible on the prints that came out of the Air Ministry mimeograph. The imagery from sortie N/860, meanwhile, was being crashed through first-stage interpretation. The high-resolution film at maximum magnification clearly showed the airfield on the western tip of the peninsula.

It was not yet understood that there were distinct air force and army experimental sites. What mattered was the rocket itself. 'Two torpedo-like objects' lay horizontally, each on some sort of transporter, inside the elliptical earthworks north of what was thought to be the development area. One was pale in colour and reflected the light. The other was 'greyish', but otherwise their dimensions were identical. The new objects measured 38 feet long and 6 feet wide, with a 'tail' of three fins.* The interpretation report on sortie N/860 was ready on the 28th. Another sortie, N/867, was flown on the 27th in conditions that were not quite so benign.

The Sandys report, completed on 27 June, began by reviewing the evidence received from all sources relating to the German long-range rocket since the beginning of the year. It incorporated the Luxembourg reports as well as the apparent leak from 'inside a technical department of the OKW [Supreme Command of the Armed Forces]' mentioning an 'air-mine with wings'.

There was some very recent news, including the fact that movements of civilians on the Danish island of Bornholm appeared, for some mysterious reason, to be subject to rigorous security checks

---

* Ironically, modern image-enhancement techniques have cast doubt on whether the objects were in fact rockets at all. The 23 June mission actually picked up several FZG 76 pilotless aircraft, but these would not be identified until much later. Nor were rockets standing in vertical positions identified as such. The assumption still was that they must be connected with some sort of projector.

and restrictions. But Hauptmann Cleff's outpourings were given the most prominence. His statement ran for page after page, fifty-nine numbered paragraphs of ever stranger revelations.

What was London really facing?

Cyclostyled copies of Mr Sandys's report and duplicate photographs were bundled into neat packages. Stereoscope viewers had been sent from Medmenham, and it was time to take a view on what was really going on in the Baltic. The meeting was scheduled for 29 June at 22:00 in the Cabinet War Room. Sentries in battle order guarded the sand-bagged entrance. The directors of Britain's war effort arrived late on this midsummer evening in the blackout gloom, to descend into the humming underground labyrinth.*

The formal minutes of the fifth meeting of 1943 of the War Cabinet Defence Committee (Operations) are on record, but the bland transcript cannot convey the drama that attended this, the first set-piece political dissection by Britain's war leaders of the alleged German rocket threat to London. Sides had already been taken, Sandys and his supporters versus Cherwell and his. Which side would Dr R. V. Jones, take?

Sandys spoke first. The rocket was a fact. 'Remarkable photographs [have] been obtained,' he said, 'which [show] quite clearly specimens of the rocket lying on the ground in proximity to the apparatus from which it [will] be launched.' The rocket might be used at any time in the near future. The Ministry of Home Security was predicting that four thousand casualties, killed and injured, would be caused in London by the explosion of one such rocket. He invited inspection of the photographs, commenting: 'Two objects which appear to have the external characteristics of very large rockets can be clearly seen in the oval emplacement next to one of the tall structures ... from their dimensions it has been calculated that the total weight of the projectiles is between 80 and 100 tons, the probable HE [high explosive] content between 2 and 8 tons.' One of the 'rockets' appeared to have been painted white. Hitler, he warned, was pressing for them to be used

---

* Present were Churchill, Attlee, Oliver Lyttelton (Minister of Production), Anthony Eden, Herbert Morrison, Stafford Cripps, Duncan Sandys, Colonel Kenneth Post, R. V. Jones, Findlater Stewart, William Cook, Lord Cherwell and the chiefs of staff.

at the earliest possible moment, whatever technical problems might still be met with.

The best countermeasure was to attack Peenemünde, urged Sandys. The Air Staff had recommended a heavy attack but not until the nights were long enough which meant early August at the soonest. The latest news was that photographs which had arrived that very day showed a train with unusually long coaches whose nature was unexplained.

After a ripple of questioning from Attlee and Morrison, Cherwell spoke next. A nod to Mr Sandys's 'valuable work', then he opened his counter-offensive. The greatest service he could perform, he said, was to argue the precise opposite to what had just been advanced. The rocket was a carefully designed *cover plan*, he insisted, although what it was covering he did not say. Manipulating such a rocket would require outsize cranes, as well as huge pits to conceal something that big. Where were the projector sites? The prisoner-of-war evidence in Sandys's report was scientific nonsense.

The photographs they had just been invited to inspect showed a single-stage rocket, and it was his understanding that the maximum range for such a device was forty miles. 'It seems curious that a rocket should have been painted white and left lying about so that we should see it.' What was it covering up? From what was it distracting attention? Pilotless aircraft, perhaps jet-propelled? To develop such a thing would be entirely logical and technically feasible. Bomber losses beyond 10 per cent were unsustainable, the Prof explained. If you could somehow make a one-way disposable bomber for 10 per cent or less of a manned aircraft's cost, you were in business. Nevertheless he thought it prudent to attack Peenemünde and continue photographic coverage of northern France for suspicious projectors, and he recommended 'keeping watch for the signs of radio developments which would indicate preparation for the use of pilotless aircraft'.

Churchill thanked Cherwell, but had to disagree. 'Although his points deserved the greatest attention, nevertheless the idea of a cover plan hiding something else could not be made to fit the facts.' Now he would like to hear from Dr Jones, who had detected and defeated the enemy's beams for controlling his night bombers. Having heard his son-in-law and one of his best friends contradict each other, 'Now I want the Truth!' he said.

The physicist looked grave. He thought the rocket was genuine. Peenemünde was, after Rechlin, the most important German experimental establishment. Serious precautions had been taken to preserve secrecy. The photographs showed conclusively that the rocket existed. There was a white rocket on the image, and also a black one. The Germans were not at all adept at deception; and, moreover, a deception that could bring down an attack upon one of their two most important experimental sites would be from their standpoint sheer folly.

Cherwell was not about to change his mind, but Sandys had won and Jones had cheered him over the line. The meeting agreed that Sandys and his committee's work should press ahead, that Peenemünde should be attacked with heavy bombers on the first suitable occasion, while reconnaissance should be avoided and immediate attack by Mosquitos ruled out. The bombing of an apparently connected bunker site at Wissant should be delayed until it was determined what it might really be.

There was, however, a final victory of sorts for the Prof. Sandys was now to 'examine pilot-less and or jet propelled aircraft in Germany', and was to report in a month's time on his discoveries. 'Dr R. V. Jones should be associated with him in the inquiry, in view of the special interest of the Air Intelligence Staff in this matter.' As Jones recalled years later, these concluding remarks were a deliberate marker that what had happened over the rocket, with all the time-wasting and the failure to confer with his directorate at the Air Ministry, should not be allowed to happen again.

Dr Jones's own report, completed on 25 June, was not formally presented to the full Defence Committee (Operations) meeting. It went out under Air Ministry cover to a very small group – Cherwell, the Chief of the Air Staff Air Marshal Sir Charles Portal, Air Vice Marshal Frank Inglis (Assistant Chief of the Air Staff (Intelligence)), the Director of Military Intelligence and Sandys. Concerning the rocket exclusively, the report reprised the intelligence that had arrived in London since the end of 1942 and the statements of prisoners of war, but with a much more informed and expanded commentary on what was being said.

The recordings of Denys Felkin's Cockfosters bugs had been

given another airing. This time General von Thoma, 'the most technically informed of our galaxy of German generals', was further heard to have said in the snooped-on encounter: 'The major at Kummersdorf was full of hope. He said "Wait until next year and the fun will start. There is no limit to the range"!' In his report Dr Jones re-emphasised that it was the generals' conversation above all that had convinced him that the rocket was real.

The report of rocket research at the Adam Opelwerk, meanwhile, could no longer be pursued as the informant, according to Jones, 'was now imprisoned for immoral practices'. He did not say what they were, nor by whom he had been imprisoned, but no more would be heard for a while from the Danish chemical engineer who had triggered the Great Rocket Flap.

Jones's report moved on to an analysis of the doings of the Experimental Signals Regiment which, as 'an agent had reported recently', had sent a detachment to Rügen just to the north of Peenemünde. A similar 'agent' had reported the construction of four new radio stations earlier in the national park in the south-east of Bornholm in German-occupied Denmark, which might be associated with the RDF [radar] following of rockets fired from Peenemünde,' Jones noted. He pointed out that one of the latest types of Würzburg radar sets had been sent to Peenemünde. It had, but he did not say how he knew. Also, according to Jones, intelligence had arrived in London on 2 June that gave specific details of rocket launches from Peenemünde between 16 October and 30 December 1942. The first fell in the sea near the Gulf of Danzig; the second and third were partial flops. All were launched from test stand 7. The Luxembourg reports were mentioned in his paper, as was the source from within the Waffenamt (War Ministry weapons department), identified more specifically by Jones as someone on the staff of Generalmajor Hans Leyers who held a key ordnance-production post in Berlin. The staff member's name was not given.

Dr Jones's paper mentioned reconnaissance sortie N/853 flown on 12 June, and how the discovery on the prints of a missile had ended conjecture about the shape (Kenny's addendum). He did not say that it was he who had found it, or how he had humiliated Sandys in the process. There was no countermeasure available unless the rocket turned out to be radio-controlled, in which case it might be jammed. Jones concluded: 'A possible sidelight may be obtained by watching German RDF organisations as it is possible that a special one would be set up to watch the flight of the rockets. The successful collection of a suitable prisoner from Peenemünde might improve our appreciation of this aspect of development.' Cherwell had said that the rocket was a deliberate distraction from something else. Like an illusionist making his audience look in the wrong direction, Jones was doing the same. There were no 'agents'. Someone on the very small distribution list for his paper* was not Ultra-indoctrinated.

London, June–July 1943

Committees and subcommittees continued to proliferate. Duncan Sandys's investigation now acquired the cover name 'Bodyline'. The stream of alarming reports increased. The Legation in Berne reported on 29 June: 'The Germans are announcing a devastating air attack on Great Britain for the month of August. Liquid air bombs of terrific destructive power will be used. Gas is not specified. Attack will be novel and irresistible in intensity, effect probably decisive Axis victory.'

There were plenty more similar yarns. Large numbers of dead fish had been found on beaches between Danzig and Stettin. Six thousand prisoners were toiling on deep excavations at a place near the village of Watten. London was to be wiped out by gliders packed with explosive.

Which of these stories were true? On 2 July there was a meeting at Shell Mex House, with Sandys in the chair, to review the latest intelligence and assign the tasks that the War Cabinet meeting of three days before had decreed. Perhaps Cherwell was right about there being another weapon. Air Vice Marshal Bottomley promised to let Sandys have everything the Air Ministry knew about jet-propelled and pilotless aircraft. Squadron Leader Michael Golovine, a technical expert 'who has been working on

---

* 'Up to this date there had been no factual contribution from Source and this paper [by Jones] was the basis from which we started,' wrote Professor Norman in 1945.

this problem for a considerable time', would be made available, 'as would the assistance of Dr Jones'.

Bomber Command HQ, July 1943

Informed by Sir Charles Portal of the Cabinet decisions of 29 June, Air Marshal Sir Arthur Harris convened a conference on 7 July at Bomber Command headquarters in the Chiltern Hills, twenty miles north of London. The subject under discussion was an experimental station on the island of Usedom. Mr Duncan Sandys, a junior minister, had indicated that it might be important.

It would be five weeks before the nights would be long enough for an eight-hour transit from eastern England to the Baltic and back. In the interim, the secret must be tightly guarded. No one who knew about Peenemünde must be risked in the air. In fact, it was better that no one knew anything at all.

That first meeting thrashed out an outline operational plan. And although it would keep evolving in the weeks to come, it remained true to a new principle: there was to be a precision attack by the whole of Bomber Command by night – a return, in other words, to the early days of RAF wartime bomber operations. And the attack would be made by moonlight.

It was what was going on in the Forêt d'Éperlecques that now began to vex the Sandys inquiry as much as Peenemünde itself. Everyone agreed there had to be 'projectors'. This one looked like the most substantial projector imaginable. According to an MI14 retrospective report (compiled in 1945) the site had been chosen and surveyed in the last week of 1942 by Oberst Georg Thom, Dornberger's senior staff officer. 'Speer was to have been in the reconnaissance party but failed to appear,' according to Thom, whose fate would be wrapped up with the rocket to the very end.

Plans for the Watten site were drawn up by the Organisation Todt-Zentrale in Berlin. The model was bigger than the one shown to Hitler in November. Survey work was begun in early 1943. The Führer had given his approval for construction on 29

March at a meeting with Speer at Berchtesgaden, according to the MI14 report. It would swallow 120,000 cubic metres of concrete and was to be completed within four months. Within its massive flanks they intended to install a railway station, a missile-handling vault and a substantial liquid-oxygen plant.

Thousands of men toiling on a gigantic building would be hard to keep secret. The first report from an agent to mention Watten had been logged in London early in April 1943: 'enormous trenches' were being excavated, with a concrete floor three metres thick. The report was passed to the War Office.

The Central Intelligence Unit had issued their first report on mysterious clearings in the Forêt d'Éperlecques on 14 May, but at the time Medmenham had not been informed that these were being linked with secret-weapon activity. All that the air photographs might imply was evidence of 'a large rail- and canal-served clearing in the woods, possibly a gravel pit'.

On 4 July a much more focused report reached London describing 'bricklayers building walls all over the place'. A new photo-reconnaissance effort mounted in mid-July showed what had previously been observed only as 'a shapeless hole' now 'completely shuttered and scaffolded' – almost ready for concrete-pouring to begin on a massive scale. It was suggested that some sort of raid might discover what these cryptic structures were really for. Five days later, the chiefs considered a paper from Lord Louis Mountbatten, Chief of Combined Operations (Commandos), for a drop by '190 all ranks paratroops' including ten intelligence specialists. But although the planning was detailed, it was emphasised from the start that this was 'not a normal operation of war'. It would be a suicide mission. Mercifully, it was shelved.

There were other ways of finding out what was going on. An Air Intelligence report of 15 July had noted that 'secret arms were [being] positioned between Wissant and Ardres beneath 8 metres of concrete. In a very few days these weapons will be used for bombarding London ... an agent is being sent to this area to investigate.' Within four weeks 'Source Holinshed' transmitted a very detailed report, plus a sketch map, about what was going on in the Forêt d'Éperlecques. The Organisation Todt kept it all 'absolutely secret', but the source 'had been able to establish relations with a French foreman' who had revealed:

Immense foundations 40 metres deep are being laid ... Several
major German building firms are involved ... Civilian convicts
are employed under armed [Organisation Todt] guards. Other
men have been obtained by round-ups in Belgium and
Northern France and are working under the same conditions.
Ten hours a day, under electric light at night. Very few volunteers are left. A motor coach luxuriously equipped with a salon
and dining room has made visits.

The War Cabinet meeting of 29 June had called for whatever information they might have on rockets to be solicited from Britain's
allies. A subcommittee of the Joint Intelligence Committee, on
which Dr Jones was invited to serve, was formed to do just that. So
much information about rockets seemed to be coming from
Germany itself that the new JIC subcommittee had to assume that
much of it was planted. Could the Americans or Russians throw any
light?

When the JIC obtained a summary of what Washington knew of
German rocket developments, they found it contained little new
apart from a mention of an anti-shipping weapon. The rest was 'a
garbled version of reports already utilised by British intelligence
departments', and an alarming description of a 'sleep inducing
bomb made of plastic with a clockwork fuse'.

In fact, American intelligence did have their own tiny window on
the rocket. In Switzerland Allen Dulles, the Berne station chief of
the Office of Strategic Services, had nurtured a number of sources
within Germany. In February 1943 the businessman Walter Boveri
had reported that his firm was contracted to make a small machine
part for a 'flying torpedo' being developed in Darmstadt by a scientist called Buchwald (this speck of information was in fact
included in the US report sent to London and would turn up in War
Cabinet intelligence reports). The scientist turned out to be one
Buchold, the chief engineer of the Darmstadt-based Wagner
Company which was developing something they called an
'accelerometer'. Its significance was obscure.

The Air Ministry was striving to get Medmenham back under its
control. As Dr Jones said in a memorandum on 13 July, the 'Sandys
Committee with little photographic intelligence experience has

been ordering unjustified sorties on no rational basis', including 'one of the Cherbourg peninsula including Pointe St Mathieu which only [makes] sense if a rocket attack on America [is] envisaged'. An interesting observation. 'The Committee is now spreading its interest to pilotless aircraft and long range guns,' Jones complained, which had resulted in a '150 mile trawl of the Baltic coast for possible artillery ranges.' The junior minister's 'desire to cover every phase of ... activity, however remotely connected with rockets', was out of control, he said. 'Similar fears have been aired about our agent cover.'

Dr Jones was rocking the boat. He was a civil servant, a lowly scientific officer, but he could be dangerous. He could also be useful, if handled properly. As far as Sandys was concerned it was far better to have him inside his Bodyline tent than out. On 16 July Dr Jones received an oleaginous letter inviting him to appear on what was now being called the 'DS-Bodyline committee'. 'Very anxious to have your help in this matter ... Mr Sandys has asked me to extend a cordial invitation' – an invitation, in fact, to join yet another subcommittee to give scientific advice to the ministerial inquiry as and when required, 'at short notice if necessary'. Dr Jones could hardly refuse.

By now the flow of agents' reports on Jones's SIS watch had become a torrent. No wonder he didn't want Sandys taking control of that. 'Source JX/Knopf'* sent a report dated 10 July 1943:

> The Germans have constructed a rocket weighing 5 tons with a range of between 200 and 300 kilometres. The projectile is fired from light mobile steel mountings ... The high explosive content is alleged to destroy all life within a radius of 500 metres from the point of explosion.
>
> ... Serial production is hoped for by the Germans in September 1943. At present individual parts for the rocket are being manufactured in various armament plants under conditions of the strictest secrecy ... Initial tests which were carried out in the Baltic proved very satisfactory.

---

* A still mysterious source within the German Army High Command, who reported to London via the Polish consul in Berne. He had provided MI14 with excellent material on German intentions in the Mediterranean and south Russia from early 1942.

Nine days later the same source could reveal that the army experimental station at Peenemünde was under the technical direction of Hans von Braun, son of the former minister of agriculture. 'The technical and experimental sites are practically completed as well as underground plants at Friedrichshafen for serial production,' according to Source Knopf. No other information on production could be learned as it was guarded by too much secrecy. The means of steering was not clear – was it automatic or controlled from a distance?

On 15 July the British Legation in Berne reported that an intermediary representing 'certain unnamed German generals who are convinced that the war is inevitably lost and that Hitler's secret weapons will uselessly prolong it ... is offering information on new German weapons, places of manufacture, details of trials etc.' There was also a report of radio trucks on Bornholm, to where the eminent inventor Professor Dr Ernst Steinhoff flew regularly from Peenemünde.

Another report, this one of 25 July and arriving through 'diplomatic channels', stated explicitly for the first time that two weapons were being developed, a rocket and a pilotless aircraft – 'something of the Queen Bee type'.* Amid an abundant tide of gossip and rumour, this was quite useful to know.

Military intelligence, meanwhile, got in on the prisoner-eavesdropping act when it conjured up a copy of the *Daily Herald* in which was inserted a bogus article from a 'Swedish correspondent' referring to the 'rocket weapon'. It was left within reach of German senior officers at the Trent Park camp. Generaloberst Hans-Jürgen von Arnim seemed to have taken the bait, revealing in a bugged conversation that he had heard 'from competent quarters that great things were in the air, in particular huge rockets'.

Why, suddenly, this abundance of information? On 13 July Sandys asked the JIC for their opinion, and they in turn consulted the black-propaganda practitioners of the Ministry of Economic Warfare. Was it a huge bluff? Was it a double-bluff to conceal something else? Or was it just a crude way of boosting home-front morale? The JIC had it both ways, reporting on 24 July:

* British radio-controlled gunnery target drone.

There are signs we are receiving *too much* information about a rocket or long range weapons and there are therefore grounds for hope that German experiments in this direction are proving unfruitful. On the other hand ... there are not unreasonable explanations why we should be receiving so much and therefore we would not be justified in relaxing any precautions.

CHAPTER 10

Peenemünde-Ost, 29 June 1943

The same day that Churchill had demanded the truth in Cabinet, the army experimental station on Usedom had a visitor. As Dornberger recorded it, 'Himmler announced his second visit would take place on 29 June ... towards evening he arrived unaccompanied.' There was a cosy session in the snug of the officers' club with a number of key figures, including Wernher von Braun. 'Hitler's recognition of us was still in the balance,' wrote Dornberger; 'von Braun told Himmler of our hopes and aims ... The hours slipped by. We talked about the prospects of space travel and the steps towards its realisation.' Oh really? Himmler was attentive and unemotional, he went on, 'and although we engineers were not used to political talk, the question was asked – what are we fighting for?'

The conversation turned to the 'luck' of Europe's conquered peoples in being able to join the fight against 'the danger from the east'. 'We must bear in mind the greatness of our vision and simply force people to accept their good fortune,' said Himmler reportedly. Dornberger then delivered a pointed defence of his own role, in words composed for posterity. According to his account, he replied: 'Reichsführer – I have never employed foreign labour for my work, on security grounds. In the Berlin U-Bahn nowadays you hear practically nothing but French or some eastern tongue.* The danger of sabotage or spying in armament factories is immense.'

'Sabotage can be eliminated by employing German overseers,' Dornberger has Himmler responding. 'Spying can be reduced to a minimum by close supervision and severe punishments.'

The next morning after a few hours' sleep they gathered to witness a test launch. The A-4 rose a few hundred feet, tilted over and flew off horizontally to impact on the Luftwaffe airfield a few kilometres away at Peenemünde-West. Perhaps it was symbolic. That afternoon Dornberger and Himmler set off by boat. The artilleryman became lyrical: 'We stood together on the foredeck looking . . . into the haze, beyond which lay the blue grey silhouette of the Greifswalder Oie' with its launch pad and radar tracking station. The second launch of the day 'went off without a hitch'.

As the Reichsführer was outlining his geopolitical visions in his homeland and Churchill was demanding 'the truth' about the rocket in London, Dr Carl Krauch, Reich Minister for Chemical Production, wrote to Albert Speer outlining a fascinating prospectus for a German victory:

> The air war against our population centres is at present the only effective war weapon of the enemy . . . Those adversaries in England of air terror should be encouraged.†
>
> Rocket factories have to be established and dispersed in the east. The Wasserfall** apparatus will fundamentally change our air defence. The aim of operating with the offensive rocket weapon is obtained if the enemy, owing to our superior air defence, abandons the air terror against our population and armament centres and is forced to attack by land where we have a sure superiority.

---

* One of the factors advanced when Churchill called for an examination of the practicality of using gas against the civilian population of German cities in summer 1944 was the large number of foreign workers.
† Presumably those such as George Bell, Bishop of Chichester, who in the House of Lords in 1943–4, attacked the 'obliteration' of German cities as 'not justifiable acts of war'.
** Wasserfall (Waterfall) was a visually guided nitric-acid-fuelled anti-aircraft rocket under development at Peenemünde-Ost, aided by a Luftwaffe engineering team.

By baiting England with a rocket-delivered terror of Germany's own making, the enemy would be lured into an invasion and a land battle in which they would be defeated. There was indeed such an intention on the part of the Allies, but they did not plan to lose.

Rastenburg, July 1943

A week after Himmler's visit Walter Dornberger got a phone call. It was Reichsminister Speer with instructions to take the whole rocket show and get himself and his technical director onto an aircraft. The Führer wanted to see it. 'We had packed it all up, the files, the model of the big launching shelter on the Channel coast, the little wooden models of vehicles, the coloured sectional drawings, the maps, the manual for field units, the trajectory curves,' wrote Dornberger.

He and von Braun were going east. If the Führer would not come to the rocket, the rocket would come to the Führer. The guidance specialist Ernst Steinhoff piloted the aircraft, a Heinkel He 111, to the airfield in East Prussia south-west of the complex at Rastenburg and on to the 'Wolf's Lair', Hitler's Wolfsschanze. It was high summer and the midges were biting. The men waited at the army guesthouse, then were summoned to the cinema block. As Dornberger recalled, 'It was in the innermost prohibited area . . . it grew later and later, suddenly the door opened and we heard someone call out, the Führer!' He sat down in the front row of the tiers of seats between Speer and Keitel.

The film, entitled by von Braun *And We've Done It After All*, clattered through the projector. It depicted the successful launch of 3 October 1942 – in colour but with no soundtrack. Von Braun provided a live commentary, explaining the devastating power of the one-ton warhead arriving on its target at three times the speed of sound. Hitler wanted ten tons, but he was enraptured all the same.

According to an MI14 report of October 1945 based on the captured Dornberger's interrogation that summer, Hitler addressed him in the following terms: 'If only I had had faith in you earlier . . .

If we had the Gerät [device] A-4 earlier and in sufficient quantities it would have had decisive importance in the war. I didn't believe in it. Now that the long range rocket has been developed, Europe is too small for war.' Dornberger's 1952 memoirs gave the encounter much more emphasis and whole new chunks of dialogue. 'If we had developed these rockets in 1939 we would never have needed to go to war ... I want annihilation, complete annihilation!' he recorded Hitler as saying, as a 'strange, fanatical light flared up in [his] eyes. I feared he was going to break out into one of his mad rages.' Actually the Führer turned out to be more interested in the model of the launch bunker than in anything else.

Albert Speers's deputy Karl Otto Saur had also undergone a conversion from rocket sceptic after the 'comparison shoot'. On 16 July he overruled the Degenkolb programme and set out his own. It projected an output of 900 missiles in October 1943, rising to 1500 by January 1944 and a staggering 1800 a month by April. A fourth production site would be created at the Deutsche Maschinenfabrik AG (DEMAG) in Berlin-Falkensee.

When Saur issued his decree, the pilot assembly lines at Peenemünde and Friedrichshafen had yet to produce a single rocket, and the Henschel-Rax works at Wiener Neustadt was months away from being finished. Dornberger had to inject some realism. There would not be enough liquid oxygen. The supply of alcohol, as mentioned earlier, was dependent on the potato harvest, and there would barely be enough for even nine hundred rockets per month. At first Saur would not hear of any objection, but Speer put an end to his ambitious deputy's fantasy. At the beginning of August he postponed the Saur plan, effectively reinstating the Degenkolb production target of nine hundred A-4s a month at three sites by December.

Late in July, Degenkolb assigned a four-man team to Peenemünde to bang heads together, led by Albin Sawatzki, a thirty-four-year-old engineer who had energised Tiger tank production at the Henschel plant in Kassel. Under the impression that they would take over the factory, the delegation started giving orders, sending Dornberger into yet another swoon. On 4 August the interested parties, none too happy, met by the Baltic to plot the way forward. A representative of General Fromm attended. The meeting's most important decision concerned who would actually make the rocket. Although Hitler had determined on 7 July that only German workers be used, for security, that demand had to be quietly ignored. Dornberger's minutes read: 'As a basic principle, production in all four assembly works will be carried out by convicts.' The production specialist Arthur Rudolph had seen the Heinkel factory at Rostock-Oranienburg in April 1943 where concentration camp prisoners worked on the production line, crammed into bunkers within the factory surrounded by an electrified fence. The use of 'mixed nationalities' meant they did not form secret resistance groups, Rudolph had noted; he was also convinced that, for reasons of secrecy, the conscripted French labour force that was building the pilot production plant at Peenemünde should be replaced by prisoners with no eligibility for leave.

Heinz Kunze, Degenkolb's deputy on the A-4 Special Committee, agreed immediately, ordering that all indented labourers, not merely the French, be replaced by prisoners: this meant the slaves on offer from the concentration-camp leasing system, who would toil night and day and never be able to leave the confines of a factory patrolled by the SS-Totenkopfverbände.* Rocket assembly would be done overwhelmingly by the slaves, a concept that Dornberger fully accepted. The artilleryman, so keen otherwise to protect the honour of the army, had sent a note to Speer's deputy before the meeting on 4 August which would formally agree to their use. It said: 'Production by convicts – no objections.'

Oberst Gerhard Stegmaier, the ardent National Socialist previously in charge of the development works, was posted to Köslin (Polish, Koszalin), a hundred miles east of Usedom, to found the A-4 training establishment – eventually to be known as Kommandostelle Siegfried (a name that would take on importance for the Park). In mid-July the Lehr und Versuchsbatterie (demonstration and experimental battery) 444 commanded by Stegmaier was created from soldiers drawn from Versuchskommando Nord, to be the prototype mobile battery. It remained to be seen whether ordinary soldiers could operate the rocket successfully. The bunker plan proceeded in parallel.

---

* Death's-head units, concentration camp guards.

Peenemünde-West, summer 1943

In spite of the German air force's flop at the April 1943 fly-off, it had been decided to proceed with both weapons. The airmen had been busy. The firing ramps at Peenemünde-West had been complemented by new launchers at Zempin–Zinnowitz and a chain of radar tracking stations set up along the coast stretching eastwards – on the Greifswalder Oie, on Bornholm, at Jershöft, Horst and Stolpmünde as far as Leba, about 155 miles down-range. Bletchley Park had picked up the network's origin with the arrival of Leutnant Muetze at Göhren in May, even if Hut Three had still to discover its significance.

Early production had begun at the Fieseler works in Kassel. The Luftwaffe were keen to beat the army to getting their weapon operational, and they needed men to do it. Airman Josef Esser was aged eighteen, a proud member of the Flak. Years later he set down his memories. In the spring of 1943 he was in a unit near Königsberg. 'They came round asking for volunteers for a special command. Actually the sergeant just designated the men who were going to join.' He arrived on Usedom on 5 June and was billeted behind the dunes at Zempin.

> Proper training began on 17 June. Our main job was to use a crane for lifting the bomb onto the ramp and connecting the steam generator to the pressure system of the ramp. The generator was nicknamed the 'perambulator'. A concrete pill-box housed the senior staff and the control station. From there the actual ignition was made. After the bomb had been lifted onto the ramp, I hid behind the pill-box. You just did not know what would or could happen.

Life by the Baltic was good. Fliege Esser acted as batman to one Leutnant Preuss: 'He always returned to quarters very late. I often learned private and secret stuff from him. I thought it could go on like this for ever.' The CO was not doing badly either. Esser recalled: 'Oberst Wachtel lived at the Preussenhof Hotel. There, and at the Schwabes Hotel nearby, there were constant meetings of scientists, engineers and senior officers. It was a most beautiful area and on most evenings it was delightful to walk through the pinewoods and along the wide deserted beach to the most prohibited area.'

But getting the bird to fly was only the start. It would need a huge ground organisation in northern France. At the outset, General von Axthelm had favoured dispersed launchers only. Erhard Milch favoured Führer-pleasing bunkers. Now they had to decide. A meeting in Berlin on 17–18 June drew up an initial programme of four sites (reduced from the original six), plus sixty-four dispersed and thirty-two reserve sites in an arc across France that would lie within 250 kilometres of London. The locations must be far enough inland to be immune to seaborne commando raids and naval gunfire. They would be organised in four Abteilungen (I–IV) each with four batteries, controlling four firing sites apiece. Four by four by four – sixty-four sites in total. Each Abteilung would have two supply batteries, eight in total, each with its own supply depot. Then there were the four super-bunkers planned to hold a thousand missiles each.

Day and night construction shifts would begin in August. Forty thousand workers would be employed. The military intelligence station (Abwehrstelle) at Arras, headed by the energetic Oberstleutnant Heidschuch, was in charge of 'defence against agents'. The Berlin meeting also heard that the Fieseler works were not capable of turning out missiles on the scale now envisaged: they would carry on with prototype development, but mass production would be the responsibility of the VW works at Fallersleben, where a huge new assembly line was to be installed.

The missile's development and flight trials would go forward in parallel. Designs for a standard launch site were drawn up by the construction office at the German Air Ministry, with technical advice from Peenemünde-West. Its basic components were an angled ramp shielded on each side by a concrete wall, a 'non-magnetic' building for final alignment of the FZG 76's compass, a half-buried launch-control bunker, the long missile-storage buildings with their kinked ends, a water cistern and several smaller buildings for fuel and spares.

There could be no woodland or other obstacle in the first five kilometres of the missile's path. And it must point at London – which tended to rule out forest rides and natural clearings. For camouflage, orchards and woods in open country were the best prospect, although many launch sites were to be laid out on the fringes of villages and farms. The sites were surveyed in late June by two Luftwaffe engineering special staffs (Sonderstab) named for the commanders, Fritsch and Beger. They could choose as they found, evicting the population as they wished, although farming would be allowed to continue for deception purposes.

Renewed prototype-testing had been under way since April. Of fifty missiles so far launched, thirty-five had functioned perfectly. Robert Lusser, director of Fieseler, spelled out the Cherrystone's semi-magical qualities at a Berlin conference: it took just 250 man-hours to make, burned the lowest-grade petrol, required no fighter cover; it could operate in summer, winter, rain and fog – only icing up might present a problem. 'It can be built by foreigners and women almost exclusively.' But security was not tight enough. According to Major Stahms, commandant of Peenemünde-West, 'in Kassel people were talking in the street about the weapon, and in Berlin even the servant girls knew about it'.

Goering, as commander of the Luftwaffe, was bursting with excitement. He foresaw fabulous production figures – fifty thousand a month. At this von Axthelm shrugged: that was a production task, Speer and the labour chief Fritz Sauckel's responsibility. The crews were a different matter – they would be drawn from his Flak units. Three days later the first successful Walter catapult launch was made. Meanwhile development must continue, moving from prototype to pre-production testing. In Oberst Wachtel, von Axthelm could promise the Berlin meeting, they had just the man to take the Cherrystone to war.

On 9 July the first distance test shoot from Peenemünde-West reached a range of 243 kilometres and was only one kilometre off its theoretical impact point. There was jubilation – but it did not last long. Speed and altitude were markedly lower than had been hoped for, and as the tests continued they would not get much better. Furthermore, the new launch method was proving as unreliable as it was dangerous. As one prisoner would tell his British interrogators: 'The so-called Dampferzeuger, the [Walter] steam generator, was a constant cause of trouble ... The result was a death toll almost as high as that [which would later result] from British and American bombing.'

But they had to assume that one day it would all come right. An advance party left for France on 8 August to reconnoitre the area of operations. On 15 August an excuse was found for a little bit of military pomp at Zempin, when Colonel Wachtel reviewed his men. A band played stirring marches. He read out the order of the day before heading for a jolly reception at the Hotel Preussenhof: 'The staff of Flakregiment 155 (Werfer) is formed in Zempin by special top secret order No. 1/43. The regiment is now independent of the [experimental] Lehr und Erprobungskommando Wachtel. Under special order No. 1 with immediate effect, personnel from the Fliegertruppe [flying troop] assigned will wear red collar patches. Signed: Wachtel, Oberst.'

Red was the artillery colour, as opposed to the flying branch: Wachtel's men were proudly declaring themselves to be gunners. The flashy yellow-tabbed Fliegertruppe, darlings of *Signal* magazine and the Propagandakompanien, had failed to subdue England. They could not even protect the Fatherland from the terror bombers. Now the men of the air force Flak artillery would have the honour of wrecking London from end to end.

CHAPTER 11

London, July 1943

The German plan to attack London with a barrage of technically unproven projectiles would take at least six months to put into effect. Meanwhile, the British and Americans were assembling an ever growing fleet of four-engined bombers capable of reaching deep into Germany. The Casablanca Conference of January 1943 had agreed to mount the Combined Bomber Offensive with the USAAF operating from England once the airfields and bomber fleets were ready, in a strategic partnership with the RAF.

The British had been trying for months to persuade the American air commanders to paint their aircraft black and join night area bombing; but they resisted, arguing the military case for retaining the ability to hit small targets from high altitude. From mid-1943 Bomber Command, with its technical advances in target-finding, the introduction of Pathfinders (see p. 113, footnote) and the bomber-stream technique (both used in the moonlit attack on Peenemünde), could operate with dramatically increased lethality – if the attrition rate inflicted by enemy defences could be borne.

The Casablanca directive had made no mention of the system of command under which the combined offensive was to be conducted, although General George C. Marshall, speaking for the US joint chiefs, suggested that the American bombers in England should be under the operational direction of the British, while insisting that operational procedure and techniques should remain the prerogative of an American commander.

And that is how it was, to begin with, plus the extra proviso that in attacking objectives in occupied countries air commanders would conform to 'such instructions as may be issued from time to time for political reasons by His Majesty's Government through the British Chiefs of Staff'. Not until March 1943 was the US 8th Air Force consistently able to put more than a hundred bombers into the air. Meanwhile his 'piddling little force of Fortresses' (Lt-General Ira Eaker's description) could merely conduct experimental missions over occupied France.

The balance of the wartime partnership was shifting as COSSAC (originally meaning 'Chief of Staff to the Supreme Allied Commander' but also used to refer to its HQ), the planning cell for the invasion of Europe established in April 1943, took on an ever more American aspect. There was more intermingling of war-coarsened Brits and confident newcomers. By summer 1943 the CIU at Medmenham had a large number of American personnel, while photo-reconnaissance operations were being flown by USAAF F-5 Lightnings of the7th Photographic Reconnaissance and Mapping Group from Mount Farm airfield, south of Oxford.

Then came the sharing of the greatest secret of them all, in the form of the Brusa Agreement, signed in great secrecy on 17 May, which lifted the veil on the Park, at least for a tiny group of American specialist intelligence officers. They would be accompanied in their stay at Bletchley by the veteran cryptanalyst William F. Friedman.

In Hut Three Friedman found a middle-aged academic surrounded by young uniformed WAAFs. It was Professor Frederick Norman. On his wall 'was a very large map on which had been charted the location of German radar stations as determined from an intelligence analysis of their E traffic, largely on the Cockroach and Brown cryptonets – a marvel of precision and accuracy,'* Friedman reported.

Another group of American intellectuals-in-uniform were already

---

* The bomber stream technique was devised to channel the attacking force in a continuous close-formation ribbon through the radar networks' weakest points, as revealed by Ultra and plotted on Professor Norman's wall chart in Hut Three.

in London. At 40 Berkeley Square, within the purlieus of the Ministry of Economic Warfare at Lansdowne House, the Americans had in September 1942 established the Enemy Objectives Unit, dedicated to planning the dismemberment of the German war economy. Arguments would shift between going after oil-hydrogenation plants, ball-bearings or transportation. In summer 1943 the loudest voices advocated hitting enemy aircraft plants, which happened to be concentrated in central and south-eastern Germany. Take the means to resist out of the skies of central Europe, and Allied airpower must prevail. On 10 June 'Operation Pointblank' was formally adopted. The same day, an Anglo-US Combined Operational Planning Committee was set up, but this would turn out to function as more of a tactical liaison body than an operational command.

The cream of British scientific intellect was likewise engaged in pursuing the area bombing offensive by night, which, although it allowed for little subtlety in choice of target (it must be big and combustible), called for intense technical ingenuity in ways to beat the German defences. The simplest but most dramatically effective of these was called 'Window', comprising reflective foil strips that blinded ground-based fighter control radars. By early 1942 the enemy's defensive system was well understood, aided by the capture and retrieval of the core electronic components in the raid on a coastal 'Würzburg station' at Bruneval in northern France.

The countermeasure of dropping bundles of foil strips was perfected soon afterwards, but the decision to employ it was much more problematic – the Germans could copy it. The argument rumbled on through 1942 and into 1943. As Bomber Command grew bigger in striking power but took an ever greater mauling by the Luftwaffe defences, the use of Window became irresistible. It was at the Staff Meeting (Technical Devices) in Downing Street on 23 June, which Dr Jones had been asked to attend, that the decision was made that it should be.

Hamburg, 24–27 July 1943

The Window secret would not be revealed lightly. It would be employed for the first time in support of a series of attacks by RAF

Bomber Command which would wreck Hamburg, the north German port with a population of 1.8 million. The plan for its destruction envisaged four massive night raids in the space of ten days.

The first attack was on the night of 24–25 July. With their radar blinded, the defences were overwhelmed, whereas the loss rate of the bomber force was 1.5 per cent. A second, daylight, raid at 16:40 by the Americans, the first time they supported the RAF in city attacks, was inconclusive: smoke made it impossible to attack the industrial targets that had been designated. A second daylight raid was conducted on the morning of the 26th by the USAAF.

Then, on the night of 27 July, shortly before midnight, 739 RAF aircraft returned to the port on the Elbe. This time the concentration of the bombing, the use of Window, the paralysis of the fire-fighting and rescue organisations on the ground – and especially the unusually dry, warm weather conditions – culminated, extraordinarily, in a 'firestorm'. The conjoined fires rose into the night sky in a superheated vortex a kilometre high, supposedly forcing two billion tons of fresh air up through the air chimney and sucking in air at its base at gale force to feed the greedy flames, burning and asphyxiating everything and everyone in its path. Seeing the city like lava below, an airman recalled hearing his captain sigh into the intercom: 'Those poor bastards.'

There are many accounts of Hamburg's Calvary. Forty to fifty thousand perished, seven thousand of them young people. Ten thousand children were orphaned. The rubble took ten days to cool. A million people fled the city.

Most of the deaths attributed to 'Operation Gomorrah', as it was called, occurred on that night of 27–28 July. When it was over, more than eight square miles (twenty-one square kilometres) of the city were incinerated. The scale of this devastation by fire had not been foreseen by the raid's planners – 'We had no idea of what we had done until a few weeks afterwards', according to Dr Jones's memoirs.

On the night of the first attack Speer was at Rastenburg. Hitler flayed the Luftwaffe for their failure to defend Hamburg. An unfortunate air force adjutant vainly tried to explain about the tin foil that had blinded the radar. 'They will only give in when we start killing their civilians,' raged Hitler. 'Smash terror with counter-terror!'

CHAPTER 12

London, August 1943

When the epic scale of destruction in Hamburg had started to become clear in Whitehall, it was not a cause for exultation. But there were some who believed that, with radar-directed night fighters apparently beaten by Window, German cities could now be rubbed out one by one until Hitlerism expired in the embers. Surely Berlin would burn as Hamburg had done.

It was a happy vision. According to Dr Jones, 'The question now was whether area attacks would ultimately destroy the German will and ability to fight. Apart from a few who clung to the immorality of area bombing, most of us answered this question in terms of how many bombers would be required.' The Americans could keep their moral high ground and pursue their doomed daylight operations. But even Arthur (Bert) Harris could be persuaded that an attack on the Usedom peninsula was necessary. If the target was unequivocally military, the primary object as articulated by Duncan Sandys was the killing of as many scientists and technicians as possible, as they slept. How might this be achieved? 'Trench shelters are said to be available and the standard of discipline of key workers segregated in a closely guarded community may be considerably higher than that of the average town-dweller,' it was noted. The document estimated one worker per thousand square feet of target area, giving a kill rate of 0.8 persons per ton.

The RAF heavy bomber force was not a precision instrument. The US 8th Air Force flying in daylight had pretensions to be so, but it was going to be difficult asking them to attack an obscure Baltic peninsula without a comprehensive explanation of the reason why. What to tell the Americans about the rocket was extremely sensitive. Tizard's earlier suggestion that they be fully informed had not been acted upon. Washington had been sent a copy of Mr Sandys's Bodyline report of 27 June – and nothing since. The Ultra alliance was in its earliest stages (there would be nothing about 'secret weapons' in William Friedman's 12 August report of his time at the Park with Professor Norman).

US operational air commanders remained almost entirely in the dark. Nevertheless, Air Marshal Evill could tell the chiefs on 9 August that Bomber Command's planned night attack on Peenemünde would be followed by a daylight attack by American heavy bombers 'if necessary'. This time there were no old buildings to torch – the targets were of brick and concrete, mounds and excavations dispersed among sandy heaths. But maybe the RAF could do it on their own — this was unique, the only time in the war that the entire bludgeon of Bomber Command (all that were available on the day) would be used in a closely confined attack on a comparatively small target by night. It would have to be done at medium level, eight thousand feet with an intricately orchestrated target-marking plan. And it would be done at full moon.

Bomber Command's No. 5 Group, commanded by Air Vice Marshal the Hon. Ralph Cochrane, had the previous month mounted a comparatively successful attack ('Operation Bellicose') on a confined target – the Luftschiffbau Zeppelin at Friedrichshafen – a target chosen because Dr Jones had suspected it was where Würzburg radar dishes were being manufactured.

The raid had had a further significance (as yet unknown to Air Intelligence), because the factory on the shores of Lake Constance, specialising in light aerostructures, was also earmarked as a major subcontractor for the rocket production programme and had already assembled a number of A-4 centre sections. But Bellicose was especially significant because it was not an attack by RAF Bomber Command on an area target: it was an attempt to mount a precision attack by night, using the 'master bomber' technique for the first time, with a 'raid commentator' who stayed airborne in the target area directing the Pathfinders and the main force by wireless telephony throughout the attack.

For Bellicose the Pathfinders* used a novel technique for the first time: 'offset marking', which placed marker flares beyond the target area. The main force also used 'time and distance bombing', a speciality of No. 5 Group, which picked up visible waypoints on the ground, then employed compass and stopwatch and close cooperation by pilot, navigator and bomb aimer to determine bomb release. An outline plan proposed by Cochrane to employ a strengthened No. 5 Group in order to mount a raid on Usedom similar in scale to that on Friedrichshafen was turned down in the early stages of planning. Harris would rather employ the whole of Bomber Command's front-line striking force in one crushing attack.

Medmenham had worked hard to turn photo-reconnaissance covers into briefing material. A fine model of test stand 7 was ready by 11 July, complete with buildings, firing stands, vehicles and 'vertical columns'. The plans were examined by the chiefs at a meeting with Herbert Morrison, a still sceptical Cherwell and the Prime Minister on the 14th. The enthusiasm of the airpower exponents was unstoppable.

An attack would be made as soon as darkness, the moon and weather conditions would allow. There had to be little cloud over the target and the island of Rügen north of it, where the time-and-distance bombers of No. 5 Group would pick up their waypoints. A Mosquito sortie over Peenemünde on 26 July brought back clear photographs of the whole eastern edge of the peninsula. Photographic interpreters found a row of six smoke-generators with blast marks showing that they had been tested since the previous sortie, and there was proof of the recent arrival of new anti-aircraft guns. The hours of darkness would have to get longer, but the wait must not be long.

---

* The elite target-marking Pathfinder Force (PFF) was first formed in August 1942 and became No. 8 Group (Pathfinder Force) in January 1943. Initially it was the brainchild of Group Captain Sidney Bufton, an officer against whom Harris held a special animus.

RAF Wyton, 16–17 August 1943

There was unremitting cloud over the Baltic. The twelve-night moon phase began on 11 August. On the night of the 16th–17th cloud conditions improved. At an early-morning meeting at High Wycombe on the 17th, 'Operation Hydra' was ordered for that night. A Mosquito took off at 10:55 to make a last-minute weather reconnaissance.

The timing of the operation was fortunate. During the day the US 8th Air Force would coincidentally be making deep penetration raids on the Messerschmitt plant at Regensburg and Schweinfurt, centre of the ball-bearing industry, thereby distracting the Luftwaffe daytime fighter defences (the Americans would be torn to pieces in the process).

At thirty-eight airfields stretching in an arc from north Yorkshire to Essex, 596 aircraft were mustered with the 4241 men who would fly them. Briefings began in the early evening. Duncan Sandys went to the Pathfinder HQ at Wyton in Cambridgeshire to hear the 'Master Bomber', Group Captain John Searby, explain what he knew to his crews – which was just a little more than anyone else.

The target maps, once they were revealed, showed the routes in and out to somewhere called Peenemünde. No one had ever heard of it. The target, they were told, was 'a radar development station' that 'promises to improve greatly the German night air defence organization': it was to be an extension of the radar-wrecking raid on Friedrichshafen. The lives of bomber crews on missions yet to come depended on its success. 'If the attack fails ... it will be repeated the next night and on ensuing nights regardless of loss,' insisted the briefers. A trek across north Germany by the light of the moon. Total flight time would be seven or eight hours. If the planned Mosquito feint at Berlin did not draw off the night fighters, it would be a massacre.

The raid, with its novel force-concentration techniques, balletic target-marking, three-wave attack and late rallying (the Mosquito feint worked), against ferocious German defence by day and night fighters, was an epic of air fighting. Forty bombers failed to return.

As in all war-making plans, some things went right, but many went disastrously wrong.*

Duncan Sandys stayed up through the night at Wyton, waiting for the aircraft to return from the mission he had inspired. The Pathfinder crews seemed cheerful enough as they clambered down from their cockpits, although Group Captain Searby would not commit himself until he had seen the first bomb damage assessment photographs. A Mosquito covered Peenemünde a little before noon. Sir Douglas Evill told the chiefs on 19 August that 'preliminary photo-reconnaissance showed good results'. The Americans were willing to carry out a further daylight attack but were under no obligation to do so, he said. He doubted whether it would be necessary. He hinted at the heavy casualties the USAAF had just taken in their own missions the day before. The set-piece opening of Operation Pointblank had been a disaster.

Medmenham's interpreters gave the most important critical report of all on the 20th, the bomb damage assessment for Operation Hydra: 'There is a large concentration of craters in and around the target area, and many buildings are still on fire. In the north manufacturing area some twenty-seven buildings of medium size have been completely destroyed; at least four buildings are seen still burning.' The two lofty buildings in the second target area, the pilot production works, had escaped serious damage, one being completely unscathed. The housing complex had suffered most severely.

The next day, 21 August, Sandys presented the Central Interpretation Unit's diagrams at the chiefs' meeting. 'It seems unlikely that any appreciable production will be possible ... for some months,' he said. 'A large part of the living quarters was annihilated ... and many buildings in the main factory area were destroyed.' There was a rumble of approval.

But a wider intelligence summary by Sandys for the chiefs, dated the same day, was full of dread. It led with a seriously

---

* For the best account of Operation Hydra and its aftermath see Martin Middlebrook's masterly *The Peenemünde Raid*, as good for its accounts from the ground as for those of the airborne attackers. A Pole confined in Trassenheide told the author that the first he knew of the raid was the camp being bathed in bright light, as Pathfinder parachute flares floated down. 'The German guards ran, we followed them, but too late, it was too far to get to the gate.' A 4000-lb Blockbuster bomb detonated as the prisoners scrambled to climb the chain-link fence.

alarmist agent report of a forty-ton rocket with a warhead said to be 'of the atom-splitting variety'. Its range was 270–500 kilometres. 'One million such projectiles are said to be in the first delivery batch.' Although, noted Sandys, it 'seems improbable that the Germans have found a means of harnessing atomic energy'. There was, however, the prospect of a 'new chemical warfare agent based on the bacteria of botulism ... In view of the success of our own scientists working on "N" [Anthrax] the possibility that the Germans have been working on similar lines cannot be excluded.' His own ministry was carrying out this work and would in due course prepare 'an appreciation of the effect and likely method of use of such substances'. These acutely alarming references were deleted from any wider circulation of the report to avoid 'dangerous speculation'.

The vice-chiefs (the chiefs were in Canada for the Anglo-US Quadrant Conference, which began discussions on an invasion of France) reviewed the paper and its recommendation that the mysterious building site at Watten be attacked as soon as possible. Watten, in spite of its gargantuan concrete flanks, was not an area target. From the first, therefore, consideration had been given to making it a precision objective for the Americans. And here was the bonus – it was in occupied France. Under the Combined Bombing Offensive directive, it could be directly assigned as a target by the UK Air Staff, without telling the Americans why.

In the week before the Peenemünde mission, on 11 August, the 8th Air Force planning chief Colonel Richard D'Oyly Hughes had attended a meeting of the Air Ministry's Bodyline coordinating committee chaired by Air Vice Marshal Bottomley to discuss the Watten conundrum. Lt-Colonel Kenneth Post gave the briefing. He was disarmingly honest: the structure's purpose was as yet unexplained – 'There is no evidence to show it is in any way connected with rockets.' It was just a theory. The Americans were hooked.

An extraordinary conversation had followed, which resulted in Air Commodore Sidney Bufton, Director of Bomber Operations, being invited to write a letter to C-in-C Bomber Command asking him to prepare a plan in consultation with the commanding general of the US Army Air Force, to consider 'a night attack by Lancasters using Oboe [the navigation aid], a day attack by

Lancasters under fighter cover ... a day attack by Lancasters using Oboe, and a day attack by Lancasters accompanied by American aircraft equipped with the Norden bomb sight with which aircraft would control the bomb releases of the Lancasters'. Bufton seemed to be leading Bomber Command back to the righteous path of precision bombing and taking a step towards a unified Allied bomber command, something that Bert Harris abhorred. He vetoed it. It was the Americans who would fly the mission, without a written directive and without even telling Washington. Bottomley and Lt-General Eaker were going to war on their own.

And so it was agreed. 'All target maps will be forwarded to Col. Hughes ... but no further instructions will be issued to 8th Air Force except the executive order to attack which will be issued by the [British] Air Ministry,' the minutes of the 11 August meeting had determined. American crews were told they were attacking an 'aeronautical facilities station'.

Casualties were light. The mission flown on 28 August was escorted by a large number of P-47 Thunderbolt fighters of which one was lost and the pilot listed missing. On Tuesday 7 September the Americans hit Watten again. Weather was a problem and three groups aborted. But the target was plastered. Medmenham described what was left on the ground as 'a desolate heap'.

CHAPTER 13

London, August 1943

Through the second two weeks of August, a stream of intelligence of exceptional interest arrived in London. Dr Jones was away for two weeks' leave in Gloucestershire so Charles Frank handled it. The 'Waffenamt [weapons department, German War Ministry] source' had come live again in a series of telegrams received from Geneva. The first was dated 19 August 1943. 'Source Z.178/B' could reveal that there were two different rocket secret weapons under construction. One was a pilotless aeroplane officially known as 'PHI 7'. The second was a rocket projectile officially known as 'A-4'.

Dr Jones would later describe the motive of its sender as 'pure treachery', but that sender was not a bogus agent covering an Ultra source. Jones scribbled down: 'Very important. First mention of A-4' on the copy of the signal that survived in his personal papers. A second telegram from the same source arrived in short order, giving the range of the A-4 as 200 kilometres. The bombing raid on Friedrichshafen had destroyed a guidance equipment factory, the source revealed, and the German High Command 'believed the British must have discovered this important work'. The next day Z.178/B reported that ten A-4s had been test-fired in the Baltic with another hundred on hand. Accuracy was very poor, and without radio guidance they could be used only for 'aimless destruction'. The launcher was a 'simple sledge with rails' which could be 'used in open fields if necessary'.

The source also reported that Hitler had told his military leaders that Germany had to hold out only until the end of 1943, and London would be levelled to the ground. The Führer insisted on reprisal for Hamburg: 20 October was the date for launching thirty thousand rockets – something the source said was beyond the bounds of possibility. He dismissed all talk of long-range guns as irrelevant.

So what was PHI-7? It was not the rocket. That there was some sort of pilotless aircraft in the background was clear, but where it was being made and tested, how it worked and who would operate it, was all still utterly mysterious. It was little better with the rocket itself. Deep puzzlement remained in London concerning everything other than the external dimensions gleaned from glimpses of cylindrical objects from thirty-five thousand feet. Its range, fuel and weight, its guidance principle and manner of basing, the weight of its warhead and the potential date of its operational debut were all conjecture. Cherwell, meanwhile, remained sceptical as ever, gleefully attacking the report when it was copied to him, taking its technical principles apart line by line.

On 25 August Jones was presented with another agent report full of new information, in French. Professor Norman was sent a copy. It purported to be the statement of a 'captain on the active list attached to the test station in question'. It began with intimate details of security arrangements at Peenemünde and 'Zemfrin' and the nature and colour of the passes needed to get in.

A stream of highly detailed information followed, a jumble of facts and hypotheses about new weapons that did 'not obey the laws of ballistics' and about the use of 'bacteria as a weapon'. Then it got more specific: 'A final stage has been reached with developing a stratospheric bomb of an entirely new type ... The bomb is provided with "Racketten" (ailettes) and could be guided to specific targets. Trials are said to have been made from Usedom towards the Baltic.' This might be understood to refer to the rocket. But the trials, according to the source, seemed to be both an army and a Luftwaffe affair.

The trials have been made by the Lehr und Erpro-bungskommando Wachtel. Oberst Wachtel and the officers he has collected are to form the cadre of a formation (16 batteries – 220 men) called the 155(W) Flak Regiment which is going to be stationed at the end of October or beginning of November with HQ near Amiens and batteries between Amiens, Abbeville and Dunkirk.

The army artillery will have more than 400 catapults sited from Brittany to Holland. Major Sommerfeld, Colonel Wachtel's technical adviser, estimates that 50–100 of these bombs would be sufficient to destroy London. The batteries will be so sited that they can methodically destroy most of Britain's large cities during the winter.

The report had been sent to Kenneth Cohen, SIS controller for Western Europe, by a French Resistance operative called Georges Lamarque with a covering note that said, in effect: 'This material looks preposterous. But I have total faith in my source.' Who this was would not be revealed for many years. The story of how the report got to Broadway is as remarkable as its contents.

In 1942 Lamarque, a thirty-year-old former tank officer, had joined the Alliance network. It was right-wing and patriotic, and its members were known to each other as birds or animals, hence the alternative name for the network, 'Noah's Ark'. In early 1943 a sub-network called Les Druides was recruited among former members of the Compagnons de France, the patriotic youth organisation that had been dissolved by the Vichy government. One of these recruits was codenamed Amniarix. She was Jeannie Rousseau, the Parisian-born daughter of a civil servant. Twenty-year-old Jeannie became a translator for the Germans in Brittany. In 1941 she returned to Paris and worked with an industrial syndicate supplying the German war effort. One day she had met by chance on a train an old friend from her student days, ten years older than her, a math-ematician. Now he was putting together a new network, he told her. His name was Georges Lamarque. Did she meet Germans in her job for the industrial syndicate? he asked her. She did.

The German officers would often gather in the evenings at a house on the fashionable Avenue Hoche in the eighth arrondisse-ment. They would drink and talk freely among themselves about their work. 'I had become part of the equipment, a piece of furniture,' she told an interviewer in 1998. She did no more than tease and flatter her new friends.* 'I insisted that they must be mad when they spoke of the astounding new weapon that flew over vast distances, much faster than any aircraft. I kept saying: "What you are telling me cannot be true!"' Afterwards she would make her way to Lamarque's lodgings near Les Invalides. She would sit down at the kitchen table and write out what she had heard, word for word. 'I would absorb it, like a sponge. I wasn't asked to paraphrase, or to understand,' she told an interviewer. 'When the Germans referred to *Raketen*, for example, [I] had no idea what they were talking about.' Jones noted in pencil on his copy: 'Amazing report from a French girl but she wasted time because she mixes up Rockets and Flying Bombs.' The Waffenamt source had made a clear distinction between the PHI 7 and the A-4 rocket, but the French source had jumbled them up again. However, it had introduced the names Wachtel, Sommerfeld and Flak Regiment 155(W). All, it would turn out, were intimately concerned with the Cherrystone.

Bornholm, summer 1943

Very soon afterwards a third source was to produce unequivocal evidence of the existence of the pilotless aircraft. It came from Denmark. Invaded by the Germans in 1940, Denmark was supposedly the Reich's model protectorate. But Danish military intelligence services had continued to operate after the Nazi takeover, and had stayed in contact with London via Sweden. In the spring of 1943, an ever more active and open resistance led to German demands for a crackdown. By August the crisis had come.

On the morning of Sunday the 22nd something fell out of the sky

---

* In a closed postwar lecture on the wartime work of the SIS, Jones revealed somewhat ungallantly: 'It is only fair to mention that during the war there was one outstanding report obtained ... when a young French girl in August 1943 seduced a German officer attached to Peenemünde ... and got a remarkably detailed account of the embryonic flying bomb organisation although she much confused the issue by telling us that it was for the rocket.'

into a cabbage field on Bornholm. The island, given its strategic position in the Baltic, was much more militarised than the rest of the country. The local policeman went to investigate. He telephoned his headquarters in the town of Rønne, the administrative capital and seat of the German Kommandantur. Police superintendent J. Hansen got into his car, having informed the Kommandantur by phone of the incident and contacted Lt-Commander Christian Hasager Christiansen, the senior Danish military official on the island. The aircraft, if that is what it was, had crashed two kilometres north-west of Bodilsker church, twenty kilometres away at the other end of the island. Christiansen and Hansen got there at around 2:00 p.m.

The two Danes learned from local inhabitants that whatever it was had arrived at great speed and had given a loud whistling during its flight. It was 'in many pieces'. Christiansen got out his camera and took photographs of what seemed to be a miniature aircraft with no cockpit and a tube strapped somehow underneath its fuselage. 'V83' was marked on the tail and the words 'fuse – careful – do not pull', in pencil. A cylinder that seemed to house its motive force had what looked like a car radiator at its front end. It was said to be 'very warm an hour after the crash'.

Various hatches had sprung open revealing curious wire-wound spheres, and what appeared to be a guidance mechanism 'operating valves with compressed air which in turn operate the rudder', according to the subsequent report. In his dark-blue uniform the policeman posed with the object, to show the scale. As well as taking photographs, Lt-Commander Christiansen managed to make a sketch. Fifteen minutes later, two Germans turned up. They had no idea what the object was but it was clearly of German origin. It was covered in tarpaulins and dispatched to Rønne. When Christiansen reported to the Kommandantur, as he was obliged to do, he was asked if he had taken any photographs. He answered no.

Christiansen then sent an initial report by teleprinter to the head of Naval Intelligence, Commodore Paul Mørch, at the Ministry of Marine in Copenhagen. As Mørch told the story over thirty years later: 'The denial of taking any pictures meant sufficient time was won to get the copying and photographic work done in Rønne, including the sending of the main report with the enclosures to the Marine Ministeriet in Copenhagen and copies to England.'

> Copies of the main report [were] sent from me, in cooperation with the Danish General Staff Intelligence Organisation (LIGA), to the British Legation in Stockholm, to Mr [Ronald] Turnbull [SOE, Danish liaison], to Captain Denham the Naval Attaché and from there to the Air Ministry, Admiralty and SOE. A copy also went to the Swedish Defence Staff with which we were in close connection. The matter there was evidently sensational.

On 29 August the Germans declared martial law and the dissolution of the Danish government. The Danish naval commander ordered the fleet to go to Sweden. When he got to Stockholm, Mørch went straight to the British Legation with more of the story.

The Bornholm object marked V83 was a Fi 103 on a test flight from Usedom, which had flown beyond its planned range. Now it was about to fly straight into the brewing intelligence feud in London. There was to be a renewed Chiefs of Staff Committee at Downing Street at 17:00 on the 31st. Deputy Prime Minister Clement Attlee would chair it, as Churchill was on his way back from the Quadrant Conference in Quebec. The primary briefing document was a summary of the Waffenamt leak.

Dr Jones was summoned from holiday to add what he could, with just a few hours to absorb the three reports – from Geneva, from the Danish Ministry of Marine and from the French section of the SIS. His two bosses would be there, Sir Stewart Menzies and Sir Charles Portal. Lord Cherwell was sure to be peppery. Which way would the wind be blowing for Duncan Sandys?

Cherwell was as deprecating as ever, then Portal shifted the discussion onto a different plane when he referred to Cherwell's previous warning of the rocket being camouflage for something else. The photographs of the Bornholm object (it had only arrived out of the clear Baltic sky eight days before) seemed to show a pilotless aircraft – perhaps that was the PHI 7 mentioned in the report before them? Might it be of more immediate concern than the rocket? Lord Cherwell commented sourly that it would be an expensive way of conveying what seemed to be just a thousand pounds of explosive. Dr Jones said very little. But the pilotless aircraft had at last swum into view.

The question now was: Could Britain's fractious politicians and intelligence chiefs get it as wrong as thus far they had got the rocket?

PART II

'WE WILL FORCE ENGLAND TO HER KNEES'

CHAPTER 14

Peenemünde-Ost, August 1943

Peenemünde tended its wounds and took stock of what was still functioning. The measurement house and the wind tunnel had not been hit by the British bombs. Hall F1 of the pilot production facility was relatively undamaged: 80 per cent of the bombs had fallen in the woods. One hundred and seventy-eight German technicians were dead, including the engine specialist Dr Walter Thiel. Seven hundred Russian prisoners, Polish workers and prisoners from the camp at Trassenheide were dead or missing. No more whispers from the Baltic would come this way.

The spy-finder general, SS Obergruppenführer Ernst Kaltenbrunner, head of the the SS security service, hurried from Berlin to find out 'just how England might have gained information about the activities at Usedom'. The day after the Peenemünde raid, intending to blame spies and traitors, Himmler in turn rushed to the Führerhauptquartier at Rastenberg. When Albert Speer arrived in East Prussia that evening, the news from Usedom was grave: the secret work so vital to the Reich had surely been betrayed. Himmler had already proposed that the rocket programme be given the protection of the SS and move to a place where its security could be guaranteed.

According to Speer, 'We discussed the damage at Peenemünde … at some point Hitler brought up the manufacture of the A-4 and the necessity of keeping it secret. In this respect he said he had had a suggestion from Himmler. It was to reduce concern about security to a fraction by the use of prisoners from concentration camps [already being used already before the raid].' Skilled workers and even scientific specialists could be found. Himmler had already lined up 'a young and dynamic engineer' to take charge of the enterprise in case Hitler should agree with the proposal.

The next day, 25 August, Speer saw Himmler at his own head-quarters east of Rastenburg, to be given a pompous account of how Hitler had entrusted him with the stewardship of the rocket pro-gramme. Himmler had 'one of his most capable SS commanders ready to carry out the task'. He expected Speer to assign 'a first class staff or your engineers, with [Gerhard] Degenkolb continu-ing in some managerial capacity if he proved capable'.

All this was 'the express wish of the Führer who had already agreed to everything', recorded Speer. 'Finally [Himmler] told me that the Führer had requested that we continue the discussion with him that very evening.' So it was back to Rastenburg. Speer recalled the meeting at the Wolfsschanze:

> Hitler gave free rein to his imagination. He demanded an absolute minimum of 5000 A-4 rockets within the shortest pos-sible time ... My argument that the assignment could be compared only with the attempted mass production of a recently developed racing car made no impact. My anxieties were caused not only by the thought of all kinds of technical dif-ficulties, but also by the predictable conflicts that, as experience taught me, would come from working with the SS.

But Hitler could not be stopped. 'This will be retribution against England. With this, we will force England to her knees. The use of this new weapon will make any enemy invasion impossible.' Speer's minutes further noted: 'The Führer orders that all efforts must be made to once again speed up the con-struction of suitable production plants as well as production of the A-4 in cooperation with the Reichsführer-SS [Himmler], with heavy use of inmates from the concentration camps. He wants caves and bunkers for final production. According to a pro-posal of [Himmler's], the permanent factory shall be erected in connection with the training area belonging to [Himmler] in the Generalgouvernement.'* The training area in Poland was the Truppenubungsplatz Heidelager, sixty kilometres north-east of Cracow, a closed military zone run by the SS. It was big, remote and secure, even if the still far-away front line to the east was moving closer. In the middle of it was the abandoned village of Blizna. This was where trial rocket shoots and field training would be conducted.

At a meeting on 25 August in Degenkolb's Berlin office, Walter Dornberger first learned of Hitler's decision on underground production. He phoned Peenemünde, precipitating a meeting of key technicians chaired by von Braun which agreed that technical development must remain centred on Peenemünde. The rocketeers, however, were perfectly willing to move production plus its existing prisoner workforce. The man in charge of production, Arthur Rudolph, seemed especially keen to get manufacture under ground as soon as possible. Test-firing and troop training were another matter.

'Heidelager' had started appearing in Bletchley Park decrypts in 1942 as an SS 'recruit depot'. The whole site had been created, and ringed by a double wire fence, by slave labour. The work was overseen by an SS Zentralbauleitung (central building authority) of the sort that operated throughout the camp system, under the aegis of the Ministry of Economic Warfare head office in Berlin. The experimental area itself was in the heart of the forest close to the railway line, with barracks built for the four hundred army troops under the command of Oberst Gerhard Stegmaier. To begin with, the officers would be housed in a train parked on the railway spur.

The operational plans for the rocket were still evolving. The War Ministry's first scheme, of 1 September, gave Dornberger control of the A-4 both at home and in the field. It directed that he become something called 'Beauftragter zur besonderen Verwendung (Heer)' – 'Officer for Special Duties (Army)' – under Generaloberst Fromm, and that he be responsible for rocket development, production and training. Dornberger's headquarters as BzvB (Heer)

* Occupied Poland, the part not incorporated into the Reich.

would be at Schwedt-am-Oder, between Stettin and Berlin, with Oberst Georg Thom as his chief of staff.

To train the rocket troops, a rocket school was to be set up at Köslin in western Pomerania under Oberst Stegmaier. There would be a course for officers and technicians and one for soldiers, each lasting six weeks. Walter Dornberger, as well as being the Commissioner, was appointed to oversee preparations for actual operations in the West, for which post he was entitled Artillerie Kommandeur 91 – to be ready, presumably, to personally direct the rocket troops when the great day came to open fire on London, optimistically scheduled for the end of the year

The search for a bomb-proof factory site had begun after the raid on the Zeppelin works in June, which was coincidentally making rocket fuel tanks. The Peenemünde raid had confirmed the need for such a site. The whole of the German war economy was going under ground. And if there were not enough miners or other workers, there was the inexhaustible supply of prisoners. A certain Paul Figge of the A-4 delivery subcommittee found an obscure government agency that had been using old gypsum workings deep in the Kohnstein, a mountain north of the town of Nordhausen, for the strategic storage of petroleum and chemicals. In October 1940 the Armaments Ministry in Berlin had approved expansion of the site, creating two parallel S-shaped tunnels connected at regular intervals by cross-tunnels. It was for storage rather than industrial production. How could Germans be expected to work in such a place? The answer was soon forthcoming. By mid-1943 forty-six cross-tunnels existed, and each of the main tunnels was wide enough to accommodate double standard-gauge railway tracks.

On 26 August, Albert Speer called Karl Saur, Dornberger, Degenkolb and one Hans Kammler into his office for 'very secret negotiations'. Here they settled on the tunnels as the site for the main A-4 production. Then, by command of the Führer, they were ordered to expand further. Two days later the first truckloads of prisoners arrived from Buchenwald, where extensive SS-controlled armament production was already operating. A sub-camp was set up, at first inside the tunnels themselves. That camp would later be known as 'Dora'.

The 'young and dynamic engineer' that Himmler had

mentioned was forty-one-year-old SS Brigadeführer Dr Hans Kammler, who represents a paradox in his role as master-builder in the service of the mass destruction of human life. Born in Stettin, he studied civil engineering in Munich and Danzig, was awarded a doctorate, and joined the Nazi Party in 1932. From the time the Nazis came to power he held a variety of ever advancing positions, latterly in the new Reich Air Ministry. In 1940 he had been one of the planners of the Luftwaffe airfields in northern France from which the air assaults on Britain were mounted.

In 1941 he joined the SS, and it would the making of him. He quickly became head of the building and works department of the SS Economic and Administrative HQ in Berlin. Its head, Obergruppenführer Oswald Pohl, gave him the job of building the infrastructure for the mass extinction of the Jews. The site at Auschwitz in Upper Silesia, with which he would become intimately involved, was originally intended to be a model city, a regional capital of the SS empire in the east with a concentration camp attached. The family homesteads and cultural monuments were never built. Instead, in 1941–2 Kammler set about creating a sub-camp for thirty thousand prisoners, employing as his assistant one Karl Bischoff, a Luftwaffe officer who had worked on the airfields project in 1940. It would be the origin of Auschwitz-Birkenau, the main site for the implementation of the Final Solution. Rudolf Höss, the Auschwitz commandant, would describe Kammler as 'a tireless worker, with many good ideas. He hoped to achieve the impossible by force and finally had to admit that the war was stronger than he was. He lived a very simple, humble personal life and had a good family.'

Speer noted that Kammler was 'in many ways my mirror image. He too came from a solid middle-class family, had gone through university [and] had been "discovered" because of his work in construction.' Walter Dornberger compared him to a Renaissance warrior-prince, indifferent to the normal need for rest, who would fire a sub-machine gun during a meeting to keep staff awake. Within a year, Kammler would bring the baleful breath of the Holocaust to the people of London. The demon-king had appeared on stage.

Peenemünde-West, September 1943

The Luftwaffe's enclave on Usedom had not felt Hydra's wrath on
the night of 18–19 August. Max Wachtel told an RAF officer a little
after the war that 'the camp woke to find not one bomb dropped
on it'. But the Cherrystone trials would have to proceed, like the
rocket, in the knowledge that the secret establishment on the
Baltic was no longer immune. The completion of the operational
training site at Zempin–Zinnowitz eight kilometres along the
shore to the east would be delayed by the evacuation of prisoner
labour.

A reserve testing range had been quickly found at a naval air station at Brüsterort on the coast of Samland in East Prussia (from 1945
in the Russian enclave of Kalingrad). It was codenamed Windeck,
and Polish prisoners were drafted in to build three firing ramps.
More emergency sites had been surveyed, at Deep in Pomerania
south-west of Kolberg and at Rosenhagen south of Rostock. By 10
September the three Brüsterort batteries were complete and technical training had started under instructors from Fieseler, Argus and
Siemens. Then operational training, three weeks of learning the
firing procedure and about the special dangers of the 'perambulator' (the steam generator). Training proceeded with a further two
weeks at Zempin, with its mock-up firing site identical to the one
they would find in northern France.

At first the firing rate was steady, at thirty a day, but it fell to only
fourteen at the beginning of September as the stock of trial bombs
was used up. The first of the new prototype batch then arrived
from Kassel for testing, and there was an experimental air drop
over the Baltic from a converted He 111 bomber. A number of
bombs were equipped with the Funkgerät 23, a simple radio
device transmitting a single letter in Morse continuously via a trail-
ing aerial which could be picked up by a direction-finding array.

The arrival on 13 September of Generalleutnant Werner
Prellberg, commander of the Flak artillery school, gave Wachtel a
chance to relay news of progress in the theatre of operations:
'40,000 workers are at present engaged and no fewer than
178,000,000 bricks are required. But French workers often don't
turn up – can you believe it because they are afraid of air raids?'

Nevertheless Wachtel could report on the 16th: 'Rapid progress is being made ... the regiment has taken all measures to ensure that operations can begin by the date fixed, 1 December 1943.'

Leutnant Dr Wilhelm Pohl, the regimental security officer, visited Paris during 10–15 September when it was noted that the air fleet, Luftflotte 3, supplied a 'large quantity of maps of Great Britain which will be used by the regiment in compiling a target atlas' (the Flakregiment's map of London survives in Dr R. V. Jones's personal papers).

At the end of September the regiment's HQ war diary noted that 'security is especially important as enemy agents have been more active recently'. An oath of secrecy had been imposed on 1 July so that now 'men going on leave or being posted will be required to sign a further oath ... [and] Colonel Wachtel himself will personally censor all mail.' Meanwhile, the drink was flowing in Paris at the apartment on the Avenue Hoche, where oaths of secrecy did not seem to count for much.

CHAPTER 15

London, September 1943

It was Duncan Sandys himself who realised his committee was perhaps out of its depth hunting what were now clearly two weapons. He proposed at the beginning of September that Bodyline would continue to pursue the rocket but that the German air force's activities should be an Air Ministry concern. On the 10th, the chiefs readily agreed.

Dr Jones and his small staff were no longer concerning themselves with the rocket business – for the time being. He noted thankfully in his memoirs how they retreated while Cherwell and Sandys were still arguing, 'an argument so trivial that we thought ourselves well out of it'. His department was now to concentrate on 'jet-propelled or gliding bombs, pilotless aircraft and jet aircraft', and produce intelligence summaries to be presented as annexes to Mr Sandys's periodic reports.

The Bodyline report of 13 September carried the first such summary. It assumed that the pilotless aircraft, as it was now understood, could be countered by standard interception techniques as long as it did not fly exceptionally fast or high. If some sort of barrier defence was to be created, it was imperative to find out the device's range, speed, operational altitude and accuracy. The Air Ministry suggested that 'from very limited information based on unconfirmed intelligence ... [it appeared that] the

Fieseler Company [of Kassel] are working on an aircraft launched by catapult, afterwards propelled by a rocket unit with an explosive charge of several thousand kilograms. [It] has an automatic pilot with compensation for atmospheric conditions [and] is not controlled by wireless and therefore cannot be jammed.'* Apart from the means of propulsion and the size of the warhead, this account was pretty accurate.

On 14 September Dr Jones circulated a 'special note' with just four listed recipients, the service intelligence directors and Brigadier Stewart Menzies (C). It did not go to Sandys. It consisted of two telegrams, both sent on 7 September by a staff officer in Luftflotte 3 to a subordinate unit, plus some commentary from Jones. The copy surviving in Jones's personal papers is not marked 'Ultra', but uses bracketing & signs to indicate unfamiliar terminology in the Bletchley procedure. It had clearly come from the Park. Dr Jones would later tell an interviewer that it was 'the first really good piece of solid evidence about the pilotless aircraft'.

The signals were concerned with a banal-seeming piece of housekeeping. The sender chided the unidentified recipients for venturing outside the 'chain of command' to try to get extra anti-aircraft protection, which they had already been told was unavailable. The telegrams mentioned the 'ground organisation of Flak Zielgerät [Flak target apparatus] 76'. There was also a report of the capture of an enemy agent 'who had the task of establishing at all costs the position of the new rocket weapon. The English, it is stated, have information that the weapon is to be employed in the near future. And they intend to attack its positions before this occurs ... Five reception stations have up to now been attacked [by the RAF], some repeatedly.'

Jones's note suggested that, on this evidence, the Flak target device referred to was not a Queen Bee-style gunnery training drone as might first be deduced, but an offensive weapon. He concluded: 'The Germans are installing under the cover name FZG 76 a large ... ground organisation in Belgium and northern France which is probably concerned with directing an attack on England

---

* This was a report from the 'anti-Nazi Abwehr officer' Johann Jebsen, alias 'Artist', one of the few Double Cross agents to operate in Germany. He was arrested by the Gestapo in April 1944.

by rocket-driven pilotless aircraft.' In his memoirs he describes cheerfully informing Cherwell about the telegrams because it 'would let him off the hook for any blunders he might have made about the rocket. He was right about the pilotless aircraft.' But the cantankerous Cherwell would not be appeased: what was being referred to as Flak Zielgerät was indeed an 'anti-aircraft aiming device', he insisted.

The episode did not serve to make the Prof any less grumpy, but what happened next would have made him very happy indeed: the humiliation of Duncan Sandys.

Frank Inglis had circulated Jones's paper within his own intelligence directorate at Monck Street. Originally with a distribution list of four, it was doing the wider rounds of secure Whitehall in-trays. Within a week it would blow up in one.

The Chiefs of Staff Committee was still transfixed by the rocket. And it was the rocket that concerned Sandys in his report presented on 13 September, to which Jones's reflections on the pilotless aircraft were included as an appendix. Committee members were treated by Sandys to a rambling intelligence summary which reported, among much more besides, that a special unit had moved into Watten wearing grey-green uniforms with red flashes and was operating 'delicate instruments on tripods'. Since the 'undoubtedly most successful bombing of Peenemünde' there had been a notable soft-pedalling of German secret-weapon propaganda, Sandys told them.

The two long-range weapons had at last been largely disentangled from one another, but they each held many mysteries yet to be solved. According to Sandys the rail-served mortar-projector was still at the heart of the rocket-launch technique. And the Medmenham interpreters could now produce a diagram, serial number CIU D/353, based on aerial photography, that showed a 'rocket' projectile with three fins and a curiously blunt rounded nose.

The War Cabinet Defence Committee meeting the next day made a number of decisions based on the latest intelligence. They concluded that a further attack on Peenemünde was not yet necessary. They also agreed that the so-called Black Move, an operation devised in early 1941 for the evacuation of twenty-five thousand civil servants from London in the event of invasion or devastating bombing, was not to be revived – although every option would be kept under review, including preparations to put all vital government departments in underground 'citadels'.

The Committee agreed that the Minister of Home Security, Herbert Morrison, should put in hand the construction of a hundred thousand of the home air-raid shelters that bore his name. In the matter of the rocket, a Scientific Coordinating Committee should be set up to assist the inquiry. Sandys accordingly drew up a list of sixteen scientists including ten Fellows of the Royal Society to be on this committee. If intelligence from agents and photo-reconnaissance was confusing, a picture of the threat might be built up from first principles by clever minds in London.

Lord Cherwell saw this as a mistake as big as appointing Sandys had been in the first place. Such a large committee was hardly practical, he said. Again he consulted Dr Alwyn Crow, and a very short time later he informed Sandys brusquely that he was going to consult a panel of his own on the matter. It would have just four members: Professor G. I. Taylor, Sir Frank Smith (chief engineer of armament design at Fort Halstead in Kent), Professor Sir Ralph Fowler and Dr Alwyn Crow. Cherwell listed his own questions for his panel and sent them copies of the Medmenham sketch. Was it possible that this object could be a multi-stage rocket with a range of 130 miles? Could it be a single-stage rocket? What calorific-value fuel would it require? The feud would now be played out with rival scientific spear-carriers in support (although Professors Taylor and Fowler were also on Sandys's committee). Dr Jones remained serenely aloof.

At about this time Jones's special note of 14 September had made its transit of the Air Ministry and had reached Group Captain Lawrence Pendred, Director of Intelligence (Operations). On the 24th he sent a memo to Jones to say he had 'seen an MSS [Most Secret Source] in which complaint had been made that five "reception depots" in northern France had been attacked recently which had made the Flak authority responsible for their safety ask for more guns'. The inconveniently initiative-taking group captain had compiled a list from operational records of the locations of ground attacks by the RAF made between 25 August and 9 September. He had, he said, given it to Flight Lieutenant Kenny at CIU who was told to 'minutely examine these aiming points to see if any sinister object or construction had been missed by previous investigations'.

The resourceful Pendred sent Dr Jones a copy of Kenny's report, which in fact had found nothing, together with 'some extra copies for Mr Duncan Sandys'. Then this: 'Normally I would send such reports direct to him but I'm concerned with security aspects because I do not think that [Sandys] is in the picture. If you give him copy ... he will doubtless wish to know why this special investigation was made and if you say it was on account of a special report he will obviously want to know why he did not receive it himself.' Dr Jones seemed to know for certain that Sandys was not. He wrote in pencil on the letter: 'D-S may have received the report as a bogus agent's report.'

So that is how it stood in September 1943. Sandys, charged with ministerial powers since April to investigate the threat of the German long-range rocket, was not in the picture. Nor was he about to be. Cherwell and his protégé Jones were. Their battle to keep Mr Sandys ignorant of Ultra was only just beginning.

Dr Jones next drafted a paper for the chiefs entitled (ironically, it might seem, in the circumstances) 'Report on Reliability of Intelligence'. Formally presented by C and sanitised of Ultra references, it assured its readers once again that the evidence for the rocket could be considered reliable, but the rocket being a fact did not preclude the pilotless aircraft being developed by the German air force 'in keen rivalry' with the army. The paper emphasised the separateness of the air force establishment on Usedom, and concluded that it was 'certain from such disinterested witnesses as clerks compiling distribution lists, that the GAF [German air force] station ranks second only to Rechlin [the experimental station in Pomerania, the Luftwaffe's main testing ground for new aircraft]. This evidence is not only a key point in the picture but provides a touchstone on which other evidence can be tested.' It was very possible that the pilotless aircraft would arrive first, concluded Jones.

If Sandys was being told untruths, an equally sensitive question was looming: what to tell the Americans? On 20 September a signal from the British Joint Staff Mission in Washington arrived in London with the alarming news that the US War Department had asked for a summary of the information now available on the rocket. The military attaché, informed only via the general gossip, had started digging around the subject and had cabled the Pentagon that he could not get anything worthwhile 'from anywhere official as it is confined to Cabinet and Chiefs of Staff Level'. His signal was copied to the UK Air Ministry. A very sensitive row was simultaneously playing out between Bletchley Park and Whitehall as to how much Ultra material generally the Americans should be given.

Air Intelligence replied that they were averse to circulating papers such as the ones in question merely for information. So that was it. The matter of the rocket was for UK eyes only. After the Peenemünde raid of the month before, it might have seemed that some time had been bought. The Americans had been twice induced to attack the mysterious site at Watten, and they had done so under British command with no directive beyond a telephone conversation. But the Americans, it turned out, had already been sent a document dated 3 July headed: 'German Threats of Air and other Means of Attack upon Great Britain', which had been based on Sandys's Bodyline Committee report of a week earlier. It contained the information from the gossiping engineers in Berlin, the Luxembourg labourers and page after page of Panzer captain Cleff's imaginings. In fact, it must have been deeply baffling. After that the Americans had learned nothing more.

Lord Cherwell remained as resolute a rocket denier as ever. Aided by his fellow diehard Dr Crow, the Prof argued that the Peenemünde object as presented in the Medmenham sketch CIU D/353, with its blunt nose and three fins, could not contain enough fuel possessing enough energy to make it fly fast and far enough and carry sufficient explosive to be in any way dangerous. The supposed 'super-fuel' was a distraction. The crucial comparison was the weight of fuel carried as a proportion (the more the better) to all-up weight. Factored with the amount of thrust delivered as the propellant burned, the range of the missile and the size of the warhead could be determined. To understand it better, the Scientific Coordinating Committee appointed a 'fuel panel' of experts who were first obliged to consider 'whether a rocket with a range of one hundred miles or more carrying a warhead of one ton or more was a reasonable proposition'.

The Shell Petroleum scientist Isaac Lubbock was in America, so his chief assistant Geoffrey Gollin was summoned to the first fuel-panel meeting held at Shell Mex House on 20 September. He reported something both amazing and alarming – that the latest information from the US showed it was possible to reduce a liquid-fuelled rocket's physical weight to effectively less than half the weight of the fuel itself. The exploratory work had been done by a company called Aerojet, formed in March 1942 by a group of California Institute of Technology scientists led by the Hungarian-American Dr Theodore von Karman. To Dr Crow, still thinking in terms of solid propellants that needed a heavy casing, this proposition seemed impossible. Referring to the Peenemünde rocket sketch, Crow suggested: 'It seems possible that it might be a large torpedo.' Then, after considerable argument and having consulted Lord Cherwell, he bulldozed through this conclusion: 'We are of the opinion that the necessary range cannot be achieved by a single-stage rocket, and that the possibility of such a development in Germany can be ruled out.'

Cherwell was invited to attend the panel's next meeting, to be held on 11 October. To Geoffrey Gollin it was clear that this would be a tipping point. He suggested that Sandys visit the petroleum warfare experimental station at Langhurst in Sussex beforehand to see the petrol-oxygen rocket motor in action for himself. Lord Cherwell was still hoping for a reply from his chosen four – Taylor, Crow, Fowler and Sir Frank Smith – to his detailed questionnaire sent to them on 21 September. A reply was surely due, but by the first week of October he had still received none. He accused Sandys's office of deliberate obstruction. Relations remained icier than liquid oxygen.

Isaac Lubbock, back from the US, called along with Geoffrey Gollin on Sandys's loyal assistant Lt-Colonel Kenneth Post on 1 October. Together with two ballistics experts from the Ministry of Supply they began to design a liquid-fuelled rocket to conform to the Peenemünde object's outline, using the American-pioneered oxygenator-fuel combination of nitric acid and aniline. But the real news from America was how fuel and oxidant were fed into the combustion chambers by mechanical pumps. The Aerojet Corporation was employing an automobile engine to drive them, much lighter than the pressure bottles used thus far for the gas expulsion of propellant in experimental rockets. According to Dr Charles Ellis, making his view felt a little later, the information brought back by Lubbock from America 'completely altered the picture'.

That afternoon Lubbock and Post drew up a tentative design for the Peenemünde missile, based on a single-stage liquid-fuelled rocket. The design provided for 42 tons of fuel to be expelled from the rocket's tanks either by gas pressure or by gas-turbine-driven pumps. Six combustion chambers would deliver a theoretical thrust of 150 tons from the nitric acid/aniline combination. The 54-ton rocket would probably carry a 7-ton warhead to 140 miles.

Just then Mr Sandys got a glimmer that there might be a higher intelligence agenda. C had presented the Prime Minister with his daily personal harvest of diplomatic decrypts. On 7 October, Baron Oshima, the Japanese ambassador in Berlin, had some strange stuff to transmit from the Reich capital to Tokyo about an artillery weapon of 'enormous explosive force to be used against London by mid-December at the latest'. The Prime Minister scribbled in red ink that 'this should go to Mr Sandys'. The decrypt was annotated in return, 'shown to Mr Sandys by CSS in separate typed form on 11/10/43'.

That day, 11 October, the fuel panel met as scheduled. Cherwell was there, reluctantly, to declare that nobody could teach him anything about rockets. Enlarged photographs of the Peenemünde object were distributed. In spite of its obscure-seeming subject – the imaginary fuel for something that might or might not exist – the exchange was as tense and passionate as any of the many rocket discussions held in London that autumn.

When Lt-Colonel Post described the tentative design prepared by Lubbock and himself, there were protests that this was being introduced as new evidence before anyone had had the opportunity of examining it. Turning to each panel member individually, Sir Frank Smith inquired whether they now felt the object seen at Peenemünde might be a rocket. Each signified that it could indeed be. Crow and Cherwell thought not. According to the Prof the 'rockets' were inflated barrage balloons. Post asked drily why the German army found it necessary to transport barrage balloons on heavy-duty railway wagons. Smith then declared that he would record their agreed opinion that, 'having seen the sketch submitted to us, we are of the opinion that it may be a rocket'. Cherwell rose from his chair and left the room. Crow dissented. It was a fragile kind of unanimity.

Sandys was due to report to the War Cabinet after a meeting of his own scientists on the 22nd. Lord Cherwell's experts were planning to counter-attack at the upcoming Defence Committee (Operations) meeting, scheduled for the 25th. The fight was about to get even more acrimonious. Both sides would need more ammunition.

CHAPTER 16

If Churchill's most trusted scientific adviser could claim the Peenemünde objects were 'balloons', in Poland they were becoming a military reality. Activity at the Heidelager range was intense. On 28 September Himmler had arrived to inspect progress. The great rocket plan with its simultaneous technical development, field trials and operational training, along with the colossal construction work going on in the Harz Mountains and in northern France, was all supposed to proceed together.

On 6 October, A-4 test firing had resumed at Peenemünde with the first experimental field battery launch. It was a success. At Köslin, at a former imperial artillery barracks, the first operational unit was completing its preliminary six weeks of classroom training. Lehr und Versuchs [Demonstration and Experimental] Battery 444 would be sent to Poland at the end of the month just as two more launch units, artillery battalions 836 and 485, began their training.

As a German prisoner would much later tell his British interrogators, elaborate mock-ups were provided at Köslin, and the colour film of the rocket – the one shown to Hitler, with the von Braun-drafted title *And We've Done It After All* – was obligatory viewing. Then it was on to Heidelager to observe a launch by the demonstration battery before actually shooting the rockets. 'We were told we were firing into partisan territory,' said the prisoner. And of Professor von Braun: 'Despite his Nazi convictions and the

fact he often appeared in uniform indicating he had some honorary
SS rank, he was not greatly enamoured of the operational possibilities of the A-4.'

As far as London was concerned, nothing new about the nature
of the rocket or other long-range weapons had emerged from
Poland or anywhere else. But there was a tiny glimmer of light. On
12 October, Professor Norman set the scrambler and telephoned Dr
Jones in London. There was an interesting decrypt on the Brown
(Enigma key) watch. Having gone quiet in June, the XIV
Kompanie of the Luftnachrichten-Versuchs (Experimental
Signals) Regiment had come live again. Feldwebel (Sergeant)
Beyer at Köthen airbase had a simple message: 'To Zempin. Traffic
can begin from 08:00 tomorrow.' The whispers from the Baltic were
back on air.

Lausanne, 20 October 1943

A middle-aged Frenchman picked up a public phone in a Swiss
border town and put a call through to the British Legation in
Berne. He announced to his contact in a prearranged code that 'he
had bought the tickets for the performance at two'. He had, he
said, some very good seats. The man was Michel Hollard, commercial traveller in the gas-producing charcoal-stove business
which powered petrol-less motor vehicles. He was a French
patriot, and agent extraordinary. He had come this way before –
many times – crossing the border illicitly from the Jura mountains
into neutral Switzerland. As usual he would head for the meeting
place in Lausanne by bus. He had a story to tell, taken down by his
contact, an officer of the British Secret Intelligence Service who
had returned from Berne. Hollard knew him only as 'OP'.

The story he had to tell this time, to be sent as a cipher telegram
to London that night, was sensational. But what was really exceptional was a sheaf of drawings – builders' plans of construction
works under way in northern France. How this anonymous-
looking, Paris-based travelling salesman had come by them was
the real story. They too would be on their way to London, by
diplomatic pouch, that night.

M. Michel Hollard had built up a *réseau* of volunteer observers – railwaymen, telephone linesmen and the like – a network that had no connection with any wider Resistance group. It was called 'Agir' (meaning 'to act'). His commodity was information, gossip, any observations at all about what the German occupiers were up to. His ability to get in and out of Switzerland, where he had first made contact with the SIS station in 1942, meant that wireless didn't need to be used, with its risk of detection in getting its messages to London. It was all done by personal contact, by word of mouth.

That summer of 1943 a railway engineer, a contact of Hollard's, had overheard a conversation between contractors in a Rouen café discussing large-scale projects demanding a high degree of accuracy in the way the buildings were laid out. Hollard went himself to the Seine-Inférieure department to track them down. At a little place called Bonnetot-le-Faubourg he got onto a building site by simply picking up a wheelbarrow. There he found a clutch of low buildings newly built with modest roadways leading to a central strip, the orientation of which by judicious use of a concealed compass he managed to fix. It was pointing at London. The Germans had told the French workmen they were garages. According to George Martelli's very readable biography, published in 1960:

> Collecting a team of reliable agents, [Michel] provided them with a bicycle and allocated them a zone covering a stretch of the coast to a depth of twenty miles. Each agent was also provided with a map, and a description of what to look for. All he had to do, when he discovered a site, was to mark the exact position.
>
> The results surpassed Michel's wildest expectations. After three weeks his team had located over sixty sites, distributed along a corridor nearly two hundred miles long ... running roughly parallel to the Channel.

By the end of October a hundred sites had been discovered – mysterious closed areas, workers' huts, trial convoys of building materials – Hollard travelling weekly to Switzerland to update OP (named much later by Hollard's son Florian as James Kruger, an SIS desk officer in Lausanne). About the same time Hollard

recruited a young draughtsman, one André Comps, who managed
to get work on a building site at a place called Bois Carré, near
Yvrench in the Somme region. Comps then did something amaz-
ingly brave: he diligently copied the Luftwaffe construction-office
plans left each lunchtime in a German engineer's coat pocket. This
was the package that arrived at the British Legation, Berne, in
Kruger's hand, to be put in the diplomatic bag on its way to
London. It would take a little while yet to reach SIS headquarters
at 54 Broadway.

London, October 1943

Lord Cherwell was unbending in his dismissal of the rocket.
Duncan Sandys was banging his head on a wall of bowler-hatted
scientific obscurantism. After the frustrations of the fuel-panel
meeting, Isaac Lubbock was directed by Sandys to prepare a fuller
theoretical blueprint for a long-range, liquid-fuelled rocket of the
size of the Peenemünde object. Starting on 14 October, he had finished by the evening of the 18th. The next day, he showed the
blueprints to Sandys.

Lubbock had allowed for accelerations up to 16G, and this
meant a pretty robust construction. To expel fuel from the tank he
proposed using gas pressure from burning cordite, a technique that
was impossible with liquid oxygen. It would explode. He did warn
Sandys, though, that it was possible the Germans had perfected a
centrifugal-pump system.

Sandys had copies of the Lubbock blueprint dispatched to
Fort Halstead on the 20th for an independent opinion on the
rocket's practicability from the chief engineer, Sir Frank Smith.
Smith found that 'there was no single major engineering factor
which had not been considered and for which an answer was not
forthcoming', then got down to some theoretical designing of his
own. Lubbock was instructed to bring the drawing personally to
the committee meeting next day. The only dissent arose over the
way in which the liquid fuels could be introduced into the combustion chamber. Dr Crow complained that he had had hardly
any time to study the Lubbock design. Professor Ellis agreed

that pumps (rather than expulsion by cordite) appeared to be the key.

At last it seemed there was agreement. The Scientific Coordinating Committee reported to the War Cabinet thus:

> We consider that a rocket projectile ... could have the dimensions of the object seen at Peenemünde. Whilst there is no reliable basis for calculating the accuracy of such a projectile, we consider it reasonable to assume that half the rounds fired would fall within a circle of about five miles radius around the mean point of impact at a range of 100 to 150 miles. Depending on the variables as outlined, the warhead could be anywhere between one and twenty tons.

Sandys circulated the report on the 24th as an annexe to his 13th interim report to the chiefs, which opened with the statement that in view of the new technical information from America, 'previous estimates for range and weight of warhead [may have been] *rather too low*'.

'Rather' was not the word. The projectile as currently perceived might deliver a warhead of between ten and twenty tons over a range of 130 miles. This bruiser, furthermore, said Sandys, 'had reached a state of development where it can be used operationally'. Intelligence evidence, he warned, strongly suggested that the Germans might have manufactured five hundred already and that an offensive was possible by the end of November, thus 'making possible the delivery of the equivalent 10,000 tons of bombs in London in a single week'.

The paper was considered at a meeting late on 25 October in the Cabinet War Room. The gathering was as argumentative and bad-tempered as any that had gone before. Churchill was in the chair. Dr Jones was there and so, this time, was Isaac Lubbock.

Sandys presented his summary, and explained how Mr Lubbock had been invited on his return from America to prepare a tentative study of a rocket motor with outside dimensions matching the object photographed at Peenemünde. Lord Cherwell insisted that if experiments were continuing 'we [can] be sure the weapon, whatever it might be, [is] 8–12 months away from being operational'. Turning to Lubbock's design, he remarked that it was a great pity that Dr Crow, who knew more about rockets than anyone else in the country, was not present. The Lubbock device was a leap too far: 'It is unlikely that [German rocket] development would jump suddenly from a relatively small projectile to one of the size which we are now informed is nearing completion. There are many reports of secret weapons, and the only reason that the rocket has attracted such attention is the fact that objects assumed to be long-range rockets have been photographed at Peenemünde.' Even if the device could be made to work, his view remained as always: that its low initial acceleration and large fins meant it would simply be blown off course by the wind in the first seconds of rising from the ground. He ended his tour of the rocket horizon thus: 'At the end of the war, when we know the full story, we should find that the rocket is a mare's nest.'

Dr Jones was now called on to speak. The evidence had led him to a very different conclusion. Rumours had turned into firm reports, and the objects photographed at Peenemünde 'tallied closely with reports received from foreign labourers employed at the experimental establishment concerning large rockets'. He could assure the committee that the rocket was not a hoax. The Germans had invested a lot of work in a long-range rocket, but to what extent they had succeeded he could not say.

Isaac Lubbock spoke about his design, which, he said, was a reasonable approximation of what could be done. The pump for such a device needed to generate 4000 horsepower, but given 'the knowledge of the work going on in this country [Frank Whittle and Power Jets Ltd]', a gas turbine producing the required horsepower would not present any great difficulties. Cherwell spluttered. He had been at a meeting of the Scientific Coordinating Committee which, he understood, had concluded the rocket was not practical. Professor Ellis was quick to correct him. It was his recollection that Cherwell had left the meeting before consideration had been given to the new American fuel-pump technique as reported on by Mr Lubbock'.

Cherwell could not bear it. Getting that amount of power out of such a small mechanism (even for a few seconds) just could not be done. If the Germans had somehow mastered it, why did they not use the aircraft? But it could be done. Few people knew the secrets of Wing Commander Frank Whittle's jet engine, but Lubbock (who had helped develop it) did.

To save face all round, Cherwell was directed to arrange a meeting with the four scientists (Prof-friendly, he might assume) to whom he had wished to send his questionnaire, and Mr Churchill himself would hear a reprise of the scientific discussion afterwards.

It was past midnight, but the acrimonious exchange was not yet over. In the final summation Sandys's view just about prevailed. The Chief of the Air Staff was directed to continue attacks on the suspicious structures discussed at such length and on factories. Photographic reconnaissance of northern France should be intensified. In view of the rumours circulating, consideration should be given to the advisability of making a public statement.

Cherwell retired, bruised, to plot his next move. He wrote a blistering memorandum for the Cabinet Secretary, recording the arguments to date and the dangers of letting scientific amateurs loose on such matters. Mr Sandys had first been seduced by 'a mendacious prisoner', he said, who with his tales of super-fuels had bypassed the laws of physics. 'When it was pointed out that [super-fuels] would heat the combustion chamber to a temperature that no material in the world would stand, a new hare was started – that the Germans could make a rocket two-thirds of whose weight was fuel. We were told that Dr Lubbock had this brainwave on hearing of some American plans,' he remarked acidly. 'Now we are told that a certain German Colonel ... is working on pilotless aircraft, bacteriological war or long range rockets. From the fact that this colonel really exists it seems a long way to concluding that long range rockets really are practicable.'

Cherwell's meeting with his own four scientists was duly held at noon on 28 October in the Prof's room at the Cabinet Office; a further meeting, with Churchill, was scheduled for later. All the now familiar objections were rolled out again: gyroscope guidance was impractical, the combustion chamber would melt, a monster launching mortar would be required, and a fuel pump as described by the ludicrous Mr Lubbock would need an engine of 4000 horsepower to power it. The blunt round nose of the object at Peenemünde was supposedly the top of a fuel tank to which a warhead would be fitted, but no such warhead had been observed. The ratio of fuel to overall fuelled weight was said to be as high as 70 per cent. This was impossible, thought Cherwell, if the structure was to be robust enough to withstand firing. Sir Ralph Fowler quite reasonably inquired what the Prof thought the objects seen on the photographs might be if they were not rockets.

'They might possibly be some sort of kite balloon.' There was a moment's silence. Or they might be a cover for some other activities, Cherwell added.

The meeting ended with a formal agreement that 'many formidable difficulties still stood in the way of accepting the objects photographed at Peenemünde as being long-range rockets'. It looked as if the Prof had won.

Cherwell went into the evening meeting at No. 10 on the 28th believing his own favoured panel of experts were loyal rocket-sceptics to a man. With Churchill in the chair and the Minister of Aircraft Production Sir Stafford Cripps in attendance, once again the Prof banged on about an 'outsize mortar'. And if the Germans really had devised a wondrous gas turbine to power the rocket's fuel pump, why did they not use it in aircraft? he asked, not unreasonably. He still contended that pilotless aircraft would be far easier and more cost-effective to manufacture than rockets.

The scientists made their points, gradually veering towards Lubbock's presentation as being both practical and possible: 'no means of judging' ... 'a matter of speculation' ... 'by no means improbable' ... 'no insuperable engineering difficulties'. Cherwell's flag was drooping, Churchill looked baffled. Professor Ellis summed it up: 'All that it was necessary to show was that the difficulties in making such a device could be overcome and no natural law would have to be violated in the process.'

Churchill indicated wearily that it was pointless to go on debating scientific theories for month after month. A decision would have to be taken. He announced a special committee of inquiry to recommend further steps and proposed that Cherwell himself take the chair at its first session, to be held the following morning. But Cherwell rose and declined, saying that he had another engagement. The Prime Minister turned to Sir Stafford Cripps. The cerebral minister and ascetic socialist lawyer undertook to hold the first session in the Cabinet Office the next day.

CHAPTER 17

London, October 1943

The conundrum of what to tell the Americans was unresolved. It could not last. On 25 October Major-General Francis Davidson, Director of Intelligence at the War Office, told the chiefs that 'certain American officers were pressing for information on the rocket'. The chiefs ordered the Joint Intelligence Committee to look into the matter. Their response, two days later, revealed some extraordinary goings-on.

They wanted guidance because 'there is at present a divergence between official policy and what is happening in practice'. It was clear that Americans in London were picking up odd bits of information from Stockholm and other legations in neutral countries, from 'agent reports of a general nature' and from 'P/W interrogations to which they have access'. The Americans were not stupid. The JIC surmised that they might have realised by now the purpose of the Peenemünde raid and could have worked out the reason why the 8th Air Force had been sent a little later to attack Watten in Norman Bottomley's freelance bombing war. The report of two escaped USAAF officers had given the game away, said the JIC document. This was an astonishing admission. Shot-down aircrew who had managed to evade and get back across the Channel were telling high-up US commanders just what the British were up to.

The report pointed out that London's reticence had backfired.

When asked to find out more, the US military attaché's reply to the Pentagon that the subject was so secret that it was not worth pursuing had caused even greater excitement in US intelligence circles, 'their appetite no doubt having been whetted by the fragmentary reports from their office in [20 Grosvenor Square] London'. The current position was clearly untenable. The commander of the European Theater of Operations, United States Army (ETOUSA) and his intelligence chief '[are] starting to take an interest ... furthermore US scientists have been consulted by Mr Sandys's committee and it is reasonable to assume they passed on [to Washington] what they knew,' said the JIC.

What was to be done? The Americans might take fright. The cross-Channel invasion, planning for which was advancing rapidly after the decisions reached at the Quadrant Conference, might be compromised. 'It must be stressed that there is a propaganda aspect to the secret weapon story which is one of the principal methods by which German morale is being maintained,' the JIC report went on. The three service intelligence directors who made up the committee recommended compiling a list of the most senior US officers in Washington and England, including the Commander of the 8th Air Force, who should be put in the picture as far as long-range weapons were concerned. 'Above all [the Americans] must not undertake *independent* inquiries,' they stressed. There was little chance of ensuring that.

The chiefs, however, were not going to open the gates entirely. Having received the JIC's recommendations, they agreed that rocket intelligence could 'be given orally and under the strictest security conditions' to competent US authorities. The UK's Ministry of Economic Warfare (responsible for bombing-target intelligence) was brought into the mix a week later. But the new flow of information would be just a trickle.

The actual arrangements were extraordinary. Thus it was that in the last weeks of 1943 a lonely officer from ETOUSA, a certain Colonel Jackson, went each day to the Air Ministry to be given an account of the latest intelligence about rockets and pilotless aircraft. It was 'the responsibility of this officer to keep the Americans in this country and in Washington in touch with current developments'. Poor Colonel Jackson found it just a little difficult to keep it all in his head.

Churchill, though, seemed prepared to be more open with the Americans, and he sent a long telegram to President Roosevelt on 25 October summarising the rocket story since the beginning and promising to send the latest information as it was obtained. Thus Sandys's super-alarmist summation of the 24th would soon be on its way to the Pentagon. 'The expert committee who are following this business ... think the main attack would be attempted in the new year,' Churchill told the President. 'Your airmen of course are in every way ready to help.'

And the American airmen indeed were. A mysterious construction site on the coast at a place called Marquise-Mimoyecques, south of Calais (see p. 162), picked up by air reconnaissance was twice bombed in early November by the US 9th Air Force after a telephone conversation between Lt-General Eaker and Air Vice Marshal Bottomley, but 'with no official directive'. A bunker under construction at Martinvast on the Cherbourg peninsula would receive the same treatment. A leaflet was prepared for dropping on the sites before the attack in the name of the 'Inter-Allied Command', ordering 'every workman in the region working for the Germans to take to the maquis at once'.

Since the meeting on 28 October from which Cherwell had huffily withdrawn, Sir Stafford Cripps was now de facto Long-range Weapon Grand Inquisitor. Duncan Sandys seemed slightly superfluous. There had been a whispering campaign against him ever since his doom-filled report of the 24th. In closed session, the patrician Victor Cavendish-Bentinck, chairman of the Joint Intelligence Committee, told the chiefs of staff that 'the tone of the report ... might be considered rather too alarmist'. He implied, more damningly, that its author had been duped by the enemy. An attack was not imminent. Not one of the chiefs disagreed.

But Sir Stafford's first task was to bring order to the squabble among the scientists. The fractious intelligence services and Sandys's outfit would get the same treatment a little later (and much good would it do any of them). The Cherwell camp was dwindling but Churchill was not going to sack his friend. Before starting the formal proceedings, Sir Stafford shrewdly invited informed figures in the affair to his flat for background briefings. Dr Jones was one of them: 'I did not attend the inquiries in the sense of sitting with Cripps,' he would recall twenty years after the events. 'I had two interviews with him, one was a private one in which the situation about the radar plots and the flying bomb was explained.'

And so the minister was drawn into the fringes of Ultra. It was timely. There had been that flicker on 12 October from Feldwebel Beyer that went 'Traffic can begin ...' From mid-October the Brown-key breaks began to deliver the chatter of the Baltic Insect radar tracking stations about the airborne 'body'. There was mention of 'departure and impact', 'angle-shots', 'explosive trials'. And on 2 November from a Luftwaffe officer attached for some reason (it would become clearer later) to the SS artillery school at Glau, south of Berlin: 'To Lehr und Erpr. Kdo [Erprobungskommando] Wachtel Zempin. I am still to receive soap for October from the Lehr [und Versuchs] batterie. Please send it. Pay I receive here. From Nelz. Obegfr.'

A plea for a soap ration to be sent thus confirmed the location of the demonstration and experimental command: it was at Zempin, and its commander was one Wachtel. Long strings of barely encoded numbers had begun to turn up from 28 October onwards, and Jones was pretty sure what they signified. They were the measures of bearing, height and distance (the system would later change to grid squares) flown by some kind of pilotless aircraft taking off from the said Zempin, near Peenemünde. The aircraft was flying in an east-north-easterly direction along the Baltic coast and being plotted by a chain of radar stations. The data could be transposed onto maps and charts in London just as was being done on Usedom. They could plot the range, the speed, the accuracy. It was a miracle.*

From their efforts Air Intelligence had thus obtained, as Jones would say later, 'a ringside seat at the trials'. The distribution list for the reports that would follow was just four people.

---

* According to the internal history of Section 3GN at Hut Three, Bletchley Park, much of 'the working out of the daily trial plots' was done by Miss Rhoda Welsford, otherwise librarian of the Courtauld Institute in London (where one of her colleagues was the wartime MI5 officer Anthony Blunt). Another source describes the bespectacled Miss Welsford, a veteran of naval codebreaking during 1914–18, keeping up her Mayfair standards by wearing white gloves as she toiled over the decrypts amid vases of freshly cut flowers. Jones in his memoirs also credits David Arthen Jones, a 'young Welsh physicist from Ebbw Vale', a junior member of his own tiny directorate.

Zempin, October 1943

The Baltic weather stayed fine and clear. The season was turning. The date for the promised bombardment of London by the Flak Zielgerät (FZG 76) was getting closer. Immune to fog and rain, it could fly by day and night whatever the weather – that was its special trick, and one that the people of London would come to loathe.

The flight trials continued. The experimental Kommando must achieve longer ranges. The trouble was, the hand-built prototype V-series would soon be exhausted. One hundred pre-production units had been promised but by mid-October only thirty-eight had arrived at Zempin from the Fieseler Works at Kassel-Bettenhausen. Test firings were restricted to two a day. The regiment had been optimistically informed that the mass-production series, to be built at the Volkswagen plant at Fallersleben, would reach five thousand monthly by the end of the year. No chance. VW, in fact, had not even started production until late September, and major structural problems remained unsolved.

Who should have the honour of commanding the destruction of London? On 14 October Feldmarschall Gerd von Rundstedt proposed the creation of an interservice corps under his authority to command all long-range weapons.

That same day the first 'hot bird', as Wachtel described it, arrived on a camouflaged truck at Zempin – the first G-series pre-production missile from VW Fallersleben. Two days later the war diary recorded: 'On a fine, mild autumn Sunday at No. 1 Ramp everyone waits tensely. The power unit roars. A flare signal for the chase-plane rises into the sky, the launcher goes into action, and with a long exhaust flame the missile takes off smoothly, rising slowly then quicker and quicker – the FZG 76 gains height and takes course. Very quickly it disappears from sight.' The regimental lead party had already left for France two days before. That afternoon of 16 October Hauptmann Suss and his men of 1 Batterie I Abteilung boarded the train at Zinnowitz on the first stage of their journey west. There was singing and joking. The regiment would all be heading the same way soon enough.

The next bird off the Zempin ramp crashed, but the following day's shoot was successful. They continued through October, the 'weather fine and clear, for weeks now it has been extremely mild but it cannot be speeded up until the VW works deliver more than six a day, but still they need modifications and tinkering with – at least two hundred working hours needed per unit,' recorded the war diary.

They were now production testing. The mass-production-series airframes, spot-welded, proved faulty: two thousand wings and mid-sections had to be scrapped at the factory as unfit. G-series airframes broke apart on the catapult. The VW works was damned for every flop. And when the craft actually got airborne there were plenty more faults.

Kassel, October 1943

A report that the Gerhard Fieseler aircraft company was making pilotless aircraft had been sent from Berne in August and given to the chiefs. On 21 October a Luftwaffe prisoner had stated that the Fieseler Storch works was being equipped for the manufacture of the 'same secret weapon as was being made at Peenemünde'. The next night Kassel was gutted by an RAF-laid firestorm. The medieval old town was the target, not the Fieseler factory in the eastern suburb of Bettenhausen. This was a Cherwell–Harris exercise in 'dehousing' that killed at least ten thousand, most of them sheltering in cellars, by carbon-monoxide poisoning. One survivor, returning to find her home a mass of charred rubble, reported: 'We thought first of all we could get some air. Air air air. All round us was a picture of horror ... We hoped at least our things in the cellar were safe. We had carried everything down there, blankets and clothes and hats and shoes and furs ... Churchill took everything, the bastard!'

After Hamburg, after Kassel, how could the Nazi regime keep the German people believing in Final Victory? How could it deflect their rage from those so signally powerless to defend them on to those who were burning their homes, their children? The prospect of making the British pay might restore the semblance of a battle fairly joined. For a while it worked. 'There is almost unanimous agreement among the national comrades in their demand that the British people be exterminated,' said a security police home intelligence report. The German historian of the bombing, Jörg Friedrich, recorded public sentiment: 'Revenge cannot be strong enough.' 'Gas them before they gas us.'

Goebbels turned the wonder-weapon rumours off and on, as required. He did not have to try too hard. Even the servant girls in Berlin seemed to know that the Führer had sanctioned the means of retaliation, as the Peenemünde-West commandant put it. An intelligence department in London did little else but count the references to 'revenge' in the German newspapers as an indicator of likely attack. And rumours would soon turn to specifics. Hitler would make a sulphurous speech at the Löwenbräu beer cellar in Munich on 8 November that year, the twentieth anniversary of the Beer Hall Putsch. Germany's hour for revenge was coming, he proclaimed: 'Even if for the present we cannot reach America, thank God that at least one country is close enough to tackle!'

Hitler saw treachery behind the Kassel attack, and ordered the Fieseler works to dismiss the non-Germans (mainly French and Dutch) who made up 45 per cent of the workforce. The delivery of M-series serial-production airframes slowed to a trickle. But enough were reaching Zempin for the flight-test programme to continue.

The tests were progressing from simple flight trials to plotting the fall of shot at extreme ranges. Through late October the Park picked up messages about a detachment of XIV Kompanie under a certain Leutnant Kubitza being sent with geological instruments to the Danish island of Falster. Their task was to find out whether microseismic waves were being caused by ground detonations carried out at the Luftwaffe test centre at Rechlin, 120 miles to the south. The SS artillery school at Glau was involved with the explosive experiments. Obergefreiter Nelz, the officer in want of soap, had been the first clue. This exercise puzzled Professor Norman, until he realised that the geology of water and land formation between the two locations was broadly similar to that between southern England and the French coast. The experiments aimed to discover whether bangs heard in London could be plotted by detecting tiny seismic tremors in Abbeville. It would turn out, in the end, that they could not – when the time came the Luftwaffe would need other means to determine where its missiles were falling.

The Kassel raid also put paid to any doubts about moving long-range weapon production under ground. By October eight thousand slaves were labouring at the Mittelwerk to expand the tunnel system. Skeletal men in rags ceaselessly pushed hopper trucks of rock against the deadline of the production equipment arriving. They ate and slept within the pharaonic ant-hill, thousands of them crammed into bunks stacked four high and slithering with excrement in an atmosphere thick with dust and fumes from the blasting. They died where they laboured.

At the end of September, Degenkolb pressed the A-4 Special Committee to establish a new industrial combine to make the rocket under ground, once the cave system was ready. Called the Mittelwerk (Central Works Ltd), it was headquartered in Berlin and effectively financed by the Armaments Ministry, but run along the lines of a private firm with directors drawn from existing industrial companies. Dornberger was on the board, as was an ex-Buchenwald guard, Otto Förschner, who would become the commandant of concentration camp Dora. He would act as Obergruppenführer Kammler's representative.

The most important member of the Mittelwerk would turn out to be Albin Sawatzki, the engineer who had energised Tiger tank production and who, although not an SS member, would soon supplant Förschner as Kammler's most important operative there. The Peenemünde production specialist Arthur Rudolph was in charge of the technical division under Sawatzki.

The grisly Harz Mountains complex was just the beginning. The search had begun for an underground site for the Peenemünde development works itself, not to be located with the factory. South of Salzburg, a vast underground factory codenamed 'Zement' would eventually be tunnelled out of the Austrian Alps. From September slaves began preparing a slate quarry at Lehesten in the mountains of southern Thuringia about 128 kilometres south-east of the Mittelwerk, for use as a test-firing site and for the calibration of rocket engines and turbo-pumps. The Lehesten quarry had its own small concentration camp, known as Laura, in the village of Schmiedebach, which was also administered as a sub-camp of Buchenwald. Caves hollowed out by slave labour would later house a liquid-oxygen plant which could produce eight metric tons of lox an hour, shutting down for three days out of thirty in order to thaw out. There were more such plants, created in the same way – at Raderach near Friedrichshafen and Wuittringen in the Saar. At Dernau-Marienthal near Bonn, two railway tunnels were turned into an underground factory where seven thousand Russian and Italian prisoners were set to work on making ancillary vehicles for rocket operations; an SS-run camp, Rebstock, was installed there. This archipelago of labour camps put Hans Kammler at every nodal point of long-range weapon production and testing.

The Mittelwerk was formally founded on 24 September as a limited company – 'GmbH'. The first director was Dr Kurt Kettler, lately of the Reichsbahn and Rheinmetall-Borsig locomotive works. It was Albin Sawatzki who set the pace, however, with plans for 1800 rockets per month produced by eighteen thousand workers toiling without cease. The project was soon judged unrealistic, though, and on 8 October a new one was adopted, to produced nine hundred units a month. Now at last a production order could be given to the Mittelwerk by order of the Army High Command, represented by General Leeb as chief of the army weapons development branch. The order for the monthly production of nine hundred A-4 units, to reach a total of twelve thousand, was signed on 19 October.

By now the whole region was becoming a security zone, including the towns of Nordhausen and Niedersachsenwerfen. Already plans had been made for moving production machine tools into the mountain. The slave-labourers would do that, and then civilian technicians and supervisors from the Baltic would come to work in the Harz, at first in their hundreds, later by the thousand. Some were already there. Pay was good (Arthur Rudolph trebled his Peenemünde salary), and child allowance and life insurance were available. In view of the 'difficult working conditions', Speer's deputy Karl-Otto Saur acknowledged that they should get extra leave. They would need it.

CHAPTER 18

Central Interpretation Unit, autumn 1943

In London, the Great Rocket Flap was subsiding. A mysterious pilotless aircraft was now calling for attention, along with some sort of dispersed organisation on the ground. A startling new fact was about to be revealed. This time it would come from Medmenham.

The Sandys imperative to re-photograph the entire French coast had been put in hand on 28 October. They were still looking for some sort of rocket and an associated projector based near a main railway line. Over a hundred sorties would be flown, each returning with up to a thousand exposures, all of which had to be printed, sorted, distributed and worked over with the stereoscope. But this time there was a new clue as to where to look – and it was not near any railway line.

Wing Commander Douglas Kendall, head of the Technical Control Section, was in a unique position at Medmenham. He was 'indoctrinated into Ultra', and since 1942 had been cleared to see CX 'agent' reports. He was about to be apprised of something very interesting that had reached the Secret Intelligence Service from Switzerland and it had landed on Dr Jones's desk early on the 28th. The package transmitted by Michael Hollard via James Kruger to Berne had got through. Dr Jones was to call it 'a brilliant piece of espionage'.

Contained in the package were builder's drawings in both plan and section, to 1:100 scale, with French-language annotations as to what the constructions were called on site, if not their actual function. One, called the Maison R, had a broad arched entrance and a wide arc inscribed on the interior floor. The structure was made of *béton non armé*, concrete without the standard iron-rod reinforcement. The Maison R was reported, curiously, to contain no metal parts whatsoever – no latches, door handles or air vents; even the door hinges were made of a synthetic material called *Zinqaut*, and the path leading from the platform to the building was fitted with wooden rails and rollers. The sketches also showed curious long, low constructions with curved ends and a network of roadways that seemed to focus on some sort of linear structure. Six such sites were mentioned.

Later the same day, Flight Officer Hosking took off from Benson in Oxfordshire in a photo-reconnaissance Spitfire to take advantage of what daylight remained to get covers of the site named in the report. It straddled a small wood, ten miles northeast of Abbeville, and was called Bois Carré. The images were processed, and when the covers and the plans from Switzerland were compared, they matched. The strange long, thin buildings with the kinked ends (one of them slightly shorter than the other two) were especially prominent in the photographs, two of them in open fields. They could be measured from the imagery as ten feet by 260 feet, with a distinct shallow curve at one end. Viewed from above, each one looked 'like a ski laid on its side'. There was also a row of concrete plinths about 150 feet long overall, with an apparently associated square building offset from these but on the same alignment and to which the whole complex, including the 'ski' buildings' curved ends, were connected by narrow concrete tracks.

'Everything seemed to point to the skis being used for storage,' wrote Kendall afterwards. The kinked end was curious – it seemed to be some sort of anti-blast precaution. Rockets of the scale seen at Peenemünde could surely not negotiate the curve, though? Cloud obscured the remaining targets mentioned in the agent report and Medmenham would have to wait until 3 November when all six sites were photographed. When the covers were compared, it was clear that each had the same structures, as if they had derived from some common plan modified so as to fit the local topography. None was near a railway line and each was in a small wood. They were still under construction, but clearly close to completion. What sort of 'rocket projector sites' were these?

The images of the Bois Carré type of site were compared again. By setting up their compass alignment to read true north, the lines of concrete plinths could be correlated. Kendall and Major Norman Falcon came to the same conclusion: these were ground footings for some sort of inclined ramp or catapult. And they were all pointing at central London.

London, 2–10 November 1943

Sir Stafford Cripps had moved, as requested by Churchill, to deal with the squabble that had engulfed the rocket. He opened his first paper, dated 2 November, on the scientific row by stating that there was 'a unanimous opinion that a rocket of the range and size supposed is both possible and practicable'. Cherwell's took the opposite view. His critique of the Cripps scientific report was so long that he did not think it worth Churchill's while to read it, he wrote on the covering note when he sent it to the Prime Minister.

Duncan Sandys presented his latest summary to the chiefs the next day. Among the broadly correct suppositions was that the bombing of Watten had been successful. Intense building activity was also continuing at Wizernes near St Omer, where a huge bunker had first been reported as under construction in late summer. 'The nerve centre of rocket production at Peenemünde [has] been paralysed, according to a downed Luftwaffe airman,' he could report. Amid a rag-bag of intelligence snippets news had come in that at the town of Tôtes, south of Dieppe, 1500 men were toiling on a site for the launching of '15-ton rockets'. Two huge tunnels were being dug into a hillside at a place called Mimoyecques for an unknown purpose. Air reconnaissance had found a Watten-style excavation at Martinvast on the Cherbourg peninsula.

And then there was this: an SIS source known as Ishmael had reported at the end of August that a 'rocket bomb with a range of 450 kilometres and a 6500 kg warhead of "Ekresit" was being developed for production at Peenemünde, at Wiener-Neustadt and by the IG Farben industrial concern at Auschwitz-Monowitz'. According to Ishmael: 'In Auschwitz the IG Farben works manufactures the high explosive content of the rockets ... There are 65,000 workers here, kept closely confined; they include 32,000 Jews.'* Sandys incorporated this in his summary for the chiefs without further comment and amid many more wild-sounding reports from prisoners of war, diplomats and over-imaginative agents.

What might Sir Stafford Cripps make of all this? Were the mysterious goings-on in northern France about rockets, or, as Cherwell was still insisting, were they cover for something else? When the Medmenham model-makers started putting the information from the Bois Carré reports into 3D form, they dressed the set with miniature rockets.

At 10:00 a.m. on 8 November the experts summoned to Cripps's renewed inquiry assembled in the Cabinet Office. To act as assessors, Cripps had appointed the railway engineer Sir William Stanier and the chemist Dr Thomas Merton, Scientific Adviser to the Ministry of Production. They would hear some diverse stuff – from the photographic interpreters at Medmenham, from the psy-war experts at the Ministry of Economic Warfare, from Dr Jones (who was supposed to talk only about the pilotless aircraft) and from members of the JIC, not to mention some bizarre diplomatic chatter. Cherwell and Sandys sat beside Sir Stafford at the head of the table, their feud unabated. And there were new faces in the room: Wing Commander Douglas Kendall was there to give the latest from Medmenham, aided by Flight Lieutenant André Kenny and Captains Robert Rowell and Neil Simon.

Would German propaganda provide a clue? The expert from the Ministry of Information concluded: 'It is beyond reasonable doubt that Germany possesses [a weapon which] its leaders believe will create in British cities havoc at least as great as that in German

---

* The huge chemical works at Monowitz, six kilometres from Auschwitz-Birkenau, began operating in early 1943. In spite of source Ishmael's (in fact inaccurate) report, it was not put on any long-range-weapon target list, although Monowitz would be attacked by the USAAF in August 1944 as an oil target.

cities, probably much greater.' Bulging files of cuttings were produced, including this from the SS newspaper *Das Schwarze Korps*: 'Against the terror from the air there is a counter-measure whose effectiveness is determined solely by us. By the skills of our research workers and constructors.' There was plenty more: references to 'tools of our revenge', 'laboratories and factories', then: 'the enemy air terror will end under the burning ruin of English towns'. By means of keyword analysis a compelling graph showed stops and starts in the ferocious editorialising and in the accounts of the timing of the predicted day of judgement, with a gap immediately following the raid on Peenemünde and the one on Watten.

Douglas Kendall was asked to give an exposition on the 'rocket', if that was what it was. The 'bunker' sites remained menacingly cryptic. All were served by standard-gauge railway and most were aligned on London or Bristol. And there was something else. With a minimum of drama Kendall announced the discovery of 'a new sort of installation, almost certainly a launching site of some kind. A whole system of them is being built in the Pas-de-Calais.' Up to midnight just past, nineteen sites had been found.

The meeting was electrified. 'They are not like any known military installation,' Kendall said, giving an outline of the 'ski' structures and the evidently associated square building. 'They were all started at once. Each of them is apparently going to have a firing-point aimed at London.'

Sir Stafford adjourned the meeting for two days so as to give the photo-interpreters a day and two nights to continue the search and to prepare a detailed analysis. On 9 November a low-level photo-reconnaissance mission brought back clear oblique photographs of Bois Carré and its strange ski-shaped structures, which seemed to be made out of pre-cast concrete blocks.

The inquiry's second session opened on 10 November. In the interval, more photographs from northern France had gone through third-stage interpretation. The Central Interpretation Unit had now detected twenty-six ski sites. There was no evidence of heavy handling gear. Kendall proposed without prevarication that the sites had nothing to do with the handling and projection of a forty-five-ton rocket. So what were they for?

On the 12th, Dr Jones submitted a short paper to the inquiry on the pilotless aircraft, with details of range, speed, flying height and

At Bletchley Park in 1939 the physicist Dr R. V. Jones (*left*) met Frederick 'Bimbo' Norman (*right*), professor of German at King's College London. A scientist with no German and a linguist with no understanding of science – they proved the perfect partnership in interpreting German 'secret weapon' message traffic.

Churchill's son-in-law Duncan Sandys, MP (*left*) was appointed in spring 1943 to investigate the missile menace. Professor Frederick Lindemann (Lord Cherwell), Churchill's scientific adviser, fought hard to keep the junior minister outside the Ultra-secret circle. *Right:* The bowler-hatted 'Prof' and Churchill witness a demonstration of anti-aircraft rockets in 1941. Sandys had commanded an experimental battery in Wales and judged them useless. Their developer, Dr Alwyn Crow (in trilby), was Britain's top rocket expert but was very slow to understand how the German liquid-fuelled rocket worked.

Top left: Winston Churchill at an ill-starred photo-call in July 1944, with his daughter Mary and General Sir Frederick Pile, head of Anti-Aircraft Command, when not one flying bomb flew over the gun site in Kent. *Top right:* Deputy Chief of the Air Staff, Air Vice Marshal Sir Norman Bottomley, was the airman-bureaucrat in the middle of the whole revenge-weapon drama. *Below:* US strategic bomber commander Lt-General Carl Spaatz (*centre*) would rather bomb Germany than V1 launchers. Air Chief Marshal Sir Arthur Tedder (*right*) struggled to keep the Americans on side. Air Marshal Sir Arthur Coningham (*left*) would command the 2nd Allied Tactical Air Force in winter 1944–5, whose ground attack aircraft would prove powerless against rocket launches.

Generalmajor Walter Dornberger (*above left*), director of the German army rocket programme in his office at Peenemünde-Ost. Dornberger's ambitions to command the rocket in action were thwarted by the SS engineer Dr Hans Kammler (seen *above right, on left* at a rally in Berlin, 1934), who seized operational control in September 1944.

In happier pre-Kammler days (*below left*) Dornberger (on steps) stands to the left of Wernher von Braun (in dark civilian suit) as General Erich Fellgiebel, the army signals chief, congratulates Peenemünde commandant Oberst Leo Zanssen after the successful launch of the fourth test A-4 on 3 October 1942. To the right are Dr Rudolf Hermann and the telemetry expert Dr Ing Gerhard Reisig. *Bottom right:* Oberst Max Wachtel, the artilleryman who was put in charge of the air force's experimental flying bomb in 1943. A year later, masquerading as Oberst Wolf, he led the campaign against London.

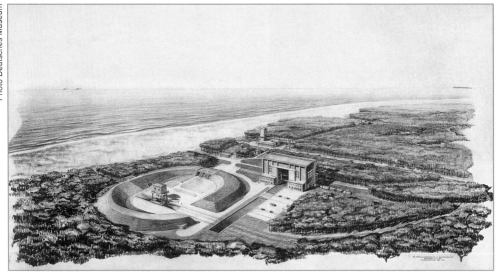

The development of Peenemünde on the Usedom peninsula began in 1936 – a scientific city by the sea for a Nazi technical elite. Hindenburgstraße (*below right*) in the Karlshagen *Seidlung* (settlement) featured flats, shops, even a beauty parlour. The rocket test stands (*above*, shown in a building plan of 1937) were first interpreted by British aerial snoopers as 'neolithic remains'. When something that might be a rocket was spotted on test stand VII (*left*), things got more urgent.

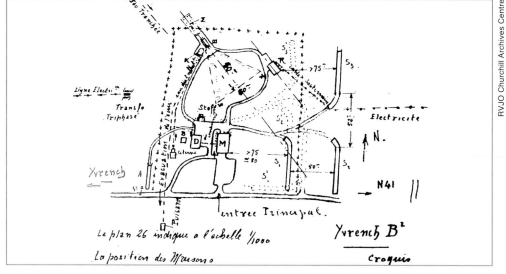

Reports about Peenemünde arrived in London from the end of 1942, including this sketch map (*right*, from a smuggled microfilm) that clearly shows the test stands and prisoners' camp.

More agent reports arrived of giant bunkers and construction sites in northern France. A photo-reconnaissance effort was mounted with no real idea of what to being looked for until sketches arrived via Switzerland in late October 1943 (*above*). The detailed drawings came from draughtsman André Comps via the resistance organiser Michel Hollard. Photo-reconnaissance (*below*) would confirm the existence of almost a hundred of them – and highlight the buildings that looked like 'skis on their side'. Ultra nudged it all along.

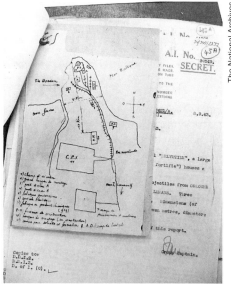

Feind Hört Mit! The Enemy is Listening! The German exhortation engraved on all military microphones was all too true. The Luftwaffe's signals discipline (*above*, a three-man air force team with an Enigma machine, and their field radio out of shot) was especially lax.

The XIV Kompanie of the Luftnachrichten Versuchs (experimental signals) regiment were responsible for the Baltic missile range, and from 1943 gave an abundant harvest of information to the interpreters in Hut Three at Bletchley Park (*below*), where Professor Norman's Section 3G(N) bundled them up for a tiny Ultra-cleared readership in Whitehall.

The flying bomb (*top right*) on its *Zubringerwagen* handling trolley under test in Poland was designed for launch from fixed catapults. The offensive against London only ended when the breakout from the D-Day lodgement pushed the firing units out of range.

A-4 rocket (*right*) at Blizna, Poland, on wheeled trolleys. The post D-Day capture of such trolleys in Normandy gave Air Intelligence vital clues on the size of the rocket.

The transporter-erector vehicles – *Meillerwagen* – under test at Peenemünde towed by a half track (*below*) deposited the missile on a firing table called a *Bodenplatte*. In action these mobile launchers would prove almost impossible to detect.

Below: Propaganda Minister Joseph Goebbels and Armaments Minister Albert Speer (wearing Organisation Todt armband) witness an A-4 launch from test stand VII at Peenemünde, early summer 1943 (*above*). Goebbels well understood that to promise the German people too much of the revenge weapons might backfire. Albert Speer conceded after the war that making the rocket at the expense of defensive fighter aircraft had been a catastrophic mistake.

accuracy: 'The present rate of trial is about two flights per day. The aircraft can be made to turn in the air although straight runs are normal.' Where the detailed figures came from was not revealed.

Cripps had completed his information-gathering, and withdrew to write up what he hoped would be his definitive report. Meanwhile, Duncan Sandys was looking ever more exposed. When the pilotless-aircraft investigation had been removed from the Sandys Bodyline investigation and taken over by the Air Ministry in September, it looked as if the intelligence professionals might be regaining control. But the junior minister had continued to review the evidence on the rocket threat, and his conclusions had been more flawed than ever. Sandys's alarmist report of 24 October had been especially unhelpful.

Since late summer the JIC had been getting truculent, suspicious that it was not being given everything it should be given, and at the same time wanting more control over what Sandys was getting. At the end of October it had gone so far as to set up its own subcommittee 'to sift SIS, diplomatic, consular and prisoner reports' – in essence, to question what Sandys was telling them and to seek its own answers.

It was an impossible situation, and it was Sandys who blinked first. He suggested to a meeting of the chiefs on 11 November that either the Joint Intelligence Committee should take over his operation, or he take over theirs – this second option was a little ambitious, perhaps. The chiefs politely suggested that it should be the former, and by lunchtime it was all agreed. Portal, Chief of the Air Staff, told Sandys that the JIC would certainly wish that some of the people who had been working for him continue to assist. It was the beginning of a very polite humiliation of those who had fought the good Bodyline fight under the Sandys banner. Dr Jones was not displeased.

On 15 November, just as Sir Stafford Cripps's report was nearing its final draft, Brigadier Ian Jacob, Assistant Secretary to the War Cabinet, wrote to Churchill explaining why it had come to this:

The Chiefs of Staff have formed the opinion that the inquiry stage has passed ... A further reason for making this change is that much of the evidence now comes from Most Secret

Sources, the knowledge of which it is undesirable to extend beyond a wider circle than that of the regular intelligence organizations.

The Chiefs accordingly discussed the matter this morning with Mr Duncan Sandys ... it was agreed ... Mr Sandys should relinquish his responsibility in the matter.

There were soothing words for the junior minister, references to his 'work of value', his long association; he would 'continue to sit with the Chiefs', 'he should in his personal capacity receive copies of reports'. Nevertheless, he was out. The thrusting modernists of Shell Mex House were stood down.

Thus that same day the Air Ministry at last took effective charge of the Great Rocket Flap – as it had already done with the lesser threat of the pilotless aircraft. And henceforth a new JIC subcommittee would bring together the intelligence strands, itself supervised, as the *Official History* of British wartime intelligence described it, 'by an ad hoc interdepartmental committee chaired by the DCAS [Deputy Chief of the Air Staff, in the substantial shape of Norman Bottomley], on which were represented the JIC, the Air Ministry, the Ministry of Home Security and the Home Defence Executive'. As the *Official History* explained, 'Within the Air Ministry, a new Directorate of Ops (Special Operations) [would be] formed to handle offensive counter-operations and defensive countermeasures. Its head would [also] be chairman of the new JIC subcommittee [yet to be appointed] in order to facilitate co-ordination between intelligence and operation staffs.'

It all seemed perfectly sound. That same day Bodyline was retired and the codename 'Crossbow' substituted for intelligence on the enemy's long-range weapons and everything that went with them. In the secret crevices of Whitehall there were sighs of relief at Sandys's departure. 'It is pleasant to think that outside of this office we shall have only one body to deal with in the future,' wrote Claude Dansey, Vice-Chief of the Secret Service, on 15 November in a memo to his boss: 'I understand that S.I.S. has acquired great merit outside on account of its information on sites and [secret] weapons. I think this merit is deserved. Now, unfortunately, the subject has become one which might be termed "fashionable" and various committees are at work.' The Air

Ministry seemed to be hogging the show. Dansey urged that 'similar steps should be taken in this office, otherwise we shall have the forces at our disposal ... dissipated or wrongly directed. This direction can only be given by someone who is acquainted with all the various sources.'

And who should that be? The answer was obvious: Jones. 'All reports which directly concern rockets, pilotless aircraft and firing sites should be sent to Section II(D) [Dr Jones's title in SIS nomenclature] – Dr Jones – who in turn would be responsible for transmitting copies to the service Directors of Intelligence, the Ministry of Economic Warfare etc.' It was also noted that 'CX [agent reports] connected to Bodyline were now to be known as PINGPONG', each with a serial number starting from 1. With Jones at the centre of their own intelligence switchboard, in combination with Professor Norman at the Park (the Government Code and Cipher School was under the nominal control of the SIS), there was every chance the service would emerge from this secret-weapons business with even greater merit.

But Dr Jones was most unhappy with the new arrangements. As a civilian, he could not head the proposed joint intelligence and operational directorate, to which he would be a mere provider of raw information. Once again he had been pushed aside. For two days he brooded. Another politician, meanwhile, was to get it badly wrong.

Sir Stafford Cripps circulated his second report on 17 November. The science had supposedly been dealt with – this was about intelligence. He noted at the outset that Mr Sandys had seen the whole paper, including its Most Secret aspects, and was in 'broad agreement with its conclusions'. Then followed a summarised list of conclusions, with the evidence presented in six appendices according to its origin. There was no doubt the Germans had been experimenting with long-range weapons for a long time. These were of three types: the glider bomb, the pilotless aircraft and the rocket.

A long and unenlightening review of the photographic covers of the Baltic reported that activity was continuing at the earthworks at Peenemünde, but there was no sign of operational prototype launchers of the Watten or of the ski-site type that had been found very recently via agents' reports. The tunnel site at Mimoyecques was suspicious, but its purpose remained unknown. The ski sites of which by now thirty had been found by photo-reconnaissance 'could not yet be linked by causal evidence to the A-4'. The Bois Carré report was given special prominence, Cripps concluding that 'the large square building devoid of metal fitments was presumably for the handling of explosive or corrosive material'. 'The 14th Company [RDF] of 155(W) Flakregiment had been following the flight of a large airborne body in the Baltic,' he said. 'Its rate of descent was 20 metres in 40 seconds indicating that it had wings.' This was given as a bald statement, with no mummery about 'infiltrating agents'. But in spite of the sanitised evidence from the Park and agent Amniarix's revelations, this crucial information was thrown away. 'W' stood for *Werfer* and thus related to the rocket, he wrongly concluded.

The significance of the Luftflotte 3 telegrams was discussed. How internal messages had been miraculously obtained was not commented upon. But surprisingly, the ground organisation for the FZG 76 mentioned in them was connected with a rocket.

Apart from the discussion of the importance of the Bois Carré site and the revelation of the testing of an 'airborne body', Cripps's conclusions were an intelligence disaster. He was still confusing the rocket with the pilotless aircraft, and failed to link the just discovered ski sites in northern France with the winged projectile that he teasingly revealed was being tested in the Baltic. The pilotless aircraft needed no special launcher but the rocket did, the report wrongly concluded. Then it suggested that the ski sites might be launchers for a smaller version of the A-4, as yet to be detected: the rocket was being reinvented to fit the evidence.

Cherwell was jubilant. 'I think it is clear from [Cripps's] conclusions that even he was not impressed by the evidence. I of course am even more sceptical,' he told Churchill on the 23rd. He gave a crushing line-by-line critique of his Cabinet colleague's work: it was all nonsense – including the pilotless aircraft.

Why not assume that the torpedo-shaped objects evident in the Peenemünde photographs are just that? said Cherwell. The small A-4 was not worth considering. The bunkers were anti-invasion fortifications, and the ski sites based that far back from the coast could not possibly be part of an offensive plan aimed against

London. The experimental Flak company was doing acoustic or seismological research to ascertain where bombs of *any* type might fall, said the Prof. The Luftflotte 3 telegrams about the captured agent and air attacks on 'five reception stations' were too vague as evidence on which to make suppositions. The so-called Flak Zielgerät was an 'aiming gadget' possibly connected to an anti-air-craft device, he argued. And what did the existence of a Colonel Wachtel prove?

The Prof had an answer for everything – even the bugged generals. 'We are told that a German general passing through London was heard to say "Well they don't seem to have destroyed this town with their rockets yet." … a soldierly remark which might be expected from a general who had been led up the garden path by some wild inventor.'

Jones could see the mess the politicians were making of it. First Sandys, then Cripps. Now the Air Ministry were looking to appoint someone who would both lead the operational side and chair the proposed intelligence-coordinating operation. It would not be him.

On 19 November he wrote to the secretary of the JIC and copied the letter to his Air Ministry boss. 'It has been my duty since the beginning of the war to anticipate new applications of science to warfare by the enemy … once again a committee has been formed … to perform a function which I believe to be largely my own,' he told him. This apparent display of lack of confidence in him, he went on, might have led him to resign. 'My section will continue its work, regardless of any parallel committees which may arise, and will be mindful only of the safety of the country. I trust that we shall not be hindered.'

His arrogance was breathtaking. The survival of the country depended on *him*.

Dr Jones's finest hour was yet to come. On 23 November the new JIC Crossbow subcommittee had its members assigned and received its terms of reference from the chiefs. It could order air reconnaissance and recommend targets for attack. Otherwise, its functions were to monitor and advise. To general surprise, instead of the ambitious thirty-six-year-old Group Captain Jack Easton, newly appointed Director of Intelligence (Research) at the Air

Ministry, the chairmanship fell on Air Commodore Claude Pelly, a forty-three-year-old career officer, who was whisked from an obscure administrative desk in Cairo. Pelly was 'pleasant to work with', but he had no previous experience of intelligence, according to Jones.

The secretary of the new subcommittee was Paymaster Lieutenant A. L. Bonsey RN. There would be eight members including Dr Jones (who would 'hardly bother to turn up to meetings'), Squadron Leader Golovine the jet aircraft expert, and Major Matthew Pryor of MI14,who had set the whole thing in motion with his overture to Medmenham in January. Some were Ultra-cleared, some not; there would be difficulties. The physicist Dr E. C. Bullard, scientific adviser to the Admiralty, was the sole survivor of the Sandys team. They were to report weekly to the Deputy Chief of the Air Staff, the ubiquitous Air Vice Marshal Norman Bottomley, who would chair the interdepartmental oversight super-committee, to meet 'as and when it was felt necessary'.

Meanwhile, Jones received no reply to his letter from the JIC, a body for which the physicist was developing an ever greater contempt. Then a sudden illness intervened. He went down with influenza and a raging temperature and was confined to bed in his flat at Richmond Hill Court, south-west of the capital. He missed, therefore, the circulation of a report sent to Sandys on 26 November by the Ministry of Supply's Chief Engineer of Armament Design, Sir Frank Smith, who had been working on a hypothetical rocket since the Lubbock–Cherwell rumpus of October. The device was quite fantastic, according to Smith's paper, weighing eighty tons, mobilised by a multi-wheel trailer – the accompanying illustration in the Air Ministry file looks like a Soviet intercontinental ballistic missile from a 1970s May Day parade – and propelled from a giant launching tube in an underground cavern redolent of Hauptmann Cleff's fantasies.

The Cambridge physicist Sir George Thomson reviewed it for the Air Ministry. 'It's a good paper,' he concluded. 'It is impossible to say for certain whether a rocket of the type considered is possible or not. But in view of the intelligence reports we must, I think, assume that it is. The mortar method of launch is most probable ... The ski sites are for pilotless aircraft.' Sir George added perspicaciously that these last 'represent the main threat. The giant rocket is a second string developed for its spectacular character.' Sandys wrote to Bottomley on the 26th: 'This paper is an example of the contribution that our research and development establishments have been making during past months. As I explained to you their ability to continue to assist in this way must depend upon their being kept fully in the picture.'

'Lunch next Tuesday,' he suggested.

Jones was bedbound for a fortnight. When he recovered, he returned to the intelligence fray with enthusiasm, only to find plenty of enemies close to home. A whole new Whitehall feud was shaping up.

CHAPTER 19

Blizna, autumn 1943

There were no eighty-ton rockets being made ready for an attack on London. But the command organisation for the operational A-4 was certainly all set. Feldmarschall von Rundstedt had moved in mid-October to assume authority over both weapons. On 1 November Hitler signed a warrant for the preparation and execution of the projects. The Feldmarschall now made a proposal that suited the military mind: he recommended to the High Command the establishment of a Special Army Corps to assume control of all long-range weapons; it would be subordinate to himself as Oberbefehlshaber-West.* Candidates to command the Corps were discreetly assessed.

It was to be a single formation under the Oberkommando der Wehrmacht, the Supreme Commander of the Armed Forces, but superior to the three existing tactical commanders Dornberger, Wachtel and Generalleutnant Erich Schneider who commanded the high-pressure pump project at Mimoyecques. Long-range naval guns on the Channel coast were to be part of the Corps's remit. To lead them all into glorious action against England the choice fell on sixty-two-year-old Generalleutnant Erich

---

* Army Commander in the West.

Heinemann, lately commander of the army artillery school. Von Rundstedt made it clear that he wanted Dornberger, an 'armchair general', relieved of tactical control of the rocket and restricted solely to development and production and to overseeing troop-training.

But General Alfred Jodl insisted that Dornberger remain as Artillerie Kommandeur 91, nominally in charge of the operational preparations in France – in fact, he was still spending most of his time in the wilds of Poland. If Dornberger believed he would lead the rocket troops into action, he would soon be disillusioned. For now, there were grave doubts as to whether the rocket would work at all.

The leathery Heinemann, who had joined the imperial army as a cadet in 1900, embarked on a month-long tour of inspection to try to get a grip on the sprawling secret-weapons complex – something of which, other than rumours, he had previously been unaware. There was a training range in Poland under the control of the SS, called Heidelager, he discovered. He arrived there on 5 November in time for the first launch from the forests by the army's Lehr und Versuchsbatterie 444.

Anticipation must have been intense. The Peenemünde-made A-4 was raised from its *Meillerwagen* (multiple-axle transporter) onto the firing platform and then fuelled. Countdown. Ignition. Then the exhaust flame immediately thawed the frozen sandy soil – into which, according to Dornberger, 'one leg of the firing table slowly sank'. The rocket rose diagonally and crashed into the forest two miles away.

Heinemann was dumbstruck. He insisted thereafter that rockets be fired from hard standing. According to Dornberger, 'for six months, manpower and material were wasted on the erection of these concrete emplacements in the battle area ... a false start entirely due to the inexperience of one man in charge of the launch'. But soggy soil was not the only problem. Launches from Blizna were routinely exploding either in the air after take-off or on the way down, a few hundred metres above the target. As Dornberger put it in his memoirs:

Shot after shot went wrong and faced us with apparently insoluble problems. Some rockets rose barely 60 feet. Vibration would cause a relay contact to break and the rocket would fall back to earth destroying firing tables and cable sets. Others exploded at 6000 feet destroying all evidence of the cause of what was wrong.

Others would make a perfect flight, then emit a white cloud of steam. There would be short sharp double bang, and a shower of wreckage fell to earth after covering 160 miles. I was in despair. Was our flying laboratory too much for the soldiers to handle? . . . Whether rockets came from Peenemünde or from the Central Works it was the same.

Dornberger and von Braun hopped around the range in their Fieseler Storch trying to find answers. Von Braun went to the impact area. During re-entry into the atmosphere the rockets broke apart, seemingly because of fluttering of the fuselage's middle segment. He could actually see it. In late 1943 in no way did the rocket seem fit for military purpose.

Zempin, November 1943

Colonel Wachtel's Baltic operation too, already in the process of being decanted to France, would be under the control of the Special Army Corps. On 12 November the regimental war diary gave a snapshot of progress: 'Gentlemen from FHQ arrived to inspect the Zempin installation and also watched a successful shoot. Oberst Wachtel gave them 1 March as the operational date, blaming the slow drafting of specialist personnel for the delay. But the sites in France are almost ready, eighty-eight of them plus eight in the Cherbourg area by December as well as eight supply positions.'

The delegation from Führer headquarters brought the news that, for the present, the number of missiles coming from VW was to be fifteen hundred a month – the full five thousand would not be attempted until June 1944 at the earliest. And the giant bunker sites? There were serious doubts as to their viability. Oberst Berg from FHQ pointed gloomily to the attacks on the site in the Cherbourg peninsula – the enemy's superiority in the air was indisputable, and there was no infallible camouflage available.

Through the foggy days of November the units from the naval air station at Brüsterort arrived one by one at Zempin, to be smartly passed through their final training. The last of the Flakregiment's battalions entrained for France on the 18th. Soon it would be the HQ's turn to join the trek westwards. At the Hotel Preussenhof there was a little diversion, a competition to produce a regimental emblem. As the diary recorded, the first efforts were too obvious in their depiction of the moment of retribution: a fist, flashes of lightning, a stylised FZG 76 crashing down on a map of Britain – in one case even 'a hammer battering a top-hatted Churchill'.

Then Stabsarzt Hans Soblik, the regimental doctor, came up with a coat of arms with a large W and a figure 8 below it W-Achtel – 'Wachtel'. It really was quite clever. So it was adopted, and soon it would be flying from the staff-car pennants of Oberst Wachtel and his battery commanders as they plied the wintry roads of northern France. At the end of the year, a sketch of it would arrive on Dr Jones's desk.

On 19 November Hermann Goering demanded imperiously that flying-bomb operations, rather than coming under the planned Army Corps, be directed by a special air force division. When the joint command was established, the Army Corps would supposedly be compensated by the appointment of Luftwaffe Oberst Eugen Walter as Heinemann's deputy commander, and reassured that duplicate staff officers would be provided by the army and air force at every level.

But Wachtel was still dissatisfied. According to the Cabinet Office history based on post-surrender interrogations:

> He was personally at enmity with Oberst Walter, chief of the air force component. The rivalry appears to have been inspired by the fact that LXV Armee Korps lacked technical knowledge of the weapon and sought to camouflage their weakness under a screen of authority and red tape ... the bomb was to be used as a form of artillery in support of diminished air power ... Wachtel opposed this on the grounds that the accuracy of the weapon and the nature of its delivery and explosive charge made its use

as a pure terror reply to the enemy's mass bombing of German cities the only logical application.

On 26 November Hitler attended a demonstration of new aircraft types at Insterburg airfield in East Prussia. Himmler was in eager attendance. The FZG 76 was there, but without a live-firing catapult. This was Hitler's first view of the air force's long-range weapon. When he was told it would not even be fully developed until the end of March the following year, the mood turned frosty.

Zempin was emptying. Wachtel and his technical adviser Sommerfeld flew back and forth to France to attend yet more conferences. The demonstration unit would continue firing from the Baltic seashore for a few months yet. On 24 November the diary noted the detachment of specialists to 'Falster, Denmark, where preparations are being made to measure the fall of shot', a move picked up by the Park. Four days later it was noted that 'a high flying Mosquito seems very interested in Usedom, especially the north-west part of the island, circling at 9000 metres' until it was driven off by flak.

The staff of LXV Armee Korps assembling near von Rundstedt's HQ at St-Germain-en-Laye north-west of Paris, meanwhile, found it difficult to comprehend what was required of them. And only by visiting Peenemünde, Zempin and Blizna did Heinemann and Oberst Walter learn how woefully behind schedule both projects really were. No serious attempt had been made in the Baltic trials to hit specific targets, Heinemann discovered, while for the A-4's anguished developers the main concern was how to stop them breaking up in mid-air. Germany could not produce enough liquid oxygen to launch more than perhaps fifty rockets a day, and of these fifty fewer than half would come within ten miles of their target, assuming that the air-burst problem could be fixed.

Heinemann made one attempt to close down the whole A-4 project in favour of the FZG 76. Then he made a tour of the launching sites in France, finding them 'insecure, conspicuous, needlessly elaborate and vulnerable to air attack'. Not one of the large sites, in his view, was either capable of being camouflaged or worth camouflaging. The latest report from the construction super-intendent bewailed the slowing of progress at the sites, for which 'leaflets dropped regularly from the air' were responsible. 'The French are no longer interested in bonuses ... It is suspected that the workers are being paid compensation by enemy organisations.' Any excuse would do.

CHAPTER 20

London, autumn 1943

Employing 'deception' in some way against the long-range weapon threat had been on the agenda since almost the beginning of the bid to understand it. In late July the Twenty (Double Cross) Committee had been asked to report on any indications of forthcoming 'rocket' attacks that might reach it through double agents under its control. On 5 August one of them, agent Tricycle,* had been sent a questionnaire by his Abwehr controllers in Berlin asking about an 'unusually wide runway' being built at Sutton Common near Woodbridge in Suffolk. In fact it was built to receive damaged bombers returning from raids on Germany. He reported the interest to his London masters.

This approach by the Germans inspired the Twenty Committee to go on a wider offensive. On 8 September Colonel Bevan, head of the London Controlling Section, informed C of a 'little deception plan' he had in mind. The chosen instrument was agent Garbo, otherwise a Spaniard called Juan Pujol who had arrived in Britain in April 1942. He lived in Crespigny Road in suburban Hendon, north London, as a 'Republican refugee' in a stormy ménage with Señora Pujol. According to his cover story, he had a

---

* So called for his liking for three-in-a-bed sex; otherwise the Serbian-born double agent Dušan 'Duško' Popov.

part-time job at the Ministry of Information while running an entirely invented nationwide ring of informers.

Colonel Bevan's original plan had been to induce the Spanish ambassador in London, the Duke of Alba, to inquire of the Germans whether he should take a house north of London in view of the threat of the rocket. But perhaps agent Garbo should do something similar, the Twenty Committee thought, as well as offering to supply information on the rocket and its effects on London when it actually arrived. Bevan had outlined this plot to Duncan Sandys, so he told the SIS chief, but the junior minister felt that the approval of the chiefs of staff would be necessary first. 'You will remember that the Chiefs shot down Mr Sandys's plan to start rumours in neutral countries because it might give away the fact we have knowledge of the rocket,' Bevan reminded C. 'The Germans must surely appreciate [by now] in view of the attacks of Peenemünde and Watten that we are concerned over a new weapon,' he added.

The Duke of Alba plan fizzled out. Whatever might be coming London's way, the Duke seemed minded to stay put. But Garbo, meanwhile, drafted a long letter telling his controller in Madrid that the Ministry of Information was expecting soon to have to deal with the fall-out from 'a radio-controlled plane' and an 'enormous explosive rocket' arriving on the capital. His wife had been alarmed by press reports and she wanted to take the children to Spain. What was the truth of the matter? If it really existed, he suggested he would stay in London and report on how the rocket fell. 'We could make use of this weapon to liquidate all these English dogs.'

This letter 'went astray'. The plan must be given a nudge, so under the instructions of the Twenty Committee an article appeared in a Stockholm newspaper written by its Berlin correspondent who had 'recently been expelled' from the Reich capital (the Swedish article, according to the accompanying file, had been placed by Anthony Blunt, the MI5 officer specialising in neutral embassies). The wheeze worked. A translation appeared in the *Daily Telegraph* of 27 September mentioning an 'enormous rocket gun' buried underground somewhere within a radius of fifteen miles of Calais and ready to bombard London whenever a German city was attacked by the RAF.

The planted article had unintended consequences. Herbert Morrison, the Home Secretary, expressed acute alarm in a memo to Churchill on 5 October and suggested background briefings for newspaper editors before 'certain preparations became known to members of the public and lead to questions'. The briefing was arranged for 11 October. Michael Foot, as its editor, represented the London *Evening Standard*. The briefing was bland enough – the rocket was very probably a fact – as were 'sensational rumours of eminent military scientists meeting their deaths in an attempt to accelerate the perfection of such weapons'.

'Do not give the secret weapon too much prominence,' Morrison told the eminent journalists, but he asked them to continue to reprint stories from neutral countries, German-planted or not, to 'familiarise the public with the possibility'. Fleet Street pushed it as far as they might. The *News Chronicle* on 13 October, for example, wrote about 'Swedish reports of mysterious events on the Danish island of Bornholm'. It was 'widely believed in Stockholm that the raid on the Peenemünde research station in the Baltic was connected with work done there with secret new devices'.

On the day the original *Telegraph* 'rocket gun' article appeared, Señora Pujol suffered another fainting fit. 'I would like you to tell me by radio the truth,' Garbo demanded of his controller. He said he would willingly stay in London to report the fall of shot by wireless, while his wife, 'who loathed England and found everything about it unpleasant and tiresome', would go to the countryside. On 18 November Garbo was assured there no cause for alarm, but on 16 December he was told to leave London – and to ensure the safety of his transmitters. Agent Tricycle had been warned, meanwhile (by agent 'Artist'), to go and live in the Midlands or even Scotland 'because of the rockets which are going to be fired'. Tricycle duly passed all this to his London controllers.

The Tricycle connection was bearing strange fruit. He had reported in August that the Abwehr had asked him at all costs to discover the purpose of the runway being built in Suffolk, 'facing in the direction of Berlin of which [the Germans] have an aerial photo and believe to be associated with a catapult for rocket bombs or a new form of chemical warfare'. ('This is being sent

to Sandys via C as an unchecked report' was minuted on the
message.)

An idea had been planted. A mischievous light went on in the
head of Lt-Commander Ewan Montagu RNVR of the Twenty
Committee, veteran of black operations past including the
Operation Mincemeat deception, the planting of phoney plans on
a dead body drifting in the sea off the coast of Spain in April–May
1943. He wrote to Bevan on 28 October suggesting that 'we get
the Germans worried and gain many advantages by threatening
them with a Reverse Bodyline'.

It was simple enough: it would be suggested through 'Most
Secret Channels' and by building suitable structures that Sutton
Common with its outsize runway was in fact Britain's very own
missile base aimed at the Reich capital. Just how this was to help
get to grips with the German long-range rocket was not explained.

The plan gathered momentum. Dennis Wheatley suggested to
Sidney Bufton, Head of Bomber Operations at the Air Ministry,
that the runway should be revealed to the enemy by 'special
means' (double-cross agents) as the base of a 'super-long-range
rocket or large radio-controlled aircraft carrying twenty tons of high
explosive aimed at Berlin'. Professor Edward Andrade, Scientific
Adviser to the Ministry of Supply, devised a bogus 150-foot control tower. Wheatley proposed that 'mystery signals' be broadcast
from the nearby Martlesham Heath aerodrome while a general
'atmosphere of mystery' should be generated in the neighbourhood.* But it was not to be. Reverse Bodyline bounced around the
Air Ministry for weeks. In December it would be put out of its
misery as a 'waste of effort'.

The bright new JIC Crossbow subcommittee put out its first
report on 24 November. Dr Jones was down with flu, so it might
be assumed that he had not colluded in the blunder on the very
first page: 'The activities of Colonel Wachtel link the ski sites
beyond all reasonable doubt with some large weapon, probably a
large rocket.'

The ever multiplying intelligence committees were going

---

* Goering did order the Luftwaffe to consider defences against an Allied pilotless aircraft,
but not until November 1944.

round in circles. Sandys had blown himself up. Sir Stafford Cripps had got it even more wrong. Medmenham was building models of ski sites bristling with rockets, while Jones fretted from his sickbed in Richmond that his talents as a scientific sleuth had been over-looked once again. The professional airmen, Norman Bottomley and Claude Pelly, were running the show.

Lord Cherwell, all this time, was laughing up his sleeve. Dr Jones in his memoirs makes no apologies for his apparent arro-gance in believing that he and his tiny directorate had been supplanted once again by bumbling amateurs. His outrage was stoked, he implied, by the bravery of the agent sources whose devotion was in danger of being squandered. Jones was in such a sulk, in fact, that Bottomley ordered that he be watched and reported on lest he and his team might 'not be pulling their full weight'. He expressed the hope that it was merely a clash of per-sonalities that would 'quickly be forgotten, if senior officers make generous use of Dr Jones's very high ability in his own particular line'.

But it was clear that the feud between career airmen, self-regarding scientists, waspish civil servants and ambitious politicians was hobbling the intelligence effort. 'The situation was so serious that I would have gone straight to Churchill if anyone had got in our way,' Jones recalled. There were quite a few who thought that Jones was the problem.

If only the pilotless aircraft could be disentangled from the rocket then, a practical counter-plan to meet the threat of both might be devised. And where was the mystery projectile being launched from? Why had it never been seen?

Central Interpretation Unit, November 1943

Douglas Kendall explained the conundrum in an unpublished postwar memoir:

> Up until now no one had seen this secret weapon. However, we reached the firm conclusion that the weapon facing us was a flying bomb with a wing span of less than 20 feet (based upon

measurements of the buildings in France) ... We had at the PI unit a section which focused on the German aircraft industry and its products. We instructed them to re-examine all likely areas in Germany to locate the missing flying bomb. It was a measure of their capability that they were successful in finding what we wanted within 48 hours.

The Air Section was the preserve of its head, Flight Officer Constance Babington Smith. Although engaged from the start in attempts to unlock the mysteries of Peenemünde, she had no knowledge whatsoever of Bodyline. Then on 13 November, having returned from some urgent meeting at the Air Ministry, Douglas Kendall asked her to take another look at some covers of 'a very small plane, smaller than a fighter'. Something very small – that would only show up on good-quality images. The most recent mission over Usedom, flown on 30 September, had added little. There was no apparent activity in the elliptical earthworks at Peenemünde-Ost associated with the rocket, but a P-30 (Me 163 rocket fighter) had been spotted in a revetment on the Peenemünde-West airfield.

The two covers of the earlier 23 June Mosquito mission from Leuchars, made half an hour apart, were by far the best to date. They were now methodically re-examined right down to the very grain of the film emulsion, Miss Babington Smith squinting through a stereoscope in search of no one quite knew what. The work took days. Then she found something. As she told the story afterwards: '[It] was sitting in a corner of a small enclosure some way behind the hangars immediately adjoining a building which I suspected, from its design, was used for testing jet engines.' It was, she said, 'an absurd little object'.

And all this in the shuttered winter darkness of a hut in the grounds of a crumbling stately home on the banks of the River Thames. But in her mind she was prowling the sandy heaths of the Usedom peninsula in high summer. The veteran photo-interpreter Colonel Roy M. Stanley, USAF Retd, described that first sighting of the FZG 76 at Peenemünde-West as 'one of the great PI achievements of the war'. From that moment on, Medmenham photo-interpreters knew they were looking for 'a tiny plane and, thanks to Constance Babington Smith, they knew its shape'. The new aircraft was dubbed 'Peenemünde-20' from its assessed wingspan, twenty feet. According to her memoirs, 'during the next two weeks I got out more back covers, intent on probing into all the most unlikely corners'.

Eye-wateringly close-up re-examinations of imagery from the sorties of 22 July and 30 September disclosed a second cruciform object. Of the two seaside resorts south-east of Peenemünde itself, Zinnowitz and Zempin, Zempin had been covered on 24 April and 26 July. A re-examination of the prints showed a clutch of barrack-like buildings a quarter of a mile north-east of the railway station. A long concrete platform and four or five objects previously reported as guns could be observed. These were seemingly served by a crane running on rails. It was time to take another look – and on 28 November 1943 two camera-carrying aircraft famously did just that.

The postwar internally compiled air-reconnaissance account is of two Mosquitos leaving Leuchars at 09:55 and 10:45 that day, ostensibly for Berlin on damage assessment, but which diverted from their primary target because of cloud over the Reich capital so as to cover Usedom peninsula instead. But Dr Jones told the JIC Crossbow subcommittee in an Ultra-sanitised paper of 23 December that 'consequent to the discovery of the radar tracks in October [by those mythical infiltrating agents], a photographic sortie was ordered to Peenemünde and Zempin'. He even specified the best time of day, deduced from 'daily habits', to 'catch an aircraft on its catapult – 1100 or 1400 hours'. The Berlin diversion was another cover story.

Jones said in his memoirs that it was he who originally ordered the mission earlier in the month, but bad weather kept it on the ground. Then he got flu. It was Medmenham that put Zempin down as a 'radar-related' target, not him, he later told an interviewer – 'a lucky thing because it meant [the information] came to Claude Wavell . . . a man I could really trust'.

Squadron Leader John Merifield departed Leuchars in his Mosquito with his observer, Flight Officer W. N. Whalley, early on a bitingly cold late-autumn day, flying towards Usedom. At 54°N the November sun was low and the shadows long. The airfield at Peenemünde-West was covered first, followed by a couple of runs over Zinnowitz and Zempin. The Mosquito was then engaged by flak. Six hours and five minutes after take-off they were back at base. The film had to come down from Scotland, be printed at the

CIU, then the prints distributed. Dr Charles Frank took a set to Jones's bedside at Richmond.

The results were stunning. At Medmenham the prints had indeed gone first to Claude Wavell, the RDF specialist and Jones's confidant. But if there was radar, there was something even more interesting. A little inland from the foreshore between the two bathing resorts, a long thin structure pointed out to sea – a launch ramp. And there was the square building, the Maison R of the builder's plan copied by the draughtsman André Comps. It was aligned with the ramp. As Douglas Kendall remembered:

> We had never photographed Zinnowitz before, so imagine our satisfaction at finding a complete Bois Carré type site minus the skis [there was no need for storage – just launch facilities]. The importance of the Zinnowitz site was that it not only gave us a link back to the Peenemünde area, but it revealed a site in a finished state ... We could see the firing ramp in detail. By using a stereoscope, we took three-dimensional measurements. I calculated the ramp incline at about 10 degrees and length at 125 feet. Everything fitted our theories.

Those theories had been crowding in since the riddle of the ski sites had first presented itself. What powered the catapults? Could it be some sort of pressurised piston? The metal-free building orientated towards London was possibly where some form of magnetic compass might be set. The pre-launch procedure could be imagined as a routine whereby the partially assembled, maybe wingless, projectiles from the ski-shaped stores were brought via the R-House with its broad doors, then onto the ramp. The discovery spurred another trawl through old covers. The tiny Peenemünde-20s seen thus far on Peenemünde-West had been associated with engine testhouses. They were not on ramps. 'Unidentified rails' mentioned in previous interpretation reports took on new significance.

Flight Officer Babington Smith's speciality was aircraft and associated structures and vehicles. But a 'launch ramp' opened up new territory. She decided to extend her search, criss-crossing the mosaic of prints of Peenemünde-West with her stereoscope. She recorded of her Lilliputian adventure: 'This first excursion beyond the official bounds of the airfield encouraged me to try my luck in the other direction and I decided to follow the dead-straight road which led northward along the eastern boundary of the airfield towards the Baltic shore. I passed the limits of the airfield towards the extreme edge of the island.'

She found four 'strange structures. Three of them looked very much like ... cranes. But the fourth seemed different, and it was the one that drew my attention most. It was evidently a sort of ramp banked up with earth – you could tell that from the shadow – supporting rails that inclined upwards towards the water's edge.' Kenny had already interpreted it as something to do with 'dredging equipment'. Babington Smith, however, 'being more aircraft-conscious than her colleagues in industry', as Wing Commander Kendall noted – although at that stage she knew nothing about Crossbow – 'might come up with a different answer'. She did. On 1 December she told Kendall of her suspicions that what she had found were launch ramps, not at Zempin but at Peenemünde-West. 'That's it! I know it is!' she recalled Kendall blurting out, interrupting her delightfully breathless description.

Babington Smith went over all the old covers again. 'I cast my eyes further afield than usual, towards the no man's land which lay between the area I was officially watching and the woods that marked the edge of the main experimental station,' she wrote. Among the blobs of light and shade in the emulsion she found 'four rather fancy modern buildings set by themselves in the open, which I was sure housed some sort of dynamometer test beds. I had made a close study of test beds, because Walt Rostow [see p. 275] and the American target experts had wanted to know the numbers at each German factory, as evidence of potential output.' There they were – more Peenemünde-20 airframes. She had found the pilotless aircraft – several of them, in fact, in her retrospective search – and she had found the ramps on the airfield at Peenemünde-West. Add to that the fact that Claude Wavell had found a Bois Carré lookalike site not far away at Zinnowitz. What would be the most convincing evidence of all, though, would be a Peenemünde-20 actually *on a launcher*.

But even after an exhaustive examination, as Kendall put it, still there was no real live Peenemünde-20 discoverable in the latest 28 November imagery of Usedom. Babington Smith could not get a look at the images before various other sections at Medmenham had gone over them. When they were released to her, she returned to the area where in the old covers she had already distinguished four ramps. In her 1958 account she tells how 'even with the naked eye I could see something that had not been there before, a tiny cruciform shape set exactly at the lower end of the inclined rails, a midget aircraft ready for launching'.*

So there it was – irrefutable proof, a pilotless aircraft ready for launch on a test ramp at Peenemünde-West; and down the coast at Zinnowitz, a prototype operational launch site which, minus the 'ski' buildings, matched the cryptic sites around Abbeville exactly. Soon afterwards a cover of Brüsterort on the Baltic, further to the east, would reveal three ramps, this time with the ski units and other buildings.

The pilotless aircraft had flown into plain view.

On 3 December Lord Cherwell was told the news. He wrote at once to the Prime Minister, who was in Cairo for the Sextant Conference:

I have heard today that recent photographs at and near Peenemünde have disclosed sites resembling closely the ski sites in France, of which there are now sixty to one hundred under construction. Since they showed gentle ramps, one with a pilotless aircraft on it, and since we know quite definitely that successful experiments with pilotless aircraft are being made in that region, it seems almost certain that the ski sites are intended for this weapon.

If the Peenemünde trials were acceptance trials, attacks might start within one to three months, Cherwell considered. The projectiles 'might have an accuracy of, say, five miles. The launching of 1000 of these aircraft fired off within a day or two could produce very unpleasant concentrated effects.'

Suddenly there was a new scare: the Secretary of State for Air, Archibald Sinclair, had got into a state about the prospect first raised by Mr Sandys in the summer, of the 'enemy employing some new and exceptionally powerful explosive in connection with

* Professor Jones wrote in his memoirs: 'All credit to the interpreter who, not knowing the story behind the [28 November] sortie, found a V1 and thought it was accidental.'

Crossbow'. Norman Bottomley asked Claude Pelly on 6 December
whether this had been investigated, and if not, perhaps Dr Jones
could study the matter. An alarmed Pelly replied that no such consideration had been given by his committee, but while the prospect
of 'atomic disintegration' warheads on rockets had been raised
before, the mass of launch sites apparently under construction
across the Channel must mean that the enemy was not investing in
one single big bang.

Nevertheless, he said, employing Dr Jones to investigate was a
good idea. Very soon, a dedicated team of US intelligence officers
would arrive in London – but, as Jones would discover, the path
henceforth of Anglo-American intelligence cooperation into a supposed German atom bomb would prove a very tortuous one.

But within a few days of the scare Cherwell was about to show his
contrary streak all over again. On 13 December he wrote to Churchill:
'I think the threat is real but I believe its scale to be comparatively
insignificant.' He had 'consulted with Jones who has obtained some
excellent detailed plans of one of the sites'. Jones had also shown the
Prof the latest Baltic-flight trial plots. Cherwell concluded: 'The reliability of the aircraft is low, one third go the full range ... one third
go three quarters of the way and one third crash soon after launching.
Of those that do go the course, accuracy is poor.'

On the northern course, flying towards London from France
using gyro-cum-compass, accuracy would be even lower than the
trials were currently demonstrating, he predicted, invoking an
aspect of geomagnetism that he did not explain further. With a
warhead of one ton, the absolute maximum in his view, 'casualties
would be two to four persons per aircraft reaching London'. If the
offensive were sustained, he added, it was 'unlikely that more than
three aircraft per site will be dispatched per twenty-four hours'. In
his view, therefore, 'precipitate measures to plan for the evacuation
of London were uncalled for'. The Prof was back to his don't-panic
best.

In contrast, Claude Pelly's JIC Crossbow subcommittee was getting into the most tremendous flap. The air commodore had
somehow found out about the flight-trial plots (but not yet about how
they were obtained). On 15 December he sent Jones a pompous
memo briskly asking for 'a note of what you know of the range, speed
height and tracks' so that it might be given to 'people planning the

various countermeasures'. So far he had been given these details orally by Dr Jones and Dr Frank. He wanted them in writing.

Pelly's second report of 17 December estimated that the German programme comprised 'one hundred ski sites from which a 2000 bomb raid could be launched in 24 hours'. Or, he added unhelpfully, 'it could be four or five times as great'. The enemy would be able to repeat this operation for as long as their firing sites, supply system and production centres remained operational. A chiefs-of-staff paper of the same date predicted a full-scale attack could be made as soon as February, assuming no attempt to frustrate it by counter-bombing. 'The current RAF raids on Berlin* might induce premature use of the weapon,' they concluded.

The use of gas as some sort of countermeasure had first been considered during the Sandys-induced rocket panic of late October. With the pilotless aircraft now generating the same sentiments, a report by the Joint Planning Staff (a resource for the Chiefs of Staff Committee made up of the three Directors of Plans from the Admiralty, the War Office and the Air Ministry) was timely. In a paper of 29 November the Joint Planning Staff had argued that it would be hypocrisy to denounce Crossbow as 'indiscriminate warfare' – it was just a new method of attacking long-range targets. A threat to use gas in retaliation 'even if made through black and unacknowledgeable channels', might bring embarrassing political repercussions if it was not followed through.

The means to wage chemical warfare had been on the British agenda since the start of the war (followed by biological weapons), as a deterrent threat should the Germans use it first. But now here was a suggestion of Allied *first* use, provoked by a conventionally armed if novel weapon. The means of doing so were real. Many thousands of tons of First World War-style chemical agents had been manufactured and stockpiled. A chain of 'forward filling depots' were under construction close to bomber bases in eastern England.†

---

* Harris had launched the first of sixteen huge raids on Berlin on 18–19 November. The Battle of Berlin would continue until March 1944, with punishing losses to RAF bomber crews and no buckling of German morale.
† Five installations were built in 1943–4 to charge aerial bombs with mustard gas brought in tank-cars by rail from ICI factories in Manchester, Runcorn and Rhydymwyn, North Wales. Two FFDs were operated by the USAAF.

Numbers 15, 149 and 214 Squadrons of No. 3 Group were trained in accurate delivery. On 27 September there was a full-scale demonstration at RAF Lakenheath in Suffolk. An operational plan for attacking German cities with chemical weapons was emerging.

But in their extensive November report, the Joint Planning Staff concluded that using gas against the German population, although it would cause a panic, would not be enough to bring about an unconditional surrender; nor would the use of gas against the 'projector sites' in France be effective. Gassing the enemy's construction workers might work, but this was not certain, either. Their camps were too dispersed. High explosive remained the only answer, if still an unknown quantity. 'The effort required to neutralise a ski site is considerable', it was noted in an intelligence summary, while bombing-effects experts from the Ministry of Home Security estimated it would take '150 tons delivered in 37 Lancaster sorties by night using [the navigation aid] Oboe or 47 Fortress sorties by day', to deal with each site effectively.

On 1 December Air Vice Marshal Bottomley went to see the US air commander Ira Eaker, accompanied by Air Chief Marshal Trafford Leigh-Mallory, commander of the recently established Allied Expeditionary Air Force, to discuss hitting the ski sites. Eaker agreed that the tactical airpower being assembled for use in the planned invasion of Europe could begin immediate attacks against ski sites that were identified as being more than 50 per cent complete. The targets were given the codename 'Noball', each to be allotted a specific number. The attacks by medium bombers of the US 9th Air Force began on the 5th, to be quickly grounded by bad weather. When they did operate, the results were thin.

It was now clear that there was an existential threat to London – and by extension a threat to the mounting of an invasion of Continental Europe. It came from mysterious locations dispersed in farms and orchards. Could they be blasted into submission from the air? To save London needed US strategic airpower. It needed the heavy bombers. The trouble was, the Americans would have to be told the full reasons why.

CHAPTER 21

Oise, December 1943

Max Wachtel had his orders: to get his men to France, occupy the launch sites, endure whatever the enemy might do to stop them, and prepare the means for the destruction of London. In a bid for even tighter security the 155 Flakregiment was renamed Flakgruppe Creil (after the French town on the Oise, a bland cover-name). As for the battalions, I Abteilung became Zylinder (top hat); II Abt, Werwolf; III Abt, Zweiback (biscuit); and IV Abt Zechine (sequin). The Signals Abteilung became Vandal.

The headquarters began its move west on 9 December, embarking from Zinnowitz on a stop-start rail journey that took four days. The kitchen car was left behind, mourned the war diary, to arrive at last at the village of Merlemont, eight kilometres south-east of Beauvais and midway between Amiens and Paris. Max Wachtel noted: 'With my staff I decamped to the Château Merlemont, a small Schloss, about a mile from the Paris–Beauvais road set in the middle of a park. We are also assigned No. 56 Avenue Hoche, near the Arc de Triomphe, to where our officers go if there are meetings to attend in Paris.'

The security scare was general. On 18 December, for example, the Park picked up signals within the 'Insect' radar tracking detachment inquiring into the national origins of members of XIV Kompanie: 'Obegrf. Faltten, home address in Holland. Off. Mede, mother Danish. Gefr. Speer, grandmother Danish'. 'It seems as if inquiries are being made on any foreign connections of men belonging to Muetze's detachment,' noted Professor Norman. The Park soon decrypted a cheerier signal from the Leutnant: 'Merry Christmas and a Happy New Year to all comrades of the detachment.'

The Mittelwerk, December 1943

The horrors in the Harz Mountains had not abated. Albert Speer saw it for himself on 10 December. He quoted his own ministry diary in his book *Der Sklavenstaat*, published in 1981: 'The Minister went to inspect the plant in the Harz. The implementation of this tremendous mission required the maximum strength of the men in charge. Some had reached the stage of having to be forcibly sent on leave to restore their nerves ... The visitors were guided either by Director Degenkolb or Brigade Commander Kammler.' Speer managed to stand it for just an hour. 'The air in the cave was damp and stale and stank of excrement ...' He saw 'exhausted bodies, dull eyes, the expressionless faces of men who, at the approach of our group or at the sound of a cutting command, stood at attention, holding their caps in their hands. They seemed incapable of any reaction.'

The tunnels were nearly finished. The transferring and installing of the industrial plant from Peenemünde and the Rax Works were set in hand with no slackening of the brutality, as trainloads of machine tools and jigs were unloaded and hauled into the mountain. Transports of new prisoners arrived as the dead were pulled out on barrows. It has been computed by the historian Michael Neufeld, of the National Air and Space Museum in Washington, that of the seventeen thousand prisoners who toiled at the Mittelwerk in the truly appalling period between August 1943 and March 1944, six thousand died in the course of expanding the tunnel system and in moving and installing twelve hundred trainloads of factory equipment. It was Kammler who wielded complete power. Rudolf Höss recalled it in his strange memoirs (he himself was hanged at Auschwitz in 1947): 'Kammler had incredible powers over the mining operation. He had his own police force with special courts which proceeded rigorously and without mercy ... It made no difference if the delay was caused by saboteurs, directors, engineers, construction chiefs, skilled German workers, foreign workers, or prisoners.'

Along with machine tools from Peenemünde came civilian technicians and managers – men like the production engineer Arthur Rudolph. The survivor Yves Béon, in his famous memoir *Planet Dora*, remembered as a relatively new arrival 'the civilian technicians continually measuring the galleries according to the plans they carry. They move about, climbing the piles of rubble, going round machines and reels of cable, past churning concrete mixers, but never looking at the tattered men around them nor even hearing the ... screams of pain.'

By 17 December Albert Speer had recovered enough from the shock of his first inspection of the tunnels to return for another look. He personally congratulated Hans Kammler on the progress made. 'The director of the Sonderausschutz [special directorate] A-4, Degenkolb, tells me that you had succeeded in transforming the underground facilities at Niedersachswerfen within the almost incredible time of two months,' he said. 'From its original rough beginning it has been turned into a plant which has no equal in Europe ... I therefore take this occasion to express my deepest appreciation to you for this truly outstanding action and ask you to continue supporting Herr Degenkolb in this tremendous way.' It was indeed an achievement, and one secured by the brutal exploitation of thousands of slaves.

The intense Anglo-American photo-reconnaissance effort ordered after Mr Sandys's report of 24 October had gone on through the fog-shrouded autumn. By 21 December the airborne eyes had revealed, in addition to the seven large sites, a belt of ski sites ten to twenty miles deep, extending more than three hundred miles along the French coast. They might declare themselves in unusual ways.

SOE, for example, picked up rumours from an agent of a 'concrete runway' being built at Auffay in Normandy, which had been a restricted area since October: 'One possible significant indication was that sometime in December, a man he knew in Paris had abruptly ceased to receive his regular supplies of butter ... without any explanation.' Air Intelligence could think of one.

The missiles themselves would come on special trains from Germany and across the frontier into France, to be delivered to the Feldmunitionslager, or Feldmulag (field munitions depot). Then, it was planned, on to the 'fortress stores', connected by rail spurs and each holding 250 missiles (destined never to be used – by February 1944 Air Intelligence would have discovered seven out of eight of them).

The problem was not only how to bomb these targets, but how often. Douglas Kendall invented a point system of assessing the readiness of each site, so that attacks could be timed for the moment when construction was far advanced but not too danger-ously near completion. That's how it was supposed to work, but the Germans would prove cleverer than that. After ten days of attacks it was becoming clear that the medium bombers were not effective. Cloud obscured the targets on the short winter days. On 15 December the chiefs moved to ask the Americans to use the 8th Air Force's heavy bombers. Portal urged an all-out attack that might serve, he said, to lure German dayfighters into air battles with escorting fighters over France, something they had hitherto avoided.

Lt-General Ira Eaker was certainly willing, but the days of the USAAF being sent on mysterious missions by Norman Bottomley were over. On 20 December the joint chiefs in Washington ordered an urgent inquiry into the whole business. General George C. Marshall, US Army Chief of Staff, sent a curt memorandum to the chief of the British Joint Staff Mission in Washington, Field Marshal Dill, declaring that the USAAF could offer no help until it was spelled out fully why attacks on the Noball sites were so urgent. Marshall could understand that the British might be being coy because of their own continuing disagreements. But if the threat was so acute, why had British intelligence not told their US counterparts about it long before? Soon there would be a great army of young Americans mustered in southern England. What were they facing? Gas, bacteria, atom-splitting munitions, revolu-tionary explosives of 'unusually violent character' – all had appeared in the fragmentary intelligence that had been supplied so far.

Rumours of the Germans delivering gas by long-range weapons could be safely ignored, said the chiefs on 8 December, while so far as was known the enemy had no new gases for which the defences would prove inadequate (they had, but Allied Intelligence had signally failed to detect the new nerve agents). The OSS and US Military Intelligence, by contrast, were raising an acute alarm in Washington. Fantastic rumours were beginning to circulate.* The Germans were going to bombard London with something called 'Red Death', to shoot 'enormous tanks of poison gas and destroy every living creature in the British Isles'. According to the US air attaché in Madrid, they were preparing refrigerating apparatus along the French coast for the 'instantaneous creation of massive icebergs in the Channel'.

On 22 December Marshall asked Lt-General Jacob Devers, the London-based commander of US army forces in Europe, to get answers. Devers arranged for a courier to fly to Washington that night with Medmenham-drawn sketches and photographs of a 'ski site' supplied by Claude Pelly's committee. The Americans bought it. On the 24th more than 1300 aircraft participated in Mission Number 164, the biggest 8th Air Force operation yet. Six hundred and seventy bombers escorted by swarms of fighters dropped 1700 tons of explosives on twenty-three ski sites. Their crews had no idea what they had been sent to hit; in the briefing they had been described as 'mysterious constructions'. At the end of the raid, only three sites had been destroyed. Colonel Wachtel's regiment had suffered no casualties, thirty French workers had been killed.

This was going nowhere. Marshall recommended to Henry L. Stimson, US Secretary of War, that he should appoint a committee to investigate the German long-range weapon threat independently of the tricky Brits. The choice of chairman fell on General Stephen G. Henry, director of the War Department's recently-established New Developments Division. Henry, a former tank commander, was to make sure that everyone – the War Department, the US navy, and especially the British – cooperated. On 29 December Field Marshal Dill cabled the Air Ministry from

---

* Not so fantastic to those who had been working on the US's own very secret bio-weapon research at Fort Dugway, Utah.

Washington to tell London the news. The US War Department
could not offer assistance unless the fullest information was forthcoming, he had been told.

Liaison existed already in London, with Air Commodore Pelly's
committee, he noted, and the DMI and the Military Intelligence
Department in Washington 'enjoyed the warmest relations', but
thus far there was not enough data on whether the attacks would
be limited to London and Bristol. What about the airfields in East
Anglia, the Channel ports? What about the use of 'toxic agents or
other munitions'? There was a New Year scare that 'the enemy
might be planning to use ... radioactive powder' in the threatened
long-range weapons. It was clear where this was going. There was
a grand panic brewing in Washington that swarms of pilotless aircraft would dish the planned invasion of Europe before it had even
started and a million young Americans were in the line of fire. The
chiefs of staff in London had already very discreetly raised this
issue with Lt-General Sir Frederick E. Morgan, Chief of Staff to
the Supreme Allied Commander-designate, General Dwight D.
Eisenhower (who would be formally appointed on 17 January
1944).

Was the threat, as it was understood, enough to jeopardise the
invasion of France planned for the spring of 1944? Yes it was, Lt-
General Morgan replied, but not enough to prompt a change of
plans or a postponement. The long-range weapons had to be considered as 'a reintroduction of German air power, limited and
cumbersome to wield and likely to cause the Allies grief, but
unlikely to ruin the invasion'. The threat, however, was still capable of prejudicing an assault mounted from the south coast ports.
A decision would have to be taken at once if the preparations were
to be shifted to the West Country and the Bristol Channel rather
than the Thames estuary.

Morgan thought that the threat of a bombardment of London
and Portsmouth would prove a greater political problem than a
military one. The potential impact must not be exaggerated, but
neither should it be played down if US support for a sustained
aerial counter-offensive was to be secured.

A bizarre new factor was about to intervene. A certain Brigadier
Arthur Napier of the Ministry of Supply had been sent independently to Washington in late November to discuss rocket

developments in the US itself. He reported news of his journey to the Cabinet Office on 28 January. On the 4th of that month he had met Dr Vannevar Bush, the President's science adviser. Bush outlined to the startled brigadier just how seriously this thing was being taken in Washington – indeed it was the most serious threat so far because the use of 'bacterial warfare' was on the agenda. The small payload in such a sophisticated and expensive vehicle as the German rocket could not be explained in any other way.

Napier had then seen Field Marshal Dill, still reeling from the pounding he had received at the hands of General Marshall and his intelligence team. There had been an uncomfortable meeting at the Pentagon on the 14th, with General Henry and General Strong, Marshall's intelligence chief, at which Brigadier Napier learned that the Americans had 'conducted a series of trials in Canada'. Bacteria had been sprayed from low-flying aircraft on unfortunate goats and rabbits, and lethal effects had lasted on the ground for up to six weeks. It was all very alarming. Furthermore, American Intelligence had information that the Germans appeared to have 'converted forty of their biggest sugar refineries to the production of the bacteria yeast'. This was what London was facing, this was what the armies gathering in southern England were up against.

But then, consider how the Americans might help. US scientists had made great strides with airborne magnetic anomaly detectors. These land-based experiments for detecting submarines were being carried out by US Navy PBY-5 Catalina aircraft in the Arizona desert, so Brigadier Napier was informed; and there were new infrared devices that could prove enormously useful. But without information from London they could do nothing. 'The whole party was extremely peeved,' said Napier.

But peeved or not, it suited British purposes that General Henry's committee initially assumed the worst. US Crossbow investigators would go through precisely the same panicky reasoning process as had Duncan Sandys's Bodyline investigation six months earlier, and to begin with would reach similar alarming conclusions. It looked all too possible that massed pilotless aircraft attacks could overwhelm Allied anti-aircraft defences; and if the rumours of the supersonic A-4 were true, there was no defence. London might be wrecked, and with it the plans for a cross-Channel invasion of Continental Europe.

Oise, Christmas 1943

Airman Josef Esser had arrived in the Pas-de-Calais with the first wave from Zempin. All through the autumn he was on 'boring' guard duties at a construction site. He was billeted with an old lady in St Omer, he recalled, and that Christmas of 1943 he and Leutnant Preuss were invited to lunch by a French farm worker. 'There were air raids nearly every day,' he said. A horse-drawn column of building supplies was shot up by English fighters. There were seventeen dead most of whom were workmen, but with no casualties in his regiment. The teenage Flak gunner watched the bombardment of the Watten site by Allied heavy bombers from a nearby hill. 'Each bomb here is one less dropped on the homeland,' he recalled thinking at the time.

Life at the headquarters of the Flakgruppe Creil at the Château Merlemont was also quite agreeable. On Christmas Eve there was a party, with the 'table stacked with presents, no shortage of good French red wine, plenty of biscuits, chocolate and cigarettes, and books inscribed by Oberst Wachtel for everyone'. That afternoon a single-seat aircraft had crashed nearby, thought to be American. 'The pilot had been burned to death strapped in his seat.' The festivities were undiminished.

On New Year's Eve, the Herr Oberst posted his order of the day:

All ranks!

Once more we stand at the threshold of a new year. The war still rages inexorably around us, a war forced on us by those countries who, as in 1914, could not tolerate the rise of our nation ...

And so this gigantic struggle must go on to the end, which must be victory for Germany ...

I therefore wish all officers, NCOs and men of my regiment all luck for the coming year which will bring us much nearer to final victory and peace.

Signed Wachtel, Oberst and CO of the Regiment

CHAPTER 22

A new year had arrived, a year in which an Anglo-American army of liberation must cross the Channel and engage the enemy by land. Where so recently it had been the U-Boat, now the pilotless aircraft looked more of a threat to that great endeavour than anything else. The biggest question was when it might be considered operationally ready. Would it be before or after the invasion had begun? Would a landing and a breakout from the beaches neutralise the sites anyway? Bombing the ski sites seemed the only prophylactic. Or should they prepare a defence? The device might, presumably, be shot down.

The first plan for the defence of London, Bristol and the Solent against pilotless aircraft was issued by Air Marshal Sir Roderic Hill on 2 January 1944 at the headquarters of Air Defence of Great Britain (ADGB), as the defensive component of Fighter Command had been renamed on 17 November. Although subsequently revised, many of the plan's fundamentals would be incorporated in what would be done six months later.

Cherwell kept to his previous form, insisting that the threat of the midget aircraft had been 'much exaggerated'. That is what he told the Defence Committee (Operations) meeting of 22 December. He presented the scientific case, drawn from the data presented in a masterly intelligence analysis of the pilotless aircraft that Dr Jones had drafted and would circulate around the Air

Ministry the next day. The scientific adviser's keyword was 'precipitancy', describing the Luftwaffe's rush to get a long-range weapon into action in the heat of their rivalry with the army and its A-4. Their haste had brought with it a rash of technical problems, which were not yet solved. Of the organisation itself Jones could say that the proving unit was now probably operational. 'The IV Abteilung has been located at Brüsterort [information gleaned via the Ultra decrypt of 24 October 1943] which indicates the regiment is a large one of four Abteilungen.' The mathematics of it pleased him – 108 launchers, 27 per battalion, three batteries, each of three sections. Three by three by three.

'The 155 is some sort of super-regiment,' he concluded, 'which means the rank of Oberst for its CO is too low.' There was a connection with the SS artillery school at Glau near Kummersdorf, south of Berlin, and Wachtel's operation was known to have absorbed an airfield-servicing company associated with the Hs 293 rocket bomb. Everything in the intelligence summary came from the Park, although its provenance was carefully disguised. As Jones explained:

Our sources soon reported that in April 1943 the [German Air Experimental Signals Regiment] 14th Company had sent a Würzburg D [ground-based radar] to the Flak Experimental Station at Peenemünde, and during the summer they told us that sections of the same company were deploying around the shores of the Baltic ...

Towards the end of October 1943 one of our sources managed to penetrate the organization ... and from his report it was obvious that they were plotting pilotless aircraft.

He explained how 'the stations originally broadcast their observations as ranges and bearings', but had lately changed to other systems of plotting. The first problem had been to locate the stations themselves. 'This could be done in several cases merely by timing the plots along the tracks, and by extrapolating from one station to another, their relative positions could be worked out ... When we had fixed one station, that on the Greifswalder Oie, the others could be fixed station by station, thus we could build up the plotting framework.' On the sad story of Aircraftsman Wilde, whose suicide on 20 November 1943 had alerted Bimbo Norman to the tiny Baltic island, he was silent.

Jones outlined the story of finding the midget aircraft on its ramp at Peenemünde-West and the parallel discoveries by photo-reconnaissance Mosquito at Zempin. Thus it was finally established that the ski sites would develop into pilotless aircraft projectors. Detailed performance figures from the trial plots could be included in the report. What he and everyone else got wrong at the time was the method of propulsion. The 'Pingpong' (agent-derived) material seemed to feature storage for two different fuels at each Bois Carré site. Jones had described a fuel store (*Stofflager*) with compartments divided off by a wall as part of 'elaborate precautions to ensure that any liquid or solid in one compartment should not come into contact with the other'.*

This pointed to the propulsion not being via an air-breathing jet turbine.† And if the engine did not get its oxygen from the air, it must carry its own supply with it. The payload would therefore be comparatively small – perhaps half a ton. And from the performance data presented on the Baltic plots, of the aircraft launched only a third would reach their target anyway. 'If my assumptions are correct,' said Cherwell at the Defence Committee meeting, 'one aircraft fired will result on average in one casualty in London.' But the Prof's assumption, at least about the fuel, was not correct. Jones had not said what the two fuels were for. Cherwell thought they were the projectile's main propellant.

Jones's analysis was, in fact, a model of precision. Having congratulated once again the mysterious agents who had so bravely infiltrated the XIV Kompanie and those who had removed the ski site plans, he built his conclusions on all-source intelligence. He correctly identified the already much bombed Fieseler company of Kassel as the most likely original developer of the pilotless

---

* The fuel store in fact was configured to store hydrogen peroxide (*T-Stoff*) and sodium permanganate (*Z-Stoff*), which when mixed generated steam under high pressure to punch the launch piston up the catapult. The principle, developed by Professor Hellmuth Walter, was also used in the Hs 293 rocket glider, the A-4 fuel turbo-pump, the Me 163 interceptor and the small, fast, air-independent Type XVII U-Boat. Whereas the Allies had the atom bomb, along with the rocket this was the Germans' most important novel technology of the war.
† Of the type that had been developed in Britain with Air Ministry funding since 1938 by Frank Whittle.

aircraft, and Argus of Berlin as being associated with its power plant. But where series production might be undertaken was still a mystery. 'The rate of production is even more obscure than the factories,' said Dr Jones. 'At Peenemünde an average two aircraft a day have been fired, for testing the projectiles and possibly for training ground crews. It is reasonable to deduce that the production figure is at least 20 per day.'

What sort of a threat did it add up to? Dr Jones was in the Cherwell no-need-to-panic camp. He concluded:

> Despite the Zempin trials and errors, the programme proceeds at the Führer's impatient demands and so it will almost inevitably result in pilotless aircraft being projected at this country. Probably Oberst Wachtel is more nervous than anybody here about the success of his operations, and some good bombing now of the ski sites might enable him to furnish the Führer with sound excuses for indefinite delay ... [T]he trials recommencing in October are still showing the missiles to be so unreliable that only one in six would hit London. In the meantime a hundred operational sites are being constructed in France ... Perhaps the surest sign of precipitancy [is]that the sites [are] under construction before the prototype [has] fired its first missile.

Jones considered there would be no serious threat until March. The maximum load that could be delivered within a radius of ten miles of Charing Cross would be forty tons an hour, which the enemy would be unable to sustain. It would therefore 'take a long time to do serious damage to the capital'.

The scientist's oversight of German activities seemed magical – too magical for some. On the day of the report, 23 December, Air Commodore Pelly wrote to Frank Inglis, the Air Ministry intelligence chief, to express his anguish. The most valuable and reliable source that his committee had was Most Secret Source, said Pelly. But it was exclusively in the hands of ADI (Science). 'We are asked to commit ourselves to estimates of scales and dates of attack ... it is most important that the committee should at least know what the results of this particular analysis may be [based on].'

There was a heated meeting with Pelly on the morning of Christmas Eve. Jones told some of it to Inglis in a letter dictated that afternoon. He reminded him how he had objected to 'intelligence by committee', and how nothing he had seen of Pelly's committee at work had changed his mind. He was being regarded simply as 'experienced in handling MSS material', which the air commodore was now demanding to see 'in parallel' and in its 'raw' state, without comment from ADI (Science). That could not be. It was a declaration of war: 'My section ... regards itself as holding a post of honour in the front line of this country's defences,' said Jones. 'We shall only surrender this position when it is shown that another organisation can do better.'

He brooded through two days of an austerity Christmas. On the 27th he asked Inglis for his permission to resign. Pelly's committee should preferably be abolished, he declared. 'Whatever happens I trust you will not stop me working on Crossbow problems.'

Again Jones was too good to let go. It was the JIC Crossbow Committee that would be abolished, although Pelly himself would survive. After briefly considering a move to split responsibility for the rocket and the pilotless aircraft between the War Office and the Air Ministry, on 3 January the chiefs of staff resolved to turn the lot over to Air Vice Marshal Arthur Bottomley, while Frank Inglis was made responsible for forwarding reports to the chiefs. The faintly absurd Pelly would stay on as Bottomley's deputy, with special duty for coordinating intelligence work and for directing the offensive effort against the ski sites.

Brigadier Ian Jacob wrote to General Sir Hastings Ismay, Military Secretary of the War Cabinet, with a very shrewd summation of what was wrong: 'I understand that part of the difficulty is the personality of Dr Jones ... a very clever and capable man, but a man who likes working on his own and has all along disliked the Crossbow subcommittee. His mode of procedure has been to disagree with all they do and to brief Lord Cherwell privately in the opposite sense' – thus enraging Mr Sandys and the hapless Pelly. But 'we will get over this difficulty, because I imagine that Dr Jones will now be handling the Intelligence side in the Air Ministry, and, presumably [his] reports will ... be less subject to criticism by Lord Cherwell [whose] technical objections are, of course, most incomprehensible to Ministers and they do not get resolved one way or another,' Jacob went on. 'The [Defence Committee] meetings are entertaining but unprofitable because Ministers are left wondering whether Lord Cherwell is right or not ... It so happens that throughout this business, Lord Cherwell has been, on the whole, far more right than the Investigation.'

Cherwell's influence with Churchill was undiminished, and Jones was still the Prof's protégé. Pelly did not get his way. On 8 January the chiefs decreed that the radar plots should remain Dr Jones's exclusive preserve. It seemed a bureaucratic reshuffle of exquisite pettiness, but to those who understood it meant that Jones had kept the keys to the Ultra castle. On 10 January he gave Cherwell a summary of the previous month's trials in the Baltic. Accuracy had improved from the month before to three out of four of the shoots being within ± 4° of the declared bearing. Greater London, he pointed out, was 8° wide, at 200 kilometres. The two most recent shoots had achieved ranges of 258 and 270 kilometres – exceptionally long. A third of the shoots failed to start at all. The chances of hitting London were now three in eight. Cherwell sent a note to Churchill with these figures the next day, and they were incorporated into the Inglis report to the chiefs on the 15th.

That same day came an instruction from the Air Ministry under the Crossbow mantle, giving two new codenames – 'Big Ben' for the rocket and 'Diver' for the pilotless aircraft. 'Noball' was to become a 'codeword of convenience', it said. American air commanders, meanwhile, were more convinced than ever that it was all a trick. Why had the ski sites been designed with a signature so visible from the air?

The bombing ground on relentlessly. Churchill was shown a set of moonscape post-attack photo-reconnaissance covers, but was unimpressed. 'What really surprises me about the photographs is how little harm we have been able to do with ordinary explosive bombs,' he wrote to Charles Portal on the 10th. 'Are you attacking all camps or hutments where labour may be accommodated for constructing these places? The photographs certainly show that a liberal drenching with mustard gas would make all work, especially firing, very difficult.'

It was not the response the Air Staff were expecting. The PM seemed mustard-keen on gas. And the Germans were behaving in an unpredictable way, camouflaging some sites and seeming to abandon others. 'The enemy's policy for the repair of damaged sites is not yet apparent,' Bottomley told an Air Ministry meeting. But the Germans did have a policy – and that was to cause as much consternation as possible. They were getting very good at it.

Northern France, December–January 1944

Jones had been right to use the word 'precipitancy' in his description of the FZG 76 programme. The rush to get the novel weapon developed, flight-tested and into series manufacture, while at the same time building a complex ground organisation and supply chain and training the men to operate it (all under aerial bombardment), was a feat of management at the limit of even German organisational talents.

On 1 December the Führer headquarters had formally announced the activation of LXV Armee Korps zur Besonderen Verwendung – the 65th Army Corps for Special Employment – with a mandate to 'prepare and execute the long-range engagement of England with all such secret weapons as might come into consideration for that purpose'. At the same time Dornberger was struggling on at Blizna amid a shower of air-bursting rockets, and Wachtel's launch sites were being pummelled from the air.

Clearly the enemy had detected the Flakgruppe and its site system, of which, said the war diary, seven firing positions had now been destroyed and three completely obliterated. Foreign workers were to blame. As the regimental diary put it:

> More attacks, progress nil. At the slightest suspicion of the sound of aircraft, workers throw up work and leave. No protecting fighters, and Flak is useless. From 1 January four-engine bombers have been dropping 500 kg bombs several times a day. Roads and convoys are being shot up by low-flying aircraft. Electricity and telephone lines are frequently cut, sites are turning into a sea of craters. The best result of the raids for the enemy has been the sudden flight of the workers who do not return for hours.

II Abteilung Werwolf further noted that 'some of the German foremen had lost control and – at the sound of aircraft engines themselves ran away'.

General Heinemann had made his tour of the embattled ski sites, and gave his woeful summary to Keitel in an encounter at the HQ of 15th Army at Tourcoing, thirteen kilometres north-east of Lille, on 10 January. But there was a way out of this – and there was indeed a Plan B. The Walter works of Kiel had developed a clever prefabricated launch ramp, still using their own magical steam-generation system, that could be erected in a matter of days. The surveying and making ready of a parallel network of sites with simple concrete plinths began in early January. The work was done by convict labour under close guard.

Security was reaching new levels of paranoia. The headquarters guard of 'Flemings' (Belgian collaborators) was dismissed. A special court martial tried the case of Leutnant Busse of No. 1 Battery Abteilung Zylinder, accused of high treason. Billeted with a French family, he had left a technical drawing in his room. The court ruled that Busse had not done so deliberately, but sentenced him to death anyway. The sentence was posted in regimental orders as a 'strict warning'. When agents of the secret field police (Geheime Feldpolizei) tested security 'incognito', they found that 'the guards were only too willing to give out information and some of them actually acted as guides'. More alarming still was the discovery by No. 5 Battery Werwolf of a mysterious container dropped by an enemy aircraft by parachute near Hauvin. It carried propaganda material in French 'inciting the civilian population to spy ... A pencil for taking down notes and a bag of corn completed the equipment which has been passed to the security office at ... Arras.' The mysterious snack would be ideal for a homing pigeon.

Max Wachtel himself had already become convinced that somehow his telephone conversations from Zempin had been intercepted. When summoned to Arras, he was informed that an intercepted radio message revealed that enemy intelligence 'had put a price on the person of Oberst Wachtel'. Immediately a paybook was prepared in the name of Oberst Martin Wolf: 'I was also classified as one-armed and told not to shave. Colonel Wolf has to have a short beard and moustache,' he wrote. On 7 January the new CO's name was solemnly announced to the headquarters personnel on parade at Merlemont.

Wachtel stayed undercover in Paris, growing his beard. By his account he then took the Paris–Berlin sleeper train from which he jumped down at a spot where a car was waiting. He drove to Zempin to find the demonstration unit lined up on the beach path under the pine trees for inspection, and announced his new name. It all amused his men greatly.

Beards were not enough to cloak the regiment in mystery, though. On 9 February the whole staff of Flakgruppe Creil, as the regiment was now styled, 'changed uniforms in taxis in the streets of Paris in the best E. Phillips Oppenheim tradition',* wrote a British intelligence officer when he put the story together – from which they emerged dressed as Organisation Todt engineers and set off for their new headquarters at Auteuil, six kilometres south of Beauvais. A small staff was left at Merlemont to channel instructions from 'Colonel Wolf'.

The deception pantomime seemed to work. December's clear horizon, when the link was made in London between the Peenemünde-20 midget plane, the ski sites and the Zempin ramp, was now swathed in fog. Wachtel was lost to sight, and the rather more significant LXV Armee Korps headquarters had been invisible from the start. The Park had nothing to say. Bombing of the Noball targets continued with unrelenting ferocity – and futility.

The Germans knew, now, that London knew. The Luftwaffe would not repeat their mistake of declaring their presence on the ground so obviously. They had a new plan.

---

* A prolific English international adventure-thriller writer of the pre-war period.

CHAPTER 23

Valparaiso, January 1944

The American interest in the pilotless aircraft had now become an obsession. They were turning their best scientists to it, and were as anxious as ever to know what the British knew. Jones recorded getting a phone call from Portal telling him that 'an American' was coming to London to whom he should turn over his files. Jones wanted this expressed as a direct order – not just informally by phone – because 'it would reveal all our intelligence methods'.

The person who turned up at 54 Broadway by urgent transatlantic flight was a 'quiet, bulky man', H. P. 'Bob' Robertson, lately professor of mathematics at Princeton, now of the Office of Scientific Research and Development in Washington, DC. A get-to-know-you meeting at Broadway was followed by an agreeable lunch at St Ermin's Hotel. 'Within Bob Robertson's first hour in the office, he was convinced by our work, and we became the closest of friends,' Jones told an American lecture audience many years later. The Princeton professor's report back to his superiors was positive. US airpower and technical assistance should be eagerly applied in the cause of saving London from robot bombardment. It should be done rapidly and on a scale which only American resources could provide.

On 12 January General George C. Marshall had approved the

suggestion of the War Department Committee that the Army Air Force should undertake a 'technical and tactical inquiry into the means, methods, and effectiveness of air attacks against Crossbow targets in France'. The task was assigned to the AAF Proving Ground Command at Eglin Field, near Valparaiso in the sunny western Florida Panhandle. General Henry 'Hap' Arnold, the USAAF chief of staff, telephoned the commander, Brigadier General Grandison Gardner: 'I want some buildings reproduced. I want to make simulated attacks with a new weapon. It will take a hell of a lot of concrete ... give it first priority and complete it in days.' It would be done.

On the 23rd a renewed aerial reconnaissance of the threat zone was ordered. It showed attempts to disguise the sites with farm buildings – especially the give-away curved bomb stores. Craters had been left ostentatiously unfilled – 'probably,' it was assumed in an Air intelligence report, 'with the intention of deluding us into thinking that work had been abandoned'. It was also reported that a number of weather balloons with radio transmitters of Luftwaffe origin were found during December on the south coast of England. Somebody was interested in the weather over Kent and Sussex. The outlook was blustery.

London, January 1944

A new piece of intelligence arrived at 54 Broadway in mid-January. Pingpong No. 394, as it was numbered, was from 'Source B.3'. It was headed 'France, Air, Informations Diverses' and was circulated by Kenneth Cohen's French section of the SIS. Date of information: end December 1943. Place of origin: Paris.

It was clear to Dr Jones that it came from the same source as the autumn report that had mixed up the pilotless aircraft with the A-4. This did exactly the same – but never mind, it brought news of the latest doings of Colonel Wachtel.

'Following numerous air reconnaissance flights and bombing, the HQ of the AA Wachtel regiment has moved from Doullens [thirty kilometres north of Amiens] to a château at Creil, 55 km from Paris,' it revealed. 'Colonel Wachtel himself will not be in continual residence ... for he makes frequent visits to Berlin, Paris and Zempin to supervise the finishing touches to the stratospheric rocket. The guns will be set up at their emplacements in March. The officers of this HQ expect commando raids or even a landing.' 'Strong defensive measures' were being carried out and visits by Goering 'or even Hitler' were expected in the near future.

The last line of the report gave a clue to its source: 'It might be possible for the translator in charge of the purchasing for the account of the unit, and acting as liaison with the French authorities, to gain access into the HQ,' it said. Someone working as a translator for the French contractors, perhaps?

The Oberst was right to expect a commando raid. Assaults on the large sites had been considered in London since the summer past, but ruled out as being suicidal. Now the Americans were talking of a major airborne operation. It was still about intelligence-gathering. If operational units were shortly to arrive in France, was there a chance of snatching one of the weapons or its vital components?

On 25 January the chiefs considered the options. Agents would soon be unable to get into the sites in the guise of labourers. 'When crews arrive, and the end of February looks likely, the only method of getting information would be by small commando raids.' Combined Operations sought reassurance that all this was for intelligence-gathering, not an attempt to blow the sites up or otherwise disable them; but the Special Operations Executive had also been drafting plans since December for Resistance networks to attack power lines and telephone cables on receipt of a coded announcement from the BBC. And there was another way to gather intelligence: SOE had also hatched a plan to kidnap and drug a suitable technician from a construction site, then 'deliver the body to England'.

Lord Cherwell had an even stranger scheme. He drafted a pamphlet to be dropped on German cities revealing that the British knew all about the goings-on in France, and mocking the 'puny weapon' as a 'toy aircraft' that would have no effect on London or on the war – then, the idea was, the enemy would counter by revealing the weapon's true potential. Ismay thought the suggestion 'unhelpful'.

The Mittelwerk, January–February 1944

The process of installing a rocket factory in the Harz tunnels had been as grisly a task as expanding the caverns had been. By the onset of 1944 parts of it were ostensibly ready, with civilian technicians all set to instigate a new phase. The camp Dora outside the tunnel itself was now complete down to its gallows.

Three newly made rockets had emerged from the tunnels on flatcars in the last hours of the old year. But the first production models were of such poor quality that they could not be used, even for static tests. Cracks, leaks, faults – the Peenemünde technicians sent to correct them despaired. The first slave-made missile was fired from test stand 2 on the night of 21 January, rose a few feet, toppled, then exploded. 'Saboteurs' were blamed. After a visit to the Mittelwerk in mid-January Hans Kehrl, head of planning at the Speer ministry, recorded: 'This is in no way a wonder weapon. In fact it does not even seem wise to continue its production. The expenditure involved in sending a small quantity of explosive to a place which is so difficult to accurately target is simply a useless waste. It is true that I am a civilian and not an expert, but common sense must see the chance for success of no matter what kind, as nonexistent.' There were others in London and Berlin of the same opinion. The Luftwaffe aircraft production chief Erhard Milch thought the people behind the rocket 'should be put in a lunatic asylum'.

It was Walter Dornberger's flag that was drooping now. Having survived the attempt in October to sack him, still shuttling between Peenemünde and Blizna, he was summarily dismissed as operational commander by Erich Heinemann and supplanted as Artillerie Kommandeur 91 by Generalmajor Richard Metz, an artilleryman with no rocket experience. The veteran artilleryman still had his work cut out trying to make the rocket work at all.

Valparaiso, February–March 1944

The bombing of the ski sites continued with a futile ferocity. Newspapers on both sides of the Atlantic served up triumphal accounts of the 'Rocket-gun Coast' being pasted by Allied bombers. The scale and technical competence of American air-power must surely prevail. In the second week of February, Bottomley and Inglis flew to Florida as guests of General Arnold to see for themselves the live experiments being conducted at Eglin Field, including B-17s dropping 'television-controlled glide bombs' from stand-off ranges of twelve miles. Air Vice Marshal Bottomley was said to be 'deeply interested'.

General Gardner's report on the Eglin trials concluded that minimum-altitude attacks by tactical fighters were the most effective against the ski sites. Medium- and high-altitude bombing attacks were the least effective. It was not necessary to divert heavy bombers from strategic missions. Within a week Gardner was in England to spread the word about the Eglin findings with General Eisenhower and with leading British and American air commanders. But could what was true in Florida also be true in the rainy skies over northern France?

The British thought not. Leigh-Mallory had already written to Lt-General Spaatz, commander of US Strategic Air Forces on Europe, on 4 March to say: 'I think it is clear now that the best weapon ... is the high altitude bomber.'

London, March 1944

The bunker sites had also been under heavy attack since late January. The chiefs heard the latest at their meeting on 16 March. Martinvast was devastated and need not be attacked again. The large sites at Siracourt and Sottevast would take two to six weeks to repair, the one at Lottinghem longer. No serious further damage had been inflicted on Watten, Wizernes or the mysterious site at Mimoyecques – which photo-reconnaissance showed was being developed on different lines from the others. An agent report mentioned a 'rocket launching cannon', which seemed a throwback to the misconceptions of mid-1943. In fact it was correct.*

---

* Work on the underground installation near Cap Gris Nez of the *Hochdruckpumpe*, the multi-barrelled cannon aimed at London, had begun in October. The workings of the V3 weapon itself would remain more or less hidden from Allied intelligence until late 1944, but not the site.

By the same date as that report, 16 March, the Air Ministry could give the chiefs a revised estimate of the scale and timing of an attack by pilotless aircraft. In the first fifteen days of an offensive, beginning at the end of the month, an assault could deliver only 160 tons of bombs in ten to twelve hours at forty-eight-hour intervals – the equivalent of a mission by twenty Lancasters.

The propaganda experts from the Ministry of Economic Warfare, meanwhile, found enemy pronouncements much more muted. The best the Kreisleiter – the Nazi party boss – of Innsbruck could come up with was 'Our sharpest weapon of retaliation is our belief in the Führer.' 'It is unlikely anything sensational will happen within the next four weeks,' the analysts suggested.

By 18 March the chiefs were able to tell the War Cabinet that the scale and weight of any predictable attack were a third to a half of what they had looked like at the beginning of February, and that if the counter-bombing continued at its current tempo all the sites would have been knocked out by the end of April. This sunny assessment was welcome. The Baltic flight trials as now being reported by Jones showed a big improvement in range and accuracy: 40 per cent of launches would hit London, and there were few non-starters. But that meant nothing if the means of launching had been obliterated.

Oberst Wachtel was ahead of everyone. On 1 March the Flakgruppe headquarters held a 'paper command exercise' in Paris, which wargamed a revenge attack made on England in response to imaginary raids made by RAF 'terror bombers' the night before on Leipzig and Dresden. The orders from LXV Armee Korps arrived about twelve hours before operations were due to begin. Transmission from regiment to launcher took about three hours, during which orders to fire were radioed to the officers in charge of the battalions, sent in writing by dispatch rider to the batteries, and telephoned in code to the sites.

According to the war diary, 'the administrative exercise was judged to have been a success'. Wachtel claimed that his sixty-four operational launch sites could have sent up to 960 missiles to their targets on the night of 1–2 March. The Herr Oberst was jubilant.

Three days later the Park decrypted a message: Leutnant

Muetze, their old friend from the Greifswalder Oie radar station, had had a lucky escape from a crashed aircraft. He was returning from a 'survey trip to Poland'.

What was he doing in Poland?

CHAPTER 24

Blizna, February–March 1944

The rocket trials at Blizna were in trouble. There were the usual misfires, but of those that reached the height of their planned trajectory, on the return earthwards most of them 'burst' on re-entry into the atmosphere. Von Braun blamed the alcohol tank, which, although practically expended of fuel after the initial boost phase, could explode through overheating or increased air pressure as it re-entered the Earth's atmosphere. Dornberger, still in charge of development, took station in an observation trench at the impact site 115 miles from Blizna (the well-rehearsed joke was that the theoretical spot on the map marked as the centre of the target was where the rocket would not fall).

His description was lyrical: larks trilling in the shimmering sunlit air, and a cloudless blue sky in which the veteran artilleryman saw 'a tiny dot, lengthening into a short streak'. Suddenly there was a cloud of steam. One part of the rocket – the warhead and the instrument compartment – flew on, raising a huge dust cloud two hundred yards ahead of him, while other large parts of the rocket slowly fell from the sky. Surveying the damage, General Josef Rossman, in charge at Peenemünde-Ost, suggested packing the carcass interior with 'glass wool' to absorb and disperse the heat of re-entry.

A-4 launches continued by the Baltic, as part of the effort to find a fix for the air-burst. There would be four launches in January and twelve in February. The insulated rockets did seem to work: six impacts in one day were all successful. When the glass-wool modification was introduced on the production line, overall success went to 70–80 per cent. But Dornberger wanted better than that.

Hochwald, March 1944

The all-hearing Himmler picked up the more optimistic noises coming from Blizna. The SS now made a renewed bid for control of the whole A-4 affair. In an episode much rehearsed in von Braun biographies Himmler summoned the scientist to come, alone, to meet in his impressive command train in the forest near his Hochwald headquarters. He had flown there piloting himself in his little Bf 108 liaison aircraft. The Reichsführer-SS had similarly summoned Hans Kammler a few days earlier, on 18 February. There was much to discuss with both men.

Von Braun himself told the story of the visit to Hochwald in a 1949 deposition to American interrogators: how he felt 'jittery' on meeting Himmler, who had promised to 'free him of Army bureaucracy' and turn the rocket, which nad 'ceased to be an engineer's toy', into an instrument of destiny for the German people. Now there was no Albert Speer* around to act as a counter to the Reichsführer's wonder-weapon takeover ambitions. 'I replied coolly that in General Dornberger I had the best chief I could wish to have, and that it was technical trouble and not red tape that was holding things up,' von Braun reported. The date of the meeting was 21 February according to several accounts but the NASM historian Michael Neufeld, consulting von Braun's pilot's log, concluded there was no evidence that the meeting even happened. There are several sources, though, for what happened next – the strange story of von Braun's arrest.

---

* In mid-January the armaments minister had succumbed to a knee condition (which seriously worsened when complicated by a pulmonary embolism) and was entrusted to the care of Himmler's personal physician, the SS doctor Karl Gebhardt. Speer would later become convinced that the bespectacled medical experimenter was trying to kill him. Speer managed to get to a convalescent home in northern Italy where he was comparatively safe, but he would be out of Hitler's inner circle until the end of April.

All the leading Peenemünde personalities had been under surveillance by agents of the Sicherheitsdienst (the SS intelligence service) for many months. In the early hours of 22 March von Braun was taken to the Gestapo post at Stettin and put into a cell for 'protective custody'. His brother Magnus von Braun, Klaus Riedel and Helmut Gröttrup (Dr Ernst Steinhoff's chief assistant in the guidance division) joined him in the holding cells on the top floor of police headquarters.

The nominal cause for the arrests was remarks that they had supposedly made at a party in Zinnowitz early in March, which had been recorded by a duplicitous female dentist (who appears in other Peenemünde memoirs) and relayed to the Gestapo. Von Braun was 'building a spaceship' and was 'plotting to fly to England with plans of the rocket', while Riedel did not want to be associated with 'a murder instrument'.*

Dornberger pleaded for their release. Speer gave support from the sidelines, and a 'surprisingly benevolent' Hitler visited his convalescent bedside. Von Braun would be protected, the Führer had indicated, as long as he was indispensable. Himmler's drawn-out takeover bid had failed, for now. For von Braun, his arrest for 'dreaming of space flight' would prove to be very fortunate in the long term. By late spring he and the other interplanetary enthusiasts were back hard at work by the Baltic plotting the destruction of London.

Bletchley Park, March 1944

At the Air Ministry and at the Park the rocket seemed to have slipped out of view. But not entirely. Brown-key messages warning the air force 'Insect' radar stations to expect rocket trials had been intercepted by the Park six times in January, three times in February and the same in March. They said nothing about the rocket's performance, its technical nature, where it was made or how many there were. Bletchley must try harder.

---

* Klaus Riedel, instrumental in developing the mobile support equipment for the V2, was killed in a car accident on 4 August 1944. In 1970 a crater on the moon was named after him.

Section 3G(N) had instigated a keyword-alerting system the summer before on the routine watch of enemy 'development and training', where mention of the rocket might be expected to occur. But what words were they? As Bletchley's own account put it: 'No names of commands or units were known, not even the type of unit or the service. No place names except Peenemünde, very few personal names, and none of the operational ones – not even the name of the missile itself.' The exercise began with a few 'scarcely intelligible' scraps which contained 'further names and characteristic ideas'. In December a mention of 'A-4' rising from 'Ost' had popped up. It was a start.

The second way in was to 'look out for names of organisations for which there was no known explanation'. Thus it was that wildly elusive 'rocket traffic' began to show up in spring 1944 as 'isolated texts on routine military district W/T [wireless telegraphy] links.' The Park needed help. It would have to get it unofficially. Intelligence of varying usefulness had come from prisoners captured in Tunisia in mid-1943. Now prisoners taken in the grindingly slow Italian campaign were throwing up more scraps. Front-line intelligence officers had been briefed to screen out technical personnel – anyone with a link to a research station in the Baltic attracted immediate special attention. Based on the interrogation of two captured German Flak gunners, a report was circulated in early April 1944 which gave an insight at least into the topography of the missile range: 'The Germans have used the Island of Ruden primarily for installing equipment to photograph and measure the flight of rocket projectiles. From the old lighthouse tower they photographed the projectiles with motion picture cameras. The projectiles were fired north of Peenemünde on the Island of Usedom and were aimed to travel about halfway between the Island of Ruden and Oie.'

It was all useful, but a much more intimate view was essential. Photo-reconnaissance covers of Usedom taken on 5–7 January 1944 had shown 'three columns' standing in a triangular formation on the foreshore at Peenemünde-Ost. Were they rockets? Everything remained enveloped in the impenetrable Baltic mist. Then a window opened up – in Poland. Reports from occupied Poland showing a possible long-range weapon connection had begun in October 1943. Villages were being forcibly evacuated around Debica, north-east of Cracow, an area already identified as an SS training area. A new rail line was being built, at the midpoint of which was a village called Blizna.

The reports got more detailed. According to the Polish author and Auschwitz survivor Jozef Garlinski, the underground Home Army (Armia Krajowa) intelligence in Warsaw was receiving information from 'forestry workers, almost all the personnel of which belonged to the underground'. They spoke of the building work at Blizna, of mysterious transports, of exceptional security. A car had crashed in Warsaw killing all the passengers, and 'Home Army counter-intelligence was able to state a few days later that the passengers were experts working on the secret German weapons and that they had come from Mielec [airfield] situated not far from Blizna,' said Garlinski.

A report of 15 February was said to have given a description of 'a rocket fourteen metres long with a weight of seven tons'. Another, on the 22nd, described a projectile 'twelve metres long, [with] a diameter of one and a half metres and a weight of twelve tons'. Missiles were being fired regularly by day and by night. 'Sometimes they exploded quite near Blizna, sometimes they travelled to the north, as far as the river Bug ... making huge craters in the ground.' A peasant had been blown off his feet by an explosion a kilometre away, which had also left a number of dead hares.

From the beginning of 1944 there had been fitful breaks into a 'police' key that the Park called 'Quince'. A message of 9 February to the SS leadership main office in Berlin mentioned a 'special construction project' at 'Blytna'. Another decrypt, of a 10 February message, snatched by a keyword search of routine military district traffic, mentioned both 'Versuchsstab [experimental staff], Kommandostelle Siegfried' and 'SS Truppenübungsplatz [troop exercise area] Heidelager'. It was sent by someone signing himself as 'Oberleutnant Geller Chief of Staff for Special Representation of the Army'. There was no previous use of that term in the Bletchley index. Professor Norman quickly pinned the location down. 'There is a place called Blizna about 50 12 N 21 46 E, 12 miles NE of Debica' was appended to the signal before it was copied to its tiny list of recipients.

The Park decrypted a Luftwaffe signal of 4 March from one 'Klehnert' (for whom no rank or service was given) to

Peenemünde-West complaining that 'completion of the building was delayed on account of experiments by the Army'. What experiments? Equipment had arrived, including a *Zubringerwagen* (shuttle trolley) and a *Dampferzeuger* (steam generator), as requested. The signal had originated from somewhere also signing as 'Heidelager'.

Blytna – Blizna – Heidelager – the SS training camp – Command Post Siegfried – they all seemed to be the same. On their different keys they were entered in sequence into the ever-expanding J Series (see p. xv) with Professor Norman's annotation. 'This camp is at Debica in Poland on the railway line from Cracow to Lwow,' he commented. 'This is the first time that activity of this type has been noted – however, Leutnant Muetze's trip to Poland [and the aircraft crash on his return] may be connected.' The mysterious Klehnert, meanwhile, was asking for a fuel allocation request to be forwarded from Zempin. He was therefore something to do with Wachtel, Norman deduced.

The Professor was right on both counts. Muetze, the radar tracking expert, had gone to Poland to sketch out a new test range for the FZG 76. And Wachtel's air force officers, of whom Klehnert was clearly one, were indeed preparing for a sequence of test shoots.

More reports emerged. A Luftwaffe decrypt of 4 March, again from 'Klehnert' this time messaging from 'ZBL [Zentralbauleitung] Heidelager' to 'Erprobungstelle Karlshagen' (Peenemünde-West), reported that construction of further facilities was being delayed by the 'army's secret command project'. What was that?

The catapult base and command stand were finished, it was reported. There was something called a 'T-Fuel depot' and an 'adjusting house'; 'kitchens and lavatories are 10% complete', it was stated on the same channel on 13 March in a signal routed jointly to Oberst Wachtel at Zempin and to somebody called 'Inspizient 76' at Bernau-bei-Berlin.

A near identical progress report was sent the same day on the Quince key from a certain SS Obersturmführer Thode, also declaring himself to be of the 'Zentralbauleitung.' It was sent to a personality in Berlin – SS Gruppenführer und General der Waffen SS Dr. Ing. Hans Kammler. His address was given as 'Taunusstrasse 8 Berlin-Grunewald.'

Professor Norman noted on the decrypt: 'Kammler is new to J.*
He is however, well known for his control of an interest in various
and varied construction projects within the SS, of which he is most
probably the chief engineer of the Waffen SS.' The demon king
had made his entry.

By 21 March, Norman was assuming from the flurry of
Luftwaffe messages coming from Blizna that Oberst Wachtel was
associated with both 'A-4 and FZG 76 and the same seems to be
true of the Waffen SS'. He was wrong; but what was true was that
Hans Kammler, having powered forward the Mittelwerk construction, was now energetically concerning himself with the
long-range weapons themselves. He had been stalking the rocket
for months: according to Dornberger, 'from November 1943 Dr
Kammler frequently attended our launching tests. He took part in
conferences as Himmler's representative and came to tests without being asked.'

Here was an acute irony. The slave labour doing the work in
Poland for the Luftwaffe had brought Kammler's attention back to
Blizna. But now, in the spring of 1944, the SS engineer seemed to
hold the army's rocket and those in charge of it in utter contempt.
According to Dornberger again: 'Kammler's stay at Heidelager had
given him some insights into our domestic disputes ... von Braun
he dismissed as "too young, too arrogant ... Degenkolb was a hopeless alcoholic."' As for Dornberger, he should be
'court-martialled ... for tying German armament potential to so
hopeless a project ... a chimera without hope of realisation ... a
crime against the German people.' But Kammler's estrangement
from the rocket was not to last long.

* Kammler had been in the Park's files for two years via the decrypts of German 'police'
keys. In a partially garbled decode on 4 June 1942 SS-Brigadeführer Dr Hans Kammler, the
head of construction for the SS Economic and Administrative Main Office, in a sequence
of messages concerning Auschwitz-Birkenau alluded to a chimney for a 'crematorium'. The
transcripts had gone to MI14.

CHAPTER 25

There was a sense of powerlessness in London, as if in the face of some overwhelming menace. The more Ultra revealed, the more there was to know. The British held on to American bombing like a child holding tight to hand of nurse. The US air commanders would not put up with it much longer. Their public language was polite but the backroom talk was pretty rough. General Spaatz did not conceal his increasing dissatisfaction. There was no cohesive controlling organisation, he declared. For now they would carry on bombing the brute-force British way.

On 18 April Ismay would inform Eisenhower of the War Cabinet's view that the bombing was still not enough. The chiefs of staff invoked 'the security of the British Isles' and requested the Supreme Allied Commander 'to direct that Crossbow operations be accelerated and be given priority over all other air operations except Pointblank [the attack on the German fighter aircraft industry] until such time as the threat is overcome'. But the Crossbow 'diversion', in the opinion of Army Air Force headquarters in Washington, had reached such proportions that 'it may well make the difference between success and failure' in accomplishing their pre-invasion objectives (as embodied in Operation Overlord).* It was all a damn Kraut trick.

* The cross-Channel invasion of France, now in advanced preparation.

General Eisenhower, however, anxious to fend off bombardment by weapons of still unknown power while launching the great Allied seaborne invasion from ports in southern England and the Thames estuary, bent to British sensitivities. On 4 March the 'Overlord/Diver Concurrent Plan' was finalised by Air Marshal Roderic Hill: it was flexible enough, hopefully, to meet the needs of protecting the embarkation ports for the invasion, the timing of which Allied commanders could determine, and to contend with the start of the pilotless aircraft offensive, Diver, which was at the enemy's whim. Either could come first. Fighters would defend the front line with anti-aircraft guns spanning the North Downs behind them. Barrage balloons would be the final physical barrier protecting the capital.

In the month of March 2800 sorties and 4150 tons of bombs were expended in Anglo-American offensive operations against Crossbow targets. In April the effort would be increased to 4150 sorties and 7500 tons of bombs. And there was a darker factor. After the alarms of late 1943, the US joint chiefs had ordered the USAAF to draw up retaliatory plans should the Germans initiate chemical warfare. It identified Germany's thirty-eight largest cities for inundation with poison gas; Bomber Command was working in parallel. A gas-weapon-handling infrastructure was under construction.

News from France, meanwhile, was thin. The military intelligence station at Arras had the Resistance in its grip. The Flakgruppe's war diary recorded on 10 March: 'The enemy is dropping agents and explosive on unprecedented scale, according to Field Command Beauvais, eleven British officers have been apprehended with 105 canisters of arms, radios etc.'

Air reconnaissance presented repair of the ski sites as a giant puzzle – some were being worked on, some had been abandoned outright. The suggestion that the 'launch sites' had been dummies all along was dismissed, but there was still a frisson of suspicion that the enemy efforts might just be a mask for something else.

The clandestine construction of the 'simple' launch system was proceeding under its thus far impenetrable security cloak. And mass production of the projectiles now looked much more viable. Hitler himself had directed at a conference on 5 March that FZG

76 production should go underground, in a parallel factory to the rocket within the Mittelwerk. Feldmarschall Erhard Milch was keen to open the attack as soon as possible. General der Flakartillerie von Axthelm told him at a meeting on 28 March that output would probably reach 1700 in April and 2500 in May, rising by about five hundred monthly thereafter. Milch considered that they could now open fire towards the end of April, but the Flak general disagreed. The new site system would not be complete before June. And the proposed tactics seemed wrong. Axthelm wanted 'a really sadistic bombardment' lasting for longer than just one month – the proposed three thousand 'will all be fired within twenty-four hours,' he noted drily. Milch maintained that June would be too late. April 20th (Hitler's birthday) would be the appropriate start date. Only the Führer could decide, said Milch. In fact, he had already suggested to Hitler that a sustained drizzle of pilotless aircraft was 'the most evil burden' on a city imaginable.

The Flakgruppe continued with its drills and command exercises. A second big exercise was held in Paris in the Palais Bourbon on 13 April, involving the entire staff of LXV Armee Korps down to individual battery commanders, in a carefully choreographed war game with runners and telegraphists passing orders around imaginary firing sites. It was judged 'a success'.

There was still deep uncertainty in London as to what was really going on in Poland. As Ultra had revealed, the German air force had secured entry to Heidelager to conduct some sort of firing trials. As far as Professor Norman was concerned, the messages confirmed the connection between Wachtel and the pilotless aircraft.

But there had been several hints of an army presence at Blizna. A Polish account had arrived in London in early April of firing trials, going back to November, of something that might be a rocket. One had 'annihilated two farms' and another had allegedly made a crater fifteen metres deep. The noise could be heard from ten kilometres away. Railway tank wagons had been observed with a cold, odourless bluish gas issuing from their taps. The Poles had managed to take photographs of debris and craters. A number of shots seemed to explode prematurely, high in the air.

On 13 April, back-breaks by the Park of routine messages found via keywords divulged the existence of somebody referred to as the 'Beauftragter zbV Heer', Officer for Special Duties (Army), to whom or to which 250 men and fifty trucks had been assigned. It seemed to be the same as the 10 February mention signed off by 'Oberleutnant Geller'. BzbV Heer appeared to operate from Berlin and to be acting in conjunction with the SS leadership office.

There were more signals dating back to December which, once broken, offered snippets: 'setting up is proceeding according to plan', 'Oberst Walter is arriving in the Corps', 'please forward to Generalleutnant Erich Heinemann','Oberstleutnant Niemeyer has been given leave'. It did not yet make much sense, but it all added to the card index of personalities. There was mention of 'Waffen Prüfamt [weapon proving department] 11' and of an 'Oberst Thom' whose existing card showed him to have been previously connected with an Oberst Dornberger on some sort of weapons business in Tripoli in 1942.

Every new scrap, every name, every designation, was allotted a card and cross-indexed. Technical terms went into the Abbreviations and Equivalents index. A pattern was emerging.

Hans Kammler in Berlin was told by his SS representative onsite in Poland on 19 April that competing 'work for the Wehrmacht' meant that FZG 76 construction was temporarily held up. The Luftwaffe project must have been nearly complete because two days later thirty missiles with live warheads were fired from their ramps. Accuracy, though, was poor. The Polish Home Army reported the firings to London, but the mix-up concerning the two weapons persisted.

And news had now arrived from the intended area of operations in the west. On 29 April the Park logged a decrypt of a report from the Luftwaffe quartermaster general in Berlin sent to LXV Armee Korps two weeks earlier: in future, 'complete trains departing under cover names' would be reported direct to Heinemann's command, with the Abwehr security office at Arras in north-east France being informed of the movements. Trains carrying what?

CHAPTER 26

Central Interpretation Unit, April–May 1944

On 27 April a reconnaissance Spitfire on a routine sortie covered Belhamelin, a village on the Cherbourg peninsula. When the results were viewed under a stereoscope at Medmenham, a narrow rectangle 250 feet long and 12 feet wide plus a number of small sheds at the edge of a wood were discernible – innocent farm workings, perhaps? The rectangle, however, could just about be interpreted as a row of concrete footings. There was also a square concrete plinth. No skis, no roads, no water cisterns, no fuel store, no accommodation buildings. But the ramp, if that was what it was, pointed at Bristol.

For weeks now interpreters looking for 'skis' had gone unrewarded. But there was something in the woods and orchards here: a new network of sites, some survey points, some concrete hardening, which might be equipped later. There seemed to be a firing shelter, a test bay and a compass steering platform – just visible from the air. The work on these simple sites was being done by prisoners. There had been no leaks to follow up.

But inconclusive as it was, the Belhamelin discovery changed everything. Such simple sites were fiendishly difficult to find. It was clear, however, that a parallel network was in the making, aimed it seemed at the Overlord assembly areas as well as at

London. A new reconnaissance overflight of Zempin–Zinnowitz found a 'modified' launch site being completed on the shoreline, with 'prefabricated' six-metre-long sections of rail lying about. This new uncertainty was crippling. The bomber offensive ground on – but what was its purpose?

Dr Jones coincidentally produced his latest analysis of the Baltic trial plots in a paper dated 1 May. He had transcribed an analysis of 154 shoots since the beginning of February to an outline map of London: 'We have the results of 154 shoots at pre-declared aiming points between 1.2.44 and 30.4.44. These results are displayed on the attached map, where the error pattern has been transferred to a map of London with Charing Cross as target. 65, or 42 per cent, of the missiles would have struck built up areas. This is the most reliable figure hitherto obtained for the overall sustained accuracy.' There had been mass firings on 9 and 29 April, Jones noted, from both Peenemünde and Zempin. 'These ... imply either an increased degree of urgency in the trials, or that they have now reached the stage where sustained rate of fire is being tested, the missile itself having proved satisfactory.' The term 'FZG 76' was judged to be no longer secure. From 1 May it would be changed (reportedly on Hitler's inspiration) to Maikäfer (Maybug), the Flakregiment was ordered.

The Mittelwerk, May 1944

The Mittelwerk by now employed six thousand prisoners and half as many German civilian workers. Conditions had marginally improved – the death rate had gone down but more sub-camps had been established in April–May to supply labour for more underground plants. The best chance of survival for any prisoner was as a skilled assembly-line worker.

Layers of oversight had been put in place so as to detect sabotage. It was not the SS who policed the production line, but the civilian specialists. They would forward a signed report, according to verbal testimony, to the commandant's office, which would then be acted on by the security service office in the factory.* The Dora survivor Yves Béon told a story of having seen hundreds of Russian prisoners being forced to stand shivering on the roll-call square at Dora. He found out why: 'It appears that two Russians were surprised while pissing on some machines in the tunnel. They are now in the bunker and will be hanged in the afternoon. In reprisal, all the Russians from the night shift are going to spend the day on the square and will go back to work without having slept or having received any rations.' According to another survivor, 'The tail assembly was by far the most difficult unit to build. The sheet metal work was not especially complicated but the small control devices in the fins required precision workmanship and instrument-shop working conditions. These parts were the most difficult to manufacture. Rejections were high. Saboteurs found it easy to let dust get into the delicate apparatus.'

More effective perhaps than dust – not to mention urine – was that most dangerous commodity of all, information. Within Buchenwald, the parent camp to Dora, was an industrial complex called the Mibau. A survivor published his story in the early 1970s, in a lightly fictionalised form, changing names including his own because, as he told Professor R. V. Jones at a meeting in London in 1986, 'he did not want to identify individuals who had behaved badly' (everyone behaved badly in Buchenwald).

In the story he called himself Alain (real name, Pierre Julitte). In June 1940, as a thirty-year-old French army officer, he had followed Charles de Gaulle to England and undertaken several SOE operations before being betrayed, then was captured by the Gestapo in March 1943. He had ended up in Buchenwald and been set to work in Block 26, grinding rust spots out of metal boxes. Another Kommando was working on electrical components. In the story, Alain suspects they are part of the same device. When he at last gets to see it complete, he recognises it

---

* 'Quality-control' was the primary means of detection. A worker was obliged to sign paper chits to link him to the individual components. The chit was stamped along with the component (fragments of rocket still coming out of the ground around Blizna show a multiplicity of such die-stamps) and filed away. The production quality-control division stayed under the supervision of von Braun's development group at Peenemünde even after its formal move to the Mittelwerk in spring 1944. For an analysis of von Braun's and others' complicity see Michael J. Neufeld's definitive *The Rocket and the Reich*.

as some sort of gyroscope, if made of poor-quality metal. There is no way of resetting it – it is for one-way use only.

A sick prisoner in the hospital block tells him about another camp, Dora, and an underground factory called the 'M works' where they make enormous rockets. Alain must inform London of this. At one remove, he gets the information to a 'free' worker in Weimar, a Frenchman whom he calls Oscar and describes as 'a repentant Pétainiste'. After his obligatory labour service, Oscar can go home to his family in Caen. Alain does not know whether the message gets through, but as an act of sabotage aimed at inviting an air attack on the Mibau, as well as hinting at the existence of the Mittelwerk, it could hardly be bettered.

By mid-May, the 'M works' were producing thirty A-4s a day. One army rocket-launching battalion was ready and another was completing its final training. The huge dome at Wizernes was progressing and numerous small sites in France had been laid out. Dornberger was still wrestling with the air-burst problem, although things were improving. He, Generalmajor Metz and von Braun could agree that the weapon might be fit for task by the beginning of September. Erich Heinemann's LXV Armee Korps drew up plans for an opening attack to be launched from France on London. It was to be codenamed 'Operation Penguin'.

Polish Home Army reports still had not pinned down what was being tested at Blizna. Ultra decrypts from March onwards had revealed Leutnant Muetze's plane crash, discussed the fact that construction at Heidelager was being delayed by the 'army's secret command project', and had chanced on the name of Hans Kammler. The assumption at the Park and in London was that some sort of pilotless aircraft trial was going on, in which the SS and the Luftwaffe seemed to be working together

On 27 April a message to Berlin had revealed interest on the part of 'the experimental detachment of Waffen Prüf Amt 10' based at Heidelager in an 'impact-crater' at a place called Siedlce, 230 kilometres to the north-east. This was an army, not a Luftwaffe department, and the distance was beyond the range of the pilotless aircraft demonstrated thus far. Could there be something else hidden in the forest? The rocket perhaps? Jones said in his memoirs that it was this message that caused him to request renewed photographic cover of the Polish site.

On 19 April, after the earliest hints that there was something interesting there to investigate, a reconnaissance Mosquito flying from Italy had already made the nine-hundred mile round trip to get the first covers of Blizna. Mediocre imagery had shown a 'housing estate' laid out on a horseshoe plan, and also what interpreters suspected (correctly) were firing ramps for pilotless aircraft along with what looked like craters, possibly left by failed launches.

The next cover was flown on 5 May, in two passes and in better lighting. A train unloading on standard-gauge tracks was visible, plus passenger coaches, flat trucks and tank cars similar to those already seen on Usedom. It was a Crossbow site – that was certain. News spread along Whitehall's secret crevices. On 8 May Major-General John Sinclair, the recently appointed director of Military Intelligence, wrote to Brigadier Menzies requesting that his man in Hut Three, Major Terence Leatham, be given access to the J Series and be allowed to transmit its contents to MI14. The request was acted upon. The British army was back in the rocket intelligence business.

Bletchley Park, May 1944

On 13 May the Park got a break into a hitherto obscure German army key. It had first gone live in March, and like all new keys it had been subjected to a routine attack by the Hut Six code-breakers. They would strike lucky with this one. GC&CS's internal history of Hut Six, compiled soon after the war, told the story of the hunt led by Stuart Milner-Barry, the former chess champion, who was one of Bletchley Park's founders.

'In contrast with other keys, the breaking of which extended over many months, Corncrake [the German army Engima key] was brief but full of interesting points,' he wrote. 'About the beginning of May 1944 ... a long message was brought into Army Research for a routine examination ... This was a standard precaution specially intended for new and obscure [code] groups so that no chance of a snap break should be missed. And ninety-nine times out of a hundred nothing came of it.' But, said Milner-Barry, 'this was the hundredth time. The delighted cryptographer discovered the Cilli sequence [code-breakers' name for transmitters' mistakes] ... and the day was quickly out on a bombe menu [see p. xviii].'

The message was from a virtually unknown group and there was no indication of its significance, until the first fragments got to Bimbo Norman. As Milner-Barry recalled: 'The contents of Corncrake created an intelligence *sensation* in Hut Three. It seemed to refer to army artillery experiments. It would quickly be described as the "army equivalent of Brown III" [the air force key used by the experimental signals regiment]. Strong representations were made from the highest quarters in the Park in favour of a determined effort to break more days [days' transmissions].'

After a blank week it worked, made possible by 'the considerable reserve of bombe power we had in 1944', according to Milner-Barry. Two days in May's traffic came out, then another two. Something called a Prüfwagen for Battery 444 was mentioned, and the 'Campania' (radio guidance) installation having been sent with 'errors in the wiring' by the Technische Hochschule, Dresden. The January–February breaks on the SS Quince key had already given up the 'Versuchsstab' (experimental staff) at Blizna, which provided a 'very usable crib'. Quince had also mentioned 'Command Post Siegfried' and someone referred to as 'Commissioner for Special Duties (Army)'. Here they were back again, this time on the army key the Park called Corncrake. As the cryptographer explained:

The wireless telegraphy system of Corncrake was simple. There were three stations, Heidelager which acted as control, Peenemünde and Köslin, all distinguishable by their call signs. Practically all the traffic was run from Heidelager ... It was discovered that a number of messages to Koslin started off with the Wagnerian address 'Am Kommandostelle Siegfried' [Oberst Stegmaier's rocket school] and [using this as a crib, they] broke three days in the week ending 10 June and no fewer than eight days after that ...

Messages were broken retrospectively back to March ... from the nature of the key, these were as valuable as current breaks ... as new traffic came in.

In all, thirty-three Corncrake days' transmissions would be broken.

Personalities fleetingly revealed earlier by keyword watch were back on stage – Dornberger, Heinemann, Niemeyer, Walter, Thom, plus some additional spear-carriers. Waffen Prüfamt 10 in the War Ministry in Berlin was associated with a General Josef Rossman. There was a 'transport liaison office' at Schwedt-am-Oder. More back-breaks from May would be circulated on 1 June. On the 2nd, a Major Jahms at Heidelager had signalled Peenemünde: 'The following are asked to be ready for a conference. Professor [Wernher] von Braun, [Konrad] Danneberg, [Walther] Riedel III, [Martin] Schilling to meet Direktor Sawatzki who is leaving Mielec [the airfield near Blizna] at 06:00.'

'With today's transport please send ten sets of jet-rudders,' said one Corncrake decrypt. And there were more snippets. Battery 444 was to take over three long-distance rocket trailers. The 2nd Battery of Artillery Battalion 836 was starting training. The command structure of the German army rocket programme had been put on air – intimate technical secrets, like 'jet-rudders', had been disclosed to Britain's cleverest minds. The trouble was understanding it.

The man in charge, Claude Pelly, did not seem quite up to it. The air commodore was at the same time presiding over a countermeasures campaign that was infuriating the Americans with its ineptitude and had failed to hit a single modified pilotless-aircraft launch site. Pelly might have felt relieved, therefore, when on 14 May he relinquished his post to become Chief Intelligence Officer for the Allied Expeditionary Air Force. Air Commodore Colin McKay Grierson, 'a jolly good chap but a complete newcomer', took over.

The great bunker-technician kidnap plot had fizzled out – perhaps getting a live German to London did not seem so urgent now. SOE seemed almost disappointed. Colonel Maurice Buckmaster, head of the French Section, wrote to Pelly on 18 May to wish him well in his new post, adding: 'I'm afraid we were rather a broken reed over our exfiltration project. We were right in estimating the chances as low. It would have been great fun to have brought it off. Grierson already knows our curious ways.'

The Park, meanwhile, had seemingly bugged the enemy's

most sensitive circuit. For now, only a tiny of group of the Ultra-indoctrinated knew. And they were not in a mood to tell anyone.

The Baltic, May 1944

The Maikäfer was in the final stages of flight-testing. There was a 'special shoot' at Zempin on 10–13 May which surpassed all previous achievements, according to the regimental diary. Of twenty-nine fired, twenty-two shots could be judged successful. 'Two flew too far, two came down too soon, and three were not picked up by radar.'

One of those that flew too far caused a bit of a stir. On 11 May a German radio-controlled rocket aircraft, as a press report described it, crashed at Brostrap in the south of Sweden. The air attaché in Stockholm flashed the news to London. Two Air Ministry intelligence officers, Squadron Leader Calvert and Flight Lieutenant Heath, were flown immediately to Stockholm by BOAC Mosquito. After some diplomatic manoeuvring they were allowed to examine the wreckage, which was now in the custody of the Swedish air force in a hangar at Bromma aerodrome.

The Swedes revealed they had encountered two more like it. One had been fished from the sea in December, and another had been blown up by the navy as a mine. Both had dummy warheads. The latest missile appeared to be made mainly from pressed steel, crudely built as if for mass production, and was in the form of a small mid-wing monoplane with a 16-foot wing span. It had the standard flight controls of a rudder and elevators but no ailerons; guidance was provided by three gyroscopes, one of which was linked with a magnetic compass. There were two spherical containers around which were wrapped lots of piano wire. No radio equipment was apparent. The Swedish air force technical experts had assessed its speed at 1600 km/h and its range at 500 kilometres. 'Unused propellant (petrol) was found in the forward part.' The mysterious E1 revealed by the 7 March Quince decrypts, was just low-grade aviation fuel. It did not need to carry its own oxygen, which it got it from the air. The warhead could be substantial.

Flakgruppe Creil HQ, May–June, 1944

The LXV Armee Korps moved its headquarters on 14 May to the
Paris suburb of Maisons-Laffitte. Luxurious villas were requisitioned (No. 7 Avenue Dessaix was the Paris home of the Aga Khan,
according to a prisoner captured later, who turned out to be Erich
Heinemann's chauffeur).* Two days later Hitler gave the order that
'long-range fire against England' should begin in the middle of June.

Heinemann was informed of the codeword – 'Rumpelkammer'
(Junk Room) – for the activation of the site system and the bringing of catapults from Germany, a process that should take ten days.
The order to open fire on London would be 'Eisbär' (Polar Bear).
On the 20th the regiment was ordered to move to the 'operational
site system', which would only be fully set up with prefabricated
ramps when an attack on London was imminent.

Every German in France knew the planned Allied invasion was
coming straight for them. The men of the Flakregiment were no
different. What would come first – the invasion or Polar Bear? The
Flakgruppe's headquarters war diary recorded the mood on 2 June.
'The abandoning of Site System I had taught a valuable lesson –
that simplified construction was necessary and that technical equip-
ping has to be put on a mobile basis ... There have been tests at
Zempin on even simpler launch sites ... The question is, shall we
get in first or will the enemy be across the Channel beforehand?
Every man in the regiment is convinced that the Maikäfer will be
on the other side before Sammi and Tommi are over here.'

D-Day –1, 5 June 1944

The tide was right, the moon was right, and the weather in the
Channel might be coming right. Early on the morning of 5 June,

---

* The general's heart was perhaps not always in it. A senior rocket troop officer in a post-
surrender interrogation recalled Heinemann staring out of the window during a vital
conference at the villa, and 'suddenly going into the garden to shoot a squirrel which he had
been observing all the time'.

Eisenhower uttered his famous command: 'OK. Let's go.' The invasion was on.

The same day, Bomber Command headquarters sent out by teleprinter to Group HQs in eastern England the sublimation of a plan that had been in the making for nine months. The three type-written pages were headed simply 'Operation Instruction Number 74'. It noted: 'Should the enemy initiate chemical warfare, HM Government intends to retaliate in kind and will presumably permit unrestricted use of gas against objectives in Germany ... In this case a complete change in bombing policy is involved and the objectives for strategic attack will be selected with the object of obtaining the maximum impact on the German people.'

There were two options: Plan I, the warning codeword for which was 'Knockabout', for 'large-scale experimental attacks on selected industrial objectives'; and Plan II, codeword 'Infusion', 'employing gas as the primary weapon on the heaviest scale [against] selected centres of population in the manner best calcu-lated to bring about a collapse of German morale'. The warning period for 'Infusion' was seven days.

Instead of the familiar bomb-load codewords such as 'Normal' or 'Arson' (incendiaries), that for the loading of bombers with gas weapons was 'Vesicle'. Stations were to ensure 'the immediate col-lection and transport of chemical weapons from air ammunition parks ... once gas warfare has been ordered.' It was noted in the document that the safety orders had already been issued and per-sonnel trained.

In comprehensive discussions at the Air Ministry on 19–20 May,* with Norman Bottomley in the chair, the target cities had been chosen for all-out gas attack because they had not yet been 'heavily bombarded and thus would be more psychologically sen-sitive'. In previous appreciations 'we assumed that of the strategic bomb load, 25 per cent would be gas weapons', according to Bottomley. 'As our bomber force expanded, this seemed irrational. The latest assessment was of the amount required to neutralize activity in certain German cities,' he noted dispassionately.

---

* On 18 May, Churchill told Ismay that he wished Lord Cherwell to explain a 'certain matter to the Chiefs of Staff' after a sudden revival in Washington of the fission scare.

CHAPTER 27

The first the Flakregiment knew that the invasion had begun was when the field telephone rang in the operations room in the cellar of the Château d'Auteuil, a little after 01:30 on 6 June. It was the headquarters of 245th Infantry Division with the first tentative alert. Two hours later, Oberstleutnant Heidschuch, the regimental security officer at the Abwehr intelligence post at Arras, came on the line for Oberst Wachtel. It was true. Parachutists were reported at a depth of sixty kilometres south of Caen. Airborne landings were reported on the Cherbourg peninsula, and the enemy was ashore west of the lower Seine. They were on Alarmstruffe II, the highest state of alert. The regimental HQ was to quit Auteuil and consolidate at the original site at Château Merlemont.

On Gold Beach in the Anglo-Canadian assault sector, amphibious Sherman tanks of the 8th Armoured Brigade began coming ashore around 07:20. The defenders put up a feeble resistance. By 16:00 British tanks and infantry had reached Creully, a small town east of Bayeux and about four miles inland. Among the defenders coming out with their hands up was Obergefreiter Lauterjung of 3 Company, 220 Panzer Pioneer Battalion, an engineer unit attached to 21 Panzer Division. Before the war he had been an architect. He seemed quite relieved to surrender. Very soon he would be whisked to England and put in Denys Felkin's hands. He had a story to tell – about rockets.

D-Day, 6 June 1944, was also Oberst Max Wachtel's forty-seventh birthday. But as he recalled, 'I quickly forgot that. I shaved off my beard, hung my civilian clothes in the cupboard and put on my Luftwaffe uniform.' Thus formally attired, Wachtel took the phone call at 17:45 that afternoon from LXV Armee Korps containing the codeword 'Rumpelkammer' – the signal to move the prefabricated ramps from western Germany and arm the launch sites by moving bombs from the Nordpol and Leopold field ammunition depots. Wachtel was hesitant: 'I strongly cautioned against a hasty operation. I was convinced that the catastrophic conditions prevailing mean that delaying the opening of fire by 48 hours is essential. But the chief of staff of the Corps [Oberst Walter] would not hear my warnings. His answer was: Open fire on Target 42 [London] on 12 June. Then we headed for our operational headquarters being prepared at Saleux outside of Amiens.'

The underground battle headquarters had been dug out (by SS-guarded slaves during the preceding eight weeks) in the north face of a narrow valley stretching from Saleux village to just before the Amiens–Plachy road. The war diary describes it: 'Below the huts, there are tunnels and bunkers 18 metres deep. At the bottom of 100 steps the air is damp and cool. Some 150 KZ prisoners, Russian PoWs and convicts, are working. Security is the factor behind this hotchpotch, most of the prisoners being anti-social elements. Site System I was betrayed by foreign workers.'

The Flakgruppe headed out from their farmhouse billets to occupy site system II, toiling to erect the ramps, get the starter systems ready, lay power and telephone cabling. The bad weather, which had miraculously cleared enough on 6 June for the invasion forces to make their epic crossing of the Channel, had closed in again – to the Flakgruppe's advantage. Allied photo-reconnaissance had had to be suspended partly because of the weather and partly because of the demands of Operation Overlord. An Air Intelligence was drafted advising that although not far advanced, pre-fabricated launch sites could be completed very quickly. The Political Warfare Executive, basing its judgement on enemy propaganda, reported: 'The general inference [is] that large scale attack on this country with Crossbow weapons is unlikely to take place within the next fortnight.'

Then the SIS received a priority message from a source in Belgium (known as agent Junot) that on the night of 9–10 June a train of thirty wagons had passed through Ghent in the direction of Tourcoing: 'each wagon was loaded with three rockets ... five more are expected'. There were 'lots of soldiers everywhere with cannon and machine guns'.

On the morning of the 10th, D-Day +4, Flight Lieutenant David Nutting of Air Intelligence went ashore at Utah Beach. The chemical-testing phials in his rucksack had been 'smashed by boots above me as I came down the nets of a troopship into a landing craft'. He had been briefed to go looking for evidence of hydrogen peroxide and calcium permanganate. But on this mission a bayonet, a notebook and a camera would turn out to be enough.

Nutting had trained for this day with 30 Assault Unit, the specialist Royal Marine Commando intelligence-gathering outfit founded at the instigation of Lt-Commander Ian Fleming RN. At a farm at Neuilly-le-Forêt, fifteen miles forward of the beaches, Nutting found an expanse of newly laid turf. The village, captured the day before, was still under intermittent German fire. Protected by 'ten Marines armed to the teeth', he found himself prodding around with a bayonet, which led to the discovery of lines of 'sockets in the concrete'. A 'few tons of turf' had to be moved to reveal exactly what was hidden there. 'In the late afternoon I closed my notebook. That evening a Hurricane flew back to the UK with my notes and the photographs,' he recorded.

Nutting's poking around provided Air Intelligence with the complete ground plan of a 'modified site' and an understanding of its way of working. Then, on 11 June, at last came a break in the weather and air reconnaissance of the inland belt could be restarted. Medmenham informed Air Intelligence that evening that 'much activity' had been seen at six sites in the Pas-de-Calais area and that launch rails were identifiable at four of them. As Wing Commander Kendall recalled: 'If our predictions were correct ... installation would begin only a day or two before firing. The bombs could be expected within 24 to 48 hours. An immediate signal was sent to the Air Ministry and the next morning [12th] I had the unpleasant task of advising senior officers in person that the bombing was imminent.'

In London, Frank Inglis gave the chiefs of staff the news, adding that at least twenty of the forty-two identified sites in the Pas-de-Calais might now be structurally ready. The scale of attack was judged at 400 tons of high explosive, the amount that might be projected from twenty operational modified sites in the first ten hours, at a rate of one missile every half-hour.

After months of jitteriness, the Air Ministry reacted to the 'Diver imminent' signal from Medmenham as if in slow motion. Dr Jones, in retrospect, thought it was because 'the watchers had become tired and jaded'. Neither was agent Junot's report that a trainload of 'rockets' had two days earlier passed through Belgium a trigger for action.

USAAF headquarters in Washington was signalled on the 12th that there was no change in the situation. Air Marshal Sir Roderic Hill at the Air Defence of Great Britain (ADGB) filter room at Stanmore, who had been led to believe that the modified sites were 'not likely to be used for several weeks', heard nothing all day. In fact, after more than a year of anguish and recrimination over German long-range-weapons intelligence, Hill would get no warning until the flying-bomb attacks had actually begun. As he recalled very forgivingly after the war: 'This information [about the 'rocket train' and the alert from Medmenham] did not reach my headquarters until after the German offensive had begun, but little or nothing would have been gained if I had received it earlier, for the defence plan had been ready since March, and I should not have ordered deployment merely on the strength of these two reports.'

The ant-like activity at some of the dispersed sites might have been spotted by photo-reconnaissance, but the comings and goings at Saleux were invisible. The Park, however, was picking up all sorts of indicators from the Quartermaster's department of LXV Armee Korps. 'Flakgruppe Criel' and 'railway station Nucourt' were mentioned on 24–25 May. An SS seismologist was to be kept fully informed on the forthcoming operation.

Maikäfer Lehrgerät were to be taken from field ammunition depots L, N and R, which were to be 'guarded by infantry units from attack by paratroops', according to a message of 10 June (circulated in the J series on the 12th). Professor Norman was able to associate the location of 'Depot L' with the town of St Leu d'Esserent in the Oise valley, north of Paris. Through 10–12 June, long messages were intercepted in the command traffic of the Luftwaffe Belgium–northern France air district, ordering the issue from the depots (identified as 'Nordpol', 'Leopold' and 'Richard')

of fuses and batteries – many hundreds of them.* On 11 June LXV
Armee Korps ordered ammunition depot Leopold to 'send off
loaded columns in such a way that they arrive with the troops
during the dark. Task to be carried out by 0400/12/6.'

As those columns were rolling, in the early hours of Monday 12
June, Oberst Wachtel addressed his men:

After months of waiting the hour has come for us to open fire ...
Now that our enemy is trying to secure at all costs his foothold
on the Continent we approach our task supremely confident in
our new weapons. As we launch them, today and in the future
let us always bear in mind the destruction and suffering wrought
by the enemy's terror bombing.

Soldaten! Führer and Fatherland look to us. They expect our
crusade to be an overwhelming success. As our attack begins, our
thoughts linger fondly and faithfully on our native German soil.

Long live our Germany! Long live our Fatherland! Long live
our Führer!

Just then the object of Wachtel's salutations was at the Berghof
in the Bavarian Alps: here at Hitler's court the mood was one of
eager anticipation. The possibility that the Maikäfer attack might
force the Allies into a precipitate invasion of the heavily defended
launching zone in the Pas-de-Calais was touched upon during an
early-evening conference between Hitler, Admiral Dönitz, Field
Marshal Keitel and General Jodl. The two army commanders
described such a diversion as Germany's only chance of retrieving
the situation unfolding in Normandy.

Saleux, 12–13 June 1944

For believers in the Final Victory the command post at Saleux was
a better place to be. As the 155 Flakregiment's diary recorded:

---

* These decrypts were not circulated until the 16th.

More and more visitors arrive – engineers from Peenemünde, Karlshagen and Zempin, representatives from LXV Corps, and observers from Luftflotte 3. Late that afternoon the commanding General Heinemann arrives from Maisons-Laffitte ... Two war correspondents, Leutnant [Erich] Wenzel and Oberfahnrich Jansen, arrive with the regimental security officer who is supposed to act as their minder ... Throughout the evening reports come in via telephone from the site system to tell of incomplete or untested ramps. There is no safety procedure, with some sites there is no contact at all ...

At 23:00 Oberst Wachtel called Oberst Walter, asking for a one-hour delay. It was granted at the intervention of Heinemann, who in fact was at the colonel's side at the teeming, chaotic Saleux HQ. At 23:50 Wachtel ordered no firing before 03:30 – then sites were to fire as they became ready.

The great revenge exercise began at midnight on the 13th, when German naval gun batteries behind Calais opened fire at extreme range on southern England. Eight rounds crashed into Maidstone and twenty-four on Folkestone. Through the night the launch crews toiled as they had been trained to, to position the Maikäfer on its ramp having set its magnetic gyro-compass and the little nose-mounted propeller 'air-log', and brought the 'perambulator' charged with its volatile chemicals up to the piston tube.

At 04:00 the long-range shelling stopped, just as the first Maikäfer fired up with a roar, to be punched in a burst of super-heated steam from its ramp in the Pas-de-Calais and streak north across the dark expanse of the English Channel. Then another. Then, to general surprise, another.

PART III

DIVER! DIVER!

CHAPTER 28

A little before dawn, the crew of a Royal Navy motor torpedo boat on patrol in the English Channel saw a 'flame' in the southerly sky which 'started from a point approximately north of Boulogne'. It was flying at a height of 1500 feet, estimated speed 200 knots. The captain signalled Dover, which signalled the Admiralty: 'At 04:10 from the direction of Blanc Nez appeared a bright horizontal moving flame. The following were observed: a rocket-shaped missile, probably two little wings which gave [an] A/C [aircraft] impression. The following was heard. Steady rattling noise … when angle between line of sight and line of flight was 45 degrees.'

On duty at Observer Post Mike 2 at Dymchurch on the Kent coast, Mr Ernest Woodland, a greengrocer, and Mr Archibald Wraight, a builder, heard an aircraft approaching. It was making 'a swishing sound'. Through binoculars they could see it clearly – or rather, the bright flame that seemed to be coming from its rear. It was the German pilotless aircraft on which they had all been so extensively briefed and sworn to keep secret. No doubt about it. It was crossing their post directly above them.

Ernest Woodland immediately telephoned 'Diver! Diver!' to Royal Observer Corps No. 1 Group control room in Maidstone. To a background of clanging bells, the plotter picked up the general excitement, passing the alarm up the chain. The pilotless aircraft flew on northwards, sounding, according to Mr Woodland in a subsequently much quoted phrase, 'like a Model T-Ford going up a hill'.

Seven minutes later at Swanscombe, west of Gravesend in Kent, several eyewitnesses spotted an approaching aircraft in the night sky apparently on fire. As it passed overhead at 400–500 feet, a steady yellowish white light flaring behind it flickered, and went out. Then the object dived towards the ground. A heavy explosion and a yellow flash followed, then it fell on a field bordering the A2 Rochester–Dartford road. When a baffled civil defence warden arrived at the impact site he found 'a large corona of metal fragments surrounding . . . a three feet deep crater shelving to a wide saucer'.

Two minutes later something fell at Mizbrook's Farm near Cuckfield in Sussex, where a Miss Atkinson was awakened by a whirring sound. A third object fell at 05:06 at Crouch near Sevenoaks, Kent, in a strawberry field. An airman sent to guard the wreckage found 'some dead chickens lying around and it had made a terrible mess of two rows of greenhouses'.

An Air Ministry official was in his bed in suburban Sussex when the Cuckfield missile passed overhead. He rushed to his telephone in the hall, eager to be the first to yell the secret word 'Diver!' into the mouthpiece. According to his account, given in the 1970s, the GPO operator readily accepted his urgent request for a priority call to the Air Ministry, only to tell him after a few minutes that it was no use – 'The switchboard operators at the ministry are all taking shelter.'

As in some Wellsian fantasy of attack by aliens, fiery objects were falling from the heavens into the fields of Kent and Sussex. One of the strange incomers was now flying over the sprawling southern suburbs of the blacked-out city, its propeller-driven air-log spinning down to the point when it would fire two detonating bolts that would send it into a dive. It flew on, over the mock-Tudor semis and huddled Blitz-scarred terraces of the capital. Night-duty policemen in Croydon cheered the sight of an enemy aircraft on fire. London slept below, while the Maikäfer's auto-pilot sent puffs of compressed air to the little rudder, straining to swing it into line with its notional target, Tower Bridge. The Flakregiment armourers had set this one up well.

At his early-morning post a little east of Liverpool Street Station

Inspector Manning of the London and North Eastern Railway 'heard a noise ... like the beat of a two-stroke motorcycle engine in the sky'. He looked up and saw 'what appeared to be a tiny monoplane approaching at low level with a brilliant illuminated tail'. In Mile End Park in east London, the anti-aircraft guns opened up with tracer but the little aircraft took no evasive action. The fire went out, then the raucous noise stopped. Silence. It was hard to see in the not yet quite brightening sky. At around 04:30 the Maikäfer detonated in a violent explosion on the brick-and-steel railway bridge running east–west over Grove Road, carrying the line from Chelmsford and Essex into Liverpool Street Station.

Bethnal Green Civil Defence Group quickly set up an incident post, and higher officialdom began to take notice of what might have happened. The first two messages that went to Civil Defence Group headquarters referred to both a 'bomb' and a crashed aircraft. The first senior official sent to the site was instructed to confirm 'if possible from the bits and pieces what it actually was' and to determine whether the wreckage had in fact originated from a pilotless aircraft. He could report early that morning that whatever it was that had fallen from the sky was not a bomb and that 'sizeable portions of light metal casing of tubular form were strewn about'. A Royal Engineer bomb-disposal squad turned up. Regional Civil Defence HQ arrived at lunchtime, plus officials from the Ministry of Home Security who were concerned to find out whether the mysterious arrival had been a projectile falling vertically or in the manner of an aircraft coming in at an angle under power. There was no evidence of gas.

Six Londoners were dead, twenty-eight injured and two hundred homeless. Air Intelligence officers later reported recovering 'a fin and rudder in reasonable shape' near the impact site, as well as 'a Bosch sparking plug model W.14'.*

From the disruption to commuter railway lines from the east it was clear to thousands of disgruntled passengers that morning that something big had happened, but there was no indication of what had caused it. The Air Ministry actually broke the strict wartime censorship rules by mentioning London as the target in its first

---

* For schoolboy plane-spotters the spark-plug would become the totemic souvenir from a doodlebug crash site.

communiqué, issued that afternoon. Later editions of the *Evening Standard* told readers: 'The first air raid alerts since 27 April were sounded earlier today' – several people had been killed when 'bombs fell in a working-class area'. A single enemy raider was reported shot down* somewhere over London, according to the BBC. Nothing about pilotless aircraft.

At 04:40 Oberst Eugen Walter at Army Korps headquarters at Maisons-Laffitte ordered a ceasefire and all sites to be camou-flaged. A stream of Teutonic oaths went back and forth along the phone lines as reports of the night's efforts were collated. The four battalions that had been in action early on 13 June had between them managed to get ten Maikäfer into the air, from five ramps. Five of the missiles crashed on launch, one disappeared. Four had flown on, destiny unknown.

It was a fiasco. The words 'court martial' hovered in the air. Wachtel said later he would have welcomed it. Instead, he was ordered to convene an immediate investigation. He wrote a mournful report. 'Dislocation of supply routes by enemy action' was to blame. They would try again.

---

* There had been a Luftwaffe 'raider' in the air that night, which was indeed shot down – an Me 410 reconnaissance aircraft sent to snoop around which was engaged by ground fire flying up the Thames estuary at 04:00. It came down at Barking Marshes. Both pilot and co-pilot were found dead.

CHAPTER 29

London, 13 June 1944

The chiefs met in London in a state of bewilderment on the morning of the 13th. Switchboards buzzed with the news of Diver's arrival. There had been some sort of incident in east London. Norman Bottomley could tell them, from information he had been given, that nine 'aircraft' had made landfall and four had penetrated to the Greater London area. They were 'about the size of a Spitfire' and had approached the coast at 1000 feet and then been seen to climb. Their speed was estimated at around 250 mph, and they 'could be clearly seen as a large white flame was emitted from the tail'. Ministry experts, he could tell them, were being sent to the sites of the explosions.

Portal thought it was 'a response to Overlord', as the Germans had to be seen to do something – they had not really been ready. Bottomley confirmed that intelligence experts were being sent to France to examine two suspected sites captured in the Cherbourg peninsula. Air Marshal Hill had assured him that the measures taken thus far were adequate. A more considered report issued by Portal early that afternoon spoke of twenty-seven airborne arrivals overnight, which might have been employed in three waves, bad weather making visual reporting by observer posts difficult. The figure was soon reduced to eleven, then to four, as was now being reported that evening by the Ministry of Home Security. It was a pinprick.

Radar plots showed them coming from the Pas-de-Calais. Portal recommended, in view of the difficulty of attacking the modified sites, an immediate bombing effort against supply sites – which in fact had been evacuated by the Germans weeks before.

'The public should not be told the enemy had used a new form of attack', it was agreed. German propaganda was saying nothing. Air Marshal Hill did not even think it merited putting the Overlord/Diver anti-aircraft gun and fighter defence plan of March into effect. The chiefs, still riveted on the outcome of the invasion, were not going to disagree. A full War Cabinet was convened to consider the reports of the inconsequential-seeming opening attack of the night before. They had been expecting the delivery of four hundred tons of explosives within the first ten hours – perhaps all that could still arrive at any minute.

Dr Jones went to see Cherwell at the Cabinet Office. The Prof in fact had just returned from grimy Grove Road to see for himself the results of the first German long-range weapon falling on the capital. 'The mountain hath groaned and given forth a mouse!' he said famously. Jones recalled in his memoirs that he reminded the Prof that during their daily Baltic firing trials the Germans had been launching many more bombs than had fallen on London that night. Worse was certainly on the way – 'For God's sake don't laugh this one off!' he pleaded.

Gräsdals Gård, 13 June 1944

That same afternoon, an A-4 rocket was fired from Peenemünde. It was a test vehicle for the radio-control of the experimental Wasserfall (Waterfall) anti-aircraft rocket. The take-off was perfect but, it was explained later, the spectacle so overawed the operator, who was using an experimental joystick, that he lost control. The rocket turned to the north and vanished into cloud.

At Gräsdals Gård close to Bäckebo in Småland, Sweden, a farmer called Robert Gustavsson and his son Ivar were tending their horses out in the fields when there was a great bang above them, the sky went dark and metal fragments started raining down. Ivar's horse, Daisy, ran off. Locals reported hearing 'not one but three or four consecutive blasts'.

The next day a flash telegram arrived at the Air Ministry in London from the air attaché in Stockholm: 'Following from Swedish press. Reaction-propelled German projectile crashed at 14.15 on 13 June at Gren Farm Knivin, Backebo ... Violent explosion made crater several metres wide. Windows reported broken 14 kilometres away. Pieces found over area four kilometres ... Do you intend sending experts?' The ministry most certainly did, but first, as with the earlier arrival of flying bombs in Sweden, the diplomatic minefields would have to be negotiated, then the wreckage found and secured.

A senior policeman turned up from Bäckebo, as well as the Home Guard. It might be assumed that a bomber had crashed, but where was the crew? There was a general scramble to get to the place, which the newspapers had found with admirable speed, then had published the story without it being censored. Swedish air force officers arrived to collect the more obvious remains. Bits of wiring hung from the trees. An appeal was made for rocket parts to be put out on the steps of houses for collection, to be taken to Bromma airfield in Stockholm. The Air Ministry in London, meanwhile, was very keen to get its hands on whatever it was that had so startled Daisy the horse.

Combined Services Detailed
Interrogation Centre, June 1944

There was rocket intelligence to be had closer to home. On 22 May during the intense fighting in Italy that broke the Gustav Line, a prisoner had been captured who had ended up in England in the hands of Denys Felkin. Feldwebel (Sergeant) Helmut Müller was a chemical warfare specialist. He had also done a course at Peenemünde on rockets.

Felkin's report was issued on 9 June. The prisoner, who had studied chemistry at a technical high school, was 'highly intelligent'. He had arrived at Peenemünde in August 1943, three days before the RAF attack there, for a fortnight-long course on rockets.

The bombing had destroyed the admin building, but Müller assumed that it was in operation again as a friend had been ordered to report there four months ago.

In August, the workers in his department had all been German civilians, he said. Girls were employed in the offices. Work was supervised by army personnel but many of the leading posts were held by civilians using cover names. There were two shifts, a day one and a night one. Müller had seen enough to give a pretty good description of the fuel load: one tank was filled with 96 per cent ethyl alcohol, the other with liquid oxygen, and they were connected by a 'very complicated pump system'. He could also reveal that the casing was thin aluminium or steel. The range was between 300 and 350 kilometres. The rocket was fired from a metal base, a *Bodenplatte*, onto which it was transferred via a trolley that elevated it into the firing position. No support was needed. The rocket rose vertically and was steered by wireless from a ground station.

He gave a very workable illustration of the multiple-axle transporter, the *Meillerwagen* (although he did not call it that). Nearly all the experimental shots had been made at Peenemünde but he had heard a rumour that one of these rockets, in December 1943 or thereabouts, had fallen in the Lublin area. It carried about one ton of explosive. The explosive was secret and very powerful, and would produce a five-kilometre zone of destruction. He had no idea what it was – but it was not a chemical agent. He should know.

Saleux, 15–16 June 1944, 22:00–05:00 hours

The Flakgruppe tried again with their Maikäfer. The Saleux command post was packed anew with vengeful bigwigs. The war diary reported briskly: '15 June: Oberst Walter [at LXV Armee Korps HQ Maisons-Laffitte] relayed the launch order by telephone to Saleux at 18.45. Ten minutes later all the Abteilungen [battalions] were given the following order by radio: All launchers will fire at Target 42 [London], salvo, basic range 200 km, basic time 23.18 (target impact 23.40) Then continuous fire to 04.50.'At 23:16 the first Maikäfer left the ramp in the area of II Abteilung and so opened the salvo.

Flight time to London was a little over twenty minutes. By midnight, 217 missiles would have left their ramps. The Flakregiment's long night had only just begun: 'By 05.50 ceasefire is ordered. No. I Battery managed to launch every 30 minutes ... Since the beginning the men have worked without rest ... They have remained at their posts continuously – they are bearded like U-Boat men,' as the war diary recorded. The Flak-gunner Josef Esser described a curious feature of the revenge offensive, a canine safety measure:* 'At the launch, a toxic cloud of hydrogen peroxide emerged, and we had to depart to avoid it drifting in the wind. Two dogs were always present as we fired, as the noise of the reduced power start came and they jumped up to the missile [as they had been trained to]. Soon their fur was red – H2O2 makes hair and fur go red before bleaching it.'

It had begun to rain soon after midnight, ideal Maikäfer weather. In the space of six hours the Flakgruppe put 244 missiles into the air from fifty-five sites either side of the Somme. Forty-five crashed soon after catapulting, nine sites were wrecked by detonations on the ramp, one fell on a French village, one was seen circling. The rest flew on, roaring vengefully on their little stubby wings, towards the coast of England.

South London, 15–16 June 1944, 23:00–05:00 hours

The first of the missiles began to arrive at the southern fringes of London, flaring and rumbling out of the darkness at around 23:40. Mrs Hettie Long was in Streatham with her sister that night. She wrote in her diary:

11.45 p.m.: First plane passed over, an awful noise from the engine. We got up at once, then the alert went and before we had left the bedroom, the explosion. We got down quickly to the

---

* In London, Alsatians were trained as rescue dogs to find survivors in the rubble. They would prove very effective in the months to come.

mission shelter and remained all night. It was dreadful – the guns sounded as if they were firing over our heads.

About 3 a.m. one passed very low over the house and almost before we could speak we heard the explosion. I thought it had hit us but it had gone over the next row of houses and crashed on a house straight across from my sister's back bedroom. Killed all the occupants.

Acting Wing Commander Roland Beamont was commanding the three-squadron-strong Tempest Wing, No. 150, at Newchurch in Romney Marsh. He told an interviewer fifty-five years after the event: 'Although we knew that some sort of secret weapon was coming ... we had been unable to get any technical or operational information. All the controller was able to tell us was that the targets were flying at 2000 feet.'*

Up to midnight on the 16th, 155 missiles were counted by observers on the coast, of which 144 crossed into the inland defence belt. Fourteen were shot down by gunfire and seven by fighters. Seventy-three would reach London.

Saleux, 16 June 1944, 02:00–06:00 hours

Wachtel's men waited anxiously for news. According to the war diary: 'In the early hours of 16 June extremely satisfactory reports began coming in to the battle HQ ... a reconnaissance pilot of IX Fliegerkorps [Air Corps] has sent in the first visual observation. London was burning. At 03:30 ... he could still see the glow after he had crossed the French coast.' Erich Heinemann, commander of LXV Armee Korps, left Saleux for Paris after his night of excitement. Before he left he wrote in the visitors' book: 'It gives me pleasure to have been present on such an important day, the

---

* This was a general complaint, and represents another intelligence failure. As Dr Jones explained in his memoirs, by the end of 1943 his directorate was reporting the pilotless aircraft's operating height at 6–7000 feet from the Baltic plots. 'As the trials progressed, the heights were gradually brought down and we duly mentioned the fact ... as a matter of routine ... But AM Hill's views which were presumably sent to the Air Staff did not reach me and our information about the reduction in height did not reach him.' Hill was not Ultra-cleared.

crowning achievement of long laborious weeks. May the regiment continue to be blessed with fortune for the sake of the Fatherland.'

A stream of jubilant telegrams went out that morning as 'officers and men shake hands with all the German working comrades who have manufactured our weapons. May success crown the hope that binds front and homeland in our operations,' said Wachtel. And seal the doom of London.

London, 16 June 1944, 10:00–12:00 hours

The attack dominated the chiefs' meeting in London on the morning of the 16th and the War Cabinet meeting that followed. The mood was chastened. This was not a range-finding exercise. The pilotless aircraft threat, supposedly buried under the rubble of the ski sites, had blown up in their faces. What had Air Intelligence been up to? Air Marshal Roderic Hill recalled: 'The Air Ministry had expected to be able to give us a month's warning. In the event we had received no warning at all, apart from that provided by the Germans themselves on the 13th June.' Seventy-three bombs had come down on Greater London. Herbert Morrison told the Commons that morning that the capital was under attack by pilotless aircraft, while 'the available information does not suggest that exaggerated importance need be attached to this new development ... The enemy's preparations have not, of course, passed unnoticed.'

The long prearranged censorship rules regarding Crossbow were promulgated once again for the press: 'Refer only to southern England ... do not report the sounding of an air raid warning in the London area ... do not publish reports or photographs of damage ... do not report the change of address of any person or firm in southern England ... do not publish in any one issue of the newspaper more than three obituary notices from the same postal district ... '

Hill commanded the fighters, and Lt-General Sir Frederick Pile the anti-aircraft guns. The two chiefs were directed to redistribute and reinforce the defences as necessary within the prescription of the Overlord/Diver plan. Across southern England at 19:00 balloon and gun trains began to move into the positions allotted to them in the spring – namely, to one of three defensive zones radiating from the capital to the coast. Initial planning had predicted a minimum of eighteen days to put the gun and balloon defences in place. In fact it would take five.

The second major decision taken by the War Cabinet on the 16th was to request General Eisenhower to take 'all possible measures' to neutralise the supply and launching sites from the air. Eisenhower would respond two days later, after a personal visit by Churchill to his headquarters, with the statement that Crossbow targets had 'first priority over everything except the urgent requirements of the battle'. Lord Cherwell had again reminded the Cabinet meeting that the supply sites that had been built to succour the now abandoned ski sites should be ignored. Nevertheless, Bomber Command went after them two nights in a row. They found them empty.

London journalists laboured to make some sense of what was going on, and to discover what they could get away with publishing. The *Daily Mail*, for example, could reveal the next morning that three people had been killed in southern England, gave details of Mr Morrison's speech and reproduced an official sketch plan of the 'pilotless plane'. The paper also revealed that the BBC was liable to sudden shutdown and that the broadcast tones of Big Ben would be replaced by a recording, lest anything heard live in the background should be of use to the enemy. It also reported the news, as relayed on German-controlled Radio Oslo, that 'a good-hearted and morally inspired Führer has ordered the Luftwaffe on this course so that the air gangsters should be brought to account for their terror crimes'.

Northern France, 17 June 1944

Hitler arrived in northern France the next day. He was anything but good-hearted in his condemnation of the senior commanders in the West, von Rundstedt and Rommel, who had let the invaders come ashore and had thus far failed to evict them. But German genius had delivered the means to smash their enemies. The revenge weapon commander General Heinemann and his deputy Oberst Walter were summoned from Paris to Wolfsschlucht II, built four years before at Margival, five miles north-east of Soissons, as a command post for the planned invasion of Britain.

General Hans Speidel, Chief of Staff of Army Group B, later recalled what happened when Hitler confronted his hapless commanders in the bunker complex's tea-house: 'Hitler looked worn and sleepless ... and played nervously with his spectacles and an array of coloured pencils. He broke into a tirade about Vergeltung, vengeance. The "vengeance weapons", as he now called them, would be decisive!' Then, 'Hitler wandered away and began to dictate a press communiqué to a representative of the Reich press chief announcing the use of V-weapons to the German public and the world. The two field-marshals were being treated to an irrelevant monologue ... they seized the opportunity to insist the V-bombs should be directed at the Allied bridgeheads.'

General Heinemann wanly explained that it was impossible to launch them at the Allied invaders already ashore in France without endangering the defenders. But the invasion ports could be hit – Southampton, Portsmouth – that would make a difference. 'Hit London! Hit London!' Hitler raged, just before a stray flying bomb impacted nearby, 'arousing alarm and suspicion'. In fact the Flakregiment was on the brink of achieving a murderous success in the heart of the enemy's capital.

London, June 1944

The Flakgruppe's war diary for 18 June hailed the launch of the five-hundredth Maikäfer against England. One hundred and eighty-nine missiles had been fired in the twenty-four hours ending at noon that day. Of those last shots that morning, three made it as far as central London. One hit the side of Hungerford railway bridge that spanned the Thames at Charing Cross. A second fell in Rutherford Street, Westminster, demolishing two blocks of flats and killing ten. That morning, Churchill was at Chequers, the country house north of London. He recalled:

Mrs Churchill told me she would pay the Hyde Park anti-aircraft battery* a visit. She found the battery was in action. One bomb had passed over it and demolished a house on the Bayswater Road. While my wife and daughter [Mary] were standing together on the grass they saw a tiny black object dive out of the clouds, which looked as if would fall very near 10 Downing Street. My driver, who had gone to collect the letters, was astonished to see all the passers-by in Parliament Square fall flat on their faces. There was a dull explosion nearby.

At the Guards Chapel opposite St James's Park, a Sunday service was in progress. The venerable building was packed with servicemen and their families. A little after 11:00 the 'tiny black object' hit the roof. One hundred and twenty-one dead were found beneath the tumbled masonry. All news of it was suppressed, although rumours of a disaster soon spread.

There was a Chiefs of Staff Committee meeting at 18:00 in the Prime Minister's map room, with Churchill now returned from the country. The brooding menace of the unknown had become bloodily real a few hundred yards from Downing Street's back door. After the Guards Chapel, sudden death appeared to be stalking everybody. But feelings were mixed. Field Marshal Sir Alan Brooke, Chief of the Imperial General Staff, was half rejoicing when he wrote in his diary, 'Flying bombs have again put us in the front line.'

The Prime Minister was 'at his best and said the matter had to be put robustly to the populace', according to Admiral Sir Andrew Cunningham, Chief of the Naval Staff. 'Their tribulations were part of the battle in France and they should be glad to share in the soldiers' dangers,' he said – a theme that was widely picked up by the old warriors around the table. The meeting moved to re-establish a dedicated Crossbow committee of the War Cabinet with the Prime Minister in the chair, to deal, as Churchill put it, with the 'flying bomb and the flying rocket', a curious phrase to which he would return.

---

* Where the Churchills' youngest daughter, Mary, served with an Auxiliary Territorial Service AA unit.

The War Cabinet Civil Defence Committee met the next morning and heard the latest figures: 674 flying bombs had made landfall, of which fighters had shot down 76 and anti-aircraft claimed 101. In London, 499 men women and children had been killed and 2051 seriously injured. One hundred and thirty-seven thousand dwellings had been damaged and twenty thousand men were working on repairs. There had been no general demand for evacuation, although the use of Tube stations as night shelters, as in the Blitz of winter 1940–1, was increasing.

The committee also decided there would be no siren alert for a single flying bomb, only for 'a covey' of them approaching at night. It was noted that people had taken up residence in the Chislehurst caves and were 'demanding the supply of meals' – this should be discouraged. No action would be taken to stop people going to concerts and theatres, but restriction on attendances at greyhound racing 'would be looked at'. No encouragement should be given to the closing of schools, it was agreed, although school shelter accommodation was inadequate. Staff and pupils were recommended 'to go to the north-west corner of their school buildings' on hearing an alert. In fact, many parents kept their children at home. One south London teacher counted only eleven on her register on Tuesday 20 June, and by the following Monday it was down to six. Within two weeks (by which time the official evacuation scheme had started) she was counting 'more missiles than pupils'.

The firing of anti-aircraft guns within the built-up area was signally failing to blow up the pilotless aircraft in the air – instead when hit they fell to explode on the ground, unspent shells and shrapnel clanging onto the rooftops. Lt-General Pile admitted: 'In the districts where they fell, our troops were refused cigarettes in the local shops and even denied access to restaurants, while the very fact that the guns were firing at all was a cause of infinite offence. Many people wrote, in person or through their solicitors, complaining of the horrid noise.'

The official expression 'pilotless aircraft' spoke of some irresistible Teutonic technology that German propaganda had been hinting at for months. And thus, at Herbert Morrison's urging, it was transmuted into 'flying bomb' as being 'more understandable'. Flying bomb it would be.

CHAPTER 30

At Saleux, telegrams of congratulation for the Flakgruppe were still pouring in. What effect were their exertions having in London? 'According to an announcement on the radio [they were probably listening to the BBC] the British Air Minister has called a secret meeting of experts, scientists and military chiefs in which advice will be sought about the German secret weapon,' said the war diary.

Then early on the morning of 20 June the teleprinter clattered out a summary of reports from 'agents in the target area'. It talked of 'complete surprise ... shock effect very great ... panic in those places hit ... military authorities report serious effect on invasion ... very many dead ... drastic censorship ... telephone use restricted ... London railway stations full of crowds ... fantastic quotes for numbers of dead and injured ... public enraged at the defence's failure ... newspapers call for immediate invasion of the Pas de Calais.'

Who were these 'agents in the target area'? The answer was, they were doubles. Britain's disinformation specialists had long been engaged in the web of deception, codenamed 'Fortitude', spun around the invasion of Normandy. Agent Garbo, who had gone on a fishing trip for rockets the autumn before, had been a lead actor in pre-D-Day trickery. On 13 May, just as his torrent of plants and falsehoods about the timing and place of the invasion was reaching its peak, Garbo had been advised by his control in Madrid to expect a 'special questionnaire'. He was instructed to give his answers a prefix, 'Stichling'(Stickleback), which would ensure their priority transmission to the Abwehr station at Arras and thence on to the Flakgruppe HQ at Saleux.

A message sent from Berlin to Madrid early on the morning of 16 June was picked up by the Park: 'Arras reports Stichling is beginning.' It sounded deeply sinister. In fact, it would turn out later, it simply meant Garbo was transmitting. Two hours later, another message on the same channel retransmitted by Madrid to Garbo in London that evening. First control in Madrid apologised for not giving prior warning, declaring that he had himself only heard of the beginning of the pilotless aircraft attack on London 'through the news agencies'. Then he relayed the instructions from Berlin: 'It is of the utmost importance to inform us about the effect of the bombardments. We ... wish you to communicate results as follows. Take as your basis a plan of London by the publisher Pharus which I suppose you have in your possession and indicate how many ... missiles have fallen in determined squares.' From MI5's wireless-equipped safe-house in north London, Garbo messaged back indignantly: 'We had an alert all last night. I learned at mid-day [Morrison's statement as reported on the BBC] that we had employed a new secret arm, that is to say a pilotless aeroplane ... It has upset me very much to have to learn the news ... from our very enemies.'

But the deceivers had a problem. The special agents had been told to report on the fall of pilotless aircraft. Genuine information would aid the enemy, while false information could be readily checked by German air reconnaissance – the very dilemma the tricksters had discussed the previous summer. The double-cross agents would be blown while Fortitude was still running.

According to Dr Jones, it was he who devised a masterly solution when one morning his old MI5 chum Flight Lieutenant Charles Cholmondeley came to see him. His visitor's most successful scam to date had been Operation Mincemeat, cooked up with Lt-Commander Ewan Montagu of the Twenty Committee. Cholmondeley and Jones (who calls him 'George' in his memoirs) had already perpetrated various double-agent hoaxes on the enemy, involving electronic devices and U-Boat detection (serving as cover to Ultra).

The ground plot of flying-bomb arrivals in the first twenty-four hours, although they were widely scattered, showed a distinct grouping south and east of the city with a mean point of impact (MPI) around Dulwich, said Jones. It was close to where his parents lived in Herne Hill. He could see 'in a flash' that by giving the correct point of impact for bombs that tended to have a longer range than usual, then coupling these with the times of the bombs that fell short, they had a solution to the dilemma. If the Germans tried to correlate the results, they would think that the bombs they might otherwise consider to have fallen short were instead tending to fall in north-west London. The result should be to keep the main weight of fire falling on the south-east of the capital and spare the centre. Photographic cover of London, if the Germans could achieve it, would not alone prove the agents were lying. And the Germans might take steps to reduce the range even more. That was the theory.

When Churchill declared he would chair the new War Cabinet Crossbow Committee himself, it was a statement of urgency. But with the success of the invasion still in the balance, that was too ambitious. On the 20th he announced that Mr Duncan Sandys was back on the front line as chairman; the Air Ministry was appalled, but stayed outwardly polite.

The Park, meanwhile, had gone into self-imposed purdah. A directive was posted on 17 June: 'Anything of any importance regarding Crossbow should be passed to Hut 3 for teleprinting to Broadway for Dr Jones, and to the Air Ministry for Crossbow Watch. It is not to be passed to ministries and commands.' But the restriction was soon partly lifted: 'information on the pilotless aircraft . . . may now be included as necessary in our normal [decrypt] series,' it was decreed on the 20th. However, the channel for urgent operational intelligence on secret weapons still ran from Professor Norman to Jones. Signals indicating 'dumps or concentrations on the other side or intention to launch attacks against this country' should be sent to him direct. At night the procedure would be this: 'Phone the Broadway Duty Officer and tell him to get Dr Jones or his deputy in. Dr Jones to phone Duty Officer in

Hut 3 as soon as possible.' Was the thirty-three-year-old physicist really expected to run the secret-weapon war on his own? He seemed perfectly happy to do so.

It could not last. In London, Duncan Sandys was back on the bureaucratic case – and in 'a commanding position'. Churchill would ask Brigadier Jacob on the 22nd for suggestions as to which members of the War Cabinet, 'constant attenders and others in the secret circle', should be associated with the new committee. And just like last time, it would have a scientific subcommittee. Dr Jones, indeed, was a member. It all sounded perfectly reasonable.

At its first meeting on 22 June the new Crossbow Committee with Sandys in the chair considered the still mysterious 'large sites' – Watten, Siracourt, Mimoyecques – and the prospects for attacks on them with the new 'Tallboy' deep-penetration bombs.* They were reminded, though, that their association with long-range weapons was still based on negative evidence, in that no alternative use could be suggested. As for the rocket, it was clear from the Committee's strangulated discussions that nothing from the Park or from prisoner interrogations was being allowed near Sandys. On 22 June the Committee would hear from Colin Grierson that there was 'no intelligence about production [of the rocket] whatever' and 'intelligence about the weapon itself was still scanty'.

In fact, ever since D-Day there had been a stream of new information: the extraordinary Corncrake insights, for example, and what had transpired from the interrogation of the Peenemünde technician Helmut Müller captured in Italy – with his description of the alcohol–lox fuelling and the *Meillerwagen* trailer-erector, and what he had said about the rocket not having a chemical warhead. That intimate insight had been passed on 9 June to the tiny few who needed to know.

Sandys's next report, issued on the 29th, would not even mention the rocket. He was letting it be known that he interpreted the directive from the Prime Minister as not merely to 'report' on the

---

* Designed by Barnes Wallis of 'bouncing bomb' fame and comprising almost three tons of explosive in an aerodynamically refined armour-piercing casing, it could pass through five metres of reinforced concrete. The first Crossbow mission, against Watten, was flown on 19 June.

flying bomb and the progress of countermeasures, but to personally direct all elements of the campaign. Clearly, the junior minister's battle with Britain's air commanders was about to resume. Meanwhile the days of the Air Ministry committee chaired by Air Commodore Colin Grierson – 'on whom the strain was beginning to tell,' according to Jones – which had so miserably failed to warn of the pilotless aircraft's arrival, were numbered.

It was not only the Park that learned much from careless talk. The Luftwaffe's 'Y' (signals-eavesdropping) service was listening to the radio-telephone conversations of the defending fighter pilots, who were very talkative. By such means the Abwehrstelle at Arras had direct tactical information to give Saleux about how the man-against-machine fight in the air was developing: 'Anglo-American pilots are not having an easy time of it ... the British call them "Bitches", and the Americans call them "Bastards",' they reported on 21 June. Of more direct use, perhaps, was the fact that they were said to be arriving over the coast at an altitude averaging 900–1200 metres – vital operational intelligence. According to the war diary, Allied pilots had also given away this: 'Judging by the pilots' R/T [radio-telepathy] among themselves and with the ground, it appears very dangerous to approach the target. One British pilot reported firing at a missile and then was amazed at the explosion ... Communications by enemy fighter patrols show the Maikäfer are being shot down almost exclusively ... when they are flying singly. Dusk is a good time for shooting them down.'

So fire them in salvos and not at dusk. Defensive tactics evolved in the chase. The robotic intruders crossed the coast at 340 mph, still accelerating, to reach 400 mph by the time they got to London. Piston-engined Typhoons and Spitfires, both slightly slower than their quarry, were obliged to parallel the line of flight and fire deflection bursts as they passed, or wait for the enemy missiles to cut power. A young ARP warden in Croydon saw the aerial drama and wrote in his logbook: 'One came flying over nearby and the engine cut out over Lane Hill, then it started its glide. There was a Spitfire chasing it and as it started to glide the Spit caught it up, he was using his boost override ... you could see the smoke from his exhaust. He came up close to it and then fired, breaking away in a steep climb directly afterwards, then he came round for another burst.' The thing was very low by now and the pilot didn't get another pot at it as it crashed.

The Hawker Tempest V and the Rolls-Royce Griffon-engined Spitfire Mk XIV were fast enough to put on an impressive chase in the turbulent wake of the bomb's blazing motor. But attack within three hundred feet and the explosion would wreck the pursuer.

These were not the gallant duels of 1940. Roland Beamont tells of receiving a terse signal from higher up in the command chain saying that his pilots were not to claim the destruction of flying bombs as victories. Beamont coolly pointed out the dangers of pouring gunfire into something charged with '1800 lb of Amatol which could bring down the attacking fighter as it exploded'. And he was right: during the first six weeks of the assault eighteen fighters were substantially damaged and five pilots and one navigator killed by mid-air explosions.

Worse, certainly, in morale terms, was being shot at from the ground by your own side. Relations of airmen with gunners were brittle. When Beamont went to AA HQ at Hastings, ordered to make peace, he found 'a universally hostile atmosphere broken only by a radiant young girl lieutenant who took me into dinner. I was introduced to General Pile who was barely civil and hoped the RAF would discontinue their complaints. I said the cause of any complaints would be removed by his gunners being persuaded not to fire at our fighters.'

On 20 June Denys Felkin wrote up his first report on the statements of Obergefreiter Lauterjung, the Panzer pioneer captured on D-Day. It would turn out to be intelligence gold.

Lauterjung was described as 'a strongly anti-Nazi ex-architect who wanted what he said to help shorten the war'. He might not be able to do that, but what he had to say was of direct use in understanding the threat to London. He had been posted to the Sonderstab Beger command and 'entrusted with the selection, surveying and construction of sites for rocket installations'. (Oberst Beger himself was a regular army engineer, a Bavarian with a reputation for hard drinking.) As well as a comprehensive list of sites under survey or construction, the prisoner gave intimate information on the chain of command and the special security measures, which were under the supervision of the Abwehrstelle at Le Mans. Felkin added another detail: 'The P/W was accosted by a member of the Geheime Feldpolizei [secret field police] in a café in Isigny and ordered to break off a relationship he had made with a local French girl.'

The Panzer pioneer had personally been involved in the construction of four of the sites he described. One was at the Château Bernesq, typical of the others with its three firing platforms built along a stretch of road. 'The surface is first removed and then the road is excavated to the necessary depth,' he explained. 'The concrete is poured, specially toned to match the colouring of the road ... completely level when finished.'

He also described a supply dump at the village of Hautmesnil, a quarry where tunnels had been bored into its horseshoe-shaped sides, lined by narrow-gauge railway. The projectiles were to be stored within on special trolleys. For actual use each rocket would be hoisted into what the prisoner called a *Meillerwagen*, a multiple-axle transporter, and would then be towed to the firing site. They had seen plans for such vehicles but none had yet arrived.

The labour at Hautmesnil had been supplied by an SS punishment battalion. Other sites that Obergfreiter Lauterjung knew of which had been bombed by the RAF were 'dummies', built by local French labour with lots of Feldgendarmerie in attendance. The workers there had actually been encouraged to reveal where they were employed. In contrast, all the sites he had been involved with had been constructed in great secrecy and only by Wehrmacht personnel. Security was in the hands of the Geheime Feldpolizei and the Gestapo.

Obergefreiter Klotz was another veteran of Sonderstab Beger – a deserter – picked up near St Lô on 21 June. He was a trained draughtsman and intelligent, according to Felkin. His unit, the 94 Pionier Battalion, had been specially brought back from Russia with its two German companies and one Turkestan company – around five hundred men in total – to work on rocket sites.

At La Meauffe south-west of Bayeux, work had been progressing at some burrowed-out lime kilns to make a supply dump. Security was tight at the site: mail was heavily censored, and everyone was under the observation of the Gestapo post there, which consisted of 'one Sonderführer, a Polizeimeister, an Obergefreiter and two French girls'. According to Klotz, 'Polizeimeister Lange kept a strict watch on German soldiers associating with French civilians, especially women in local cafés'.

Thus was the plan for the destruction of London by stratospheric rocket kept on course.

In Whitehall, what mattered was the flying bomb. The official mind strove to understand it. From the moment the first one crossed the south coast, no effort was spared in evaluating its destructive power, its vulnerability, the way it worked and its effect on the population. Its in-flight behaviour during its last seconds could be observed by those with steady nerves, a shelter nearby and the ability to run fast. And what characterised the doodlebug above all was the mid-air motor cut-out, followed by the dive or glide, then the bang.

Many long glides were recorded, the longest lasting 202 seconds, and there were plenty of stories of the thing turning in flight. Running out of fuel appeared to be the main cause of the gliding phenomenon, which was quite arbitrary and could be especially terrifying. By one authoritative account: 'Bombs could float along for several miles, gradually losing height as the wind sighed in their lifeless motors. They sometimes travelled on an elliptical course, whistling quietly over the ground until they and everything near them disintegrated in a shattering explosion.' The first bombs that landed relatively intact were taken to the Royal Aircraft Establishment, Farnborough, for detailed examination. Understanding the Maikäfer construction enabled its vulnerable aspect to be quantified, although this proved of less interest to fighter pilots who had already discovered these aspects by more direct methods.

The robot lacked, of course, the vulnerable points of an ordinary aircraft: it had no pilot, no oxygen system, and no complex reciprocating engine. The airframe was small and robust, and the crude Argus pulse-jet provided enough thrust for continued flight, even if damaged. On 22 June Hitler ordered a slowdown in rocket production because the flying bombs seemed to be so successful. In Berlin the propaganda minister Joseph Goebbels was worried lest the bombs be perceived as too successful: 'People are already making bets that the war will be over in three or four or eight days. I see this as an enormous danger for us if these exaggerated hopes and illusions are not met. I fear this excessive enthusiasm will end in great disappointment.' He would be proved right, but not yet.

CHAPTER 31

London, June 1944

Juan Pujol, agent Garbo, still had to get the right map on which to plot where the Maikäfer were falling. It was proving a problem. Garbo radioed his control and bought the Baedeker guide to London from a second-hand bookshop. But Control insisted on the Pharus version. Garbo's research took him to the British Museum Library, where he found 'the only copy in existence. I learn that the German map was edited in 1907 and therefore is very antique indeed. It seems to me very strange that war plans are worked out in Berlin on such antique maps.'

But now, at least, everyone was working from the same grid. 'I am proud,' Garbo informed his control on 18 June, 'that you have been able to prove this fantastic reprisal weapon, the creation of German genius'. He reported rumours that the bombs were falling in a wide arc to the north and west of London, and promised to find out more.

The Abwehr would grow suspicious if their agents delayed for much longer in providing them with information about events that were presumably occurring under their very eyes. But was the policy in London to deceive, or wasn't it? On 18 June a meeting of the officials directly concerned was held: Sir Samuel Findlater Stewart and John Drew from the Home Defence Executive, J. C. Masterman of the Twenty Committee, the former Air

Intelligence officer Charles Cholmondeley from MI5's B1a (double-agent) section and Garbo's case officer, the Mayfair socialite and art dealer Tomas Harris of B1g (Spanish counter-espionage) section. All decided that for the time being they should treat the flying-bomb attacks as they had previous air raids, and not try to use them for deception.

There was a reason. The MI5 counter-espionage chief Guy Liddell recorded a meeting of the JIC later that day to determine whether 'if we did try to mislead the enemy ... what were the chances of being found out? ... Air Commodore Grierson, who appears to be the Crossbow expert, said that the pilotless aircraft carries some sort of wireless apparatus which would indicate its course and point of impact.' If the enemy could somehow accurately plot where the missiles fell, then the whole wider deception operation – still keeping powerful German forces in the Pas-de-Calais – would be exposed.

On 22 June the Twenty Committee agreed to suggest to the Air Ministry that their agents should give accurate reports of isolated explosions, some of them at least with times and dates to show they were still in business. That evening Garbo did in fact report by radio, although without times and dates, incidents that had occurred in the West End which could hardly be kept quiet, including the destruction of the Guards Chapel. But, he added, the general opinion in London was that the weapon was now being brought under control and that 'the nervousness of the public created at the beginning has now disappeared'.

Six days later, with his map problem now resolved, Garbo began to transmit information in the form required, but he warned that concentrating on the flying bombs would mean that his other activities would suffer. Reinforcements were on their way. In the Security Service summary for the month of June, given to Churchill on the 29th, it was noted that 'the outstanding event had been the return of agent Zigzag [from Norway] to this country'.*

---

* Durham-born thirty-year-old safe-breaker Edward Arnold 'Eddie' Chapman, recruited by the Abwehr and sent to England as a saboteur, had been 'turned' in 1942. In June 1944 he had been sent by his German controllers back to Britain, not to undertake sabotage but to report on the landing places of P-planes (pilotless planes). Chapman would emerge in the 1950s, with an autobiography and a film, as the most infamous double agent of the war.

At an ad hoc meeting of the deceivers on 28 June there was a brisk discussion of what to do. The Air Ministry assumed that the aim point was the centre of London – Charing Cross – but after ten days of bombardment it was becoming clear that most were still falling short. The mean point of impact had stayed substantially the same as in the first twenty-four hours – in the region of North Dulwich station. Should the enemy be deliberately misled as to where the bombs were falling, north or south etc., and what effects they were having? it was asked. But nobody could decide what to do, other than continue 'confusing the enemy'.

The plan to swap times and places was presented to the Twenty Committee on 29 June and approved. The next day Garbo, briefed by the deceivers, reported multiple flying bombs all falling in north London. But as he told his control: 'It is dangerous to ask questions in damaged areas since the public who lose their houses are rather hostile.' He was ordered to concentrate on troop movements. This was not what the deceivers wanted; their plan depended largely on Garbo. So he replied to his control on 1 July: 'In order to correct your aim ... the fire should be more concentrated. It is essential that you receive more exact information.' He was back on the case.

On 2 July Portal, Chief of the Air Staff, formally gave Findlater Stewart responsibility for deception with a brief to 'mislead the enemy as to the physical and psychological effects of flying bombs'. Findlater Stewart would do so with enthusiasm, but he concluded in a preliminary paper that some of the truth was worth telling. He suggested that neutral journalists should be flown over the city to belie the 'sea of flames' propaganda coming from Berlin. But he still recommended hoaxing, and more than just reinforcing the existing error: 'We should try by special means to create the impression that the bombs are overshooting the target which we assume to be central London in the hope that the range and deflection should be moved *further* to the east and south than at present.' Here was an official suggestion that the mean point of impact should be moved somewhere else – at British instigation. But deciding which Londoners should be at the bull's-eye was not just a matter for secretive civil servants.

The Park made an unusual intercept on the morning of 24 June. It was from German Military Propaganda broadcasting to its out-stations from Berlin: 'for the new German weapons ... the description "V1" will be used. V means both Vergeltung [revenge] and Victory – Sieg. The connection with the number "1" is intended, without directly saying so, to arouse expectation among our friends and terror among the enemy that there are intensifications to follow.'

German radio was using the term that evening. The Flakgruppe's war diary recorded it dispassionately the next day: 'The Maikäfer is now the V1.' It also reported in the same entry that 'Anglo-American secret services are groping in the dark desperate to know our secrets.' But there had been – 'no further incidence of treason since foreign workmen were taken off construction'. As far as Wachtel's men had been told, in London there was 'acute anxiety ... the plutocratic families in particular are leaving the capital.' Winston Churchill, plutocrat-in-chief, was not leaving. On 26 June he messaged: 'Personal and Top Secret Prime Minister to Marshal Stalin':

> You may safely disregard all the German rubbish about the results of their flying bomb. It has had no appreciable effect on the production or life of London. Casualties during the seven days it has been used are between nine and eleven thousand. The streets and parks remain full of the people enjoying the sunshine when off work or duty. Parliament debates continually throughout the alarms.

But despite Churchill's balmy depiction of a democracy under fire, the political weather in London was getting stormier. Herbert Morrison told the War Cabinet on the 27th: 'The public have so far withstood pretty well the growing loss of life ... they have been buoyed up with the belief that the situation is well in hand and that in a short time the RAF [will] have destroyed the source of mischief.' But he also told colleagues: 'This is not 1940–41. The Anglo-American Alliance is now a vast military power, and the people not unreasonably expect a quicker and more decisive defence. People are asking "where is this air superiority they talk about".'

Alan Brooke thought him 'white-livered ... he did not mind if we lost the war provided we stopped the flying bomb'. It was actually Herbert Morrison who was emerging as the Cabinet zealot, demanding direct action 'to kill the evil at its source in the Pas-de-Calais' by commando raids or by outright invasion. Very soon he would be proposing – 'saturating and re-saturating the Pas-de-Calais with gas', adding, 'There may be some French there. My answer is they ought not to be there.'

It was Morrison, indeed, who brought gassing German cities back onto the agenda in Cabinet on 27 June as retaliation for the 'indiscriminate bombing of England by flying bombs and possibly rockets'. 'This matter is not without difficulties', he noted.

CHAPTER 32

By the third week of June, 40 per cent of all Allied bombing was being directed against Crossbow sites, but they were the wrong targets. Air Commodore Grierson seemed paralysed with indecision. The target pattern must change. How did the missiles reach the launch sites, and where were they coming from?

Ultra did what it could to come to the rescue. There had been an SOE report in March of some sort of depot at a place called St Leu d'Esserent. The Park had reported in May that LXV Armee Korps was interested in a cavern at Nucourt, also in the Oise valley. On 10 June, Most Secret Source had mentioned Maikäfer being stored at St Leu, Nucourt and Rilly la Montagne, six miles south of Reims. These apparently large-scale depots might be attacked much more effectively from the air than the elusive launch sites. The USAAF were keen, and went after Nucourt on 22 June. On the 30th there was this from the Park for Grierson's attention: 'Top Secret U [Ultra] from Duty Officer Hut 3 to Dir of Ops (SO [Special Operations]) Priority ZZZ from War Station. More evidence available concerning supply of flying bombs. A large number are apparently routed to Feldmunitionslager 10/XI located at St Leu d'Esserent SW of Creil. Supply by rail from there transport to the launching sites carried out at night by road.'

This short signal would prove important. But meanwhile the

bombing campaign was sliding into greater irrelevance. A row at the highest level was about to erupt.

Those directing American strategic bombing had long sought independence. To begin with the Brits had all the target information, but a direct expression of the bid for American 'separateness' was the presence in London of the Enemy Objectives Unit, the operation run out of Berkeley Square, Mayfair, staffed by American academics in uniform from the Office of Strategic Services, Research and Analysis Branch. Their role was to plot the efficient dismemberment of the German war economy from the air, looking for weak points like oil or ball-bearings. One of them was young economic historian W. W. 'Walt' Rostow, commissioned as a captain in the US army. He had first arrived in London in 1943 and been seconded to work at AI2(a) at the Air Ministry Intelligence Directorate in Monck Street 'as a working member of the section charged with estimating German aircraft production and the location of factories for precision attack'.

In the spring he had returned to America, and now in late June 1944 he was back. It was doodlebug summer. After three weeks of fire-watching on the office roof, Captain Rostow would be pitched into the battle against the flying bomb in a much more direct way. Carl 'Tooey' Spaatz, commander of US Strategic Air Forces in Europe, had had enough of being fed nonsense by the British. He himself knew enough from Ultra to realise that there might be more intelligent ways of hitting back.

At the end of June, Spaatz made two proposals for reducing the rate of fire: attacks on factories making gyro-compasses, and more missions against the already identified storage depots. On 29 June he handed to Eisenhower in person a 'remarkably strong letter' demanding an immediate policy change. Those clever guys in the Research and Analysis Branch would do the rest. Eisenhower, leant on by his deputy, Air Marshal Sir Arthur Tedder, made up his mind to do the opposite. The day he received Spaatz's letter, the supreme commander ordered that bombing of the V-weapon launching sites should 'continue to receive top priority'. The Brits had won for now.

That same day, the two-thousandth flying bomb left its ramp. A message of congratulations came from the Führerhauptquartier. An officer and an NCO were selected to head off to Berchtesgaden to personally report on the Flakgruppe's great revenge enterprise. There was much to say.

To the Germans it was now Revenge Weapon One. British newspapers and politicians were calling it the flying bomb. To the defenders it was Diver. Churchill preferred 'the robot'. For Londoners, in saloon bar and bread queue, it was the doodlebug.*

Londoners might spend their waking hours glancing nervously upwards but it was the sound that spoke of impending danger. First a distant hum that people strained to pick up, day and night, awake or in dreams; then it might multiply as other emissaries from France joined the chugging chorus – getting louder, passing, halting. Constantly on the alert, people flinched at the sound of a labouring diesel engine, even, so it is said, a swarm of bees. These things played tricks. Sometimes, as one seemed to be drawing close, it would suddenly veer away, or circle, then return. Even field marshals hid under their beds.

By the beginning of July around fifty flying bombs a day were reaching the capital. The alerts were coming so often that most people ignored them. Unofficial roof-top spotters proved more reliable. Buzz – hush – bang – tinkle, then the ambulance bells, had become the incidental music of London's midsummer night's bad dream. 'The sky was leaden,' wrote the wartime nurse Jane Gordon describing a summer morning in Marylebone. 'There were bursts of thunder and enormous hailstones clattered down. At the same time a flying bomb chugged overhead and crashed not far away. I thought to myself that the world would probably end on a day such as this.'

A grey emulsion was smothering what colour was left in the city and its people. The novelist H. E. Bates characterised plaster dust as a lead player that monochrome summer: 'It covered streets and roofs and trees, it covered people with a ghastly great bloom that was like the mask of death, washed off [the injured] in the casualty ward to reveal only slight injuries . . . ' Plumes of plaster dust hung in the air for minutes on end, or swirled in unseasonal fogs.

---

* Norman Longmate's masterly social history *The Doodlebugs* ascribes the term's first use to an RAF flight lieutenant speaking on the BBC on 20 June: 'It was my luck to be the first pilot to get a doodlebug.'

Roused from his bed one early morning, the MP and diarist Harold Nicolson got up to find 'small crash, no sense of blast ... I put on a coat and go out into the court. There are points of torches everywhere and a warden running about ... They tell me it has fallen in Essex Street. I notice a soup-like haze in the air and all today my eyes have been red and smarting. I go back to bed and sleep.'

Provincial England, meanwhile, was alive with rumours, according to home intelligence reports fed to the Cabinet: that Queen Mary had been killed, as had Mary Churchill; that Buckingham Palace had been destroyed, that the King and Queen had been injured; that six hundred bombs a day were hitting the capital; that a proportion of them had contained gas. 'The general view seems to be,' it was reported on 22 June, 'that our technical expertise will soon find an answer although there is general criticism that no answer was ready beforehand despite our advance knowledge.' There were many in Whitehall who held that view.

It was time to leave the city. Officialdom, with a largely female face, rose to the challenge. Explaining to small children what these visitations were was difficult enough, while the 'doodlebug' epithet made them sound almost benign. They killed children in their beds just as they killed grown-ups.

By the end of June, a few days before the official evacuation began, 231 boys and girls under the age of sixteen had been killed by the Flakgruppe's attentions, and almost five hundred hospitalised. There had been a particularly grim incident in the early hours of Friday 30 June when a London County Council residential school being used as an evacuation centre, Weald House near Westerham in Kent, had been obliterated. Twenty-two of the twenty-eight children, all under five, who had been sent there for safety were dead. Eight of the eleven nursing staff were killed. After that, many mothers hung onto their children tighter than ever. One survivor, Peter Findley, then a year-old infant with measles, had been put in another house for isolation; his mother, who was at the home, was killed.

On 1 July the Ministry of Home Security asked the London County Council to start the registration of the priority classes from the metropolitan area, and to accept responsibility for those mothers and young children from the leafier districts to the south of the capital who had expressed a desire to leave. The first officially organised parties would go on 5 July. Convoys of buses waited in side streets to take their noisy cargoes of bewildered, wide-eyed children, luggage labels around their necks proclaiming their names, to the railway stations for the west and north. At King's Cross a journalist spotted a goods van full of prams coupled to a train heading north.

Some seaside towns, with their boarding houses and hotels, were requisitioned more or less entirely. On just one day, Monday the 7th, two thousand four hundred evacuees arrived in Blackpool by special trains. H. E. Bates, with a fine reporter's ear, captured knowing heads on young wartime shoulders: 'The great contrast with the evacuation of 1940 was that the great unknown was no longer such … this time they knew the ropes, some of them already knew what the country was like … They knew where they were in the scheme of things. "My Dad's in Italy", "My Mum's on munitions", "Ain't got no Dad, he was killed fighting in Africa." The tears of the children on the whole were very few.'

The flight of the timorous from London left the hardy behind. Some sort of cultural and social life continued: there were, apparently, weekend-long 'doodlebug parties' with watchers posted on a little rota. The cinemas stayed open. One teenager from Wood Green in the north-east of the capital would recall: 'We'd rather have died watching our favourite film stars than stay at home. They used to put up a notice to say that the siren had gone but nobody ever left.'*

The defence plan was not working. Sandys was moving in the background to get Hill 'removed' because, against Pile's demands to give the guns more of a chance, the air commander 'was so afraid of offending the feelings of his pilots'. Alan Brooke summed it up in his diary on 4 July: 'The fighter aircraft are not proving fast enough, the guns are not hitting them, the balloons may have their cables cut, the launching sites are not worth attacking with bombers etc. etc.' It was quite true that neither guns nor aircraft could work to their best advantage. The balloons bobbing impassively on the

---

* As Norman Longmate's history of the doodlebug summer recounts: 'The official policy of not issuing formal restrictions was vindicated by events. No disaster occurred as a result of a V1 hit on a crowded cinema or theatre.'

suburban fringe were the last chance: '1000 balloons in an area approximately 20 miles long give an impact probability of 15 per cent,' Hill informed the War Cabinet. The rate of V1 firings actually intensified during the first few days of July. And now some were mysteriously coming in from the east, flying up the Thames estuary. Where were they being launched from? Not from northern France, for sure. Gun and fighter defences must be diverted, and if the barrier defence could not stop them, they must be attacked at their source.

But the Noball bombing campaign was also in dire trouble. The Americans were moving to break the British Crossbow intelligence shackles. On 4 July the Enemy Objectives Unit sent the Air Ministry its own Independence Day preliminary report on pilotless aircraft production – 'in case any attacks were to be laid on'. Its substance, however, was an outdated list of supposed production centres largely derived from British reports.

It was clear that the countermeasures campaign was political. The anguished Sidney Bufton, Director of Bomber Operations, declared: 'I presume the present policy to continue bombing launching sites is to satisfy the public that all possible measures are being taken against the flying bomb.' The problem was, of course, that it was not working even at that level. Bufton had done his own research on the morale of the working class. A newspaper reproduction of a photo-reconnaissance cover showing a launch site plastered with bomb craters gave the impression that 'bombs were being wasted in open fields', he said (this was pretty much correct). 'The workers are disappointed when targets in France are attacked,' said Bufton. 'They much prefer them to fall on Germany.' Charles Jarman, General Secretary of the National Union of Seamen, declared: 'I hope the PM will tell the German people that for every "fly-bomb" that reaches us, a hundred bombs will fall on named towns in Germany.'

Mr Churchill was already in a mood to do exactly that. He suggested on 1 July that HMG should announce the intention of 'flattening' a selected list of 'lesser' German cities. The chiefs agreed to 'postpone action to allow for a thorough review'. When Guy Liddell met Brigadier Menzies two days later, C told him that a 'Jap BJ' (diplomatic Berlin–Tokyo decrypt) had indicated that the Germans were not contemplating the use of gas. The SIS chief thought the general talk about gas was probably due to the German belief that we would retaliate for the doodlebug with gas, or some other weapon. He personally was in favour of retaliation, though not with gas or microbes. He thought we should bomb open towns and villages, and that this might even be forced upon the government by public opinion.

While Churchill's enthusiasm for such methods was undiminished, at the Air Ministry moral anguish combined with detailed planning. The targets must be shown to have 'no appreciable industrial significance – hence the attacks could not be mistaken for anything but reprisals'. Furthermore, 'many of them will be reception centres for evacuated schoolchildren and retreats for the dependants of Nazi officials'. That was a good thing. The list of targets was drawn up. The Americans were expected to join in, although nobody as yet had consulted them. An announcement was drafted, to be declared on the BBC: 'For four weeks past the Germans have been subjecting London ... to bombardment by flying bombs ... including extensive residential areas devoid of war industry. HMG express with regret that [in return] it is intended periodically to obliterate similar areas in Germany without warning.'

Having commissioned the detailed studies, at the chiefs' meeting on 3 July Portal spoke out strongly against: such action would provide, he insisted, invaluable proof to the Germans that their campaign had succeeded. In fact, it would amount to 'opening into negotiations with the enemy'. They might resort to counter-reprisals, such as 'murdering aircrews'. It would all get even ghastlier. 'The Germans are not limited by moral scruple or public opinion,' said Portal. 'We could not hope to keep pace.' Air-launched gas was back on the agenda, for attacking the launch sites and for wider retaliation. Once again the Joint Planning Staff argued against in a paper delivered on 5 July and the chiefs, thankfully, forwarded their own advisers' negative view to Churchill.

The same day that Portal anguished, Dr Jones drove north to High Wycombe to seek out the chief of Bomber Command. 'The country-house atmosphere' of the early war had been replaced by something more businesslike. It was 'the only time Bert Harris and I have really agreed', Jones scribbled on a carbon of a note of the meeting. Attacking the flying-bomb launch sites was 'a hopeless waste of effort ... we cannot eliminate them at the rate they can be rebuilt,' they had agreed. It was better to use heavy bombers to attack hydrogen peroxide production. That was a job for the Americans in daylight. But there was room for RAF Bomber Command to do something.

The distribution depots in the Oise valley, found by the Park, were 'within range of our heaviest bombs and most accurate bombing methods', Jones went on. Harris promised 'to chase [the Germans] round till all their storage facilities are blocked', basing his proposed action on a programme of 'quick bombing on intelligence [received]'. And in the days to come Bomber Command would do just that, in a sequence of epic attacks that would prove as dangerous for the young men flying them as anything they had faced over Germany itself.

On the night of 4–5 July St Leu was attacked by No. 617 Squadron, using seventeen Lancasters which managed to drop eleven Tallboy bombs without loss. The main force arrived soon afterwards, dropping 1000-lb bombs in an attempt to block road and rail links to the caves there; thirteen aircraft were lost. The target would be hit again on 7–8 July when German night fighters gave the attacking force an even more severe mauling, and twenty-nine Lancasters went down.

As the telegrams to the relatives of the dead and missing of the St Leu missions were going out from the Air Ministry in London, an incoming message arrived from Hut Three, a decrypt of a wireless signal from Feldmunitionslager Leopold (St Leu) to the Air Ministry in Berlin: 'Roof collapsed in several places, large amounts of apparatus destroyed, rail, electric and telephone lines destroyed. All approaches endangered by delayed action bombs.' London had been brought a reprieve.

London, July 1944

The rocket seemed almost forgotten in the wider Whitehall jungle. But Lt-Colonel Matthew Pryor of MI14 had kept up his watch and was urging Jones to do the same. Military Intelligence was now included in Section 3G(N)'s Ultra-cleared distribution list, and this was timely. Professor Norman reported that, after a long break, Lieutenant Muetze's detachment in the Baltic had resumed tracking A-4 shoots on 7 June, and from then until the end of the month there had been 'references almost every day'. The rocket was back.

On 3 July, yet another long report, this one from Pryor. 'Ultra has admitted us to the fringes of a very large army organisation, possibly with the Waffen SS playing some part,' he said. 'There is very little doubt that this organisation is concerned with super-long-range weapons.'* A special outfit, referred to by one prisoner as an 'Army Corps', was 'constructing rocket launching sites in northern France under conditions of great secrecy ... [that organisation] has hitherto escaped us completely.' The enemy rocket was a semi-mobile device, Pryor concluded. The allocation of motorised tactical army Flak units to its protection greatly supported this assumption. His report made much of the revelations by prisoners that the rocket could be fired from simple concrete foundations laid along roads. 'The finding and analysing of these sites now in our hands is the most urgent intelligence task that confronts us, but communications with our experts in Normandy are slow.' They had better get a move on.

The prisoner-of-war revelations of June were beginning to be followed up on the ground. The physical evidence in France presented itself like an ancient archaeological puzzle. The cryptic bunkers and simple concrete footings posed the question: how were these temples of doom meant to operate, and by whom? There were more revelations from prisoners. The questioning of Leutnant Krumbach, for example, captured on 1 July, gave an insight into the organisation of the mysterious all-controlling 'Army Corps'. As MI19's interrogator, Lt-Colonel A. R. Rawlinson, explained: 'He has a German father and a Dutch mother, to which side of his family tree he has now decided to adhere. Unfortunately his interest in military matters [is] definitely weaker than his interest in the attractions of Paris night life, which explains the narrow limits of his military knowledge.'

---

* Dr Jones's copy of the report has all sorts of annotated niggles and spluttered exclamations. He clearly was jealous about the War Office having its own link to the Park.

All the same, Leutnant Krumbach could reveal that he had been on convalescent leave at home when in February he was directed to the special artillery headquarters known as Höhere Artillerie Kommandeur 191. There were two locations for the headquarters, LXV Armee Korps at St-Germain-en-Laye and its subordinate Harko 191 at nearby Maisons-Laffitte. He was able to draw a little map showing Generalleutnant Richard Metz's headquarters in the elegant Avenue de la Marne.

Krumbach was told by the commandant that he was too young for staff work and should have a good time in Paris. 'His diary confirmed that he had taken the advice,' noted Colonel Rawlinson. Then Leutnant Krumbach's good times had come to an end when he was posted to an active unit. While he had been at Harko 191 Rawlinson continued, 'The function of the staff was kept a well-guarded secret even in the mess. Although the prisoner gathered it was for a special secret purpose, it was not until the last evening that a brother officer under the influence of drink revealed they were working on reprisal weapons.'

A real nugget came to light during an interrogation by Felkin, circulated on 11 July, of an unnamed subject, although its significance would not be picked up quite yet: 'A very romantic Frenchman who recently arrived in this country from Germany via the Normandy bridgehead brought with him rumours of an underground factory engaged in the manufacture of secret weapons and supposedly situated within the precincts of a concentration camp either near Nordhausen or near Weimar, quite possibly at Buchenwald.' The factory was making an 'aerial torpedo', twenty-two metres long and one metre in diameter, with 'small stabilising fins or wings with a pronounced sweep back designed for the long range bombardment of England ... Forty sets were completed a day, the completed weapons being stored underground in the factory precincts.' The message was jumbled, but in retrospect it was clear where it had originated.

It had come from Pierre Julitte – 'Alain' of the Buchenwald story. His sublime act of sabotage had come good. His messenger, the repentant Pétainiste Oscar, had managed to get back to his family in the Calvados after all (and presumably found his home town of Caen flattened by Allied bombing). He had made his way through the Allied lines and across the Channel. Julitte's description of what

they were assembling in the Mibau at Buchenwald – gyroscopes
with attendant radio equipment, gyroscopes that could not be
reset – had not only reached London: it would soon be included in
a report for the War Cabinet

And there was more: a reference to the fearsome underground
factory itself, the foundry of revenge, which Pierre Julitte had not
seen but had heard of from a prisoner who had been shuttled from
Dora to the Buchenwald medical block. It was 'near Nordhausen'.

Saleux, 5 July 1944

By 5 July the two junior representatives of the Flakregiment,
Leutnant Hennenbruch and NCO Hunger, had arrived back from
their mission to Berchtesgaden to tell their story. They had been
kept waiting for two days until late at night on 28 June they were
summoned to the presence in the Berghof. The war diary recorded:

> The Führer was holding a situation conference. Top ranking
> generals were present. The great moment came at 23.30. The
> door opened and we entered the room in which the Führer, sur-
> rounded by his advisers, was leaning over a table on which a
> map of northern France marked with the Regiment's positions
> was spread.
>   We saluted. With a smile the Führer shook our hands. In his
> natural direct manner he spoke about our operations. He said he
> had been very surprised at the initial success. And then he asked
> if we had any reports of the effect on the other side. We replied:
> 'The bombing of our sites by the enemy air force is the best tes-
> timony to the effect of our weapon, my Führer!'

There were apologies for the flop of 12–13 June. 'Hitler smiled,
observing that the V1 operations were tying down hundreds of
enemy aircraft' – and on the subject of reprisal operations with
other new weapons he announced: 'A-4 is coming!'

CHAPTER 33

London, July 1944

After three weeks of bombardment, Churchill judged the time was right for 'a fuller account' of the true situation. The Chamber of the Blitz-damaged House of Commons had been relocated to Church House near by. The mood was febrile. London MPs conveyed their constituents' demands that there be 'reprisals for this illegal form of warfare'. Members generally were anxious not to say anything 'which might help the enemy', but Churchill was prepared to reveal a good deal about the German weapon and the response thus far: 'It would be a mistake to underestimate this form of attack. It has never been under-rated in the secret circles of the Government ... The probability of such an attack has, among other things, been under continuous intense study and examination for a long time.'

He gave an outline of the intelligence story and how by July 1943 they had succeeded in locating the development site at Peenemünde on the Baltic. He explained how the chiefs of staff had proposed that Mr Sandys be the chief inquisitor and how Bomber Command was sent out to attack those installations identified by his inquiry, when 'very great damage was done to the enemy and his affairs, and a number of key German scientists, including the head scientist, who were all dwelling together in a so-called Strength-Through-Joy establishment, were killed'.

According to Churchill, 'This raid delayed by many months the development and bringing into action of both [of the] weapons.' But it was the flying bomb that had turned up first. Questioned about reprisals, he told the Commons: 'The flying bomb ... is a weapon literally and essentially indiscriminate in its nature, purpose and effect. The introduction by the Germans of such a weapon obviously raises some grave questions which I do not propose to [discuss] to-day ... Might I appeal to the House not to pursue unduly these interrogatories[?]' Fatalities thus far were one person per bomb, he said. 'Will new developments, on the other hand, of a far more formidable character come upon us? Will the rocket bomb come? Will improved explosives come?' He could give no guarantee that any of these evils would be entirely prevented.

While the city suffered, the immunity of the launch sites enraged everyone. On 5 July Churchill had written to General Ismay about 'burning them out' with petrol. Still he pressed the reprisal option. The chiefs had already agreed that 'the time might well come in the not too distant future when an all-out attack by *every means at our disposal* on German civilian morale might be decisive'. They recommended that 'the method by which such an attack would be carried out should be examined and all possible preparations made'.*

Churchill took them at their word. Later on the day of his Commons statement, 6 July, he wrote an infamously ferocious memo for the chiefs' attention, demanding a 'cold-blooded calculation as to how it would pay us to use poison gas'. He proposed using chemical weapons offensively in Normandy, where the British and Canadians were still stuck on the beachhead's left flank. It was absurd to consider morality on this topic, he said. 'It is simply a question of fashion changing.' Then came the sticking point:

---

* Portal scribbled a note to Bottomley on 6 July: 'Please prepare an outline plan in due course. It would be a sort of "Banquet", a full-out attack on all towns not believed to be defended lasting say 3 days'. The list of fragile, venerable and unwarlike targets was drafted on 1 July: 'Auerbach, Saxony, tapestry, Meissen, Saxony, porcelain, Bayreuth, Bavaria, music, Bingen, Hesse, wine, Swinemunde, Pomerania, holiday resort' and so on, twenty-four in total.

If the bombardment of London really becomes a serious menace and great rockets with far-reaching and devastating effect fell on many centres of Government and labour, I should be prepared to do *anything* that would hit the enemy in a murderous place ... We could drench the cities of the Ruhr and many other cities in Germany, and if we do it, let us do it one hundred per cent. [He wanted] studies in cold blood by sensible people, not psalm-singing, uniformed defeatists ... I shall of course have to square Uncle Joe [Stalin] and the President.

The gas memo, mercifully perhaps, did not feature in the War Cabinet Chiefs of Staff Committee discussion held very late that night, which rambled on about the 'number of white men in uniform in Egypt'. The meeting was 'ghastly', according to Alan Brooke. Churchill was 'maudlin ... drunken ... and in a highly vindictive mood against the Americans'.

The chiefs squeamishly passed the Prime Minister's demand to their deputies for comprehensive examination. Portal was unconvinced: 'Concentration would be hard to achieve,' he said at the chiefs' meeting on the 8th, and 'present preparations allowed for one-fifth of our bombing effort for dropping gas'. (Norman Bottomley was in the course of changing that to 100 per cent if necessary, after the pivotal Air Ministry meeting on 18 May.)

There was something new. In the course of the discussion it was suggested, as recorded in the meeting's minutes, that the existing subcommittees on chemical and biological warfare (the latter having been set up in late April) should be consulted. Both were chaired by the ubiquitous Bottomley.

Brigadier Hollis told Churchill that night that the vice-chiefs had 'been directed to go into this matter'. In his short note he mentioned only the use of gas. But, almost casually, germ warfare had crept onto the agenda. The chiefs had put it there, although the means to wage it – via air-dropped anthrax bombs – was a long way from being operational.

Waging chemical warfare was an immediate reality. Since the chiefs had rejected threatening it as retaliation against the pilotless aircraft the year before, Bomber Command Instruction 74 had been brought to operational readiness. Churchill's demand for 'a cold-blooded calculation' had already been met on the technical side. The plan was made, the crews and armourers trained, the weapons were in dumps close to the airfields or ready to be filled. Britain's military leaders and scientists had done their duty in ensuring they were. So had the Americans. The research establishment at Porton Down had produced detailed studies on efficient delivery, optimum meteorological conditions and predicted death rates in German cities. The plan would target twenty-two million German civilians, should the enemy use gas first.

The Germans had not done so. The Allies were ashore in France, and in spite of several Ultra-raised scares in London no gas had been thrown at the beaches. The pilotless aircraft had arrived in the capital with a bang not a hiss. Ultra henceforth would report an unambiguous concern on the German side lest the *Allies* initiate chemical warfare.

Could the Allied gas-attack plan be switched to retaliation against 'great rockets'? It was ready to go. But ordering its execution was another matter. In the official documentation that survives, the acute tension between the service chiefs, the vice-chiefs, the Joint Planning Staff and the politicians in the dangerous weeks that were to come is tangible. If the Cabinet Office minutes of the chiefs' discussions on the topic are terse, the background papers show evidence of late-night telephone dramas and anguished changes of mind. It was only the first link in the chain. It would still require full War Cabinet sanction and, as Churchill said, the squaring of Roosevelt and Stalin, plus formal agreement by the Washington-based Combined Chiefs of Staff.

Driving it all was the still unknown scale of any attack by the rocket or of its destructive power. The weight of its warhead would become a matter imbued with 'raging emotional tensions', according to one who witnessed the arguments. In the context of retaliation, considering what was at stake – not just the survival of London – it becomes obvious why.

In this climate, accurate intelligence could not be more crucial. Who could be trusted to provide it? For all its Ultra-briefed and Medmenham-informed cleverness, Air Intelligence had failed to predict the actual arrival of the flying bomb. Its chief Frank Inglis had gone out to inspect for himself the damage done in south London, and had caught the gloomy mood in a letter of 3 July to the Vice-Chief of the Air Staff, saying feebly: 'I have been informed the other service ministries are being somewhat critical about [our] handling of Crossbow. This is perhaps inevitable ... it is a fact that the organisation within Intelligence to meet this menace has been inadequate.'

An understatement, indeed. Lord Cherwell too would have to explain himself. He had correctly warned of the pilotless aircraft but had described it as 'comparatively insignificant', and he still dismissed the rocket outright. Sandys's committee was too new to take any blame. Dr Jones's grumblings were just about tolerable. The rocket was surely coming.

CHAPTER 34

London, 6 July 1944

On the day Churchill addressed the House of Commons with his soothing mention of 'our many and varied Intelligence sources', an Ultra-cleared meeting took place at the Air Ministry, chaired by Frank Inglis. The mood was recriminatory. Lt-Colonel Stewart McClintic, a forty-year-old former investment banker, had been specially summoned to represent the US Strategic Air Force, of which he was deputy intelligence chief. His presence was far more than just a gesture.

'The arrival of the flying bomb demands a reorganization to meet this new menace,' explained Inglis. When Colin Grierson, Director of Special Operations, was quietly relieved of intelligence collating, he did not seem surprised. Dr Jones, the great survivor, was to be responsible for 'assessing and distributing' intelligence, and would now, crucially, 'assist in the preparation of the target list'. His little directorate would move from the SIS building at 54 Broadway to the Air Ministry in Monck Street.

The rocket got a nod at the meeting when it was affirmed that Jones would work closely with 'those army officers who were being attached to AI2(h) [a new army–air force department dedicated to the rocket] by the Director of Military Intelligence', who would be responsible for maintaining the list of operational sites, launchers dumps and depots. Section AI3(e)* of the Air Ministry intelligence directorate would be responsible for all intelligence on 'organization, supply and personalities'.

Thirty-seven-year-old Wing Commander Godfrey (John) Mapplebeck from the Air Section at the Park was to be Jones's deputy, said Inglis, whose section would be responsible for the distribution of agents' reports, decrypts concerning secret weapons, and prisoner-of-war interrogations – all at Dr Jones's discretion. The lone American, Lt-Colonel McClintic, complained that thus far information had been issued to him, as a USAAF officer, 'on a very restricted basis'. It was promised that he would now get full Crossbow intelligence promptly, once the new arrangements were in place.

Why begin to open up to the Americans at last? It was not just that they were getting ever more reluctant to bomb what the British referred to as launch sites, in France. It was also an admission that the US would not embark on undefended city-smashing or the mass gassing of civilians without the clearest oversight as to why. The whole reprisal eruption had shown the degree of desperation in London. It was a tipping point. The US air commanders hated saturation-bombing of non-military targets: it was a 'moral hazard' too far, they felt, and a further diversion of Allied airpower from its prime objectives, already prejudiced by the Crossbow diversion. General Eisenhower, the Supreme Allied Commander, was pulling back from the brink. On 6 July he sternly told the British chiefs via his deputy Tedder: 'As I have before indicated, I am opposed to retaliation as a method of stopping this business. Please continue to oppose.'

On the same dangerous day that Churchill sent his poison-gas memo to the chiefs, a paper urgently prepared by Brigadier-General Charles P. Cabell, USSAFE Director of Plans, was transmitted to Churchill's confidant, the former aircraft production minister Lord Beaverbrook. While recognising that the effect of the V1 on civilian morale justified strong measures, Cabell argued that 'retaliation for vengeance alone has no place in sound military schemes'.

---

* AI3(e) was the Air Intelligence section responsible for assessing the organisation of the German air force, and as such received all CX MSS/J and SJ reports and messages concerned with secret weapons from Section 3G(N) at the Park.

And there was another internal reason for the intelligence shake-up. According to the official history of wartime intelligence compiled by the Bletchley veteran Professor Harry Hinsley: 'It was also no doubt influenced by the fact that at a time when knowledge of the rocket remained so scanty, the prospect of the Enigma making crucial disclosures [the Corncrake break] was rapidly improving.' There was no greater secret than Ultra. Ambitious individuals who had got too close had had their wings burned. It was not made any easier by the contradictions inherent in the conundrum of who was in the picture and who was not. Bert Harris was not Ultra-indoctrinated. Nor indeed were Air Marshal Sir Roderic Hill or General Sir Frederick Pile. The argument, such as it was, was that 'home' commanders did not need to make operational decisions based on time-critical information about enemy intentions.

Lt-General Spaatz, commander of USSAFE, and Lt-General 'Jimmy' Doolittle, commander of the 8th Air Force, *were* in the picture, however. Spaatz had been since mid-1943. Here was a way of tying the ever more recalcitrant Americans into the Crossbow countermeasures campaign. Indoctrinate some key intelligence figures into the binding brotherhood of Ultra, embrace them in a Whitehall committee, and maybe the Americans would go on taking orders from the Brits for a little longer. The trouble was, R. V. Jones knew it was a sham. And neither did Bert Harris at High Wycombe need code-breaking to tell him the Crossbow counter-bombing was useless. He was in open revolt and so were the Americans. Spaatz had already made his position clear. The frustration of the US air commanders had come to a head.

In a personal memorandum written on 8 July, Brigadier-General George McDonald, USSAFE's Director of Intelligence, expressed his exasperation to Major-General Frederick L. Anderson, the force's deputy commander, over what he called the 'impractical applications of security which had always pervaded Bodyline and Crossbow'. The British had persistently failed to keep their American counterparts involved or even informed, said McDonald, and above all there was 'too little voice by this headquarters in matters of policy'.

And it was all true. In spite of the Air Ministry's promises, the British had effectively kept complete control of intelligence-gathering and analysis, and the decisions on targeting that flowed from it. The days when a single US officer was allowed to sit in on meetings at 2 Monck Street but not to write anything down had hardly changed at all. The consequence was a colossal bombardment campaign aimed (apart from the Ultra-discerned Oise valley targets) at French farmyards.

That same day, Anderson proposed to Tedder the organisation of a joint committee that would be composed of six authorities – three from the British air staff, three from USSAFE – familiar with problems of intelligence and operations 'at the working level', to take over from the now openly derided Air Ministry operation. This committee would be, in the words of the USAAF *Official History*, 'directly responsible for assuring General Eisenhower that the best possible intelligence [would guide] the assignment of the right weapons in the correct role against the proper objectives'. But what might yet another committee contribute? In fact, its input would be considerable.

Two days later, Spaatz sent Tedder a memorandum urging support of the recommendations, and on 10 July he made another direct appeal to General Eisenhower for a definitive policy statement. But patience was wearing thin.

CHAPTER 35

A real rocket, actually two, were about to fly into Air Intelligence's lap. But instead of answering the many questions still hanging in the air, they would complicate the situation even further. The rocket that had fallen out of the sky at Bäckebo on the day the first flying bomb was launched at London was now the subject of urgent examination by two Air Intelligence officers, Squadron Leaders Charles Burder and Gordon Wilkinson, who had travelled uncomfortably to Stockholm in two Mosquito flights on 6–7 July to inspect the fragments. Group Captain Jack Easton, Air Intelligence research chief, expressed himself anxious, in a first signal from London, to know whether the device had wings or fins, and whether there were any indications of the kind of fuel it employed. He also wanted them to make sure the Germans had not somehow put it there as a plant.

Wilkinson said much later: 'I must admit that the sight of the A4 wreckage was absolutely terrifying.' Confronted with a mass of fragments in a Swedish aircraft hangar, it was not surprising that the interim report sent on 8 July was more conjecture than fact. 'It is inconceivable that so many man-hours would be devoted to an expendable weapon unless very great results were expected,' it stated. 'At a mere guess [it has] a warhead not less than 10,000 pounds [4.5 tons] and it might be considerably more,' said paragraph 5. 'The electronic circuits are extraordinarily complex ... all evidence points to series production.'

Equipped with this fabulous new insight into the rocket, Group Captain Easton was clearly minded to get it out around Whitehall. The circulation list was long. Dr Jones, however, was distinctly miffed: 'Easton chose to circulate the telegram without reference to me,' he wrote on his copy of the signal preserved in his working papers. 'I would not have done so. Paragraph 5 was the cause of the rocket flap of July 1944.' Like the telegram of December 1942 about gossip in a Berlin restaurant, another cable from Stockholm, had set Whitehall aflutter. Now the rocket had a four-ton-plus warhead and was in series production.

As the two men picked over the wreckage in the air force hangar at Bromma airfield outside Stockholm, their further telegrams spoke of 'multiple radio units of a complex nature ... an Hs 293-style radio-control unit ... gyro stabilisation ... turbine-driven fuel pump ... directional control by adjustable vanes projecting into the jet stream'. It was all good, but it still did not answer the outstanding questions: what was the true weight of the warhead and the nature of the fuel?

So there in Sweden was a real rocket. Added to that the Ultra-revealed rockets in Poland, and plenty of reports from the Polish underground of frozen tank wagons, explosions and craters; fragments from these had been smuggled to Warsaw and examined by Polish scientists, the news of them reaching London by clandestine radio. On 7 July Bottomley had signalled the C-in-C, RAF Mediterranean and Middle East, Air Marshal Sir John Slessor, in Caserta, 'Would you like to consider laying on a Dakota pickup similar to operation Wildhorn* to bring back this equipment? Inquiries are being made as to exact location to enable you to select clandestine landing ground ... appreciate that hours of darkness inadequate.' The SOE link at Bari in southern Italy would handle communications with Poland.

Ultra had delivered another mystery, meanwhile. The Corncrake back-breaks had revealed lists of 'Geräte' (devices) travelling between Blizna and Peenemünde. What were they? The signals up

---

* An SOE-directed air landing in Poland on the night of 15–16 April. There was a second on 29/30 May, and this would be the third, Wildhorn III. In Poland the operation was code-named 'Most' – 'Bridge'.

to early June quoted serial numbers in a series from 17053 to 17667. Could they be rockets? And if they were, why were they going from Poland to Germany? Then a message dated 26 June from Blizna referred to the requested dispatch of 'fifty 1000-kg elephants', shortage of which was causing 'large intervals between shoots'. 'Elephants', first mentioned in a Corncrake back-break of 17 April, had been assumed to be 'tracked heavy lorries'. It now looked as if they were warheads.*

But before stating that the devices were indeed rockets, Jones wanted outright proof. As he recounted in his memoirs, he went back to the copies of the Blizna photo-reconnaissance covers taken on 4 May, on file at the Air Ministry. He spent the evening of 7 July, he recounted, poring over the one stereo pair showing what had been taken to be the flying-bomb compound at Blizna. Could there be an A-4 in there as well? 'It was not the same GAF [German air force]–Army divide as at Peenemünde,' Jones said. 'I went on looking round and round this thing and finally there it was ... There was just enough of the shadow of the fin. I rang Charles Frank [his deputy] up in the early hours of the morning and told him.'

His findings were presented on the third page of the cyclostyled typewritten report presented by Frank Inglis to the chiefs on the afternoon of 9 July. The first two pages bumbled on about flying bombs. Then under the subhead 'Rocket Bomb' it came dramatically to life:

> The existence of a V2 [sic] weapon is established beyond doubt. Parts of a long range weapon are being examined in Sweden. A report from a prisoner indicates that the launch mechanism may be much simpler than formerly thought ...
>
> A large rocket has been found on photographs of the SS camp at Debica in Poland which has been working very closely with Peenemünde.

---

* The officer in charge of rocket and fuel shipments from Germany westwards, Oberst Wilhelm Zippelius, would tell American researchers that rocket trains 'camouflaged with wood and hay' were extremely effective from the outset. 'Every one we sent reached its proper destination ... if anyone inquired what was on our guarded trains we would say "circus elephants".'

Reports have been obtained from the Polish Intelligence Service about the Debica trials and they point very strongly to a large radio-controlled rocket with a range of 200 km or more powered by hydrogen peroxide fuel.

The paper also revealed that between 7 and 30 June at least seven rockets had been fired (it did not say how this was known).

The Inglis–Jones 'V2' report of 9 July was full of dramatic revelations, but its immediate impact was muted. Very soon what it had to say would be causing explosions in the Cabinet War Room.

CHAPTER 36

Saleux, July 1944

The bombing attacks on St Leu d'Esserent were having a direct impact on the rate of fire. And because fewer missiles were coming, the defences of London were more able to concentrate on those that did. The Flakgruppe HQ's war diary reported on 9 July: 'Enemy has considerably improved and strengthened his defence in the past few days ... LXV AK reporting at least 20–25 per cent being shot down. We cannot afford this rate of loss. There is to be no more night firing until further notice.' But there was better news from agents in London, who reported the same day that 'the morale of the people is ebbing, there is a permanent feeling of uncertainty'.

At Saleux that evening there was music, wine – dancing, even – to celebrate the completion of the underground headquarters. 'The band of the Signals Abteilung and a troupe of entertainers from Paris contributed to the success of the evening,' according to the war diary. Oberst Wachtel missed the party on account of an urgent conference in Paris. His fortunes were rising. On 12 July he was authorised to raise four new batteries and to survey sixty-four new launching sites. It was directed on the 17th that a second regiment, to be called Flakregiment 255 (W), was to be formed immediately with the possibility of a third in the offing (a move picked up by the Park). The Flakgruppe now had plenty of emergency sites ready, and construction had been simplified further so that operations were now being completed within eight to ten days.

But if the Flakgruppe could dismiss air attacks on their launch sites as generally ineffective, the complex web that got the missiles to the firing points was vulnerable. 'Agents' reports indicate the enemy are aware of the regiment's supply routes,' said the diary for 15 July. 'The Maikäfer are now being sent by three different routes.' Then: 'The Arras Abwehrstelle reports the capture of an agent. Nordpol [Nucourt] and Leopold [St Leu] have been effectively bombed. Treasonable material which has fallen into the hands of our Intelligence includes a report which gives accurate details of the Leopold ammunition depot.'

In fact, the Park had found the ammunition supply sites weeks before. But why could they not break into the air force signals directing the operations of the launch sites themselves? It was not for want of trying. But the Flakregiment's Enigma key, known as 'Jerboa', proved 'for a greater part of the time unbroken', as the Bletchley Park internal history put it. It did reveal some things, however, such as the fact that some missiles were armed with the high-energy explosive Trialen.

There was another lower-level signal system that broke easily, but that did not tell the listeners much that was useful. It was a three-figure code called 'Klavier', which substituted daily changing figures for letters and phrases in common use. It did not pinpoint battery locations, allow site numbers to be matched with photo-reconnaissance, or give indications of intention to fire or of the target – other than Target 42B, assumed to be London. Nor was it handled by Section 3G(N), which meant that 'those dealing with the key had no background against which to work'. But Klavier did reveal some things. A standardised weather forecast giving wind speed, wind direction and atmospheric pressure was sent from Abteilungen to individual batteries every two hours, for example. And target-settings for the air-log were transmitted to the nearest single revolution, giving a theoretical accuracy of 56 metres in range. Autopilot settings were to two decimal places, giving a variation in latitude of 35 metres after 200 kilometres of flight, leading to the assumption that they were 'aimed at pinpoint targets to the nearest second of longitude and latitude'. That did not mean, though, that they would actually hit them.

Having revealed so much about the weapon they were developing, Luftwaffe signallers were much more secure once operations against London had started, never giving enough away to bring down air attack. The frustration was intense.

London, July 1944

When the chiefs met in London on the morning of 11 July, the rocket had been the first item on the agenda. They urged that every effort be made to get the Bäckebo fragments from Sweden, especially the radio parts, the analysis of which they considered might make countermeasures possible. They further urged that the Prime Minister 'make a personal representation to Marshal Stalin to allow a technical inspection of Debica–Blizna against the prospect of it being overrun in the next few weeks'.

In a second meeting later that day it was proposed that Air Intelligence, assisted by the Intelligence Branch of the War Office, should prepare a report on the latest information on the long-range rocket. It also recommended that radio-jamming equipment be acquired urgently from America. The meeting concluded: 'It will be up to Mr Sandys's committee to appoint a panel of scientists to examine the evidence when produced and also the remains of the missile which [has] fallen in Sweden as and when these [are] brought to England.'

Its remit would soon be extended to cover everything to do with the rocket (on the 17th it would be split in two, the flying bomb side chaired by the physicist Sir Thomas Merton and the rocket by Dr Charles Ellis). The lead authority on rocket intelligence was swinging towards Sandys and his ever-growing band of advisers, so the Air Ministry must fight back.

Churchill needed no extra urging to pursue rocket diplomacy with Marshal Stalin. On 11 July he sent a message to the Soviet leader: 'The Londoners are standing up well to the bombing which has resulted in 22,000 casualties so far. Congratulations on your glorious advance to Wilna!' A message to Moscow the next day was more practical: 'There is firm evidence that the Germans have been conducting trials of the flying rocket from an experimental station at Debica in Poland for a considerable time . . . It is very important to know more. Debica is in the path of your victorious advancing armies – in particular we need to know how the rocket is discharged.'

On 13 July came something more cryptic from the code-breakers – from the Park's watch on the signal traffic of the Abwehr, the intelligence service of the German High Command. It was a message sent the day before from the military intelligence station at Arras to Berlin. It seemed to be a copy of another message: 'To Sabine ["W/T station Madrid" is scribbled on the flimsy] Stichling [the Abwehr activation code first intercepted in May for the double-cross agent Garbo, and nothing to do with the rocket]. Bombardment will shortly be carried out on limited areas. Exact time will be announced. Particular value is placed on reconnaissance of the effect with times and places of hits. Arco.'

The cable went immediately to Churchill, personally from C. The Prime Minister, not unnaturally, assumed it referred to the rocket. He wanted urgent clarification, stressing 'the political implications if the A-4 landed unexpectedly in the London area, and wanted the Stichling message and C's reply copied to the chiefs of staff. Menzies turned to Dr Jones for his opinion.

Jones's concern that intelligence was bubbling up all over the place – he wanted to keep it all to himself – was intensified, meanwhile, when on 13 July AI3(e), the Air Intelligence section responsible for collating PoW-derived intelligence, put out a long note on 'the German Flying Bomb Organisation'. It offered a well informed breakdown of the LXV Army Corps with its 'army side' and 'GAF side', and a potted history of the abandonment of the ski sites and the development of the modified sites. It gave a clear statement about the three big storage depots, 'one in a disused quarry, one in a series of limestone caverns and one in a disused railway tunnel' (St Leu d'Esserent, Nucourt and Rilly la Montagne), from where the flying bombs were moved at night by road to the launch sites.

The paper, although largely concerned with flying bombs, stated outright: 'Trials of a weapon still under development, which will here for convenience be referred to as "the rocket", are taking place at the SS camp at Heidelager near Debica in Poland and the

SS are actively supporting these trials.' The report had a very limited distribution among the Air Ministry, USAAF intelligence officers, MI14 and Professor Norman's section at the Park. It did not go to the War Cabinet Crossbow Committee or, to begin with, anywhere near Mr Sandys.

But the intelligence was clearly acted upon. St Leu had already been pummelled, and on the night of 15–16 July Nucourt was heavily bombed by the RAF; Rilly la Montagne (ammunition depot Richard in the railway tunnel south of Reims) was also attacked by the RAF, on the 17th. Ground agents were now reporting depots elsewhere, and claiming that flying bombs were being moved from them to firing sites at an average of ninety a night.

Dr Jones's most immediate task was to calm the Prime Minister's alarm over the Stichling cable. There was some serious inter-agency liaison to do.

On the 14th Menzies, having consulted Jones, noted that they believed the cable came from the 'intelligence liaison officer with the LXV Army Corps and is one of a series of Stichling messages that referred to the V1 weapon previously ... It is impossible to determine what the message is meant to say, but clarification could come should the German Intelligence pass on more specific orders to German agents (controlled by us) in this country.' But as Menzies further informed the Prime Minister: 'In spite of all these assurances, the possibility cannot be excluded that launching sites for the rocket have not already been erected. In fact agents have already reported sites which have not been confirmed by photography.' Nerves were fraying. It was time to get a grip.

The Polish rocket pick-up plan was advancing bumpily. Slessor's staff at Mediterranean Allied Air Forces HQ in Caserta had messaged back to Bottomley on the 9th: 'Mid July in Warsaw area there are only four hours of darkness ... chances of success would be immeasurably improved if aircraft could use an American bomber base in Russia.' Bottomley, whose show this very much was, cabled back on the 11th: 'No objections to Russia if you and SOE Italy can make arrangements' – though that might prove a little beyond them. The Air Ministry was able to relay the news from SOE London on the 14th that the landing ground would be used again. 'The load to be picked up consists of 50 kilograms of equipment and one man.' The mission was on.

Château du Molay, July 1944

Flight Lieutenant David Nutting of Air Technical Intelligence was making more discoveries in Normandy. Having gone ashore looking for pilotless aircraft, he had managed in the first week of July to examine two of the apparent rocket-linked sites reported by the talkative prisoners from the Sonderstab Beger command.

One of these was on the road leading from the Château Bernesq to the Château du Molay, west of Bayeux, and the second was at some burrowed-out lime kilns a few kilometres further west at La Meauffe, south of Carentan. At Bernesq, a German artillery headquarters had clearly quit the château in a hurry. 'Considerable further searching revealed three concrete sections in the surface of the road leading to the Château du Molay,' according to Nutting's report dated 14 July. 'The three sections were identical. The road's orientation was 310 degrees compass.' Sunken terraces covered by camouflage nets were to be seen on either side of the road.

What did it mean? Local inhabitants thought the concreting was down to repair after heavy traffic and the lateral extensions were for ammunition dumps. The report concluded: 'The connection of the site with Crossbow is improbable.'

At La Meauffe Nutting found a quarry with tunnels burrowed into its face along with light railway tracks. There were signposts in Russian, German and Turkmen. No documentation was found except for 'a torn exercise book'. Again the site was judged not suitable for Crossbow. In the Bois de Baugy near by an arrangement of roadways and concealed storage huts was found in the woods, and narrow-gauge tracks on which ran some sort of trolleys configured to hold a large cylindrical object.

So were the Sonderstab Beger prisoners making it up? Jones did not think so:

The site at Château du Molay was surveyed for me ... [a] sketch showed it simply as a tree-lined road on either side of which parallel loop roads had been made ... I was reminded of a pattern I had seen months before [in photo-reconnaissance imagery] on the foreshore at Peenemünde which hitherto had made no sense ... the [same] pattern of the roads at Molay had been laid out on the sand to see whether the proposed curves and loop roads could be negotiated by whatever transporters were to carry the rockets.

Jones was right: even if the investigators on the ground could not yet see what was under their noses, all-source intelligence and an inquiring mind might solve the conundrum. There were no projectors or giant mortars. There never had been. Here at last was the unlocking of the puzzle: the 'columns' seen for so long at Peenemünde were not launch rails – they were rockets standing vertically on their firing points.

London, 13 July 1944

The vice-chiefs of staff considered the chemical-retaliation proposal with a mixture of distaste and urgency. At a meeting on the afternoon of 13 July the terms of reference for the Joint Planning Staff to once again make judgement on the 'military implications of our deciding on an all-out use of gas' were cast and recast against a ticking clock. There are multiple annotations on the typewritten summary of conclusions.

In response to Churchill's rambling demands of the 6th, the planners were asked to consider the use of 'mustard gas, or *any other method of warfare** which we have hitherto refrained from using against the Germans' as a means of shortening the war, and also 'as a counter-offensive in the event of the use by the enemy of flying bombs and/or giant rockets developing into a serious threat to our ability to prosecute the war'.

Their work should 'take the form of a thorough and practical examination of the military factors involved and should ignore ethical and political considerations,' said the summary of the vice-chiefs' discussion. Only British experts were to be consulted (the Americans must not know). The planners were asked to consider the requirements in aircraft and bomb production for 'unrestricted

* Meaning anthrax. Author's emphasis.

use of chemical and biological weapons'. And they had better get on with it because Mr Churchill wanted answers.

The next day, 14 July, a revised version of Operational Instruction 74, with an updated mix of mustard, phosgene gas and high-explosive bomb loads was sent by Bomber Command via teleprinter to Group commands in eastern England. A copy went to Bottomley. The transmission of the warning signal to set the armourers toiling, and to prepare young men to drench German cities with poison, was a coded teleprinter instruction away.

The flying bomb could just about be tolerated, but this was really about the 'great rocket'. That Air Intelligence must very soon produce a definitive statement of its capabilities was clear. That meant Jones. The first draft of what he described as an 'interim summary statement of the broad lines of our knowledge and ignorance' was ready on 14 July. He would later say it was the one report of the war he regretted, blaming Frank Inglis for the indecent haste and his own sense of panic.

'There is little doubt that the Germans have developed a technically impressive missile which they call the A-4,' his report began quite calmly, 'the performance of which is good enough at least for a desultory bombardment of London.' On the evidence of the size of the craters seen thus far in reconnaissance imagery, 'the missile's warhead would seem to be probably between three and seven tons'. The rocket's main fuel was based upon hydrogen peroxide.

The manner of launching, and the presumed associated launching device, remained a mystery. 'According to eye-witnesses ... the missile was placed on a short lattice ramp pointing upwards at 45 degrees whence it rose with a flash and a roar,' Jones reported (the fatal flying bomb–rocket confusion intruding again – this had come from brave Polish Home Army sources who had managed to observe the Luftwaffe trials at Blizna alongside the army's A-4 test-firing). And Jones said this: 'A prisoner has spoken of a fairly simple concrete slab from which the rocket can be fired – and has pinpointed such constructions in liberated Normandy.'

The report correctly understood that that looked-for launcher – 'one of the gravest gaps in our knowledge', according to Jones –

might not even exist. The combination of gyroscope and jet rudder was the answer.

From the Swedish evidence it could be assumed that the weapon was already in mass production. The Peenemünde–Heidelager 'Geräte' conundrum revealed by Corncrake was not mentioned because Jones had yet to realise the significance of the numbers quoted. 'A small-scale attack could be mounted at any time,' he said. And it was accurate to a degree that made it an effective way of attacking London. 'Wild shots still occur, but from the Polish evidence half the shots fall inside a circle twenty miles in diameter.'

So much was right but so much was still wrong. The hydrogen peroxide as main fuel confusion (it drove the fuel pump) was still disallowing a clear understanding, and thus the threat the rocket really posed. The supposed warhead was still far too big. Jones would say later that he was influenced by the declaration of Dr Charles Ellis that craters of the size observed at Blizna were the result, according to his own experts, of the 'detonation of a charge of explosive of between three and seven tons'.

His penchant for blaming others when things went wrong was becoming insufferable. On 15 July, Douglas Kendall circulated a polite but inwardly seething minute that accused Jones of not consulting the professionals at Medmenham while blithely presenting the chiefs of staff with claims that there was an A-4 rocket on the coverage of Blizna.

'Ground sources have reported experiments there,' said Kendall, 'but no warning or briefing has been given to this unit to examine this area from this point of view. There is a reasonable possibility that the object in question is merely an excavator.'

Kendall wrote a similarly outraged note to Inglis, indicating that the 'rocket' that Jones claimed to have seen was in fact 'a locomotive ... Wild statements in the past have invariably had unfortunate effects.' Dr Jones's enemies were multiplying.

CHAPTER 37

London, July 1944

Strategic deception was running into trouble. The Twenty Committee, operating the Fortitude plan in parallel, thought Garbo's exposure too great. They decided to retire him – Zigzag and others would begin transmitting in his place. But first, Garbo's MI5 minder Tomas Harris decided on some inspired prevarication.

On 5 July the mythical second-in-command reported to Madrid that Garbo was missing. Two days later Garbo had been 'arrested'. The messages from Madrid that followed showed how seriously the Germans regarded this entirely fabricated blow. On 10 July Garbo's deputy sent the welcome news that his master had been set free. Four days later, Garbo himself sent a detailed dispatch explaining his absence.

As he reported his adventure to Madrid, pursuing his duties on 4 July he had gone to lunch at a pub in London and 'overheard talk of bombs falling the previous night in Bethnal Green'. He had quizzed a man in the crowd on the time of the incident and the number of deaths; the man had then followed him and produced a Metropolitan Police warrant card. A brutal interrogation had followed, said Garbo.

While he had been in his fantasy lock-up, on 5 July Findlater Stewart had submitted a fuller proposal to the chiefs of staff. He was now going for the big move. The implications of the proposed

shift of the mean point of impact further to the south-east by
deception had now been discussed with the government departments principally concerned, he said. The Ministry of
Production had no objections, but Herbert Morrison did. Civil
defence in the outskirts would not be up to it, and the pattern of
attacks had been established to the extent that those already under
fire had become 'hardened'. Findlater Stewart's paper plus
Morrison's objections were copied to Churchill.

The chiefs considered the deception paper on 7 July. They
were not convinced and invited its author to explain more fully
what he had in mind. He did so in a long document completed on
15 July which acknowledged from the start that the deception
would be implemented 'almost wholly by double agents'. As
Findlater Stewart said:

> Practically all [the] agents, now run by us, have received urgent
> requests to report on the fall of bombs giving both time and
> place of as many incidents as possible. Two of the agents,
> Brutus* and Garbo, on whom the main burden of supporting
> the plan Fortitude has fallen, have been instructed to provide
> themselves with specific maps and to report quickly on inci-
> dents by reference to co-ordinates ... Another high agent, who
> has recently arrived here [Zigzag] has also been instructed to
> give a high priority to bomb reports, and his masters in briefing
> him were emphatic that time and place must be accurately
> given ... we know from Most Secret Sources that the highest
> priority within the German Intelligence Service is given to the
> forwarding of these reports to the force responsible for the oper-
> ation of the weapon.

Since they had to report something in order to stay credible,
Findlater Stewart continued, the only way to turn this to advantage
was to imply an error in range; thus 'the agent concerned ... should
report on actual incidents in NW London, and give as the times of
those incidents the actual times of incidents in SE London [the
Jones–Cholmondeley plan].'

* The former Polish air force officer Roman Czerniawski.

Findlater Stewart then considered the likely other sources from which the enemy might derive information: for instance, uncontrolled sources such as reports from neutral embassies and 'the inspired guesswork of freelance agents in neutral capitals' – this referred to 'Ostro', the Czech-born Paul Fidrmuc, a freelance Abwehr agent in Lisbon from 1940 to 1945 who based his reports 'on gossip, imagination and anything he could get from the newspapers'. Much of this could be monitored through signals intelligence, but the information known to have been transmitted thus far was 'vague and inaccurate and certainly not of a nature which would influence the enemy's aim'. More serious were the radio devices known to be carried by a small proportion of the weapons. The Germans' faith in the weapon's intrinsic accuracy had been revealed in the Peenemünde trials, and after more than two thousand combat launches they were still not correcting its aim. 'It would seem to follow from that,' said Findlater Stewart, 'that if the enemy has in fact radio results indicating his error, he is not relying on them as much as on the accuracy and consistency of the results established in the trials. If this is so ... our task is to work at the enemy's faith in his weapons rather than his radio results.'

The question of inducing the Germans to attack another city than London had been raised. The south-coast port of Southampton had been the notional target of air-launched flying bombs on 7 July (see p. 257), but their aim was so inaccurate that Lord Cherwell assumed the target to have been Portsmouth. On 14 July the Prof suggested to Morrison that the Germans should be encouraged to continue attacking the ports, where eighty-one flying bombs had inflicted a total of ten casualties. 'I would press you to consider the possibility of commiserating with a "South Coast town" on the heavy losses sustained, or in some other way indicating that the attack had been a success,' he wrote.

Morrison thought the idea 'at first sight attractive', but as he replied on the 17th, 'politically it would be dangerous in the extreme ... it would soon be known to be untrue and doubts would be cast upon the accuracy of Government statements generally'.

The chiefs considered Findlater Stewart's latest proposal and the Southampton–Portsmouth diversion on 18 July. This was clearly more than a military decision – the Prime Minister must be involved. But they accepted that the double agents should indeed implement the proposed policy of moving the mean point of impact – MPI – something which, Findlater Stewart admitted, they had already begun to do. Churchill was told: 'It is clear that from this insistent demand for information [on flying bomb impacts] that the agents must comply or be hopelessly compromised ... For the time being, the information imparted to them is designed to move the mean point of impact which is already short, still further to the south-east. This must inevitably increase the danger in some areas in order to reduce it in others.'

The same memo further invited the Prime Minister to consider encouraging the enemy to waste more bombs on Portsmouth and Southampton. So the MPI-moving plan was in hand, and the Prime Minister knew. But other members of the War Cabinet did not.

There was a mildly comic interlude on 20 July when Lord Cherwell suggested to Findlater Stewart that newspaper obituaries were 'allowing the enemy to plot the fall of his Crossbow shot ... It seems unfortunate that the papers have been allowed to print obituaries of those killed by enemy action which quote the borough or district. One of my people has plotted 70 from *The Times* and 80 from the *Daily Telegraph*, a definitely significant sample.' If allowance were made, as it would be reasonable to suppose the enemy would, for the overweighting of Kensington and Chelsea as the domiciles of the classes who would bother to place such death notices, the mean point of impact for *Times* deaths congregated around middle-class Streatham Hill and *Telegraph* deaths at more artisan Clapham Junction. This gave 'results dangerously close to the truth'. In other words, the bombs were not killing enough people in north, west and central London. Cherwell suggested inserting 'a score or so bogus obituaries' on the assumption that Luftwaffe intelligence officers were indeed poring over the death notices of the London dailies and sticking pins in a (Pharus) map.

The Home Defence Executive deception enthusiast John Drew expressed it well in a letter to the Chief Censor (the redoubtable retired Admiral George Thomson), who would have to police the obituarists: 'It's like long-range artillery,' he explained. Shots fell round a mean point of impact which could be computed once you had a big enough sample. The Germans' target could be assumed to be Charing Cross* but the actual MPI, having hopped around. Therefore, said Drew, 'there must be a systemic error in the weapon about which the enemy is ignorant ... the importance of keeping him in the dark about this cannot be overemphasised'. And Lord Cherwell was right about the obituaries sample, said Drew, which did indeed show that more bombs were falling south of the river. If the newspapers objected, Admiral Thomson should point out that a correction of the aim by the enemy to Charing Cross would 'bring the heaviest concentration [of fire] to Fleet Street'.

Brigadier-General George McDonald, the US Air Intelligence chief, had had enough of being given the run-around by the Air Ministry. He told Inglis on 15 July that 'a joint and balanced Anglo-American Crossbow Committee' was essential. Frank Inglis was already holding the door ajar: 'I feel that great advantage would spring from an increasing American representation in the intelligence set-up,' he told Bottomley, 'and Dr Jones has therefore asked if Dr [Bob] Robertson [professor of mathematics at Princeton] who is a member of the secret weapons committee in the New Developments Division of the War Department could help him. He would be a full working member of the intelligence team.' It was a start, but the Americans wanted much more than that.

And Jones, his relationship with Medmenham now in deep freeze, would not be deterred from making more attempts at 'amateur interpretation'. According to his memoirs, he went over the Blizna covers again. Late on the evening of 17 July, having already found a rocket, this time he spotted a modest square of concrete in the Polish forest which matched the discoveries at the Château du Molay. He later told an interviewer that this was also the moment, twenty-four hours before a set-piece meeting with Churchill, that he cracked the significance of the Corncrake-derived 'Geräte [device] numbers' and understood why the

* In fact, to begin with it was Tower Bridge, but it later notionally moved around the major London railway termini.

trainloads in question were going from east to west: they were carrying expended rockets from Blizna for technical post-mortem at Peenemünde. He knew from the decrypts, but he could not say that. Instead, the railway movements and the numbers of 'devices' in transit were supposedly revealed by mysterious 'bills of loading' obtained from some agent source.

Jones took the news of the Blizna launch pad and the Geräte series to Lord Cherwell personally. He then spent a brittle evening at dinner with Duncan Sandys, whom he informed of his intention to urge Portal to get a technical team to Blizna. 'Sandys was friendly enough but was obviously gathering ammunition for an attack on the air staff,' Jones recalled twenty years later.

An all-new Rocket Flap was in the making. But first there would be another row in London about the flying bomb.

Air Defence of Great Britain HQ, July 1944

It began as a simple idea (claimed by Air Marshal Sir Roderic Hill as his) on 10 July. Too many flying bombs were getting through. The current overlapping disposition of fighters and guns, with their complicated rules of engagement, was self-defeating: they should be given clearly delineated and separate zones, the balloons remaining as the longstops at the gates of London.

The AA chief Lt-General Pile admitted it: '[Our record in early July] was not very impressive ... Our shooting was both wild and inaccurate. Many of the claims to have destroyed flying-bombs arose from no more than the fact that the missile had reached the end of its course and, regardless of our fire, had dived to earth. At a generous estimate, I should think we were destroying perhaps 13 per cent.' Pile was already convinced of the need to separate guns and fighters completely, and Hill concurred. The artilleryman now urged the removal of the light guns from their forward coast strip and consolidating them in one rearward line on the North Downs, where the heavy guns had already 'taken root'.

Hill readily agreed; but having been asked to draw up a paper explaining the move to subordinate commands, his deputy senior air staff officer, forty-year-old Air Commodore G. H. Ambler, presented him with a radical alternative. The proposal was to move the entire gun belt forty miles *forward* to the coast, re-siting it to within the best radar conditions and with unrestricted fire over the sea.

Two examples could be cited of the benefits to be gained from such a move: the current success of the two American-manned AN/CPS-1 MEW (Microwave Early Warning) radar sets, loaned by the US 9th Air Force to help locate the direction of launching sites, and the high kill rate against flying bombs of those US army anti-aircraft units that had been moved to the coast, pending their joining the battle in France. These units were currently achieving excellent results – one bomb destroyed for every forty shells fired – with the help of variable-time-fused shells and their SCR 584 automated gun-laying radar sets, which had arrived in early June.*

Ambler and Hill thrashed out the plan on the morning of 13 July. Pile was summoned to a conference late that afternoon, while Hill studied the problem from the air-intercept viewpoint. The proposed move of the gun belt would split fighter activity into two areas: patrols out over the sea, and a second inland belt behind the guns extending up to the balloons on the southern fringe of London. And thus far it was the fighters who were in the ascendant.

At this pivotal point in the defence of London, Hill, Pile, Ambler, the radar expert Watson-Watt, Air Vice Marshal Hugh Saunders commanding the front-line fighters of No. 11 Group, a representative of Leigh-Mallory, the Air Commander-in-Chief for Operation Overlord, and other senior air force and army officers gathered at Stanmore. To their own surprise, they unanimously approved the plan. But no one had sought the air staff's approval. There had been no political consultation, although when Hill took the proposal to the Crossbow Committee chaired by Sandys on the evening of 14 July the latter had asked for a brief written appraisal of it. Hill wrapped it up as a tactical decision taken entirely within his remit. Leigh-Mallory suggested a trial in a smaller area, but Hill

---

* One of the most advanced electronic devices of the war, the origins of which went back to the Tizard mission of 1940 (see p. 77), that took British technical secrets to the US. It picked up a moving target and automatically brought 90mm gunfire to bear.

ignored him and just got on with it. The gun convoys rolled through that night, and the next.

Sir Charles Portal, Chief of the Air Staff, was not pleased. He saw the hand of Sandys behind the move. In retrospect, Pile described the episode in tribal terms, as the air force and army fought for the crown of saving London (or to avoid the blame for its destruction):

> The most tremendous beating of tom-toms took place. I think that it was considered in some important circles that Hill had been unduly influenced by myself or by Sandys, or by both of us, into agreeing to a move which would increase our successes and decrease the RAF's total. Which of course was just what it did do.
>
> ... Anyway, the Air Council were very displeased. They left Hill in absolutely no doubt that he must take the full consequences of the failure – for failure was forecast in their every word – attending upon this decision.

The great upheaval went with remarkable smoothness, in fact. The Germans never detected it. Sandys told the War Cabinet on 17 July: 'The redeployment of the anti-aircraft guns on to their new sites along the coast was carried out over the week-end and the new defence plan came into operation at six o'clock this morning.' It was something of a miracle.

But the first week following the move was decidedly wobbly, and fewer flying bombs were destroyed by the defences than the week before, 204 reaching Greater London out of the 473 that came within range. Hill recorded: 'Analysis of the week's figures showed, as critics of the new plan had predicted, [that] improved results from the guns and from an expanded and denser balloon barrage had not sufficed to outweigh a sharp decline in the achievement of the fighters.'

Mr Sandys had gambled the survival of the capital. It looked as if he had got it wrong.

CHAPTER 38

After a month of bombardment, the defence of London against the flying bombs was being conducted by trial and error. The chiefs of staff had no answers. Hill and Pile had ignored them and proceeded to move the guns while Duncan Sandys gave political cover. The toiling gun- and balloon-crews knew nothing of the mysterious process behind the great upheaval, and the public knew even less. The counter-bombing of Crossbow targets was a sham and the US bomber chiefs were in revolt, as was Bert Harris.

Detailed plans to gas millions of German civilians and the means to do so had been made ready. The Home Secretary wanted to empty the capital, Churchill was proving 'impossible', and the intelligence structure set up to confound the German long-range weapons was now at war with itself. To beat the flying bombs some put their faith in the imminent arrival of American radar, fire control and proximity fuses, and maybe even in the all-British Gloster Meteor jet aircraft about to come into squadron service.

If there was any real hope, it was that the Allied armies in France would now just get on with it. As for the rocket, no one was quite sure what to believe. H. E. Bates recorded the mood in Doodlebug Alley, the southern approach to the capital where, in contrast to 1940, 'the battle was entirely without thrill or pride ... [People] hated it, the edges of their nerves were rubbed raw by it, and they saw in it, beyond their taut day-to-day, meal-to-meal existence, all its hideous potentiality for the future.' On 9 July the Ministry of Home Security had made the symbolic decision to open London's 'deep Tube shelters', the chain of subterranean bunkers built in 1941–2 paralleling the Northern Line and the Central Line at Chancery Lane.

London, 9–18 July 1944

Nine days later the chiefs met to review Dr Jones's interim rocket report – the one he would later say he regretted for its haste and misapprehensions. Cherwell was there, now backing down from his formerly implacable rocket-denial stance. Just how ingenious the Germans had been was emerging from the Swedish remains. The first consignment had arrived by Mosquito at Leuchars on the 16th. The Air Intelligence officers Burder and Wilkinson had returned with them from Stockholm and had told Charles Frank that what seemed to be a turbo fuel-pump recovered intact from the wreckage had shown no trace of lubrication of its rotating parts – other, perhaps, than that caused by the fuel it was pumping. Dr Frank had been reminded of the Claude process for liquefying air at very cold temperatures, in which the bearings of a rotary pump are lubricated by the cryogenic properties of the medium being pumped – liquid oxygen, in this case?

A War Cabinet Crossbow meeting was scheduled for early that evening. Churchill himself was going to chair it. Dr Jones spent the day in tedious subcommittees. This was to be his first encounter with the Prime Minister since the pilotless aircraft bombardment had begun; and since the last great Air Ministry shake-up he had been formally in charge of all long-range-weapon intelligence coordination. If blame were to anyone, it would be him. He later told an interviewer: 'Claude Pelly was sitting on one side of me, now as the Chief Intelligence Officer of AEAF [Allied Expeditionary Air Force], and Colin Grierson was on the other, since he was still [having been relieved of his intelligence duties] nominally directing countermeasures. The two of them were so silent, scared stiff to say a word.'

The mood was one of emotional tension. Then Dr Jones reported, to general astonishment, his discovery of a rocket in the Blizna–Debica photographs (although in fact it had figured in the Inglis paper of the 9th). There was a brief discussion of the Swedish rocket and the fact that it seemed to be of series production. Certain of the radio parts had just been received: the wiring was of 'immense complexity'. The larger parts would have to await sea shipment, said Jones. In fact they would be flown to England by three American Liberators on 26 July, each carrying 'two crates containing rocket bomb parts consigned as diplomatic freight'.

Then came the explosion. According to Jones, reading from his paper, the rocket's warhead might contain as much as five tons of high explosive – at least, this was as Dr Ellis's crater experts would have it. Five tons! The Prime Minister growled. Why had the Air Ministry not revealed such information as it had become known? But now Jones was reeling off yet more alarming facts that were not even in the briefing paper before them. 'The crisis came when I told Churchill that from the evidence I had just evaluated, I thought that the Germans must have at least a *thousand* rockets,' he recalled. 'At this he exploded, and started to thump the table, saying that we had been caught napping. And so I respectfully thumped the table back.'

'When did this evidence become available?' demanded Churchill. 'Why has Lord Cherwell not seen it?' Because the rocket in the photograph in Poland had been found by himself personally a few days before, Jones said (actually it had been eleven days before, on 7 July), and the evidence about the rocket serial numbers had only just become available. In fact the numbers that took the 'Geräte' series from 17053 to a new peak of 18036 had been in the Park's decrypts up to 14 July.

The next shock was the manner of launching: from a simple concrete plinth. The search for monstrous constructions had been a distraction, which 'again had only become clear in the last 24 hours', Jones explained – at the moment when he had found a concrete platform in the photo-reconnaissance covers of Blizna. In fact the possibility of a minimal launcher had been in Matthew Pryor's MI14 report of 3 July and in the Air Ministry summary of 9 July, but the obsession with rails and projectors was just too strong to be overturned by statements from a few deserters and prisoners.

The awkward silence was broken by Major-General Sir Colin Gubbins, the head of SOE, saying that he had received a bit of intelligence that the rocket was to be steered to its target by a man inside it, who was to parachute out during its final ascent. Portal made avuncular noises about rockets and flying bombs having been closely watched, asserting that all action that could have been thought of had been taken.

Churchill summed up, and again raised the prospect of threatening the enemy with gas-for-rocket retaliation, should 'such a course appear profitable'.* The minutes read tersely, with no paragraph break: 'He had instructed the Chiefs of Staff to carry out a military examination of such an attack on the enemy. He directed that Dr Jones should keep Lord Cherwell fully informed on all aspects of intelligence on the long range rocket.' The young physicist had better have got it right.

The meeting ended, but the passion it had released was by no means spent. Jones picked his way through the blackout to the flat of a friend with whom he was staying in Petty France, a street a few minutes' walk from the Cabinet War Room. At 02:20 on 19 July a flying bomb fell on Monck Street just around the corner outside the Air Intelligence building, demolishing a truckload of sensitive enemy equipment captured in Normandy. Field Marshal Sir Alan Brooke, not far away in his London flat, also had what he called 'a nasty disturbed night . . . with about a dozen flying bombs in the vicinity . . . The nearest landed about 150 yards away . . . I heard it coming, so I slipped out of bed and took cover behind my bed on the floor to avoid glass splinters.'

The men of the Flakgruppe would have rejoiced had they known how close they were coming to the enemy's seat of power. The Chief of the Imperial General Staff emerged from his improvised bedroom shelter that morning to answer a summons from Churchill, whom he found 'in bed in his dressing gown in an unholy rage' after some slight from Field Marshal Montgomery. 'I

---

* Professor Jones recalled the meeting in an article published in 1987 defending the Prime Minister against allegations of promoting chemical and biological warfare: 'When [Churchill suggested] that Britain should attempt to deter the onset of the V2 campaign by threatening the Germans with gas should they launch their rockets, some of those present spoke firmly against it, and none spoke in favour. [Churchill gave way] to opposing views on the use of gas, despite his own strong support for it.'

cannot help feel [Churchill] is becoming more and more unbalanced. He is quite impossible to work with,' so Brooke confided to his diary.

Churchill composed himself enough that day to send a telegram to Stalin giving the geographical location of Debica, where 'experimental firing of large rockets takes place ... It is possible they have a thousand of these things, each of which carries about 5 tons,' he wrote. 'If this be true, it would become an undoubted factor in the life of London ... but everyone is taking it very well. Parliament will require me to convince them that everything is being done, therefore it would be a helpful if you could lay your hands on any evidence.' However impossible Churchill was proving, British army officers were not plotting to blast their political chief out of office.

The next morning, 20 July, Oberst Claus von Stauffenberg arrived by aircraft from Berlin at Hitler's headquarters at Rastenburg in the midge-ridden forests of East Prussia. At 12:50 the briefcase bomb he had primed a little before with a time-pencil fuse exploded in the briefing hut. Just to show whose side they were on, LXV Armee Korps headquarters had telephoned Oberst Wachtel just before 23:00 on the night of the bomb plot and ordered: 'Continuous fire at maximum tempo and with an unrestricted expenditure of ammunition.'

That evening, as the army conspirators went before extemporised firing squads in Berlin,* the men of RAF 150 Wing based at Romney Marsh were celebrating their five-hundredth shot-down flying bomb with a grand Doodlebug Celebration Dance at the Majestic Hotel, Folkestone.

Bletchley Park, 20 July 1944

Letting certain Americans into the Ultra picture was opening up some dramatic intelligence-gathering opportunities. The obsession

---

* Dornberger would tell his postwar interrogator that he arrived at the War Ministry in Berlin early on the morning of 21 July, after a summons by Fromm, to find 'Stauffenberg and co lying about the courtyard. I didn't know what was going on.'

with the rocket being radio-guided had already led to proposals from the Crossbow interdepartmental radiolocation committee chaired by Sir Robert Watson-Watt to get listening stations operating in the Baltic – on Swedish soil, on Royal Navy or Soviet submarines. Thus far it had proved impossible. On 20 July Bimbo Norman sent the Air Ministry Director of Signals Intelligence a proposal headed 'A-4 and the Super Fortress':

> The American scientists who are in on the A.4 story, suggested that they should obtain a [Boeing B-29] Super-Fortress. The A/C [aircraft] was to fly over Poland and stay there as long as possible. (24 hours?) It would fly higher than Flak and fighters, would be full of scientists and instruments, and would attempt to measure and get the frequencies of any A.4 shot that was going. The Americans needed a 50/50 chance. I was asked about Heidelager, and pronounced against it. My counter-suggestion was Peenemünde, because . . .

Norman then elaborated on the extraordinary plan, in which he clearly intended taking part himself, to employ the US super-bomber:* 'We could fly over south Sweden, in case of accidents; Brown[-key] security being non-existent, we usually have log-evidence 4 to 6 hours before an A.4 shoot. It would be a simple matter to get any such evidence telephoned to B.P. and handed on via Broadway to the A/C.'

So Ultra would give real-time warning of an A-4 shoot and the US bomber could take off and head for the Baltic safe in the knowledge that 'once the trial is announced, there is a good chance of its coming off, even if usually there is a delay of a few hours'. As for Heidelager and the Russians, Professor Norman noted: 'The moment the Russians reach Heidelager, our information ceases. There is a scheme afoot to get the P.M. to write to Stalin to ask for permission to examine the sites. As we have had some excellent reports from Polish Underground sources, security of our sources here [Bletchley Park] is not endangered.'

The electronic snooping plan never got airborne. But the

---

* Which would never be employed in Europe, but in the destruction by fire of Japanese cities, and eventually to drop the A-bomb.

scheme to get investigators to Heidelager most certainly did progress. On the 22nd, Stalin sent Churchill a message saying that the matter was 'now under his personal control and everything possible would be done'. So the Blizna plan was on. In light of what was to happen in the wilds of Poland, it might have been better, perhaps, if a team of Allied scientists had done what they could to unlock the rocket's secrets in their own pressurised laboratory flying at 20,000 feet.

London, 20 July 1944

Lord Cherwell was not untouched by Churchill's testiness about intelligence being 'asleep'. As he insisted in a personal note to his friend on 20 July, 'I did not assert that the rocket was impossible. I pointed out that it could not be proved to be impossible ... Since then a year has passed. Not having been shown all the secret evidence, I do not pretend today to have a view on the likelihood of attacks in the near future by long range rockets.' Thus the Prof was defending himself on the grounds of having been left in the dark. Churchill minuted in response: 'Why was this ... The Professor ... has been admitted to most of my secrets. He knows about Boniface. He even knows some that hardly anyone knows.'*

Herbert Morrison also waded in, with a note complaining that there seemed to be 'something wrong on the intelligence side' – it had been 'a surprise to me as it appeared to be to you, to be told as they had been by Jones that the scale of the attack was four or five times that which had been previously contemplated. I find it hard to understand why it has been so hard to get information'. The Home Secretary was not alone.

---

* It was Cherwell who first told Churchill about the prospects of an atomic 'super-explosive' in mid-1941. On 16 May 1944, at a meeting in London brokered by Jones, the Danish physicist Niels Bohr, accompanied by Cherwell, attempted to give a bad-tempered Churchill a briefing on the nuclear danger. The meeting proved a fiasco. The 'fission products' scare blew up two days later. On 3 July Bohr presented a lucid memorandum mentioning 'feverish activity on nuclear problems' by the Germans and an invitation for him to go to Moscow. Churchill told Cherwell that Bohr 'ought to be confined', and that he did not like the man, 'when you showed him to me with his hair all over his head, at Downing Street'.

That same day, Dr Ellis chaired the first Big Ben scientific subcommittee meeting in Room 350 at the War Office. As well as the scientists, Matthew Pryor of MI14 was there and so was Lt-Colonel Kenneth Post, Duncan Sandys's loyal assistant. Jones loftily stayed away. His representative, the Princeton mathematician Bob Robertson, attended but said nothing. Ellis declared, 'Unfortunately we are without definite evidence of any of the major facts involved.' The meeting huffed and puffed, blissfully ignorant of the harvest of intelligence sitting in the Air Ministry.

CHAPTER 39

London, 21 July 1944

The Anglo-American Joint Crossbow Target Priorities Committee met formally for the first time in London on 21 July. There were four Americans on it: Colonels Stewart McClintic and Richard D'Oyly Hughes; Colonel Joseph J. Nazzaro, Deputy Director of Operations, USSAFE; and Captain Walt Rostow of the Enemy Objectives Unit. On the British side, Wing Commander Sidney Bufton, Portal's protégé, presented Bomber Operations' view. Bert Harris had been denied a direct representative on the committee on the insistence of Arthur Bottomley. Air Commodore Colin Grierson, recovered from his fright at the Cabinet table three days before, took the chair.*

The atmosphere was distinctly brittle. In his bravura account of the campaign against the flying-bomb sites given to the Commons two weeks before, the Prime Minister had said that 'every one of them was destroyed by the Royal Air Force with the wholehearted assistance of the growing United States air power'. American officers

---

* As the *Official History* of the US Army Air Force pointed out in retrospect: 'The new committee contained American representation ... but it had only advisory powers, was still under the jurisdiction of the [UK] Air Ministry, and its recommendations could be – and frequently were – set aside by Tedder, who continued to be considerably influenced by opinion in the Air Ministry and War Cabinet.' As far as the Americans were concerned, the Brits were still running the show.

thought that a 'very unfortunate way of putting it'. Colonel Hughes
pushed Spaatz's line that it should be more than just a targeting
committee. The whole secret-weapon complex from factory to
launch pad should be reappraised and bombing priorities completely recast.

Lack of information was the problem. All through July, intelligence would be groping around after the true production rate of
the missile. Where they were being made was even more obscure.
Final assembly was at the field depots or near the firing site, but
the subcomponents seemed to come from sites all over western
Germany. The VW works at Fallersleben, attacked twice in June,
remained the only one that could be definitely associated with the
manufacture of flying-bomb components. In the light of the latest
intelligence, or lack of it, and having listened to the views of
Colonel Richard Hughes, the committee advised the suspension
of all but harassing attacks on modified sites, ending all attacks on
ski sites, and all except the 'Aphrodite' attacks on the large sites,
using old bombers packed with explosive under radio control – a
two-man crew was supposed to get them airborne before para-
chuting out.*

As soon as he heard about the shiny new committee, Duncan
Sandys wanted the omnipresent Lt-Colonel Post to sit on it.
Bottomley took the matter up with Portal. 'I feel it would be a mistake for Mr Sandys to become involved in the intelligence and
operational aspects,' said the Chief of the Air Staff. Bottomley
quoted at length the terms of reference of Mr Sandys's own committee, which had been 'charged with the responsibility of
reporting on the effects of Crossbow, i.e. the flying bomb and the
flying rocket, and the progress of countermeasures and precautions
to meet it' – but not with actually doing much about it.

The minister, Bottomley inferred, had already interfered in the
disposition of the anti-aircraft defences, at the same time plotting
against Air Marshal Hill. Portal agreed, but thought it wise to send
Sandys privately the minutes of the committee. He added in a

---

* Operation Aphrodite proved highly dangerous and ultimately ineffective. A big effort
against the heavy Crossbow sites on 4–6 August produced no useful results. On the 12th
a US Navy aircraft flying against Mimoyecques detonated prematurely, killing the pilot
Lieutenant Joseph P. Kennedy Jr, JFK's elder brother, and the co-pilot.

The A-4 liquid-fuelled ballistic missile later known as the V2 saw a number of novel technologies coming together in a weapon system. It was an amazing achievement. British scientific intelligence struggled to understand even its basic workings until the eve of its arrival. Although Ultra had captured plenty of 'rocket traffic', the complex technical German of the messages presented Jones and Norman with an almost impenetrable puzzle.

Within the Mittelwerk, rockets were put together by slave labour, alongside a smaller component of German civilian workers and managers. The factory under a mountain in Thuringia was part of the wider SS-controlled Mittelbau closed area. Dora was the principal prison camp, one of several.

For the slaves, the precision assembly work (*above*) was subject to a ferocious regime of overseeing – with brutal punishments for acts of sabotage – with fear of detection a constant deterrent. Each sub-assembly was stamped with a personal certification mark (*below*) to show its unique origin should it not pass inspection, fail under test or be returned after a misfire. Such stamped components are still coming out of the ground in Poland and wherever else the rockets fell.

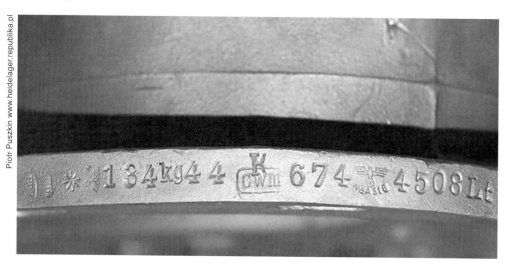

Fleet Street at 2.07 on the afternoon of 30 June 1944 as a flying bomb arrives from France to hit the Air Ministry at Aldwych with deadly effect. Passengers seem to ignore both the smoke plume in the distance and the dubious safety of the nearby brick-built street shelter as the bus carries on as normal. Churchill said of the dilemma: 'You cannot leave every bus driver to decide what to do himself, especially when his passengers may disagree with his solution.'

The Propaganda Ministry in Berlin, after a hesitant start, put out claims that London was aflame and the population fleeing under the menace of the Vergeltungswaffe-1 – as depicted in this propaganda leaflet.

Mittelwerk slaves tend the tails of splinter-camouflaged A-4 rockets. Saboteurs discovered they could make partial arc welds inside the fins that would then be sealed and hidden from further inspection.

This bizarre image is one from a sequence shot in early summer 1944 on Agfa colour stock by the film-maker Walter Frentz, commissioned by Albert Speer. The results show skilled assembly work in the caverns by relatively healthy and unguarded prisoners. Speer's motive remains obscure – to record for posterity this German managerial 'achievement' perhaps. The pictures lay forgotten until 1998 when Frentz's son discovered them in the attic.

On 24 July 1944, eleven-year-old Eileen Clements was carried unharmed from the ruins of 5 Arundel Road, Leytonstone. The drama was captured in this iconic news photograph (*above*) first published without names or location of a V1 strike on the capital. The rescuer was identified much later as Leading Fireman Bill Sayers.

Right: A grim-looking Churchill, with Admiral Edward Evans, London Civil Defence chief, inspects damage in the heart of the government district at Tufton Street, Westminster, in early July 1944. A few days later he demanded the chiefs of staff make a 'cold-blooded calculation as to how it would pay us to use poison gas' in response.

DAILY EXPRESS FRIDAY SEPTEMBER 8 1944

The whole story of how the Flying Bomb was beaten

by *Duncan Sandys, M.P.*

Chairman of the War Cabinet committee on operational counter-measures against the flying bomb

EXCEPT possibly for a few last shots the Battle of London is over. This battle against the flying bomb has been going on now for 18 months.

The inquiry stage

IT was in April 1943 that the Chiefs of Staff sent me four rather vague reports from secret agents which suggested that the Germans were developing a long-range bombardment weapon of some novel type.

I was asked to carry out an investigation to ascertain whether there was any truth in these reports and, if so, to advise what action should be taken.

Throughout this investigation I had the assistance of the intelligence machines of all three Services and the advice of many of our leading scientists and engineers.

Activities at Peenemunde

THESE four reports led us to suspect that the new

to repair them. As they were repaired they were bombed again.

Heavy and persistent air attacks were kept up all through the winter. In the end the Germans abandoned these launching sites altogether and started round about last March, constructing an entirely new series of firing points.

The design of this second series was enormously simplified. Most of the buildings, including the conspicuous storage accommodation for bombs and fuel, were entirely eliminated.

These new sites took only about six weeks to construct, and were so thoroughly camouflaged that it was practically impossible to detect them on air photographs until they had actually fired.

After the destruction of the first series of sites the Germans had to start again from scratch, and it was therefore well into the summer before the second series was completed.

The original defence plan

BY this time our intelligence services had pieced together sufficient information about Hitler's secret V1 to enable us to go ahead with detailed arrangements for the defence of London.

the bomb led us to make certain changes in our defence plans.

The balloon barrage

This is the official V-bomb map showing the range of the various defence lines. Daily Express cartographer has put in the land fighting area.

led to an improvement in the overall results of the combined defences. On the other hand, it restricted the opportunities of the fighters. So many bombs were shot down by the guns on the coast that the number of targets presented to the fighters inland was much reduced.

This is the main reason for the falling off in fighter results since the redeployment in the middle of July.

High-speed interception

IN the battle against the flying bomb our fighters were faced with a number of difficulties. The first was the speed of the bombs. Only our fastest fighters possess the high speed needed to overtake the bomb in level flight.

The other types, in order to obtain an interception, had to dive on to the bomb from several thousand feet above.

The problem of exactly hitting off the correct angle of dive was a very difficult one and could only be mastered with experience.

The flying bombs travelled so fast that it was necessary to maintain constant standing patrols over land and sea throughout the 24 hours, in readiness for any bombs that might come over.

In times of intense activity between 30 and 40 aircraft had to be continuously in the air. This imposed a great strain upon both pilots and machines.

Spotting the bomb

ANOTHER awkward prob-

Fighter Command have good reason to be proud.

Some time ago a special trial was arranged for Hitler in the Baltic. A German fighter ace flying a captured flying bomb demonstrated to the satisfaction of the Fuehrer that flying fighters did not possess the necessary speed to intercept the flying bomb.

They reckoned without the increased efficiency of our latest types and overlooked the superior skill and resource of our pilots.

Attacks from the east

I HAVE told you about our defence measures against flying bombs launched from sites in the Calais and Dieppe areas, that is to say, from the south and south-east.

However, as was noticed by many people, a small proportion of the bombs came to us by night from a due easterly direction.

This puzzled us a little at first, because, so far as we knew, there were no firing sites either in Belgium or Holland. We very soon obtained information that these flying bombs were being launched not from the ground but from aircraft.

Specially adapted Heinkel bombers were carrying the bomb pick-a-back, and launching them from the air over the North Sea. These bombs proved less accurate than those fired from the land.

To meet this new type of attack additional guns were rapidly deployed in the Thames Estuary, and intruder squadrons were sent out each night to patrol over the Dutch and Belgian coasts. At the same time attacks were made upon the sites

On 7 September 1944, Duncan Sandys hosted a boisterous press conference announcing unscripted, 'Except for a last few shots the Battle of London is over.'

The next morning there was a mysterious explosion outside 5 Staveley Road in Chiswick, West London. Three people were killed. Herbert Morrison, the Minister for Home Security, rushed to the scene accompanied by Ellen Wilkinson, MP, his parliamentary secretary – closely followed by Duncan Sandys. There was a news blackout. Six months of rocket bombardment had begun.

On 10 February 1945 Purfleet in Essex, just north of the Thames, was hit by a V2. *Top:* Two young women air raid wardens do their bit in the ruins of a demolished hotel.

Mid-morning on 8 March a rocket hit crowded Smithfield Market in central London. 110 were killed and 123 seriously injured, some of whom are pictured here (*middle*) in the aftermath, waiting to be ferried to nearby Bart's Hospital.

East London took the brunt of the rocket attacks. *Below right:* A turbo-pump by a garden shed in East Ham, on which it fell on 18 September 1944. A V2 combustion chamber survived as 'a rockery and wishing well' in Plaistow for fifty years.

After six years in the Texan desert, Wernher von Braun broke cover in New York City in 1951, at a 'spaceflight' symposium. He is pictured *above* with his young wife Maria, his first cousin, whose von Quistorp family estates had first brought him to Peenemünde. After the triumph of the Explorer I satellite in January 1958 von Braun and his colleagues were national heroes.

One result was the biopic *I Aim at The Stars*. The director was the ex-RAF pilot J. Lee Thompson (*The Guns of Navarone*, *Ice Cold in Alex*). Lionel Bart (*Oliver!*) wrote the love theme lyrics and Laurie Johnson (*The Avengers*) the music. The Jewish comedian Mort Sahl quipped: 'I aim at the stars but sometimes I hit London.'

More myths bloomed when photo interpreter Constance Babington Smith, 'the London WAAF with X-ray eyes', first told her story in America very soon after the war (*bottom*). Such yarns were a convenient cover for Ultra.

handwritten note: 'The sanctity of Ultra would in itself exclude the Colonel.' So there it was again: Ultra was determining who saw and decided what. Mr Sandys's loyal assistant could not be part of the real discussion. The Americans, however, were part of it already.

London, 23–30 July 1944

Sandys now saw the enemy clearly – the Air Ministry. He was beginning to realise, if he had not already, how far certain people would go to exclude him and his expert committee from the intelligence high table. His chief rocket adviser Dr Ellis had stumbled on the truth. He told Sandys with restrained fury on the morning of the 23rd: 'I now learn the Air Ministry had in their possession a number of reports ... no mention has yet been made to us of this vital information.' Lt-Colonel Kenneth Post would spend the next two days trying to put together a summary of what was already known in Monck Street, and had been for weeks past.

Sandys sent Portal a blistering memo that afternoon complaining about the way information had – or had not – reached him. There were the interrogations of the Normandy prisoners, for example, of which he had known nothing until 21 July, when he had heard indirectly of their existence. Then there was the aerial photograph of Blizna, taken on 5 May, showing, according to the opinion of the Air Ministry, a simple concrete firing plinth similar to the one described by the prisoners. Furthermore, 'the discovery of such platforms in the Cherbourg Peninsula was reported on 14 July, but I was not informed about this development until I enquired'.

And there was more. 'As I further learned on 21 July, there is a link between the military organisation in Normandy responsible for long range weapons and the rocket organisation at Blizna and Peenemünde,' wrote Sandys. 'I have as yet received no report on the evidence.'

Rocket reports were multiplying. That same day, 23 July, Group Captain Easton circulated more details of the first Swedish rocket fragments and their analysis thus far at the Royal Aircraft

Establishment, Farnborough. The only clues to the fuels employed were blue and violet stains found in pieces of an aluminium-alloy unit. Most of the fuel-tank fragments were stained a reddish-brown. That could indicate that hydrogen peroxide was the main fuel, but, said the report from the RAE, 'it is almost certainly used to drive the main fuel pump turbine'. The pump itself (and there was a second one, 'badly smashed') was pretty well intact. 'The rotor is splined to a gas turbine shaft. It is noteworthy that the shaft is carried in plain bearings in the pump casing. The bearing surfaces show some signs of scoring but none of seizure.'

As to the main fuel, a nitric acid-aniline combination on the US pattern seemed unlikely. 'A liquid oxygen-alcohol combination is not yet ruled out,' said the report. One very important discovery was that of 'vanes', which apparently 'projected into the jet stream at four points diametrically opposed in pairs'. Thus they might control the flight of the missile in elevation and azimuth.

Here was the golden clue to the rocket's stability. It did not need a launcher: in the first juddering seconds of ignition and lift-off, it guided itself. 'Jet rudders' had figured in the Corncrake decrypt circulated on 1 June. What controlled them? As Jones said in his memoirs: 'Almost in chorus, Bob [Robertson], Charles [Frank] and I shouted out "gyroscopes" ... because we knew that the Germans were using gyroscopic control whereby information about the altitude of the rocket is transmitted via servo mechanisms to the rudders that were placed in the main jet to deflect the stream of gases and thus turn the rocket on to a pre-set trajectory both in bearing and in elevation.' Furthermore, whereas the one intact turbo-pump from the Swedish rocket had no provision for external lubrication, the second one, in spite of being pretty mangled, seemed to have normal arrangements. It could be assumed, then, that cryogenically self-lubricating liquid oxygen was almost certainly one of the fuels.

Gyroscopes, jet rudders, servo-motors, hydrogen-peroxide-powered turbo-pumps and liquid propellants, one of which was supplied by an ingenious pump working at very low temperature: the rocket was giving up its secrets. The biggest remaining puzzle presented by the Swedish wreckage was the extraordinary complexity of the radio equipment.

Having complained that he had not seen any report on the now much-talked-about rocket set-up at Blizna and Peenemünde, Sandys was partially enlightened later in the day when he was shown a copy of the report produced by Air Intelligence's targeting section AI3(e) headed 'The German Flying Bomb Organisation', which gave details of the command connection under LXV Armee Korps of the two long-range weapons. The paper had given a full history of Wachtel's command and how its supply operation was currently working. It was packed with facts about flying bombs derived from the Normandy prisoners. But its opening remarks had concerned 'rocket trials at an SS camp in Poland' and it had given its German name, Heidelager.

Where did this information about the SS and about rockets in Poland originate? Dr Jones had stopped the Cabinet show several times with his revelations, but Sandys had had enough of theatricals. His grumpy list of complaints to Portal on the 23rd, copied to his father-in-law, seems to have brought results. The next day Sandys sent a brusque note to Frank Inglis, the Air Intelligence chief. 'Top Secret "U"' was portentously typed in the top-right-hand corner. It demanded 'as quickly as possible … the most detailed information available from all intelligence sources including MSS. It should also indicate the reasons for associating the organisations and the personnel preparing the rocket sites in Normandy with the activities at Heidelager and Peenemünde.' Duncan Sandys, it seemed, was in the picture.

Inglis passed on the poisoned chalice. The letter rattled around Whitehall and ended up with Matthew Pryor. He wrote a weary covering memo on the 25th addressed to the Bletchley insider, Wing Commander John Mapplebeck: 'It looks as if it falls to me, with the assistance and approval of [Wing Commander] Russell [of AI3(e)] and Jones, to get Prof Norman to look at the draft. I think we must set our face against listing personalities and minor units which are purely "working intelligence" and stick to basic facts … God willing. I will start this evening if you agree.'

In fact, as Professor Norman had predicted, no more Ultra intelligence would be coming out of Blizna. One of the last decrypts detailed Hans Kammler's concern at dismantling the place with his slave labour. On 24 July the last A-4 was fired, as the Red Army drew near. A new testing site in the Tucheler Heide, West Prussia, had been cleared, with a target-impact area 152 miles to the south.

But Corncrake would not be reporting from there. The fabulous bird had flown.

Sandys's latest report, cyclostyled on the 24th for presentation to the War Cabinet Crossbow meeting the next day, began with a coded statement for those who had for so long denied him the full facts. 'During the last few days I have been reviewing the evidence from all sources relating to the German Long Range Rocket,' he said. 'This picture may have to be modified as further information becomes available.' The latest rocket had a warhead of 5–10 tons, 'possibly charged with an improved type of explosive ... The fuel is certainly liquid oxygen and possibly ethyl alcohol.' There was, he went on, an indication of a second, larger rocket under development. No elaborate projector was required. In its initial period of propulsion it was radio-guided with some sort of coded device to make it unjammable.

'The enemy probably has had stocks of at least 1000 and possibly considerably more,' said Sandys. 'Although we have as yet no reliable information about the movement of projectiles westwards from Germany, it would be unwise to assume from this negative evidence that a rocket attack is not imminent.'

This report went to the chiefs' meeting on the morning of the 25th. Colin Grierson's deputy gave it a covering gloss: 'This report is based partly on theory and partly on undigested intelligence.' He advised the chiefs that Dr Jones had not yet given his views on the paper, and suggested that they consult the Air Ministry for their 'detailed comment'.

It was indeed a disastrous mix of speculation and Ultra-derived fact. The Park had delivered a figure of one thousand-plus production rockets (although how they had come to this number could not be revealed), and Sandys's Big Ben scientific subcommittee had endowed them with ten-ton warheads. Ten thousand tons of explosive was pointing at London.

Sandys presented it to the chiefs with the confidence of one who had at last reached the inner ring. He reminded them at the morning meeting of the charges that had been made by Churchill in Cabinet on 18 July. His scientific subcommittee had worked out from first principles that a rocket could be launched from a simple site exactly as was now being suggested by the Air Ministry, who had wasted his scientists' time by holding back evidence for weeks.

Portal interrupted the litany of complaints: 'Is there not a representative of Air Intelligence on your committee?'

'Yes,' said Sandys. 'But that representative cannot [or would not] supply the intelligence required.' And when Dr R. V. Jones could not be bothered to turn up to the committee meetings, Professor Bob Robertson would make an appearance. He himself could not discharge his responsibility properly, Sandys told the chiefs, if he was provided only with 'a periodic digest of intelligence'. Sight of the raw material was essential as and when it was obtained. The Air Staff should no longer permit their intelligence officers to 'delay circulating information until absolutely certain of the reliability of its conclusion on every single point'.

Brooke and Portal made conciliatory noises about moving towards a cooperative effort. Portal thought it perfectly possible that Dr Ellis's scientific subcommittee might see appropriate intelligence 'as long as adequate precautions were made to safeguard the source'.

But why was it all so sensitive? Sandys knew many very secret things from within the Ministry of Supply – about 'Tube Alloys' (codename for the atom bomb), for example, and the production of 'Agent N' (anthrax). He knew about deception. So why could he not be given the unprocessed information on long-range weapons?

One reason was within the nature of the super-secret MSS J series material itself. So much of it was the result of bending the rules, of late-night phone calls and mutual detective work. But even with its 'restricted circulation and close contact with the recipients', the results must be presented as all coming from within 'Source' to get past Park security.* 'The proper way [was] to vet and control recipients, not to interfere with the presentation of the information,' said Professor Norman. Letting others into the charmed circle would compromise the deception.

---

* Several attempts were made to 'infiltrate' junior Bletchley Park officers into Jones's tiny directorate in London, briefed to find Jones's own mysterious 'Source' who seemed to be outguessing everyone. As the German linguist Peter Gray Lucas ('who arrived in the Section [3G(N)] in July 1944 and threw himself with enthusiasm into the A-4 work') wrote in an internal history: 'The strict security placed on all information about secret weapons, while it did not affect our relationship with ADI (Science), meant a great deal of subterfuge in our dealing within and outside BP.'

Dr Jones, meanwhile, with the greatest reluctance, attended Dr Ellis's ghastly Big Ben subcommittee meeting being held that afternoon of the 25th at the Hotel Victoria, just off Whitehall. There was much discussion of the 'terracotta and violet' stains found in the fuel tanks of the Swedish remains, and what they might signify. Jones bluntly confessed that his paper of the 15th was wrong. Fuel was liquid oxygen and alcohol and the warhead was one ton. And as he had told the Crossbow Committee on the evening of the 18th, the number of rockets in existence was over a thousand.

The longest day in the Crossbow intelligence saga, 25 July 1944, was not yet over. Late that afternoon the War Cabinet returned to the existential threat of the rocket. The Prime Minister and the Home Secretary expressed extreme disquiet that a threat whose very existence had been played down by Sir Stafford Cripps eight months before should have erupted with so little warning.

London, 25 July 1944, 18:00 hours

It was time for a reckoning. At the Crossbow Committee meeting that began at six in the Cabinet War Room, Sandys looked especially purposeful. Grierson, Pelly and Jones were the naughty schoolboys caught by the head prefect. Bottomley kept his distance, waiting to see which way the wind would blow. Churchill's mood was at its blackest.

Herbert Morrison opened proceedings with a statement of his worry that the 'intelligence machine' on this subject (by which he meant Air Intelligence's oversight of the rocket) might not have shown 'sufficient consolidation'. 'Information may not have been disseminated rapidly enough to those concerned.' The Secretary of State for Air, Archibald Sinclair, defended his ministry. The important intelligence had only become available after the Swedish rocket crash, he suggested. Churchill disagreed. There had been an abundance of information, which Air Intelligence had just sat on. He was very surprised that it should suddenly have been brought to light that the Germans had a thousand of these things and that, 'instead of a bulky edifice', all that was required to launch them was a mobile mechanism that could be placed on a simple bed of concrete. Then there was the range, which meant that the missile could be fired at London from as far away as the Ardennes.

Jones explained that the Swedish and Polish evidence had become known to him equally suddenly during the week before his report was issued. It was not until certain information was received from Poland that there was any inkling of the numbers that the Germans might have. But the proper question was whether an attack was imminent, Mr Sandys was suggesting. He was doubtful whether the Germans would be able to move men and stores westwards to northern France without Intelligence learning of it.

When Churchill asked what progress Mr Sandys's scientific sub-committee was making, its chairman Dr Ellis replied that it was quite substantial. 'The conclusions from their studies fitted in with the intelligence information which has subsequently been received.' Ellis seemed to be claiming that the intelligence so hard-won by agents, by photo-reconnaissance, by the Park and by thousands of hours of analysis was actually validating their imaginary rocket as presented in Sandys's latest report – namely, a monstrous device with a warhead of perhaps ten tons.

Jones flinched. He admitted later that the expression on his face must have given away his anger. His special contempt was reserved for those advising Sandys, who had 'very little idea of how the rocket was actually designed and constructed'. In his account of the meeting: 'When the expert [Ellis] made his remark, Winston immediately turned to me and asked "Is that true"?' It was not. 'Why isn't it?' Dr Jones catalogued the errors in the statement that had just been made. 'What do you have to say to that?' Churchill asked the hapless Ellis, who 'began to flounder'.

Nevertheless, as the minutes of the tempestuous meeting recorded, Churchill urged that the scientists should get all the information available, 'as long as the source is safeguarded'; Portal added that instructions had been issued to that effect.

Churchill then asked why he had not received any report from Sir Alwyn Crow's Projectile Development Department at the Ministry of Supply. Dr W. H. Wheeler, deputy director of the department, explained that he had written a report three months earlier proving that a 50-ton rocket with a range of 150–200 miles could indeed be designed. But theory was different from practice. His department had been 'deceived by the assumption that cumbersome projection arrangements were necessary,' explained Wheeler. Only now did the evidence from Sweden show the opposite.

It was Sandys's turn to speak. According to him, the two new facts of the greatest importance were the evidence about the mobile firing points and about the employment of liquid oxygen. The thrusting junior minister was already seizing the operational reins. The minutes record that as soon as he heard the second piece of news, he had asked the Ministry of Economic Warfare for a map of production centres and had passed the information to the Air Ministry so that 'they might be made targets for a bombing attack'.

Herbert Morrison now returned to his opening theme, the lack of cooperation between the intelligence-gatherers and the scientists. Sandys assured him that he had discussed the matter with Bottomley and that the proper steps were being taken. But Dr Jones's future looked distinctly uncertain. Alan Brooke thought the whole meeting 'awful'.

Churchill was furious with everybody. His mood could be read by a terse personal minute he sent the chiefs afterwards, in which he returned to the matter of retaliation by gas attack. Where was the position paper he had asked for on 6 July? He demanded one within the next three days and then left the meeting.

Cherwell was at the meeting but said little. Nevertheless, he chose that night to write a long note to Churchill defending the actions of those who had just come in for such a pasting from the 'amateur' Sandys and his camp. He also openly underlined the Ultra background to what Jones had said:

Complaints which you have voiced to the effect that you have not been promptly and fully informed concerning the German long-range rocket by Jones ... the Air Ministry and myself indicate that you have been misled as to the facts ...

Sometime in April we received indications [from Ultra] that the SS were experimenting on flying bombs in Poland

[Kammler's prisoners building ramps for the Luftwaffe]. In May it was said that they were also testing rockets.

In June a certain cipher [Corncrake] was cracked which enabled us to establish that apparatus [Geräte] was being sent from Poland to Peenemünde ... and towards the end of the month this information, combined with agents' reports, raised a suspicion that this apparatus was concerned with rockets.

The Prof then explained how Jones carefully re-examined the photographs of the Polish station (all of which had been available to Sandys) and discovered an object which had been missed by Medmenham and which he recognised as a large rocket. 'He told me about it two days later, when I saw you, [and] when a rocket fell in Sweden many of these bits of evidence fell into place ... I do not believe that the most brilliant brain supported by a collection of inexperienced scientists, however eminent, is likely to make a better job of it than [Jones] has, especially if they cannot be given access to all the most secret evidence.' Cherwell clearly had distinct views of his own on who should be in the picture. To let 'inexperienced scientists' in on the great secret would challenge his status with Churchill.* Cherwell the unworldly boffin could be the most ruthless power broker when it came to it. And Ultra was power.

The battle was rejoined the next day with tempers still short. Frank Inglis did his bit in the morning with a note to Bottomley disparaging the contents of Sandys's report: there was almost certainly no second, bigger rocket, the suggested weight of projectile and warhead was too high, and there was no super-explosive. If there was, why was it not being used on the flying bomb? The whole tone was too pessimistic, he said.

Dr Jones had a more personal fight. On 26 July he sent a minute

---

* It was more than just jealousy. The Prof had personally clashed with Mr Sandys before in Churchill's presence, over the much-vaunted photo electric proximity fuse (it did not work) that he had championed, and which was used by the experimental anti-aircraft rocket battery the Prime Minister's son-in-law had commanded in the defence of Cardiff in 1940–1. And R. V. Jones later indicated that the pre-war Official Secrets rumpus over air defence had also not been forgotten: '[Cherwell] did not like Sandys. There had been all sorts of odd things ... that shemozzle in Parliament when Sandys had used information he had gained as an army officer and exploited as a politician.' C, clearly, also had views.

to Portal: 'I am prepared at any time to answer Mr Sandys's complaints ... both vague and specific. I would be glad of an opportunity to reply in front of competent judges to complaints from any quarter ... If it is substantiated that I am not working in the best way, I will readily resign.'

The whole mess, once again, was attributable to who was or was not Ultra-indoctrinated. 'Professor Ellis has arranged for two members of his committee ... to be shown MSS evidence, contrary to the original arrangement,' complained Jones. This was 'one further step indicating mistrust of our handling of the material we have fought so hard to obtain'.

He ended even more bleakly: 'As we shall undoubtedly be blamed, should the rocket prove a disaster, we might at least be allowed a free run at the intelligence.' The letter went to Portal via Inglis. No reply was immediately forthcoming.

CHAPTER 40

Russian rocket diplomacy was looking much more serene. Everyone was scrambling to get aboard the Blizna train, including Duncan Sandys who had been making overtures ever since the Prime Minister had raised the prospect. On the 24th he informed Bottomley that he wanted to discuss 'composition of the mission', proposing Lt-Colonel T. R. B. Sanders (like himself an Old Etonian, and a Territorial Army artilleryman) of the Ministry of Supply as leader. Indeed, it seemed the whole Crossbow Scientific Committee seemed anxious to be Poland-bound. Geoffrey Vollin, the Sandys protégé, got on the list.

The question of who to send was complicated indeed. Nobody Ultra-indoctrinated could be put in jeopardy, either by capture by the Germans or by some indiscretion at a Moscow diplomatic cocktail party. Bottomley passed the hugely delicate matter to Grierson who responded with a note to Sandys agreeing with the importance of getting Professor Ellis's subcommittee associated with the visit – although the Air Commodore seemed anxious to pass the whole thing over to Inglis.

Jones was furious. 'Instead of the choice of personnel being left to me, it was taken over by Duncan Sandys,' he wrote in his memoirs. 'Air Intelligence officers were included in a balancing rather than a primary capacity.' Flight Lieutenant Wilkinson, veteran of the Stockholm mission, was one of them, and the other was Eric

Ackermann, a radio specialist. The operation had already been rendered ineffectual due to Sandys's involvement, Jones told him, but he was to continue with it as long as there seemed to be any hope.

Getting to Moscow direct was problematic. The party would have to go via the Middle East. Meanwhile, what of Blizna itself? 'We are making inquiries as to when the Russians are expecting to overrun the area concerned so that as little time as possible is wasted waiting at the intermediate post,' said Grierson in an internal memo. It was a shrewd warning.

The UK mission in Moscow cabled the Air Ministry on 26 July. It was all 'agreed at the highest level', and no delay over visas was expected. If there was a hold-up, 'the embassy would ginger up the Russians'. But they should not be accompanied by any Polish interpreter unless he was a British citizen with a British name: 'Soviets most repeat most suspicious of UK émigré Poles.'

The chiefs of staff received the next day a paper from the Air Ministry Director of Signals: 'a listening station [was] established in a suitable area outside the UK in May to intercept control signals from Big Ben ranges in the Baltic. So far no information has been recovered.' Four USAAF P-38 Lightning aircraft were being equipped with search radio receivers to fly over Poland and intercept radio control transmissions during test-firing, the chiefs were told, with specially trained RAF radio observers and US pilots. It was expected that the first flights to Russia would start shortly. But the Lightnings were never sent; the last A-4 had already risen from the Polish woods three days before.

London, 26 July 1944

As July in London neared its end amid the chug of doodlebugs, Herbert Morrison considered what might be yet to come. On the 26th he demanded an urgent examination of all defensive measures: 'If the rocket should be superimposed on the flying bomb, then civil defence could buckle within a matter of days,' he predicted. Panic was in the air.

Cherwell, who had earlier in the day conferred with Jones, sent

Churchill a note indicating that the Home Secretary, backed by the Minister of Health, was going that night to urge the War Cabinet to decide what to do. The Britain-Can-Take-It glue of 1940–1 had come unstuck: Morrison was talking of a mass exodus from London and political breakdown. He produced a six-page memorandum. His experts had concluded that each rocket would kill thirty people, resulting in eighteen thousand fatalities and with the number of seriously injured potentially five times that figure. It would be a catastrophe.

The choices were these: to order the remaining population of London to stand fast – 229,000 had gone already, according to Morrison – to leave further evacuation plans until a time when the scale of bombardment became clear, or to make immediate plans to empty the city (just as he had suggested during the first Great Rocket Flap of November 1943). He thought at least half a million people would choose to leave anyway. 'If an attack were to develop on the scale with which we are now threatened, the exodus might reach proportions such as to present a completely unmanageable problem … I fear the public will become angry [he had been booed by his Hackney constituency on a visit to bombsites] although whether their anger will be directed solely against the enemy may be doubted.'

A public announcement about the rocket was essential, he told Bottomley, 'to encourage a voluntary exodus and to discourage any tendency of people to return to London'. But Cherwell thought this a drastic measure, because, he told the Prime Minister, what little secret evidence there was pointed to a warhead very much smaller than the seven or so tons proposed by Sandys's committee and now being assumed by Morrison. And there was every prospect, he felt, of jamming the rocket's radio control. He was wrong about that, and so was everyone else. But he was right about the warhead. The Prof at last was on the side of the angels.

A grim meeting of the Crossbow Committee was held on the evening of the 28th. Sandys was on the warpath. There had been 'failures of a type we could not afford' in communicating intelligence, he told his colleagues. Was there any more news from Normandy? Jones blustered. His technical staff had not got there until D-Day +20, he said, having been 'diverted to another important installation'.

The minister's bid to control the Sanders mission was deepening with his insistence that a Polish-speaking Englishman accompany them. Professor Ellis's scientific committee appended their present view of the rocket as coming in two sizes and having a seven-ton warhead. Jones was in despair.

The Flakgruppe HQ at Saleux, meanwhile, was happier in its work. 'The devastation in London is becoming greater and greater,' said its diary for 27 July. 'A group of experienced [enemy] agents has been sent to France via Spain, the enemy is desperate to gain insight into our operations. General Heinemann expects that every man will make it his first duty to cooperate in the fight against espionage. Everyone, especially Frenchmen and foreign workers, must be treated with very great suspicion.'

CHAPTER 41

London, 28–30 July 1944

Friday 28 July was an especially tough day in London. At 09:41 a bomb exploded in Lewisham after impacting on a street-level air raid shelter outside Marks and Spencer's. Woolworth's and Sainsbury's were full of shoppers, as was the street market. Fifty-nine people died and a further 124 were seriously injured in this, as it would turn out, the deadliest single V1 incident in south London.

The capital was decanting its under-fives and their mothers to the country. There were still chaotic scenes at the railway stations, Paddington especially becoming notorious for its 'harassed, irritable and thoroughly uncivil' crowds. There was a dangerous crush on 29 July after which twenty people had to be treated at the GWR's first-aid post. Outraged questions were asked in Parliament. And all this before the rocket, of still to be determined destructive power, arrived. The War Cabinet examined 'measures to stimulate evacuation of the priority classes', which now might be extended to include mothers with school-age children; to move patients from London hospitals (without publicity); to make travel plans for the movement of two million people within a period of three or four weeks; and to deal with what was referred to as a large exodus on foot.

The Cabinet thought it appropriate to brief certain newspaper editors so as to 'make the public aware of the possible imminence of rocket attack without [somehow] causing alarm', while 'highly protected accommodation should be got ready for those whose (administrative) war-work compels them to stay in London'. The meeting proposed forming yet another War Cabinet subcommittee; this one to be called Rocket Consequences and to be chaired by Morrison, would report weekly on the rocket threat and recommend measures to deal with its effects.

A welcome rocket, or parts of one, arrived at Hendon airfield in north London on the 28th aboard an RAF transport aircraft from Italy. SOE's Wildhorn operation concerning a pick-up in Poland had come good. Earlier that day a brave Pole called Jerzy Chmielewski had made it to the landing strip near Tarnow, having cycled some two hundred miles carrying a sack of rocket parts, photographs and reports. He could speak no English, and even on touchdown at Hendon he refused to hand over his precious cargo. 'The stalemate lasted for several hours before he obtained the authority to relinquish his collection.' Still on the tarmac, and via a translator, he told one of his first debriefers, Dr R. V. Jones, that many of the rockets that observers had seen fired from Blizna had exploded in the air, something that made the Germans very angry. He brought with him a sketch map of Blizna and the impact site around the village of Sarnaki where a rocket had fallen, plus a collection of 'rumours and miscellaneous information'. It emerged that the fall of a shell was 'accompanied by an explosion on the ground and then after 1–2 seconds, a muffled explosion ... The blast operates for a distance of about 200m, enough to blow a horse six metres and to deafen a man.'

Departing London in the opposite direction almost at the same time was the party heading for the wilds of Poland via Casablanca, Tehran and Moscow. They left on the 29th, after a little Sandys-inspired drama at the airfield (see p. 341), in a USAAF C-87 Liberator transport. The first signal from HQ British Forces Middle East reached the Air Ministry that night: 'Party amalgamating well and very hopeful of good results.' Visas, they had been assured, would be waiting for them on arrival in Moscow. The Americans would be travelling via their air base at Poltava, set up in June for 'shuttle-bombing' missions over Germany flown by long-range aircraft from southern Italy to the Ukraine and back.

Perhaps it would have been better for Dr Jones's career if he had gone with the Poland party (in spite of his Ultra clearance, which meant he was grounded). His 'I will readily resign' memo to Portal of 26 July had yet to elicit a response. According to Cherwell's diary he met with Jones on Tuesday 27 July, but, it would seem, did nothing to restrain him from rocking the boat even more. Jones then wrote another memo, this one to Inglis: 'I can make no stronger protest ... Every step of acquiescence which you have taken to [enable] the invasion of outside bodies has brought us nearer disintegration. Our sources will be mishandled. Collation will be wild and incomplete. Presentation will be political.'

The memo was in his pocket ready to present at a meeting with Assistant Chief of the Air Staff (Intelligence) in Monck Street on the morning of the 30th. Sandys, meanwhile, was moving to ensure that Jones was defenestrated once and for all. He sent Portal another pompous memo moaning about his exclusion from vital intelligence, this time presenting a list of more rocket-linked sites in Normandy with their dates of capture. Why had they not been brought to his attention earlier? And nor had his 'Top Secret "U"'-headed demand of the week before to see the evidence connecting Blizna with Peenemünde been acted on.

Furthermore, his man Sanders, about to fly off to Moscow, had not been informed that 'a Polish expert had arrived in this country bringing rocket parts and photographs', Sandys complained. 'On hearing of this, I informed ACAS (I) who agreed that the head of the Mission should see the Polish expert and arranged a last minute meeting at the aerodrome. The mission had left without any instructions as to whether the Americans were part of it or not. This may lead to friction and confusion.'

Jones did not get a chance to resign – he was sacked. The notification, sent by Inglis to the Crossbow cognoscenti, was brutal in its bureaucratic terseness: 'In view of the number of meetings requiring information on Crossbow and the number of ministries that ADI (Sc) [Jones] has to attend, I have decided that from Tuesday 1 August, [Director of Intelligence (Research)] shall assume responsibility for coordinating the work of those sections in the Branch responsible for Crossbow and providing all external agencies with intelligence they require.' So the newly promoted Air Commodore Jack Easton, D of I (R), who was perceived to have done well with the Swedish rocket business, got the job. But Jones still had his small staff and office in the SIS building, and Professor Norman and Section 3G(N) were still at the Park. He would still see sensitive Medmenham covers under the guise of wireless telegraphy. And, ironically perhaps, he was still on the War Cabinet Crossbow Committee.

According to Jones himself, the fact of his dismissal 'drove any further thought of resignation [as ADI (Science)] from my mind because it brought home to me the mess that might result if I ceased to watch the rocket'. His country needed him. And he was arrogant enough to believe that its capital city, the city of his birth, needed him even more. As he would write: 'I told Inglis that whatever else he might do, he could not remove from me the function of discovering the scientific and technical nature of the rocket . . . I proposed to take my investigation as far as that and write up the account to that stage, come what may.'

Jones cleared his desk at the Air Ministry and went back to 54 Broadway. Inglis would henceforth brief the loathed Scientific Committee. Mr Sandys had won. And, it might appear, he was now in the picture, but to what degree seems to have depended on his father-in-law. On 30 July C sent Churchill a diplomatic decrypt of a cable from the talkative Japanese naval attaché in Berlin discussing the latest gossip on V-weapons. The Prime Minister scribbled on the typescript flimsies: 'Mr Sandys to see these'.

Menzies forwarded them to Sandys with a request that they 'be returned in the enclosed envelope'. The news sent to Tokyo was scrappy but tantalising: 4200 enemy aircraft had been counted attacking V1 installations in a single day, but damage was very slight. Meanwhile, the effect of the revenge-weapon bombardment of London had 'exceeded German hopes, the enemy are doing their best to conceal and censor the effects, and at the same time are beginning to disperse the inhabitants of the capital – seven million of them'.

But the junior minister's clearance went no further. As the *Official History* of wartime intelligence put it: 'Mr Sandys's demand that he and his scientific advisers be shown the raw intelligence, as and when it was obtained, could not be granted. It took no account of the dangers of reaching premature conclusions or of the rules which restricted the circulation of such of the intelligence that was derived from high-grade signals intelligence.' Cherwell had won that point, even if Reginald Jones had been sacrificed in the winning of it. Greater losses were borne to preserve the Ultra secret.

Jones and Cherwell had won that battle, at least. On the evening of the day he left Monck Street, 30 July, Jones wrote his 'First Weekly Summary of Crossbow Intelligence', a kind of Ultra-informed tipsheet for super-insiders. He did it, perhaps, just to show that he was still in business. Its distribution was tiny: Portal, Bottomley, Inglis, Cherwell, Menzies (C) and Sinclair (Director of Military Intelligence). Not Mr Sandys. It reported the latest discoveries in Normandy, the resemblance between the ground works at Château du Molay and those on the Peenemünde foreshore, and the fact that Blizna had shut down because of the Russian advance ('no more MSS Intelligence can be expected from there'). It mentioned a diplomatic decrypt of a cable from the Japanese naval attaché in Berlin saying that the '[German] Army's new torpedo would come into use within 2–3 months'.

The matter of the Blizna–Peenemünde train movements was set out on paper for the first time: 'It will ... be seen that the conclusion that 1000 rockets [were in existence] could not have been drawn before the 14 July [when it hit 18036]', and this had been reported to the War Cabinet Crossbow Committee on 18 July, said Jones. There was no discussion of the weight of either rocket or warhead. Commander Harry C. Butcher, Eisenhower's naval aide, was also writing up his diary. It was pretty wide of the mark but it characterised the way those directing the war at the highest level were thinking and the kind of information they were getting. His entry for 31 July read: 'A special crew in one of our Flying Fortresses [the Wildhorn mission] flew to Poland, landed and picked up pieces of one of the rockets obtained by our agents. Our intelligence people deduce that it really weighs fifty tons and presumably carries some ten tons of explosive which would wreck a five mile area. This would play hell in London.'

Dr Jones would have despaired at the wild exaggeration, but he was now in exile. His self-proclaimed mission 'to continue to watch the rocket', however, could not have been better timed. Churchill was still thrashing around: memos flowed from No. 10 about using butane on the launch sites, while the Air Ministry laboured over various plans on how to tip German civilian morale over the edge or to somehow go after the Nazi leadership.

Churchill's brusque note to the chiefs on 25 July demanding answers on an offensive gas attack was rewarded three days later with a report based on the advice of the Joint Planning Staff. Attacks on German cities with phosgene would kill 5–10 per cent of the population and civil defence personnel, it stated starkly, and mustard-gas attacks would induce wholesale evacuation (which might not be effected in time), resulting in many casualties.

Should the Allies *initiate* chemical warfare, the enemy would respond at once in the field and against the United Kingdom with aircraft, flying bombs and rockets. Public morale in England in those areas that might be affected was less resilient than it had been, said the report.

Cherwell a little later reported stocks of 14,000 tons of mustard gas on hand, plus 12,000 tons of mustard in US hands in Britain, as well as 6000 tons of phosgene – 'enough to achieve effective contamination of 900 square miles, more than the areas of Berlin, Hamburg, Cologne, Essen, Frankfurt and Cassel put together'. On paper all this looked like a dry statistical exercise, but in fact, for months past thousands of chemical-factory workers had been toiling, tanker-trains running day and night, and many hundreds of British and American air ordnance personnel had been preparing the filling depots and bomb dumps close to bomber airfields in eastern England. As an exercise in industrialised lethality, the gas-attack plan had none of the rocket's technical elegance, but in terms of the numbers it held under deterrent threat it was far more deadly.

There was an annexe to the chiefs' paper headed 'Biological Warfare', which added another dimension. 'If the claims of "N" [anthrax] are substantiated, its use would probably make a material change in the war situation,' said the analysts. 'If it can be used in practice, its effect on morale will be profound. It would cause heavy casualties, panic and confusion. It might lead to a breakdown in administration with a consequent decisive outcome on the outcome of the war.' But there were practicalities to consider.

Anthrax was not yet ready to use as a weapon although it would be within six months, when American production had peaked.* 'On balance,' concluded the chiefs, 'we do not believe that for us to start chemical or biological warfare would have a decisive effect on the result or the duration of the war against Germany.' The chiefs' committee secretary General Ismay reinforced the view that although the Germans might keep control of their population under gas attack, the 'same cannot be said for our own people'. Look at the efforts necessary to alleviate '*the very light scale of attack of the flying bombs*', he said.

Churchill, very grudgingly, accepted this conclusion. He wanted the matter brought up again 'when things get worse'.

Three days later, C sent the Prime Minister one of his special personalised selections of that day's Ultra traffic. Churchill in turn bid the SIS chief send it to Ismay, just so that everyone should be of the same mind. It was a diplomatic decrypt of a signal from the Reich Foreign Ministry to all stations, sent six days before:

England started this bombing war against the civil population, killing tens of thousands of German women and children. We are resolved to continue operations without pause during the coming months and, if must be, years, to reduce all southern England to ruins.

---

* Guy Liddell, Director of MI5 B Division, would write in his diary for 24 August 1944: 'I saw C today about the uranium bomb and put it to him we use the suggestion that it should be used as a threat of retaliation to the Germans if they use V2. C said that he could see no reason to think V2 was imminent although it was possible to think it might start in the near future. He felt however there was nothing to be lost and he would put this suggestion to the PM.'

CHAPTER 42

London, July 1944

The deceivers' plan to shift the Flakgruppe's target had been advanced. On 22 July, John Drew of the Home Defence Executive told Ian Jacob, Military Assistant Secretary to the War Cabinet: 'We have drafted a report proposing a shift of the Mean Point of Impact from North Dulwich to a point six miles to the south east.' In fact it ended up in suburban Beckenham.

Two days later, Sir Samuel Findlater Stewart produced a report showing how the density of shot falling in the Whitehall area would go down from 2.8 to 0.7 per square mile. In Bromley it would rise from 1.7 to 2.3, but there were no ministries in Bromley. He dutifully rehearsed the Ministry of Home Security's counter-arguments in his paper for the chiefs of staff, while insisting that they had no objection to leaving the MPI where it was – in poor old Dulwich – or trying by any other means to prevent it moving north to central London.

This time the chiefs agreed with the plan to move the MPI and Ismay informed the Prime Minister accordingly. But in view of the confidentiality of the matter (the special agents' role), he advised that only Herbert Morrison and the Minister of Production Oliver Lyttelton should be consulted. Mr Churchill duly did so on 28 July. The ministers, however, were not prepared to accept responsibility for deliberately redirecting the enemy attack against a specific part of London. This did not inhibit the deceivers, who would not give up. They were going ahead anyway. On 31 July Stewart insisted that mere uncoordinated confusion 'would compromise our agents'. The same day Drew wrote to Jacob urging him to get the chiefs to make up their minds, as they were getting into serious difficulties 'keeping our special agents supplied with material'.

Agent Garbo, meanwhile, after his invented brush with the Metropolitan Police, had been told by his control to stay away from the V1 investigation and take no more risks. Brutus had been similarly instructed, it might have been recalled. On 29 July Señor Pujol was informed by radio that the Führer had awarded him the Iron Cross for his 'extraordinary merit'. Agents Zigzag, Tate and Treasure (otherwise Eddie Chapman, Danish-born Wulf Schmidt aka Harry Williamson, and Nathalie Sergueiew, a Frenchwoman born in St Petersburg) now took up the flying-bomb burden. As the only agent not directly involved in the Fortitude deceptions, Zigzag spent July and August recording the fall of flying bombs; or rather, an MI5-provided driver called Jock Shortfall did, taking pictures of bomb damage with a Leica camera that Chapman had brought with him from Germany – a pub damaged in Windsor, rubble-strewn street corners, that sort of thing. Actually sending the photographs on to Lisbon was later deemed too useful to the Germans.

Duncan Sandys intervened dramatically with a paper to Churchill on 2 August. It contained tables and statistics (provided by Cherwell's researchers) showing that if the Germans corrected their aim to Charing Cross, casualties would increase by four thousand a month, but if they shortened their range they might fall by twelve thousand. The enemy should therefore be persuaded to roll back their target to the limit of the other southern suburbs. Poor old Beckenham was back in the firing line.

Bansin, August 1944

The aftermath of the failed plot to kill the Führer spun the rocket's fate into a new trajectory. Generaloberst Friedrich Fromm, head of the Reserve Army and the Army Ordnance Department (the Waffenamt), had been fatally compromised by the events in Berlin as the coup unravelled. To humiliate the army, whence the conspiracy derived, Fromm was replaced by Himmler. The Reichsführer-SS was now the titular head of the Waffenamt and thus of the rocket's development.

On 1 August the army made a counter-move to protect their most prestigious project by giving the Peenemünde operation a new name: it was now the Elektromechanische Werk, with Paul Storch of Siemens at its head and Wernher von Braun as his deputy – a private company effectively owned by the armaments ministry. On the 4th Himmler promoted Hans Kammler to the rank of SS Gruppenführer. Two days later he made him A-4 Plenipotentiary with a portentous message: 'I am putting you in charge of all of the execution of all preparations for achieving the operability of the A-4 ... you are responsible only to me.' Albert Speer protested in vain.

Blizna had been evacuated. The air-burst problem was unresolved, and work had been transferred to a new range, the Heidekraut in West Prussia, where operations were run from the same train that had been at Blizna.

But poor old Walter Dornberger – as if air-bursts were not enough to worry about, he had already been removed from control of the rocket in the field and now seemed to be losing his life's work to this SS superman. 'I felt like a man who has devoted years of toil and affection to making a superb violin,' he wrote in his 1952 memoirs, 'a masterpiece which only needs tuning, and then has to look on hopelessly as the instrument is grabbed by an unmusical oaf.'

He took a few days' leave at breezy Bansin, the bathing spa on Usedom, to consider his position – and drafted his resignation. But it was not to be: 'That afternoon von Braun and Steinhoff came to tea,' he wrote. 'They lectured me for hours, telling me I ought not to leave with the crisis just coming on. Not to desert the ship ... stick at it ... to assure our place in the history of technology ... help Kammler ... save what could be saved. The A-4 had to be developed to perfection and delivered fit for action.'

London, 1–14 August 1944

While the Germans squabbled and Dornberger considered his position at his seaside villa, egos in London were proving just as fragile. The issues at stake were existential – not least, the argument over the weight of the rocket. The perception by Mr Sandys's scientists of a warhead of as much as ten tons put the survival of the capital at the centre of the direction of the war. The chiefs of staff, their advisers, the air staff and Lord Cherwell laboured on their plans to retaliate with mass gas attacks. The grim mood was reinforced by the stalemate at the invasion bridgehead in northern France.

Then on 26 July the Americans had begun their epic breakout, Operation Cobra, at the western end of the Normandy lodgement. After intense fighting, the Anglo-Canadian grind into Caen at last seemed to be working. Churchill's mood was brightening by the hour. On the 29th his attention was drawn to London bus drivers and what they should do when caught in a doodlebug alert. Abandon bus or drive on? 'You cannot leave every bus driver to decide what to do himself, especially when his passengers may disagree with his solution,' he told the Home Secretary. Admiral Cunningham recorded the bus conundrum in his diary, along with the observation that the more he saw of Herbert Morrison 'the more I despise him'.

The Rocket Consequences Committee met again on 3 August with Morrison in the chair. The Health Minister confirmed that mothers with school-age children (five-plus) were now to be encouraged to leave. Ernest Bevin, the Minister of Labour, expressed concern that this would lead to 'a serious loss of juvenile labour', suggesting that hostels could be provided for boys and girls aged fourteen or more who had to remain in London. And the evacuation of mothers 'would make difficulties in obtaining women to work in catering establishments, laundries etc.' But a potential lack of waitresses seemed inconsequential when viewed in the context of the Health Minister's prediction that two million people might soon be on the move – on foot, if necessary. Although a stand-fast policy should be publicly proclaimed, there must be some organisation to cope with what he called an 'unofficial panic exodus'.

No one doubted the rocket was coming – not even Cherwell. 'There is some evidence that a thousand things connected with rockets (which may be rockets) have been made,' he wrote to Brendan Bracken, the Information Minister, on 1 August. 'The intelligence evidence ... indicates one ton or a bit more. The more pessimistic scientists ... claim they could make a rocket carrying five to seven tons [although] none of them has made a rocket that ever flew at all.'

But the assumption of a five-ton-plus warhead was still driving higher policy. Sandys's Crossbow Committee considered the evidence from the Bois de Baugy on 4 August, to be informed that the retrieved trolley, when examined at Farnborough, indicated that the rocket it was designed to handle might weigh twelve tons. The reconstituted Swedish fragments, however, were now pointing to a warhead of four tons. The scientific subcommittee hesitated to go lower when they met on the 1st. Why would the Germans go to such trouble to make something so complicated and expensive with a warhead no bigger than the flying bomb?

In the first week of August, Medmenham threw a new ingredient into the intelligence mix. Interpretation report No. BS 780 released on the 4th was a reappraisal of past covers in the light of the disclosures from Normandy, specifically to 'obtain information covering the vertical firing of the A-4 rocket'. All sorts of interesting things had turned up at Blizna – a little tank, lots of cylindrical objects, and 'a contraption 20 feet in length which resembles the trolley reported at Bois de Baugy'. But by 27 July all the evidence pointed to the site having been totally abandoned, the CIU reported. Wreckage seemed to be strewn at random. Given the new understanding of vertical launch and of the *Meillerwagen* (transporter-erector), going over old Peenemünde covers (of which there were many more than of Blizna) also gleaned plenty of retrospective evidence of rockets in vertical positions, plus trolleys 'previously referred to as "cradles"' pointing away from 'the upright objects'. One horizontal object earlier labelled 'cradle' was now identified as 'a dazzle-painted rocket' lying on its trolley.

Two sets of road layouts like that at the Château du Molay were discernible at Peenemünde, 'marked out for demonstration or training purposes', according to the CIU. Identical rail tanks and flat wagons could be seen at both locations. All this was helpful, but did not answer the warhead question.

Then came a piece of luck. A prisoner turned up, a Waffen-SS Rottenführer (corporal) captured in France, who turned out to have been an electrical fitter at Peenemünde. Unusually, in the report of what he had to say to the expert interrogator Denys

Felkin, he was not named – perhaps because the information he gave was so exceptionally revealing. Felkin scribbled a note on the Vice Chief of the Air Staff's copy: 'This is about the best and possibly most authentic report on the V2 yet to hand.'

It was indeed pretty good. The prisoner had worked in the wind-tunnel section. The rocket structure was like a Zeppelin, made of light alloy, he said. There were two propulsive fuels, alcohol and liquid oxygen. On test, the rocket was fuelled at the last minute to avoid the valves icing up. The high-explosive warhead, he said, weighed only *one ton*. A six-wheeled lorry raised the missile to the vertical on a cone-shaped firing platform, the *Bodenplatte*. He had never actually seen the rocket on its firing stand, but when it was about to take off a deep droning noise was heard, then a cloud of steam was seen to rise above the woods between the firing point and the point from which the prisoner had observed what he could of the spectacle.

The rocket then rose slowly on a line close to the vertical, somewhat wobbly as it left the ground but within a few seconds all instability had gone. The power burn lasted 50–60 seconds, the entire flight 5–6 minutes. Guidance was by a wireless beam device, the *Leitstrahl*, aided by synchronised frequency changes in the ground transmitter and in the on-board receiver to make it immune to jamming.

When he had been there, the corporal continued, half the launches had failed. After the August 1943 air raid the Luftwaffe took their flying bomb to Brüsterort near Königsberg, he added. The wind-tunnel section was going to move to somewhere near Munich.

He listed Peenemünde personalities including Stegmaier, von Braun, Hermann who was in charge of the aerodynamic section, a certain Dr Reidel, 'a fattish man of 38 in charge of the firing points'; there was also a second Reidel, whose function was uncertain, and a Professor Oberth, the elder statesman of the whole business. Police were constantly on patrol, he said; 'Gestapo agents mingled in civilian clothes with the workmen, and a word out of place resulted in a visit to the concentration camp.'

Of all the intelligence that had emerged in July, the fact that liquid oxygen could be one of the rocket's fuels was perhaps the most significant. Up to the 16th even Dr Jones had still been proposing hydrogen peroxide as the primary propellant. The Waffen-SS electrical fitter had said it used liquid oxygen, as had the chemical warfare specialist Helmut Müller. Reading across the reports that mentioned 'liquid air' or something similar, they all pointed to much more modest weights for both the rocket and the warhead than those favoured by Duncan Sandys's experts.

The answers to every outstanding mystery might yet lie in the debris of Blizna. The Sanders mission's journey had taken them via Cairo to Tehran, where they were now waiting in dusty frustration for the promised visas. Within a couple of days most of them had gone down with dysentery.

Moscow, August 1944

Rocket diplomacy had thus far been conducted directly between Churchill and Stalin. Like many of the A-4 launches themselves, it was about to lurch off into the unknown. Alerted by the stream of messages from Churchill, on 4 August Stalin had ordered Aleksei Ivanovich Shakhurin, the People's Commissar for the Aviation Industries, to get his staff to Debica before the British showed up. Boris Yevseyevich Chertok, a young engineer with NII-1, the principal Scientific Research Institute in Moscow (the nearest Soviet equivalent to Peenemünde or Farnborough), recalled fifty years later:

> In July 1944, we Soviet missile specialists who had been working at NII-1 knew nothing about the test range in Poland and had virtually no idea about the A-4 missile. [It could be inferred] from Churchill's letter [of 12 July] to Stalin that the English only had vague notions about the missile ... Our troops had the opportunity to capture the Germans' most secret weapons, about which the English intelligence service knew more than ours. We could not allow that, and our specialists received an order to inspect everything that could be inspected before the English would be allowed in.

That same day, 4 August, the Soviet State Defence Committee ordered Major General P. I. Fedorov, the director of NII-1, and members of his staff to get to the Blizna area as soon as possible. Military intelligence reported that it was still occupied by SS troops, but they seemed to be evacuating. The group departed Moscow by air the next morning. Also on his way to south-east Poland on Stalin's orders, to keep an eye on things, was General I. A. Serov, Deputy Minister of Internal Affairs for Counterintelligence.

There was another way of beating the British – delay them. Accordingly, the Sanders team stuck in Tehran were granted visas only on 4 August, then the Russians failed to provide an aircraft. The Foreign Secretary Anthony Eden cabled the embassy in Moscow to express deep concern at the delay, as he had 'hoped that Marshal Stalin's personal interest in the mission would have facilitated the Soviet authorities in issuing the necessary instructions'. It worked. The following day, the Foreign Office was able to instruct Sanders to prepare to fly his mission from Tehran to Moscow.

But meanwhile, General Federov's experts were going to need some help in interpreting the few cryptic remains the Germans had left – if they could find anything at all in the woods around Blizna. So far, nothing. There were those in Moscow who suspected the whole rocket alarm was a trick to get a team of Anglo-American observers onto 'their' front line.*

London, 7–10 August 1944

Dr Jones had huffily decried the Sanders mission as a Sandys-inspired stunt. He would rather pursue the existing intelligence, the fuel clue especially. As he put it in his second weekly newsletter on 6 August: 'Every source which has given liquid oxygen and alcohol as the fuels has put the warhead at 1–2 tons.' This was

---

* In one distinguished Soviet rocket scientist's considered view: 'In many respects for our future [rocket building] activities, Churchill's appeals to Stalin were truly decisive. If not for his letters, our victorious army would have moved right past these Polish marshlands and forests without investigating what the Germans had been doing there.'

supported, he said for his Ultra-cleared readers, by 'J evidence [Section 3G(N)'s output] from Blizna'. There had been the Corncrake-derived clue of the one-tonne 'Elephant' warheads, and on 12 July the Park had circulated a decrypt mentioning 'measure for 4300 kilograms of *A-Stoff*. If this was indeed liquid oxygen, the rocket's total fuel weight would be around eight tons. Hut Three had cut the rocket down to size.

An Air Intelligence report on the 7th gave news of Flight Lieutenant David Nutting's discovery of plans of rocket storage sites at Hautmesnil: 'A plan of a light railway through one of the galleries showed the outline of a rocket 45 feet long in trolleys similar to those found at the Bois de Baugy ... Other documents give details of a dismountable steel and timber base plate.' It was all getting clearer.

The Joint Crossbow Committee on which sat the cerebral Americans Dr Bob Robertson and Captain Walt Rostow, plus Wing Commander John Mapplebeck from the Park now transferred to London, represented a collection of diverse brainpower as robust as any directed at the whole secret-weapons matrix. Their job was not to find ways of attacking it, to find targets for bombing, but to find some choke point or weak link in the production chain. Was there, perhaps, some particular factory?

One of their first recommendations was to suspend attacks on flying-bomb launching sites altogether, a move immediately overruled by Norman Bottomley. He could not allow the enemy to have freedom of action at the sites, he said, while the hunt went on for some magical way of disrupting the flow of flying bombs based on what he called 'hypothetical assumptions and inadequate intelligence'. Politics, as ever. Churchill had told the Commons on 2 August: 'We press to the utmost our counter-offensive measures'. Something must be seen to be being done. What about bombing gyroscope production? What about electronics? The intelligence was too slight, their manufacture too fragmented. The same went for alcohol production, dispersed around fifty plants in northern France alone (it was distilled from potatoes). Hydrogen peroxide had been briefly fashionable as a target, but liquid oxygen was a different matter. It was difficult to make and difficult to transport. Was it the weak link?

On 10 August the Joint Committee drafted its first list of

liquid-oxygen production and transport targets. Most of them were in Belgium. At the same time the Special Operations Executive was working on its own counter-liquid-oxygen campaign, to be effected by air-drop-aided Resistance groups. When he saw the target list, Air Vice Marshal Alan Ritchie, SOE's air adviser, asked for the bombing of one plant in Belgium to be deferred: 'We have already briefed and sent in a special agent to undertake sabotage in this factory.' But a note scribbled on the document reads: 'Ritchie has agreed to withdraw this agent at once.' SOE longed to get to grips with the Crossbow target in France, in Belgium, in Holland, in Poland, but there was nothing it could do in the heart of darkness itself – Germany

But perhaps something *could* be done. The same Joint Crossbow meeting that had examined liquid oxygen as a target on 10 August also recommended a high-priority attack on the 'believed rocket factory at Weimar–Buchenwald'. It noted that 'extremely circumstantial reports have for some time located the manufacture and assembly of the large rocket in the Weimar–Nordhausen area'.

One of these circumstantial reports came from the Frenchman that Denys Felkin had interrogated in early July, the emissary of Pierre Julitte (see p. 228) who had reached the Normandy beachhead and got his precious scrap to London. An aerial torpedo, twenty-two metres long and one metre in diameter, 'designed for the long-range bombardment of England' was being made, it said. It incorporated radio equipment and small swept-back fins: 'The torpedoes are stored underground, near the factory.' 'Probable underground facilities are noted on the analysis of aerial photographs,* and the entrance to these facilities can be recommended as one aiming point for attack,' said Captain Walt Rostow, who as committee secretary signed off the report. To reinforce the point about a possible underground factory the Park decrypted a message of 12 August that looked obscure, but was of great significance: 'Unterscharführer Erich Becker is to be sent at once to Sonderbauvorhaben [special building project] SS Fuhrungsstab

---

* The Nordhausen–Niedersachswerfen area had been covered by RAF photo-reconnaissance missions on 6 March and 7 July. Renewed analysis of the prints in August showed two railway lines going into the hillside 'with no exit on the SE side', plus a 'large hutted camp to the west of the camouflaged entrances'. This was Dora.

B13 Nordhausen, by order of SS Gruf. und Generalleutnant der Waffen SS Dr Ing [Engineer] Kammler.'

They did not quite know it yet, but the Park had found the Mittelwerk. All-source intelligence had discovered the rocket foundry under its carapace of gypsum even before the first A-4 was directed at London.

CHAPTER 43

The complete understanding of the rocket, from its point of manufacture to its method of operation, was tantalisingly close. Since the invasion of Normandy, a huge contribution had been made by the interrogation of prisoners.

The British army's chief rocket sleuth, Lt-Colonel Matthew Pryor of MI14, suggested on 10 August that as the rocket was emerging as a German army–Waffen SS operation, it was right that any prisoners should be interrogated by the War Office's MI19. The Air Ministry had no objections to such an arrangement. Pryor added this comment about the 'anti-Nazi architect' who had put his hands up on the afternoon of D-Day: 'The report on P/W Lauterjung has been the cornerstone of the whole structure which we have now built up concerning the mobile operation of the big rocket, and was therefore as near to be being a war winner in a single report as I have yet met.' So Dr Jones was not as indispensable as he thought – but the opportunity for him to show that he still might be was looming.

The War Cabinet Crossbow Committee, of which he was still a member, met on the evening of 10 August (this was the big political committee – not the 'Joint Crossbow' gathering of Anglo-US airmen and analysts which had met earlier in the day).

Herbert Morrison took the chair. Air Commodore Easton representing Air Ministry (Intelligence) made 'a limited and factual

statement'. Then Dr Ellis, Jones's special *bête noire*, made some
small concession towards reducing the weight estimate, but still
would not go below twenty tons overall. The weight of the missile
was again the subject of discussion. Opinion seemed unchanged,
until Jones spoke: his description of a rocket of twelve tons total
including a one-ton warhead met, he said, with a 'generally incredulous reception'. Once again he had stopped the show. Now it was
Air Ministry orthodoxy. 'The best secret intelligence on the warhead gives a normal weight of one ton,' Frank Inglis told the chiefs
on the 12th, and his report got more or less everything else right –
including the launch technique.

The 14th saw a comeback for a casualty of earlier feuds.
Norman Bottomley brought back Air Commodore Claude Pelly to
the Air Ministry as Director of Operations (Special Ops), while
Easton was moved sideways to be Frank Inglis's representative on
the Joint Crossbow Committee. Jones, who had managed to alien-
ate almost everyone, stayed on the fringes.

But Jones was right about the warhead when almost everyone
else was still wrong. Cherwell, whose own conversion was complete after a visit to Farnborough to see the Swedish rocket, fed his
protégé's one-ton-maximum warhead conclusion to Churchill on
15 August in a note headed 'Big Ben'. The Prof also noted: 'When
it is remembered that each rocket carries a 1000 hp turbine, at least
two gyros working servo motors to control vanes in the jet and on
the fins, two radio receivers, three transmitters etc and all for the
sake of bringing the same warhead to London as does the flying
bomb, Hitler would, I think, be justified in sending to a concentration camp whoever advised him to persist in such a project.'

But thus far the rocket's rationale had defeated attempts at
understanding it by any logical analysis. Toiling on a long position
paper, Dr Jones was now attempting to do just that. It would turn
out be his masterwork, but it would hand the victory to his
enemies.

The deception issue was still not resolved. Morrison dug in even
more: 'If the gravity of what [is] being done should ever come out,
there might be most serious political consequences,' he minuted.
When Sandys's own deception paper had gone to the War Cabinet
on 9 August, discussion had turned on how poorly built south-east

London's houses were and thus how heavy the casualties might be. The proposal came up again two days later, but no conclusion was reached other than that there should be no change from the policy of leaving the enemy thinking his aim was more or less correct.

At the Cabinet meeting of the 15th, Attlee took the chair. Slowly the truth trickled out: the deceivers had been manipulating the position all along. Present were Morrison, Sandys and Anthony Eden, the nominal political head of MI5, but not Jones. Morrison was especially passionate in his opposition. The deceivers won a compromise. Sir Samuel Findlater Stewart was informed by W. S. Murrie of the War Cabinet secretariat afterwards: 'You should continue to convey to the enemy information that will confirm his belief that he has no need to lengthen his range. You are at liberty, within limits, to take what steps you may judge safe to intensify this belief.'

At a meeting of the Twenty Committee on 17 August, the super-deceiver John Drew (who would head Britain's postwar deception operations) was more explicit. A directive, he said, had been obtained, 'namely to prevent the enemy from moving his aim towards the north-west and, to a slight extent, to attempt to induce him to move it towards the south-east'. So the deceivers had their charter after all, even if it was only a partial one. They had been acting all along as if they had one anyway.

Was it really to be hoped that the flying bomb might be being beaten? As Churchill had told the Commons on 2 August: 'We are sure that our defences are gaining in power ... I fear greatly to raise false hopes but I no longer feel bound to deny that victory may come perhaps soon.'

In fact, the beginning of August had seen the Flakgruppe's finest hour. Their greatest single effort had culminated in thirty-eight sites opening fire. As the war diary for 2–3 August had crowed: '316 missiles fired overnight, heaviest attack to date'. The results of the onslaught took four days to come through from the agents in London and from the press reports, the diary explained, but Wachtel's men were jubilant. 'The bombs came in waves, the defences had one of their worst days since the beginning of operations, especially as the attacks were favoured by a heavy cloud layer over the Channel' (in fact only 107 out of the 316 launched during the period reached their target).

For 10 August the diary reported: 'Waffen-SS General Kammler appointed by the Führer as representative for special weapons paid a visit to the Regiment to orient himself on V1 operations.' There was a Propagandakompanie cameraman on hand to record the immaculately uniformed Kammler strutting around the Saleux headquarters, built by concentration camp labour, with SS aides and Luftwaffe officers beaming at the rosy prospects of the new Revenge order.

But they had better get a move on. The Allied armies in France were pressing in from the west. The Park got a fleeting break into Luftwaffe messages via the Jerboa key and on the 15th circulated a decrypt showing a comprehensive movement of launch units eastwards. There were mentions of 'the demolition plan'; and an infantry officer veteran of the Russian front 'who had been sworn to secrecy' was on his way to teach defensive infantry tactics and 'the use of light Flak in ground fighting'. It was clear where this was going.

On the 16th Mr Sandys told the War Cabinet:

Since 14 August there have been practically no launches from south of the Somme. The pressure of the battle front has forced the enemy to concentrate his flying bomb effort exclusively in the Pas-de-Calais. But thanks to the flexibility of his organisation he has effected this reorientation without any apparent restriction of his scale of effort. The HQ is being moved from Amiens [Saleux] to a place near Brussels.

The Air Ministry reported the next day: 'Following a week of the maximum flying bomb activity, the scale of attack ending at 06:00 on the 15th was the lowest level yet recorded. London had its quietest week since the attacks began with only 20 per cent of those launched penetrating to the area.'

The July arrivals that had come in over the Thames estuary were also giving up their secrets. On 1 August, Dr Jones had put out a one-page report for his tiny readership. It apologised for circulating a judgement in April in which radar tracks associated with a device being tested at Peenemünde had been ascribed to a glider weapon. This was now revealed to be nothing less than an air-launched flying bomb. (No wonder, then, that photo-reconnaissance had found no ground launch sites for flying bombs in Belgium or Holland.)

And here was the proof. In the past few weeks the Luftwaffe bomber unit III/KG 3 had been 'advised of flying bomb activity'. Moreover, post-damage assessment photography of the previous week's raid on Peenemünde (attacked by the US 8th Air Force on 18 July and on 4 and 25 August) showed three aircraft plus a flying bomb, all clearly associated with airborne launching trials. On 3 August, the Park delivered this seemingly inconsequential scrap: 'Now known that a Heinkel 111 at present at Verrelsbuch with third Gruppe KG3 underwent structural alterations at Stuttgart–Boeblingen at beginning August. Comment from DDI3 [Deputy Director of Intelligence]. Believed that Heinkels are modified at this airfield to take flying bombs.' There could be no doubt after that.

Dr Jones did another piece of retrospective detection by re-examining earlier Ultra decrypts. Transmissions from the Insect radar station showed air-launch trials over the Baltic beginning in April. These had become most intense from mid-May to mid-June, then had slackened off when whoever was working up the technique had presumably been declared combat-ready, in Jones's opinion. He was right.

London, 25 August 1944

The day Paris was liberated was a day of yet more grinding committee meetings in London. On 25 August Mr Sandys chaired two Crossbow Committee meetings in succession at the Cabinet Office. The first concerned the rocket; the second, flying bombs. Air Commodore Easton reported that a senior German prisoner had revealed it was intended to launch rocket attacks by mid-September or possibly earlier. Lt-Colonel Pryor thought that no detectable early warning would be given by the movement of stores or personnel. Jones was at both meetings, but said nothing.

Cherwell stressed the importance of establishing an electronic listening-post in Sweden to establish codes and remote-control techniques (he was pursuing the wrong hypothesis – that the rocket was radio-controlled). In an interesting exchange about what the public should be told, the Prof pointed out that various authorities were progressing plans on the basis of a ten-ton warhead, and asked: 'Should not some publicity be given to the one-ton warhead thesis so as to reassure the public?'

But Sandys pointed out that the Civil Defence Committee's presiding anxiety was to '*prevent* evacuees returning to London ... and the rocket threat was to some extent useful from this point of view'.

On that day too, the tiny speck of intelligence about air torpedoes being made at Buchenwald expanded into an attack by the 8th Air Force in which seven out of ten prisoner-operated workshops were destroyed; they then attacked Peenemünde for the third time. Test stand VII was damaged, and five liquid-oxygen plants in Belgium and northern France including the one at Tilleur-Liège were also attacked by the 8th on the 25th. In its turn, the RAF attacked that old rocket chimera, the Adam Opelwerk at Rüsselsheim near Frankfurt.

The next day, 26 August, Dr Jones circulated his big rocket report – thirty thousand words, and a month in the making. Forty cyclostyled copies were made, number 1 for the Prime Minister, number 21 for Mr Sandys. Unlike with Jones's weekly newsletter, Ultra-derived intelligence was carefully concealed.

The report comprised a history of the intelligence attack, a discussion of technique, a history of development and production, a discussion of the rocket in operation; organisation, deployment, scale and date of attack, plus a note on policy and an epilogue. It stated its purpose as being 'to assemble from the many fragments of information gathered by the intelligence services a general and truthful picture of what the enemy has done'.

It began with a brisk romp through the intelligence story, from the great secret-weapon scare of 1939 to April 1943, 'when our best potential source in the German Air Signals Experimental Regiment fortuitously became active once again'. Then Jones précised all the false trails and misinterpretations, instanced the eighty-ton cordite-powered rockets, the flying bombs referred to as rockets by the French source, then described the breakthrough

when the hunt for a flying-bomb installation at Blizna put them on
the trail of a second long-range weapon in the Polish forests. He
recapped the stories of the Swedish rocket, of the fragments that
came from the swamps of the River Bug in Poland, the information
from prisoners, the capture of documents and sites in Normandy,
the dual-fuels question, the turbo-pump, the firing from simple
sites, the tactical mobility, and at last an accurate prediction of the
weight of the warhead at around one ton.

The report gave a speculative list of supposed production centres, with as many as five hundred widely dispersed subcontractors.
'There is also said to be an "M" works somewhere in central
Germany which is a main assembly point,' he said. 'Ground sources
have reported that there is an underground factory named Dora in
central Germany engaged in making secret weapons. An extensive
new factory which corresponds well with the ground information
has been found in a wood four and half miles NW of Weimar. This
may well be connected with A-4 construction.'

Towards the end his paper changed mood, presenting a philo-
sophical discourse on what the enemy might really be up to:

The Germans have produced a weapon which, at the cost of
years of intense research, throws perhaps a one or two ton warhead into the London area for the expenditure of an elaborate
radio-controlled carcass consuming eight or so tons of fuel. Why,
then have they made the Rocket?

The answer is simple ... The German Army has produced a
great technical achievement in the Rocket, and the Nazis have
been carried away by the romantic prospect of operational consummation. There is no deeper policy behind the Rocket.

The epilogue dwelt in ill-disguised code on the dangers of
expert advice (but not his). He was pushing his luck: the pillory-
ing of scientific 'experts' was a clear attack on their political patron.

Jones's successor was already in place, appointed the day before
in the person of his one-time deputy, the Ultra-cleared Wing
Commander John Mapplebeck running section AI(h). This RAF
Volunteer Reserve officer might prove less troublesome than the
civilian Jones. Two days later Jones got a phone call from Frank
Inglis: Portal had ordered his paper's immediate recall. Every copy.

Mr Sandys had insisted. Jones had thought he was running the war, and for a little while he had been.

Northern France, late August 1944

The Allied breakout was rolling up the 'German Flying Bomb Organisation' (see p. 301) from the west. On the 18th, Oberst Walter and the rump of LXV Armee Korps quit Paris for Belgium. The Park picked up its move with a message on the Jerboa key. The launching ramps were dismantled for transport; all movement to the railhead dumps was at night, and trains were compelled to wait, loaded, until darkness before they could move.

After the assaults on St Leu in July, the counter-bombing of the Feldmunitionslager had gone on through August, while the intelligence effort and the bombing that followed were more and more shifted to the rocket. For example, there were attacks on liquid-oxygen production that had no relevance to the flying bomb. Attacks by heavy bombers on dispersed launch sites, having been suspended by the Joint Crossbow Committee as useless, had been resumed under pressure from Norman Bottomley and would continue until the first days of September. But in the end, what would the bombing have achieved? The *Official History*, in a judgement delivered in the 1950s, said: 'Offensive countermeasures brought no direct return commensurate with the great effort devoted to them.' The French who died in the bombing, and the fate of vanished villages such as Tôtes, Siracourt, St Leu and St Maximin, are hardly recorded in the popular narrative of the war.

The attacks on the storage sites north of Paris in their caverns and mushroom farms (found by the Park) did bring returns, though. While Londoners in the doodlebug summer nervously scanned the sky, in the Oise valley the Germans were doing the same. M. Vincent Claude of Nucourt told an interviewer sixty years after the events that he well remembered V1s being transported through his town from the storage caves to the firing sites. As a teenager, he and his friends would spook the Germans simply by all looking straight up at the sky whenever they drove past. 'We used to get shouted at and got into a lot of trouble,' he said.

After 20 August, no more flying-bomb trains got out from west of the Seine. Equipment from south of the Somme was more or less safely extracted; at the north-easterly sites crews continued to fire for as long as they could. General Heinemann's deputy, Oberst Walter, sent orders to battery commanders to carry on firing until the enemy actually arrived. They duly did, and the guns on the south coast of England kept shooting them down.

Air Marshal Sir Roderic Hill, who had taken to flying his personal Hawker Tempest around the front line of No. 11 Group airfields (to Acting Wing Commander Roland Beamont's scorn), recalled graphically:

Flying towards the south coast on 28 August, I could see over Romney Marsh a wall of black smoke marking the position of the Diver barrage ... On the far side fighters were shooting down flying bombs into the Channel; on the nearer side more fighters waited on its fringe to pounce on the occasional bomb that got so far ... That day 97 bombs approached these shores. The defences brought down 90 and only four reached London.

Still the RAF harried them as they retreated. Airman Josef Esser of 155 Flakregiment recorded:

Another move, reconnaissance planes had found us and flew over our new site.

We ran for cover as a huge formation could be seen approaching us. It was a case of running for our lives. Bombs rained on our positions. On our return the V1 was still ready but the cone was damaged and there was a hole in the fuselage. Once more we [were] off to a new site.

A long march began. I had no knowledge of the demolitions of the firing sites. Special units did that.

An Ultra-informed Air Intelligence report of 30 August indicated that the depots at St Leu, Nucourt and Rilly were pulling out. The fuel dump in a railway tunnel at Le Coudray, south of Beauvais, was being evacuated. The last flying bomb launched from France left its ramp at 04:00 on 1 September. It was over. The war diary commented, without irony, 'The question now arises as to the future of the Regiment.'

Brussels, 31 August 1944

The future was the rocket, and Obergruppenführer Hans Kammler was in the process of seizing it. On the last day of August he turned up in Brussels to announce that he was in operational command. At issue was a message sent to LXV AK by Kammler that the teleprinter had deposited in the early hours of that morning. The Armee Korps in turn had sent it to the Army High Command (West) for clarification. Headed 'Operation Penguin', it read:

> The following teleprint received 23:55 hrs 30th August from SS Gruppenführer und Gen-Lt. Der Waffen SS Fegelein* of the Führerhauptquartier. The Führer on the evening of 29 August ordered provision of sufficient firing places to bring half the fire on each of London and Paris. Please take necessary action. (sgd) Kammler.

Operation Penguin was the codename for the use of the A-4 rocket against the enemy. Never mind the implications of the message itself, what outraged Oberst Walter was that Kammler had insinuated himself into the chain of command, seemingly under Hitler himself. There followed a flurry of outraged messages invoking the army's honour, which culminated in General Heinemann being told by Supreme Command that henceforth his command would be responsible only for the rocket's 'supply system and for guard troops'.

British tanks were approaching Brussels. Who was in charge of what did not seem to matter. On 5 September Supreme Command signalled: 'In view of urgency Führer has ordered that Kammler should command.' The Armee Korps was to be responsible for no

---

* Hermann Fegelein was Himmler's protégé, married since 3 June 1944 to the sister of Fräulein Eva Braun, Hitler's mistress. According to Dornberger's memoirs, Fegelein was a 'good friend of Kammler and his quickest route to Hitler'.

more than 'providing sufficient information to enable defensive measures to be taken'. It would, however, stay in charge of flying-bomb operations – which were suspended anyway, but not yet terminated.

Kammler had won. The SS were in control. But France was lost and Belgium about to be. If the Netherlands were evacuated, the day of the rocket would never arrive. Even the slaves of Dora knew – informed by clandestine radio – and the 'whole camp began rejoicing in secret', according to Yves Béon. The irony was that Dornberger at last seemed to be mastering the air-burst problems that had punctuated the skies over Blizna. When testing had been evacuated to the Heidekraut camp in West Prussia in late July, the problem had still not been fixed (although packing the front end with glass wool had brought some improvement). Then, on 30 August, test launches had begun at Heidekraut of eighty 'sleeved' rockets (comprising a metal tube riveted round the fuel-tank section). Dornberger called them 'tin trousers'.

There were no more air-bursts. The rocket worked. London was just a few days away from finding out.

CHAPTER 44

Blizna, 1 September 1944

On 1 September, over a month since Major Sanders and his team
had set off in hope from London, the Air Ministry at last heard from
the Russian capital with news of the now somewhat forgotten expedition. With boy-scoutish enthusiasm the signal announced: 'We
leave Moscow 05:20 tomorrow morning ... we are all thrilled to be
off at last and intend to do our best.'

They journeyed via Poltava, the strange US airbase in the
Ukraine set up for bombing the Reich from the east, where they
enjoyed a huge luncheon according to Geoffrey Gollin, the nearest thing to a British liquid-fuelled rocket expert, with caviar,
vodka, champagne 'and speeches'. They reached the Blizna area
on the 3rd, a collection of not terribly soldierly Englishmen and
Americans in battledress headed by the Old Etonian Major
Terence Sanders, who a long time before had been an Olympic
oarsman. Deputy head of mission was Lt-Colonel John 'Jack'
O'Mara, Carl Spaatz's technical intelligence officer. Their accommodation was a row of villas where formidable female Russian
soldiers acted as batmen, with 'clinking medals to show how many
Germans they had killed in combat'.

When they found the front line, only about five miles away, it
seemed that the Germans had evacuated everything. The
Russians had apparently discovered nothing among the abandoned

buildings and test stands – indeed they were 'sceptical about the existence of large rockets'.

According to Boris Chertok's memoirs, 'The British specialists arrived, including a representative of their Intelligence who had a detailed map of the area showing the coordinates of the launch site and numerous sites where the missiles had fallen.' The Russians were awestruck. Now the Anglo-Soviet-American examination of Heidelager could proceed with all the intelligence that had been so painstakingly assembled since the first whispers about rockets in Poland had turned up at the Park in February. And the information turned out to be remarkably accurate. 'Upon his return [to Moscow] M. K. Tikhonravov* told us that our military intelligence officers had driven all over the test range and had confirmed that the British map was correct in every detail,' wrote Chertok.

They found an area one mile square in the midst of the forest, surrounded by a wire fence. At the centre of this experimental area was 'a large open space surrounded by forest with buildings on its fringes. On the west side [was] the old village of Blizna which [had] been completely demolished. All the buildings were left standing but were completely emptied of contents' and done in such a methodical way as to suggest strongly to Sanders that the 'evacuation was made with a view to the equipment being re-erected elsewhere'.

For five more days they poked around in the forest, finding the foundations for two prefabricated flying-bomb launchers pointing in the general direction of Lublin, then two 'rocket'-firing points were identified. Gordon Wilkinson found scorched tree trunks on paths barely wide enough for a transporter to pass.* This would be all but impossible to spot from the air.

One Polish peasant, Wilkinson recalled, had rushed to the wreckage of an A-4 that had crashed about four miles from its launcher: 'his hand [had] frozen to his tongue as he tried to taste the liquid oxygen rather than the methyl alcohol'. Ten craters were

---

* Mikhail Klavdievich Tikhonravov, who would later supervise the design of Sputnik I and the Luna programme.
* Dornberger had always emphasised the importance of being able to fire the weapon from 'a bit of planking on a forest track, or the overgrown track itself'.

located within a radius of five miles, from which one and a half tons of fragments were eventually recovered, including a tail fin with an aerial, a crumpled fuel tank, a complete 'burner unit' and a 'battered venturi'. The bits of radio and servo motor would need further analysis.

But had the Germans *really* taken everything with them? Nigel Tangye, the aviation writer, had a drink with Jack O'Mara on his return to London. He wrote in his diary:

> When the party reached the site, they soon realised the Russians were sceptical ... it was two miles from the front line and [they] thought it was just another excuse to get a military mission near the fighting. Three days were spent fitting together odd bits found in the woods ...
>
> Then one of the party [Gollin] observed in an old field latrine some bits of paper with figures on them. He fished them out and found that they were test sheets of the V2. The party went in search of more latrines and found more scraps from which the whole story could be gained.

One of Gollin's retrieved documents referred to one fuel as O_2 and the other as *B-Stoff*, of which the amount was given as 3900 kilograms, which was exactly the capacity of the fuel tank found – if the fuel was alcohol. According to O'Mara, 'From this moment the Russians were converted from apathy and distrust to enthusiasm. Messages went to the Kremlin. At that point the mission went smoothly and much headway was made of a tremendously valuable nature.' The hunt in craters and latrines went on.

Western Holland, September 1944

The day of the rocket's warlike debut was getting closer. On 2 September Himmler reconfirmed Kammler's authority as his personal 'plenipotentiary'. The Armee Korps would still, nominally, conduct operations.

Walter Dornberger, meanwhile, must bear his perceived humiliation. 'I had to endure a chaotic flood of ignorant contradictory orders, 100 telegrams a day. In those two months I reached the limits of a man's endurance,' he wrote in his memoirs.

It was now that Kammler set up a Gruppe Nord (North) and a Gruppe Sud (South), under the control of the Division zur Vergeltung (Revenge Division) with Oberst Thom as chief of staff. On 5 September from his headquarters near Nijmegen, not far from the German border, Kammler ordered the rocket troops – some six thousand men and 1500 vehicles – to deploy in readiness to open the attack on London. The army command was ignored. The rocket was going to war.

CHAPTER 45

London, September 1944

For days the Klavier watch on flying-bomb message traffic had shown minimal activity. On 31 August only the most northerly Abteilung was transmitting. At 15:15 it signalled that something was to be 'blown up', but whether this was a flying bomb or the battery headquarters was not clear, the Park watchkeeper noted. Nothing after that. The second day of September in London was doodlebug-free. So was the third. The Diver plot at the ADGB filter room at Stanmore showed nothing. On 4 September the Park decrypted a message announcing the endgame in the Oise valley: 'Feldmulag [field munitions depot] Leopold blown up. Engagement with armoured spearheads. Terrorists shot and houses blown up. A battle group has been formed to break through the ring.'

The same day there was a signal from LXV Armee Korps to an unknown recipient. It reported that Undertaking Erzwerk at Thil-Villerupt near Longwy in north-east France required urgent instructions concerning 'the entire machine park of Volkswagenwerk Fallersleben stored underground and whether to close the gallery entrances by demolitions'. Moreover, 'instructions were required as to what to do with several thousand foreign workers including Serbian insurgents and concentration camp prisoners, an outbreak by whom is feared'.*

The end of the ordeal – of the war itself – seemed tangibly close. The slaves would be freed. London would be saved. It was publicly announced in that glad, confident first week of September 1944 that the blackout was now a 'dim-out', Civil Defence was to be wound down, daytime fire-watching was to cease and the 'public spirit was to be relied on at flying bomb incidents'.

It was the military drama unfolding across the Channel that was grabbing all the attention. After the bloody grind through the hedgerows of Normandy, the onward rush of the Allied armies since the last week of August had made V-weapons yesterday's news. *Flight* magazine, enraptured with anything possessing wings, reported sadly: 'So many launching sites for air torpedoes have been overrun that war correspondents now hardly trouble to stop their jeeps and have a look at them.' The British army entered Brussels on 3 September, then Antwerp was captured without resistance the next day. The war was won.

Euphoria was sweeping through the Air Ministry. But despite all the hard-won insights there were still gaps in understanding just where the rocket and its fuel were made, where its transport and flight-control systems were located. But what did that matter now? Portal told Bottomley and Inglis: 'It is now a reasonable certainty that the German rocket has an operational range of up to 200 miles. The only preparations we know of are centred in much the same area as that containing the flying bomb sites ... the whole of this area is already occupied by our land forces or is likely to fall into our hands very shortly.'

The next day Air Marshal Hill was ordered to stand down fighter patrols. Portal proposed that air attacks 'against rocket targets and the flying bomb organisation (except those connected with airborne launchings) ... should cease forthwith'. The Joint Crossbow Committee was wound up. The only dissenting voice, according to the *Official History*, was Hill's chief intelligence officer Group Captain Vorley Harris, who pointed out that London

---

* The Erzwerk was an underground factory set up in early 1944 in a former iron mine with SS-supplied prisoner labour from the KZ Natzweiler-Struthof concentration camp in Alsace. A US army technical team got there on 25 September.

would still be in range from west Holland – and that even if no launch sites had been found there by air reconnaissance, that proved nothing. Discoveries in Normandy and Poland had already shown how elusively minimal they were. His view was ignored.

On Brendan Bracken's suggestion, Sandys set to drafting a press statement to proclaim the victory. But if all was peace in Doodlebug Alley, it was not so in Whitehall. The Air Ministry, already planning their own show with a script by their man Claude Pelly, caught wind of the Sandys move. Norman Bottomley turned up himself at Shell Mex House demanding sight of the draft, insisting that their top political figure (or his deputy) face the press.

Churchill, however, forbade 'the slightest change in the arrangements ... A statement to the press can only be made by the chairman of the committee set up by me with Cabinet authority'. Victory was to be proclaimed by its architect. The chiefs at their 5 September meeting declared: 'There is no further danger to this country from either flying bombs or rockets. Our intelligence staff consider the airborne launching of flying bombs may continue for a short period but in a dwindling scale.' Action to stand down the defences would go ahead – 'in anticipation of the War Cabinet's approval'. When Sandys's draft statement to be presented to the press was reviewed, the chiefs had no objections.

The Rocket Consequences Committee met for its fourth session the same day. There was no panic now. Their report opened: the 'latest intelligence and the progress of the Allied armies means a fundamental change in the position'. The latest estimate had given the likely scale of rocket attack as '80 tons of HE [high explosive] per day in the London Region compared to 48 tons per day during the worst week of flying bomb attacks'. But the Germans would not be able to launch rockets after the Allied armies cleared Belgium and west Holland, as seemed to be imminent. Thus, said the report, signed off by Herbert Morrison, 'plans to meet the consequences of a severe rocket attack should be kept on a paper basis'.

Instead of mass evacuation the watchword was now 'Stand fast'. It was imperative to maintain the seat of government and continue war industry production in the capital, even under rocket attack, which now promised to be 'limited in effect and duration'. But contrary to the normal instincts of government, perhaps, publicity was to be prepared to 'counter any rapid growth of optimism about the end of the war'.

Ardennes, 6 September 1944

Through the day and into the night of 5–6 September, the men of Lehr und Versuchsbatterie 444 (demonstration and experimental) had moved to a forward site near St Vith in Belgium. In the glimmer of dawn they were preparing for the first combat launch of an A-4 rocket.

The target was Paris, liberated two weeks before. Eight tons of alcohol and liquid oxygen were pumped into the rocket, hoar frost blooming on its splinter-camouflaged flanks. The projectile came to full power, lifted slowly off its firing-table – and the engine cut. Like a film playing backwards, the rocket fell back onto the firing-table, tottered, stayed upright. Hauptmann Kleiber of the technical battery ordered it defuelled at once. Forty minutes later the second rocket was fired – and performed identically, wobbling from its launcher, only to fall back after a couple of seconds. Two days of intense technical investigation followed. Faulty integrating accelerometers were responsible. The long-anticipated great rocket drum-roll had opened with a whimper.

Bomber Command HQ, 7 September 1944

'Great rockets', should they arrive in London at all, might now seem inconsequential. The gas retaliation plan, however, had not been stood down. On the morning of 7 September a teleprint signal went out from Bomber Command HQ at High Wycombe to the five front-line groups plus the Pathfinder, flagged Top Secret and marked 'attention armament officer'. It informed them that because of the 'utmost strain on station transport' expected in getting 65-lb Light Case bombs* to the airfields in the event of Operational Instruction 74 being ordered. The components for 500-lb LC bombs (the phosgene gas delivery method) had already been moved forward to air ammunition parks.

'Demands may now be made,' said the signal, of bomb components: tail units, arming pistols and fuses – enough for 'two initial sorties as laid down in BCOI Operational Instruction 74'.

Arrangements had also been made to bring initial supplies of the 500-lb phosgene gas weapons themselves forward, '*well within the seven days warning period*' according to the message. The short note seemed a piece of prudent housekeeping. In fact it was an indication that Plan II, 'Infusion' – the all-out city attack with gas – was more than ready to go. The bomb trucks were already rolling.

London, 7 September 1944

The toilers of Fleet Street, so used to having their flying-bomb yarns torn to bits by the censor, gathered at the Ministry of Information on the evening of 7 September to hear at last the facts about the doodlebug summer. Inside the ground-floor conference room it was standing-room only.

Brendan Bracken, Information Minister, was in the chair. This was ostensibly an air force–army affair. Mr Sandys – pinstriped, waistcoated, watch-chained – was flanked impressively by Air Marshal Sir Roderic Hill, Air Vice Marshal W. Gell of Balloon Command, and army anti-aircraft chief General Sir Frederick Pile. Norman Bottomley, the *éminence grise* of the whole business, stayed in the shadows. Major-General Frederick Anderson represented the USAAF.

An American magazine that week described 'tall, young Duncan Sandys ... facing a packed press conference in London ...

---

* The standard mustard-gas weapon was the fragile 65-lb LC bomb, effectively a petrol can fitted with a crude tail unit, which was notoriously difficult to transport without incurring 'leakers'. Hence the bulk storage of mustard gas in the forward filling depots close to the bomber stations.

MP and husband of Churchill's daughter Diana – who has been in charge of Britain's defense against buzzbombs ... gave the facts of the robot blitz, now ended'. Which is what he did, in a detailed account of the effort mounted against what he called 'Hitler's secret V1'. In his opening unscripted remarks he said: 'Except possibly for a few last shots, the Battle of London is over.' Newspaper sub-editors loved that – it gave them the perfect splash headline for tomorrow morning. It would be repeated around the world. They would come to love it in Berlin too.

Mr Sandys described the discovery of the ramps at Peenemünde in the Baltic, the implementation of the defence plan, its recasting in mid-July, the offensive countermeasures and the contribution by the Americans 'who had thrown themselves into the job of beating the bomb as if New York or Washington had been the victim of the attack' [applause].

> The latest American equipment for use with British heavy guns was ordered earlier in the year when flying bomb attacks began to look imminent. The necessary priority was accorded by the President as a result of a personal request by the Prime Minister [more applause]. Intelligence, agents, air reconnaissance and photo-interpretation units warned us in the first place what Hitler was preparing for us, 'and since then we have directed our bomber forces with remarkable precision onto the weak links and bottlenecks in the enemy's organisation. The visitation which London has so bravely borne has been painful enough. Had it not been for the vigilance of the intelligence services and the unrelenting efforts of the British and American air forces, her ordeal might have been many times more severe.

One well-informed reporter (not named in the Air Ministry verbatim transcript) asked: 'Is there a V2 weapon, sir?'

Sandys replied in measured tones. 'I think we've got enough to deal with if we stick to the V1 ... we do know quite a lot about it ... but in a very few days' time I feel the press will be walking over these places in France and they will know a great deal more about it than we do now. It would be very dangerous for anyone to make a statement now.' Then followed a jostling photo opportunity on the steps of Senate House with Squadron Leader Joseph

'Night Hawk' Berry DFC, the incomparable night-flying Tempest ace of the Fighter Interception Unit based at Newchurch in the Romney Marsh 'who had blown sixty robots out of the sky including seven in one night'. Bracken sent Churchill, who was heading for the Octagon Conference in Quebec aboard the *Queen Mary*, an effusive telegram:

> Duncan Sandys to-day held the largest Press Conference I have seen since I came to this Ministry. His account of how the Government handled the flying-bomb menace was beyond praise ... at the end he was cheered by the Press, and as you know the Press are a hard-boiled lot. The newspapers are full of Duncan's praise and his speech has been reported in every part of the world.

Telegrams of congratulation poured in. A smart cocktail party was held that evening at Mr Sandys's flat at 67 Westminster Gardens in Marsham Street. The flying bomb was beaten, the rocket pushed out of range. The Battle of London was over.

PART IV

THE REVENGE EXPRESS

CHAPTER 46

The London morning newspapers for Friday 8 September led approvingly on Sandys's statement. That same day, eight Germans implicated in the 20 July plot to kill Hitler, one of them a woman, were guillotined in Plötzensee Prison. Liège was liberated, the Canadian 1st Army captured Ostend and Bulgaria joined the Allies.

Lehr und Versuchsbatterie 444 was also about to make its mark on history. Hauptmann Kleiber believed he had fixed the fault with the accelerometers. At around 08:40 hours the battery set up and fired their first combat rocket from the village of Petites Tailles near Houffalize in Belgium. It seems to have exploded at high altitude. Just under three hours later they fired rocket number two, which fell at Maisons-Alfort in south-east Paris. Six people were killed and thirty-six injured. It was the first ballistic-missile attack in history.

Around 16:00 the second battery of 485 Artillerie Abteilung took up position in a street in the leafy suburb of Wassenaar just north-east of The Hague, the Dutch capital. They had trained hard for this. Two launchers 150 feet apart were positioned at points surveyed the day before and were marked with white crosses painted on the trees (according to Resistance reports), amid the secluded villas at the point where Lijsterlaan, Konijnenlaan and Koekoekslaan met, then a little further on at the intersection of Lijsterlaan and Schouwweg. Electricity would be drawn from the municipal supply.

After the *Meillerwagen* had pulled back, only the armoured launch-control vehicle remained. At 18:37 the bases of two dazzle-painted A-4 rockets erupted into flame. Both grazed space after their integrating accelerometers had automatically signalled fuel cut-off and brought the trajectory arcing towards the sprawling target of London. Six minutes after launch, rocket number 1 impacted in the middle of Staveley Road, W4, outside no. 5, a modest semi-detached in Chiswick, just north of the Thames.

Ada Harrison, who had been sitting by the living-room fire with her husband at no. 3, crawled out of her wrecked house and died in the arms of the local school caretaker. At no. 1, three-year-old Rosemary Clarke was suffocated in her cot in the front bedroom, her body unmarked. A young soldier on leave, Sapper Bernard Browning, on his way to meet his girlfriend at Chiswick station, was killed outright.

The crater was thirty feet wide and eight deep. No doodlebugs, no gas. It was caused by 760 kilograms of Amatol high explosive. A double crack – of the explosion and of the rocket breaking the sound barrier as it re-entered the lower atmosphere – was heard all over London. Duncan Sandys, on hearing it, sped westwards by car. Harry Butcher, Eisenhower's naval aide, heard a 'double har-rumph'. Dr Jones and Charles Frank, in the Broadway office, also understood immediately what it was. They too would head for Staveley Road to see for themselves.

Newspapermen arrived at the scene through the evening and into the night. Everything they wrote would have to go to the censor. A *Daily Sketch* photographer had his intended caption stamped forbidding the picture's publication or any mention of the location. The original read:

In West Area London 18 houses of which 6 are destroyed and the others severely damaged by a mystery explosion. Mr (Herbert) Morrison, the Home Secretary, rushed to the scene of the explosion accompanied by Admiral Edward Evans of the Civil Defence and Miss Ellen Wilkinson MP [Morrison's par-liamentary secretary]. Mystery fragments of the container of the explosion were inspected by high officers of the National Fire

Service who were unable to identify the form of the explosive. To all officers concerned the explosion is a total mystery.

A crowd gathered in Staveley Road, curious, speculating. Was it a gas main?

To the Brentford and Chiswick Air Raid Precautions depot the arrival of the stratospheric visitor from Wassenaar was Incident 636. The logbook recorded simply: 'Eleven houses demolished, 15 seriously damaged and evacuated. Blast damage to 516 houses. St Thomas rest centre opened to house sixteen. The WVS [Women's Voluntary Service] incident inquiry point opened to the 10th. 14 families re-housed, three billeted.'

Sixteen seconds after the first, rocket number 2 fell on the village of Epping, north-east of the capital, demolishing some sheds. The log was written up: 'Incident Pardon Wood, Epping Long Lane ... the enemy missile fell in a wooded part of open country. Blast caused considerable damage to undergrowth and trees but there were no casualties.'

It had begun. Portal, who was on his way to Canada with Churchill, was messaged by the Air Ministry late on the evening of the 8th:

Two incidents occurred today at 1843 hours, one at Chiswick and one near Epping. There were none of the normal indications of aircraft or flying bombs, and examination of relics indicates they were doubtless rockets and probably much of the size we had estimated.

Blast relatively local and much less than from flying bombs. Casualties small and damage local.

Nothing visually observed on radar but sound ranging indicates likely area of discharges near Rotterdam. Home Secretary would be grateful if you would inform Prime Minister.

Field Marshal Dill was cabled in Washington: 'Two rockets arrived in London last night, apparently from Rotterdam area. We are keeping matter dark until we see how things develop, but you can of course inform US Chiefs of Staff.' Field Marshal Montgomery at 21st Army Tactical HQ near Brussels was told: 'Two rockets so-called V2 landed in England yesterday ... Would you please report most urgently by what approximate date you consider you can rope off the coastal area contained by Antwerp–Utrecht–Rotterdam. When this area is in our hands, the threat from this weapon will probably have disappeared.'

Montgomery had already formulated a plan at the beginning of the month, Operation Comet, to do more than that: it was to use the 1st Airborne Division, with no ground troops, to seize the bridges spanning the Meuse and the Rhine. Poor weather kept Comet grounded, but it was soon replaced by a more ambitious plan. Called Market Garden, it was designed to seize the same bridges by airborne attack and push large ground forces across them, then trap the German Fifteenth Army, open the way to the Ruhr and win the war. According to Montgomery's memoirs: 'So far as I was concerned that [roping-off of the coastal area] settled the direction of the thrust line ... it must be towards Arnhem.'

When on 10 September General Sir Miles Dempsey, commander of the British Second Army, raised doubts, Montgomery replied that he had just received a signal from London that something needed to be done to neutralise the V2 launch sites and that Market Garden must therefore proceed. Montgomery went to see Eisenhower aboard his B-25 transport at Brussels airport that afternoon (the Supreme Allied Commander had injured his knee and was practically immobile). In an ill-tempered meeting inside the converted bomber, Montgomery explained his new imperative. 'I told him about the V2 rockets and whence they came,' he recalled in his memoirs, and urged a concentrated northward thrust with the crossing of the Lower Rhine at Arnhem as the goal. Eisenhower was equally adamant that the advance should be on a broad front. However, he did consent to Market Garden, giving it 'limited priority' in terms of supplies.

The War Cabinet met at Downing Street at noon the same day, with Clement Attlee in the chair. The agenda comprised a single topic: 'attack by rockets'. It was explained that because there was no radar trace, no warning had been received. Meanwhile, the meeting was told, Montgomery had been asked for the earliest time by which the launch areas in Holland could be captured. The chiefs, by now in Canada for the Second Quebec Conference (Octagon), were still optimistic, expressing the view that 'no serious attack could be developed by the enemy, whose organisation in Holland must have been hurriedly improvised'.

What to tell the people? Herbert Morrison argued that no publicity should be given for at least twenty-four, and perhaps forty-eight, hours, but that information could be passed confidentially to the press. Admiral Thomson sent sugar-coated gagging orders to newspapers. In the end it was agreed there should be no public statement of any kind – and nor would there be, in fact, for weeks to come.

Norman Bottomley relayed the intriguing news from the Chiswick crater that 'some parts of the casing were too hot to touch for a considerable time after impact ... some other parts had a coating of ice and it was thought that the rockets had reached the height of approximately 30 miles'. In his opinion the circumstances did not warrant very drastic measures of censorship 'because of the military situation which would shortly see the launching sites overrun'.

But where *were* the rockets coming from? Radar was useless, sound ranging and flash spotting not up to it. Photo-reconnaissance of Holland had thus far found nothing. Ultra was silent. But the launch of a rocket could not be concealed from those close to it. It was directed that SOE should try to obtain what information it could from the Resistance movement in Holland.

And it came good quickly. A stream of messages was passed to both Air Defence of Great Britain headquarters and the War Cabinet in the next forty-eight hours giving the likely places and map references for the rocket-launch sites – Duindigt and Wassenaar north of The Hague, 'where a strip had been evacuated between the beach and Ryksweg [Rijksweg]. Probably three mobile firing places.' Battery 2/485, in fact, was taking up new positions in the Dutch capital, while 1/485 was taking up positions in Wassenaar. Battery 444 had departed Houffalize in Belgium and was heading for a pre-surveyed site on the island of Walcheren to join the attack on London. They would be in position by the 15th. The stream of Resistance messages ended when German security forces clamped down, forcing people from their homes at gunpoint.

In the wilds of Poland the hunt continued. That same 10 September, Sanders signalled Jones (jointly with Sandys) at the Air

Ministry that 'many fragments have been found and we have good results. Soviet officers cooperating well.' It was established that no special launching mechanism was required, and that the fuels were of the types expected. 'From fragments of exploded rockets and bits of paper we can confirm the following items are certain,' messaged Sanders who, following on from Gollin's latrine discoveries, was able to give a very practical and accurate account of A-4 technology and technique. Having finished their search, it was the mission's intention to move on to the impact areas to the north-east which were now in Russian hands.

At 21:29 hours a third rocket landed near Maldon in Essex, forty miles east of London; there were no casualties. The next morning around 09:05 a fourth 'exploded on impact with trees' near Orpington in Kent, sixteen miles south-east of the capital. Again, no casualties. Half an hour later a fifth impacted at Magdalen Laver near Harlow in Essex, this one with no effect either. Then, early on the morning of the 12th a rocket fell on the Chrysler vehicle works in Mortlake Road, south-west London, killing eight and injuring fourteen. Still it was all put down officially to exploding gas mains. People believed it because they wanted to. Dagenham in the east of the capital was rocked by an explosion two hours later, then at 15:55 something blew up in the sky just north of Southend. The Air Section at Bletchley Park was messaged with a report the next day: 'A-4 in SE England. On the evening of the 12th patrols from ADGB watched the 1555 leave for Southend. Pilots reported a black missile emitting red flames accelerating at 60 leaving vapour trail up to possibly 15,000 feet. Pilots dived down and saw nothing but a puff of black smoke.'

The political alarm went down a notch. There was no need, as had been suggested earlier, to shut down the Tube lines running under the Thames. The Ministry of Home Security put out vague warnings of possible danger, but these did little to discourage the many who had decided to return to the capital after all they had heard about the Battle of London being over. Even as the bombardment began the queue for taxis was said to be half a mile long at Paddington Station. Twenty thousand were estimated to be returning each day, but Londoners were still left guessing about the sudden blasts and alarms. Anxious parents shooed their children to bed with fanciful tales and just fretted the more themselves.

An army of telephone eavesdroppers and MI5 busybodies went into action. Newcastle, Cardiff and Tunbridge Wells were reported to be 'full of rumours' by the snoopers. On 12 September an unnamed woman at the Ritz Hotel was heard to say 'we have had a couple of these second things' by phone to a friend in Lismore, County Waterford, before the call was cut off.* MI5 estimated a delay of six days before the German Legation in Dublin could get the detailed information to Berlin. But for now, neutral Eire seemed buttoned up tight.

The Germans were still saying nothing. The V1 offensive, once it got into its stride, had been reflected in an orgy of gloating propaganda. It was better to be more cautious this time. Battery 444 was now in position in the gardens of the Villa Vrederust on Walcheren Island, within range of London. The daughter of the local black-smith discreetly took photos of a splinter-camouflage-painted rocket rolling through the main street on its trailer. The images, shot through a gap in the lace curtains of a ground-floor window, later reached London. They remain full of sinister immediacy, a child's innocent glimpse of something dark and very dangerous.†

Sarnaki, 15–25 September 1944

With schoolboys finding chunks of rocket in the streets of London, the Sanders mission might now have seemed a little irrelevant. By the 15th they had decided they had had enough of Blizna. Sanders had supplied documents and maps to his hosts showing the supposed impact areas of the test rockets 150 kilometres to the north-east.

But there was one other place to look – around Sarnaki on the

---

* The penalty for careless talk was different by the Baltic. According to a veteran, a female telephonist at Peenemünde was summarily executed in autumn 1944 when she was detected, by Gestapo eavesdroppers, mentioning 'V2'.
† They would end up in the hands of Air Intelligence officers when Walcheren was liberated in October.

River Bug. Sanders and his team were on their way. First they went to Lublin where the Soviet-backed provisional government had just been installed and where they attended another banquet. Then on to Sawin, a hundred miles from Blizna, which had been bombarded by flying bombs for four days in April. It was near Sarnaki 150 miles down-range, they were informed by witnesses, that most of the rockets arriving over this area had 'burst in the air'. Some had landed, to form craters of varying size, and others had not blown up at all. The Waffen-SS threatened to burn the village of anyone found hoarding fragments. Nevertheless, parts were offered that had been hidden in farmyards, and other parts that had been concealed under water when the river was in flood.

Mikhail Tikhonravov had pulled a combustion chamber from a swamp, the location of which had been indicated on a British intelligence map, he said, while the coordinates had been supplied by Polish partisans. 'Not far away they had found blown up aluminium tanks, pieces of the exterior steel casing, and white shreds of prickly fibreglass.'* The rocket had few technical secrets left, but the launch sites and supply routes were a different matter.

Southern Holland, 17–25 September 1944

Just after noon on 17 September, twelve Spitfire XVIs of No. 229 Squadron took off from Coltishall in Norfolk with an ill-defined mission to scan a stretch of the Dutch coast. At twelve thousand feet over north Holland, several pilots witnessed what looked like a V2 rising in the distance, too far away to discern the launch location other than that it was near the coast, possibly The Hague.

It had been decided that once the Germans claimed publicly to be bombarding London, some form of statement would have to be made. On the 18th the enemy undertook what Admiral Thomson considered to be a fishing expedition with a Berlin Radio story that an unspecified secret weapon had destroyed Euston Station. It was

---

* The heat-insulating partial cure for the air-burst problem. It was especially loathed by slave labourers in the Mittelwerk because, according to Yves Béon, handling it 'turned men into bleeding hedgehogs'. Tons of it would be shipped to America along with captured V2s.

agreed; however, that this hardly qualified. According to the blue-pencil admiral: 'Mr Morrison pointed out that the rockets were causing no panic nor any real anxiety among the population ... Complete silence mystified the enemy and he could not be sure even that his rockets were landing in England.'

There was reason for optimism. On 17 September Operation Market Garden had dropped an airborne army, with the result that the two batteries of Abteilung 485 were at immediate risk of being cut off. Their anti-tank platoon was briefly captured British paratroops, before their captors were in turn captured. The rocket units were withdrawn to north-west of Münster, within Germany itself; then Kammler moved his headquarters from Nijmegen to the same area. On 20 September Generalleutnant Metz of LXV Armee Korps resigned his meaningless command.

Battery 444's stay on Walcheren lasted just three days. The Park tracked its movements via an order on the 15th for it to withdraw because 'it would be jeopardised by measures the enemy was expected to take'. Landing craft would be sent to Flushing if they could not get out via the causeway to the mainland. The battery withdrew on the night of 15–16 September and headed for Zwolle, thirty-six miles north of Arnhem.

The wandering Battery 444 ended up on the IJsselmeer polder north of Zwolle. It set up operations in a small forested area, the Rijsterbos. Kammler opened fire on the only British population centres in range, the cities of Ipswich (where only one rocket fell) and Norwich. On 25 September at 20:00 hours Battery 444 launched its first rocket towards eastern England. Around five minutes later it impacted near the small village of Hoxne in Suffolk.

On the faraway banks of the River Bug all was optimism in the Sanders camp. London was messaged: 'The Russians were undoubtedly sceptical until they saw us recovering and recognising parts of a large rocket. This has made a deep impression on the Russian officers with us. We may cause another sensation when we return to Moscow with the parts. All to the good regarding the future relations between our three countries.' But Major Sanders might have been getting along a bit too well. Air Commodore Easton replied: 'You may discuss the German rocket with Russians but not go out of your way to disclose detailed functioning.' There was also the fact that London had been under rocket bombardment for the past ten days, although that was all meant to be very secret. Sanders did not know.

Sandys advised that Sanders should indeed share his knowledge with the Russians but thought it right for the sake of face that he be told of the V2 attacks on the capital. 'It would be humiliating to be told by the Russians, who no doubt have already been informed by their diplomatic staff in London,' he said.

When, on the 21st, the mission arrived back in Moscow, Sanders began to write his interim report. Their precious crates of salvage had yet to catch up with them. He signalled somewhat desperately on the 23rd: 'The Americans want a duplicate set of everything as soon as possible ... can one be provided from parts falling on England?' The rocket components did get to Moscow, to be laid out in the Institute's assembly hall where at first only General Fedorov was allowed near them, apparently. The British had gathered several large cases of parts, according to Chertok. Upon their arrival in Moscow, 'we were given the opportunity to inspect the contents the night before they were transferred to the British Mission. Three other engineers and I did just that at the Khoroshevskiy barracks.' Which is where they were destined to stay for a little while yet.

CHAPTER 47

The Arnhem gamble had failed. Early on the morning of Tuesday 26 September the survivors of the 1st Airborne Division were extricated from the far side of the Rhine. The mood in London was bleak. The war was going to continue for another winter. The launch sites seemed invisible. Radar gave no warning. After the Blizna evacuation, all that Most Secret Source had contributed to the rocket question were some scraps concerning mobile army Flak units. Then, quite suddenly, the code-breakers got lucky. A message from the SS Commander for the Netherlands, Hans Rautner, to Himmler was intercepted, saying that he had been present on Walcheren with Kammler and that the Hague and Gruppe Süd batteries had each fired three shots.

On the 25th there had been jubilation at the Park when a back-break into Corncrake revealed the existence of a 'Gruppe Nord' and a 'Gruppe Süd', along with a connection between them and that old friend of Hut Three, the Commissioner for Special Duties (Walter Dornberger). Individual sub-units were identified, as well as broad geographical locations in Holland and western Germany, all apparently under the command of 'Special Plenipotentiary No. 2 of the Reichsführer-SS' – none other than Hans Kammler. But with the rocket batteries as mobile as U-Boats roaming over the Dutch polders, knowing who was in command was of no tactical value.

Kammler now decided to move at least a part of Group North back into the firing line in south Holland. On 2 October a rocket convoy of Battery 2/485 departed Burgsteinfurt in darkness and headed back to The Hague, setting up in the south-west suburbs, so as to be within range once again of London. Late on the evening of the 3rd they opened fire, and six minutes later a rocket fell on Wanstead in east London. A second rocket exploded in mid-air soon after launch. The Battle of London had been rejoined.

Battery 444, shooting and scooting around the woods and polders of Friesland, was proving immune to detection. On 1 October a rocket had fallen on Sycamore Farm, fourteen miles south-east of Norwich and a mile east of the main runway of Hardwick, a USAAF bomber airfield; four people had been wounded. Three days later a rocket fell at Crostwick close to another 8th Air Force base. Battery 444 would keep firing for another ten days. If the battery firing at Norwich could not be pinned down, at least Group North's move back to the Dutch capital was picked up by Air Intelligence. As Hill saw it from Air Defence headquarters at Stanmore:

On 3 October an agent reported that the firing troops might be in the process of returning to The Hague. Sure enough, late that evening a rocket [the Wanstead one] fell at Leytonstone, the first in Greater London for a fortnight. So far as we could judge, the Germans were now firing at London from ... wooded parks within the built-up area of The Hague ... Possibly a few sites elsewhere were being used ... a lunatic asylum in the suburb of Bloemendaal ... in a wooded park adjoining the Hotel Promenade.

Thus it was that from 3–12 October both London and East Anglia were under fire, until Hitler ordered that the V2 offensive should concentrate solely on London and Antwerp.

Having completed its training, one entirely new regiment, SS Werferbatterie 500, moved into position at Burgsteinfurt on 10 October. The Park had picked up its existence in a decrypt of messages from Kammler on 30 September ordering the move of its technical battery. Moreover, a German army prisoner of war had described the training of SS rocket troops at Heidelager – so, Hut Three concluded, 'the existence of further SS rocket units cannot be excluded'.

The rocket attacks on Continental targets necessitated new command arrangements among those at the receiving end, as Hill had demanded. But what materialised was not necessarily what he had had in mind. On 9 October, Eisenhower asked the UK Air Ministry to transfer intelligence operations on Crossbow to his headquarters. On the 15th, Air Defence of Great Britain reverted to the title Fighter Command (see p. 199) with Hill still in charge, 'responsible at least in theory for both defence and offensive countermeasures of both flying bombs and rocket', as the *Official History* puts it. There remained the special problem of air-launched flying bombs and the question of going after their airfields in Holland, 'but without the aircraft to do it ... [Hill] was limited in practice to making representations to other commanders'.

And it was the same with the rockets rising from The Hague. Hill wrote afterwards: 'Officers from my headquarters visited Brussels to give Air Marshal [Sir Arthur] Coningham's [Second Tactical Air Force] staff the benefit of such experience as we had gained in the first three weeks of the campaign ... we stressed the desirability of confirming by visual reconnaissance the intelligence obtained from other sources.' But Coningham's mind was on the wider tactical battle, and the rocket was being more or less ignored. Hill considered this a grave mistake. 'The Second Tactical Air Force was obliged to rely on its general programme of armed reconnaissance over the enemy's lines of communication,' he wrote. 'This method ... left us without any means of judging the effect of so indirect a counter-measure. Nor did it throw any light on what the enemy was doing.'

Writing his official report four years after the events, Hill blamed Coningham for effectively doing nothing to stop the rockets: 'Indeed, from the date when the Second Tactical Air Force assumed responsibility for armed reconnaissance up to the 17 October, when this issue came to a head, we were without any report to say that pilots of that Command ... had seen or attacked anything on the ground which could be associated with long-range rockets.' But on the 17th a deal was struck. Hill's pilots would go after sites seeming to endanger London, and Coningham's would engage those further east that were firing at Continental targets. No. 12 Group of Fighter Command operating bomb-carrying Spitfire XVIs flying from airfields in East Anglia took up the watch on the Dutch capital in the third week of October. Over the next five weeks they would fly six hundred sorties – with mixed results.

Flattening the Dutch capital with heavy bombers was not an option (although it would increasingly be considered). Hill wanted a more muscular approach for his fighters turned ground-attack air-craft, especially as 'civilians were said to have been removed from those parts of the city which they were likely to attack'. A confer-ence on the 23rd chaired by Tedder, Deputy Supreme Commander, considered the options. It was a question of life and property in The Hague weighed against the same in London, argued Hill. Representatives of the Dutch government in exile reluctantly agreed. Hill could let his UK-based fighter-bombers loose as long as he regarded them as 'reasonably discriminating' in their attacks.

The Germans, of course, had their own ideas. After three weeks, Battery 444 departed the Rijsterbos in Friesland just as quickly as it had arrived, having fired its last rocket in the direction of Antwerp on the morning of 20 October. The battery packed up and began to move south that same day, heading for The Hague.

Ever since the first rocket had been fired from the Rijs area, radar plotting had fitfully tracked the path of incoming missiles. An RAF pilot reported sighting the contrail of an ascending rocket coming from somewhere near Gaasterland. After several weeks of finding nothing, a photo-reconnaissance mission brought back a photograph showing fresh clearing and a turning loop in the Rijs forest. But what use was that? Douglas Kendall at Medmenham expressed his frustration: 'The photographic evidence was of no value and would not have been found at all without some evidence to direct it to the spot from other sources. Nevertheless in a vain attempt to get some clue for countermeasures, we continued throughout September and October to examine thousands of pho-tographs without any positive results.'

On 21 October Tempest fighters from Second Tactical Air Force, seven aircraft attacking in line, shooting up everything on the ground, found the launching sites in the Rijs forest that photo-reconnaissance had confirmed. But the elusive Battery 444 had already pulled out and was well on its way south, reaching the Dutch capital the next day to join Battery 2/485. They set up first at Duindigt, from where rockets had been launched in the opening days of the campaign. Battery 444 established a new firing point just inside the Rijs forest.

In London the official silence on the rocket stayed unbroken, but American newspaper reporters proved increasingly hard to keep quiet. The War Cabinet felt increasingly uncomfortable, but the ban held. Home-intelligence reports, meanwhile, compiled by the Ministry of Information, listed all sorts of rumours among the wider population whatever Churchill might say to the contrary: that the mysterious explosions in the capital were made by a stratospheric shell that would 'devastate anything within a square mile', that they had fallen in Leeds, Scarborough and Birmingham, that they arrived noiselessly and coated with ice, that whole districts of the capital had been obliterated. It was reported from provincial England that in the face of this menace the Prime Minister was constantly drunk and had been hissed at in the street.

On 30 October Churchill told the War Cabinet that 'the balance of advantage' lay against making a statement. MPs were growing restive, but it would be the Germans who would break the silence.

Oberst Wachtel and his men had extricated themselves from France with much of their equipment intact. On 2 September he had been ordered to prepare a new offensive aimed at the Mons–Brussels–Antwerp region. Three days later he was advised by Field Marshal Walther Model, recently appointed C-in-C West (his reign would last from 17 August to 4 September), to find a launching zone between the Ruhr and the Westerwald on the eastern side of the Rhine.

Wachtel was to set up thirty-two launchers. He sent two batteries to the Eifel region, where eight sites had been under construction since late summer, and it was from these that he would eventually reopen attacks on Allied targets by flying bomb, though not on London.

The V1 was coming back into the battle. Hans Kammler made a bid to take over the air-force weapon as well as the rocket. Armaments minister Speer discussed the move with Hitler on

12 October, the same day his leader ordered via the C-in-C West, von Rundstedt – back in charge after the Model interregnum – that the firing of the V2 should concentrate solely on London and Antwerp. Speer observed afterwards: 'The Führer does not concur with the plan for Kammler to take over the flying-bomb offensive in addition. It has been run perfectly satisfactorily under its present leadership.' So Kammler was not quite, yet, the all-round SS superman.

Kammler was now beginning to step up the rate of rocket fire. In the week ending midday 1 November, twenty-six V2s landed in London against only eight elsewhere – a success rate of 76 per cent, though several shots were very far off target. One fell in Windsor Great Park, but more than ever were landing in densely populated areas – Walthamstow, Bermondsey, West Ham, Camberwell – and a few, via the great cosmic lottery, had done real damage to transport and industry. Two months into the attacks from the stratosphere 235 Londoners were dead.

Deception had been a highly contentious issue when the flying bombs were landing on London that summer. In the first six weeks, no more information was put over through 'special channels' than was necessary to maintain the credibility of the double agents. Censorship had remained absolute. It really did seem London was locked up tight.

Then a message from agent Treasure on 25 October reporting (real) damage in London was quoted back almost verbatim in a German High Command wireless communiqué. A potential deception channel was still open: so the Twenty Committee considered on 9 November whether it should not once again somehow induce the Germans to shorten their range.

Sir Samuel Findlater Stewart, still in harness at the Home Defence Executive, discussed the matter with the Air Ministry. They calculated that the rockets were being fired at their extreme range of some two hundred miles and with an aiming point at Wapping, but in fact most were falling short. The east London boroughs were still taking most of the punishment, less than 10 per cent falling west of London Bridge. It was akin to the V1 campaign of the summer past – an apparent bias to the east. What to do?

CHAPTER 48

London, November 1944

Still the government kept the official silence. One late-autumn evening, an informed group of observers were gathered in a flat in the Gray's Inn Road, Holborn, home of Flight Officer Arthur C. Clarke, wartime radar technician and future president of the British Interplanetary Society. As he would write in his memoirs:

> There was nothing in the papers, but for several weeks large holes had suddenly been appearing in southern England. We were holding a meeting in London to discuss our post-war activities. The speaker was A. V. Cleaver, an aero engineer working in America for the Ministry of Supply. He had just returned from the US, where Willy Ley* had assured him that tales of large German war rockets were pure propaganda. Who could handle thousands of tons of liquid oxygen in wartime? We were still laughing when crash! The building shook and we heard that curious unmistakable rumble of an explosion climbing backwards up into the sky from an object that had arrived from space.

---

* Space pioneer Willy Ley, one of the first members of the Verein für Raumschiffahrt (Space Travel Society), wrote extensively for its journal. With the rocket pioneer and Peenemünde scientist Hermann Oberth he had been a consultant on *Frau im Mond* (see p. 21). In 1935 he left Germany for Britain and the USA.

The heavenly visitors did not come in peace. On 1 November south-east London took a hammering at the hands of 444 Battery firing from Scheveningen, a district of The Hague. During the first week of the month twelve V2s hit London; during the second week, thirty-five; during the third, twenty-seven. When the first few rockets had landed on England in September they had been little more than a nuisance, but no longer.

The rockets streamed in from central Germany to the firing sites uninterrupted, whatever optimistic noises the Allied airmen were making. The Germans had changed their way of operating. Under a supply system called Warme Semmeln ('Hot Cakes') introduced in October, the rockets were transported to the launch-ing area by rail, then on by road to an assembly point where they were immediately inspected, then on to the launching sites. By firing them only a few days after they came off the assembly lines at the Mittelwerk, any deterioration in the fragile control and elec-tronic systems could be prevented.

The failure rate was indeed falling, and of those that crossed the North Sea almost as many were hitting London as not. The first week of November would prove the toughest so far: up to the 8th, fifteen rockets landed outside the capital and twelve inside. The calculation of a mean point of impact showed that accuracy, if Tower Bridge were taken as the theoretical aiming point, was improving. It was certainly more accurate than during the fitful campaigns of September–October. On Sunday the 5th seven rock-ets fell killing thirty-two, all but one of the deaths in a single early-evening incident at Grovedale Road, Islington. By the 8th, rockets had killed 235 people and injured 711, a casualty rate of more than seven per rocket and a death rate of 1.6. No warning was possible. There was no reason why the number of casualties should lessen – indeed, it was likely to rise.

The strange compact of mutual silence continued, until the Germans broke the spell. On 8 November the War Cabinet were told in the regular daily communiqué broadcast picked up by the BBC monitors: 'German High Command announces that the V1 bom-bardment of the Metropolitan area of London, which has been carried out with varying intensity and only brief interruption since 15 June, has been joined in the last few weeks by another and more effective explosive missile, the V2.' The statement was complemented soon afterwards by a morale-boosting commentary about the new weapon by one Heinz Rieck, described as a reporter at the front:

> Not quite five months ago, the High Command communiqué startled the world on the employment of a novel explosive missile, V1. This is the case again today. Once again everyone is asking: 'What is it?' ... The thanks of the homeland today go out to the innumerable hands which have worked on V2. To the German inventors and workers who, despite the enemy air terror, in unending and self-sacrificing labour and by the strength of their organising ability created this weapon, tested it ... and finally, with the help of our soldiers, put it into use.

Peenemünde, 8 November 1944

By the Baltic Sea there was jubilation. According to Werner von Braun's thirty-two-year-old technical assistant Dieter Huzel, writing thirty years later:

> One day Magnus [von Braun, Wernher's brother] and I were going over some correspondence together. The door was closed so that we could work undisturbed. His secretary, Fräulein Beise, acted as watchdog. The date was 8 November, 1944 ... Suddenly, the door burst open, and Fräulein Beise stood there, a newspaper in her hands.
>
> 'I'm sorry, Herr von Braun, but ... look!' She held the paper so that we could read the headlines. Vergeltungswaffe-2 Gegen London im Einsatz, it declared. 'The V2 in Action Against London.'
>
> Magnus and I rose quickly and hurried across the hall into his brother's office. The news had also arrived there and the room was rapidly filling. A dozen excited conversations were going on at once.

Some good champagne had been kept for this moment. The rocket was toasted along with who knows what else besides – 'To the stars', perhaps, via the ruins of London.

London, 10–24 November 1944

At last the fact of the rocket was admitted. But not all reporting restrictions were lifted. Mentions of times and places were forbidden: there was a big fuss, for example, when a V2 fell on the car park of a public house in Bromley and the name of the pub was given in a press report, even though the name of the district was not mentioned. Some thought that a little work by the enemy with a guidebook might have given him the location of the incident. German intelligence may not have been interested in pubs in Bromley, but the newspapers were letting rip. A report containing information gleaned from British sailors in Lisbon declared: 'Southern England is in an indescribable state of chaos – the morale of the population has sunk very low. England will not be able to carry on in this war for much longer.'

There was indeed anguish in the streets of London, in the War Cabinet and at Fighter Command HQ at Stanmore. As Roderic Hill wrote in his official dispatch published in 1948: 'In November the scale of the German attack rose sharply ... Six rockets a day was not an intolerable weight ... for an individual rocket was not appreciably more destructive than a flying bomb. Yet I became uneasy about the fact that the scale of attack was rising and that comparatively little was being done to check it.'

Hill wrote formally to tell Bottomley what he already knew, that armed reconnaissance over the elusive firing sites was not enough. Defensive fighters had been modified for ground attack, and he wanted his Spitfire XVIs* flying from Coltishall, carrying bombs and equipped with extra fuel tanks, to freely attack 'such targets as could be accurately located and were situated in areas from which the inhabitants were known to have been removed'. He got his way when the new rules of engagement were agreed by the Combined Chiefs of Staff on the 21st at a conference chaired by

---

* Hill noted: 'The Spitfire XVIs were each capable of carrying two 250 lb bombs and an overload tank which enabled them to fly to and from bases in England without refuelling on the Continent. By refuelling in Belgium – which became possible on a limited scale at the end of November – they could dispense with the tank and carry twice the load of bombs. The Spitfire IX could carry at most one 500 lb bomb, and that only by refuelling in Belgium.'

Tedder at Supreme Headquarters. But the scale and success of the missions would now depend more on the weather than on any political sensitivity to blasting an occupied ally's capital city.

The heavy bombers would stay out of it and, as Hill noted sourly, 'any assistance I could expect to receive from the Second Tactical Air Force would be virtually limited to that provided by their current rail interdiction programme'. In fact, at the end of November Coningham's fighter-bombers shot up two trains carrying forty missiles between them. It was a rare success. The day that the rules of engagement changed, 21 November, Duncan Sandys delivered his seventeenth report to the chiefs: 'The rocket before fuelling is light and easily transportable. It is mobile and easily concealable. From the time it leaves the factory there appear to be no effective counter-measures. It has proved impossible to jam the rocket's radio guidance system.' It was an admission of powerlessness.

The prospect of devising a warning system seemed equally remote, said Sandys, for 'although, very occasionally, the survey teams installed on the Continent or the Channel coast have managed to identify rockets by radar as they took off ... [they] cannot be intercepted by an existing method of air defence'. The factory, too, seemed invulnerable: 'The only assembly plant about which we have conclusive information is one in Thuringia, at Nordhausen,' he said, 'the output of which is thirty rockets per day. The depth of the tunnels meanwhile makes a successful attack most difficult.'*

Lord Cherwell then made an unfortunate intervention, informing the Prime Minister with his magisterial grasp of science, that the chances of being killed or injured by a rocket bomb on experience thus far were 384,000 to 1. 'The odds in the Whitehall area are increased by the tendency of the rocket bombs to fall on east London,' he had noted in a similar calculation three days earlier.

On Saturday 25 November, Battery 444 once again proved

---

* On 5 November Denys Felkin had circulated a detailed prisoner-of-war interrogation of what he called a 'muddy-minded Pole', who had been at Peenemünde and then at the Mittelwerk from March to July 1944 as a fuel technician. He described the tunnels – '*Hallen*' – with their railway tracks reaching deep into the mountain and the arrival of Junkers jet-engine manufacture alongside rockets. The entrances had 'strong steel doors that opened inwards' and were 'guarded by a dug-in tank and pillboxes' manned by the SS. Thousands of components arrived from outside for final assembly in the tunnels, he said.

London's bane. The first rocket arrived at 11:15, shattering a block of flats and offices in High Holborn close to Chancery Lane. Six people were killed and a large number seriously injured. A witness recalled: 'Windows fell out of the shops I was passing and ... a small piece of metal, almost certainly part of the V2, landed at my feet. After it had cooled down I picked it up ... I remember seeing a man with blood streaming down his face and a little boy clinging to an empty pram, crying uncontrollably. But no one seemed to be comforting him. Perhaps because no one knew what to do.'

The Holborn rocket, exploding in the centre of the capital, was the most visible incident so far, but within the space of a few minutes it would be overshadowed in its murderousness by a second rocket from The Hague. It landed on Woolworth's in New Cross in south-east London. That Saturday morning it was full of housewives drawn by rumours of a consignment of saucepans. One hundred and sixty-eight people died. After that, simply enduring was getting politically difficult. On the 29th, the Conservative member for Croydon South let it be known in a letter to the Chief Whip that the incident 'has given rise to a great deal of apprehension. It is being suspected rightly or wrongly that we are not paying enough attention to the sources of the rockets because of the objections of the Dutch Government [in exile].'

The Park could not help and Dr Reginald Jones had 'left the fray', in his words. After the visit to the Chiswick crater he had gone on 'a family holiday to Cornwall'. A friendly RAF pilot flew them there. The bustling Wing Commander Mapplebeck of Section AI(h) now personally briefed the chiefs: for the Section it was now about obeying security rules and answering questions about the basic reliability of the information they did manage to produce. 'Our service deteriorated', Bletchley's own history confessed. Reg and Bimbo had routinely broken the rules to get results. 'Section AI(h) had a traditional programme and authority and it is doubtful whether they would have acknowledged that we had any right or obligation to make interpretations ... Further, they belonged to the opposite political camp from ADI (Science) to whom our old allegiance bound us,' recorded Professor Norman's deputy Peter Lucas.

Jones's attention had turned to jet fighters and German nuclear developments, but he was not out of the V-weapon business altogether. Although he was off the J-Series distribution list, teleprint messages from Hut Three were still copied to him flagged 'Air Ministry for Crossbow Watch'. He was also briefed to pursue the rocket's supposed radio guidance. That the range control was all on board and automatic did not become clear until the integrated accelerometer was understood in November. But the fluency of the old Bimbo–Reg relationship had gone. Also, the Section was brooding on past mistakes. Because it had failed to realise in summer 1944 that Heidelager was also a training organisation – they thought it was purely experimental – 'we refused to write up the operational traffic in the West which was equally fragmentary and obscure'. The back-break into the Corncrake key, meanwhile, while revealing some of Kammler's order of battle, could say neither where his highly mobile batteries actually were nor reveal anything useful about their means of supply.

Traffic in a new Enigma key that the Park would call 'Ibis' had been logged in October, but it was not at first recognised as anything to do with V-weapons. Then forward listening units in Belgium picked up wireless traffic apparently between dispersed HQs and army sub-units 'with no other apparent parent.' This in itself was significant. The information (not Enigma) was transmitted each evening in a 'Double Playfair' code, and seemed to be a summary of rocket launches made during the day. It would be handled by the Army Section at the Park. Charles Frank worked through the material of 22–24 November to compare indications of launch with radar plots of fall of shot, and from the timings he could see that this was indeed a live V-weapon messaging system. No location for a firing site was given but 'intention to fire' clearly was. 'Occasionally a long dash is sent – this invariably accompanies a launching and on clear days a well placed operator can look out of the window and see a condensation trail in the sky,' it was reported on 14 December. Urgent requests went out to get extra listening power on the ground – from the Americans, if necessary.

Was this the breakthrough? Listening stations at Cheadle and Broadstairs were earmarked to intercept the traffic on the relevant frequencies, and Park watches were briefed to be on the alert for it in the form of short messages. What they decoded was an indication of time followed by a 'bigram', two letters indicating the launch site. The messages were being sent by the batteries of

Gruppe Nord with its launchers based around The Hague firing at London, as well as by those of Gruppe Süd (located around Kaiserslautern) firing at Antwerp, to and from an unidentified control located by Allied direction-finding near Solingen, south of the Ruhr. The code changed fortnightly.

A conference was held on 26 November involving Frank, Jones and Norman to discuss what to do. The new signals key could not be used to give public warnings in London, but it might be used to bring down offensive action. Although it was not Enigma, it was proposed that the security classification should be Ultra. As Air Commodore Jack Easton informed Portal and Bottomley on 27 November:

> [A] German Army code has been broken into by our cryptographers. This code is used by the rocket organization, and the firing batteries use it to report in advance the times at which they intend to launch rockets. They also report to Headquarters each time a rocket has been fired.
>
> The advance notice given by the firing battery so far has varied from ½ an hour to 1½ hours. As far as can be seen, they have adhered to their anticipated firing times within about 10 minutes either way ... So far we can identify only two out of eight [launching sites], these being north and south of The Hague.

It all looked so promising. Meetings with Fighter Command and Second Tactical Air Force were scheduled to take advantage of the 'new intelligence' that might make it possible 'to take tactical countermeasures . . . before a rocket is due to be launched'. The new information seam was codenamed 'Vera' by the Park.

But there was a problem. Grading Vera as Ultra meant it could not circulate low enough to be tactically useful to Fighter Command. 'If they are going to be effective in their counter action,' it was noted, 'they cannot perform the necessary preliminary photo-reconnaissance demanded by Ultra regulations.' Professor Norman promised to take it up with Mapplebeck, and Vera was duly taken down a notch.

Although London was hit eighty-two times in November, the crews of 444 and 485 Batteries had no real idea where their missiles were impacting. They could only set their gyro mechanisms and hope they were accurate. Air reconnaissance was impossible. The 'best' reports came from 'German spies' in London. After the inactivity of the first two months the Twenty Committee decided on 16 November to send out bare information, just to keep the special agents credible, and that is what was minuted. But according to the *Official History* 'subsequent events make it clear that some of the members took matters into their own hands'. The evidence, as presented in 1990, works backwards from the results apparently achieved, as follows.

Out of a hundred A-4s that fell between 26 October and 17 November thirty fell north and east of a line running south-east from the Lea Valley to the Thames at Erith, just short of the big built-up areas of east London. Of the next hundred to arrive, between 18 November and 8 December, the number falling short of this line had risen to forty-five. There seemed to have been a change of aim.

But was this induced by the trickery going on in London? The deception channels were still in place – notably special agents Brutus, Tate and Rover. Any success depended on the continuing censorship of the times and places of 'incidents', and this would remain the case until the end of the campaign. The information blackout went to the highest level: for instance, when on 19 January 1945, General George C. Marshall requested information on flying bombs and rockets for a morale-boosting talk to US senators, Churchill declared himself willing only to 'give the senators a false pattern ... representative of London's ordeal. There will be a great outcry here if the truth leaks and the aim improves.' A transparency was made showing impact points, 'to be superimposed on a map of New York'.

London, December 1944

After the catastrophes of November it seemed that the scale of the attack on London might actually be going down, from an average of nearly seven rockets a day to four by mid-December. Most of them now came by night; Hill would claim that this was because

of Fighter Command's aggressive daylight patrolling of the launch
sites. Night-time also meant less chance of mass casualties, he said,
as Londoners were dispersed, sleeping in their pockets of domes-
ticity. And then there was the fact that rockets being moved by
road at night in blackout had accidents. They were harder to prepare and align, and they were therefore less accurate.

After New Cross, the matter of the launch sites' apparent
immunity had become even more political. The Chief Whip sent
the Croydon MP Sir Herbert Williams a soothing confidential
letter agreeing that the Woolworth's toll was 'as you say very
heavy', while explaining that the launch sites in Holland were not
large concrete structures but 'small and fleeting and virtually
impossible to detect'. Was that what Sir Herbert was meant to tell
his jittery constituents?

The sixth Christmas of the war was approaching, a politically
grim and uncertain one made worse by comparison with the optimism of three months before when peace had seemed so close.
The dim-out revealed how war-coarsened and shabby everything
and everybody was – the fabric of the city, people's clothes, hair,
skin. The randomness of the attacks, the fact that they killed rich
and poor alike, fell on both grimy tenement and leafy suburb,
engendered a certain sense of solidarity. The people of London,
like those of Antwerp and The Hague, must simply endure.
Dodging doodlebugs had at least allowed an adrenalin-pumping
awareness of the imminence of death and the possibility of avoiding it. The unsporting rocket gave no such chance.

Polite society kept calm and carried on. The editor of *Woman's
Own* recalled entertaining her ATS sister: 'We heard the unmistakable crump of a V2 ... we didn't mention it in case, perhaps,
it bothered the other. We just kept on talking and had tea.'
Exactly – one did not mention the rocket. There were whispers,
of course – stories of freakish survivals, skeletons stripped of their
flesh and body parts sailing through the air, sudden disappear-
ances. Professionals just had to deal with it. As the Borough of
Hackney's post-VE-Day report on the work of its Incident
Inquiry Team would explain, the 'morbid and gruesome' work of
identifying remains required unrelenting effort. It also needed
extreme sensitivity when, for example, a parent was unable to
identify the body of a son or daughter. Showing a body part with

a ring or fragment of clothing to a relative for identification was 'inadvisable', according to the official advice, although occasionally it was possible to arrange a selection of remains 'suitable for viewing by relatives'.

German propaganda was claiming that the city the V1s had already razed to the ground in the summer was being flattened all over again: 'The centre of London lies in ruins ... every building within 500 metres of Piccadilly Circus has been devastated ... in another month there will be nothing left of London.' Such reports from German newspapers were gathered and reproduced in the Ministry of Home Security intelligence summary, of which a weekly reading would show that most of the hits were still falling to the east of the capital.

All the same, London was taking a general hammering. A rocket fell near Selfridges store in the West End on 6 December. Eight Americans in two passing taxis were killed and thirty-two injured, ten Londoners were dead and seven injured. The blast was heard all over central London. Nineteen were killed in Hackney the next day, then six more in Southwark on the 12th. The same day saw a direct hit on a primary school in Greenwich which, although it killed just one, sent a special tremor through the Ministry of Home Security. Eleven people died in Southgate on the 13th.

In a wintry essay published in *Tribune* on 1 December, George Orwell pointed up another truth:

> V2 (I am told that you can now mention it in print so long as you just call it V2 and don't describe it too minutely) supplies [an] instance of the contrariness of human nature. People are complaining of the sudden unexpected wallop with which these things go off. 'It wouldn't be so bad if you got a bit of warning' is the usual formula. There is even a tendency to talk nostalgically of the days of the V1. The good old doodlebug did at least give you time to get under the table.

CHAPTER 49

Antwerp, December 1944

The main focus of Kammler's grim enterprise was being directed elsewhere – on Antwerp, the Belgian port that had first come under a ranging shot in early October. There was a good reason: the German armed forces, so long in retreat, so strategically moribund, had a vicious surprise in store. And it was not some new wonder weapon but a full blown counter-offensive on the Western Front.

On 16 December thirty German divisions fell upon a largely US-held sector of the front in the Ardennes. Communications, largely by landline, had cut Ultra out of the German Command conversation, but the Park had caught hints of an offensive build-up. The weather had grounded reconnaissance aircraft, and would keep the overwhelmingly superior Anglo-US air forces out of the battle for the first few days and thus unable to support a weakly defended section of the Allied line. The Germans advanced with shock and surprise on their side; their objective, Antwerp.

The Belgian port had been captured with its docks relatively intact, but it was not until the last German forces had been cleared from the mouth of the River Scheldt that the Allies were finally able to take advantage of its vast facilities. On 28 November the way to the sea was at last open.

Antwerp had been battered by rockets for almost as long as

London. On 27 November one had fallen at a major road junction near the Central Station. The dead numbered 126 (26 of them American and British soldiers) and another 309 were injured. But much worse was to come. On that first day of the Ardennes offensive, 16 December, the Rex cinema on Avenue De Keyserlei was packed full. It was mid-afternoon. At 15:20 a rocket fired by the launching unit SS Werfer 500 impacted directly on top of the cinema. It was a catastrophe three times the scale of New Cross. The blast killed 567 people, 296 of them British, US and Canadian soldiers, and injured 291. The bodies were laid out at the city zoo for identification.

Seelbach, December 1944

An old acquaintance, Oberst Max Wachtel, had returned to the battle. At 05:00 on 16 December, his men opened fire from their new sites in central Holland with a salvo of flying bombs aimed at Antwerp – the German air force's contribution to the Ardennes offensive. In another security move, the command had meanwhile been renamed 'Flakgerätepark West'. After a gloomy Christmas, Oberst Wachtel issued his New Year's message from his new headquarters at Seelbach, east of Bonn. He had lost none of his National Socialist bombast: 'After years of reverses Germany is on the attack again! We enter the New Year in a spirit of cheerfulness and hope, all the stronger in our conviction that under Adolf Hitler's leadership we shall see the victory of our cause.'

The war diary admitted, however, that the bombardment of Antwerp and Liege by the revenge weapon had not so far produced militarily useful results. But there was now a promise of using it – politically – by reviving London's torment. According to the diary: 'At the moment, new wooden wings are being tested at Zempin and these will probably meet the requirements for greater accuracy, greater speed, and longer range.' Tests on a long-range V1 had continued through the autumn. Unlike Max Wachtel, military realists in the shrinking Reich might have long since conceded the war was lost, but plans for new weapons of defence and attack progressed with undiminished managerial zeal.

Leutnant Muetze and the merry men of XIV Kompanie were still operating their tracking radars in the wintry Baltic, reporting on the long-range flying bomb's experimental progress. Their codenames had now metamorphosed from insects into birds – 'Fasan' (Pheasant), 'Taube' (Pigeon), 'Habicht' (Hawk), 'Kondor', 'Kuckuck' (Cuckoo), 'Moewe' (Seagull) and 'Bussarsd' (Buzzard). And they were still messaging to control at Köthen airbase about domestic matters such as sore throats, lost boots and bedlinen. The Park lovingly recorded it all. It did not seem quite so menacing as it once had.

Wachtel might well have been prepared to go into 1945 full of cheerfulness and hope, but on the Ardennes front the great gamble of the offensive that was to recapture Antwerp and turn the Western Allies to flight had juddered to a freezing stop. On 23 December, when the weather had cleared, Allied tactical air forces were unleashed. By the 26th the German advance had stalled well short of the Meuse.

London, Christmas 1944

The rocket was grinding itself into the life of the capital. It had earned no pet-name like 'doodlebug'. The partial lifting of censorship had long since ended the gas-main jokes. The newspapers had published technical drawings in the second week of December as well as explanations of how the horrible things worked – which just underlined how clever the Germans were. The men of the Fernraketentruppe meanwhile presented the children of Dr Kammler with a pet pony and miniature coach as a Christmas gift.

London schoolchildren were by now routinely collecting bits of rocket where they fell. Large chunks were guarded by the police until the Royal Engineers came to make sure they were safe. A combustion chamber buried itself in the back garden of 27 Redriffe Road, Plaistow, where it would survive for decades as 'a rockery and wishing well'.

A few people claimed they had seen the things before they arrived, either rising from across the North Sea or descending at five times the speed of sound. It was possible, according to one account, 'if one looked down the River Thames at the right time, to see what appeared to be a shooting star climb upwards'. There were tales of people momentarily glimpsing what they could only describe as 'telegraph poles' as the rocket descended; of psychic premonition, of pets behaving hysterically moments before an impact. Like a lightning bolt, the first physical evidence was a flash of bright light followed in a matter of seconds, depending on how close you were, by the soundwave.

The vagaries of the way the blast propagated and variations in the local geology created strange phenomena. Vacuums suddenly generated could suck the soot out of all the chimneys in a road at once, cause glass to quiver like flowing water, blow clouds of plaster dust or feathers from mattresses into curious blooms. As the Ministry of Home Security noted: 'Sound seems to be no indication of either the distance or direction of the explosion ... Explosions have been heard thirty miles away. Yet to people within half a mile of the incident, it has sounded too far away to be of concern.' Air-bursts – and there were plenty of them – added another dimension to the pyrotechnic display: puffs of smoke by day, strange 'orange moons' by night.

At twenty minutes to midnight on New Year's Eve, when brave revellers were out in the cold streets of central London, there was a loud explosion. A rocket fired from Wassenaar had landed on Stroud Green in the north of the capital. 1945 had arrived.

CHAPTER 50

London, January 1945

The gloom among those entrusted with the defence of London was deep. Having considered Herbert Morrison's call for heavy bombers to attack The Hague, the chiefs had decided against it at a meeting on 23 December – because it would divert '1500 Lancaster sorties to counter *small scale rocket attacks whose results have no military significance*'. This is how they judged London's peril. And they might be justified, but it did not feel like that.

On 16 January they returned to the theme: bombing The Hague 'would suggest to the enemy that the present scale of attack on London is producing favourable results'. It was noted, however, in the same discussion that a long-range attack on the revealed source of all the torment – the underground plant at Niedersachswerfen 'where documentary and other evidence has suggested that it is the sole final assembly centre for the long-range rocket' – remained an option. Although it would require special weapons, it could be done if necessary without requiring the sanction of the (Anglo-US) Combined Chief of Staffs. Because, as Ultra had revealed, Niedersachswerfen was where the jet engines were made, and jet engines came under the pre-scribed targets for any attack on Germany's fighter-aircraft industry.

*

The Russians were coming. Peenemünde kept on launching. There were still bow-tied waiters at the Hotel Preussenhof, but the inhabitants of the scientific city by the sea knew they were on borrowed time. Since the previous autumn it had been compulsory for all able-bodied male civilians from sixteen to sixty to join the Volkssturm.

On 18 January von Braun is said to have hosted a discreetly treasonable meeting at which he suggested they vote on what to do next, proposing that they go somewhere likely to be in the path of the Americans. On the 25th, Generalmajor Rossman, the base commander, ordered everyone to stay put. Then on the 31st, according to Dieter Huzel, evacuation orders arrived. The first came from Kammler, another from the armaments ministry. Even on the question of abandoning ship they were still squabbling over who was in charge.

Dornberger got a message through to von Braun to tell him that his own organisation was evacuating to the mountain village of Bad Sachsa, ten kilometres north-west of Nordhausen. The loyalists sought confirmation of what they should do from the Army Ordnance Department in Berlin. General Leeb gave his approval the next day, 1 February, but there was little chance that he could have defied Kammler even if he had wanted to. There was no choice of whether to stay or go. It was go.

'This is not a rout,' von Braun assured his colleagues. In fact the Russians would not arrive for months yet. Kammler's extraordinary intention, it would seem, was to pack everything up and start again in the Harz Mountains.

Production at the Mittelwerk hummed on. Components arrived and rocket trains departed for Holland. But that winter, transports were arriving in Thuringia with a different cargo – thousands of prisoners evacuated from the east, most notably from Auschwitz, as the Red Army advanced. The situation in the Mittelbau camp in Thuringia was already catastrophic. Bodies were piling up faster than they could be taken to the crematoria. The SS created a particularly horrific situation at the Boelcke Kaserne, a former Luftwaffe barracks in Nordhausen, making it a 'dying camp' for the hopeless cases from the incoming transports.

Von Braun himself surveyed the Harz area in early February. Not far from Bleicherode, a small town seventeen kilometres south-west of Nordhausen, was a potassium mine which seemed suitable for the new research centre. Kammler had made fantastic plans for his slave labour to drill ten miles of galleries there. The Park picked up a signal from Dornberger via the High Command that the Bleicherode outpost of the mining enterprise Preussag was now charged with carrying out an unspecified task as a 'Führer emergency'. Something was up.

What remained of the Luftwaffe operations at Peenemünde-West would be evacuated to the area south of what was now being called Fortress Cuxhaven, the port at the mouth of the River Elbe. On 22 January Goering commissioned Kammler to be responsible for all of the 'rocket-propelled, self-steering and remote-controlled weapons of the Luftwaffe'. He was to be in charge not just of the rockets but of the continuing Vl operations in Holland and the production of flying bombs in the Mittelwerk. In addition he was to attempt to develop a long-range flying bomb as well as the Flak rockets and jet fighters that were going to somehow put a roof over Germany. Final victory was virtually embodied in his person.

And Max Wachtel was back, convinced that Britain would tremble at his return. He wrote on 21 January: 'Reports by German agents indicate that England will surrender ... should the bombardment of middle and northern England continue with the V1.'*

Delusion was widespread. Heinrich Himmler issued an order on 29 January incorporating the Army–SS rocketeers of the Vengeance Division and the Luftwaffe Flak-gunners of 5 Flak Division (W) into the Armeekorps zur Vergeltung (Army Corps for Revenge – AKzV). Hans Kammler, of course, would command this gruesome sounding formation with Oberst Georg Thom as chief of staff. The Reich's long-range weapons had a united command once again. Walter Dornberger in his very readable memoirs describes Kammler dashing between the Mittelbau, Berlin, Holland and the Rhineland – 'on the move day and night, calling conferences for one in the morning, sometimes on the side of the Autobahn'. And in the operational area: 'The convoys still moved

---

* Early on the morning of 24 December forty-five flying bombs had been air-launched off the Yorkshire coast from Heinkel He 111s aimed at Manchester in 'Operation Martha'. Only one missile fell within the city's Civil Defence area. Forty-two people were killed and 109 injured.

without respite, convoys of motor vehicles bridging the gap in the railways. Kammler's supply columns, equipped with infra-red devices that enable them to see in the dark, rumbled along the Dutch highways.' So that's how it was done.

On 9 February, Oberst Wachtel was promoted to command 5 Flak Division (W) and reverted to his pantomimic *nom de guerre*. Thus it was Colonel 'Wolf' who was ordered by Kammler to prepare for the renewed attack on 'Target Area 0101' (London) from ground launchers in Holland. The reconnaissance and preparation phase was codenamed Operation Pappdeckel (Pasteboard).

The War Cabinet in London did not yet know that the ground-launched flying bomb was back. The continued fall of rockets fired from Holland was their concern at the moment. On 26 January the Defence Committee met to review Herbert Morrison's revived proposal to go after the launch sites with heavy bombers. The tonnage dropped on The Hague thus far has been trifling, he said. 'We have been very fortunate ... so far really serious incidents have been few ... One rocket fell on a school on the day before the holidays ended – 300 children might have been killed or injured.' But Morrison feared London's luck would not last. The Defence Committee still thought the use of heavy bombers was inappropriate but agreed to sanction precise attacks on selected targets in the Dutch capital by the medium bombers of Second Tactical Air Force. The seeds of a new tragedy had been sown.

The deceivers were still in business. Ronald Wingate, the London Controlling Section deputy chief, told Brigadier Hollis on 25 January that he wanted a planted question asked in the House of Commons that would convince the Germans that strict censorship was continuing, thereby indicating why there were no press reports of rockets hitting central London. According to Wingate:

No definite deception plan is in operation. We have been obliged to adopt a policy ... that is to deceive the enemy that V2s have fallen in the west and south-west with a view to preventing him moving his aim westwards to central London ...

During the last fortnight there have been signs of success since V2s have tended to land more to the east and the north of

London. The [real] MPI for the week ending 21 January has been Stapleford Abbotts [in Essex, twelve miles from Charing Cross].

Hollis reminded Ismay of the Cabinet's reaction last time round, that 'it would lead to incalculable difficulties if it were to become known that such deception had been the cause of shifting the damage from one part of London to another'. Ismay replied: 'We got our fingers badly burnt last time by bringing ministers into this business. I for one do not wish to risk doing so again. The only possible course is to let the Controlling Officer do the best he can, referring to the Chiefs of Staff [only] when absolutely necessary.'

So it was clear: the chiefs would stay aloof and the ministers would stay out. Wingate was told to drop his proposed House of Commons stunt. As they had been allowed to do in late summer 1944, the deceivers just got on with it. On 18 January the Twenty Committee chairman indicated that signals intelligence was showing that the Germans were paying great attention to agents' reports. A week later the committee cautiously concluded that, since the experts could give no technical explanation for the evident eastward shift of the MPI, it was 'possible that it was due to deception'.*

Could the Park do any more than keep oversight of the deception channels? The Vera decrypts, although they gave an hour's notice of intention to fire, had proved no kind of breakthrough because the bigram code indicating which launchers within a battery were going into action was still not very productive. The higher-level 'Ibis' Enigma key, suspected all along to be concerned with rockets, still had not broken. According to the Hut Six codebreaker Stuart Milner-Barry: 'Ibis in contrast with Corncrake was now attacked in full knowledge of its nature.' It proved very difficult – 'We were up against a blank wall.'

But by the end of January Ibis began to break – back-messages at least – providing, Milner-Barry called it, 'a rocket Bradshaw' (the famous railway timetable). German army signallers were using

---

* An AI(h) Ultra-cleared summary for 3 February announced an average range error of 9.9 miles and line 6.4. The MPI had moved three miles E-NE, and 53 per cent of incidents were in the London area.

stereotyped phrasing such as 'faulty start', 'burst where it stood', along with long lists of launch times. But by now the launchers had long departed. The struggle to break Ibis in time for it to be useful was especially anguished. It would prove a cryptanalytical challenge too far.

Deception was proving an uncertain shield. Rockets still fell on central and west London just as they did, if a little more thickly, on the east. The first half of February was especially bloody. In the meantime Fighter Command must do what it could offensively with dive-bombing Spitfires – now six squadrons strong rather than four – 'for exclusive use against rocket targets'.

For a little while it worked, but the reprieve was short-lived. Batteries 1/485 and 3/485 moved to Duindigt just north of The Hague with its elegant racetrack. Their accuracy was improving. There were fewer wild shots, fewer air-bursts. Sending Spitfires against them was nonsense, although no one would admit it. General Sir Frederick Pile proposed a loopy scheme to put barrages of shrapnel in the path of the projectiles as they approached the earth. Sir Robert Watson-Watt assessed the chances of success at a thousand to one.

There was, however, something that guns and fighter aircraft *could* do – namely, meet the threat of the return of the flying bomb. Park decrypts in mid-February made it clear that the threat was growing. A summary for Churchill on 12 February revealed that 'Himmler [was] in entire agreement with the V1 programme put forward on 8 February' and that Lt-General Kammler seemed to want to set up an observation post in Dunkirk, where a hold-out German garrison was surrounded. Then came this decrypt: 'On 16 February plotting of FZG [Flak Zielgerät] 76 being transferred to North Sea. Range of 370 kilometres distance between London and Amsterdam envisaged for next week.'

Putting it all together, Section 3G(N) at Hut Three could conclude: 'It is now clear that AKzV [Revenge Division] under Lt-Gen. Kammler is a new creation to control both rockets and flying bombs. In the absence of further evidence we can assume the chain of command down is still through division z.V. and 5 Flak Division (W) for flying bombs … it seems clear that high-level interest in the V-weapon campaign has not abated.' The purpose of an observation post at Dunkirk was unclear but it might be assumed that it was 'related to some form of new tactics envisaged against England from Holland starting on 1 March'. Churchill himself stickered that date in his diary with a red-and-black 'Action This Day' label.

Leutnant Muetze's Baltic tracking units were pulling out. The Park picked up orders from the airbase at Köthen to their Bird codenames to retreat west of the Oder, 'unobtrusively so as not to alarm the [German] population'. Köthen ordered that the sites should not be demolished, as work at each site would start again 'after reconquest'. An Ultra summary for 24 February discussed trial launchings over the North Sea at ranges of 230 miles; this was collated with a report of 'instructions to a German agent in London to regard reporting flying bomb incidents as an immediate task'. In light of these, concluded Wing Commander Mapplebeck, 'the revival of flying bomb operations is considered not unlikely'.

The ground stations were in place with their radars and radio direction finders, and the Luftwaffe signallers were ready to relay the plots. Hut Three's old friend from the very beginning, Leutnant Muetze, seemed to be still in charge, this time based at Cuxhaven with his detachments strung out along the west coast of Denmark.

On 7 March, Ultra would further report the move of what was left of the air-force experimental stations at Zempin and Peenemünde-West to Nordholz–Cuxhaven. It might have been a shadow of what it had been before, but whatever the Germans did, they always did it thoroughly. They were testing a long-range flying bomb, and all over again they were telling the Park everything there was to know about it.

It seemed prudent to inform the War Cabinet, Ismay suggested, of the 'recrudescence of a ground-launched flying bomb attack on London combined with a concerted rocket attack' at the end of February or the beginning of March. That same day RAF reconnaissance aircraft at last found two of Wachtel's launching ramps – one on the edge of the abandoned airfield at Ypenburg near The Hague and another next to a soap factory at Vlaardingen, near Rotterdam. Both were aligned on London. A third at Delft escaped detection.

Ismay had told Churchill: 'The Chiefs of Staff wish to emphasise that all our information about the flying bomb comes from the Boniface [Ultra] source and they therefore hope that when, and if, the information is divulged to the War Cabinet, it may be given in such a way that may lead Ministers to believe that it was acquired through prisoners of war and agents.'* Even now, at this climactic moment in the prosecution of the war, most of the politicians directing it were excluded from its greatest secret.

The renewed flying bomb offensive, if that was what it was, could be met by guns and fighter aircraft, it was thought. Pile and Hill moved to meet the bombs coming in from the east by reinforcing the gun batteries between the Isle of Sheppey and Orfordness on the Suffolk coast, and by allotting six Mustang fighter squadrons to fly daylight patrols – three working seaward of the guns and three more together with Meteor jets to operate between London and the gun line. Two Mosquito and Tempest squadrons were allotted for night interception.

Against the rocket there was no defence, but something must be done. On 23 February the Chiefs of Staff Committee reviewed a paper, which also went to Churchill, from Norman Bottomley about how to scale back the 'increase in attacks on London'. There was the option of going after the underground factory identified at Niedersachswerfen, but at three hundred feet under a mountain, even Tallboy deep-penetration bombs offered 'little hope of success', said the Deputy Chief of the Air Staff. The visual conditions required to find the target would necessitate a daylight attack by the Americans, 'who, it is understood, are already considering a form of incendiary attack against the entrances'. He further informed the chiefs of a prisoner-of-war camp on top of the factory – 'an attack on the buildings housing the factory workers has been considered but was not [thought] promising'.

Wing Commander Mapplebeck gave 'certain information' (all of it derived from Ultra) to the Committee about the suspected long-range flying bomb, which might soon become operational 'from launching sites located among the present rocket operations'. But using bombers against The Hague, even if the heavy loss of life

---

* They would be told a flying bomb that crashed without exploding in Antwerp on 25 February was found to have a wooden nose and other modifications, indicating that a longer-range version could be used against London.

among the Dutch population were accepted, would not bring any decisive result, wrote Bottomley. The only answer was to cut Holland off by land.

But how long would that take? The political pressure to do something immediately was becoming irresistible. How could Fighter Command's precision attacks on military targets in the Dutch capital by puny-seeming Spitfires be weighed against the hammering of London by rockets, most of which still seemed to be falling on the embattled east?

Throughout February, the daily toll of relatively minor incidents claiming ten or so dead and injured had ground on. The Prime Minister's own parliamentary constituency on the fringes of Epping Forest, prosperous Woodford, had felt the rocket's wrath late on the evening of Saturday 20 January when one fell on Cowslip Road. Churchill's private office informed him on the 26th: 'The daily post contains a growing number of letters about rocket attack from your constituency and from Ilford.' Various points had emerged, among them: 'If the weight of the attack had not been falling on the East End but on Whitehall and Buckingham Palace, far more vigorous attempts would have been made to stop it.' Correspondents would rather the citizens suffering casualties were Dutch than English – Geoffrey Hutchinson, the Conservative MP for Ilford, informed the Secretary of State for Air that he had heard from pilots on leave that the RAF was refraining from bombing certain sites because of their proximity to Queen Wilhelmina's palace. The good folk of the north-east London suburbs would welcome a public announcement to show that the government was taking the situation seriously.

'If Whitehall were in Essex these attacks would cease,' Hutchinson's constituents were grumbling. 'Steps must be taken, even if it destroys North Holland', so people were saying – and 'these pin-point attacks referred to in the press are in fact useless'. Which was the truth of it.

CHAPTER 51

The Hague, 2–3 March 1945

The Defence Committee of the War Cabinet had given its sanction at the end of January to use the big stick. After a flurry of late-night arguments between operational headquarters and the Air Ministry in London as to who had given authority for the mission, fifty-six medium bombers took off in the early hours of 3 March. The target chosen was the Haagse Bos, a wooded park in The Hague.

This was, in fact, a disaster that outdid New Cross, even the Rex cinema in Antwerp. The lead aircraft dropped its bombs south-east of the woods instead of north-west, following the mission briefing to the letter. The entire Bezuidenhout quarter was soon burning, crowded as it was with evacuees from the coastal zone of The Hague and Wassenaar. Around five hundred civilians were killed and about twelve thousand had lost their homes and all their possessions. The rockets had been moved from the wood more than a week earlier.

'Unfortunately the bombing was not sufficiently accurate,' Hill recorded bleakly. 'After this unhappy experience, Air Marshal Coningham decided to make no more attacks on targets at The Hague.'

That something had gone wrong only started to become clear in London several days later. Churchill wrote a furious note to the chiefs about the RAF's 'feeble efforts to interfere with rockets' and the extraordinarily bad aiming that had led to the slaughter of so many Dutchmen. Bottomley, in a spirited defence, pointed to Herbert Morrison's urgings that the rocket sites should be subject to a concentrated attack by heavy bombers. The chiefs responded by blaming 'an unfortunate lapse by one or more officers', currently the subject of an inquiry that might result in court martial proceedings'.

A hurried inquiry found that HQ Second Tactical Air Force had supplied 'inadequate and inaccurate intelligence' when it claimed that the houses within five hundred yards of the target area had been cleared of inhabitants, and that an (unnamed) intelligence officer had given an incorrect aiming point because of 'a mistake in computing the co-ordinates'. It was astounding to discover, said the inquiry report, that Coningham's command had not consulted Fighter Command in any way on their techniques and priorities in avoiding civil casualties.

As the tragedy at Bezuidenhout was unfolding, Wachtel's men opened fire with their long-range wooden-winged flying bombs against London. But Operation Zeppelin, as this assault was called, was not quite the triumphal comeback that Wachtel had promised. Mapplebeck gave an intelligence summary of its effects soon afterwards: 'Between midnight and 0600 hours 13 flying bombs launched against England, of which two crossed coast and one landed London area [Bermondsey]. Attack divided into four fifteen minute phases. Method of launching not yet definitely established but none of usual Ultra indications for [air-launched attack] by KG [Kampfgruppe – bomber squadron] 53. Staging of attack suggests ground launching.'

More Ultra-derived intelligence, meanwhile, 'might lead to the assumption that [Kammler] intends to keep firing to the bitter end'. Indeed, the rocket crews had simply moved back to the Haagse Bos to begin the vengeance campaign all over again. On the morning of 8 March the firing platoon of 3/485 Battery toiled to make ready their latest messenger. It rose from its platform and six minutes later impacted on central London – Smithfield meat market on the corner of Charterhouse Street and Farringdon Road. A rescue worker reported: 'As luck would have it, a consignment of rabbits had come on sale and the information had spread around the neighbourhood, so the market was ... thronged with women shoppers, many of them accompanied by their children.' It was several days before the final toll was assessed: 110 dead, 123 seriously injured and 243 with lesser injuries.

Clearly, the Germans' shooting was improving. Mapplebeck issued a report noting sixty-five rocket incidents in England in the week up to 10 March: 'Performance showed an improvement. MPI moving 4 miles south-west ... line error decreased 4.6 miles. Improvement particularly noticeable in range error which decreased to six miles.'

But within the gigantic dartboard of London the rockets' fall was bruisingly random. There was nothing to be done but bear the ordeal. There would be no repeat of the Bezuidenhout disaster. As Bottomley had told Churchill the month before, the only way to end it was to cut Holland off by land.

Hans Kammler's review of the February operations dwelt on the impotence of Allied airpower:

The counter-measures of the enemy increased considerably, especially as far as bombing and attacks by fighter bombers were concerned ... Supply lines were broken 44 times ... This damage was remedied very quickly ... so that contrary to enemy air force statements reporting success, only negligible disturbance occurred, but never any definite stoppage in launching. From time to time it was necessary to stop operations during the day and launch only by night.

Peenemünde, March 1945

By now Peenemünde was almost empty. The Birds had also deserted their nests. Ultra listened to their departure. 'Baltic stations engaged in following rocket and flying bomb trials (now apparently under direct control of Kammler) were withdrawn west of Oder in early February,' said an Ultra-based summary for 13 March. Station Kuckuck on Bornholm was told: 'Get to Germany any way you can.'

Dieter Huzel and his driver were among the last to get out. On

14 March they left Usedom for ever to travel south for two days in an Opel staff car, 'honking our way through crowds of frightened old men, women, and children [until] we arrived at Bleicherode [in Thuringia] late in the evening ... I saw many familiar faces, and the general impression I got from conversations was that everybody felt about it as I did. I asked where von Braun was and learned, to my shock, that he was in hospital. He had been in an automobile accident and had broken his right arm.'

It had happened early on the morning of 12 March on a mission in pursuit of one of Kammler's 'special tasks'. Because of the threat of American long-range fighters shooting up all traffic, von Braun had travelled only at night. Sleep had been fitful. As he would explain to his parents in his first long postwar letter, his equally exhausted driver fell asleep at the wheel.

Central Germany, March 1945

Huzel was about to be reunited with an old friend at the school at Bleicherode, where he found one of the Peenemünde secretaries, Fräulein Klinger, who told him he could use one of the compartments on the Vergeltungs-Express (Vengeance Express), the train of sleeping-cars that had been stationed at Heidelager and Heidekraut as 'a hotel on wheels'. Its purpose had puzzled the photo-interpreters at Medmenham. 'Now it was parked on a railroad siding at the potassium mine two miles outside of Bleicherode,' wrote Huzel.

Just a few miles further on were the tunnels of the Mittelwerk. That March saw the SS-inflicted horrors peak. SS-Sturmbannführer Richard Baer, late of Auschwitz I, began a new round of executions. On the evening of 9 March a group of Soviet prisoners in the bunker, the camp's internal prison, had broken out. After killing some guards, all the escapees were hunted down. The SS then began to liquidate the other bunker inhabitants in mass executions – fifty-seven on 11 March and thirty each on the 21st and 22nd. The victims were hanged inside the tunnels from the overhead crane.

In their spa-town outposts not far away, the rocket technocrats were holding their fantasy conferences about new, improved ways to destroy London.

On the evening of 23 March, 21st Army Group began the operations that would carry three Allied armies across the Rhine. The Revenge Division, meanwhile, were ordered by Field Marshal Keitel to withdraw to Germany with as much equipment as they could carry. There were plenty of rockets left, and time to launch a number of them. Whitfield Street Tabernacle off the Tottenham Court Road in central London took a direct hit that day, killing nine. In the evening a rocket fell on Stepney, killing twelve. On the 24th, nine more rockets rose from The Hague heading across the North Sea.

The onslaught continued. Fourteen minutes after midnight on 27 March a rocket was fired, to land six minutes later in Edmonton; one died. Four minutes later a launch went rogue, sending its missile off into the unknown. Cheshunt, north-east of London, was struck at 03:03; ill-fated Ilford again at 03:24; Hutton, in Essex, five minutes later. Just after 07:00 the men of 3/485 Battery had their fourth rocket of the night fuelled and ready for ignition in the Haagse Bos. The dawn chorus in the woods gave way to the wail of the firing siren.

London, 27 March 1945

The Haagse Bos rocket grazed the stratosphere, its motor cut on the signal from the integrating accelerometer, and arcing towards London it began its descent. It landed at 07:21 on a five-storey block of working-class tenements, Hughes Mansions, in Vallance Road, Stepney. The central block of three was demolished. The block to the east was half flattened, the one to the west badly damaged, all forming a hazardous jumble of masonry from which to extricate both the living and the dead. Bloody mayhem in the early-morning light. As a fireman from Whitechapel Fire Station recalled almost forty years later: 'The bells went down and we heard of the incident at Hughes Mansions in Vallance Road. I remember one chap covered in blood carrying what once had been

a whole live baby, calling his wife, and some people grabbing him
and leading him away. The rocket had dropped in the middle of
the block and the inside wall had been sheered away. Bedding and
people had all dropped into a large mound.'

The casualties were still being dug out of the rubble when
around 16:30 on the 27th the firing siren sounded in The Hague
where 1/485 Battery had set up to shoot. The rocket landed at
16:37 on a bungalow in Orpington, a commuter suburb on the
south-east fringe of London. Fifteen houses in Kynaston Road
were demolished. At no. 88, thirty-four-year-old Ivy Millichamp
had gone into the kitchen to boil a kettle. She was killed outright.
Her husband, who had remained in the front room, survived.
Seventy people were injured overall. A fourteen-year-old girl living
at no. 51 said afterwards that she did not even hear the explosion.
Her sister was with a friend in the Embassy cinema at Petts Wood
in Kent when a message on the screen summoned her from her
seat and she was given instructions to meet her father at Orpington
Station. Together they went to their home: '[we] saw it by moonlight ... glass shattered, all the fish in the garden pond dead and
a neighbour's pyjama trousers flying from a chimney.' Thus did the
Second Battle of London end.

On the far side of the North Sea the men of the Vengeance
Division were wiring up for demolition the equipment they could
not take with them.

The last flying bombs to fall on Greater London arrived from
their launch site near Delft on the 28th. One came down at
Chislehurst, one at Waltham Cross. There were four casualties.
The *Official History* recorded the last few shots: 'A few minutes
before ten o'clock ... the last bomb to elude the defences came
down at Datchworth, a village near Hatfield. An hour after that one
succumbed to anti-aircraft fire and descend near Sittingbourne in
Kent. Finally at 12.25 p.m. that day ... a bomb approached the
coast at Orfordness and was successfully engaged by guns of the
Diver Strip* and crashed into the sea.' It was over.

---

* The easterly anti-aircraft defence established against the V1s, coming from North Sea air
launches.

CHAPTER 52

The Hague disaster was kept secret from the British public. A Lancaster flew over the Dutch city to drop leaflets expressing regret. When the Secretary of State for Air was reported in the newspapers to have sung, mildly, the RAF's praises at the opening of an exhibition, Churchill sent a poisonous memo: 'You have no grounds to claim that the RAF frustrated the attacks by the V-weapons . . . in my opinion, their effort ranks definitely below that of the AA artillery, and still farther below the achievements of the Army in cleaning out all the establishments in the Pas-de-Calais. As to V2, nothing has been done or can be done by the RAF.'

Nor would the Revenge Division be holding a press conference to declare that, from its point of view, the Battle of London was over. Their tenure of the Dutch capital, however, was. The Park decrypted this message on 28 March: 'Army Corps z.V has urgently requested release of its own lorries from the motor transport repair park having regard to the present special task. The lorries are marked WL (Luftwaffe) but are subordinated to the command of the Reichsführer-SS.' Dr Jones's copy of the teleprint has 'special task' underlined. He knew exactly what that was – 'Getting Out' is written in the margin. In the smoke-blackened parks of The Hague Battery 485 still had sixty rockets on hand. There always had been plenty. As Dornberger would later tell his British inter-rogators, getting rockets to the firing sites had never been a problem. Air attacks were inconsequential. Only the liquid-oxygen supply had affected the rate of fire.

Air Intelligence would a little later produce a digest based on the statements of a prisoner of war who had been in the Revenge Division's teleprinter Truppe, namely that on 31 March Kammler had ordered that all rocket units be withdrawn north of Hanover, for use as infantry on the River Weser line.

The security detachments in Holland had already been made into an infantry unit in January, said the prisoner, and sent to fight the Russians. They had suffered heavy losses: 'About 100 men [out of 1000] had returned under Oberst Hohmann in mid-March to an area around Suttrop [Westphalia].'

What happened next was not in the prisoner's statement – and would only emerge many years later. Hans Kammler himself had turned up in the area on 20 March. His car was held up by columns of 'foreign workers' trying to get home. Among the officers from the Revenge Division he found in the little Westphalian town was an SS lawyer, Obersturmbannführer Wolfgang Wetzling. When Kammler saw some foreigners cooking chickens in the woods, he flew into a rage. They must be 'decimated', he ordered. Wetzling rounded up those he could in the Suttrop schoolhouse, selected those to be killed and organised the firing squads (made up of SS, Wehrmacht and locals). Over the next two days in three mass executions in the woods around the small town of Warstein, 208 mostly Russians, including women and children, were shot.

The Americans were nosing into central Germany in a bid to cut the Reich in half. Berlin would be left to the Russians. Von Braun rejoined Dornberger at Bad Sachsa to plan anew for a rocket-filled future. They would soon be on the move again.

It was Kammler who transmitted the operational order from Berlin late that Easter Sunday night, 1 April, to Dornberger's chief of staff: his four hundred 'top men' should be gathered together and prepare for an immediate move south – to somewhere around the Messerschmitt aircraft-design facility, already evacuated to Oberammergau in Bavaria, where he would be waiting. It would be a little while yet before this second exodus could be completed. None of the classified material – the plans and test results, the crates of blueprints that had been shipped south from Usedom – would be going to the Alps. Around 3 April von Braun ordered them to be hidden (as a temporary measure – to one day advance rocket technology in the West, his apologists would later claim). It took three Opel Blitz trucks to carry the fourteen tons of papers and a platoon of VKN soldiers to move them into a disused mine gallery.

The Vengeance Express steamed out of Bleicherode, heading south, on the 6th; it would take six days to make the journey. Its sleeping cars clanked on a roundabout route through the Reichs protectorate of Bohemia before ending up in Bavaria. Bad Sachsa was evacuated the same day. Von Braun had already got out by car.

North-central Germany, March–April 1945

The slaves of Dora too were about to embark on a final journey. The SS prisoner from Kammler's teleprinter Truppe would provide his interrogators with a commentary on events. 'An order was sent out on 31 March by teleprinter from AKzV [Army Corps for Revenge] presumably on instruction from Kammler at the Führerhauptquartier [Hitler's bunker in Berlin since January] thatV-weapon production should be stopped at once and workers employed on other tasks. To be available for continuing V-production if and when required.'

Kammler's order was addressed to the Mittelwerk. The notion of restarting production was not as fantastical as it might seem. Subcomponents had kept arriving, the power station still had coal. The lights burned and the ventilation fans hummed. In February the toilers in the tunnels had managed to assemble 617 V2s and some 2275 V1s. Records are only available for the V2 up to 18 March, by which time the plant had loaded another 362 rockets onto trains heading for Holland. But the message of 31 March from the Berlin bunker really did signal the end

The Allies had known about the Mittelwerk since August 1944. Sparing the lives of those who toiled there was not a consideration. Norman Bottomley had told the War Cabinet in late February that a plan 'to attack the buildings housing the factory workers has been considered but was not promising'. The Americans were considering the use of newly developed napalm on the tunnel

entrances. On 2–3 April the RAF attacked nearby Nordhausen in
two fire-raising raids that destroyed the medieval centre of the city
and killed an estimated 8500, including 1500 prisoners confined in
the grisly Boelcke Kaserne, the former air force barracks used to
accommodate those who were terminally too weak to work. These
attacks did not then trigger the immediate evacuation of the
underground factory and attendant camps. There was still a
chance, it was thought, that the Harz might be defended. At the
same time Kammler ordered all offensive rocket operations to
cease forthwith – they had, anyway – and the army and air force
units of the Revenge Division to be reorganised as an artillery
corps to protect jet-fighter factories.

Bletchley Park reported on 4 April the Supreme Command's
latest decree: 'The protection of important industrial installations
in Thuringia will be taken over by GOC of Corps z.V.,
Obergruppenführer Kammler ... It is henceforward forbidden to
send his troops anywhere else.' It looked as if the rocket troops
would be making a last stand at the gates of the Mittelwerk.

There was nothing left to defend in Thuringia but piles of
corpses. The only way was out. Hans Kammler had no intention
of going down fighting, machine-pistol in his hand, with the rest
of the Revenge Division. He summoned Oberst Georg Thom to
Berlin to tell him that, from now on, he was in charge. Thom,
apparently, wanted it in writing. As Albert Speer wrote thirty years
later:

> [Kammler] came to see me [in Berlin] in early April in order to
> say goodbye ... and made vague hints about why I should go
> with him to Munich. He said efforts were being made by the SS
> to get rid of the Führer. He himself was going to contact the
> Americans and in return for his freedom he would offer them the
> entire technology of our jet planes and rockets including the
> intercontinental rocket.* For this purpose he was assembling the
> development experts in Upper Bavaria in order to hand them
> over to the Americans. He offered me the chance to participate.

---

* The A10, development of which was halted in 1943, was according to a post-surrender
MI14 report a two-stage rocket with a range of 1800–2500 miles – enough to hit New York.

The evacuation of Dora and the satellite camps intensified the inmates' suffering. Railway sidings where rocket trains had been loaded were now occupied by cattle trucks, SS guards urging into them those who could still move for 'transport' to Bergen-Belsen.

The Park had no oversight of the human catastrophe unfolding in central Germany, but the continuing Crossbow Watch mounted by Norman and Jones kept abreast of Hans Kammler's continuing rise. Any message mentioning Himmler's Plenipotentiary was brought immediately to Churchill's attention. On 6 April the Quince key brought news that Himmler had ordered all chief SS and police commanders to ensure that their signal staffs give 'every assistance to the Special Plenipotentiary No. 2 of the Reichsführer in the execution of his special tasks'.

A long administrative message about Kammler's 'special task as General Plenipotentiary of the Führer for Jet Aircraft' was decrypted on the 7th. This led the Park to assume, correctly, that the SS were taking over all responsibility for air armaments, jet air-craft manufacture and operations. It was all a little late.

The next day at 17:00 Ultra intercepted something rather different: an urgent message from C-in-C West to Chief of Staff, Army Group B, about a train 'with undamaged V2 apparatus said to be standing near Bromskirchen'. It was essential that this train be destroyed, went the message: 'report the possibilities of dem-olition and sabotage and offer special honours in event of success'. At 01:30 on 12 April the Park picked up a signal from Supreme Command to Air Fleet Reich to get aircraft into the air to destroy the train at whatever cost.

High drama followed. The hard-driving American Third Armored Division had got there first, and what they found amazed them. General Eisenhower went to see for himself. The British and the Americans filmed newsreels of it. The missiles from the Bromskirchen train were then loaded onto tank-transporters and taken to Antwerp. They would be shipped to America – the prop-erty of the nation whose army had captured them, even if Ultra had told them where to look.

The Revenge Division was still intact, but any notion that it might function as an artillery corps was sheer fantasy. The former rocket and flying-bomb troops were going to be thrown into a stand on the Elbe as infantry against the Americans, or so it seemed. Hans Kammler would not be with them.

On 10 April an American infantryman, Private First Class John Galione of the 105th (Timberwolf) Division, had made a discovery on a railway track in Thuringia. He had been reconnoitring the line for several days, working alone, drawn along it by a strange smell. He could not have imagined the full horror of what he was about to encounter. In a memoir for his daughter that he wrote many years later: 'I followed the trains all the way for miles and found a train car filled with dead bodies.' From where he was standing he could see a tunnel coming out of the side of a mountain. He moved further on, and entered some sort of camp. Dawn was breaking, the low-angled rays of first light falling on what looked like piles of logs. These too were bodies. A skeletal figure emerged to say: 'There are people in here.'

Private Galione had found Dora. He had found the wretched of the earth, those already dead or so close to dying that there was nothing to be done for them. He had found the anteroom to Hell.

The transports had left. The entrance to the tunnels themselves was beyond the SS compound a few hundred metres up the line. In the shambles of evacuation since 4 April, around four thousand prisoners had been herded in their grimy concentration-camp stripes into cattle trucks and dispatched north. Two trainloads had ended up six days later in a siding at a town called Gardelegen a hundred miles to the north; the rail line had been destroyed by air attack. Some prisoners had managed to escape and a number of guards deserted. But over a thousand had been herded into a large barn full of straw, which those in charge had doused with petrol and set alight. Any who tried to escape had been machine-gunned.*

Ultra had already reported in early March the move of what was left of the Luftwaffe experimental station at Zempin and Peenemünde-West to the area around Wesermünde and Cuxhaven on the North Sea. On 7 April came a message that

---

* American newspapers carried horrifying illustrated reports of the discoveries in Nordhausen and at Dora, some of them making the connection with V-weapon production. These were excised from the Cold War missile-race narrative, to resurface in the mid-1980s.

Flakgruppe Zempin had 'ceased work and was awaiting transport to the front'. Panic was reported in Cuxhaven – the arrival of the English was expected at any moment.

And what was the Park to make of a message sent on 10 April by the Wesermünde experimental centre: 'Responsibility for affairs already commenced in Munich can no longer be taken over. Request to be released from task.' Kammler must have concurred with the request, because on the Brown key on 11 April there was an intercept from Leutnant Muetze, now at reporting station Bussard, now sited near Bremen, wanting further instructions for itself and for the rest of the stations, as 'General Kammler had ordered that experiments end with immediate effect'. The message suggested the 'destruction of all documents concerning trials [and] incorporation in Fortress Cuxhaven as rail transport to Köthen is no longer possible'.

Hut Three's long watch on XIV Kompanie that had begun with the arrival of Leutnant Meutze at the Villa Sirene on the island of Rügen so long ago was over. As one by one the stations that had sustained the intelligence flow went off the air, a list was compiled entitled 'Births, marriages and deaths and other notable fun events in the Brown Family – April–May 1945'. It ended mournfully: '30 April Baltic Group heard for the last time, 2 May Danish group heard for the last time.'

It was a testimony to the camouflage skills of the Revenge Division that air reconnaissance had not spotted the German withdrawal from The Hague. Neither had the Dutch Resistance. The absence of rockets falling on London might have indicated something. An Ultra-informed intelligence summary reported on 16 April: 'There is no further information on the location of rocket units operating in the west and no satisfactory evidence of a withdrawal from west Holland, although [there is] nothing against this.'

Bottomley's summary for the chiefs of staff on 14 April reported eighty incidents in England during the month before (including the Stepney disaster), but none since 27 March. He could report that 'the SS launching unit [Werfer 500] in east Holland moved into Germany in the last few days of March, to receive further orders to proceed to Nordhausen, but it is not known if it got through'. It had not. The SS were heading for a last stand in

Berlin. And it was time for the army rocketeers to make up their minds.

On 10 March, while the bombardment of London was still at its height, several officers including Oberst Georg Thom had conducted a meeting at the divisional HQ, where in great secrecy they had agreed that they should surrender as soon as practical – so one of the plotters would tell British interrogators later. The move was inspired by SS-Obersturmbannführer Wetzling, the division's 'field judge', who (according to a post-surrender deposition given by him to British interrogators) had 'recognised for a long time that final defeat could not be avoided'.

When Hans Kammler disappeared from the Revenge Division's affairs around 7 April, Oberst Thom, now de facto divisional commander, reasoned that if the division surrendered as a whole the Allies might be interested in what they could tell them about rockets. They could make a deal. After all, they represented 'a great number of highly qualified engineers ... their practical experience could be used for the welfare of Western civilisation', according to Wetzling's account. He was not the only one to have such thoughts occur to him. According to Wetzling, Thom went off to Berlin, ostensibly to seek higher permission for his surrender plan; in the general chaos, no one seemed to notice his departure.

The Revenge Division was ordered on 14 April to cross to the eastern bank of the Elbe. They were, it seemed, to be expended as infantry in a last-ditch fight with the Russians.

Bavaria, April 1945

As the Revenge Division contemplated its last stand, the men who had put the rocket in their hands were making their own exit. In 1947 during an American interrogation von Braun described the flight south from Thuringia: 'Dornberger ordered 450 key men to go to Upper Bavaria, the rest to remain at Bleicherode ... I asked him not to desert the men left in the Harz.' Dornberger argued that it was Kammler's order, and if they did not obey it the SS would shoot them all. He also told his questioners: 'No chemical, biological or atomic warhead charges had even been considered at

Bad Sachsa [Dornberger's last functioning headquarters] either before or after. I have never heard of any such plans.'

In fact, while von Braun and the Dornberger group were heading for the Alps, most of the Peenemünde technicians stayed in Thuringia to glumly don Volkssturm armbands. For those who made it to Bavaria, a last stand in a mountain fortress was an illusion. But Kammler seemed to think it possible. A civilian electrical engineer would later tell British interrogators that in the first week of April Kammler had ordered preparations 'to launch V2s from the vicinity of Oberammergau against Allied-held German cities and considered that the Redl-Zipf [liquid-oxygen] plant near Vöcklabruck in Austria would be a suitable supply base'.

Dornberger's group had ended up in a hotel at the ski resort of Oberjoch on the former Austrian–German border, where all they could do was 'stare at the sky and play cards'. But where was Kammler? An Ultra report on 17 April located his whereabouts at 19 Muspillistrasse, Munich. From his agreeable suburban villa the Plenipotentiary was transmitting Enigma-coded commands by radio across what was left of the Reich to conjure vengeful swarms of jet interceptors out of underground factories. But there was nobody left to receive them.

The men of the Revenge Division waited for their fate on the east bank of the Elbe. Then an order arrived that from 17 April they would operate as the motorised Infanterie-Division z.V. and be assigned to General Walter Wenck's 12th Army. It was Hitler's last hope. On 22 April, Wenck was ordered to disengage from the Americans to the west and attack the Soviet armies encircling Berlin. Thus the Revenge Division began a weary sixty-mile trek eastwards through the shrinking corridor. On 26 April its acting commander Oberstleutnant Schulz, the former commanding officer of Gruppe Nord, was persuaded by Wetzling to sign an order authorising talks with the Americans.

The same day in London Geoffrey Hutchinson, MP for Ilford, asked a planted question in the House of Commons: Was the Prime Minister now able to make any statement with regard to enemy rockets attacks? Churchill replied: 'Yes, Sir. They have ceased.'

Late on the 28th, General Wenck reported that no attack to

relieve Berlin was possible. Wetzling, meanwhile, was making good his plan to surrender: in a white-flagged parley he declared that he and his men would cooperate in the further development of the rocket 'for the good of the Western civilisation'. The Americans bought it.

The Revenge Division boarded their vehicles at dawn on 30 April, quietly stole out of the line facing the Russians and headed in convoy on the refugee-clogged roads towards the Elbe crossing.* They were deserters. At 22:30 the next day, Hamburg Radio announced the news from Admiral Dönitz's headquarters that Hitler was dead. Dieter Huzel was in Bavaria when he heard (he had joined Dornberger and von Braun at the hotel at Oberjoch, where Bletchley Park found them in a decrypt message of 9 April): 'The Führer was killed in combat in his headquarters in Berlin … The announcer's voice was quite matter of fact,' he said. 'We all looked at one another. Nobody said much. Wernher von Braun summoned several of us to his room. He seemed more relaxed than for many days. I knew immediately that the waiting was over. He spoke simply: "Magnus [von Braun's brother], who speaks English, has just left by bicycle to establish contact with the American forces … We cannot wait here for ever".' It was 2 May.

To the north-west on the east bank of the Elbe, American reception posts for disarming the surrendering Revenge Division were set up. There were interpreters, blankets, coffee. It was rumoured that the Russians were demanding the Germans be handed back. They would indeed be going west, but not to be led through the streets of London for baying crowds to demand their version of revenge. They thought they were going to America, and some of them indeed would be.

As the Revenge Division headed for captivity, in the Bavarian Alps another surrender negotiation was playing out. Magnus von Braun had met a sentry and been ordered to dismount from his bicycle and come forward with his hands up. 'The arrangements with the Americans had been made,' wrote Huzel, who was waiting for the news. 'Wernher listened quietly, then turned and

---

* The Division's escape, according to one account, was 'later looked upon as selfish and possibly even cowardly by some'. One of the locations where the Russians later broke through was where they had pulled out of the line.

ordered three BMW passenger cars to be readied with drivers.' Fragments of the German command system were still functioning smoothly.

That early May afternoon in the mountains was dull and rainy. Seven men dressed in a collection of battered military greatcoats and trilbies assembled at the entrance to the Haus Ingebörg in Oberjoch. As Huzel recalled: 'Shortly, the convoy of BMWs pulled up and we loaded the material we were taking with us, and then climbed in. We were all tightly jammed among an assortment of suitcases, trunks, briefcases, and boxes. I had the uneasy sensation that this was now all that remained of one of the greatest engineering adventures of modern times.'

They wound their way down the Adolf Hitler Pass. An American soldier waved the convoy to a stop. 'Magnus got out and briefly showed a piece of paper to the guard, who then motioned us all into a nearby building, which many years ago must have been an Austrian customs station,' Huzel continued. They posed for a group photograph. Flanked front and rear by jeeps, the convoy drove to the town of Reutte in the Tyrol where in a candle-lit mansion other rocket refugees had been assembled. 'The face of a US officer, sifting through the papers, was ghostlike in the semi-darkness. Then US personnel, speaking excellent German, started to record our names. The next morning ... we were all led to a temporary building ... and given an American-style breakfast. We were told to pick up our luggage and board a US Army truck in front of the house. I noticed immediately that Wernher von Braun and Dornberger were missing.'

EPILOGUE

Walter Dornberger and Wernher von Braun had been taken by their captors fifty kilometres to the east, to the Olympic ski resort of Garmisch-Partenkirchen. They were being held for an interrogation to be mainly conducted by Dr Richard W. Porter, a thirty-two-year-old systems engineer of the US General Electric Company.* This was not about war guilt, slave labour or plans to destroy London. It was about making rockets in America. Meanwhile, in early June an intrepid reporter from the *Daily Express* tracked them down in their Alpine captivity. It was the first time the name von Braun reached the British public, when the interviewee recalled a stay in London in 1934, including a trip to the British Museum and lunch at the Savoy. So how did he feel about trying to 'smash it up'? 'You know how it is,' the rocket scientist replied. 'You have to suppress your feelings a bit in wartime.'

The rest of the former Peenemünders would soon follow. The stripping of the Mittelwerk by the US army and the transshipment of its contents via Antwerp to America against the rival claims of the British, French and Soviets were being carried out at the same time with D-Day-like determination.

On 3 September von Braun was flown to Britain – to be 'loaned

---

* Which had been contracted in November 1944 by the US army to research guided missiles under the codename 'Project Hermes'.

to the Ministry of Supply for seven days', as a Whitehall official put it at the time. He was held in a requisitioned school ('Beltane'), otherwise Queensmere House near the All-England Lawn Tennis Club in Wimbledon, codenamed 'Inkpot', where he was supposed to provide a 'list of experts for future British employment'. He and several other Peenemünde veterans – Dornberger had been flown in to join them – were shuttled daily through the battered southern suburbs across the Thames to Shell Mex House for chats with Sir Alwyn Crow at the Ministry of Supply. When interviewed by an American journalist in 1951, von Braun commented on the fate of the 'undercover' Abwehr agents who had reported the fall of shot. 'I never did find out [what happened to them], but one thing I know is that we had some good ones. Our battery commanders ... used to have reports on V-2 effectiveness within an hour after a rocket had been launched.' So deception did work.

MI14, meanwhile, was doing its best to spy on the Americans, who had long since claimed von Braun and the others as entirely theirs. By the end of the year they would be working as employees of the War Department at a Peenemünde remade by the US army 'midst the yuccas and the thistles in the Texan desert. Britain did get Walter Dornberger, for a couple of years at least, who after some mutterings about a war crimes prosecution would also be heading for America, and lucrative employment with the Bell Aircraft Corporation. He told his British interrogators some remarkable things along the way, according to the Combined Services Detailed Interrogation Centre report of August 1945: not least that he and von Braun had realised at the end of 1944 that things were going wrong and so had been in touch with the General Electric Company via the German embassy in Lisbon 'with a view to coming to some arrangement'. How different things might have been if they had cut such a deal. On its publication in 1954, Dornberger's book *V2* was reviewed in the *Times Literary Supplement*. The (anonymous at the time) reviewer was Bimbo Norman. He was pretty tough on the author. The book sold well.

The story of the machinations to get the rocket scientists working in the US (Operations Overcast and Paperclip) has been told many times over – some accounts in outrage at the cynicism of it, others keen to proclaim the benefits to the Free World of getting

Nazi rocket secrets. Of the Soviet side less has been written. Of Britain and France there is not much to say.

By the mid-1950s the wartime story of the 'Rocket Team' had been repackaged in America as a Cold War fable of patriots-for-science seduced by evil Nazis. After the Explorer satellite launch in 1958, von Braun became a national hero. The US army willingly cooperated with the biographical movie *I Aim at the Stars* with a British director, the ex-RAF fighter pilot J. Lee-Thompson, and the German star Curt Jurgens to play a suitably boffinish von Braun. Duncan Sandys was approached by Columbia Pictures to act in a private capacity as consultant (the file on the matter is noted 'missing on transfer' at the National Archives). Music and lyrics for the main title song were by the Jewish composer Lionel Bart. The Jewish comedian Mort Sahl effortlessly encapsulated the bizarre confection when he suggested the movie's title be changed to 'I Aim at the Stars, but Sometimes I Hit London'.

The fuss did nothing to harm von Braun's extraordinary career. His greatest achievements still lay ahead. Londoners' memories were fading, and all the Americans wanted was to trounce the Russians in the space race. Senator Kennedy won the presidency and promised to put Americans on the Moon. Von Braun would prove instrumental in doing that. When he died aged sixty-five in 1977, NASA proclaimed that he was 'without doubt, the greatest rocket scientist in history ... His crowning achievement ... was to lead the development of the Saturn V booster rocket that helped land the first men on the Moon in July 1969.'

The Revenge Weapon story touched millions. The involvement of some of the individuals involved has been the concern of this narrative – politicians, grandees in uniform and scientists who would become world-famous. Still largely unknown are the civil servants and the accidental heroes such Jeannie Rousseau, 'Amniarix', who was captured after a blown attempt to exfiltrate her from Brittany to London, and who survived Ravensbrück. Alongside Dr R. V. Jones, she was honoured at a rare public cere-mony in 1993 in Washington by the US Central Intelligence Agency (the CIA Director named his yacht after her).

Michel Hollard, who got the Bois Carré plans to London, was betrayed to the Gestapo in February 1944. He survived Neuengamme concentration camp. R. V. Jones recommended him for the CBE, which he received in autumn 1945. He died aged ninety-five in 1993. A Eurostar train was named after him. Lt-Commander Christian Christiansen, the Danish officer who got photographs of the pilotless aircraft from Bornholm to London in summer 1943, was arrested by the Gestapo that September. He survived torture, was broken out of a Copenhagen prison, and safely reached Sweden.

The desk warriors in London prospered on their rocket record. Air Commodore Jack Easton became assistant chief of MI6. Sir John Sinclair, who as Director of Military Intelligence had advanced the War Office's stake in Ultra's rocket watch, became the service's chief. Air Chief Marshal Sir Norman Bottomley, Grand Panjandrum of the whole affair, supplanted Bert Harris as AOC Bomber Command in 1945 and later became a powerful figure at the BBC.

Dr Reginald Jones had an unhappy year in a deflating Whitehall intelligence establishment before heading for the Chair of Natural Philosophy at Aberdeen University. He published his fabulously revelatory book *Most Secret War* (*Wizard War* in the US) in 1977, and it became a deserved best seller, made a compulsive television series and turned its author into a global celebrity. Unlike some of the German wartime scientists brought to America, the enthusiastic hoaxer proved the most reliable of narrators. He turned down a knighthood and a proposed peerage proved abortive. He advised Margaret Thatcher during the Falklands War. He died in 1997.

Walt Rostow (died 2003), the youthful secretary of the Joint Crossbow Committee, became Special Assistant to President Johnson and the most vocal Vietnam War 'hawk', directing B-52 strikes on the North. Dwight D. Eisenhower, who had urged the utmost restraint in the gas-retaliation drama of July 1944, became President of the United States in 1953. The Air Intelligence officer Brigadier-General Charles P. Cabell, who had underpinned the no-first-use-against-civilians policy, became Deputy Director of the CIA.

Winston Churchill won the general election in October 1951 and returned to office, with Lord Cherwell once more as Paymaster-General. Duncan Sandys became Minister of Supply. Cherwell continued the feud, according to R. V. Jones, by ensuring that atomic-energy research was taken from Sandys's ministry to be placed under the new UK Atomic Energy Authority, something the Prof had been instrumental in creating.

When in 1956 the Cabinet Secretary sent Sandys the relevant chapters on the V-weapons from the first draft of *The Defence of the United Kingdom: Official History of the Second World War*, he complained that he was being sneered at and belittled throughout, even though he 'had larger responsibility than anyone else for this aspect of the war ... The part played by Dr Jones ... a technical officer ... has been magnified beyond all recognition.' The author, the former RAF officer Basil Collier, was obliged to produce a revised text, very different in tone. A year later Sandys became Minister of Defence. In 1963, three years after he divorced Diana Churchill, he was suspected to be the 'headless man' in a Polaroid photograph that featured in the Duchess of Argyll divorce scandal, along with Sigismund von Braun, Wernher's diplomat brother. Sandys denied it was him. He was not in the picture. He was made a life peer in 1974, dying thirteen years later.

Max Wachtel, Oberst Wolf, never faced trial, and nobody after the war was interested in the secrets of his flying bomb; the US army had already built a copy from crashed parts.

In 1965 he told a strange story of his immediate postwar doings. One day a car drew up in bombed-out Hamburg. A British officer got out and asked, 'Are you Mr Wolf?' It was André Kenny, latterly of RAF Medmenham, now a Squadron Leader of Air Technical Intelligence, who was leading Operation Windfall, a belated attempt by a British investigative team in north-west Germany to find those few rocket secrets the Americans had not already taken. Wachtel, who had once been of such pressing concern to Air Intelligence, might be useful again. Kenny, in this strange tale, took a letter from the colonel to a Belgian nurse in Brussels called Isabella de Goy, with whom Wachtel had fallen in love. As he told it: 'In autumn 1947 British officers came to look for me. They had been sent by Kenny to get me to London. We drove to the Hook of Holland and set off for England. In London I stayed in the [training] camp in the suburb of Hampstead. There is Isabella ...! On 9 December 1947, we were married at Hampstead Registry Office. The witnesses were Squadron Leader Kenny and his secretary.' Guests at the reception, held in Kenny's flat, were 'people from the British Abwehr', said Wachtel. The marriage certificate is real enough and Air Intelligence did have a training school at Caen Wood Towers in Hampstead. Wachtel died in Hamburg aged eighty-five in 1982. His obituary called him 'Kommandeur der V1 Raketendivision'.

The fate of the lead player in the drama's second act remains contentious. On 9 July 1948 Frau Jutta Kammler petitioned a Berlin court to have her husband Hans declared dead. Her evidence included a sworn statement by his driver, SS-Oberscharführer Kurt Preuk, who had personally seen the corpse of Kammler, apparently, and been present at his burial outside Prague on 9 May 1945. He had taken cyanide. Albert Speer tells a similar story. Internet conspiracy theorists still have him variously in America working on anti-gravity devices, in Antarctica or on the Moon.

Kammler made many postwar appearances as the necessary monster on whom to fix the blame. Dornberger told his British inquisitors that the SS chieftain had 'ordered 6000 prisoners to be blown up under the rock at Nordhausen' and had 'Dutch girls in a brothel for his rocket troops in Holland, then had them shot after a fortnight and new ones brought along so they could not divulge what they might have discovered from the soldiers'. Kammler was scarcely mentioned at the Nuremberg Tribunal but his name cropped up during the trial in October 1960 of the Revenge Division lawyer Wolfgang Wetzling for the Warstein massacre (he got life). Three defendants were acquitted when the court considered 'the cruel, brutal and fanatic character of SS-General Hans Kammler, their superior, who was not present [when the massacre took place] but who had given the execution order. He constituted a permanent danger that they could not disobey.'

At the height of the panic in London in summer 1944 R. V. Jones had said that behind the rocket lay 'the romantic prospect of operational consummation'. It seems as good a reason as any. The weapon's random murderousness summarised the whole madness of Hitlerism, but it jolted human history into a direction in which it is still travelling.

STATISTICAL NOTE

A little over half of the circa six thousand A-4 rockets produced were actually fired operationally. Of which, 1402 reached the United Kingdom and 1760 fell on continental targets. In London an estimated 2754 civilians were killed and some 6500 injured in 1358 V2 attacks.

The most rocket-afflicted London municipality was Ilford in the east (thirty-five rockets) followed by Woolwich in the south-east (thirty-three). On Saturday 25 November 1944, at Woolworth's in New Cross, 168 people were killed and 122 injured in the deadliest single rocket incident.

Some thirty-two thousand flying bombs were manufactured. Between 13 June 1944 and 28 March 1945 10,492 were launched at London, of which 4261 were destroyed by fighters, anti-aircraft fire and barrage balloons. The 2419 that reached the target area killed 6184 and injured 17,981. Of the most afflicted areas, 121 fell in Croydon in the south and 122 in the Metropolitan Borough of Wandsworth in the south-west.

A total of 107,000 houses were destroyed, and over 1,500,000 damaged, by V-weapon attacks.

In the twelve months from August 1943, 15 per cent of Allied bomb tonnage dropped was on Crossbow targets. By March 1945 120,000 tons of bombs had been expended. The reconnaissance effort was proportionally similar, with approximately four thousand sorties flown by British and American aircraft. 2917 British servicemen were killed by or in pursuit of the V-weapons and 1939 seriously injured

ACKNOWLEDGEMENTS

Of the original papers and memoirs on which this work has substantially been based, transcripts from Crown Copyright documents in the National Archives at Kew appear by permission of the Controller of HM Stationery Office. I am grateful for the use of copyright unpublished material to the Trustees of the Churchill College Archives Centre, the Liddell Hart Centre for Military Archives, the library of Nuffield College, Oxford, the library of Bristol University, the Cabinet Office Historical and Records Section, the Imperial War Museum Department of Documents, the Trustees of the Medmenham Collection and the Bletchley Park Trust.

Every effort has been made to trace the copyright holders of further unpublished documents from which quotations have been made. I am grateful to Penguin Book Group and the Random House Group for permission to quote from the published works of Dr R. V. Jones and Norman Longmate.

There are many individuals I wish to thank for help and guidance along this dusky path, including: John Gallehawk; Mike Mockford; Sir Arthur Bonsall; Mrs Jean Loudon; Bryan Oakley; Alan Glennie; Stephen Ovens; Hans Christian Bjerg; Patrick Bishop and Michael Smith; David Monaghan, Felicity Blunt and Vivienne Schuster at Curtis Brown; at Little, Brown, Tim Whiting, Claudia Dyer and Zoe Gullen; Alexis and Andrew Nicol in Bacqueville-en-Caux, Seine Maritime; Ludovic and Grégoire

Dufour for showing me their very own V1 ski site at Belleville-en-Caux, now a thriving dairy farm; former OT forced labourer M. l'Abbé Norbert Dufour, author of *L'enfer des V-1 en Seine-Maritime* (Bertout, 1993); Albrecht Kurbjuhn; Dr Udo Schaper and Frank and Monika Rontgen for making us so welcome by the Baltic; and my sister Rosheen Finnigan, keeper of the family secrets. And to my wife Clare, my son Joseph and daughters Katy and Maria Campbell, thank you for putting up with those damn silly rockets.

A NOTE ON SOURCES

Primary sources

The UK National Archives at Kew provided an abundance of documentary material. Particularly revelatory were the CX/MSS J series of secret weapons related Bletchley Park decrypts in the HW 5 series and the Ultra-informed wartime working papers of R. V. Jones in the DEFE 40 series. Beyond the real-time Ultra decrypts, much of the German side of the story is told in the English language by contemporaneous prisoner-of-war interrogations and the transcripts of extended post-surrender interviews. I am grateful to officials at the National Archives and the Cabinet Office for helping with the opening of a number of CAB and HO files following Freedom of Information requests.

The Churchill College Archives Centre in Cambridge, houses the papers of R. V. Jones and Lord Duncan-Sandys. The University of Bristol Library has the papers of Sir Charles Frank. The Cherwell papers are in the library of Nuffield College, Oxford. All have extensively been drawn on. Bletchley Park's own archive provided material, as did the Liddell Hart Centre for Military Archives at King's College London and the Medmenham Collection at RAF Brampton.

The Imperial War Museum Department of Documents provided letters and diaries from Londoners, the recollections of

Flieger Esser, a copy of the original Oslo report as received by the Admiralty in 1939 and (held at Duxford) the War Diary of HQ Flakregiment 155 (W).

Secondary sources

A number of those who have told this story in print over the past sixty years were direct participants. The autobiographies of such disparate personalities as Walter Dornberger and Constance Babington Smith first appeared in the mid-1950s, joined to two decades later by the magnificently boastful memoirs of Reginald Jones, the great hoaxer who turned out to be the most reliable of narrators. Churchill, Pile, Hill et al. had already produced stately narratives. Many such first-hand accounts have been drawn on.

Of those investigators who set out to capture the recollections of participants on both sides, David Irving led the way in 1964 with his book *The Mare's Nest*, which stumbled on the Park's contribution but was restrained by the government from revealing it. Mr Irving, so lauded then, so damned later, kindly let me consult his research gathered by correspondence and interviews at a time when the events were barely twenty years past. Transcripts of interviews with R. V. Jones are in the physicist's personal papers (RVJO B.341–346) at the Churchill Archives Centre.

In two landmark books of the early 1980s the social historian Norman Longmate captured the voices of those the V-weapons fell upon, while in America Frederick Ordway and Mitchell R. Sharpe's *The Rocket Team* (1979) caught the twilight memories of those who devised them. It was the last of the 'Huntsville school' eulogies before a new investigative wave of writers set the Mittelwerk at the dark heart of the story. The National Air and Space Museum historian Michael J. Neufeld's The *Rocket and the Reich* (1995) became and remains the defining analysis of the development and production of the German wartime liquid-fuelled rocket along with the late Heinz Dieter Hölsken's *Die V-Waffen* (1984), which also covers the flying bomb. T. D. Dungan's 2006 book *V-2, a Combat History* and website www.v2rocket.com, and Murray R. Barber and Michael Keuer's *Hitler's Rocket Soldiers*

(2011), delivered remarkable first-hand accounts from both Dutch civilians and surviving members of the Fernraketentruppe.

Of the UK official histories, the *Defence of the United Kingdom* (1957) is businesslike but Ultra-sanitised. The Cabinet Office row over its depiction of Duncan Sandys's role can be accessed at the National Archives. The V-weapon chapters in the multi-volume *British Intelligence in the Second World War* (1979–1990) make much use of agent and photo-reconnaissance derived intelligence as formally presented to the chiefs of staff but not the original sources, while at the same time giving tantalising glimpses of Bletchley Park's input but little of the content.

Special note

Decrypts of Enigma traffic could take many days to move from initial intercept to circulation. Where they might have directly informed decision-making in real time, the time of transmission ('message stamped at') is given along with the date of their circulation to the Ultra-indoctrinated through the medium of the J series. The Abbreviations and Equivalents index at Bletchley Park used the German originals for ranks, units and technical expressions as followed here and in the glossary (pp. xx–xxi).

NOTES

Abbreviations

BL   British Library
BP   Bletchley Park
CCAC   Churchill College Archives Centre
IWM   Imperial War Museum
LHCMA   Liddell Hart Centre for Military Archives, King's College London
NCO   Nuffield College Oxford
TNA   The National Archives

Epigraphs

vii   'In their obsession ...': *The History of Hut 6*, vol. II, TNA HW 43/71.
           'Those damn silly rockets': Hastings, *Bomber Command*, p. 343.

Preface

xiv   'unwise arrangement': *Los Angeles Times*, 29 October 1992.
xv   'Most Secret Source J Series': TNA HW 5/708-17.
xv–xvi   'Under the ill-considered belief ...': P. G. Lucas, *A-4 Intelligence*,
           TNA HW 43/69.
xvi   'Source found a circular ...': CX/MSS/2438 T16 TNA HW 5/249.
xvi   'The German Army has produced ...': TNA AIR 20/1661.
xvii   'because of the extreme ...': Overy, *The Air War*, pp. 186–7.
xvii   'The wide dispersion ...': Zveginstov to Delmer, 20 October 1944,
           MEW, TNA FO 898/352.
xviii   'The extremely strict security ...': TNA HW 43/69.
xviii   'There was intense ...': Ibid.
xix   'According to RAF regulations ...': Watkins, *Cracking the Luftwaffe
           Codes*, p. 149.

PART I: WHISPERS FROM THE BALTIC

Chapter 1

4 **Self-inflicted wounds:** Such a desperate act could mean a sentence of five years' penal servitude according to the Luftwaffe penal code. By way of comparison, 'sleeping with a French female' brought five months; 'infecting a German girl with VD and failing to report to Medical Officer' seven months; and 'onanism' nine months (with loss of rank). Edith Rose Gardner (Capt. USAF), 'Military Justice in the German Air Force During World War II', *Journal of Criminal Law, Criminology, and Police Science*, vol. 49, no. 3 (September–October 1958), pp. 195–217.

10 **'Operators ... constantly address ...':** *Notes on the Brown Group*, 24 December 1940, BP Archives.

11 **'astounded at the vast congregation ...':** Churchill to Ismay, 16 October 1940, TNA HW 1/3794.

11 **'the number of recipients ...':** There is no official archival statement as to exactly who was in the picture in Britain's wartime leadership and who was not. According to the *Official History*, 'the ranks of the indoctrinated ... included the three directors of intelligence, and *we must assume*, the Chiefs of Staff and the War Cabinet. But ... it does not appear that these authorities had any way of distinguishing the Enigma from any other ingredients that went into the briefings.' (Hinsley et al., *British Intelligence in the Second World War, Vol. 1*, p. 138.) In an interview with the author in 2011 the departmental historian at GCHQ said: 'The question is difficult. My guess is that ministers who were Privy Counsellors were not indoctrinated as they would be considered bound to secrecy by their Privy Council oath.' Lord Cherwell was sworn a PC in 1943 and Duncan Sandys on 8 December 1944. BP's link to the War Cabinet from May 1944 was Captain G. H. Oswald RN, who served as secretary to a number of very sensitive subcommittees. See 'Security', TNA HW 64/80.

11 **'It is impossible to imagine ...':** Calvocoressi, *Top Secret Ultra*, p. 64.

12 **'Even when German words ...':** Jackson (ed.), *The Secret War of Hut 3*, p. 75.

13 **'she is to go by train ...':** CX/MSS/ J 90, 16 May 1944, HW 5/709.

15 **'For Abt[eilung] via 14th Company ...':** Message stamped at 1805/21/11 in J 17, 2 December 1943, TNA HW 5/708.

15 **'At the top of the small cliff ...':** *Interpretation Report, Greifswalder Oie*, 18 June 1943, TNA AIR 20/9190.

15 **'NOTES (1) ...':** J 17, 2 December 1943, TNA HW 5/708.

16 **'Traffic can come live ...':** Message stamped at 0930/12/10 in J 3, 29 December 1943, TNA HW 5/708.

16 **'Hotel Baltic':** Message stamped at 0830/24/10 in J 3, 29 December 1943, TNA HW 5/708.

16 **Afrika cuff title:** Message stamped at 1115/24/10 in J 43, 2 January 1944, TNA HW 5/708.

16fn **'caused more log chat, not less':** *The History of Hut 6*, vol. I, TNA HW 43/70.

16fn   'no operator was ever …': Ibid. The Park's in-house analysis of the
       Brown-key operators' many faults is a fascinating study of how cock-ups
       can drive history. The Third Reich entrusted its greatest technical secret
       to the electronic equivalent of the Walmington-on-Sea Home Guard.
       Because the traffic was confided to an in-group that hardly changed from
       1939 to 1945 its security became fabulously lazy, while it was not made
       subject to external checks because its comparatively low level of traffic
       made it seemingly immune to code-breaking attack, which depended on
       bulk material.
17   'To the usual four outstations …': Message stamped at 0900/26/10 in
       J 5, 3 November 1943, TNA HW 5/708.
17   'Fi 76 flew past …': J 17, 2 December 1943, TNA HW 5/708.
17   'When we had fixed …': *The Pilotless Aircraft*, 23 December 1943, TNA
       AIR 40/3009. In spite of 3G(N)'s initial assumption, reporting station
       Heuschrecke was later to be plotted at Zempin, and Grille on the
       Greifswalder Oie. See *Brown III Callsign Identities 13/12/44*, TNA HW
       14/93.
17   'ascended vertically': Message stamped at 0600/26/11 in J 20, 10
       December 1943, TNA HW5/708.

Chapter 2

19   'I stood on the stand …': Barth, *Hermann Oberth*, p. 156.
21   'My first job with Herman Oberth': Ibid.
22   'the most ambitious …': *The Times*, 25 October 1929.
23   'Rocketry offered an approach …': Wernher von Braun,
       'Reminiscences of German Rocketry', *Journal of the British Interplanetary
       Society*, May–June 1956, reproduced in Arthur C. Clarke (ed.), *The Coming
       of the Space Age* (London: Gollancz, 1967), pp. 37–9.

Chapter 3

25   'Most of the things …': Norman to Jones, 19 March 1958, RVJO B.525
       CCAC.
25   'a born rebel': A. T. Hatto, introduction to Frederick Norman, *Three Essays
       on the 'Hildebrandslied'*: (London: Institute of Germanic Studies, 1973).
25   'There is a sense …': Jones, *Most Secret War*, p. 120.
26   'horrified': Jones, op. cit., p. 486.
26   'rough': Ibid., p. 5.
27   'it was this personal connection …': A. J. P. Taylor, 'Lindemann and
       Tizard: More Luck Than Judgement?', *Observer*, 9 April 1961.
27   'how the Germans [are] applying …': Jones, op. cit., p. 52.
28   'Whatever you do …': R. V. Jones, 'Enduring Principles: Some Lessons
       in Intelligence', remarks at a symposium at CIA Headquarters, 26 October
       1993, <https://www.cia.gov/library/center-for-the-study-of-intelligence/kent-
       csi/vol38no5/pdf/v38i5a05p.pdf>.
28   'the last deception operation …': Richard J. Aldrich, 'Policing the Past:
       Official History, Secrecy and British Intelligence since 1945', *English*

Historical Review, 119(483), September 2004, p. 927. See also David Reynolds, *In Command of History: Churchill Fighting and Writing the Second World War* (London: Allen Lane, 2004), pp. 452–3.

29 'the use of special intelligence ...': *Guidance for Historians in the Use of Special Intelligence Material*, TNA CAB 103/288.

29 '[It must be] ensured ...': Friedman, TNA HW14/85.

29 'British Intelligence': Bernard Newman, script for his play *Now It Can be Told: A Secret War*, broadcast on BBC Home Service 25 February 1951, original in LHCMA. Newman's 1957 novel *Peenemünde Spies* (published under the pseudonym Don Betteridge) embroidered the story when British agent Bruce Dangerfield and the sexually charged Elsa infiltrate the secret (by means of running a snack bar on Usedom island) and get the vital information to 'Colonel Duncan' in London. The story was filmed in 1957 as *Battle of the V1* (*Missiles from Hell* in the US), which was filmed at Brighton Studios and Elstree. The 1965 MGM film *Operation Crossbow* took the spies-at-Peenemünde yarn into a whole new orbit.

30 'Another intelligence section ...': R. V. Jones, 'Scientific Intelligence', *RUSI Journal*, 92, 567, August 1947, pp. 361–2.

31 'We in scientific intelligence ...': Jones to Churchill's private secretary, March 1951, RVJO B.222 CCAC.

32 'von Braun and his fellow rocketeers ...': Wernher von Braun, 'Space Man – The Story of My Life', part 1, *American Weekly*, 20 July 1958.

33 'Dear Reg ...': Norman to Jones, 20 January 1958, RVJO B.525 CCAC.

33 'He had an almost pathological ...': Sir Edward Bullard, review of Jones, *Most Secret War*, *Nature*, 13 July 1978.

34 'the full force of the V1 ...': *The Times,* 9 February 1946, and *New York Daily News*, 6 October 1946, cuttings in Constance Babington Smith papers, Medmenham Collection DFG 5748.

35 'a book by you ...': 13 February 1958, RVJO B.525 CCAC.

35 'Getting a little dreary ...': 4 March 1958, RVJO B.525 CCAC.

Chapter 4

37 'This was a great ...': Jones, *Most Secret War*, p. 59.

37 'The following day ...': Ibid., p. 60.

37 'It was possible to prove ...': TNA HW 43/69. See TNA AIR 20/8535 for the German-language original.

38 'A long range rocket ...': TNA DEFE 40/12.

38–9 'Remote-controlled missiles ...': Oslo report, IWM 2417 Ger Misc 19.

39 'The place was far ...': Dornberger, *V-2*, p. 50.

42 'In Peenemünde ...': Todt to Fromm, 30 June 1940, quoted in Petersen, *Missiles for the Fatherland*, p. 64.

42 'on a cloudy overcast day ...': Dornberger, op. cit., p. 71.

42 'laughing and roaring ...': Ibid., p. 72.

44 'showed old films ...': Huzel, *Peenemünde to Canaveral*, p. 130.

44 'festive parties ...': Ibid.

44 'No Poles or Dogs': Middlebrook, *The Peenemünde Raid*, p. 31.

45 'Proposals for Employment ...': Hölsken, *Die V-Waffen*, p. 32.

47 'To space travel': Dornberger, op. cit., p. 29.

47 'Soon your work ...': Ibid., p. 173.
48 'seriously wonder[ed] whether one ...': Hölsken, op. cit., p. 89.
48 'I expected that Speer ...': Dornberger, op. cit., p. 78.
49 'completely bald ...': Ibid., p. 79.
49 'Hitler's enthusiasm or lack of it': MI14 report, *The German Long-Range Rocket Programme 1930–1945*, October 1945, TNA WO 232/31.
49 'the Führer had had a dream ...': Ibid.
49 'returned [from an inspection ...': Ibid.

Chapter 5

51 'Source overheard conversation ...': Original dated 18 December 1942, RVJO B.123 CCAC.
52 Aage Andraesen: Ibid.
52fn 'solemnly stressed ...': Norman to Travis, 28 January 1942, TNA HW 14/27.
52 'a new source ...': *Evidence of the Existence of a Long Range Rocket*, TNA AIR 40/1884.
53 'I regarded myself ...': Jones, *Most Secret War*, p. 332.
53 'Source 36966': *Germany, New Weapon – Rockets*, original dated 12 January 1943, RVJO B.123 CCAC.
53 'On the peninsula of Usedom': *Evidence*, TNA AIR 40/1884.
53 'Experiments are being made ...': Ibid.
53 'All the information ...': Jones, op. cit., p. 334.
54 'a by-pass route for requests ...': Powys-Lybbe, *The Eye of Intelligence*, p. 38.
55 'Something unusual caught my eye ...': Babington Smith, *Evidence in Camera*, p. 200.
55 'heavy constructional work': Ibid. Hugh Hamshaw-Thomas reminded Babington Smith, when she was researching her book in 1956, that 'the possibility that the rings were prehistoric sites being adapted for modern use was explored but didn't lead to anything ... an archaeologist in the Army section advised on this'. She noted, meanwhile, that 'HH-T was one more person who doesn't care for Duncan Sandys – says he was "rough" but "served his purpose well".' Constance Babington Smith papers, Medmenham Collection DFG 3831.
55 'Detailed interpretation ...': *Interpretation Report No. D.S 3*, issued 27 May 1943, p. 5 paragraph (iv): Sortie N/709 of 19 January 1943, TNA AIR 40/1884.
55 'scaffoldings rising ...': Douglas Kendall, 'A War of Intelligence', unpublished ms, Medmenham Collection MHP-16, pp. 85–6.
55 'poor and much obscured by cloud': *Interpretation Report No. D.S 3*, issued 27 May 1943, p. 5 paragraph (v): Sortie N/756 of 1 March 1943, TNA AIR 40/1884.
55 'two stage compound rocket': Kendall, op. cit.
56 'projectors, which might ...': Ibid.
56 'suspicious erections of rails ...': MI14(h) to APIS, 13 February 1943, TNA AIR 34/80.
56 'No evidence has been found ...': *Peenemünde* pt 1, 22 April 1943, TNA AIR 20/9190.

56 'propelled by hydrogen': MI10 report, 26 March 1943, TNA CAB 120/748.

57 'Frankenstein personality ...': 4 April 1943, TNA CAB 120/748.

57 'blast effect was considerable': Ibid.

58 'There's a special proving ground ...': TNA CAB 120/748.

Chapter 6

59 'within the Prof's circle ...': Birkenhead, *The Prof in Two Worlds*, p. 259.

60 'should be made aware ...': TNA PREM 3/110.

60 'they are part of the general ...': TNA AIR 20/2629.

60 'were a number of other agencies ...': TNA CAB 120/748.

61 'The Chiefs of Staff feel ...': TNA CAB 120/211.

61 'young Sandys ...': TNA CSC 11/236.

61 exceptionally good-looking: David Kendall and Kenneth Post, 'The British 3-Inch Anti-Aircraft Rocket. Part One: Dive-Bombers', *Notes and Records of the Royal Society*, July 1, 1996, vol. 1, no. 2.

61 'My Dear Winston': Letter dated 1 September 1940, TNA PREM 3/119/1. Sandys's Welsh rocket battery appointment was outright Churchill cronyism. Since his return to the Admiralty as First Lord in September 1939, with Lindemann as scientific adviser, Churchill had shown a vigorous interest in anti-aircraft rockets – known as 'unrotated projectiles' – for the defence of naval bases and warships, just as he had done in his membership of the pre-war Air Defence Research subcommittee of the Committee of Imperial Defence. As well as rockets, that body had also considered the photo-electric (PE) proximity fuse and 'aerial minefields', both championed by Lindemann for defeating the bomber. Both would prove dead-ends. Sandys's first report from Aberporth on the PE-fused rocket was damning, blaming the director of rocket development at the Ministry of Supply – Dr Alwyn Crow. Kenneth Post was secretary of the oversight committee. See Kendall and Post, op. cit.

62 'verbally by telephone': Jones interviewed by David Irving, 6 January 1964, RVJO B.341 CCAC. According to Jones, his favourite photo-interpreter, Claude Wavell, and PRU pilots from Benson would also come surreptitiously to the London office for briefings.

62 'as useful as telling ...': Powys-Lybbe, *The Eye of Intelligence*, p. 189.

63 'everything to meet your wishes': Capel-Dunn to Sandys, 22 April 1943, TNA CAB 120/748.

63 'required and requested': Anthony Cave Brown, *'C': The Secret Life of Sir Stewart Graham Menzies, Spymaster to Winston Churchill* (New York: Macmillan, 1987), p. 516.

63–4 'So far as the intelligence ...': TNA AIR 20/2629.

64 'German Long Range Rockets ...': 22 April 1943, CHER G410/1-2.

64 'The experts from the Ministry ...': Powys-Lybbe, op. cit., p. 189.

65 '[A]t the extreme NE ...': *Flak and target maps etc., Peenemünde, Germany*, TNA AIR 40/1192.

65 'no sign of activity ...': *New Developments at Peenemünde*, 29 April 1943, TNA AIR 34/196.

65 'A large cloud of white smoke ...': TNA AIR 40/1192.

66 'Sandys must have ...': Jones, *Most Secret War*, p. 340.
67 'I am anxious to guard ...': TNA AIR 20/2629.
67 'Also sent at your request ...': TNA AIR 34/626.
67 'Along the shore line ...': TNA AIR 34/626.
68 'The plan of attack ...': BP archives.

Chapter 7

69 'Kommando Rügen': Message of 28 April circulated in CX/MSS J1, 26 June 1943, TNA HW 5/708.
69 bicycle-tyre repair kits: Ibid.
69 'An orderly interrupted ...': Max Wachtel, 'Unternehmen Rumpelkammer', *Der Spiegel*, 1 December 1965.
70 'In Peenemünde on Usedom ...': Ibid.
71 'The spa hotel ...': Ibid.
71 'it seems unlikely ...': MI14 report, *The German Long-Range Rocket Programme 1930–1945*, October 1945, TNA WO 232/31.
73–4 'German industry works ...': Petersen, *Missiles for the Fatherland*, pp. 102–3.
74 'We did not doubt ...': Dornberger, *V-2*, p. 165.
74 'when one of my employees ...': Ibid.

Chapter 8

75 'The Germans have ...': TNA CAB 121/211.
76 'with other appropriate authorities ...': Ibid.
76 'those parts that had not ...': Ibid.
76 'long-range guns ...': Sandys to Evill, 24 May 1943, TNA AIR 20/2629.
76 'a new kind of fuel ...': TNA AIR 20/3424. In early May 1943 Harold Phelps turned several times to fragmentary reports of a 'special explosive being tested in connection with the Peenemünde experiments' at a Heinkel-owned factory at Jenbach in Tyrol. It seemed inconsequential, but was in fact where the A4's turbo-pumps were manufactured. Jenbach was never targeted. TNA AIR 20/9190.
76 'wasting bomber effort': Evill to Bottomley, 25 May 1943, TNA AIR 20/2629.
76 'no direction over mounting ...': TNA AIR 20/3424.
77 'generally aware of locations': Ibid.
77 'dealt with in conjunction with ...': Ibid.
78 'A large object can be observed ...': *Peenemunde, Photographs and Interpretation Reports: part 3*, TNA AIR 20/9190.
78 'A train of first class main line ...': Ibid.
78 'ginger up': Ibid.
79 'generally in the picture ...': Sandys to Hollis, 23 May 1943, TNA CAB 121/211.
79 'could be tricky ...': TNA CAB 121/211.
79 'hydrogen fuel experiments': TNA AIR 20/2629.
79 'I am anxious ...': TNA AIR 20/3424.

79 'The previous statements ...': Ibid.
80 'experimental establishments ...': Evill to Bottomley, 4 June 1943, TNA AIR 20/2629.
80 'reason to suppose ...': *Attacks on 'Crossbow' (Rocket Projectiles) Sites*, TNA AIR 40/1884.
80 'kill or injure technical personnel': Ibid.
80 'a remote contingency ...': TNA PREM 3/110 and CHER G410/6.

Chapter 9

81 'dirty and ragged': Jeffery, *MI6*, p. 533.
81 'a cigar-shaped projectile ...': *Germany* from Source B.3, 4 June 1943, TNA AIR 2/14508.
81 'anything further on this subject ...': Jeffery, op. cit., p. 534.
82 'started from a catapult ...': *Air Scientific Intelligence Interim Report German Long-Range Rockets*, 26 June 1943, TNA AIR 20/1681.
82 It spoke of winged rockets: TNA CAB 121/211.
83 'five to six weeks ...': *Minutes of a Meeting at ADI (PH)*, 3 June 1943, TNA AIR 21/14508.
83 'Suddenly I spotted ...': Jones, *Most Secret War*, p. 340.
83 'Lord Cherwell has asked ...': Jones to Sandys, 19 June 1943, RVJO CCAC.
83 'André Kenny assured me ...': Powys-Lybbe, *The Eye of Intelligence*, p. 202.
84 'This object is thirty-five feet ...': *Addendum to Report No. D.S. 9*, undated, TNA AIR 34/196.
84 'The Air Ministry will receive ...': *Division of Responsibilities in Connection with the German Long-Range Rocket*, TNA AIR 20/2629.
85 'Has Mr Sandys seen you yet?': RVJO B.341 CCAC.
85 'In fact, from what Churchill said ...': Ibid.
85 around eighty tons: Ibid.
86 'They say it's sixty ...': Ibid.
86 'inside a technical department ...': *Meeting of Defence Committee (Operations)*, 29 June 1943, TNA CAB 121/211.
87 'Remarkable photographs ...': Ibid.
87 'Two objects ...': Ibid.
88 'It seems curious ...': Ibid.
88 'keeping watch for the signs ...': Ibid.
88 'Although his points ...': Ibid.
88 'Now I want the Truth!': Jones letter to David Irving, 23 August 1963, RVJO B.339/340 CCAC.
89 'examine pilotless and or jet propelled aircraft ...': TNA CAB 121/211.
90 'The major at Kummersdorf ...': *German Long-Range Rocket*, 26 June 1943, TNA AIR 20/1681.
90 'was now imprisoned for immoral practices': Ibid.
90 'an agent had reported recently': Ibid.
90 someone on the staff of Generalmajor Hans Leyers: Ibid. Dr Jones said later that the treacherous German staff officer definitely existed, and

was not some sort of cover for another intelligence source, 8 July 1964, RVJO B.346 CCAC.

91 'The Germans are announcing ...': 1 July 1943, CHER G410/9.
91 dead fish: TNA CAB 121/211.
91–2 'who has been working on ...': *Investigation of Jet-Propelled and Pilotless Aircraft*, TNA CAB 111/36.
92 'Speer was to have been ...': MI14 report, *The German Long-Range Rocket Programme 1930–1945*, October 1945, TNA WO 232/31.
93 'enormous trenches': *German LRR Summary of Evidence*, 7 August 1943, TNA AIR 20/2629.
93 'a large rail- and canal-served clearing ...': *Watten (France): Suspected Long-Range Rocket Site*, part 1, TNA AIR 40/2526.
93 '190 all ranks paratroops': TNA CAB 121/211.
93 'secret arms were [being] positioned ...': *Development of Long-Range Rocket*, TNA AIR 2/14508.
94 'Immense foundations ...': Ibid.
94 'a garbled version of reports ...': TNA DEFE 40/12.
94 'sleep inducing bomb ...': TNA CAB 121/211.
94 'flying torpedo' ... Buchwald: *Secret Weapons*, 5 February 1943, Allen W. Dulles papers, Princeton University Library digital files.
94–5 'Sandys Committee ...': Jones to Portal, 13 July 1943, DEFE 40/12.
95 'Very anxious to have your help ...': TNA CAB 120/748.
95 'Source JX/Knopf': TNA AIR 2/14508.
96 Hans von Braun: Sandys report to chiefs of staff, 7 August 1943, TNA CAB 121/211.
96 'The technical and experimental sites ...': TNA AIR 2/14508.
96 'certain unnamed German generals ...': CHER G410/9.
96 'diplomatic channels': TNA CAB 121/211.
97 'There are signs ...': 24 July 1943, TNA CAB 121/740.

Chapter 10

98 'Himmler announced ...': Dornberger, *V-2*, pp. 178–9.
98 'We must bear in mind ...': Ibid., p. 184.
98 'Reichsführer ...': Ibid.
99 'Sabotage can be eliminated ...': Ibid.
99 'We stood together ...': Ibid.
99 'The air war against our population ...': 'Bemerkungen zum R-Programm', notes of a meeting, Berlin, 28 June 1943. Original in Bundesarchiv, quoted in Ralf Schabel, *Die Illusion der Wunderwaffen: die Rolle der Düsenflugzeuge und Flugabwehrraketen in der Rüstungspolitik des Dritten Reiches* (Munich: R. Oldenbourg, 1994), p. 268. See also Speer, *The Slave State*, p.493fn, for a somewhat garbled version.
100 'We had packed it all up ...': Dornberger, op. cit., pp. 101–4.
100 'It was in the innermost ...': Ibid.
100 'If only I had had faith ...': TNA WO 232/31, p. 16.
101 'If we had developed these rockets ...': *Dornberger's Homework*, TNA WO 208/3121.
102 'As a basic principle ...': Neufeld, *The Rocket and the Reich*, p. 155.

102 'mixed nationalities': Petersen, *Missiles for the Fatherland*, p. 149.
102 'Production by convicts ...': Neufeld, op. cit., p. 155. The NASM historian noted the studied use of the term *Sträflinge* (convicts) by Dornberger and others in the discussions, rather than the SS term *Häftlinge* (meaning prisoners or detainees held without judicial process).
103 'They came round ...': Esser, IWM 13210 Ger Misc 25 (197).
103 'Oberst Wachtel lived ...': Ibid.
105 'It can be built ...': Hölsken, *Die V-Waffen*, p. 48.
105 'in Kassel people were talking ...': Irving, *The Mare's Nest*, p. 102.
105 'The so-called Dampferzeuger ...': Hilary St George Saunders, *The Royal Air Force 1939–1945. Vol. III: The Fight is Won* (London: HMSO, 1954), p. 149.
106 'The staff of Flakregiment 155 ...': Kriegestagbuch [KTB – war diary] HQ Flakregiment 155 (W), Zempin, 15 August 1943, IWM Enemy Document Section MI14/10389.

Chapter 11

108 'piddling little force of Fortresses': Craven and Cate, *The Army Air Forces in World War II*, vol. 2, <www.ibiblio.org/hyperwar/AAF>, p. 296.
108 'was a very large map ...': TNA HW14/85
110 'Those poor bastards': Middlebrook, *The Battle of Hamburg*, p. 344. See also Friedrich, *The Fire*, pp. 165–9.
100 'We had no idea ...': Jones, *Most Secret War*, p. 302.

Chapter 12

111 'The question now ...': Jones, *Most Secret War*, p. 303.
111 'Trench shelters ...': *Appreciation of the Return to be Expected from Bombing the Target at Peenemünde*, 7 July 1943, TNA AIR 40/1884.
114 'a radar development station': *Draft Target Information Sheet, Peenemünde 8 July 1943*, TNA AIR 40/1192.
115 'preliminary photo-reconnaissance ...': TNA AIR 40/1884.
115 'It seems unlikely ...': TNA CAB 121/211 6871.
116 'of the atom-splitting variety': *New Explosives*, 21 August 1943, TNA CAB 121/211.
116 'new chemical warfare agent ...': Ibid. On the subject of 'N', Cherwell would tell Churchill in early 1944: 'This appears to be a weapon of appalling potentiality, almost more formidable, because easier to make than Tube Alloys [the atom bomb].' He outlined the 'present proposal' for ordering the manufacture of enough anthrax bombs to 'render uninhabitable thirty square miles (the size of Berlin's erstwhile built-up area)'. It would require 180 Lancaster bombers to do so. 25 February 1944 TNA CAB 127/200.
116 'dangerous speculation': Hollis to Attlee, 24 August 1943, TNA CAB 118/48.
116 asking him to prepare a plan: TNA AIR 40/1884.
117 'All target maps ...': Ibid.

Chapter 13

118 'Source Z.178/B': TNA DEFE 40/12 and TNA CAB 121/211.
118 'Very important . . .': TNA DEFE 40/12.
118 German High Command 'believed . . .': Ibid.
118 ten A-4s had been test-fired: Ibid.
119 'captain on the active list . . .': TNA AIR 40/3009.
121 'I had become part of the equipment . . .': David Ignatius, 'After Five Decades, a Spy Tells Her Tale', *Washington Post*, 28 December 1998.
121 'I insisted that they must be mad . . .': Ibid.
122 'fuse – careful – do not pull': TNA AIR 20/2631.
122 'operating valves with compressed air . . .': Ibid.
122 'in many pieces': Statement by Christian Hasager Christiansen c. late 1945, RVJO B.168 CCAC.
122 'The denial of taking any pictures . . .': Paul Mørch, 'Notes on V-1's Visit to Denmark', 4 February 1977, RVJO B.574 CCAC.

PART II: 'WE WILL FORCE ENGLAND TO HER KNEES'

Chapter 14

127 'We discussed the damage . . .': Speer, *The Slave State*, p. 205.
128 'one of his most capable SS . . .': Ibid., p. 206.
128 'This will be retribution . . .': Ibid., p. 207.
130 'very secret negotiations . . .': Neufeld, *The Rocket and the Reich*, p. 206.
131 a tireless worker: Höss, *Death Dealer*, pp. 293–5.
131 'in many ways my mirror image . . .': Albert Speer (trans. Richard and Clara Winston), *Inside the Third Reich: Memoirs* (London: Weidenfeld & Nicolson, 1970), p. 374.
132 '40,000 workers . . .': IWM KTB HQ Flakregiment 155 (W), Zempin, 13 September 1943.
133 'Rapid progress is being made . . .': IWM KTB HQ Flakregiment 155 (W), Zempin, 16 September 1943.
133 'large quantity of maps . . .': Ibid.
133 'security is especially important . . .': IWM KTB HQ Flakregiment 155 (W), Zempin, 28 September 1943.

Chapter 15

134 'an argument so trivial . . .': Jones, *Most Secret War*, p. 357.
134–5 'from very limited information . . .': Enclosure to Annex B, *Pilotless Aircraft*, 13 September 1943, TNA CAB 121/211.
135 'special note': *The Flakzielgerät 76*, RVJO B.87 CCAC.
135 'who had the task of establishing . . .': Ibid.
135–6 'The Germans are installing . . .': Ibid.

136   'would let him off the hook ...': Jones, op. cit., p. 453.
136   grey-green uniforms: TNA CAB 121/211.
137   'seen an MSS ...': 'Bodyline', Pendred to Jones, 24 September 1943,
       TNA DEFE 40/12.
138   'D-S may have received ...': Ibid., handwritten annotation.
138   'Report on Reliability of Intelligence': 29 September 1943, TNA
       PREM 3/110.
138   'certain from such disinterested witnesses ...': Ibid.
139   averse to circulating papers: Air Ministry to Britman, Washington, 25
       September 1943, TNA CAB 121/211.
139   'German Threats of Air ...': TNA CAB 121/211.
140   'it seems possible ...': Irving, *The Mare's Nest*, p. 155.
140   'We are of the opinion ...': Ibid.
141   'completely altered the picture': *German Long-Range Rocket*, 25 October
       1943, TNA CAB 121/211.
141   'enormous explosive force ...': C/4581, 11 October 1943, TNA HW
       1/2807. Baron Oshima's revealing messages to Tokyo in the so called
       Purple code (broken by Professor Norman's American visitor William
       Friedman in 1940, the product of which was codenamed 'Magic') were
       handled by the GC&CS's diplomatic section at 7–9 Berkeley Street in
       London and not at Bletchley Park. Their largely unelaborated product
       (variously called 'Blue Jacket' or 'Black Jumbo') derived from enemy, neu-
       tral and friendly sources, had a very much wider circulation that the Park's
       and had been a Whitehall staple for decades. (See Robin Denniston, *Thirty
       Secret Years: A. G. Denniston's Work in Signals Intelligence 1914–1944* (Clifton-
       upon-Teme: Polperro Heritage Press, 2007).
              The day before Sandys got the Oshima transcripts he had ruffled C's
       feathers with a bid to get his own man, Harold Phelps, to Stockholm to
       debrief a certain Müller, an engineer who had offered information on
       German long-range weapons to the legation. Jones was copied in on the
       move.
              In a bid to keep the minister quiet, Menzies met Sandys to 'explain the
       gist of certain information known to be enemy planted and drew the com-
       parison between this and certain information obtained in CX [agent]
       reports and in B J [Black Jumbo diplomatic] material, of which latter CSS
       left a note [the typewritten extract of the Berlin–Tokyo report] for Mr
       Sandys's personal information only', as an internal SIS note of the
       encounter put it. *Notes of a Meeting with Mr Duncan Sandys on the 11th October
       1943*, TNA DEFE 40/12. Thus the first hint to the minister that there
       might be signals-derived intelligence as well as agent reports and photo-
       reconnaissance on the matter he had been so earnestly investigating for six
       months was that it tied in with deliberate disinformation by the enemy.
141   'inflated barrage balloons': 11 October 1943, TNA CAB 121/211.
142   'having seen the sketch submitted ...': Ibid.

Chapter 16

143–4 'Despite his Nazi convictions ...': 'ADI (K) report 16 March 1945:
       Appendix II', TNA AIR 20/7698.

144   'To Zempin ...': CX/MSS/J 3 TNA HW 5/708.

144   'he had bought the tickets ...': Martelli, *Agent Extraordinary*, p. 179.

145   'Collecting a team of reliable agents ...': See ibid., pp. 153–8 and 172–7.

145   OP: Ibid., p. 158. It was explained that the bag reached London from Switzerland in the custody of a neutral courier.

146   'there was no single major engineering factor ...': *German Long-Range Rocket Development*, 24 October 1943, TNA AIR 20/2631 and see also CHER G417.

147   'We consider that a rocket ...': Ibid.

147   'previous estimates for range ...': Ibid.

147   'had reached a state ...': Ibid.

147   'we [can] be sure ...': TNA CAB 121/211.

148   'It is unlikely that [German rocket] development ...': Ibid.

148   'At the end of the war ...': War Cabinet Defence Committee (Operations), *The German Long-Range Rocket*, 25 October 1943, TNA CAB 121/211 and CHER G417.

148   the objects photographed at Peenemünde: TNA CAB 121/211.

149   'a mendacious prisoner': CHER G421/2.

150   'They might possibly be ...': *The German L R R*, 24 October 1943, TNA AIR 20/2631.

150   'no means of judging': TNA CAB 121/211

Chapter 17

151   'certain American officers ...': Chiefs of staff meeting, 25 October 1943, TNA CAB 121/211.

151   'there is at present ...': *German L R R, Report by the JIC Sub-Committee*, 26 October 1943, TNA CAB 121/211.

151   Americans in London: Ibid.

151   two escaped USAAF officers: Ibid.

152   'their appetite no doubt ...': Ibid.

152   '[are] starting to take an interest ...': Ibid.

152   'be given orally ...': Chiefs of staff meeting, 29 October 1943, minutes sent to JSM, Washington, TNA CAB 122/333.

152   'responsibility of this officer ...': Lt-Col. L. J. Carver to Ismay, 28 January 1944, CHER 425/20.

153   'The expert committee ...': TNA CAB 120/748.

153   'Inter-Allied Command': TNA AIR 20/2631.

153   'the tone of the report ...': TNA CAB 121/211.

153   'I did not attend the inquiries ...': 6 January 1964, RVJO B.341 CCAC.

154   'To Lehr and Erpr. Kdo ...': Obergfr. Nelz to Zempin, CX/MSS J 7, TNA HW 5/708.

154   from 28 October onwards: *Report on Brown Group to 13 12 43*, TNA HW14/93.

154   'a ringside seat at the trials': Jones to Churchill, c. 20 April 1951. In his typewritten critique, Jones also reminded Churchill that 'by that time we had [blank] about the performance of the weapon ... which was of course given without delay to the Chiefs of Staff and Lord Cherwell'. RVJO CCAC.

155   'On a fine, mild autumn Sunday ...': IWM KTB HQ Flakregiment 155
       (W), Zempin, 16 October 1943.
156   'same secret weapon ...': *Report No. V: Dr Jones's report on German pilot-
       less aircraft*, TNA AIR 40/3009.
156   'We thought first of all ...': Friedrich, *The Fire*, p. 336.
156–7 'There is almost unanimous ...': see Ibid., pp. 425–44 for a discussion
       of the expectations raised in the German public by the V-weapons and the
       reality once the campaign began.
157   'Revenge cannot be strong enough': Ibid., p. 427.

Chapter 18

160   'indoctrinated into Ultra': That is, according to Kendall's own statement
       in 'A War of Intelligence', p. 49. He was not on CX/MSS J circulation.
160   'a brilliant piece of espionage': Jones, *Most Secret War*, p. 364.
161   *beton non armé*: Annotation to plan for 'Maison R' copied by Andre
       Comps, original in Jones papers. RVJO B.176 CCAC.
161   looked 'like a ski laid on its side': The famous phrase pops up in many
       documents from November 1943 onwards. According to the Curator of the
       Medmenham Collection, it was most probably coined by an anonymous
       photo-interpreter.
161   'Everything seemed to point ...': Douglas Kendall, 'A War of
       Intelligence', p. 97.
162   'a unanimous opinion ...': TNA AIR 20/2631.
162   did not think it worth Churchill's while: TNA PREM 3/110.
162   'The nerve centre ...': TNA AIR 20/2631.
162   '15-ton rockets': Ibid.
162–3 'rocket bomb with a range ...': TNA AIR 2/14508 0020.
163   'In Auschwitz ...': TNA AIR 20/2631.
163–4 'It is beyond reasonable doubt ...': TNA CAB 120/748.
164   'Against the terror ...': Ibid.
164   'tools of our revenge': Ibid.
164   'They are not like any known military installation': Kendall, op. cit.,
       p. 99.
165   'The present rate of trial': *The German Pilotless Aircraft, Draft*, 12
       November 1943, TNA DEFE 40/12.
165   'to sift SIS ...': TNA CAB 121/211.
165   the JIC would certainly wish: TNA AIR 20/2632.
165   'The Chiefs of Staff have ...': TNA CAB 120/740.
166   'work of value': TNA AIR 20/2632.
166   'by an ad hoc interdepartmental committee': Hinsley et al., *British
       Intelligence in the Second World War, Vol. 3*, pt 1, p. 411fn.
166   'Within the Air Ministry ...': Ibid.
166   'It is pleasant to think ...': TNA DEFE 40/12.
166–7 'I understand that SIS ...': Ibid.
167   'All reports which directly concern ...': Ibid.
167   'CX (agent reports] connected to Bodyline ...': TNA DEFE 40/12.
167   'broad agreement with its conclusions': TNA AIR 20/2631.
168   'the large square building ...': Ibid.

168   'The 14th Company ...': Ibid.
168   'Its rate of descent ...': Ibid.
168   'I think it is clear ...': CHER G420/4.
169   'We are told that a German general ...': CHER G421/13.
169   'It has been my duty ...': 15 November 1943, RVJO CCAC.
170   'pleasant to work with': Jones, op. cit., p. 365.
170   'hardly bother to turn up ...': A. L. Bonsey letter to the editor, *The Times*, 17 April 1961.
170   'as and when it was felt necessary': Bottomley to Stewart, 24 November 1943, TNA CAB 113/37.
170   'It's a good paper': *V-Weapons 1943–45*, TNA AIR 20/3437.
171   'This paper is an example ...': Sandys to Bottomley, 26 Nov 1943, TNA AIR 20/3437.
171   'Lunch next Tuesday': Ibid.

Chapter 19

173   'for six months ...': Dornberger, *V-2*, pp. 204–5.
173–4 'Shot after shot went wrong ...': Ibid., pp. 209–10.
174   'Gentlemen from FHQ arrived ...': IWM KTB HQ Flakregiment 155 (W), Zempin, 12 November 1943, IWM Enemy Documents Section MI14/1038/1:2.
175   'he was personally at enmity ...': TNA CAB 101/30.
176   'Falster, Denmark ...': IWM KTB HQ Flakregiment 155 (W), Zempin, 24 November 1943.
176   'a high flying Mosquito ...': IWM KTB HQ Flakregiment 155 (W), Zempin, 28 November 1943.
176   'insecure, conspicuous, needlessly elaborate ...': Hölsken, *Die V-Waffen*, pp. 118–19.
177   'leaflets dropped regularly from the air': KTB HQ Flakregiment 155 (W), Château Merlemont, 12 December 1943.

Chapter 20

179   'You will remember ...': TNA CAB 154/49.
179   'a radio-controlled plane': Ibid.
179   'We could make use ...': Ibid.
179   'enormous rocket gun': Ibid.
180   'certain preparations became known ...': Morrison to Churchill, 5 October 1943, TNA INF 1/967.
180   'Swedish reports of mysterious events ...': newspaper cutting, TNA CAB 113/38.
180   'I would like you to tell ...': *Translation of Reference to Rocket Guns in Garbo letter No. 244*, TNA CAB 154/49.
180   'because of the rockets ...': London Controlling Section, *Plan Crossbow*, TNA CAB 154/49 3931.
180   'facing in the direction of Berlin ...': Ibid.
181   'We get the Germans worried ...': Ibid.

181 'super-long-range rocket . . .': Ibid.

181 'mystery signals': Ibid.

181 'waste of effort': Ibid.

181 'The activities of Colonel Wachtel . . .': JIC Crossbow Sub-Committee, 24 November 1943, TNA CAB 121/211.

182 Bottomley ordered that he be watched . . .: Bottomley to Inglis, TNA AIR 20/2632.

182 'The situation was so serious . . .': Jones, *Most Secret War*, p. 366.

182–3 'Up until now . . .': Kendall, 'A War of Intelligence', p. 100.

183 '[It] was sitting in a corner . . .': Babington Smith, *Evidence in Camera*, p. 160.

183 'one of the great PI achievements . . .': Stanley, *V Weapons Hunt*, p. 79.

184 'consequent to the discovery . . .': *The Pilotless Aircraft*, TNA AIR 40/3009.

184 'daily habits': Ibid.

184 'a lucky thing . . .': 6 January 1964, RVJO B.341 CCAC.

185 'We had never photographed Zinnowitz . . .': Kendall, op. cit, p. 100.

185–6 'This first excursion . . .': Babington Smith, op. cit., p. 221.

186 four 'strange structures . . .': Ibid., p. 222.

186 'That's it! I know it is!': Ibid., p. 223.

187 'even with the naked eye . . .': Ibid.

187 'I have heard today . . .': CHER G 420/16.

187 'might have an accuracy . . .': Ibid.

187–8 'enemy employing some new . . .': TNA DEFE 40/12.

188 'atomic disintegration': Ibid.

188 'I think the threat is real . . .': CHER G420/23.

188 'consulted with Jones . . .': Ibid.

188 'a note of what you know . . .': TNA DEFE 40/21.

189 'one hundred ski sites . . .': *Scale of Attack*, TNA CAB 121/211.

189 'The current RAF raids . . .': TNA AIR 20/2631.

189 'even if made through . . .': *JPS Report*, TNA AIR 8/1222.

Chapter 21

191 'The kitchen car . . .': IWM KTB HQ Flakregiment 155 (W), 7 December 1943.

191 'With my staff . . .': Wachtel, 'Unternehmen Rumpelkammer'.

191–2 'Obegrf. Faltten . . .': J 28, 24 December 1943, TNA HW 5/708.

192 'Merry Christmas . . .': Message stamped at 0615/23/12 in J 31, 2 January 1944, TNA HW 5/708.

192 'The air in the cave': Speer, *The Slave State*, p. 211.

192–3 'Kammler had incredible powers . . .': Höss, *Death Dealer*, p. 295.

193 'the civilian technicians . . .': Béon, *Planet Dora*, p. 24.

193 'concrete runway': *Crossbow: sabotage and bombing*, TNA HS 8/301.

195 so far as was known: TNA CAB 120/748.

195 'Red Death': Craven and Cate, *The Army Air Forces in World War II*, vol. 3, p. 92.

195 'instantaneous creation . . .': Ibid.

196 'enjoyed the warmest relations': JSM Washington to Air Ministry, TNA CAB 121/212 f.261.

196 'the enemy might be planning ...': Hinsley et al., *British Intelligence in the Second World War, Vol. 3*, pt 2, p. 587.

196 'a reintroduction of German air power ...': 9 January 1944, TNA CAB 121/212.

197 'bacterial warfare': Letter dated 28 January 1944, CHER G425/18.

197 'conducted a series ...': Ibid.

197 'converted forty ...': Ibid.

197 'The whole party ...': Ibid.

198 were invited to lunch: Esser, IWM 13210 Ger Misc 25 (197).

198 'There were air raids ...': Ibid.

198 'table stacked with presents ...': IWM KTB HQ Flakgruppe Creil, Merlemont, 24 December 1943.

198 'All ranks! ...': Ibid.

Chapter 22

199 'much exaggerated': TNA CAB 121/211.

200 'The IV Abteilung ...': *The Pilotless Aircraft*, 23 December 1943, TNA AIR 40/3009.

200 'The 155 is some sort ...': Ibid.

200 'Our sources soon reported ...': Ibid. The Luftnachrichten-Versuchs Regiment used Würzburg radars for height finding and long-range Freya radars for distance tracking. See post-surrender prisoner-of-war interrogation of Feldwebel Klussendorf (whose name had already served to give Hut Six a crib) for a full description of how the telemetry range operated. TNA AIR 40/2875.

200 'This could be done ...': Ibid.

201 'If my assumptions ...': War Cabinet Defence Committee (Operations), 22 December 1943, TNA CAB 121/212 f.252.

202 'Despite the Zempin ...': TNA AIR 40/3009,

202 valuable and reliable source: Pelly to Inglis, 23 December 1943, TNA DEFE 40/12.

203 'intelligence by committee': Jones to Inglis, 24 December 1943, TNA DEFE 40/12.

203 'My section ...': Ibid.

203 permission to resign: Jones to Inglis, 27 December 1943, TNA DEFE 40/12.

203 'I understand that part ...': Jacob to Churchill, 2 January 1944, TNA CAB 120/749 8775.

204 'The Defence Committee ...': Ibid.

204 'Big Ben': Air Cdre K. Buss D of I (Security), 29 December 1943, TNA DEFE 40/12.

204 'What really surprises me ...': Churchill to Portal, 10 January 1944, TNA CAB 120/749.

204 'Are you attacking all camps ...': TNA CAB 120/749.

205 'The enemy's policy for the repair ...': TNA CAB 121/212.

205 'More attacks, progress nil ...': IWM KTB HQ Flakgruppe Creil, Merlemont, 7 January 1944.

206 'some of the German foremen ...': Ibid.

206 'strict warning': IWM KTB HQ Flakgruppe Creil, Merlemont, 5 February 1944.

206 'inciting the civilian population ...': IWM KTB HQ Flakgruppe Creil, Merlemont, 10 January 1944.
206 'had put a price ...': Wachtel, 'Unternehmen Rumpelkammer'.
206 'I was also classified': Ibid.
207 'changed uniforms ...': ADI (K) summary of KTB HQ Flakregiment 155 (W) in LHCMA LH15/15/59.

Chapter 23

208 'it would reveal ...': Jones, *Most Secret War*, p. 378.
208 'quiet, bulky man': Ibid.
209 'with the intention of deluding ...': TNA CAB 121/212.
209 weather balloons with radio transmitters: *Enemy Meteorological Activity*, 15 January 1944, TNA CAB 121/212.
209 'Source B.3': *Pingpong no. 394*, RVJO B.176 CCAC.
209 'Following numerous air reconnaissance ...': Ibid.
210 'When crews arrive ...': 25 January 1944, TNA CAB 121/212.
210 'deliver the body to England': SOE, *Crossbow, Sabotage and Bombing*, TNA HS 8/301.
210 'puny weapon': TNA CAB 120/749.
211 'This is in no way ...': Hölsken, *Die V-Waffen*, p. 206.
211 'should be put in a lunatic asylum': RLM meeting, Berlin, 13 March 1943. Original in Bundesarchiv, quoted in Horst Boog, Gerhard Krebs and Detlef Vogel (trans. Derry Cook-Radmore), *Germany and the Second World War: Volume VII: The Strategic Air War in Europe and the War in the West and East Asia, 1943–1944/5* (Oxford: Oxford University Press, 2006), p. 455. Milch further told his US interrogators in 1945: 'No one with any sense believed that England could be brought to her knees with such devices [including the V 1]. I don't think they believed it even in Government circles. It was hopeless.' TNA WO 208/4341.
212 'television controlled glide bombs': TNA CAB 121/212.
212 'I think it is clear now ...': Leigh-Mallory to Spaatz, 4 March 1944. Craven and Cate, *The Army Air Forces in World War II*, vol. 3, p. 100.
212 'rocket launching cannon': Hinsley et al., *British Intelligence in the Second World War, Vol. 3*, pt 1, p. 435.
213 'Our sharpest weapon ...': PWE report, 10 February 1944, in *Crossbow, Summaries of Attacks on Ski Sites*, TNA AIR 20/8127.
213 'the administrative exercise ...': IWM KTB HQ Flakgruppe Creil, Merlemont, 1 March 1944.
214 'survey trip to Poland': J 56, 14 March 1944, TNA HW 5/709.

Chapter 24

215 'a tiny dot ...': Dornberger, *V-2*, p. 209.
216 'free him of Army bureaucracy ...': von Braun, 'Reminiscences of German Rocketry', in Clarke, *The Coming of the Space Age*, p. 52. See also TNA F0 1031/128.
216 'I replied coolly ...': von Braun, op. cit.

216   there was no evidence: Neufeld, *The Rocket and the Reich*, p. 126.

217   'building a spaceship': Ibid.

217   'surprisingly benevolent . . .': See Speer, *The Slave State* pp. 230–3.

218   'No names of commands': TNA HW 43/69, p. 20.

218   'further names and characteristic ideas': Ibid.

218   'A-4' rising from 'Ost': CX/MSS J 20, paragraph 6, circulated 10 December 1943, TNA HW 5/708.

218   'look out for name . . .': TNA HW 43/69, p. 22.

218   'The Germans have used . . .': 10 April 1944, TNA AIR 20/9191.

219   'forestry workers . . .': Garlinski, *Hitler's Last Weapons*, pp. 115–16. See also the long digest of intelligence reports in 'Poland: Air, Rockets Feb–July 1944', dated 31 July 1944, in TNA DEFE 40/18.

219   'Blytna': Message stamped at 1035/9/2 in J 59, 23 March 1944, TNA HW5/709.

219   'Versuchsstab . . .': Message stamped at 1300/10/2 in Ibid.

219   'There is place called Blizna . . .': Ibid., note 5.

220   'completion of the building . . .': Message stamped at 1810/4/3 in J 58, 21 March 1944, TNA HW 5/709.

220   'This camp is at Debica . . .': Ibid., notes 8 and 9.

220   'adjusting house': Message stamped at 1600/13/3 in J 58, 21 March 1944, TNA HW 5/709.

220   'Taunusstrasse 8 Berlin-Grunewald': Message stamped at 0800/13/3 in J 58, 21 March 1944, TNA HW 5/709.

221   'Kammler is new to J . . .': Ibid. note 1.

221   'A-4 and FZG 76 . . .': Ibid. note 7.

221   'Kammler's stay at Heidelager . . .': Dornberger, op. cit., pp. 200–1.

221   'court-martialled . . .': Ibid.

221fn   chimney for a 'crematorium': 'German Police Decodes 4.6.42', item 10, TNA HW 16/19.

Chapter 25

222   the Crossbow 'diversion': Craven and Cate, *The Army Air Forces in World War II*, vol. 3, p. 100.

222   'it may well make the difference . . .': Ibid., p. 103.

223   'The enemy is dropping . . .': IWM KTB HQ Flakgruppe Creil, Merlemont, 10 March 1944.

224   'the most evil burden': Irving, *The Mare's Nest*, p. 210.

224   judged 'a success': IWM KTB HQ Flakgruppe Creil, 10 March 1944.

224   'annihilated two farms': Hinsley et al., *British Intelligence in the Second World War, Vol.* 3, pt 1, p. 438.

225   'Beauftragter zbV Heer': Messages of 11/12, 20/1, 3/2 and 5/2 in J 64, 13 April 1944, TNA HW 5/709.

225   'setting up id proceeding . . .': Ibid.

225   'Oberst Thom': Ibid.

225   'work for the Wehrmacht': Message stamped at 1120/19/4 in J 76, TNA HW5/709.

225   'complete trains departing under cover names': Message stamped at 0022/14/4 in J 76, TNA HW5/709.

Chapter 26

227   'We have the results ...': TNA DEFE 40/12.

227   Maikäfer: IWM KTB HQ Flakgruppe Creil, Merlemont, 30 April 1944.

228   'It appears that two Russians ...': Béon, *Planet Dora*, pp. 130–1.

228   'The tail assembly ...': Ibid., p. 174.

228   he 'did not want to identify ...': R. V. Jones, 'The Intelligence War and the Royal Air Force', *Proceedings of the Royal Air Force Historical Society*, No. 1, January 1987, p. 13.

229   There is no way of resetting it: Julitte, *Block 26*, pp. 163–5.

229   'a repentant Pétainiste': Ibid., p. 221.

229   'the experimental detachment': Message stamped at 1505/27/4 in J 87, 11 May 1944, TNA HW5/709 9425.

230   Major-General John Sinclair: TNA HW 14/103.

230   'In contrast with other keys ...': *The History of Hut 6*, vol. II, TNA HW 43/71.

231   'The contents of Corncrake ...': Ibid.

231   'Campania': CX/MSS J 91 circulated 16 May 1944, TNA HW 5/709.

231   'The wireless telegraphy system ...': *The History of Hut 6*, vol. II, TNA HW 43/71.

232   'The following are asked ...': J 101 circulated 4 June 1944, TNA HW 5/710.

232   'With today's transport please send ...': Ibid.

232   'a jolly good chap but a complete newcomer': 8 July 1964, RVJO B.346 CCAC.

232   'I'm afraid we were ...': TNA HS8/301.

233   surpassed all previous achievements: IWM KTB HQ Flakgruppe Creil, Auteil, 21 May 1944.

233   'Unused propellant (petrol) ...': AA Stockholm to Air Ministry, 18 May 1944, TNA AIR 20/2631.

234   Erich Heinemann's chauffer: TNA WO 208/4292,

234   'The abandoning of Site System I ...': IWM KTB HQ Flakgruppe Creil, Auteil, 2 June 1944.

234fn   'suddenly going into the garden ...': Oberstleutlant Zippelius statement, *V2 Organisation, War Establishment and Supplies*, September 1945, TNA WO 208/3155.

235   'Operation Instruction Number 74': 5 June 1944, TNA AIR 14/1878.

235   'Should the enemy initiate ...': Ibid.

235   'Vesicle': Ibid.

235   'the immediate collection ...': *Attack on Cities with Gas*, TNA AIR 14/1721.

235   'heavily bombarded ...': Plan II, Annex to BCOI 74, 5 June 1944, *Retaliatory Gas Attack on Germany*, TNA AIR 14/1721.

235   'As our bomber force expanded ...': *Minutes of a Meeting at the Air Ministry*, 19 May 1944, TNA AIR 20/612.

Chapter 27

237   'I quickly forgot that ...': Wachtel, 'Unternehmen Rumpelkammer'.

237   'I strongly cautioned ...': Ibid.

237   'Below the huts ...': IWM KTB HQ Flakgruppe Creil, Saleux, 9 June 1944, 2067.

237   completed very quickly: Report by ACAS (I) to chiefs of staff, 12 June 1944, TNA CAB 121/213 f.536.

237   'The general inference ...': PWE TNA CAB 121/213.

238   'each wagon was loaded ...': See French language original teleprint of 8 and 10 June 1944 in TNA AIR 40/1773 and translated summary in CAB 121/213 f.536.

238   'smashed by boots ...': Nutting, *Attain by Surprise*, pp. 159–60.

238   'sockets in the concrete': Ibid.

238   'much activity': *Modified Pilotless Aircraft Sites*, 12 June 1944, TNA CAB 121/213 f.536.

238   'If our predictions ...': Kendall, 'A War of Intelligence', p. 107.

239   'the watchers had become tired and jaded': Jones, *Most Secret War*, p. 527.

239   'This information ...': Air Chief Marshal Sir Roderic Hill, 'Air Operations by Air Defence of Great Britain And Fighter Command in connection with the German Flying Bomb and Rocket Offensives, 1944–1945', supplement to *London Gazette*, 19 October 1948, p. 5591fn.

239   Maikäfer Lehrgerät: Message stamped at 1205/10/6 in J 109, 12 June 1944, TNA HW 5/710. See TNA HS 8/302 for the SOE-French contribution to the Oise Valley campaign.

240   'send off loaded columns ...': Message stamped at 0942/11/6 in J 115, 17 June 1944, TNA HW 5/710.

240   'After months of waiting ...': IWM KTB HQ Flakgruppe Creil, Saleux, 12 June 1944.

240   Germany's only chance: Speidel, *We Defended Normandy*, pp. 108–10.

241   'More and more visitors ...': IWM KTB HQ Flakgruppe Creil, Saleux, 12 June 1944.

PART III: DIVER! DIVER!

Chapter 28

245   'At 04:10 from ...': TNA AIR 20/2631.

246   'like a Model T-Ford going up a hill': Longmate, *The Doodlebugs*, p. 90.

246   'a large corona ...': See TNA HO 192/19 for the track of the Swanscombe Diver, 12/13 June 1944.

246   'some dead chickens ...': Longmate, op. cit., p. 94.

246   'The switchboard operators ...': Ibid.

247   'heard a noise ...': TNA HO 192/492 and HO 186/2369 for 13 June 1944.

247   'if possible from the bits ...': Longmate, op. cit., p. 96.

247 'sizeable portions of light metal ...': Ibid.

247 'a fin and rudder ...': *Crashed Enemy Aircraft*, 14 June 1944, TNA AIR 40/1656.

247 'a Bosch sparking plug ...': Ibid.

248 'Dislocation of supply ...': IWM KTB HQ Flakgruppe Creil, Saleux, 13 June 1944.

Chapter 29

249 'about the size of a Spitfire': TNA CAB 121/213.

249 'a response to Overlord': Ibid.

250 'The public should not ...': Ibid.

250 'The mountain hath groaned ...': 8 July 1964, RVJO B.346 CCAC.

251 'Following from Swedish press ...': TNA AIR 20/2649.

251 'highly intelligent': TNA DEFE 40/17.

252 'very complicated pump system': Ibid.

253 'By 05.50 ceasefire ...': IWM KTB HQ Flakgruppe Creil, Saleux, 16 June 1944.

253 'At the launch ...': Esser, IWM 13210 Ger Misc 25 (197).

253 '11.45 pm: First plane ...': Mrs Hette Long, Diary, IWM Misc. 180 mem 2723.

254 'Although we knew ...': Roland Beamont, *The Years Flew Past: Forty Years at the Leading Edge of Aviation* (Shrewsbury: Airlife, 2001), pp. 38–9.

254 'In the early hours ...': IWM KTB HQ Flakregiment (W) 155, Saleux, 16 June 1944.

254–5 'It gives me ...': Ibid.

255 'officers and men ...': Ibid.

255 'The Air Ministry ...': Hill, 'Air Operations', p. 5592.

255 'the available information ...': 'Air Raids (Pilotless Machines)', *Hansard*, 16 June 1944.

257 'Hitler looked worn ...': Speidel, *We Defended Normandy*, p. 106.

258 'Mrs Churchill told me ...': Winston Churchill, *The Second World War*, vol. vi, book 1, galley proof in RVJO B.223 CCAC.

258 'Flying bombs have again ...': Alanbrooke, *War Diaries*, p. 560.

258 'at his best ...': Cunningham papers, BL Add. Mss 52577.

259 'a covey': TNA CAB 121/213.

259 'would be looked at': Ibid.

259 'more missiles than pupils': Longmate, *The Doodlebugs*, p. 228.

259 'In the districts where they fell ...': Pile, *Ack-Ack*, p. 345.

259 'more understandable': TNA AIR 2/9653.

Chapter 30

260 'According to an announcement ...': KTB HQ Flakgruppe Creil, Saleux, 20 June 1944.

260 'agents in the target area': Ibid.

261 'Arras reports Stichling ...': Tómas Harris *Garbo: The Spy Who Saved D-Day* (Barnsley: Pen & Sword, 2000), p. 248.

261   'It is of the utmost importance . . . ': TNA KV 2/69.

261   'We had an alert . . . ': TNA KV 2/69.

262   'in a flash': Jones, *Most Secret War*, p. 420.

262   'Anything of any importance . . . ': TNA HW 14/106.

262   'information on the pilotless . . . ': Ibid.

262–3 'Phone the Broadway Duty Officer . . . ': Ibid.

263   'constant attenders and others . . . ': TNA CAB 21/775.

263   'no intelligence about production . . . ': 22 June 1944, TNA CAB
       121/213.

264   'on whom the strain . . . ': Jones, op. cit., p. 537.

264   'Anglo-American pilots . . . ': IWM KTB Flakgruppe Creil, Saleux, 21
       June 1944.

264   'Judging by the pilots': Ibid.

264   'One came flying . . . ': IWM Documents 11946, papers of R. Wills.

265   '1800 lb of Amatol . . . ': Beamont, *The Years Flew Past*, p. 40.

265   'a universally hostile . . . ': Ibid., p. 43.

265   'strongly anti-Nazi . . . ': TNA DEFE 40/17.

266   'The P/W was accosted . . . ': Ibid.

266   trained draughtsman: Ibid.

267   'Polizeimeister Lange . . . ': Ibid.

Chapter 31

269   'only copy in existence . . . ': TNA KV 2/69

269   'I am proud': Ibid.

270   'if we did try . . . ': Guy Liddell, Diary, vol. 10, 18 June 1944, TNA KV
       4/194.

270fn to report on the landing places: *Special Agents*, TNA KV 4/83.

271   'It is dangerous to ask . . . ': TNA KV 2/69.

271   'In order to correct . . . ': 2 July 1944, TNA KV 2/69.

271   'mislead the enemy . . . ': Chiefs of staff meeting, 30 June 1944, *Crossbow
       Deception Policy*, TNA CAB 113/35.

271   'We should try . . . ': *Crossbow Deception*, note by Sir Samuel Findlater
       Stewart, 4 July 1944, TNA CAB 113/35.

272   'for the new German weapons . . . ': Message stamped at 1426/24/6 in
       J 133, 1 July 1944, TNA HW 5/710.

272   'The Maikäfer is now the V1': IWM KTB HQ Flakgruppe Creil,
       Saleux, 25 June 1944.

272   'You may safely disregard . . . ': Churchill to Stalin, 25 June 1944, CAB
       121/213.

272   'The public have so far . . . ': TNA CAB 121/213.

272   'This is not 1940–1 . . . ': Ibid.

272   'white-livered . . . ': Alanbrooke, *War Diaries*, p. 563.

273   'to kill the evil . . . ': *The Flying Bomb and the Rocket*, memorandum, 27 June
       1944 TNA CAB 121/213.

273   'This matter is not without difficulties': *Memorandum*, TNA CAB
       121/213.

Chapter 32

274　'Top Secret U ...': TNA HW 5/730.

275　'continue to receive top priority': Craven and Cate, *The Army Air Forces in World War II*, vol. 3, p. 527.

276　'The sky was leaden': Longmate, *The Doodlebugs*, p. 129.

276　'It covered streets ...': H. E. Bates, draft of pamphlet on flying bombs, TNA AIR 20/4140.

277　'small crash, no sense of blast ...': Harold Nicolson (ed. Stanley Olson), *Diaries and Letters, 1930–1964* (London: Penguin, 1984), p. 270.

277　'that our technical expertise ...': TNA CAB 121/107.

277　'The great contrast ...': Bates, op. cit.

278　'We'd rather have died ...': Longmate, op. cit., p. 156.

278　'The fighter aircraft ...': Alanbrooke, *War Diaries*, p. 565.

278–9 '1000 balloons in an area ...': *War Cabinet Crossbow Committee Weekly Report*, Annex II, 20 July 1944, TNA CAB 121/213.

279　'in case any attacks ...': TNA AIR 40/1882.

279　'I presume the present ...': *Public Opinion in Relation to the Flying Bomb Attacks on London*, 8 August 1944, Bufton papers CCAC.

279　'bombs were being wasted ...': Ibid.

279　'I hope the PM ...': 'Give Hun 100 bombs for every buzz-bomb here', newspaper cutting, TNA AIR 40/1882.

279　He suggested on 1 July: Evill to Portal, 2 July 1944, *Reprisals*, TNA AIR 8/1229.

279　the general talk about gas: Liddell, Diary, vol. 10, TNA KV 4/194.

280　'no appreciable industrial significance ...': *Annex, Reprisal Targets*, 5 July 1944, TNA AIR 8/1229.

280　'For four weeks past ...': *Draft of Possible Announcement by the BBC*, 5 July 1944, TNA AIR 8/1229.

280　invaluable proof: *Crossbow, Question of Retaliation*, War Cabinet chiefs of staff meeting, 3 July 1944, TNA AIR 8/1129.

280　'murdering aircrews': Minutes of chiefs of staff meeting, 4 July 1944, TNA AIR 8/1129.

280　the Joint Planning Staff argued against: See *Chemical Warfare in Connection with Crossbow*, 5 July 1943, TNA CAB 121/213 f.625.

280　country-house atmosphere: Jones, *Most Secret War*, p. 281.

280　'the only time Bert Harris ...': TNA DEFE 40/12.

281　'within range of our heaviest ...': Ibid.

281　'Roof collapsed in several ...': Message stamped at 0350/16/7 in J 149, 19 July 1944, TNA HW 5/710.

282　'Ultra has admitted ...': *The Second German Reprisal Weapon*, TNA WO 208/4116.

282　'He has a German father ...': TNA DEFE 40/17.

283　'A very romantic Frenchman ...': *Suspected Doedel Factories and Other Stories*, TNA DEFE 40/17.

283　'aerial torpedo': Ibid.

284　'The Führer was holding ...': IWM KTB HQ Flakgruppe Creil, Saleux, 5 July 1944.

Chapter 33

285   'It would be a mistake ...': *Hansard*, 6 July 1944.

286   'burning them out': TNA CAB 21/775.

286   'the time might well come ...': Chiefs of staff minute to Prime Minister, 5 July 1944, TNA CAB 121/213 f.632.

286   'cold-blooded calculation ...': *PM's Personal Minute Serial no. D.217/4 W.S.C. 6.7.44*, TNA CAB 120/775.

286fn 'Please prepare an outline plan ...': Portal to Bottomley, 6 July 1944, TNA AIR 8/1229.

287   'ghastly': Alanbrooke, *War Diaries*, p. 567.

287   'Concentration would be hard ...': *Chemical Warfare*, extract from chiefs of staff meeting, 8 July 1944, TNA CAB 121/101.

287   'In the course of the discussion ...': TNA CAB 121/101.

287   'been directed to go ...': Ibid.

288   Ultra-raised scares: The Brest garrison in Brittany for example requested 'urgent supply of anti-gas respirators' late on 8 June. The top secret U decrypt of the signal was circulated on the evening of the 10th. TNA HW 1/2925. Jones's Air Ministry papers contain several diplomatic decrypts from the Japanese consul in Vienna, at the same time reporting the urgent manufacture of gas masks for the civil population. TNA DEFE 40/12.

288   'raging emotional tensions': W. W. Rostow letter to F. I. Ordway, 23 October 1972, RVJO B.526 CCAC.

289   'I have been informed ...': TNA AIR 20/2632.

Chapter 34

290   'The arrival of the ...': TNA DEFE 40/12.

290   'assist in preparation ...': Ibid.

291   'on a very restricted basis': Ibid.

291   'As I have before indicated ...': Craven and Cate, *The Army Air Forces in World War II*, vol. 3, p. 534, quoting pencilled note, Eisenhower to Tedder on copy *COS Brief and Action Report*, 6 July 1944.

291   'retaliation for vengeance ...': Ibid., p. 535, quoting report with notation by Gen C. Cabell, *Integrating Flying Bomb and Rocket Counter-Measures into the Final Offensive vs. Germany*.

292   'It was also no doubt ...': Hinsley et al., *British Intelligence in the Second World War, Vol. 3*, pt. 1, pp. 444–5.

293   'directly responsible for assuring ...': Craven and Cate, op. cit., p. 535, quoting Anderson to Tedder, 8 July 1944.

Chapter 35

294   wings or fins: TNA AIR 20/2649.

294   'I must admit ...': Gordon Wilkinson letter to David Irving, 24 January 1965.

294 'It is inconceivable ...': *Counter-measures against 'Big Ben'*, TNA AIR 20/2649.

295 'Easton chose to circulate ...': TNA DEFE 40/14.

295 'multiple radio units ...': Signals of 7–9 July from air attaché, Stockholm, TNA AIR 20/2649.

295 'Would you like to consider ...': TNA AIR 20/2649.

296 'fifty 1000-kg elephants': Riedel 3, Heidelager, to Director Maus, Peenemünde, message stamped at 1100/26/6 in J 145/6, 14 July 1944, TNA HW5/710.

296 'It was not the same ...': Jones, op. cit., p. 550.

296–7 'The existence of a V2 weapon ...': 'Large Rocket', *Seventeenth Report by ACAS (I)*, 9 July 1944, p. 3, TNA HW 5/730.

296fn 'camouflaged with wood and hay': Ordway and Sharpe, *The Rocket Team*, p. 139.

Chapter 36

298 'Enemy has considerably ...': IWM KTB HQ Flakregiment 155 (W), Saleux, 9 July 1944.

298 'The band of the Signals ...': IWM KTB HQ Flakregiment 155 (W), Saleux, 11 July 1944.

299 'Agents' reports indicate ...': Ibid.

299 'for a greater part ...': *GC&CS Special Studies, Chaper III: V-Weapons*, TNA HW 11/11.

300 'make a personal representation ...': *Information on Flying Rocket*, 11 July 1944, AIR 29/2649 3044.

300 'It will be up to ...': TNA AIR 20/2649.

300 Air Intelligence: Chiefs of staff meeting, 11 July 1944, TNA CAB 121/213.

300 'The Londoners are standing up ...': TNA CAB 121/213.

300–1 'There is firm evidence ...': Ibid.

301 'To Sabine ...': TNA HW 14/107.

301 stressing 'the political implications ...': Reported in C note to Ismay, 14 July 1944, TNA HW 1/3069.

301 'the German Flying Bomb Organisation': TNA AIR 40/2882.

301 'Trials of a weapon ...': Ibid.

302 'intelligence liaison officer ...': C to Churchill, 13 July 1944, TNA HW 1/ 3065.

302 'In fact agents have ...': Ibid.

302 'Mid July in Warsaw ...': TNA AIR 20/2649.

302 'The load to be picked up ...': Ibid., 14 July 1944.

303 'Considerable further searching ...': TNA AIR 40/2452

303 'a torn exercise book ...': Ibid.

303 'The site at Château du Molay ...': Jones, *Most Secret War*, pp. 432–3

304 'as a counter-offensive ...': *Gas Warfare Policy*, vol. II, TNA CAB 121/101.

304 'take the form of a thorough ...': Ibid.

304–5 'unrestricted use of chemical and biological weapons': Ibid.

305 'interim summary statement ...': *Report on the Long Range Rocket by ADI (Sci)*, circulated 16 July 1944, RVJO B.92 CCAC.

305 sense of panic: 8 July 1964, RVJO B.346 CCAC.

305   'There is little doubt ...': *Report on the Long Range Rocket by ADI (Sci)*, circulated 16 July 1944, RVJO B.92 CCAC.
306   'with claims that there was an A-4 ...': TNA DEFE 40/1.
306   'a locomotive ...': Ibid.

Chapter 37

307   'overheard talk of bombs ...': *Garbo Traffic*, 14 July 1944, TNA KV 2/69.
308   'Practically all [the] agents ...': *Crossbow Deception*, note by Sir Samuel Findlater Stewart, 15 July 1944, CAB 113/35.
308   'the agent concerned ...': Ibid.
309   'vague and inaccurate ...': Ibid.
309   'It would seem to follow ...': Ibid.
309   'I would press you ...': Cherwell to Morrison, 14 July 1944, CHER G428/10 NCO,
309   'at first sight attractive': CHER G428/11 NCO.
310   'It is clear that ...': *Draft Minute by Chiefs of Staff to Prime Minister*, 18 July 1944, DSND 2/3/8 CCAC.
310   'allowing the enemy to plot ...': Cherwell to Findlater Stewart, 20 July 1944, TNA CAB 113/35.
310   'It's like long-range artillery ...': Drew to Thomson, 25 July 1944, TNA CAB 113/35.
311   'bring the heaviest concentration ...': Ibid.
311   'a joint and balanced ...': TNA AIR 2/9280.
311   'I feel that great advantage ...': Ibid.
312   'Sandys was friendly ...': 8 July 1964, RVJO B.346 CCAC.
312   '[Our record in early July] ...': Pile, *Ack-Ack*, p. 329.
314   'The most tremendous beating ...': Ibid., p. 334.
314   'The redeployment of the ...': *New Plan for the Coordination of Fighters and AA Guns*, 16 July 1944, DSND 2/3/8 CCAC.
314   'Analysis of the week's figures ...': Hill, 'Air Operations', p. 5598.

Chapter 38

315   'the battle was entirely ...': H. E. Bates, draft of pamphlet on flying bombs, TNA AIR 20/4140.
316   'Claude Pelly was sitting ...': RVJO B.346 CCAC.
317   three American Liberators: TNA AIR 20/2649.
317   'The crisis came ...': Jones, *Most Secret War*, p. 438.
317   'When did this evidence ...': Ibid.
317   'again had only become clear ...': Ibid., p. 439.
318   steered to its target: RVJO B.346 CCAC.
318   threatening the enemy: War Cabinet Crossbow Committee, *Minutes of a Meeting, Tuesday 18th July at 10.00 p.m.*, TNA CAB 121/213.
318   'He had instructed the Chiefs ...': Ibid.
318   'a nasty disturbed night ...': Alanbrooke, *War Diaries*, p. 571.
319   'experimental firing of large rockets ...': Churchill to Stalin, 19 July 1944, TNA CAB 121/213.

319   Doodlebug Celebration Dance: Longmate, *The Doodlebugs*, p. 436.
319fn 'Stauffenberg and co ...': *Interrogation of Walter Dornberger*, TNA WO 208/4178.
320   'The American scientists ...': *A4 and the Super Fortress*, Norman to DDI1, 20 July 1944, TNA HW14/108.
320   'The moment the Russians ...': Ibid.
321   'now under his personal control ...': TNA PREM 3/111A.
321   'I did not assert ...': Cherwell to Churchill, 20 July 1944, CHER G428/18 NCO.
321   'Why was this': *PM's Personal Minute Serial no. D(K) 6/4*, 23 July 1944, TNA PREM 3111A f.831.
321   'something wrong on the intelligence side': TNA PREM 3/111A.
321fn 'super-explosive': TNA CAB 21/271.
321fn 'feverish activity on nuclear problems': 3 July 1944, TNA CAB 126/39.
321fn did not like the man: 20 September 1944, TNA CAB 126/39.
322   'unfortunately we are without definite evidence ...': *Hypothetical Long Range Rocket Mk. 1*, TNA CAB 98/60.

Chapter 39

323   'every one of them was destroyed ...': *Hansard*, 6 July 1944.
324   more than just a targeting committee: *Minutes of a Meeting held at the Air Ministry*, 21 July 1944, TNA AIR 20/9280.
324   'I feel it would be a mistake ...': Bottomley to Portal, Ibid.
325   'The sanctity of Ultra ...': Note by Portal, Ibid.
325   'I now learn the Air Ministry ...': TNA PREM 3/111A.
325   Lt-Colonel Kenneth Post: See *LRR Summary of Evidence*, undated, DSND 2/3/8 CCAC.
325   'As I further learned ...': TNA AIR 40/2452.
326   'it is almost certainly used ...': *German Long Range Rocket Projectile*, AI2(g), 22 July 1944, TNA AIR 20/4370.
326   'badly smashed': Ibid.
326   'Almost in chorus ...': Jones, *Most Secret War*, p. 447.
326   no provision for external lubrication: Ibid., p. 434.
327   copied to his father-in-law: See TNA PREM 3/111A.
327   'Top Secret "U"': TNA DEFE 40/12.
327   'It looks as if it falls to me ...': Pryor to Mapplebeck, 25 July 1944, TNA DEFE 40/12. In a somewhat farcical move, in answer to the minister's complaint about only now discovering the existence of the Normandy PoW interrogations, Inglis demanded a report from Mapplebeck by '16:30 hours today' as to '[why] was Mr Duncan Sandys *not* informed', so that the air intelligence chief might give Portal the reason. Ultra was not mentioned.
328   'During the last few days ...': War Cabinet Crossbow Committee, *Eighth Report*, TNA CAB 121/213.
328   'The enemy probably ...': Ibid.
328   'This report is based ...': TNA AIR 20/2649.
329   'Is there not a representative ...': TNA CAB 121/213 f.755.
329   moving towards a cooperative effort: TNA CAB 121/213.

329   'restricted circulation and close contact ...': TNA HW 43/69.
330   'terracotta and violet': TNA CAB 98/60.
330   'intelligence machine': War Cabinet Crossbow Committee, *Notes of a Meeting*, 25 July 1944, TNA CAB 121/213.
331   'instead of a bulky edifice': TNA CAB 121/213.
331   'began to flounder': Jones, op. cit., p. 444.
331   'as long as the source is safeguarded': War Cabinet Crossbow Committee, *Notes of a Meeting*, 25 July 1944, TNA CAB 121/213.
332   he had discussed the matter: War Cabinet Crossbow Committee, *Notes of a Meeting*, 25 July 1944, TNA CAB 121/213. Admiral Cunningham recorded the turbulent meeting in his diary: 'It came out that the temperamental Dr Jones, a scientist attached to the Air Ministry, would not attend Mr Sandys's science committee meetings.' The documents produced by Mr Sandys had 'no doubt been kept away on purpose on account of the intense jealousy at the Air Ministry, perhaps to some extent justified', according to the Chief of the Naval Staff (BL Add Mss 52577). Alan Brooke's version of the same meeting was that 'Portal loves to show off his scientific knowledge, Cherwell must show his mathematical genius and Duncan Sandys insists on letting everyone know he has a great political future. All this bores me to death.' Alanbrooke, *War Diaries*, p. 576.
332–3 'Complaints which you have voiced ...': CHER G428/19 NCO.
333   Jones carefully re-examined: Ibid.
333–4 'I am prepared at any time ...': Jones to Portal, 26 July 1944, TNA DEFE 40/12.
333fn '[Cherwell] did not like ...': Jones to David Irving, 6 January 1964, RVJO B.349, CCAC.
334   'Professor Ellis has arranged ...': Ibid.
334   'As we shall undoubtedly be blamed ...': Ibid.

Chapter 40

335   'composition of the mission': TNA AIR 20/4370.
335   the importance of getting Professor Ellis's: Ibid.
336   'Instead of the choice of personnel ...': Jones, *Most Secret War*, p. 441.
336   'We are making inquiries ...': TNA AIR 20/4370.
336   'agreed at the highest level ...': Ibid.
336   'a listening station ...': *Radio Countermeasures against Big Ben*, 27 July 1944, DSND 2/3 CCAC. Hut Six's internal history reported that 'black' listening posts in Sweden relayed some of the Insect group's wireless traffic to Bletchley Park. Getting supposed rocket control signals was a different matter. In May 1944 the Air Ministry had proposed supplying neutral Sweden with British-civilian-operated air defence radars (against US and German counter offers) in return for interned downed Allied airmen in a clandestine bid to get an electronic watch on the rocket. It became an obsessive intelligence priority for the next six weeks, the 'one chance of countering this threat in advance' as it was stated, information on which was not made available at TNA until 2012 (TNA AIR 20/8072). At first a lonely RAF intelligence agent, Flying Officer

Ingham, operated under cover without success, then it was decided to put a bigger clandestine team of listeners into the city of Malmö without telling the Swedes, an idea very much opposed by C. Duncan Sandys, inevitably, was not informed of the Air Intelligence plan because of the 'confidential nature of the placing of this watch'. After much diplomatic manoeuvring a British Army radio surveillance team would arrive at Ottenby on the island of Oland in October 1944 in a protracted attempt to track non-existent V2 guidance signals from continuing tests at Peenemünde.

336   to fly over Poland: Ibid.
336   'If the rocket should be superimposed ...': *Long Range Rocket, Need for Re-examination of Government Plans*, 26 July 1944, TNA CAB 121/214.
337   'If an attack were to develop ...': Ibid.
337   'to encourage a voluntary exodus ...': 26 July 1944, TNA PREM 3/111A.
337   what little secret evidence: 27 July 1944, CHER G 428/22.
337   failures of a type we could not afford: *Intelligence and Offensive Counter Measures*, 28 July 1944, TNA CAB 121/214.
338   'diverted to another important installation': Ibid.
338   'The devastation in London ...': IWM KTB HQ Flakgruppe Creil, Saleux, 25 July 1944.

Chapter 41

339   'harassed, irritable and thoroughly uncivil': Longmate, *The Doodlebugs*, p. 215.
339   'measures to stimulate ...': WM Committee of War Cabinet, 28 July 1944, TNA CAB 121/214.
340   'make the public aware ...': Ibid.
340   'accompanied by an explosion ...': *Poland, Air, Rumours*, TNA DEFE 40/18.
340   'Party amalgamating well ...': Jones, *Most Secret War*, p. 441.
341   'I can make no stronger protest ...': Jones to Inglis, copy letter in typescript of *Most Secret War*, Franks papers, University of Bristol Library.
341   'On hearing of this ...': *Draft Minute to Sir Charles Portal*, 1 August 1944, DSND 2/3/9 CCAC.
341   'In view of the number of meetings ...': TNA DEFE 40/12.
342   'drove any further thought ...': Jones, op. cit., p. 443.
342   'I told Inglis that ...': Ibid.
342   'Mr Sandys to see these': ZIP/SJA/593 TNA HW 1/3129 and ZIP/SJA 594 TNA HW 1/3120
342   4200 enemy aircraft: Ibid.
342–3 'Mr Sandys's demand ...': Hinsley et al., *British Intelligence in the Second World War, Vol. 3*, pt 2, p. 455.
343   'First Weekly Summary of Crossbow Intelligence': 30 July 1944, RVJO B.93 CCAC.
343   '[German] Army's new torpedo ...': Ibid.
343   Blizna–Peenemünde train movements: Ibid.
343   'A special crew ...': Butcher, *My Three Years with Eisenhower*, p. 539.

344 'resulting in large scale casualties': JPS report, *Military Considerations Affecting the Initiation of Chemical and Other Special Forms of Warfare, Annex 1*, 28 July 1944, TNA CAB 121/101.

344 Public morale in England: Ibid.

344 **14,000 tons of mustard gas:** Cherwell to Churchill, 4 August 1944, TNA PREM 3/89.

344 'If the claims of "N" ...': TNA CAB 121/101.

345 'same cannot be said for our own people': TNA CAB 120/775.

345 'when things get worse': *PM's Personal Minute Serial no. D 238/4*, 29 July 1944, TNA CAB 120/775.

Chapter 42

346 'We have drafted a report ...': TNA CAB 113/35.

347 'keeping our special agents ...': Drew to Jacob, 31 July 1944, TNA CAB 113/35.

347 a pub damaged in Windsor: See photograph package and Cholmondeley letter dated 1 Sept 1944, TNA KV 4/260.

348 'I am putting you in charge ...': Speer, *The Slave State*, p. 213.

348 'I felt like a man who has devoted ...': Dornberger, *V-2*, p. 222.

348 'That afternoon von Braun ...': Ibid., pp. 222–3.

349 'You cannot leave every bus driver ...': TNA CAB 120/749.

349 'the more I despise him': Cunningham diary, BL Add Mss 52577.

349 'a serious loss of juvenile labour': *Minutes of War Cabinet Rocket Committee*, 4 August 1944, TNA CAB 98/39.

349 'unofficial panic exodus': Ibid.

349 'There is some evidence ...': CHER G431/2 NCO.

350 a little tank: TNA AIR 20/9194.

350 all the evidence pointed: Ibid.

350 'marked out for demonstration ...': Ibid.

351 'This is about the best ...': TNA AIR 20/2649.

351 structure was like a Zeppelin: Ibid.

382 'In July 1944 ...': Chertok, *Rockets and People*, p. 259.

353 'hoped that Marshal Stalin's ...': TNA AIR 20/3437. See TNA FO 954/26B for the continuing diplomatic frustrations of August 1944.

353 'Every source which has given ...': *Crossbow Second Weekly Summary*, 6 August 1944, RVJO B.94 CCAC.

354 'measure for 4300 kilograms of *A-Stoff*': Message stamped at 1600/22/6 in J 142, 12 July 1944, TNA HW 5/710.

354 allow the enemy to have: TNA AIR 2/9280.

355 'We have already briefed ...': Ibid.

355 aerial torpedo: *Joint Crossbow Working Committee Minutes of 3rd Meeting*, 10 August 1944, TNA AIR 2/9280.

355 'Probable underground facilities ...': Ibid.

355–6 'Unterscharführer Erich Becker ...': J 182/8, circulated 12 August 1944, TNA HW 5/711.

355fn 'with no exit on the SE side': *Interpretation Report D.127*, 31 August 1944, TNA AIR 40/2522.

Chapter 43

357 'The report on P/W Lauterjung . . .': TNA WO 208/3437.

358 'generally incredulous reception': Jones, *Most Secret War*, p. 442.

358 'The best secret intelligence . . .': TNA HW 5/730.

358 'When it is remembered . . .': CHER G431/8 NCO.

359 'You should continue to convey . . .': TNA CAB 113/35.

359 'namely to prevent the enemy . . .': Howard, *British Intelligence in the Second World War, Vol. 5*, p. 177.

359 '316 missiles fired overnight . . .': IWM KTB Flakgruppe Creil, Saleux, 2–3 August 1944.

360 'Waffen-SS General Kammler . . .': IWM KTB Flakgruppe Creil, Saleux, 10 August 1944.

360 'who had been sworn to secrecy': Message stamped at 1230/9/8 in J 188, TNA HW 5/711.

360 'Since 14 August . . .': 16 August 1944, TNA CAB 121/214.

360 'Following a week . . .': 17 August 1944, TNA CAB 121/214.

361 'advised of flying bomb activity': TNA DEFE 40/12.

361 'Now known that a Heinkel 111 . . .': HW 5/772.

362 'Should not some publicity . . .': *Minutes of War Cabinet Crossbow Committee 15th Meeting*, 24 August 1944, TNA CAB 121/214.

362 '*prevent* evacuees returning to London . . .': Ibid.

362 'to assemble from the many fragments . . .': *Air Scientific Intelligence Interim Report, A4*, TNA AIR 20/1661.

363 'There is also said to be an "M" works . . .': Ibid.

364 'Offensive countermeasures . . .': Collier, *The Defence of the United Kingdom*, p. 388.

364 'We used to get shouted at . . .': <http://redtarget. pagesperso-orange.fr/ Nucourt.htm>.

365 'Flying towards the south coast . . .': Hill, 'Air Operations', p. 5599.

365 'Another move, reconnaissance . . .': Esser IWM 13210 Ger Misc 25 (197).

366 'The question now arises . . .': IWM KTB HQ Flakgruppe Creil, Croix, 2 September 1944.

366 a message sent LXV AK: See TNA WO 208/3121 for a full account of the Kammler takeover drama.

366 'The following teleprint . . .': TNA WO 208/3121.

366 'supply system and for guard troops': Ibid.

366 'In view of urgency . . .': Ibid.

366fn 'good friend of Kammler . . .': Dornberger, *V-2*, p. 225.

367 'whole camp began rejoicing in secret': Béon, *Planet Dora*, p. 113.

Chapter 44

368 'We leave Moscow . . .': TNA DEFE 40/12.

368 caviar, vodka, champagne: Ordway and Sharpe, *The Rocket Team*, p. 112.

368 'clinking medals . . .': Ibid., p. 113.

368 found the front line: *Preliminary Report on Anglo-American Mission, issued 22 Sept 1944*, TNA HW 5/730.

369 'sceptical about the existence ... ': 18 September 1944, TNA DEFE 40/12.

369 'The British specialists ... ': Chertok, *Rockets and People*, p. 260.

369 'Upon his return ... ': Ibid.

369 'a large open space ... ': TNA HW 5/730.

369 'evacuation was made with a view ... ': Ibid.

369 'his hand [had] frozen ... ': Wilkinson letter to D. Irving, 24 January 1965.

370 'burner unit': TNA HW 5/730.

370 'When the party reached ... ': Nigel Tangye papers, LHCMA, and 'B-Stoff Betankungsmenge 3900Kg' in Sanders for D of I (R) and Mr Duncan Sandys via 30 Mission Moscow, 22 September 1944, TNA AIR 20/3437.

370–1 'I had to endure ... ': Dornberger, *V-2*, p. 224.

Chapter 45

372 'blown up': *Summary of Klavier Decodes of 31/8/44*, BP Archives.

372 'Feldmulag [field munitions depot] Leopold ... ': Message stamped at 0915/4/9 in J 213, TNA HW 5 /712.

372 Undertaking Erzwerk: Message stamped at 1655/4/9 in J 216, TNA HW 5/712.

373 'So many launching sites ... ': *Flight*, 14 September 1944, <www.flight-global.com/pdfarchive/view/.../1944%20-%201884.html>.

373 'It is now a reasonable certainty ... ': *Future Policy for Crossbow Countermeasures*, 4 September 1944, TNA CAB 121/214.

373 'against rocket targets ... ': Ibid.

374 'the slightest change ... ': TNA CAB 120/749.

374 'There is no further danger ... ': TNA CAB 121/214.

374 'latest intelligence and the progress ... ': *Rocket Consequences Committee*, 5 September 1944, TNA CAB 98/39.

375 'counter any rapid growth ... ': Ibid.

375 'attention armament officer': TNA AIR 14/1721.

376–7 'tall, young Duncan Sandys ... ': 'World Battlefronts: Battle of England: The Score for Robots', *Time*, 18 September 1944.

377 'Except possibly for a few last shots ... ': *Notes of a Press Conference on the Flying Bomb*, TNA AIR 20/6016. In his address Sandys for some reason introduced a subsequently oft-repeated story that Hitler himself had witnessed a demonstration of a 'captured Spitfire flown by a German fighter ace' chasing and failing to intercept a flying bomb at a special trial in the Baltic. The press loved that yarn. *Flying Bomb Draft Statement*, 5 September 1944, TNA CAB 121/214 f.940. Among the letters and telegrams of congratulation that morning, Ellen Wilkinson, the Labour MP and Parliamentary Secretary at the Home Office, said, 'I admire the courage you showed with dealing with the civil and brass-hated Great. I know my Minister [Herbert Morrison, with whom she was having an affair] thinks the same.' General Frederick Pile thought it 'historic', and looked forward to seeing the junior minister at his party later that evening. R. V. Jones was also on the guest list. DSND CCAC

377   'Is there a V2 weapon, sir?': *Notes of a Press Conference on the Flying Bomb*,
       TNA AIR 20/6016.
378   'Duncan Sandys to-day ...': TNA PREM 3/111A.

PART IV: THE REVENGE EXPRESS

Chapter 46

382   'double harrumph': Butcher, *My Three Years with Eisenhower*, **p. 564.**
382   'In West Area London ...': Cal McCrystal, 'Wallop in Staveley Road',
       Independent, 4 October 1992.
383   'Eleven houses demolished ...': <http://brentfordandchiswicklhs.org.uk/
       local-history/war/commemorating-the-chiswick-v2/>
383   'Incident Pardon Wood ...': Longmate, *Hitler's Rockets*, p. 169.
383   'Two incidents occurred today ...': VCAS to CAS, TNA CAB
       121/214.
383–4 'Two rockets so-called V2 ...': TNA CAB 121/214.
384   'So far as I was concerned ...': Montgomery, *The Memoirs of Field-
       Marshal Montgomery* (London: Collins, 1958), p. 274.
384   'I told him about the V2 ...': Ibid., p. 275.
385   'no serious attack ...': TNA CAB 121/214.
385   'some parts of the casing ...': Ibid.
385   SOE should try to obtain: Jacobs to Attlee, 11 September 1944, TNA
       CAB 121/214.
385   'where a strip had been ...': TNA CAB 121/214.
386   'many fragments have been found ...': DCAS files, *V-Weapons, techni-
       cal data*, TNA AIR 20/3437.
386   'A-4 in SE England ...': TNA HW14/111.
387   'full of rumours': 12 September 1944, TNA CAB 113/39.
387   'we have had a couple ...': Ibid.
388   most of the rockets arriving: TNA AIR 20/3437.
388   'Not far away ...': Chertok, *Rockets and People*, p. 261.
388   fishing expedition: Longmate, op. cit., p. 177.
388fn 'turned men into bleeding hedgehogs': Béon, *Planet Dora*, p. 152.
389   'would be jeopardised ...': Message stamped 1412/14/9 in J229, TNA
       HW 5/712.
389   'The Russians were ...': *V-Weapons*, TNA AIR 20/3437.
389   'You may discuss ...': Ibid.
390   'It would be humiliating ...': Ibid.
390   'The Americans want ...': Ibid.
390   several large cases of parts: Chertok, op. cit., p. 261.

Chapter 47

391   Hague and Gruppe Süd: TNA HW6/6 and J 266, 10 October 1944, TNA
       HW 5/722.

391   'Special Plenipotentiary No. 2 of the Reichsführer-SS': TNA HW
       5/722.
392   'On 3 October ...': Hill. 'Air Operations', p. 5609.
393   'the existence of further SS ...': Dr. Ka., Berlin to Münster. Message
       stamped at 0710/30/9/44 in J 313, 8 November 1944, TNA 5/714.
393   'Officers from my headquarters ...': Hill, op. cit., p. 5609.
393   'Indeed, from the date ...': Ibid.
394   'The photographic evidence ...': Kendall, 'A War of Intelligence', pp.
       122-3
395   Home-intelligence reports: See sequence of reports in *Home Intelligence
       Weekly Reports, Vol. II Mar–Dec 1944*, TNA CAB 121/107.
395   'the balance of advantage': TNA CAB 121/214.
396   'The Führer does not concur ...': Irving, *The Mare's Nest*, p. 294.

Chapter 48

397   'There was nothing ...': Clarke, *Astounding Days*, p. 153.
398   'German High Command announces ...': TNA PREM 3/111.
399   'Not quite five months ...': Longmate, *Hitler's Rockets*, p. 201
399   'One day Magnus ...': Huzel, *Peenemünde to Canaveral*, p. 118.
400   a little work by the enemy: 1 December 1944, TNA CAB 113/41.
400   'Southern England is in ...': *Home Security Weekly Appreciation*, 6
       December 1944, TNA CAB 113/41.
400   'In November the scale ...': Hill, 'Air Operations', p. 5611
400   'such targets as could ...': Ibid.
401   'any assistance I could expect ...': Ibid.
401   'The rocket before fuelling ...': TNA CAB 121/215.
401   'The only assembly plant ...': Ibid.
401   384,000 to 1: Cherwell to Churchill, 23 November 1944, TNA PREM
       3/111A.
401fn 'muddy-minded Pole': TNA AIR 34/626.
402   'Windows fell out ...': Longmate, op. cit., p. 206.
402   the incident 'has given rise ...': TNA AIR 20/2652.
402   'left the fray': 6 January 1964, RVJO B.341 CCAC.
402   'Our service deteriorated': TNA HW 43/69.
402   'Section AI(h) had ...': Ibid. Jones's watch on Japanese signals to Tokyo
       from Berlin produced a fascinating account of a morale-boosting demon-
       stration at Rechlin on 3 December of new secret weapons including jet
       fighters and assault rifles that shot round corners, with which the Germans
       would snatch victory. Jones's analysis covered the V1 (of which no radically
       improved version could be expected, according to the continued Ultra
       watch on Baltic trials) and the A-4, its autonomous internal guidance
       system now confirmed. The most serious threat, however, was of new-gen-
       eration snorkel-equipped high-speed electric U-Boats (the Type XXI)
       armed with acoustic-homing torpedoes powered by hydrogen peroxide. Of
       'Tube Alloy' (atomic research) there was no sign of any large production
       effort thus far. Jones concluded that although the enemy was consistently
       fertile in weapon research, production of synthetic fuel would decide the
       outcome. 22 December 1944 TNA DEFE 40/12.

403 'we refused to write up ...': TNA HW 43/69.

403 'with no other apparent parent': TNA HW 14/117.

403 'Occasionally a long dash ...': TNA HW 2/85.

404 '[A] German Army code ...': TNA AIR 40/2639.

404 The new information seam: 24 November 1944, TNA AIR 8/1231. Annotation shows Portal asking Inglis about the nature of the 'new intelligence'.

404 'If they are going to be ...': 2 December 1944, TNA HW 14/117.

405 'subsequent events make it clear ...': Howard, *British Intelligence in the Second World War, Vol. 5*, p. 182.

405 'give the senators a false pattern ...': Churchill to Ismay, 19 January 1945, TNA CAB 121/215.

405 'to be superimposed on a map of New York': Chiefs of staff to JSM Washington, 20 January 1945, TNA CAB 121/215.

406 'as you say very heavy': Sir James Stuart to Sir Herbert Williams, TNA AIR 20/2652.

406 'We heard the unmistakable crump ...': Longmate, op. cit., p. 218.

406 'morbid and gruesome': Ibid., p. 344.

407 'The centre of London ...': *Ministry of Home Security Intelligence Summary*, TNA CAB 114/21.

Chapter 49

409 'After years of reverses ...': IWM KTB HQ Flakgerätepark West, Seelbach, 31 December 1944.

409 'At the moment ...': IWM KTB HQ Flakgerätepark West, Seelbach, 2 January 1945.

410 'Fasan (Pheasant) ...': J 295, 16 October 1944, TNA HW 5/713.

410 Christmas gift: Barber and Keuer, *Hitler's Rocket Soldiers*, p. 104.

411 'if one looked down ...': Longmate, *Hitler's Rockets*, p. 230.

411 'Sound seems to be ...': See Ibid., pp. 176–7 and 230–6 for more on the physical phenomena associated with the rocket's arrival.

Chapter 50

412 '1500 Lancaster sorties ...': TNA CAB 121/215.

412 'would suggest to the enemy ...': *Countermeasures against Long Range Rocket Attack on United Kingdom*, 16 January 1945, TNA CAB 121/215.

412 'where documentary and other evidence ...': Ibid.

413 'This is not a rout': Ordway and Sharpe, *The Rocket Team*, p. 180.

414 'Führer emergency': TNA HW 5/722.

414 'Reports by German agents ...': KTB HQ Flakgerätepark West, Seelbach, 21 January 1945.

414 'on the move day and night ...': Dornberger, *V-2*, p. 250.

414–15 'The convoys still moved ...': Ibid.

415 'We have been very fortunate ...': TNA CAB 121/215.

415 'No definite deception plan ...': TNA CAB 154/49.

416 'It would lead to incalculable ...': Hollis to Ismay, 26 January 1945, TNA CAB 154/49.

416 'We got our fingers ...': TNA CAB 154/49.

416 Germans were paying great attention: Howard, *British Intelligence in the Second World War, Vol. 5*, p. 182.

416 'possible that it was due to deception': Ibid.

416 'Ibis in contrast ...': *The History of Hut 6*, vol. II, TNA HW 43/71.

416 'a rocket Bradshaw': Ibid.

417 'Himmler [was] in entire agreement ...': 18 February 1945, TNA HW 1/2704.

417 'On 16 February ...': TNA HW 5/722.

417 'It is now clear ...': Ibid.

418 'unobtrusively so as not ...': Message stamped at 1105/1/2 in J 421, 23 February 1945, TNA HW5/716.

418 'instructions to a German agent ...': AI1(h), *Ultra Crossbow summary*, 24 February 1945, TNA AIR 40/2114.

418 'recrudescence of a ...': Ismay to Churchill, 26 February 1944, TNA CAB 120/749.

418–19 'The Chiefs of Staff wish to ...': Ibid.

419 little hope of success: *Crossbow: Intelligence & Countermeasures*, TNA AIR 8/1232.

419 'who, it is understood ...': Ibid.

419 gave 'certain information': Ibid.

420 The only answer: Ibid., handwritten annotation.

420 'The daily post contains ...': TNA PREM 3/111.

420 heard from pilots: TNA CAB 121/215.

Chapter 51

421 'Unfortunately the bombing ...': Hill, 'Air Operations', p. 5613.

422 'feeble efforts to interfere with rockets': TNA CAB 120/750.

422 'an unfortunate lapse ...': Ibid.

422 HQ Second Tactical Air Force: *Bombing of The Hague: Protest by Netherlands Ambassador*, TNA AIR 8/1225.

422 'a mistake in computing ...': Ibid.

422 'Between midnight and 0600 ...': TNA AIR 40/2114.

422 'might lead to ...': Ibid.

422–3 'As luck would have it ...': Longmate, *Hitler's Rockets*, p. 365. See also *Incident at Charterhouse Street 8–12 March*, TNA HO 186/2388.

423 'Performance showed an ...': TNA AIR 40/2114.

423 'The counter-measures ...': *Division z.V. Report on Experience Feb 45*, 23 March 1945, IWM Enemy Documents E281/20.

423 'Get to Germany any way you can': See, for example, J 466 of 10 March 1945, TNA HW 5/717.

424 'honking our way through ...': Huzel, *Peenemünde to Canaveral*, p. 145.

424 'Now it was parked ...': Ibid., p. 146.

425 'The bells went down ...': Fireman John Dann interviewed in 1981, Ramsey, *The East End Then and Now*, p. 468. See also *Incident Reports, Stepney*, TNA HO 186/2420.

426   '[we] saw it by moonlight': Longmate, op. cit., p. 369
426   'A few minutes before ...': Collier, *The Defence of the United Kingdom*, p. 395.

Chapter 52

427   'You have no grounds ...': TNA CAB 120/550.
427   'Army Corps z.V ...': CX/MSS/T504/126, 31 March 1945, TNA HW 5/722.
428   'cooking chickens': Herbert, *Hitler's Foreign Workers*, p. 375.
429   'An order was sent out ...': TNA AIR 40/2144.
430   'The production of important ...': Message stamped at 0100/3/4, TNA HW 5/722.
430   wanted it in writing: TNA WO 208/3121
430   '[Kammler] came to see me ...': Speer, *The Slave State*, pp. 243–4.
431   'every assistance to the Special ...': TNA HW 1/3683.
431   'with undamaged V2 apparatus ...': TNA HW 5/722.
432   'I followed the trains ...': <http://www.johngalione.com/timber-wolf415b003.htm>.
433   'ceased work and was ...': J 485/9, TNA HW 5/717.
433   'Responsibility for affairs ...': TNA HW 5/722.
433   'destruction of all documents ...': J 487/2, TNA HW 5/717.
433   'Births, marriages and deaths ...': BP archives.
433   'There is no further information ...': AI1(h) to Duty Officer Hut 3, *Long Range Rocket*, 17 April 1945, TNA AIR 40/2114.
433   'the SS launching unit ...': *Intelligence – Flying Rocket*, 16 April 1945, TNA CAB 121/215 f.1183.
434   'recognised for a long time ...': Oberfeldgerichter W. Wetzling, *My Account of the Surrender of the V2 Division*, TNA WO 208/3155.
434   'a great number of highly ...': Ibid.
434   'Dornberger ordered 450 ...': TNA FO 1031/128.
434   the SS would shoot them: Ibid.
434   'No chemical, biological or atomic ...': Ibid.
435   in the first week of April: *Military Aspects of V2 Weapons*, TNA WO 208/3121.
435   'stare at the sky and play cards': Dornberger, *V-2*, pp. 253–4.
435   19 Muspillistrasse, Munich: TNA AIR 40/2114.
435   'Yes, Sir. They have ceased': Parliamentary Report, *The Times*, 27 April 1945, p. 8. Churchill's remark was greeted with 'laughter and applause'.
436   'We all looked at ...': Huzel, *Peenemünde to Canaveral*, p. 187.
437   'Shortly, the convoy of BMWs ...': Ibid., p. 188.

Epilogue

438   lunch at the Savoy: *Daily Express*, 18 June 1945.
438–9 'loaned to the Ministry ...': MI4 to DDMI, 2 September 1945, TNA FO 131/85.

439   'I never did find out ...': David Lang, 'A Romantic Urge', *New Yorker*, 21 April 1951, p. 75.

439   he and von Braun had realised: Dornberger interrogation, TNA WO 208/2178.

440   private capacity as a consultant: *Duncan Sandys, Defence Minister: Request for his assistance and approval of his portrayal in the film 'I Aim at the Stars'*, 1959, TNA TS 54/21.

440   'without doubt, the greatest ...': <http://earthobservatory.nasa.gov/Features/vonBraun/>.

441   Cherwell continued the feud: See R. V. Jones, 'Lindemann Beyond the Laboratory', *Notes and Records of the Royal Society*, vol. 41, no. 2, June 1987, pp. 191–210.

442   sneered at and belittled: Sandys to J. R. M. Butler, 29 February 1956, TNA CAB 101/90.

442   'had larger responsibility ...': Ibid.

442   produce a revised text: J. R. M. Butler to Sir Norman Brook, 8 March 1956, TNA CAB 103/454.

442   'In autumn 1947 ...': Wachtel, 'Unternehmen Rumpelkammer'.

443   'Kommandeur der V1 Raketendivision': <http://forum.axishistory.com/viewtopic.php?f=5&t=148669&start=0>

443   'ordered 6000 prisoners ...': Dornberger interrogation, TNA WO 208/2178.

443   'the cruel, brutal and fanatic ...': 'Wetzling and Others' in Antonio Cassese (ed.-in-chief), *Oxford Companion to International Criminal Justice* (Oxford: Oxford University Press, 2009), p. 972.

BIBLIOGRAPHY

Electronic Sources

www.astronautix.com
www.v2rocket.com
www.df.lth.se
www.heidelager.com
www.sitesv1du-nord-de-la-france
www.johngalione.com/timberwolf
www.ibiblio.org/hyperwar

Newsaper and Periodicals

The Times, Daily Mail, Daily Telegraph, Daily Mirror, Daily Express, Time, Washington Post, New Yorker, Der Spiegel, Nature, Observer, Pariser Zeitung, cuttings of wartime German newspaper and magazines in Ministry of Economic Warfare reports held at the National Archives, *RUSI Journal, Tribune, Intelligence and National Security, Bulletin of Atomic Scientists, Cryptologia, Encounter, Flight, After the Battle, Defense Analysis*

Books

Alanbrooke, Field Marshal Lord [Alan Brooke] (ed. Alex Danchev and Dan Todman), *War Diaries 1939–1945* (London: Weidenfeld & Nicolson, 2001)

Babington Smith, Constance, *Evidence in Camera: The Story of Photographic Intelligence in World War II* (London: Chatto & Windus, 1958)

Barber, Murray R. and Michael Keuer, *Hitler's Rocket Soldiers: The Men Who Fired the V2s against England* (Pulborough: Tattered Flag Press, 2011)

Barth, Hans, *Hermann Oberth: Der Wirkliche Vater der Weltraumfahrt* (Düsseldorf: VDI Verlag, 2008)

Beamont, Roland, *Phoenix into Ashes* (London: William Kimber, 1968)

Béon, Yves (trans. Yves Béon and Richard L. Fague), *Planet Dora: A Memoir of the Holocaust and the Birth of the Space Age* (Boulder: Westview Press, 1997)

Birkenhead, Earl (F. Furneaux-Smith), *The Prof In Two Worlds: The Official Life of Professor F. A. Lindemann, Viscount Cherwell* (London: Collins, 1961)

Butcher, Harry C., *My Three Years with Eisenhower: The Personal Diary of Captain Harry C. Butcher, USNR, Naval Aide to General Eisenhower, 1942 to 1945* (New York: Simon & Schuster, 1946)

Calvocoressi, Peter, *Top Secret Ultra* (London: Cassell, 1980)

Chertok, Boris (ed. Asif Siddiqi), *Rockets and People* (Washington, DC: NASA, 2005)

Clarke, Arthur C., *Astounding Days: A Science Fictional Autobiography* (London: Victor Gollancz, 1989)

Craven, Wesley F. and James Lea Cate, *The Army Air Forces in World War II*, 8 vols (Chicago: University of Chicago Press, 1948–58)

Dornberger, Walter, *V-2* (first pub. *Der Schuss ins Weltall* 1952; New York: Viking Press, 1954)

Downing, Taylor, *Spies in the Sky: The Secret Battle for Aerial Intelligence during World War II* (London: Little, Brown, 2011)

Dungan, T. D., *V-2: A Combat History of the First Ballistic Missile* (Yardley: Westholme Publishing, 2005)

Friedrich, Jörg (trans. Allison Brown), *The Fire: The Bombing of Germany, 1940–1945* (New York: Columbia University Press, 2008)

Garlinski, Jozef, *Hitler's Last Weapons: The Underground War against the V1 and V2* (London: Times Books, 1978)

Hastings, Max, *Bomber Command* (London: Michael Joseph, 1979)

Hautefeuille, Roland, *Constructions spéciales: Histoire de la Construction par l'Organisation Todt, dans le Pas de Calais et le Cotentin, des neufs grands sites protégés pour le tir des V1, V2, V3 et la production d'oxygène liquid (1943–1944)* (Paris: Selbstverlag, 1985)

Heitmann, Jan, *The Peenemünde Rocket Centre* (London: After the Battle, 1991)

Herbert, Ulrich (trans. William Templer), *Hitler's Foreign Workers: Enforced Foreign Labor in Germany under the Third Reich* (Cambridge: Cambridge University Press, 1997)

Hinsley, F. H. and Alan Stripp, *Codebreakers: The Inside Story of Bletchley Park* (Oxford: Oxford University Press, 1993)

Hinsley, F. H. et al., *British Intelligence in the Second World War, Volume 3: Its Influence on Strategy and Operations*, parts 1 and 2 (London: HMSO, 1984–1988)

Hollard, Florian, *Michel Hollard: le Français qui a Sauvé Londres* (Paris: Le Cherche-Midi, 2005)

Hölsken, Heinz Dieter, *Die V-Waffen: Entstehung – Propaganda – Kriegseinsatz* (Stuttgart: Deutsche Verlagsanstalt, 1984)

Hoss, Rudolf, *Death Dealer: The Memoirs of the SS Kommandant at Auschwitz* (Buffalo: Prometheus, 1992)

Howard, Michael, *British Intelligence in the Second World War, Volume 5: Strategic Deception* (London: HMSO, 1990)

Huzel, Dieter K., *Peenemünde to Canaveral* (Eaglewood Cliffs: Prentice-Hall, 1962)

Irving, David, *The Mare's Nest* (London: William Kimber, 1964)

Jackson, John (ed.), *The Secret War of Hut 3* (Milton Keynes: Military Press, 2002)

Jeffery, Keith, *MI6: The History of the Secret Intelligence Service, 1909–1949* (London: Bloomsbury, 2010)

Jones, R. V., *Most Secret War: British Scientific Intelligence 1939–1945* (London: Hamish Hamilton, 1978)

Julitte, Pierre (trans. Francis Price), *Block 26: Sabotage at Buchenwald* (London: Harrap, 1972)

Kreis, John F. (gen. ed.), *Piercing the Fog: Intelligence and Army Air Forces Operations in World War II* (Washington, DC: Air Force History and Museums Program, 1996)

Longmate, Norman, *Hitler's Rockets: The Story of the V-2s* (London: Hutchinson, 1985)

——————, *The Doodlebugs: The Story of the Flying-Bombs* (London: Hutchinson, 1981)

Macintyre, Ben, *Agent Zigzag: The True Wartime Story of Eddie Chapman – Lover, Betrayer, Hero, Spy* (London: Bloomsbury, 2007)

Martelli, George, *Agent Extraordinary: The Story of Michel Hollard, DSO, Croix de guerre* (London: Collins, 1960)

Middlebrook, Martin, *The Battle of Hamburg: Allied Bomber Forces against a German City in 1943* (London: Cassell, 2000)

——————, *The Peenemünde Raid: The Night of 17–18 August 1943* (London: Allen Lane, 1982)

Neufeld, Michael J., *The Rocket and the Reich: Peenemünde and the Coming of the Ballistic Missile Era* (New York: Free Press, 1995)

——————, *Von Braun: Dreamer of Space, Engineer of War* (New York: Knopf, 2007)

Nutting, David C., *Attain by Surprise: The Story of 30 Assault Unit Royal Navy/Royal Marines Commando and of Intelligence by Capture* (Chichester: D. Colver, 1997)

Ogley, Bob, *Doodlebugs and Rockets: The Battle of the Flying Bombs* (Westerham: Froglets, 1992)

Ordway, Frederick Ira and Mitchell R. Sharpe, *The Rocket Team* (London: Heinemann, 1979)

Overy, R. J., *The Air War 1939–1945* (London: Europa, 1980)

Patzwall, Klaus D., *Vergeltung: Das Flakregiment 155 (W)* (Norderstedt: Militär-Verlag, 1984)

Petersen, Michael B., *Missiles for the Fatherland: Peenemünde, National Socialism, and the V-2 Missile* (Cambridge: Cambridge University Press, 2009)

Pile, Sir Frederick, *Ack-Ack: Britain's Defence against Air Attack during the Second World War* (London: Harrap, 1949)

Powys-Lybbe, Ursula, *The Eye of Intelligence* (London: William Kimber, 1983)

Ramsey, Winston G. (ed.), Ramsey, *The East End Then and Now* (London: After the Battle, 1997)

Speer, Albert, *The Slave State: Heinrich Himmler's Masterplan for SS Supremacy* (London: Weidenfeld & Nicolson, 1981)

Speidel, Hans (trans. Ian Colvin), *We Defended Normandy* (London: Herbert Jenkins, 1951)

Stanley, Roy M., II, *V-Weapons Hunt: Defeating German Secret Weapons* (Barnsley: Pen and Sword, 2010)

Stirling, Tessa, Daria Nalecz and Tadeusz Dubicki (eds), *Intelligence Co-operation Between Poland and Great Britain during World War II, Volume 1: The Report of the Anglo-Polish Historical Committee* (London: Vallentine Mitchell & Co., 2005)

Stubbington, John, *Kept in the Dark: The Denial to Bomber Command of Vital ULTRA and Other Intelligence Information during World War II* (Barnsley: Pen and Sword, 2010)

Tinschert, Carlo, *Boodschap aan de Bevolking van Den Haag* (The Hague: Sdu Uitgevers, 2005)

Watkins, Gwen, *Cracking the Luftwaffe Codes: The Secrets of Bletchley Park* (Barnsley: Pen and Sword, 2006)

INDEX